W0234660

Why India is Not a Great Power (Yet)

Other Books by Bharat Karnad

Strategic Sellout: Indian-US Nuclear Deal (2009), co-authored with P.K. Iyengar, A.N. Prasad, and A. Gopalakrishnan.

India's Nuclear Policy (2008).

Nuclear Weapons and Indian Security: The Realist Foundations of Strategy, Second edition (2005, First edition 2002).

Future Imperilled: India's Security in the 1990s and Beyond, editor (1994).

Why India is Not a Great Power (Yet)

BHARAT KARNAD

OXFORD
UNIVERSITY PRESS

OXFORD
UNIVERSITY PRESS

Oxford University Press is a department of the University of Oxford.
It furthers the University's objective of excellence in research, scholarship,
and education by publishing worldwide. Oxford is a registered trademark of
Oxford University Press in the UK and in certain other countries

Published in India by
Oxford University Press
YMCA Library Building, 1 Jai Singh Road, New Delhi 110 001, India

© Oxford University Press 2015

The moral rights of the author have been asserted

First Edition published in 2015

ISBN-13: 978-0-19-945922-3
ISBN-10: 0-19-945922-3

Typeset in Adobe Garamond Pro 11/13
by The Graphics Solution, New Delhi 110 092
Printed in India by Rakmo Press, New Delhi 110 020

For
my daughter Riti
and son Ketan

Contents

Preface and Acknowledgements

A thumbnail history of this book: It has taken longer to materialize than planned. The inertia of the Indian system, the confusing welter of ideas driving India's policies generally, and the bureaucracy-dominated policy-making and implementation account for the country's slow and unsteady rise. Fortunately for this book, it meant the original draft needed only updating. A small detail: most of the URLs listed in the book were accessed from 2010 to 2015.

I must here express my accumulated gratitude to the Centre for Policy Research, New Delhi—my professional home for almost 20 years—and especially to the late K.C. Sivaramakrishnan, Chairman of the Board, July 2006–May 2015, for resolutely guarding the freedom and integrity of the Centre, its intellectually gifted President, Pratap Bhanu Mehta, and colleagues, and to the helpful staff (too numerous to mention), for sustaining a milieu for policy wonks and scholars to read, ruminate, argue, and write. I would also like to thank Oxford University Press for evincing interest in publishing this book and shepherding it through its publication.

Bharat Karnad
New Delhi, August 2015

Abbreviations

A2AD	anti-access, area denial
ADM	Atomic Demolition Munition
AESA	Active Electronically Scanned Array
ASBM	anti-ship ballistic missile
ASEAN	Association of Southeast Asian Nations
AWACS	Airborne Warning and Control System
BECA	Basic Exchange and Cooperation Agreement
BEL	Bharat Electronics Ltd
BMD	ballistic missile defence
BJP	Bharatiya Janata Party
BRICS	Brazil-Russia-India-China-South Africa
CCOS	Chairman, Chiefs of Staff
CDS	Chief of Defence Staff
CISMOA	Communications Interoperability Security Memorandum of Agreement
COCOM	Coordinating Committee for Multilateral Export Controls
DCS	Defense Commercial Sales
DNDSDG	Directorate of Naval Design–Submarine Design Group
DPSU	Defence Public Sector Unit
DRDO	Defence Research & Development Organisation
ERD	Engineering Research & Development
EU	European Union
EUM	end-use memorandum
FDI	foreign direct investment
FGFA	fifth-generation fighter aircraft
FMS	Foreign Military Sales
GST	Goods & Services Tax

GPS	global positioning system
HAL	Hindustan Aerospace Ltd.
IAF	Indian Air Force
IBSA	India-Brazil-South Africa
ICBM	Inter-Continental Ballistic Missile
ICF	inertial confinement fusion
IMET	International Military Education and Training
IONS	Indian Ocean Naval Symposium
IOR	Indian Ocean Region
ITeS	Information Technology-enabled Service
IPI	Iran-Pakistan-India
IPR	intellectual property rights
IRBM	intermediate-range ballistic missile
ISRO	Indian Space Research Organization
ISIS	Islamic State of Iraq and Syria
IT	information technology
LAC	Line of Actual Control
LCA	light combat aircraft
LoC	Line of Control
LSA	Logistics Support Agreement
MDL	Mazgaon Dockyard Ltd.
MEA	Ministry of External Affairs
MIRV	Multiple Independently-targeted Re-entry Vehicles
MMRCA	medium multi-role combat aircraft
MoD	Ministry of Defence
MR	maritime surveillance
MRBM	medium-range ballistic missile
MTC	mountain corps
NHQ	Naval Headquarters
NIA	National Intelligence Agency
NSA	National Security Adviser
NTRO	National Technical Research Organization
OFB	Ordnance Factory Board
PLA	People's Liberation Army
PLAAF	People's Liberation Army Air Force
PLAN	People's Liberation Army Navy
PLASASF	PLA Second Artillery Strategic Force
PSU	Public Sector Unit

R&D	research and development
RFP	Request For Proposal
RIC	Russia, India, China
SAARC	South Asian Association for Regional Cooperation
SAFTA	South Asian Free Trade Association
SAM	surface-to-air missile
SATIS	SAARC Agreement on Trade in Services
SATHI	Situational Awareness to be Handled by Infantry
SFC	Strategic Forces Command
SSBN	Hull classification of a nuclear powered ballistic missile-firing submarine
SSM	Surface-to-Surface Missile
SIBAT	Israeli Defense Export and Defense Cooperation Agency
SLOC	Sea Lines of Communications
SRBM	short-range ballistic missile
SSN	Hull classification of a nuclear powered general purpose attack submarine
RAW	Research & Analysis Wing
UAV	Unmanned Aerial Vehicle
UNCLOS	United Nations Convention on the Law of the Seas

THE WORLD CENTRED ON INDIA

EQUIDISTANT MAP OF THE WORLD
SHOWING TRUE BEARING FROM DELHI

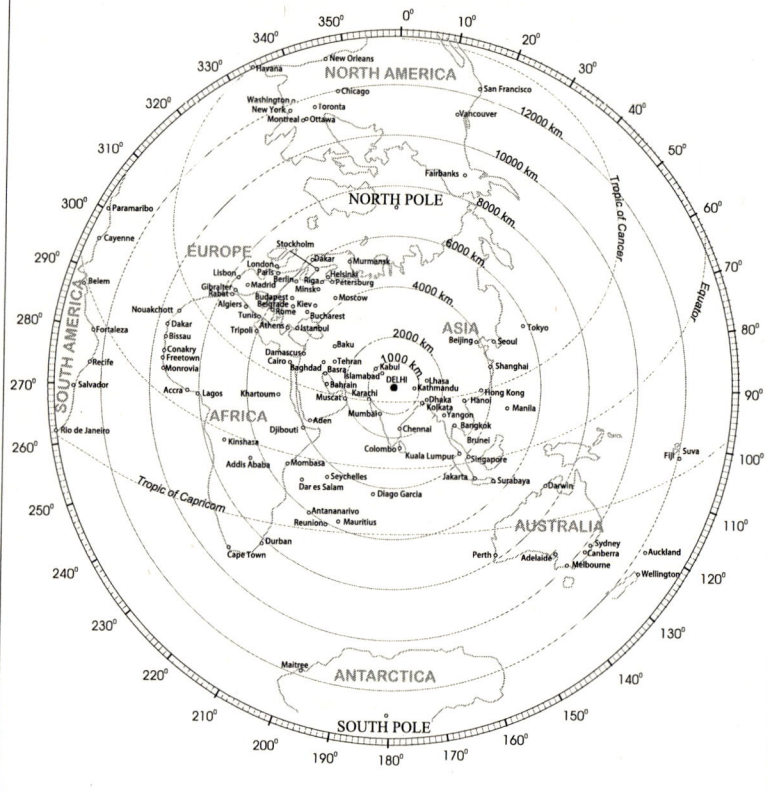

Projection : Lambert Azimuthal Equidistant (Oblique Aspect)
Origin : Delhi, India
Longitude : 77 ° 13' E
Latitude : 28 ° 35' N

Map not to scale

Source: Author.

Introduction

Great power is not a standing achieved easily or by many countries. With a modicum of economic strength, and natural
attributes of size, population, and location apart, what separates
great powers and would-be great powers from the rest are a driving
vision, an outward-thrusting nature backed by strong conviction and
sense of national destiny and matching purpose, an inclination to
establish distant presence and define national interests within the
widest possible geographic ambit, the confidence to protect and
further these interests with proactive foreign and military policies,
the building up of meaningful conventional armed forces backed by
a proven and tested thermonuclear arsenal, and the willingness to use
coercion and force in support of national interests complemented by
imaginative projection and use of both soft power and hard power
to expansively mark its status in the external realm. The United
States did not become a globe-girdling country by staying behind the
moats of the Pacific and the Atlantic Oceans nor Britain 'Great' by
restricting itself to the Dover Strait; Czarist Russia obtained strategic
weight after extending its reach to the Pacific; Prussia was a truculent
Central European kingdom until Bismarck used the Prussian Army
to unify the Germanic states and elbow Austria and France out of
the pivotal position in continental Europe; and Japan would have
remained a small group of islands in the Asian Far East but for the
Meiji Restoration and the vigorous policies it sparked. Great power-
wise, the twenty-first century is no different than the previous ages
in that a combination of widely defined interests; an outgoing, agile,

and proactive foreign policy backed by economic might and military prowess; and the ability and, especially, the will to power and the determination to use it still matters.

There is physicality to great power. Demographic and territorial bigness are consequential, the reason why China and India are expected to replace the United Kingdom and France (middling states shorn of their overseas colonies), and join the United States in the top tier. China has proved its druthers; India has yet to step up. Whether India is motivated enough, can summon the necessary political will, muster a grand vision, and begin deploying its resources beyond the subcontinent, including its growing soft power strengths (in information technology, 'frugal' engineering evidenced in everything from low-cost automobiles to Mars probes at a tenth of the U.S. price tag for similar space missions, and popular Bollywood films and music) to achieve a larger geostrategic goal, will decide if India eases into the great power groove, or is left behind (Newman 2013). India can have a huge impact if it thinks and acts big, its foreign policy is friskier, its armed forces organizationally sprightlier and strategically geared, and the defence budget is used judiciously to secure capabilities for distant contingencies and to meet China's challenge, rather than to fight yesterday's wars with a lesser foe (Pakistan).[1] This book will reveal why, owing to systemic constraints, a passive-defensive mindset, and narrow perceptions of national interest combined with a strangely diffident view of India's capacity to impact the external world entrenched over the past 50 odd years these things may not come to pass any time soon. The problem in a nutshell is that the Indian government, military, and the policy circles are habituated to aiming low and hitting lower (Karnad 2005).

Unlike other would-be great powers India has been a reticent state. Shivshankar Menon, Prime Minister Manmohan Singh's National Security Adviser (January 2010–May 2014), described the 'overriding purpose of India's foreign policy' minimally, as merely enabling 'the transformation of [the country] into a modern, prosperous and secure nation' and specifically denied that 'status, prestige…or any other goal that may appear momentarily popular or attractive' is the end-state India is striving for (Menon 2014). India has gained relative economic heft and importance (Nayyar 2014). But it has not been accompanied by a commensurate increase in its ambitions and enlargement of its policy horizons. In fact, such moves as India has made as a quasi-great power seem prompted by friendly states, such as the United States and Japan, with New Delhi apparently being prodded and pushed into assuming an expanded role as 'net security provider' in the Indian Ocean Region (IOR), as a Big Emerging Market and economic player (BRICS, G-20), and as part of the strategic quadrilateral of the US, Japan, India, and Australia envisaged by Washington and Tokyo to hem in China and stabilize the security situation in Asia. It is also American and other Western companies that put India on the map as a Research & Development (R&D), engineering, and manufacturing hub and hoisted it as a potential economic competitor to China. India's ambition in the new millennium appears less a product of its own strategic visioning and assessments and schemes for assertion conjoined to a high degree of self-belief and self-confidence than, ironically, to plans drawn up by friendly external powers. This is reflected in the fact that between Nehru's semi-articulation soon after Independence of an 'Asian' Monroe Doctrine (elucidated in Chapter 1) and President George W. Bush's hailing India as a 'major power' in the first decade of the twenty-first century, there was an ambition void. What ambition was evident was a meager one of an India striving to fit into the existing global order rather than seeking to remake it into one where it has a major say, its interests are maximized, and opportunities for advancing its interests increased—the tack taken, say, by China.[2] This reluctance to becoming a great power by beginning to act as one lingers and is among the reasons why India is proving to be its own worst enemy and obstacle in reaching that threshold, despite boasting of all the necessary attributes.

This is in the main because of lack of appreciation of geography and an aversion to geopolitics and strategic partnerships from Jawaharlal Nehru's long tenure as prime minister when most of the country's foreign and military policy lines were set almost as if in stone (Karnad 1994). Geography shapes national vision, dictates strategy, and suggests appropriate policies. Balancing power and the evolving correlation of forces in the external realm remains the key driver of foreign and military policies for would-be great powers. India has been less attentive to these basic verities of a system of sovereign nations, its policies being driven instead more by inertia than imagination, its attitude growingly suffused over the decades with a curious and unaccountable loss of nerve and conviction of the country's place in the world until by the end of the Congress party rule under Prime Minister Manmohan Singh in May 2014, the country had lost so much political, economic, and military ground that great power rather than being seen as something to be achieved with the dint of its own efforts, came to be considered a status obtained at the sufferance of extant big powers, which required placating and pleasing them and accommodating their interests. Moreover, because of its seemingly intractable internal problems, India is being written off even before it has properly embarked on its pursuit of power (Schmidt 2014).

If poverty alleviation and the economic uplift of the masses are the stock concerns of the Indian government at home, its foreign policy has stayed stuck to the myths fostered by Nehru during his long years at the helm, such as the 'Hindi-Chini Bhai-Bhai' or brotherly India–China relations.[3] On the other hand, it has lacked his genius for subverting the status quo to advantage the country. Nehru, for example, conceived the Nonalignment Movement during the Cold War to at once curtail the power and influence of the United States and the Soviet Union and benefit from the competing attentions of both super powers. Nehru also championed nuclear disarmament to firm up the country's peaceful image and divert attention from an India decanting the U.S. President Dwight D. Eisenhower's 'Atoms for Peace' programme for its Bomb-making knowledge as part of the weapons thrust he provided his larger, 'Janus-faced' nuclear energy programme from its start.[4] Undermining the existing order is what revisionist powers do to better their relative position, and gain diplomatic leverage even if only by increasing their nuisance value. China has been a successful practitioner of such policies. Being party to treaties has not deterred Beijing from weakening them. Thus, its status as a 1968 Non-Proliferation Treaty-recognized nuclear weapons state did not inhibit it from brazenly proliferating nuclear weapons technology, designs, materials, and expertise (to Pakistan, North Korea, and Iran). It is precisely the confidence to upset the extant international order owing to the conviction that the new order that will be realized as a consequence will serve the country's national interest better, which India needs to rediscover. Because otherwise, as has been the case in the last several decades, it will stay stuck to the shell of Nehruvian policy and rhetoric, while missing out on its subterranean intention and thrust.

The problem here is New Delhi's being overwhelmed by its supposed limitations coupled to conservative, risk averse, instincts that dovetail with both how powerful friendly states view the country and how Indian policymakers perceive their country's image, as a 'responsible' power.[5] A 'responsible' power by definition is not one to rock the boat or advantage itself by destabilizing the extant order. And because such self-advertisement was taken a little too seriously especially by the Manmohan Singh government, the country found itself unable to exploit opportunities and gain from the range of options afforded to India when its standing in the world improved as a nuclear weapons state, an economic giant in the making and, as U.S. Secretary of Defence Chuck Hagel visiting New Delhi stated, its 'growing global influence and military capabilities including its potential as a security provider from the Indian Ocean to the greater Pacific.' (Reuters 2014). The absence of strategic imagination, verve, and ambition may be attributable to a muted national vision, lack of self-confidence, and the inability to translate the country's many strengths into diplomatic leverage. It has marked India's gradual loss of significance in the global arena until now when Indian policies seem mainly geared to reacting, responding, and generally getting along with initiatives taken by the U.S., China, and other countries. India's steady and substantive decline as an independent player is what this book will try and analyse.

A big reason for India's diminution is its over-bureaucratized system of government where generalist civil servants implement policies, of course, but also envision them, which is unlike the case in talent-driven governments in Western democracies. Naturally then Indian foreign, military, and economic policies have tended to be status-quoist, cautious, conservative, and risk averse. And, notwithstanding the Indian government being otherwise awash in paper and strangled by red tape, documents of a seminal nature, such as those articulating a national vision and defining a typology of national interests to help configure policies, guide the work of the various arms and agencies of state, and provide continuity in the attitude, approach, outlook, and policies of the government at various levels, are entirely missing and, in fact, have never been drafted. Thus, every new government elected to power in theory starts out with a clean slate, except the 'permanent secretariat' manned by career civil servants running individual ministries, agencies and departments of the Indian government and foreign service officers manning the Ministry of External Affairs (MEA) feel free to define the national interest as they go along in their own bureaucratic light, and to act independently of each other, resulting in ad hoc policies and a maze of often incoherent, uncoordinated, and cross-cutting decisions and actions. The super fragmented structure of the government of India and of the ministries within it thus result in indeterminate strategies which have little impact. Because in such a system confusion is preordained, actual policies often subside to the deeply embedded default positions on issues from the Nehru-era. Even if there were singular documents articulating a strategic vision, the national interests, and grand strategy available as guidelines for crafting strategy and policies, there's no guarantee in a complex of clashing bureaucracies that 'The baronies of officialdom', as Colin Gray observed in another context, would behave 'cohesively, coherently, and comprehensively' (Gray 2010: 28). However, overturning the existing bureaucratic order or injecting radical administrative reforms is an option but only until new congeries of interests coalesce into new baronies which would end up reasserting the old ways of doing government business. This tendency is, perhaps, why the newly elected Bharatiya Janata Party Prime Minister Narendra Modi decided he would try and whip the existing system into shape rather than replace it or radically restructure it (Chawla 2014). The solution of minimizing the government's role while desirable and feasible in the economic and social welfare and government services-delivery fields, is not possible in the foreign policy and national security spheres. Hence, it is all the more important that the government gets things right, which it may be inherently incapable of doing, considering it relies not on experts available outside the government but on careerist civil servants and diplomats, who are the main cogs in the system as-is and inclined to carry on doing things in the manner they are accustomed to.

Whatever the systemic and other domestic constraints, the international conditions for India's consequential rise couldn't be more propitious. In the context of the decline of the United States as the preponderant power, the global milieu is in severe flux, the settled order in virtual breakdown, and the millennial belief that closer economic interlinks between nations had made old style power politics and inter-state conflicts obsolete stands debunked. Fear and uncertainty grow in a world which is likely to become more anarchic, forcing the more technologically capable nations in Asia to be attracted by the psychological comfort offered by the nuclear bomb, and weaker states to search for strategic allies and partners able to afford them overarching security (Karnad 2008: Ch 1). The lightning-fast Russian campaign to annex Crimea in eastern Ukraine in March 2014 left the United States and the North Atlantic Treaty Organization (NATO) stuttering for a military response. The Western economic sanctions imposed on Russia have revived the period of 'cold peace' between Washington and Moscow and may not dissuade President Vladimir Putin from drawing in outlying republics on its borders into forming a latter day version of the Soviet-era security system in Eastern Europe of dependent states with close military and economic relations with China as a backstop.[6] At the other end of Eurasia is a fast rising China with its burgeoning economic prowess fueling large scale military modernization and pushy policies that have Asian states in a tizzy in the context of U.S. armed services chiefs expressing fear of 'slipping behind' and America's manifest inability to prosecute a 'From the Sea'–type of amphibious strategy or even project power against the Chinese military. The revival of rivalry between Russia and NATO, on the one hand, and a sparking of one between America–Japan and China, on the other hand, opens up opportunities for India to milk the evolving situation. It can develop economic relations with China to draw greater investment from the United States and Japan, and balance it with strategic military cooperation with countries on the littoral and offshore Asia, including Australia.[7] More specifically, India can, for instance, increase its leverage in several dyadic situations, siding with (1) the U.S. and the West against a comprehensively powerful China, (2) a still apprehensive Russia against China in Asia, (3) Southeast Asia, East Asia, and Australia against China, and (4) Iran, Russia, and China against the United States and its allies in Middle Asia.[8] The increase in its maneuvering space and policy latitude will permit New Delhi to act the regional and international balancer more effectively now that there has been considerable accretion in its own power and capabilities, than Nehru ever could or did with his nonalignment policy. Indeed, it can position itself as the pivotal power able to tilt the balance decisively this way or that in the above-mentioned power balancing scenarios in the manner Britain did vis-à-vis the continental powers in the nineteenth century. With Asia witnessing a reordering of the correlation of forces, India can at once stoke and capitalize on the anxiety of America's allies about the political will and capacity of a retrenching United States to protect them from Chinese depredations.[9] It helps that Washington has expressed its eagerness to pursue a conciliatory policy with Beijing, which cannot be very reassuring to America's Asian partners.[10] New Delhi can use these circumstances to place itself at the centre, it will be argued in this book, of an alternative system of collective security. With the eye firmly on China as the main adversary and security challenge, India can synergize its engagement and role with the military, political, and economic capabilities of countries feeling threatened by Beijing to keep China at bay. It is precisely to try and head India away from such a role that Beijing sought preemptively to establish a good working relationship with the new BJP government by proposing a Shanghai Cooperation Organization-based 'Asian security' architecture which, an instinctively geostrategic-minded, Modi turned down preferring to concert with Japan and other countries such as Vietnam in rimland/offshore Asia instead, in the larger scheme of turning India's ineffectual 'Look East' policy into a more vigorous 'Act East' policy.[11]

To the west of India, notwithstanding the periodic eruptions on the Line of Control in Jammu & Kashmir, the conditions are actually brightening. Pakistan is consumed by domestic political turmoil, its army battling Taliban offshoots on the frontier with Afghanistan and Islamist militancy at home, the longstanding freedom movement in Balochistan shows no sign of abating, and it is facing alienated neighbours on three sides—Afghanistan to the north, India to the south and east, and an Iran threatening to wage hostilities if Pakistan-based Islamic militants creating disturbances on its territory are not reined in, to the west. Its paramilitary forces, moreover, are bogged down in containing home-grown Islamic extremists. The unsettled situation at home and the desire to normalize relations with India persuaded Prime Minister Nawaz Sharif to ratchet down the acrimonious rhetoric, speak of improving trade and cultural relations with India, attend Narendra Modi's investiture as Prime Minister, use the end-November 2014 SAARC (South Asian Association of Regional Countries) Summit in Kathmandu to reconnect with his Indian counterpart (after the low of a break-off of Foreign Secretary level dialogue), and even permit talks to realize the Turkmenistan-Afghanistan-Pakistan-India gas pipeline.[12] The friendly government in Kabul of President Ashraf Ghani, successor to Hamid Karzai and supported by his political rival Dr. Abdullah Abdullah, will try and play all the sides against each other, but eventually reaffirm an Indian presence in Afghanistan and, via the north–south road and rail grid radiating outwards from the Iranian port of Chahbahar and the Zaranj–Delaram highway to points connecting the erstwhile Soviet transportation network in Central Asia, and a sea outlet for Indian mining interests in the Hajigak region of Afghanistan, which the newly formed economic union of Russia, Kazakhstan, and Belarus will assist (MacFarquhar 2014). It will reduce the importance of transit rights for Indian trade through Pakistan, which loss of leverage may prompt Islamabad in fact to be more conciliatory towards India. The added gain to India from getting close to Tehran, which is at odds with Islamabad, is that, by putting Pakistan in a potential pincer, it will dampen the latter's tendencies liberally to use terrorism as an asymmetric means of unconventional warfare and to take conventional and nuclear military risks.[13] This quadrilateral of India, Iran, Afghanistan, and the Central Asian Republics could become an important geostrategic grouping with nuanced tilts towards the West and Russia to limit the Chinese thrust in Central Asia, and in the direction of Moscow to contain the U.S. influence in the extended region. Both Beijing and Washington may welcome this scheme for fear that an alternative arrangement could skew the game against them individually even more. Such a quadrilateral also promises India an expanded economic sphere to operate in, and a comprehensively beefed up presence in those parts, including a military presence in the Ainee-Farkhor air force base in Tajikistan and in Chahbahar to outflank both China and Pakistan, landward and seaward. This middle-Asian quadrilateral complements the 'security diamond' of India, Japan, the U.S., and Australia mooted for the Indo-Pacific region by the Japanese Prime Minister Shinzo Abe.

The emerging situation in Asia is, therefore, tailor-made for India to vault into prominence as one of the two nodes, along with Japan, in a rimland maritime security architecture, which will be detailed in subsequent chapters, that the countries on China's periphery can join in and the U.S. and the West, and even Russia, as extra-territorial actors, can support. This grand geopolitical design will only be realized if New Delhi does not continue squandering strategic opportunities as it has done in the past. Thus, India lost the chance to resolve the boundary problem with China as late as 1983 when New Delhi failed to respond expeditiously to a Beijing initiative that might have converted the Line of Actual Control into a formal border with the added bonus of some portion of the Aksai Chin under Chinese control being returned to India.[14] In 2007, fearing attack from the Right, Prime Minister Manmohan Singh did not sign the agreement with Pakistan President Parvez Musharraf that, while creating a fig-leaf mechanism to oversee affairs over the divided province and save Islamabad's face would have, for all intents and purposes, converted the ceasefire line or Line of Control in Kashmir into international border and resolved this festering dispute once and for all. And in the last decade, instead of beefing up India's trade and other relations with Iran, solidifying an energy supply source, and investing whole-heartedly in the land corridor to Central Asia and Europe through Chahbahar port, which an isolated Tehran pressured by the West would have welcomed and which association would have increased India's negotiating clout in Tehran and in the Western capitals, New Delhi chose to make its Iran policy hostage to American policy whims. All is not lost though. It should foster intimate relations with each of the three main actors on the West Asian scene—Israel, Iran, and Saudi Arabia, as a way of expanding its own strategic role as the peace-ballast for a turbulent region and douser of major conflagrations, and to prevent the ultra-radical ideology of the Islamic State of Iraq and Syria (ISIS) from seeping into South Asia (Shahid 2014).

Its consistently missing strategic opportunities leads one to wonder if India is a gentle giant or simply a strategically dim-witted lug. India's rise has been the subject of study and speculation, particularly in the wake of its economic surge starting in the mid-1990s. The barriers to India's rise that have drawn attention are predictably related to internal weaknesses—high levels of poverty and illiteracy, serious socio-economic disparities, caste and faction-ridden politics, failure of statist-socialist economic policies and programmes, and a decrepit and inefficient colonial era administrative apparatus of government servicing the state according to a confusing welter of rules and regulations the British had put in place. It has institutionalized corruption, delivered meager economic development, and produced astonishingly poor results in the social welfare fields (Bardhan 2010; Gupta 2010; Luce 2008; Das 2002). Treating these ills involves contentious issues and has spawned heated debates about solutions and their ideological wellsprings.[15]

India also over-emphasizes its soft power as the means to realize great power, which is part of the public discourse on the sort of great power India should aspire to become. Relatively little attention has been paid to the hard power deficit—the more seminal reason, it will be argued in this book, for India's upward trajectory being depressed, particularly because conventional and nuclear military muscle remains the final arbiter in the realpolitik-infused international relations. It is the hard power vaccum in its foreign and military policies this book will, in the main, analyse. The fact is the accretion in India's economic heft may have fuelled great power ambition but it has not been accompanied by a commensurate enlargement of the country's policy horizon, in part because of the prevailing confusion, as will be pointed out, about whether India should be a great power and, if so, of what kind. At the heart of the infirmity in India's hard power are the grievous flaws in the software component of hard power, namely, in the absence of strategic vision, political will, credible threat perceptions, and appropriate strategy and plans. India may have a grand idea of itself in the abstract, but it is not backed by the necessary self-belief and an elevating national vision to guide policies and configure a strategic game-plan. Hence, there's no manifestation of the political will to great power, leave alone the drive to achieve it. This, as the book will show, is surprising because India, under Jawaharlal Nehru, prime minister for the first 17 years of the newly founded republic, started off in the great power race at a canter before subsiding quickly to a crawl. Ere the formal transfer of power by Britain in 1947, he articulated an 'Asian Monroe Doctrine' propped up by Indian arms but, apprehending a blowback from Third World states he was cultivating, backed off. There has been a vision-cum-ambition void ever since filled in recent times by the enervating belief in great power as entitlement. Except Nehru understood better than his successors that a mere yearning for great power without the where-withal of hard power is only pretence. Hence, he embarked on a wily and wildly successful policy—that is unknown to most Indians, including the political class and the all-powerful bureaucracy—of championing universal disarmament globally as political cover for his carefully nursed and secretive dual-purpose nuclear energy programme that, with the commissioning of the plutonium reprocessing unit in Trombay, reached the weapons threshold as early as Spring 1964—a couple of months before Nehru died and some six months before China exploded its first nuclear device. Thereafter the going was all downhill. Under subsequent regimes the nuclear weapons programme was victimized by the very disarmament rhetoric Nehru had used as a shield to protect it (Karnad 2005, Ch 3). After a full decade of doing nothing, the atomic test ordered by the Congress party Prime Minister, Indira Gandhi, in 1974 rather than being fol-lowed up by an open-ended testing regime and rapid weaponization to make up for lost time, ended with the weapons programme going back into hibernation. Twenty-five years later a few more nuclear tests were conducted but despite immediately accessible evidence that the thermonuclear device which was tested had fizzled, the BJP government of Atal Bihari Vajpayee instead of ordering new tests to correct the design flaws in the fusion weapon, announced a 'voluntary moratorium' on testing. In each of these instances India contrived the worst possible outcome for itself—suffering harsh eco-nomic and technology sanctions and failing to obtain the political and strategic heft and diplomatic leverage that accrues from having formidable nuclear forces (Karnad 2005, Ch 5). Elsewhere, to make India self-sufficient in conventional armaments, another prerequisite of great power, Nehru imaginatively imported, not combat aircraft as has become the habit with the Indian Air Force and government, but the reputed Nazi-era German designer of Fockewulfe fighter aircraft, Kurt Tank, to develop the Marut HF-24, a multi-role supersonic fighter-bomber in Bangalore. A prototype was flying by 1961—the first such aircraft to be produced outside of Europe and the United States.[16] From that high-point, India plummeted to such depths as to now claim the dubious honour of being the biggest importer of military hardware.[17] India has thus time and again reached a strategic cusp only to fritter away the advantage. It is an old Indian failing which, as this book will show, has dogged India's ascent.

If there is no national vision, and no Vision document in the Indian government, and no seminal papers delineating the preferred geopolitical system or defining the national interests, it is inevitable for the Indian state to work aimlessly to produce policies on-the-run designed to deal with immediate crisis or contingencies without a hint of the 'long view' or long term strategic goals. The country's legitimate pursuit of great power ambition is thwarted in practice, moreover, by the dependence on imported armaments, spares and servicing support that permits major military supplier nations to rein in Indian policy. This state of affairs is reinforced by an under-developed public sector-dominated defence industry that has stayed stuck at the level of licensed manufacture of foreign armaments. It hasn't helped, as this study will also show, that while its armed forces are battle-tested (especially in counter-insurgency warfare), rigidities in their structure, organization, and service culture mean troubling persistence with legacy forces, such as vast fleets of armour and mech-anized elements and dated threat perceptions centering on Pakistan to justify them, and an apparent institutional inability to consider, leave alone handle, transformative change in line with advances in technology and the need in the twenty-first century for cyber-fused, network-centric, joint military task-forces. In this respect, army, the senior service, is most resistant to transformation, navy is most receptive to it and the most institutionally geared towards indigeniz-ing design, development, and production of weapons platforms and armaments, and the air force talks big but is limited by its foreign equipment. The resulting lack of synergy in warfighting capabilities and dependence on imported military hardware has fated India to suboptimal use of force which can undermine an activist foreign policy occasionally requiring coercion.

The Indian military, notwithstanding many advanced weapons platforms and systems in its order-of-battle thus remains, by and large, industrial age in its mindset, which circumscribes its politi-cal and operational utility and effectiveness. The exercise of hard power by the country is further handicapped by, what a former naval chief, Admiral (Retd) Arun Prakash calls, 'the politician's profound disinterest in, and ignorance about defence, security and strategic affairs as well as the military ethos' and a system of civilian control of the armed services by the Ministry of Defence (MoD) and the Ministry of External Affairs (MEA) which together and separately bureaucratically stifle the military spirit and initiative. In this unique system of political control, civil servants and diplomats, with little technical acumen, make far-reaching decisions pertaining to national security and posture, and preside over the higher management of the armed forces (Prakash 2014). Predictably, it results in MEA regularly vetoing proposals for establishing military bases abroad and for arms sales and transfers, and military cooperation programmes designed to promote strategic links with countries in the Indian Ocean Region (IOR), Central Asia, and Southeast Asia proposed by the Armed Services headquarters, because Foreign Service officials, intent on ceding no policy turf to the military, are content to pursue short-term policy goals for small-time gains (Chatterjee Miller 2013).

The myriad problems with regard to hard power very early scythed India's great power promise and plans. Caution and the status quo-ist habit of mind took over, leading naturally to India choosing to fit into the existing global order rather than ensure India deals with this order on Indian terms.[18] This attitude too has put-off India's reaching the great power rank (Nagao 2014).

Complemented by a proper appreciation of the evolving geopolitics and forceful foreign and economic policies and driven by a grand strategic vision, hard power can catapult India into the upper reaches of the international pecking order, win it stature and recognition, expand possibilities for trade and commerce, and the moral space to legitimize its quest for great power. India, it is argued in this book, should adopt such an approach, using its military as a strategic multiplier. Co-opting adjoining countries with economic incentives and unfettered access to the Indian market, rather than cowing them down with military force can obtain a South Asian market and, in time, a unitary security system. Freed of its fixation with Pakistan, New Delhi will be able fundamentally to redefine its strategic situation, reorient its military north and east-wards, in the maritime sphere reaffirm India's centrality in the Indian Ocean basin, flesh out its security partnerships, and help concentrate its mind and resources on the main geostrategic challenges, namely, China and obtaining a friendly and stable eco-system for consolidating the country's rise as the premier power in the 'strategic quadrant' encompassed by the East African littoral and the Caspian Sea in the west, the Sunda Strait and western Australian coast in the eastern and the southeastern reaches of the Indian Ocean, the Central Asian Republics in the north and the waters upto Antarctica in the south, in other words, in an Indian Monroe Doctrine sphere.

In this respect India's helter-skelter military procurement programmes betraying neither rhyme nor reason are a problem and have come in for scrutiny (Smith 1994; Cohen & Dasgupta 2010). But the larger subject of the shortfalls in the country's hard power and the software attributes of its hard power (vision, political will, plans, policies) have not so far been analysed in any depth, which is what this book attempts to do. While the thicket of internal fault-lines, systemic weaknesses, and economic frailties may take some time to resolve, hard power and its imaginative uses supported by appropriate doctrines, and a nimble foreign policy tasked for strategic benefits, this study contends, offer India a short-cut to the great power threshold, a model successfully pursued by other countries in the modern era. This study points out how India has stood Frederick the Great's observation that 'Diplomacy without arms is like music without instruments' on its head. India has a whole orchestra and can, in Frederickian terms, make big music but occasionally uses just the piccolo, say, to produce small notes. Belabouring smaller, weaker, adjoining states is the staple of Indian policy, not enlarging the country's international clout, presence and influence by realizing an Asian 'correlation of forces' advantageous to India's growing global interests. Such small aims in fact accentuate the lack of grand vision and strategy. A scheme for extended security based on cooperative security relationships—an Indian Monroe Doctrine system as part of a 'triple Monroe Doctrine system' in Asia, will be defined. That the Indian government has not felt the need to have any such geopolitical system as a template for its policies suggests a lack of geopolitical savvy compounded by the absence of what Halford Mackinder, the great theorist of geopolitics, called the 'map-reading habit of mind'. The resulting failure to get a grip on how geography shapes national interests and strategy has resulted in a flawed understanding of the external reality and bad policy choices. At the heart of this problem is a big hole where strategic imagination should be. Consequently, policy keyed to breaking events is looked upon as virtue, because it is mistaken for 'restraint' and inaction is praised as 'responsible' behaviour. It is an approach, labeled 'softly-softly' by Salman Khurshid, foreign minister in the Congress Party coalition government that contrived in the decade 2004–2014 to push India to the sidelines. 'Sometimes it is said that may be India is not assertive enough. But a softly-softly approach', Khurshid explained to an audience at the University of Oxford in June 2013, 'leads to the desired change without upheavals. We do not assert ourselves by intruding, dictating, or imposing. It is an approach that has worked for us in the region and globally.'[19]

It resulted in recessive policies that valued 'strategic autonomy' as an end in itself rather than as a means to an end, in talking engagement with the world but avoiding it altogether if too vigorous an involvement became necessary. It exacerbated India's seeming incapacity to exploit the half-chances offered by an international system in the throes of severe change, because policy was simply not quicksilver enough to adjust to changing circumstances and imbalances of power, and because policymakers exhibited surprising naïvete about international power politics. In Beijing, Prime Minister Manmohan Singh, for instance, damned 'the old theories of alliances and containment' as 'no longer relevant' (Deshpande & Dasgupta 2013). It accorded with his National Security Adviser Shivshanker Menon's contemptuous dismissal of 'balance of power' furthered by strategic alliances and security cooperation, as 'very Nineteenth Century'.[20] The underlying conceit being that for a New Age power (as many Indians see their country), India can do without allies and partners and that getting to great power the old fashioned way—in Bismarck's words by 'blood and steel', is an encumbrance incurring needless effort and expenditure of national resources especially when such standing may be made available to the country by an international community impressed, as a delusional quasi-official document facilitated by the Manmohan Singh regime stated, by 'the power of its example' (Center for Policy Research 2012). In the context of India's slothful progress towards industrialization and modernity at home and its troubled ties with its South Asian neighbours, a widening gap in every sphere with its natural rival, China, and no outstanding

achievements elsewhere in the external realm to show for its endeav-
ours, the success Khurshid claimed for the 'softly-softly' approach
seems exaggerated, at best. Indeed, the Vice Chancellor, Lord Patten,
at the same Oxford event made light of the notion that India stands
for anything or even that it is a serious aspirant to great power. Being
a 'super country' and 'super democracy', he said pointedly, 'is different from being a super power', and wondered if India even 'wants to
be' one.[21]

Proving Patten right are a host of policies emanating from New
Delhi which seem bereft of strategic content, are full of mistakes,
chief among these being the civilian nuclear cooperation deal with
the United States that has hamstrung both the Indian nuclear
military and civilian programmes without gaining for the country
any of the payoffs in terms of 'the rights and privileges' of a nuclear
weapons state and membership in the Nuclear Suppliers Group
promised by the 8 July, 2005 Joint Statement signed in Washington
by Prime Minister Manmohan Singh and U.S. President George W.
Bush. And New Delhi has failed to reassure Asian states on China's
periphery and hurt its great power plans by being too submissive to
Washington and too mindful of Beijing's sensitivities even as both
these governments undermined India's interests with relish (such as
their complicity in nuclear-missile-arming Pakistan). This attitude
may fortunately be changing with an Indian Prime Minister for the
first time doing some plain talking. Modi, for example, juxtaposed
'development' that, he said, India and Japan desired with 'tendencies'
towards 'expansionism' characteristic of eighteenth-century imperi-
alism that he attributed, albeit indirectly, to China.[22] India has an
enormous fund of goodwill in Asia and the world to draw upon and a
milieu receptive to its playing a more decisive role. But a self-absorbed
and inward-turned New Delhi pursuing 'prosperity' (and then, not
too successfully—with the growth rate dipping to the 4-plus per cent
level by the time Manmohan Singh's government demitted office)
at the expense of exercising 'power' ensured a fraying image of the
country to match its shrinking ambition. India appears satisfied, by
this reckoning, to make a big splash in a small pond rather than a
big splash in a big pond, and to stick with the comforting insularity
of the *jambudvipa*—giant island of ancient Hindu coinage bounded
by the seas, the mountains and the desert, that is inclined to interact

with the world on a 'take it or leave it' basis, but desiring only to be left alone to muddle along on its own.[23]

So far in the new millennium, the United States has loomed large in Indian policy. The case will, however, be made that while military cooperation with the United States and other friendly countries has increased to counter China, there are limits on how close India and the US can, in fact, get. The traditional distrust and wariness of America persists and is reinforced by Washington's reluctance, whatever the rhetoric, to transfer advanced technology and go beyond a transactional relationship oriented to selling India high-value goods (nuclear reactors and weapons systems).[24] The relationship will be analysed at some length. With no great U.S. interest in wanting to see India develop as a military technology power, the proposed program for 'joint research and co-development of defence products' is making laboured progress, and has yet to go beyond the 'thirty-two annual dialogue mechanisms' and the increased frequency of high officials to-ing and fro-ing between the two capitals.[25] In reality, this book argues, Washington has impeded India's becoming a counterweight to China by weighing in against a resumption of Indian thermonuclear testing, which alone will enable India to obtain credible fusion weapons and achieve strategic parity with the modernizing Chinese strategic forces (Thranert 2013). It hampers the acquisition by New Delhi of high technology by pressuring third countries, such as Israel, to cap the level of technology India can buy. And it pushes New Delhi on Intellectual Property Rights, World Trade Organization, and climate issues by threatening a turning off of the H1B visa spigot benefiting the aspiring middle-class and imposition of trade sanctions. Such threats will have little effect on New Delhi—after all ensuring food security for the masses and affordable medicines wins votes, not ensuring windfall profits for the American farmer and pharmaceutical companies, but they have the potential for aggravating the distrust felt by Indians and embittering relations. In any case, it is imprudent for India, it will be argued, to depend overmuch on any outside power and especially an unreliable United States, considering the enormous cross-stakes America and China have in each other's economies and a fast-modernizing Chinese military that's inducing caution in Washington.[26] The sensible strategic course for New Delhi to follow in these circumstances, it is suggested, is to forge a strong technology-security relationship with Israel, strengthen the scheme for collaboration to produce advanced weapons systems with Russia, firm up ties with Iran as a supplier of energy and as the gateway to the Central Asian Republics, and intensify military ties with countries on Chinese land and sea borders, particularly in Southeast Asia—China's soft under-belly, and offshore—Japan, Taiwan, and Australia, while treating the United States only as an opportunistic balancer.

There are, however, many reasons, mostly internal, why India may not make it as a great power. These have to do with the characteristically Third World set of factors such as internal restiveness and turmoil due to the painful reordering underway of a society severely fragmented along traditional faultlines—caste, religion, ethnicity, language, and region, wherein large masses of the underclass are getting democratically empowered and finding their voice. Then there are the perennial shortages of water and energy, and archaic laws and plethora of confusing rules and regulations of colonial vintage overlaid by more modern concerns for ecology that prevent rapid industrialization, growth of manufacturing industry, and creation of jobs on a gigantic scale to meet the aspirations of a burgeoning youth population. The fear is real that considering the serious state of disrepair the system of education and skilling is in, the demographic dividend that many economists believe could be the country's deliverance, may in fact turn into a social bomb capable of serious social dislocation and disorder. These are problems exacerbated by a corrupt bureaucracy, horrid infrastructure, and resources-wise wasteful industrialization which can 'choke' India's rise.[27] Above all else, there is the extremely compartmentalized and bureaucratized functioning of the Indian government. With each ministry, department, and agency of government, bridled by red tape and relentlessly producing paper and more paper and, in the absence of clear policy aims and guidelines, acting as sovereigns intent mostly on preserving turf and in undercutting each other, little gets done, and is the bane of good governance and, in the external realm, makes for a reduced India. This state of affairs appalled the incoming Prime Minister, Modi. 'I was surprised by what I saw', he said in his first (2014) Independence Day address. 'It seemed as if dozens of parallel governments were running under one government. It appeared everyone had his fiefdom. I observed disunity and conflict.'[28] Whether he succeeds in removing these systemic faults and bureaucratic barriers and sprucing up procedures will decide which way India will move—up or down.

To sum up: Among the things that need to be done for it to become a great power—which will be dealt with in greater detail in the chapters that follow, India has to (1) define its security perimeter in terms of an Indian 'Monroe Doctrine' in the quadrant bounded by the East African littoral, the Caspian Sea, Central Asian Republics, the Southeast Asian nations and Antarctica, (2) assume the role of the gendarme in this area, and cobble together a pan-Asian maritime security system comprising littoral-rimland and offshore nations on China's sea border while tapping to the extent possible into the U.S. capabilities pivoting to Asia, (3) incentivize its immediate neighbours, including Pakistan, and states farther afield, such as Afghanistan and Central Asia, with generous economic grants and lines of credit to buy capital goods from India, which will spur the Indian manufacturing sector, and long term loans, development aid, and trade concessions to get them to plug into India's economic and industrial engine, thereby, establishing India as the nodal economic power and prosperity spreader to complement its role as security provider, (4) build up versatile, strategically-oriented, conventional military forces able to take the fight to China in Tibet and the distant seas, and to prosecute expeditionary missions to protect friendly governments, safeguard national interests in the seaward arc Simonstown-Subic Bay and, landward, from the Gulf to Central Asia and, in furtherance of this goal, to establish foreign bases and negotiate military basing arrangements in these regions to consolidate a three-point strategic forward presence rooted in the east in Na Thrang on the central Vietnam coast made available by Hanoi for Indian Navy's use, Farkhor-Ainee air base in Tajikistan in the north, and the North and South Agalega Islands offered by Mauritius for Indian air and naval deployment in the south-western Indian Ocean, (5) significantly reorient the military effort towards China and away from Pakistan, which will have cascading political benefits of eroding Islamabad's distrust of India, by reconstituting the three strike corps that are in excess of need into a composite corps and transferring the manpower and material resources freed up to form two additional offensive mountain corps, for a total of three such corps facing China and reorient the rest of the military accordingly, (6) erect a consequential private sector-led defence-industrial complex to fully meet the country's military needs and those of friendly countries, (7) resume thermonuclear testing to obtain a matching deterrent that is credible should nuclear eye-balling in a crisis reach the stage when Chinese megaton weapons will come into play, and (8) prosecute a tit-for-tat policy with China—strategically by nuclear missile arming Vietnam to payback China for nuclear weaponizing Pakistan, diplomatically by equating Arunachal Pradesh with a genuinely 'autonomous' Tibet, internal security-wise, by playing the 'Tibet card' to counter Chinese assistance to rebel movements in the Indian Northeast, economically by severely dissuading Indian traders and companies from importing cheap Chinese goods without an equally open market access to Indian manufacturers and producers, and militarily by deploying Atomic Demolition Munitions along the likely Himalayan passes and ingress routes as the ultimate means of deterring Chinese intrusions in strength across the 4,700 km-long Line of Actual Control separating the two countries.

This study is a factual narrative-cum-historical analysis based, other than the extant literature and other sources of information, on interviews and discussions—on record and off—with politicians and senior serving and retired civilian and military officials in the decision-making loop which, hopefully, lends the study policy immediacy, verisimilitude, and relevance. Because these interactions were held in the last few years, the analysis while of enduring value in clarifying what the Indian government thinks and how it acts, is also a sort of post-mortem on the policies of the Manmohan Singh-led Congress government and 'the lost decade' in terms of economic reforms and strategic outreach; in effect, a primer for the new BJP government on what not to do!

Briefly, the chapter-wise delineation is as follows: Chapter 1 discusses the differing notions of great power and the debate within and outside India on the subject, assesses the soft power thesis, before concluding that there's little clarity in the country about the kind of power India should be, but considerable confusion about the role hard power can play. Chapter 2 deals with geopolitics and why a coalition of littoral or rimland states can moderate China's ambitions and blunt its aggressive mien. A geopolitical and security arrangement of an Indian Monroe Doctrine structure as part of a larger Triple Monroe Doctrines system—Indian, Chinese, and the U.S.-Japanese (in the Indian Ocean, the East Sea, and the Far East and the western Pacific respectively) is explicated. Chapter 3 concerns relations with the states pivotal to India and in the working of the Triple Indian Monroe Doctrines system, especially Russia, Iran, Israel, the Gulf states, Central Asian Republics, ASEAN and particularly Vietnam, Taiwan, Japan, and the United States. Chapters 4, 5, and 6 constitute the core of this book and, as in the rest of it, the views of senior serving and retired military officers and government officials who have been part of the decision-making bodies at the highest levels will be mined for insights and information about just why Indian foreign and military polices are what they are and why the national security system is the way it is. In Chapter 4 the hard power of the state is juxtaposed against its cautious use and highlights the absence of strategic imagination. This is reflected, for instance, in New Delhi's inability to see that the soft power of classical and street culture, information technology and 'frugal engineering' backed by military capabilities and other hard power of the state will take India faster to the great power level than banking mostly on soft power can, that foreign bases are foreign policy assets, and that the failure to commit fully to security cooperation activities with Asian states in China's vicinity is a serious weakness. Chapter 5 critiques Indian military capabilities, pointing out the many strengths and the many more weaknesses—among them the organizational inelasticity and resistance to technology-related transformation, the opposition to integrating the fighting forces and to unifying command, and generally the preference for short-legged weapons platforms (with particular reference to the army and air force) to fight mainly short tactical conflicts such as those relating to Pakistan, rather than to wage long duration decisive wars that may be imposed by China. The relatively modern orders-of-battle and surprisingly aggressive plans of the navy and air force to blunt Chinese aggression, are plumbed in some detail. The conclusion is that the Indian army and air force, tilt more towards tackling the military nuisance that is Pakistan than China, the more serious military threat. How well they will fare in a running war with the Chinese land and air forces, remains a matter of speculation. The navy, while boasting of a more expansive outlook and wherewithal, is still hampered by heartland considerations of coastal security. As regards the nuclear deterrent, the strategic posture is detailed and analysed and the case made for resumption of thermonuclear testing to inject credibility into India's strategic posture, and for relying on Atomic Demolition Munitions to stifle China's itch for 'map-changing' by means of short and intense conventional hostilities across an undemarcated border. Chapter 6 analyses the fatal weakness of arms dependency, which condition should it persist, will be the single, most powerful, reason why India will never make it to the great power club. This phenomenon is examined from the perspective of an indigenous defence R&D set-up and industry that is hobbled by the government favouring the defence public sector units (DPSUs) with limited skill-sets, at the expense of the more efficient and better motivated profit-driven private sector, which is also far more effective in absorbing and innovating technology because of prospects for commercial gain. A schema is drawn up for welding the resources and capacities in the public and private sectors to obtain two competing defence-industrial combines headed by two of the most reputable industrial houses, which will serve the national interests better. Chapter 7 discusses the severe internal barriers—caste-driven politics, perennial center-state tensions, and a corrupt and malfunctioning administrative system run on the basis of 'silo-based' decision-making set up to service a 'socialist' state that has only perpetuated poverty will have to be radically reformed and overhauled to implement the free market and 'minimum government, maximum governance' nostrums Prime Minister Modi to even have a chance. And it will shine a light on Indian diplomats and why they may be the wrong instrument to wield the hard power of the state or advance the new government's trade diplomacy. The concluding chapter summarizes the main arguments in the book, and expresses doubts about whether New Delhi can easily escape the gravitational pull of its domestic problems and be persuaded by strategic logic to pursue a more outward-looking and proactive role in Asia and the world.

What'll become evident is that with arbitrariness and ad hocism dictating Indian policy, the system relies too much on *jugaad* or improvisation to pull through in crises and when pushed to produce results, and how this, in turn, puts off genuine system transformation and prevents streamlined functioning of government, more productive use of national resources, more efficient working relationship sans friction between the government and the armed services, a more integrated and effective military, and a smoother ride for India to great power.

Considering the self-inflicted problems and self-imposed limitations, and the hash New Delhi has so far made of things, and notwithstanding energetic attempts by Prime Minister Modi to get more out of the extant system, if a drastic makeover of the system does not happen, the unwieldy apparatus of government isn't reduced, and there is no culling of the large and inefficient government workforce nor reforms to ensure civil servants are held accountable for the outcomes of government programmes and policies, Great Power Lite is the most India can realistically aspire to in the decades ahead. For the country to go beyond and become a genuine great power will take some doing. Then again, an elephant-sized India, wasting a great start, has in the last fifty-odd years accomplished something equally astonishing—a disproportionately small footprint in the world! Just how it has managed this feat is what the book is about.

Notes

1. Within a fortnight of the BJP government assuming power, the new Prime Minister, Narendra Modi, said: 'The need of the hour is to think big.' See 'Focus More on Skill, Scale & Speed: PM', *Economic Times*, 8 June, 2014.

2. Shivshankar Menon talked of India and China benefitting the most from globalization and, by implication, India's interest at least in continuing with the present international order that made this possible. See Menon (2014).

3. See the review essay, Sen (2014).

4. Regarding Nehru's use of 'moralpolitik' to advantageously position India and assist the country's nuclear energy programme achieve weapons capability, see Karnad (2005: Chapter 3).

5. India, wrote Kamal Nath, a powerful member of Manmohan Singh's cabinet, 'knows its limits and plays by the rules of the game' and reiterated that India is a 'team player'. See Nath (2008: 154).

6. Beijing has stepped in as provider to Russia of capital previously sourced from Western financial institutions. See Baker (2014), Heritage (2014), and Meyer and Pismennaya (2014). Also see Tiezzi (2014).

7. In response to Tokyo announcing a potential investment of some \$35 billion in India's trillion dollar infrastructure sector during Prime Minister Narendra Modi's successful early September 2014 visit to Japan, China is expected to up the ante with still more productive investment and other proposals made by the Chinese President Xi Jinping visiting Delhi later in the same month. See Patranobis (2014). Visiting Australia, Modi signed a security framework agreement that will firm up the 'security squad' or the 'security diamond' of India, Australia, Japan, and the U.S. See Garnaut (2014).

8. Vali Nasr frames the problems of a declining US thus: '...America's troubles with Russia and China stem from the dissonance between America's wish to let economics drive foreign policy and America's need to confront those powers' embrace of old-fashioned strategic posturing.' See Nasr (2014), MacFarquhar and Herszenhorn (2014), Peel and Sevastopulo (2014), Fackler (2014), and Pant and Super (2013).

9. Londono (2014). At the hearings to confirm Max Baucus as ambassador to China, the opposition leader and former Republican Party presidential candidate, Senator John C. McCain said: 'This is a matter of a rising threat or challenge to peace and security in Asia because of the profound belief in the Chinese leadership that China must and will, regain the dominant role that they had for a couple of thousand years in Asia.' Quote in Knowlton (2014). Also see Lin (2013). Regarding the pivot, US Assistant Secretary of Defense Katrina McFarland said that it's 'being looked at again because, candidly, it can't happen.' See Getz (2014).

10. President Obama in his West Point address in 28 May 2014, urged 'restraint' in the use of U.S. military power and talked of using 'military force' only 'when our core interests demand it' but retained the escape hatch by not defining what these core interests are. See the text of his address at www.nytimes.com/2014/05/29/us/politics/transcript-of-president-obamas-commencement-address-at-west-point.html. US National Security Adviser Susan Rice in spelling out Obama's second term Asia strategy stated that 'When it comes to China, we seek to operationalize a new model of major power relations. That means managing inevitable competition while forging deeper cooperation on issues where our interests converge—in Asia and beyond.' See 'Remarks as Prepared for Delivery by National Security Advisor Susan E. Rice' at Georgetown University, 20 November, 2013 at http://www.whitehouse.gov/the-press-office/2013/11/21/remarks-prepared-delivery-national-security-advisor-susan-e-rice. Also see Elbridge Colby and Brad Glosserman, 'Asia Real "America Problem"', *PacNet*, No. 16, Pacific Forum CSIS, Honolulu, Hawaii, 13 March, 2012.

11. 'Chinese foreign minister Wang Yi holds talks with Shushma Swaraj', PTI, *Times of India*, 8 June, 2014; Roy (2014). The importance accorded

Vietnam can be gauged from the fact that a little over a month after signing a defence Memorandum of Understanding during President Pranab Mukherji's visit to Hanoi in in September 2014, a full-fledged defence pact was readied by MEA for the Vietnamese Prime Minister Nguyen Tan Dung's visit to New Delhi. See Chaudhury, D.R. (2014).

12. Chaudhry, S. (2014); Taneja and Bimal (2014).

13. Afrasiabi, (2014). Afrasiabi is former adviser to the Iranian nuclear negotiating team (2004–06).

14. This was revealed by former Foreign Secretary Shyam Saran, posted in the Beijing Embassy in 1983. See Saran (2014). 'India-China border dispute—Coping with asymmetry', *Business Standard*, April 13, 2014.

15. For a lively discussion between mainly U.S.-based renowned Indian origin economists about whether policies geared to promote economic growth or to reduce wealth disparities are best for India, see Bhagwati and Panagariya (2013), Dreze and Sen (2013).

16. On the HF-24 project, see Karnad (2002: 186).

17. On arms imports, refer 'India world's largest arms importer according to new SIPRI data on international arms transfers', *SIPRI*, 14 March, 2011 at www.sipri.org/

18. Shivshankar Menon talked of India and China benefitting the most from globalization and, by implication, India's interest in continuing with the present international order that made this possible. See Menon (2014).

19. Quote in Khanna (2013).

20. Interview.

21. 'India Day @ Oxford: Is parliamentary democracy facing credibility crisis?', *Moneycontrol.com*, 14 June, 2013 at www.moneycontrol.com/news/economy/india-day-@-oxford-can-india-match-its-economic-growthpolitical-power-89880.html. In fact, Patten echoed the doubts in a lead editorial in a leading British weekly which said, 'That India can become a great power is not in doubt. The real question is whether it wants to.' See 'Can India become a great power?', *Economist*, March 30th–April 5th, 2013.

22. Speaking before an appreciative audience of industrialists and businessmen in Tokyo, Modi described 'expansionism' as 'Sometimes encroach[ing] on a country, sometimes enter[ing] into the seas, sometimes enter[ing] a country to take it over.' The quote in 'PM warns against forces of expansion', *Hindu*, 2 September, 2014.

23. On India's *jambudvipa*-complex, a former Pakistan Foreign Secretary, Shamshad Ahmad, knowingly writes: 'Since 1947, India because of its sheer size and centrality has stood more or less alone as a regional power without having to be identified in tandem with the rest of the countries in the region.' See Ahmad (2013).

24. Washington's 'We have helped you get a nuclear deal, now buy this or that piece of military hardware'-attitude was particularly evident with the failure of the bids by Lockheed and Boeing in 2012 to sell the obsolete F-16 and F-18 aircraft respectively as medium range multi-role combat aircraft to the Indian Air Force.

25. See the talk by the National Security Adviser Shivshankar Menon, 'India and the U.S.A.', Aspen India, New Delhi, 20 September, 2013.

26. Inside of 20 years China, according to Russian sources, will have a military second to none. See 'Russian Media Say Chinese Military Will Be the Strongest in the World in 20 Years', *Huanqiu*, August 14, 2013 at http://mil.huanqiu.com/obsertvation/2013-08/4240291.html http://iranmatters.belfercenter.org/. Twining (2013).

27. 'Choke point: India', Wilson Center, 10 April, 2014 at http://wilsoncenter.org/article/choke-point-india?mkt_tok=3RkMMJWWfF9ws RojuKjLZKXonjHpfsX%2F4%2B4oWbHr08Yy0EZ5VunJEUWy34MJS tQ%2FcOedCQkZHblFnV4JQ624SrUNrKEO.

28. 'Surprised to see dozens of parallel govts at Centre', *Times of India*, 16 August, 2014.

References

Afrasiabi, K. 2014. 'The emerging Pakistani factor in the Iran nuclear equation', *Iran Matters*, Belfer Center, Harvard University, 4 April, at http://iranmatters.belfercenter.org/.

Ahmad, S. 2013. 'Monsoons and geopolitics', *The News*, 21 June.

Baker, P. 2014. 'If Not a Cold War, a Return to Chilly Rivalry', *New York Times*, 18 March.

Bardhan, P. 2010. *Awakening Giants, Feet of Clay: Assessing the Economic Rise of China and India,* New Delhi: Oxford University Press.

Bhagwati, J. and A. Panagariya. 2013. *Why Growth matters: How Economic Growth in India Reduced Poverty and the Lessons for Other Developing Countries.* New York: Public Affairs.

Center for Policy Research. 2012. *Nonalignment 2.0.* 1 February. New Delhi: Center for Policy Research at www.cprindia.org/sites/default/files/Nonalignment%202.0_1.pdf.

Chatterjee Miller, M. 2013. 'India's Feeble Foreign Policy', *Foreign Affairs*, May/June.

Chaudhry, S. 2014. 'Modi's four different avatars', *Express Tribune*, 8 June.

Chaudhury, D. R. 2014. 'India Likely to Sign Another Defence Pact with Vietnam', *Economic Times*, 21 October.

Chawla, P. 2014. 'Modi Faces Bigger Threat from Wily Civil Servants than Political Opponents', *New Indian Express*, 11 August.

Cohen, S. P. and S. Dasgupta, 2010. *Arming Without Aiming: India's Military Modernization*. Washington, D.C: Brookings.

Colby, E. and B. Glosserman, 2012. 'Asia Real "America Problem"', *PacNet*, No. 16, Honolulu, Hawaii: Pacific Forum CSIS, 13 March.

Das, G. 2002. *India Unbound: The Social and Economic Revolution from Independence to the Global Information Age*. New York: Anchor, (paperback).

Deshpande, R. and S. Dasgupta. 2013. 'PM: Old theories of alliances no longer relevant', *Times of India*, 25 October.

Dreze, J. and A. Sen. 2013. *An Uncertain Glory: India and Its Contradictions*. New Delhi: Penguin.

Fackler, M. 2014. 'Japan offers support to nations in disputes with China', *New York Times*, 30 May.

Garnaut, J. 2014. 'Narendra Modi and Toni Abbott reveal new India-Australia military agreement', *Sydney Morning Herald*, November 2014, http://www.smh.com.au/federal-politics/political-news/narendra-modi-and-tony-abbott-reveal-new-indiaaustralia-military-agreement-2014 1118-11ou05.html.

Getz, B. 2014. 'Inside the Ring: Pentagon reevaluating Obama's pivot to Asia', *Washington Times*, 5 March.

Gray, C. S. 2010. *The Strategy Bridge: Theory for Practice*. New York: Oxford University Press.

Gupta, D. 2010. *The Caged Phoenix: Can India Fly?* Palo Alto, CA: Stanford University Press.

Heritage, T. 2014. 'Russia says NATO reverts to Cold War-era mindset', Reuters, *Yahoo! News*, 2 April, at http://news.yahoo.com/russia-says-nato-reverts-cold-war-era-mindset-130230158--sector.html.

Karnad, B. 1994. 'India's Weak Geopolitics and What to do About It' in B. Karnad (ed.), *Future Imperilled: India's Security in the 1990s and Beyond*, pp. 16–84, New Delhi: Viking, Penguin India.

———. 2005 [First Edition 2002]. *Nuclear Weapons and Indian Security: The Realist Foundations of Strategy*, Chs. 2 & 3. New Delhi: Macmillan India.

———. 2005. 'Aim low, hit lower', *Seminar*, Issue No. 545, at www.india-seminar.com/2005/545/545%20bharat%20karnad3.htm.

———. 2008. *India's Nuclear Policy*, Westport, CN, & London: Praeger Security International.

Khanna, A. 2013. 'At Oxford University India Day, Salman Khurshid compares China to ATM Machine', *DNA*, 14 June.

Knowlton, B. 2014. 'McCain Calls China a "Rising Threat" in Baucus Confirmation Hearing', *New York Times*, 29 January.

Lin, J. 2013. 'Navigating US-China Relations: Complicated by China's "Unrelenting Strategy"', *PacNet*, No. 15, Pacific Forum, CSIS, Honolulu, Hawaii, 5 March.

Londono, E. 2014. 'Hagel seeks to reassure allies in Asia amid questions about U.S. commitment', *Washington Post*, 5 April.

Luce, E. 2008 (reprint edn). *In Spite of the Gods: The Rise of Modern India.* New York: Anchor.

MacFarquhar, N. 2014. 'Russia 2 Neighbors Form Economic Union That Has a Ukraine-Size Hole', *New York Times*, 29 May.

MacFarquhar, N. and D. M. Herszenhorn. 2014. 'Hostile West has Russia exploring ties in China', *New York Times*, 20 May.

Menon, S. 2014. 'This Foreign Policy Moment', Speaking Notes, *Workshop for Oxford Handbook on IFP*, 9 January. (Text emailed to the author).

Meyer, H. and E. Pismennaya. 2014. 'China Embraces a Russia Cut off From Western Capital', *Businessweek*, 16 October.

Nagao, S. 2014. 'Why Japan needs India as Strategic Partner', *Defence and Security Alert*, 4 April, at http://www.dsalert.org/int-experts-opinion/international-geo-politics/516-why-japan-needs-india-as-strategic-partner.

Nasr, V. 'A Great-Power Outage', *New York Times*, 23 May, 2014.

Nath, K. 2008. *India's Century.* New York: McGraw Hill.

Nayyar, D. 2014. 'The West and the Rest', *Economic Times*, 13 January.

Newman, S. 2013. 'Why India's Mars Mission Is So Much Cheaper Than NASA's', *Non-Proliferation Review*, 5 November, at http://www.npr.org/blogs/thetwo-way/2013/11/04/243082266/why-indias-mars-mission-is-so-much-cheaper-t.

Pant, H. and J. M. Super. 2013. 'Balancing Rivals: India's Tightrope between Iran and the United States', *Asia Policy*, 15, January.

Patranobis, S. 2014. 'China set on making Xi's visit a success', *Hindustan Times*, 3 September.

Peel, M. and D. Sevastopulo, 2014. 'Hanoi faces tricky balancing act in standing up to Beijing', *Financial Times*, 5 May.

Prakash, A. 2014. 'Life after Henderson Brooks', *Asian Age*, 7 April.

Reuters. 2014. 'U.S. urges India to step up as regional power', 8 August, 2014 at http://in.reuters.com/article/2014/08/09/india-usa-defence-idINKBN0G90FB20140809.

Roy, S. 2014. 'PM signal: sitting down with Japan, standing up to China', *Indian Express*, 2 September.

Saran, S. 2014. 'India-China border dispute—Coping with asymmetry', *Business Standard*, 13 April.

Schmidt, J. R. 2014. 'Has India peaked?', *Washington Quarterly*, *37* (3), Fall, http://twq.elliott.gwu.edu/has-india-peaked.

Sen, T. 2014. 'The Bhai-Bhai Lie: The False Narrative of Chinese-Indian Friendship', *Foreign Affairs*, 11 July, at http://www.foreignaffairs.com/articles/141630/tansen-sen/the-bhai-bhai-lie?cid=nlc-foreign_affairs_this_week-071814-the_bhai_bhai_lie_5-071814&sp_mid=46486590&sp_rid=Z29uZGVlemFAZ21haWwuY29tS0.

Shahid, S. 'Spillover Effect: ISIS making inroads into Pakistan, Afghanistan', *Express Tribune* (Islamabad), 3 September.

Smith, C. 1994. *India's Ad Hoc Arsenal: Direction or Drift in Defence Policy?* Oxford, UK: Oxford University Press and SIPRI.

Taneja, N. and S. Bimal, 2014. 'Indo-Pak gas deal is more than hot air', *Business Standard*, 7 October.

Tiezzi, S. 2014. 'China, Russia Seek Expanded Defense Cooperation', *Diplomat*, 19 November, at http://thediplomat.com/2014/11/china-russia-seek-expanded-defense-cooperation/.

Thranert, O. 2013. 'China's Nuclear Arms Build-up: Background and Consequences', *CSS Analysis in Security Policy*, No. 140, September, ETH Zurich: Center for Security Studies, at www.css.eth.ch/publications/pdfs/CSS-Analysis-140-EN.pdf.

Twining, D. 2013. 'The Future of U.S.-China Relations: From Conflict to Concert', *International Spectator*, 48 (2).

1

India, a Great Power

What Kind?

In the Hindu epic, the Ramayana, at a crucial moment when he is about to go into battle against the armies of the mighty king Ravana, the Monkey God Hanuman loses his composure and self-confidence, and finds himself questioning his own abilities even as everybody around cheers him on, expecting him easily to beat the enemy. Trying to get him out of the funk he is in, his friend Jambuwan, the Bear, reminds Hanuman of his enormous powers and how it was time for him to shake off his diffidence and use them, which he does with predictable success.

India is a latter day Hanuman, potentially powerful but dwarfed by doubts, unsure of its strengths, weighed down by a sense of its own weaknesses, hobbled by lack of political will, and tending to be slow, low key, and to playing-it-safe to avoid trouble and, unlike the Monkey God in the Ramayana, with no assurance it will rise to the occasion. India is the classic under-achiever among would-be great powers; while aspiring to do big things it is, nevertheless, unwilling and seems incapable of mobilizing the necessary conviction and effort. It boasts of all the traditional elements believed necessary for a state to become a great power—geography, natural resources, one of the largest economies, industrial capacity, population with a large and talented middle class, a meaningful military, and a potentially effective government and diplomacy (Morgenthau 1967: 108–58). The crucial issue is whether the existing Indian state can extract value and the desired outcome from these attributes of the Indian nation. A 2000 Rand report on 'Measuring National Power in the Post-Industrial Age', concluded that the ability of a country in an international milieu to exploit the underway 'science-based knowledge revolution' will depend critically on 'a nation's political direction' and that will require 'a minimally efficient state' (Tellis et al. 2000: xiii). An inefficient state unable to govern well is, however, the Indian reality; it seems incapable of giving India political direction and improving the country's great power prospects. Then again, India is not a post-industrial society, but an industrializing one that is at the cutting edge in some respects, such as information technology powering the modern knowledge-based world and 'frugal engineering'. The telescoping of the pre-industrial and post-industrial milieus has created a chasm in a society with one foot in medievalist ethos (deep-rooted feudal traditions, serfdom, women treated as chattel, honour killings, female foeticide and infanticide) and the other foot in the modern age. 'Socialist-populist' policies catering to the poor in a vigorously democratic society are at odds, for instance, with the economic measures needed to keep the manufacturing sector growing and the showpiece information technology (IT) industry at the sharp end. Indeed, the sudden spectacular surfacing of the country's prowess in the informatics/computer sector led many to assume the country could bypass the intervening smoke-stack stage of industrialization altogether and emerge as a full-blown knowledge economy and a 'geek super power'.[1] The campuses of software giants, such as Infosys are—like those in Silicon Valley, California—immaculate, while outside their gates the real India of abysmal roads and other infrastructure, haphazard traffic, and reigning chaos intrudes. Given the paucity of electricity the choice between having IT companies working at peak efficiency with uninterrupted power or distributing electricity, even if unevenly owing to antiquated transmission technology, to the surrounding villages where more voters reside, is easy for the local politicians to make in a rambunctious democracy. It is another matter that IT parks and big corporate campuses—enclaves of first worldism—resorting to captive power generation units and becoming independent of the grid only increases the development dilemma for the country. To work through such anomalous situations democratically requires more time than the six-odd decades India has so far had. On the other hand, the view of the same Rand report that national power is 'expressed ultimately in terms of warfighting capabilities' and 'projectible power' which 'in the anarchic system of international politics, constitutes [a country's] first line of defence' is more readily achievable for India (Tellis et al. 2000). But this sort of thinking is missing in government as is the desire to yoke national resources, effort and capabilities to a larger purpose.

This chapter will analyze the various notions of great power that have animated the thinking of the Indian government and the 'priviligentsia' and shaped public policy since independence, in particular the view that soft power by itself is sufficient to propel the country to the great power ranks. It is the preferred route to great power because it is an easier, less strenuous, path, at once demanding less of both the people and the government, and the reason why it won't get the country very far.

Nehruvian Paradigm

It was not always this way. In the decade after Independence in 1947, when the country was traumatized by Partition (with the rump state of Pakistan spinning away into its own orbit), weakened by the division of the previously unitary strategic and economic space, burdened by massive poverty and illiteracy, and having negligible resources, India, paradoxically, had a surfeit of vision and was visibly active in world affairs. The extent and scale of deprivation and of socio-economic disparities in the country were daunting but did little to dampen the spirit or discourage India's first Prime Minister, Jawaharlal Nehru, from laying claim to a role in the international arena as leader of the Third World.[2] Nehru matters because the policy grooves he etched are the rut India's foreign and military policies are stuck in to this day.

By the time Nehru, the widely-travelled Cambridge University-educated barrister, assumed the leadership of the interim Indian government in 1946, he had fairly strong views on the economic order the country should have, what its foreign policy should be, how India should conduct itself on the world stage and to what end. His insights into the international system helped him muscle India on to the global arena post-Second World War and to unselfconsciously assume the leadership of a multitude of nations in Asia and Africa still in colonial bondage, recently freed, or in the process of gaining independence, which grouping of states congealed into the Nonaligned Movement and was touted as a buffer between the rival super powers in the Cold War. Nehru marshaled the force of moral suasion, and pushed the United States and Soviet Union locked in ideological combat into a situation they were unaccustomed to being in, namely, on the defensive, such as on the issue of nuclear disarmament. Nehru ultimately failed to parlay India's enhanced position into great power status, in the main, because moral posturing without the wherewithal of power amounts to pretence, and the country's economic and military power then was only embryonic.

Nehru, with his background in natural sciences saw modern India as molded by scientific method that would not leave 'things to chance or fate' with development and the task of raising the country from the depths of Third World despond being reduced to a 'mathematical formula' with little room for 'ideological debate' (Priestland 2012: 158). Rationally, he assessed India's various qualities, including its then under-developed economic resources and its potential to become a leader among nations. In early 1947, a few months before formal independence from Britain, the Interim Government he headed convened what was billed as the 'First Asian Relations Conference' in New Delhi. Addressing a hall full of delegations and observers from some 28 Asian countries and new states in the process of becoming, including 'Jewish Palestine', and observers from institutions in the West, Nehru spoke feelingly and at length about the deep and abiding cultural links India had with all Asian countries and, not so subtly, its impress on the extended region, which many visiting delegations warmly acknowledged. Nehru staked India's claim to leadership of this bloc of nations, his inaugural address—delivered extempore, as he did all his speeches—mixed realism, idealism, and emotion to enunciate certain principles that have since become the stock-in-trade of Indian foreign policy (Asian Relations Organization 1948: 32–67). After stating baldly that it 'was only fitting India play her part' in, what he described as, 'a new period of history', Nehru spelled out the geographic logic of India's potential as the premier Asian-qua-great power. India, he asserted, 'is the natural centre and focal point of the many forces at work in Asia', and reminded the audience that 'Geography is a compelling factor and geographically [India] is situated as to be the meeting point of western and northern and eastern and southeast Asia.' Far from targeting the West for its colonizer role, Asian countries, he declared, appreciated their contributions to 'human progress' and sought cooperation with them. Nehru was emphatic, however, that Afro-Asian countries 'do not intend to be the playthings of others or 'pawns' and, even less, 'petitioners in Western courts and chanceller-ies'. Further, he defined the role of Asian nations in the atomic age as maintaining international peace and, as between Washington and Moscow, attachment with neither—a stance geared to avoid taking sides, keeping out of trouble, and acting as a *cordon sanitaire* pre-venting the principal powers from coming to nuclear blows (Asian Relations Organization 1948: 21–6).

Nehru's relying on geography not only underlined India's physical and cultural connectedness with the countries of Asia but, as he saw it, their inter-twined destinies. In his speech, he dwelt separately on the close historical connections and social and cultural intercourse India had over several millennia with each of the regions and major countries of Asia, which trade, religion, travel, and military con-quests had facilitated. Nehru was obviously trying to establish India's 'power of political attraction' predicated on state behaviour, which attribute the sinologist Owen Lattimore writing in the 1940s said was possessed by only three countries America, Russia, and China (Lattimore 1945: 88). Lattimore was thus the first to explicate the concept that in more recent times has been termed 'soft power' (Nye, Jr . 2004). By making much of its cultural and historical intimacy with other Asian nations, Nehru sought to project India as a natural friend, ally, and empathetic leader of this group who, as spokesman, would make the case for Asian states in world councils. Collecting 'smaller nations of the world round us,' observed Nehru candidly, is 'opportunistic in the long run' and not prompted purely by idealism (Nehru 1953: 213). Nehru's *realpolitik* was also motivated by the unfolding situation in which the two super powers having polarized the international system, the leadership of the uncommitted nations in the middle seemed up for grabs, and the state assuming leadership stood to gain enormous leverage. 'If we line up on one side [the] potential importance and bargaining power are lost', wrote Nehru, who functioned as his own Minister for External Affairs, in a Note to his Foreign Secretary. In the same document dated 14 August, 1948, he opposed the signing of the 'treaty of friendship, commerce and navigation' with the United States and explained his thinking thus. Not tying up with the US or its 'economic policy', he said, will mean 'Keeping a free hand' which, ultimately, will fetch India 'more from [America] and at the same time get the friendship and cooperation' of countries of the Soviet bloc as well (Nehru 1988: 629). He appreciated that the more India kept aloof the more its political value would increase and the more it would be wooed by powerful countries. This was in keeping with the historical precedent of other would-be great powers, including the United States, that kept away from entangling alliances in the initial period of their rise in order to secure, as Bismarck shepherding a unified Germany to pivot position in the mid-nineteenth century Europe put it, 'independence of decision...without pressure or aversion from or attraction to foreign states...'[3]

Nehru was no slouch, moreover, in apprehending competition in the Asian leadership race and for his nonalignment philosophy. He tamped down on attempts by other leaders and countries in the extended region to gain a following and form rival groups, especially those seeking U.S. assistance. He successfully squelched, for example, the effort by the Philippines to call an Asian conference in 1949 as follow-up to the New Delhi Meet, not least because its President, Elpidio Quirino, mooted a 'Pacific Union' and asked directly for the United States to help 'in this perilous hour so that Asia will not be lost to communism by default.'[4] As an arch realist, and unlike later Indian Prime Ministers, Nehru understood that India's soft power attributes would be as nothing if not stiffened with military steel. He therefore planned on discussing at the Delhi Meet a pan-Asian collective security system based principally on the capabilities of the Indian Army—the most battle-tested of the Asian militaries, but desisted from doing so owing to the sensitivities of many participating nations.[5] There was enough wariness evident at the conference about the Indian Army considering it was used by Britain to suppress local freedom movements in Southeast Asia to warrant Nehru's forsaking discussion on the 'Defence and Security questions' that otherwise were at the top of the 'preliminary Agenda' drawn up by the Indian hosts.[6] He did, however, unveil his scheme for collective security in which India would play a central role a scant three months later on 9 August 1947, six days prior to the formal transfer of power. Significantly, he called his security arrangement—the 'Asian Monroe Doctrine'. As the U.S. original 'had saved America from foreign aggression for nearly a hundred years', its analog in this part of the world, Nehru argued, would have a similar effect in Asia and needed 'to be expounded'. But he failed to follow up on the idea then, or later owing to what he perceived as continued resistance to this idea by Asian states. As will become clear, he did, however, implement the part of it to do with relying on America as the friendly distant power to lean on for overarching safety and security, much as the fledgling American republic, as part of its Monroe doctrine, had informally relied on the Royal Navy to keep a predatory Spain and Portugal away from Central and South America. While India's existing military capabilities may have made many delegations at the Asian Relations Conference wary, it inspired confidence in Nehru that the Indian armed forces could prop up his Monroe Doctrine stance to keep foreign powers out of Asia. By the end of the Second World War in 1945, the pre-Partition Indian Army had established its standing as a tried and tested fighting force, having defeated the Imperial Japanese land forces in South East Asia and, as the main force in the Allied Eighth Army, beaten Rommel's *Afrika Korps* in the Maghreb. With two Air-borne Divisions India was one of only five countries in the world at the time to have power projection capability, the others being the United States, Soviet Union, United Kingdom, France, and Turkey. India during the War, moreover, had emerged as the 'eastern arsenal', the logistics and manufacturing hub producing and supplying victuals and military hardware ranging from trucks, artillery, infantry weapons and ammunition, to fighter planes and bombers, manufactured or assembled in a host of ordnance factories and privately-owned production plants established all over India to meet the war needs. Two Allied Commands—the Cairo-based Middle East Command and the Kandy (Sri Lanka)-headquartered South East Asia Command drew on India for manpower and war materiel to fight the Axis Powers (Wainwright 1994). Nehru, in fact, hoped India would emerge as a 'self-supporting defence entity' with the wartime defence industrial base modernized and expanded to supply military goods to states within the nonaligned group and his Asian Monroe Doctrine ambit (Hiranandani 2005: 4–6).

As a keen student of world history, Nehru mooted an 'Asian', rather than a purely 'Indian', Monroe Doctrine to achieve the twin-objectives of making India a nodal military power and obtaining the collective security system as inclusive as the third bloc of unaligned 'nations' he had gathered at the New Delhi Conference without ruffling many feathers or having fellow Asian states see this as a threatening move. He hoped it would produce a result similar to the original U.S. Doctrine: An Asia freed of foreign presence and threat of European interventions (Karnad 2005: 472–3). Speaking on the subject of India's security responsibility for the extended region during his first official visit to the United States in Fall 1949 at the Overseas Press Club in New York, he envisioned an expansive role for his country. 'India cannot ignore certain responsibilities which have been thrust upon her. India's pivotal position' he said, 'made it the crossroads of that part of the world. India is the central point of the Asian picture,' and added that 'Trade and defense are bound to be common bonds amongst nations in that area'. He concluded by saying that 'India's role of leadership…is something we cannot escape' (Nehru 1992: 326). By then his belief that India had the necessary mettle to serve as the fulcrum for a continent-wide Monroe Doctrine-type system, was fortified by a 'top secret' appreciation of India's military capability dated 11 May 1946, by Field Marshal Claude Auchinleck, the British commander-in-chief of the Indian Army, which lauded the country 'as an efficient base for modern war'.[7] India began in earnest to fulfill the role envisaged for it as a friendly source of military expertise. Pilot training by the Indian Air Force (IAF), for instance, was sanctioned by Nehru for the Indonesian, Egyptian, Afghan, and Iraqi air forces in the 1950s.[8] Nehru was, however, also pulled in the opposite non-military direction by, what Jaswant Singh, Minister for External Affairs in the Bharatiya Janata Party government (1998–2004), called the 'ersatz pacifism' of the immediate post-[Mahatma]Gandhi years, which was 'excessively flaunted' as an 'attribute of new India' (Singh 2013: 8). Nehru was drawn in a third direction by the secret security commitment by the United States which, in his mind, perhaps, also provided the undergirding for the Indian Monroe system Nehru hoped to install. The U.S. Department of Defense, for example, drafted plans in the mid-1950s for the 'Defense of India' against a Chinese-assisted 'Communist revolution' to takeover India or an attack by the Chinese People's Liberation Army (PLA).[9] Nehru acquiesced in these contingency plans because he perceived by then the inability of the partitioned Indian Army to take on the PLA, the economic weakness of the country, and the gravity of the internal security threat from the Soviet and Chinese-supported Communist Party of India, which he described as 'indulging in violence and sabotage' and being 'in practically open revolt' in several parts of the country.[10] Indeed, U.S. President Dwight D. Eisenhower's National Security Council Review (NSC 5701) of January 1957 specifically stressed the importance to the United States of 'a strong India…[as] a successful example of an alternative to Communism in the Asian context' and expected 'the gradual development [by India] of the means to enforce its external security interests against Communist Chinese expansion into South and South-East Asia.' To stanch the apprehensions in Washington about a strong India negatively impacting American interests, the Review asserted that 'the risks from a weak and vulnerable India would be greater than the risks of a stable and influential India' (Karnad 2005: 134) In effect, Eisenhower was prepared to bet on an economically and militarily powerful India as the bulwark of a secure and stable Asia. It is thinking that resonated with the policy of President George W. Bush to help India become a 'major global power' in the twenty-first century, leading to the mooting of a 'strategic partnership' between the two countries (Parry 2006).

China, however, was Nehru's blind spot, and it has remained so for Indian foreign policy makers ever since. His romantic idea of India and China leading Asia did not cater for the phenomenon of natural friends and natural adversaries or rivals nor reckon with the hardboiled Communist regime. Once his Asian Monroe Doctrine concept failed to take-off, he soured on lesser, more realistic, and more practicable security configurations sought by neighbouring states as defence against China, in particular Myanmar (Burma), Sri Lanka (Ceylon) and even Pakistan under General Ayub Khan who early apprehended Chinese aggression and sought resolution of disputes and proposed a subcontinental security pact (which proposals will be discussed in the next chapter).

Nehru obviously expected Tibet's autonomy to be respected by Beijing, and hoped that the vast Tibetan landmass would continue to act as a strategic barrier separating India and China and keep the peace between them. But with Tibet under military attack from the Chinese PLA bent on annexing it, Nehru failed to make the necessary adjustments in his strategic calculus despite many warnings. In November 1950, his no-nonsense Home Minister Vallabhbhai Patel alerted him to Beijing deluding India 'by professions of peaceful intention', and urged Nehru to wake up to the 'new situation' arising from 'the disappearance of Tibet....and the expansion of China almost up to our gates'. Patel sought 'comprehensive' action 'involving not only our defence strategy and state of preparations' but also a way to deal with the linked 'internal security' problem created by Indian communists now able to access Chinese arms.[11] It is possible Patel's missive to Nehru was influenced by two official documents left behind by the departing British. The 1938 Memorandum on 'the Mongolian fringe' by colonial India's Foreign Secretary, Olaf Caroe, advised ridding the Himalayan states immediately bordering India— Nepal, Bhutan and Sikkim, of Tibetan religious and cultural influences to prevent Chinese claims on Tibet extended to these Indian protectorates and to preserving Tibet's impenetrability (Karnad 1994: 30–1). And, following up on Caroe's analysis, Lieutenant General Francis Tuker, the last British officer to command India's Eastern Army, in his 1946 paper on 'India's Mongol Frontier' forecast the emerging threat from China to the subcontinent and urged the preemptive deployment of Indian armed forces to the Tibetan plateau 'to prevent [its] military occupation' by the Chinese (Singh 2009: 564–5). Caroe's, Tuker's, and Patel's warnings went unheeded. Instead, Nehru went in for a muffled response, stressing the value of not turning Communist China into an enemy. In another context, he called this a policy of 'hedging or just avoiding pitfalls... a positive, constructive policy...of deliberately trying to avoid hostility' (Nehru 1991a: 254). He decided against ordering the Indian Army into Tibet as Tuker had recommended as also the lesser option of an immediate and rapid military and border infrastructure buildup that Patel had advised because he feared these actions would send the wrong signals, end up reinforcing the aggressive approach Beijing had adopted (Garver 2001: 48). The consolidation of the Chinese presence in Tibet and the continued absence of military preparedness of India meant that its security against China in the 1950s lay in the contingent deployment of American military forces as per the U.S. Department of Defense plans. Not only did Nehru not think that relying on the United States military was unusual for a country claiming to be nonaligned, but that it was natural for India to do so in other areas as well.[12] Nehru's acquiescence in the Pentagon's plans, for obvious reasons, is not acknowledged by the Indian government. It is another matter that these plans did not materialize as Nehru had hoped with direct military intervention when his China policy went horribly wrong and a border war ensued in 1962 (Karnad 2005: 153–9).

Divergent Paths to Great Power

Big and resourceful countries can try and become great powers in the modern day through various routes, but bulking up economically is the necessary prerequisite. China and India constituted 24.4 per cent and 22.3 per cent respectively of the world GDP in 1700 which position of near parity in economic strength was again reached only in 1950 but at much lower levels with China responsible for 4.6 per cent of the world GDP and India 4.2 per cent. By 2003, however, while the Chinese GDP hit the 15.1 per cent level, India's had crept up to only a third as much, at 5.5 per cent (Maddison 2007: 381, table A.6). The economic re-emergence of India and China in the first two decades of the twenty-first century have caused ripples, highlighting their diverging pathways to great power. Post-1945 China looked long, assessed the turbulent present, and was determined to recover the country's past greatness; its revolutionary leadership under Maozedong aiming for primacy in world affairs by acquiring the paraphernalia of hard power and challenging the US and other Western imperial powers responsible for the country's 'Century of humiliation' and the international system they dominated. Beijing played hard ball so well—acquiring thermonuclear weapons in 1967 a scant three years after testing a basic fission device, it compelled the United States, prompted by the Cold War geopolitical imperative to curb Soviet power, to sue for peace on Chinese terms in 1972. Under Dengxiaoping, the 'great helmsman', these terms extended to

the opening of American and European markets to Chinese manufactures resulting in the rapid rise of China to its current status as
an economic and trading power *non pareil* with matching political
and military punch. Further, the Chinese revolutionary leadership
steeled by the warfare they had conducted during the Second World
War against Imperial Japan and Generalissimo Changkaishek's U.S.
assisted Koumingtang armies, had better understanding of military
prowess as a political and diplomatic tool and a heightened grasp
of realpolitik and geostrategy. India, on the other hand, beneficiary
of a peaceful transfer of power, was led by stalwarts of the freedom
movement, mostly lawyers, who stressed moderation, conciliation,
compromise and maintenance of rule of law and stable order at home
and abroad even if the international order and the laws upholding it
ill-served the national interest. China went out and wrenched power
out of the hands of countries having it and, in the process, elicited
fear and respect. A gradualist India, intent on being a 'responsible'
power sought acceptance and accommodation within the prevailing system, displayed a willingness to wait its turn, and succeeded
winning admiration for its forbearance, soft power, and sense of
decorum but little else. Indian leaders, of course, expected that such
good, decent behaviour would be rewarded with great power recognition, which they believed was its natural entitlement. China's
view of attaining power as a zero sum game was in contrast to India's
view of it as recognition by consensus by the global community of
a country's worth. From the end-1970s when China and India were
about on par economically, it took China just 30 years to become a
recognized great power, with a multi-trillion dollar economy margin-
ally behind America's, and with burgeoning military and political
power. In comparison, India in the same period, meandered. It is
clear which path to great power is more efficacious and which view
of great power more realistic.

Ideas About India as Great Power

Nehru's 'globalist' ideas about great power constitute a default position
and continue to animate official Indian thinking on this and many
other aspects of foreign policy.[13] This is so also because it spares newer
generations of leaders and bureaucrats the hard work of familiarizing

themselves with history and current trends in international affairs and diplomacy, or study documents from the official archives to derive useful insights as prelude to mulling policy options, narrowing choices, and making decisions. Thus, retained from Nehru's time is the belief in India's inherent importance, whatever its material status. Describing India as 'the pivot of Asia', Nehru in a 1949 encyclical to chief ministers in the provinces, wrote that India's current strength and value could not be measured in 'gold or silver or exportable commodities, but by virtue of her present position. It is well recognized all over the world,' he added, 'that the future of Asia will be powerfully determined by the future of India (Karnad 2005: 79).' Fast forward 60-odd years and India still figures as a 'swing-state' obtaining equipoise in Asia.[14] The United States cannot counter-balance China by itself, nor can it do so by only partnering Japan and Australia. India's size, location, and resources have made it 'an influential global power' indispensable to building the future, as President Barack Obama said during the Indian Prime Minister Manmohan Singh's 2009 visit to Washington.[15] An indispensable swing-state it may be, but India has still to sort out a host of basic issues regarding its rise, like the kind of global power it wants to be and the strategy it means to use to realize that goal. Publicly, the government has said little about the country's growing military capabilities, explaining them away as necessary for the limited purpose of deterrence and defence.[16] It is less restrained in tom-tomming India's soft power. In fact, a good part of India's diplomatic capital is expended in putting a gloss on this aspect by petitioning Western governments to ease the work visa rules (pertaining to the H1B or L1 visas issued by the U.S.) for skilled Indian labour and winning votes of the growing middle class at home sourcing such labour.[17] This is not the same thing as thinking big, having an outward-looking policy, augmenting force projection capabilities, and securing bases abroad.[18] In fact, this narrowing of India's foreign policy aims in the twenty-first century is the doing of governments of differing ideological persuasions. The coalition regime of the right-of-center Bharatiya Janata Party (BJP), for instance, ordered the nuclear and thermonuclear weapons tests and weaponisation in 1998 but immediately announced a test moratorium leaving the country in the worst possible situation—facing economic sanctions and an under-developed and unproven thermonuclear arsenal (because the fusion weapon tested failed to achieve the designed yield). Next, it equated great power aspirations of the country with the globalization of its economy and, to crown this series of initiatives, negotiated the Next Steps in Strategic Partnership with Washington, which was the precursor accord to the nuclear civilian cooperation deal predicated on India not resuming nuclear testing finalized by the successor left-of-centre Congress Party regime under the economist Prime Minister Manmohan Singh.[19] Manmohan Singh on his part attempted to keep Indian policy in sync with the U.S. views in sensitive areas, such as Iran and nonproliferation, and otherwise talked up high economic growth as the all-purpose panacea for the nation but couldn't muster the political will to push the pedal on economic and administrative reforms to ensure sustained growth.[20] Ten years thus passed without anybody having any idea about how the current set of policies would promote India's great power ambition.

Three Schools of Thought on Great Power

With government not giving the lead, the sort of great power India should try and become remains a matter of conjecture and public debate. There are three schools of thought about what will fetch India great power. The first school believes in soft power as the country's passport to greatness, the second school believes that morality and morally-oriented policies will ensure the country's greatness, and the third school is of the view that India is faced with too many internal problems social and economic disparities and under-development to be distracted by the search for great power. Official programmes and the widely dispersed Indian diaspora are considered the mediums of diffusion of India's soft power. But it is only in the new millennium that governments headed by the BJP, which generates a lot of party funds from Non Resident Indians (NRIs) in the West, discovered the political leverage well-heeled NRIs and NRI organizations wield in the West, such as the America-India Political Action Committee in the United States, to pressure Western governments into adopting India-friendly policies. The acknowledgement by the Indian govern-ment of the NRIs' clout reached its acme with Prime Minister Modi's well-staged addresses, to massively gathered Indian origin-crowds in United States, Canada, Australia during his official visits in 2014.

There's always the high culture showcasing classical music and dance, drama, poetry and literature, couture, fine arts, and cuisine; this is the staple fare in well-mounted 'India Festivals' in prominent cities abroad. The Indian Council of Cultural Relations run by MEA and its newly founded Division for Public Diplomacy, are responsible for running 22 Indian cultural centers in 19 countries, amounting to a systematic use of culture to acquire global influence and promote the country's interests. There are other institutions, such as the India International Institute for Democracy run by the country's Election Commission, for example, which holds training courses for visiting officials from over 50 countries in conducting elections, and is a sophisticated means of spreading the country's democratic influence.[21] Then there's the far more effective popular culture represented by over-the-top Bollywood melodramas, and music and television soap operas, which play a far bigger role in consolidating the India brand in southern and Southeast Asia, West Asia, Central Asia, Africa, and the Caribbean.[22] In the West, the profusion of eateries serving Indian regional cuisines, the popularity of the 'bhangra beat' from Punjab, Indian writers in English winning international literature awards, and the large NRI scientific, engineering, and managerial talent in industrial, corporate, and financial circles strengthen the country's image. Such presence in strength, a onetime junior minister in the Congress government, Shashi Tharoor, contends symbolizes soft power and matters more, he claims, than India's military might (Tharoor 2012: 409). Nicolas Blarel from the London School of Economics while reporting on the undoubted successes of such programmes as the teacher- and software-training projects in Africa, schemes for Buddhist religious and cultural outreach in South East Asia, Japan, and even China, the ubiquity of Indian food, films, and music in many western countries, and the praise for Indian democratic traditions everywhere, charges that India has 'inconsistently capitalized upon these soft power resources' and the references by Indian leaders and officials to Indian culture, diaspora, democratic values, and economic development, he says, 'have mostly been rhetoric for image-polishing.' There is, however, a more fundamental reason why Indian diplomacy has failed to elementally connect with, and score points particularly in, countries in the Indian Ocean basin and states farther afield with whom India is intimately linked by culture and history, notwithstanding, as Blarel notes, 'promotion of a soft power approach through a series of initiatives framed around concepts of "non-reciprocity", "connectivity" and "asymmetrical responsibilities"' (Blarel 2011).

It is because India's foreign policy is mainly big power-oriented, the best Indian Foreign Service officers, other than South Asia are assigned to Western capitals and the Americas and West European Desks in the Foreign Office, with the focus shifting to lesser states only when there is a crisis or an impending state visit. The MEA's inattention to the developing world is ironic considering the supposedly Third World rhetoric of Indian foreign policy, and rankles developing country diplomats posted to New Delhi. Complaints by Asian and African diplomats about the insensitivity of the Indian government to their needs are legion.[23] Actually, inattention may be an improvement on the condescension with which the Indian government routinely treated Asian and African regimes during Nehru's hey-day. With respect to the less-developed countries, Nehru's alter-ego, V.K. Krishna Menon, for example, said: 'Why should we get involved with these third-rate powers; our interests lie with the great powers.'[24] This sort of superior, standoffish, attitude meshed with the proto-great power notions New Delhi entertained about India, which was perhaps also reinforced by the belief that majorly interacting with great powers would lead to some of their great power-ness rubbing off on India. It failed to capitalize on the warmth many governments in the developing world genuinely felt towards India and things Indian.[25] The glow of India's soft power notwithstanding, its political power has since dimmed also because South East Asian states, for example, however illiberal their political systems, have 1970s onwards left India behind, becoming 'little dragons'—economic success stories combining high growth rates and prosperity with good infrastructure, placid domestic politics, and bright prospects. It is hard for states such as Singapore, Malaysia, and Thailand to anymore automatically accept India's presumptive leadership, including in the cultural field. There are therefore limits on what and how much India's soft power can achieve in Asia and elsewhere. A one-time Canadian Ambassador in New Delhi, David Malone, while conceding that India 'enjoys a "soft power" pull' in modern Asia contends that 'the region is unsentimental and to meet India's expectations will continue to demand [more accommodating] Indian engagement than has yet become habitual for Delhi' (Malone 2012: 223) In any case, nobody really believes that soft power alone will propel India into the great power club or that Bollywood dance and drama, or touring sitar-strummers and classical dance troupes will make much of a difference.

It is India's startling successes, beginning in the 1980s, in the information technology field and, coincidentally, of the NRI communities in the West—students from elite Indian engineering, medical, science, and business management schools who went mainly to the United States and Britain for higher education, stayed on, and fared well enough in their professional careers to come to public notice, that led to the Indian Institutes of Technology, Indian Institute of Science, the All India Institute of Medical Sciences, and Indian Institutes of Management acquiring cachet, and for India to be trumpeted as an inexhaustible source of high-quality scientific, engineering, medical, and managerial talent (Debroy 2008). It eventuated in overly optimistic and skewed analyses about how India could wield its skilled manpower to surface as a 'knowledge economy' and great power. In such a world, the influential civilian strategist, the late K. Subrahmanyam, conceived India's grand strategy as dealing with the security threat from terrorism, while outsourcing the tackling of the more potent, strategic military threats faced by the country such as China, to the United States.[26] Such thinking actually had traction in official corridors in the mid-2000s and motivated the India-U.S. civilian nuclear cooperation deal, which its critics had warned would principally divert the Indian nuclear programme from the plutonium route based on the country's vast reserves of easily accessible thorium (some 30 per cent–40 per cent of the world's deposits in the monazite sands of the Coromandel Coast and available for surface strip-mining in the Northeastern hill states) to the imported enriched-uranium fueled reactors. That such diversion would result in depleted funding and consequent lack of development of the indigenous breeder reactor and thorium reactor projects constituting the second and third stages of the 1955 3-stage Bhabha Plan, because of resources being channeled into purchases, prompted by the nuclear deal, of extraordinarily expensive light water reactors from the U.S., France, and Russia. And that this would turn India, a potentially energy-independent state, into an energy dependency and, worse, the foreign reactors and the economy relying on the electricity produced by them, and the country at-large, would all become hostage to policy interests of the supplier states. The critics had also pointed out that should New Delhi gather the courage and resume testing to obtain proven and reliable thermonuclear weapons and a measure of confidence in strategically dealing with China, supplier country sanctions would kick in, the sale of enriched uranium fuel, reactor spares, and servicing support would cease, and the billions of dollars invested in buying and installing foreign reactors would become a dead investment and ecological hazard (Karnad 2008: 150–8; Iyengar et al. 2009). None of these very real possibilities deterred the Congress government which staked its rule on the nuclear deal and survived by the skin of its teeth (aided by some allegedly under-handed shenanigans) in the July 2008 vote of confidence in Parliament.

Such an extraordinarily blinkered policy injurious to the most strategically decisive nuclear programme was justified by Manmohan Singh with his mantra of '20,000 megawatts by 2020'. It remained a 'pie in the sky' promise by the time he demitted office. His National Security Adviser (NSA) and former diplomat, Shivshankar Menon, explained the nuclear deal and the Indian posture generally as reflecting 'strategic restraint' imposed by economic priorities. India, he elaborated, is a 'unique sort of big power' intent on improving the lot of its people. 'Eliminating poverty and realizing India's potential will be the focus of our efforts—not external entanglements, arms races or other such balance of power distractions. For the foreseeable future, strategic restraint will probably be India's strategic choice.'[27] While disavowing any desire or intention to work the country up to the level of great power, or even an influential power, he did concede the possibility that if, without really trying, the country reached that status, 'that would be fine'.[28] This view of India as an accidental great power, of this status achieved less by design than happenstance, is unique, revealing the vapid thinking and complacency that has shaped Indian policies for a long time. On the other hand, it may be that such a position was deliberately taken to avoid getting the gander up of extant great powers, who would otherwise be inclined actively to impede India's climb up the great power ladder. After all, why would the present lot of great powers want to ease the entry into their ranks of an aspirant state such as India? Thus, Washington continues to warn New Delhi against resumption of nuclear test-ing, for example, on the pain of termination of the nuclear deal and renewal of sanctions.[29] But this raises the question whether such great power recognition as India may secure at another country's sufferance actually makes India a genuine great power? What is also worrying about Menon's conceiving great power in this way is that it separates cause and effect, rendering the process of India's becoming a great power into a mysterious, even magical, occurrence. Why a straight-forward expression of great power as a national goal was eschewed is not clear. Possibly, it was a policy habit of mind of the MEA acquired after Nehru's high-strutting diplomacy crashed to the ground and the national ego was dented by the military defeat in the 1962 war with China so much so as to convince the foreign policy mandarins to, as much as possible, fly under the radar and advance national interests by stealth. The best possible spin that can be given to it is that not dwelling publicly either on India's meaningful military capability or its ramifications for the existing regional and international power balance echoes German Chancellor Bernhard von Bulow's injunc-tion from the early 1900s, when the German Navy was sought to be enlarged on the sly lest it provoke Britain. 'We must operate so care-fully,' he had advised his government, 'like the caterpillar before it has grown into the butterfly.'[30] A more trivial reading of the situation could be that it was only logical for a regime headed by an 'accidental prime minister', which is how Manmohan Singh described himself, to conjure up an India as an accidental great power (Baru 2014).

If, on the other hand, the former NSA's views are taken literally, and the great power end-state is seen as an unintended consequence of a series of events that India did not initiate, does not control, and has made no concerted effort to realize in the first place, then it is rea-sonable to conclude that, because great power doesn't happen by luck or chance, India will never become one. In the real world, countries contest every little bit of political, economic, diplomatic, technologi-cal, and military space and claw for slivers of relative advantage. The international system, moreover, does not concede much or easily, and certainly not bestow great power status on a shrinking violet of a country as an act of charity or by way of altruism. The Darwinian slant to the ascent of a country to great power highlights clear vision, iron will, military capability, and coercive policies when these become necessary (Dietl 2008). A contrary sort of expectation has, however, been nursed by many in the Indian strategic community and informs official deliberations as well.[31] The feeling that India will be a great power because, well, it is India, is a historically perpetuated idea at the heart of Indian foreign policy, which was given a fillip by the U.S. policy emphasizing the importance of India to security and stability in Asia.[32] It has stirred in the official Indian mind the sense of inevitability of India's recognition as great power, that the country doesn't have to do anything other than just be, and continue to do what it is doing to, in time, become one. This was reflected in a public lecture in August 2011 by Menon who averred that 'a country with one-sixth of humanity, a large and fast growing economy, situated in a vital spot on multiple political fault-lines, with a great civilization and a consistent foreign policy…was bound to become a great power'.[33]

The idea about the inevitablity of India as a great power, of this status as the country's natural entitlement, something there for asking, can be sourced to Nehru. It never occurred to him that India had to earn it or, if offered on a platter by a concatenation of events and circumstances, to grab it. Indeed, the entitlement syndrome merged with Nehru's benign attitude towards China to majorly hurt the country's interest in terms of formally occupying a great power seat. He obviously misread the value of Security Council membership despite India's bad experience with big power machinations in the Council on the Kashmir issue. Nehru felt little would be lost and Chinese goodwill gained by his advocacy on behalf of the then politically pariah Communist China to occupy a permanent seat in the U.N. Security Council first offered to India separately by the United States and the Soviet Union in the 1950s (to replace Koumingtang China or Taiwan). In a note written on his return from a visit to the USSR in the mid-1950s concerned with the interest of both superpowers in having India as member in the top UN body, Nehru wrote: 'Informally, suggestions have been made by the United States that China should be taken into the United Nations but not in the Security Council and that India should take her place in the Security Council. We cannot', he continued, magisterially, 'of course accept this as it means falling out with China and it would be very unfair for a great country like China not to be in the Security Council. We have, therefore, made it clear to those who suggested this that we cannot agree to this suggestion. We have even gone a little further and said that India is not anxious to enter the Security Council at this stage, even though as a great country she ought to be there. The first to be taken is for China to take her rightful place and then the question of India might be considered separately.'[34] It reflected a delusional strain in Indian policy and a profligate disregard for India's interests that showed a reckless and foolhardy generosity towards a geopolitical adversary of the first order, China, which even then missed no opportunity to revile India and Indian leaders as imperialist stooges. It was a huge strategic blunder and misjudgement among the many Nehru witlessly committed (among which was not nuclear weaponizing when the Indian nuclear programme reached the weapons threshold in early 1964) , revealing an astonishing simplemindedness. Had he not acted so willfully and grasped the opportunity to settle into a permanent seat in the highest U.N decision-making body, India could then have used the promise to help China to get on-board as leverage to ensure policies New Delhi desired, the sort of promise Beijing is now using to try and manipulate Indian policy. Nehru's magnanimity made no impression on the down-to-earth Mao whose attitude did not soften a whit. India was, however, left stranded on the sidelines. In not accepting the mantle of great power when so providentially offered as a result of a convergence of U.S. and Soviet interests (the split in the Communist bloc between the Russia and China was by then in the open) New Delhi relied on Nehru's conviction that as an inherently great country the world body would enhance its own reputation by admitting India into the Security Council at a time of its own choosing, and is today left pleading for 'structural reforms' in the U.N., buttonholing every U.N member for support to get a permanent seat in the Security Council, and periodically contesting elections for temporary membership in this body. This even as Beijing looks on, ready to veto any proposal for expansion of the Council ostensibly because Japan too is in the running. Talk of missing to catch an opportunity by its forelock!

To return to more contemporary times, Shivshankar Menon dilated on great power, particularly the prefix 'great'. Greatness, he opined was 'not merely in the U.N. [Security Council] sense of the word but great in the sense in which [the pacifist Emperor] Ashoka envisaged greatness.' Except, the third century Emperor conquered almost all of South Asia, including what is today Afghanistan by the sword, before discovering Buddhism, and spreading the message of peace (Thapar 1988). To implement the Ashokan model in the present age as means of achieving great power would be easy once all adversaries, including China, in the Indian Ocean region and landward Asia are militarily reduced which, of course, is beyond India's ken—even assuming the U.S. helps out by doing some of the heavy lifting where China is concerned, which last may be too much to expect of an America that will 'spend less [and] be able to do less' (Mandlebaum 2010: 4).

India's quest for international recognition as a great power has been narrowed down to bolstering its reputation as a responsible power. For the last decade and more New Delhi has diligently advertised itself as a 'responsible nuclear power' also to distinguish India from Pakistan and North Korea, who are given to rattling their nuclear sabers and nursing terrorists who could access these weapons or fissile material to put together radiation diffusion devices or 'dirty bombs'.[35] This stance was encouraged by the U.S. government with President Barack Obama repeatedly praising India as 'a rising power and a responsible global power'.[36] The restraint in foreign and military policies that India has come to exemplify—and which its government never fails to thump its chest about—is the result of India striving to hold itself aloof from, what Shivshankar Menon called, the 'seemingly antagonistic' (Sino-Russian) Eurasian and the Atlantic worlds while having the capacity 'to deter and dissuade' both from 'subsuming [India's] independence and undermining [its] security.'[37] Alas, the 'capacity' he is referring to is imaginary, considering the United States and West European states can at any time apply the economic and technology squeeze (by cutting off the flow of credit, capital, and technology, of skilled Indian labour, and market access to Indian goods) and, along-with Russia and Israel, as main suppliers of military equipment can, in fact, disarm India, at any time. The strategic restraint and pragmatism that New Delhi exhibits is, in other words, less a matter of choice than a function of the country's existing vulnerabilities.

Even so, the theme of a restrained and responsible India and its ambition for great power fits in with recent thinking about great power as powerful states exercising 'self-restraint' without which the littlest incident in an 'increasingly fraught international environment, it is contended, could set off a series of events culminating in 'another 1914-like crisis' and world war (Kennedy 2013). The trouble is that restraint as a great power trait fits in a little too comfortably in New Delhi's policy tool kit, legitimating the official view that nothing needs to change as far as the country's attitude, outlook, approach and policies are concerned for India to win by acclamation the great power status it craves. Except, it is precisely India's record of restrained behaviour that robs its policy of the element of unpredictability and surprise, inclining major powers and minor states alike to take India for granted and not feel apprehensive about testing India's resolve or even risk provoking it. When was the last time the United States or China shied away from actions detrimental to India's national interest?[38] Or, Pakistan and China refrained from violating the ceasefire lines separating them from India? (Karnad 2014).

But restraint has been packaged into a bland Indian policy offering as little offence as possible to major states and is a theme that gets folded into the case made by some establishment analysts about how much India's prospects of attaining great power rest on its becoming part of the 'political West' (Raja Mohan 2010). Apparently as equal-opportunity compromisers, the same persons also urge India to join the 'maritime silk route' mapped by Beijing (Raja Mohan 2014). Implicit in such analysis is the assumption that India will subsume Western or Chinese interests as its own, act to further them, and generally accept and be part of a regional and global order shaped by Washington and its NATO allies and China, to serve the respective interests of these major countries as long as India benefits, even if secondarily from such arrangements. That such thinking will never help get great power for India doesn't seem to matter because it still resonates with many in the MEA, signaling the paucity of geopolitical insights and imagination in Establishment corridors, which are tuned to not making waves. However, as Robert Kagan has observed, great power is not about obeying rules and conventions but challenging the prevailing system and upsetting established norms. Great powers, he avers, rarely obey international laws except when it suits them, disregard the prevailing norms and conventions, create their own principles of conduct, are not timid in their outlook or actions, and are disruptive by habit. He ties up these Great Power traits to the fact of abundant military power. Kagan contrasts the U.S. attitude with current European beliefs that spring from military weakness that has led, he claims, to an 'aversion to the exercise of military power [and] has produced a powerful European interest in inhabiting a world where strength doesn't matter, where international law and international institutions predominate, where unilateral action by powerful nations is forbidden, [and all countries] regardless of their strength have equal rights and are equally protected'. Such European thinking, he points out, exactly mirrors American thinking in the eighteenth and nineteenth centuries when the United States was militarily weak (Kagan 2002). In the last several decades, with China behaving in the new century much as the U.S. had done post-World War II, Kagan's thesis would seem to bear out. Except, India, with a growing military heft, is hampered by its own policymakers and strategic community sporting a 'go along to get along' attitude of a country not too eager to go beyond its presumed limitations. New Delhi's eagerness to play the game by the prevailing rules rather than to rewrite them and reshape the game is the big barrier to India's substantively attaining great power. However, India's 'don't rock the boat' bent of mind is why Washington desires it as a strategic partner (Clary 2011).

New Delhi's hard-to-pin-down grand strategy and great power plans in the decade 2004–14 can be gleaned from the five foreign policy principles reportedly conveyed by Prime Minister Manmohan Singh to a conclave of Indian ambassadors in late 2013. All foreign relations, he told the heads of Indian Missions, are to be molded by the country's 'development priorities'. Further, foreign policy, he said, should obtain 'a global environment conducive to the wellbeing of our great country' (which he described as the 'single most important objective'), and 'stable, long-term and mutually beneficial relations with all major powers'. And it ought to work with the 'international community to create a global and security environment beneficial to all nations'. Rounding out this slate was forging connectivity with the states of the subcontinent and engineering policies keeping in mind 'our interests…and [our] values', with these values defined as 'democracy and secularism'. Three of the five principles revolve around the abstract concept of 'wellbeing' and seem unrelated to tensions inherent in the relations with big powers (U.S. and China).

They understate the difficulty of translating the principle of 'mutually beneficial relations with all major powers' into practical policy tenets, and the impossibility of achieving 'global and security environment beneficial to all nations', which may serve as uplifting rhetoric but as policy may harm the national interest. For instance a nuclear weapons-free world would benefit rich countries (U.S., China) with strong conventional militaries. This mélange of unsustainable ideas was labeled, a trifle grandly, as 'the Singh doctrine' by Sanjaya Baru, one-time media adviser to Manmohan Singh. The fact that Indian leaders are easily given to abstraction in their conceptualization of foreign policy may originate in the ancient inclusivist Hindu notion of *Vasudhaiva Kutumbakam*—'the whole world is one family' that they are also fond of mouthing (Baru 2013). Narendra Modi too endorsed this anodyne concept, possibly, to tamp down the expectation he would pursue an assertive foreign policy, starting with revising the nuclear doctrine promised by the BJP's 2014 election manifesto.[39] It is the *deux ex machina* for Indian politicians who have little to say but want to sound good. After all, if international relations is reduced to a family affair, does it really matter which family member wins and which family member loses?

In this imaginary world *sans* discord, use of force, and clash of national interests, good intentions are transparent and goodwill is aplenty, and the need for a powerful military and an agile foreign policy is not immediately evident. It is the sort of vaporous thinking Nehru, perhaps, unwittingly boosted. He nursed a nuclear weapons programme, seeded a defence industry in India, and clearly understood the need for military muscle, but he also displayed palpable unease with the tools of coercion and war. This may be traceable to his years spent in England and the Whiggish belief in the perfectability of man and Kant's notion of 'perpetual peace' distilled in the writings of the pre-First World War anti-militarist Norman Angell.[40] Nehru, moreover, was affected as well by the liberal values and inhibitions the British colonials had succeeded in implanting in the politically conscious Indian elite (Griffiths 1965: 228). He imbibed the hardier British outlook on military power as a tool of strategic assertion but failed to truly appreciate just how much the international hierarchy of nations is defined 'in terms of politico-strategic power'. As the British Conservative Party politician the First Lord Birkenhead observed in

1923 'The world continues to offer glittering prizes to those who have stout hearts and sharp swords' (Clark 1989: ch. 3, 4–5, 7–8). Nehru's contemporary, Charles de Gaulle, said something similar: 'The sword is the axis of the world and its power is absolute.'[41] Nehru perceived the hard power of the state and its projection differently. Reacting to the U.S. show of force in the early years of the Cold War, he wondered 'why a man with such strong muscles should publicly demonstrate his muscles all the time.'[42] He thought this way, perhaps, because of the Hindu cultural premium on self-effacing humility, of the powerful enhancing their virtuous stature by understating their own power. But, there's also the fact that unlike many other prominent leaders on the international scene post-1945—Mao, Stalin, Eisenhower, Churchill, de Gaulle, and Ho Chi Minh, who were warlords and veterans of the school of military hard knocks, Nehru was tempered only by his own ruminations in the long years whiled away in British jails during the freedom movement about how the world should be and what India should do to make it a nicer place for everybody to live in. He failed, in the process, to accord military power its due importance. Because had he done so Nehru would not have stonewalled the great nuclear visionary and founder of the Indian nuclear programme, Dr Homi J. Bhabha's pleas 1961 onwards to approve nuclear testing and weaponization, which would have given New Delhi a telling instrument to handle Beijing and, as the first Asian nuclear weapon state, placed India among the nuclear elite with all the attendant benefits (Karnad 2008: 47–8).

The end-result of being pickled in such influences is the inclination of the Indian political class as much as the policy establishment to decide on the details of policy and to justify them on the basis that its direction and substance are already settled. But faced by the harsh dog-eat-dog reality of inter-state relations and the need to balance regional and international power on the one hand and policy abstractions on the other hand, MEA officials play it safe, preferring talk to action. Thus, Baru blamed 'the foreign ministry and the foreign policy establishment' for turning itself into 'a debating society' in which 'everyone [is] holding forth on grand principles and no one [is] devoting time or attention to getting things done the way [the Prime Minister] wanted' leading to a 'wayward' policy (Baru 2013). Moreover, such is MEA's allergy to the military and the use of force it has turned down Special Forces operations to rescue Indian sailors on merchant ships captured by Somali pirates for ransom. A ship flying the Indian flag, *MV Bhakti Sagar*, was boarded by pirates in February 2006. Naval Headquarters (NHQ) immediately diverted the missile destroyer *INS Mumbai*, with a contingent of Marine commandos, returning home from a goodwill visit to Oman to the area. Instead of an express sanction to apprehend or eliminate the pirates and free the ship and its Indian crew, 'a heated debate and discussion raged in the Cabinet Secretary's office [in New Delhi] about the advisability of sending a warship on this mission', recalled the Naval Chief at the time, Admiral Arun Prakash.

> At the end of these deliberations the MEA sent a written note to NHQ posing a set of rhetorical questions, which came as a revelation about the timidity and lack of resolve that prevails at the policy-making levels. Agonizing about how our African and Middle-Eastern neighbors would react to what was termed 'muscle-flexing' by the Indian navy, the note vividly illustrated why India has rightly earned the sobriquet of a soft state.

Elaborating on the MEA epistle, Prakash added, 'The essence of the note…was contained in one plaintive query which said "Will we sail a destroyer every time an Indian national is in trouble anywhere?" The Navy's emphatic reply [in the affirmative] went unheeded…' The warship was recalled, the ransom demanded by the pirates paid, and the Indian citizens returned home 'without the Indian state or its powerful navy', wrote the Admiral bitterly, 'having lifted a finger to protect them' (Prakash 2011). The right-of-center Bharatiya Janata Party (BJP)-led coalition government of Atal Bihari Vajpayee proved no less fallible when it came to ordering decisive action—as the appeasement of the terrorist hijackers of the Indian Airlines flight IC-814 in December 1999 to Kandahar in Afghanistan demonstrated, even if its rhetoric was more fiery. Elsewhere, it was motivated enough strategically to resume testing of nuclear weapons but did not, in the face of international criticism and threat of sanctions, have the gumption to order further tests as the only way to obtain a thoroughly proven thermonuclear weapons inventory, announcing a 'voluntary moratorium' on testing which has stranded the Indian thermonuclear deterrent short of credibility. It was apparently the price the Vajpayee regime was willing to pay for a rapprochement with the United States. It went to the extent of preparing an Indian Army Division for deployment in Iraq to please President George W. Bush, believing this action conformed, in the words of Jaswant Singh, at different times the minister for External Affairs, Defence, and Finance in the BJP government, with its policy of 'relentless pursuit of one's national interests' (Singh 1999: 34–5).

The more serious deficiency in this great power game plan is the old one afflicting Indian policy after Nehru—there's no grand vision as guidelines for policies and plans, no articulation and gradation of interests ranging from the core, vital or primary, secondary, to tertiary to inform and drive policymaking, no delineation of India's place in the world and the position it should aim to occupy in 20, 30, 50 years time, and no work-chart and detailed game-plan to attain the goals. People in government readily confess that such a vision document or even one detailing the national interests, in fact, has never been drafted; most of them see no need for them. This is notwithstanding the obvious benefits that would accrue from a host of government agencies, the military, the diplomats, and the strategic enclaves in the country, and the innumerable central and state government ministries and government departments and official agencies at all levels, taking their bearing from such documents, being on the same page, pulling in the same direction, and generally working to advance the same set of interests, in order to reach the same clearly specified goal within the set timeframe. It would preclude the usual confusion and cross-cutting policies with ministries working on their different agendas. But that's not to be because the current system is believed to work fine. Shivshankar Menon explained:

> No, there's no single vision document, we don't do that. The way the government works is that we do three levels of things. We do doctrines for different sectors—nuclear, space, cyber, etc.—we…have the operational directive, which is for the short, medium and long terms, which says what [the military] need to prepare for. Then below that [each of the agencies of government] do their own planning…. [W]here it gets integrated is at …the National Security Council level, where executive decision is taken…there's an implicit vision behind all this, but no formal vision statement.[43]

In the event, vision and national interests are assumed to be known to all concerned up and down the government's decision-making ranks.

Thus, in a schematic of 'National Security Concepts and Doctrines' diagrammed in the Indian Maritime Doctrine 2009, there is no box labeled 'Vision'—grand, strategic, or other, and no reference to it there or anywhere else in the text (Integrated Headquarters 2009: 5). The then opposition BJP leader Yashwant Sinha, who was successively Foreign Minister and Finance Minister in the Vajpayee regime, readily acknowledges the absence of a single such document, and generally of 'strategy papers' in the policymaking process as 'a big, big weakness in [the Indian] system', but explains that these documents are not sorely missed because of the immediate pressures that compel policy-makers to 'function literally from hour to hour, day to day'.[44] The policies that eventuate, in the event, tend to be ad hoc, imbued with caution, usually a reaction to some incident or unfolding event, and generally hew to precedent. Thus, the BJP government of Prime Minister Vajpayee substituted the concept of 'strategic autonomy' for the hoary Nehruvian policy of nonalignment, but it did not differ from it in practice. With the return to power of the Congress Party in mid-2004, the nonalignment idea and rhetoric officially made a comeback but was now justified in terms of 'strategic autonomy' it supposedly afforded the country. True, it tried to recapture the nuanced alignments this way and that practiced by Nehru and this was a definite improvement on Indira Gandhi's policies when the grand narrative of India was lost and the sly siding with one or the other super power was replaced by the formal confinements and predilictions of a treaty alliance (in August 1971) with the Soviet Union. 'But, strategic autonomy as an end in itself and unyoked to any grand strategic purpose or even national interest, as nonalignment was in its later years, doesn't get India very far but it has historical precedent. It is reflected, for instance, in the cynical German foreign policy of the mid to late nineteenth century of 'total freedom from prejudice or aversion from or attraction' to any country that was justified by Bismarck thus: "As far as I am concerned as soon as it was proved to me that it was in the interests of a healthy and well-considered Prussian policy, I would see our troops fire on French, Russians, English or Austrians with equal satisfaction."[45] The trouble, alas, is New Delhi is not as readily inclined to exercise hard power (except reactively against Pakistan), which reluctance doesn't further India's great power ambition if any.

All the same, the lack of a vision statement is symptomatic of the Indian establishment's aversion to thinking long term or hard power. M.K. Narayanan, National Security Adviser to Prime Minister Manmohan Singh in 2006–2010, stated baldly at a public function to release the quasi-official blueprint for grand strategy, *Nonalignment 2.0,* in February 2012, that hard power is not 'necessary', soft power is 'India's forte', and 'a too activist a [foreign] policy' should be avoided because becoming a great power requires deployment of scarce resources and, hence, is 'an unaffordable luxury' that an impoverished India cannot afford.[46] In line with such tremulous views, a junior minister in MEA, Shashi Tharoor, conceived of 'Pax Indica' not conventionally as a system of regional and international peace imposed on Indian terms but as redefining the values, rewriting rules of the road, and shaping new norms for a future world of 'cooperative coexistence' to reflect 'India's sense of responsibility to the world' (Tharoor 2012: 427–8). Embellishing such views *Nonalignment 2.0* authored by a group of mostly liberal thinkers of the Nehruvian stripe, excoriated national ambition and power politics. After analyzing the internal and external constraints on India's plans and policies, it declared that India's greatness will be determined by 'the power of its example' and by its setting 'new standards in moral and ideological leadership' and attachment to values, and by its aspiration 'to create a new and alternative universality' (Centre for Policy Research 2012: 1, 63). Trying to realize so much universal good amounts, on the one hand, to loading policy with the familiar moral and other inhibitions and, on the other hand, seeing great power familiarly as an entitlement India richly deserves and a recognition that will be conferred by a world suitably impressed by India's civilizational impact, democratic values fostered in a difficult milieu, its show of restraint and responsible behaviour in the face of provocation, and its willingness to eschew aggravating international tensions and the balance of power dynamic in which the United States and China square off against each other, by siding with neither side (Centre for Policy Research 2012: 1, 63). This is more Nehruvian than anything Nehru had ever practised. How adopting such means will get India to whereever it is headed—even if it is not classical great power position, the document does not say. It invited a riposte of the kind offered, incidentally, by a minister in the Congress coalition government itself. 'We are a self-declared great power, whether we are actually one or not, is a moot point,' asserted Jairam Ramesh, the most outspoken of Manmohan Singh's ministers. 'By all economic indices, we have far to go by way of conventional yardsticks of economic performance. Secondly, a great power recognizes its responsibility. India is yet to do that. India feels that great power is its birth right and, therefore, we feel the world owes us a favour to consider us a great power.'[47] An exalted self-image by itself, however, does not amount to national vision, leave alone strategy, whose absence is noticeable. David Malone, a senior Canadian diplomat, noted that Indian foreign policy 'has been pragmatic, but it has also been devoid of the kind of strategic vision required for India to achieve great power status' (Malone 2012: 72).

It is not surprising then that pronouncements by New Delhi usually avoid trumpeting the country's hard power, or the policy options it generates. The antipathy to the military capabilities of the state in policy circles and, even more, among the intellectual elite, may have binary sources. There was the belief of the leaders of the Indian freedom movement that their policy of nonviolence was instrumental in fetching the country independence—a questionable thesis with recent historical research suggesting it was the growing evidence of fraying discipline in the ranks of the Indian army in the inter-war years owing to rising nationalist consciousness among the soldiery, which had been used previously to subjugate the Indian people, that convinced the British to up stakes and leave (Yong 2005). And then there was the fact of the Indian officers in the largely British officer-run army being studiously kept out of the war planning and strategy-making processes. As a result after 1947, when nonviolence and pacifism became the dominant themes in the official discourse, the military did not offer the country a competing model to achieve international power. A modern nationalist tradition of Indian thinking on security and military strategy consequently was never seeded in the public culture. In this vacuum, Nehru was not merely the sole source of foreign policy but also of security policy. Lord Wavell, the penultimate British Viceroy, noted Nehru's keenness to have 'a strong, virile, active, and stable government' and, no doubt, country.[48] As regards military capabilities Nehru's thinking was molded, ironically, by a trio of Englishmen. Professor P.M.S. Blackett, a former naval person and

Nobel Prize winning physicist, Field Marshal Claude Auchinleck, an old British Indian Army-hand who was deposed by Churchill as head of the Allied Middle East Command during World War II and transferred to India as Commander-in-Chief, and Lieutenant General Francis Tuker, who led the Fourth Indian Division with success in the Allied Eight Army's campaign in the Western Desert, and returned to command India's Eastern Army, actually seeded Nehru's Monroe Doctrine-scheme premised on India's geographic centrality. The writings of this English trio, and their interaction with him shaped Nehru's idea of India as a nuclear weapon state and one that was also self-sufficient in conventional armaments. It led to the project at the Hindustan Aircraft Ltd, Bangalore, led by the reputed German aircraft designer Kurt Tank, who was commissioned by the Indian government to produce a supersonic fighter. A prototype was flying inside of five years by 1961. And to a versatile nuclear energy program that became weapons-capable as early as 1964 (Karnad 2005: 186). This stage of Nehru's thinking on security matters evolved in closed official quarters. Limited public awareness resulted in military issues being addressed by rhetorical flourishes and a muddled harping on Indian morality and non-violence propagated by iconic national political and cultural figures, among them, Mahatma Gandhi and the Bengali poet Rabindranath Tagore.[49] But their attitude almost of renunciation of power and power politics does not lie in Hindu culture and religion, as is mistakenly believed to be the case both in India and abroad.

Hinduism is not exclusively, or even largely, other-worldly philosophy, spiritual yearning, and pacifism. There is a surprisingly harsh side to it that is less well known and propagated. The original, four to five millennia-old, religious text, the Rg Veda, considered the fountainhead of Hinduism, for example, is so steeped in violence and amorality it is hard to connect it with the effete and 'bovine pacifism' (as I have called it in a previous book) of contemporary Hinduism. The Rig Veda was not only the first great treatise anywhere to imagine monstrous weapons of mass destruction, but to explicate in considerable detail their political and military utility as deterrent, and to define the situations for their use as part of Vedic *machtpolitik* that is breathtaking in its bloody-mindedness (Karnad 2005: 14–19). It features astonishingly modern-sounding armaments, with the ultimate weapon described as exploding with 'the brightness of a thousand crore suns', which description is what J. Robert Oppenheimer, director of the Manhattan Project and an amateur Sanskrit scholar, was motivated by when on seeing the flash of the first atomic explosion over Alamogordo, New Mexico, on July 16, 1945 he famously uttered the words from the Bhagvad Gita: 'I am become death, the destroyer of worlds'. The degree of detachment and distance of the Indian intellectual and policy circles from the country's ancient hard-as-nails strategic culture, was revealed by their buying into the thesis propounded by the late K. Subrahmanyam and George Tanham, the latter in a RAND monograph of the early 1990s, that India had no strategic culture. It may have alerted the Indian political class to the deficient strategic content in Indian policy but was wrong in extending the argument to the past to conclude the country had no base of traditional strategic thought to build on, when the fact was that the strategic culture lay buried in the detritus of history (Tanham 1992).

Amartya Sen, the Economics Nobel Laureate, Harvard Professor, and influential public intellectual, writing soon after the 1998 nuclear tests, pilloried the Indian government, and trivialized the underground nuclear blasts as providing 'the thrill of power'. He questioned the value of nuclear weapons for deterrence and India's security, and rued the fact that the tests had hurt the country's chances for a permanent seat in the UN Security Council.[50] While Sen has been proved wrong on all these counts—the best evidence being the desire of most major countries for 'strategic partnership' with India and the country's enhanced political status and profile in the world since the tests, his lethal, philosophical, ammunition nevertheless hit the soft spot of a susceptible Indian establishment. Calling the Indian tests a 'prudential blunder' that had created, he claimed, 'moral resentment'—where? among whom?, he was careful not to say, because the Indian masses greeted the nuclear blasts with wild jubilation, Sen asserted that India had failed on ethical grounds because, he argued, 'Our behavior towards each other cannot be divorced from what we make of the ethics of one another's pursuits, and the reasons of morality have, as a result, prudential importance as well' (Sen 2005: 251–69). His case that morality has in-built prudence may be sustainable only in an ideal world where all countries are directed by the same moral compass, or in a situation where a hegemonic power imposes its ethos in a world it has shaped and presides over. Absent these factors, the relevance of morality and ethics to international relations in which military power is prized as the *ultima ratio regum*, is questionable. But Sen played on a pet premise of the Indian priviligentsia that India and Indians are an inherently morally and ethically superior nation and people, quite different from the run-of-the-mill states and societies in the rest of the world. This is the grist of popular conceptions of uniqueness of India and of Indian exceptionalism. Sen's impact, and that of others of his ilk on the Indian political and intellectual classes, and even on hard-bitten diplomats and civil servants, is because of their conviction that ethics, morality and prudent behaviour are quintessentially Indian qualities validating their positive image of self, of the nation, and the policies they prosecute. It is a self-legitimating constraint on Indian policy.

A third intellectual stream is offered by Ramachandra Guha, a popular and personable historian with insightful things to say on a variety of topics. A theme he has been exploring over the years is that, considering its many social and economic ills, India's pursuit of great power distracts the government from tackling the enormous problems of illiteracy, poverty, and social and economic inequity. He cites seven 'objective' reasons why 'India will not become a superpower', namely,

> the challenge of the Naxalites [Maoist guerillas active in parts of central India]; the insidious presence of the Hinduwadis [Hindu extremists]; the degradation of the once liberal and upright Center [federal government]; the increasing gap between the rich and the poor; the trivialization of the media; the unsustainability, in an environmental sense, of present patterns of resources consumption; [and] the instability and policy incoherence caused by multi-party coalition governments' (Guha 2011: 15–16).

He offers three additional 'subjective' reasons why he thinks 'India should not even attempt to become a superpower'. Among these is, firstly, that India should be no part of the prevailing competitive international relations. Secondly, that the country and the people should be preoccupied with realizing the promise of the Indian Constitution, and thirdly, that the Indian system should be motivated 'to bring the practice of Indian democracy closer to the ideals of Indian nationhood' (Guha 2011: 15–16). It is hard to know what to make of this and how seriously to take Guha personally or his credentials as a historian. All rising powers have unresolved social and political issues at home and India has more of them than most countries. In the event, should a state have its aspirations dictated by the conditions of its people and society at any given moment in time? Using Guha's metric, an impecunious Elizabethan England of the sixteenth century had no business funding the enlargement of the Royal Navy or deploying it to the North Sea to help the Dutch provinces secede from Spain—the founding moves of Pax Britannica (Wheeler 1999: 23–6). And Bismarck should have concerned himself with ending serfdom in Prussia before seeking the unification of the German states and waging calculated wars in the 1860s and 1870s with Denmark, Austria, and France, resulting in the rise of the German leviathan (Clark 2009; Showalter 2004). History may be against commentators such as Guha but Indian politicians echo his views. India's great power aspiration, Jairam Ramesh, Minister for Rural Development in the Manmohan Singh cabinet, contended is 'dangerous' because it inspires 'a false sense of complacency [and] obfuscates the problems that still exist in the country.'[51]

In history, it has been normal for would-be great powers to address the manifold socio-economic challenges at home even as they acquire the means of hard power and exercise it ruthlessly in establishing their presence and acquiring and protecting their interests abroad (Tellis et al. 2000). In fact, there is no instance of a potential big power, other than India, being victimized by its own spurious ideas of 'proper sequencing'—of resolving domestic-economic development problems first before expanding the country's political and military footprint and securing great power (Karnad 2005: 310–11). Given the magnitude of its socio-economic problems, India by this standard will quite literally have to shutter itself up and give up on its ambitions altogether. This last is what is suggested for the country, in their separate ways by persons at the helm of affairs, such as the former National Security Adviser, M.K. Narayanan, and by public intellectuals, among them Sen and Guha. Indeed, as a grand gesture befitting residents of the *jambudvipa*, Guha proposes that the country cut itself off from the international mainstream and progress at its own speed and in its own way, undisturbed by what's happening in the world outside (Guha 2011: 16). Except, this is the autarchy model in extremis tried less stringently by Nehru in the 1950s. It only succeeded in pushing India to desperation, begetting reliance on foreign aid, American Public Law 480 grain, and an economy growing at what was disparagingly called 'the Hindu rate' of 3.5 per cent—hugely inadequate to finance the government's social welfare and development schemes that these same people want implemented (Williamson 2006).

Such views, however, while sitting well with the politicians do not enthuse people especially the youth and the upwardly mobile and outward-looking middle class, which is some 300 million strong and growing. A country cannot globalize its economy without the people's perspective being broadened and their ambitions for the nation getting grander. Sen's Nobel halo and Guha's humanitarian isolationism, however, tilt the Indian media and intelligentsia towards fashionable notions of political correctness derived from the West, eventuating in the fashionably bourgeois Brinda Karat, member of the politburo of the Indian Communist Party (Marxist), for instance, to declare at a media conclave that 'India will be a significant power but not in a negative sense', meaning without ever resorting to coercion or use of force.[52]

Reflecting the inward focus of the Indian establishment, the National Security Adviser, Shivshankar Menon in a speech prepared but not delivered on 15 July 2011 to the Defence Services Staff College, decried the tendency for 'much loose talk about India as a potential superpower'. He harked back to the sort of disclaimer Prime Minister Indira Gandhi issued in the aftermath of the first Indian nuclear test in 1974 ostensibly to reassure the West. Indicating that India would not wield its nuclear weapons capability to destabilize the region or the global order, she told an audience at the Royal Canadian Institute of International Studies in Toronto that 'India does not want power.'[53] Some forty years later, the countries of Asia and in the West need a different kind of reassurance that India will, in fact, pull its strategic weight, take a leadership role in resolving security problems in the extended region, and help in correcting the power imbalance. 'India's leadership will help to shape positively the future of the Asia-Pacific,' said the visiting American Secretary of State Hillary Clinton at a public lecture in Chennai in July

2011. '[T]he United States supports India's Look East policy...[W]e encourage India not just to look east, but to engage East and act East as well...' (Clinton 2011). In the hope of getting New Delhi to pick up its game, U.S. officials have been at pains to address Indian sensitivities about getting too close to the United States. Speaking on 'An Indispensable [India-U.S.] Partnership for the twenty-first century' to an audience of Indian policy cognoscenti in Delhi in April 2012, Under Secretary of State for Political Affairs Wendy Sherman pointed out that 'on nearly every matter of strategic importance the fundamental interests of the United States and India converge' but, she hastened to add that 'This is not a formula for alignment. It is, however, the basis for a sustained, productive, strategic partnership...based on ...solving global and regional problems in a complex and interconnected world' and which close relationship gives the two countries 'greater autonomy in the international system, not less, by furthering the rise of India as a global stakeholder and maintaining the United States' role as a global power. (Sherman 2012). The reassurance Washington sought was not forthcoming, however. Rather, National Security Advisor Menon voiced his suspicion that prodding India to act as a would-be great power was a ploy by its 'international partners' to push it to 'be a responsible power [doing] what they would like us to do!' in their interest.[54] Menon, perhaps, meant to convey New Delhi's intention to act 'responsibly' but according to its own lights.[55] The United States, on the other hand, expects India's positions on the more vexatious issues—Iran, climate, trade and tariff, and energy security, to firm up the Western-led international consensus, which it deems 'responsible' behaviour.

As practical policy, New Delhi apparently believes that accommodating America some, without going the whole hog, will serve the national interests better because it will keep Washington interested and engaged. In this regard, Menon alluded to two other paths available to India. It could, he said, look at its 'own interests and [see] what kind of behaviour on [its] part would make [its] pursuit [of power] most successful', or 'at how the world is evolving, and plan [India's] role and actions according to our expectations' and devise a flexible plan to account for uncertainty and unpredictable events. He indicated the Manmohan Singh government's preference for combining these two paths as the best solution 'in the evolving world situation.'

In this conception, India's great power end-state is not a fixity but a moving target that constantly adjusts its foreign and military policies, taking advantage of every turn in international affairs with the aim of maximizing interests and improving the country's relative bargaining position. In short, India will be satisfied being the global presence that the evolving situation dominated by current great powers wedded to the status quo will allow it to be. And, that it will be happy to use an essentially passive-reactive policy to harvest such benefits as come its way by supporting the existing international order. This much was made plain by Prime Minister Manmohan Singh during his state visit to the United States in November 2009. 'The edifice of the India-U.S. partnership is founded on many pillars' he told a meeting in Washington of the Council on Foreign Relations. 'It is a relationship based on pragmatism and principle'. He was refreshingly honest, moreover, in explaining India's indecisive policies as an attribute of 'many democracies [that] are short-term maximizers [and are] not able to take a long term view.'[56] 'Short-term maximizing' perfectly describes the Indian foreign and military policy in a nutshell. It is a tactician's policy blueprint to pluck low-hanging fruit, not a statesman's vision to catapult the country to the great power ranks. It is in sync, moreover, with the risk-averse, incrementalist, thinking of Manmohan Singh's immediate predecessors—P.V. Narasimha Rao (1991–1996) of the Congress Party and Atal Bihari Vajpayee of the rightwing Bharatiya Janata Party (BJP), 1998–2004. The one big idea—the thawing of relations with the United States and the ensuing nuclear deal that Dr. Manmohan Singh successfully pushed, had its antecedents in the Vajpayee regime which made the breakthrough in terms of initiating a 'strategic dialogue' that resulted in the Next Steps in the Strategic Partnership (NSSP)—the prelude to the nuclear deal.[57] But this uptick in relations was, in turn, based on the previous Congress party Prime Minister Narasimha Rao's efforts to globalize the Indian economy by reforming it, a policy implemented by Manmohan Singh as Finance Minister in the early 1990s.[58] So the absence of grand goals for Indian foreign and military policy is not unusual, nor viewed as a liability. Except the Congress Party coalition government of Manmohan Singh voted out of power in May 2014 chose to shroud it in the rhetoric of nonalignment with its carapace of legitimacy acquired from Nehru's time. Menon described the 'essence' of such policy as avoiding 'external entanglements or outside restraints on our freedom of choice and action'—an aim, he said, that has been accorded 'overriding priority' from the 1950s.

Nonalignment 2.0, (*NA 2.0*) elaborates on the tactical orientation of Indian policy. Nonalignment is designed, it says, to retain 'maximum strategic autonomy'. The NSA to Prime Minister Vajpayee, Brajesh Mishra, called nonalignment 'the default policy stance [which] has been difficult to shed.'[59] Consequently, India's 'global engagement', *NA 2.0* suggests, should be seen less as a 'boxing match' than 'a constant wary game to stay a few moves ahead of competitors and opponents' (Center for Policy Research. 2012: 2–3). In this supposed 'chess grandmaster's game', comprehensive hard power is nowhere given its due. 'Air/cyber' and naval capabilities that are more amenable to restraint and control are stressed and, even after acknowledging the growth of Pakistan's and China's nuclear arsenals and their collusion in nuclear and conventional military sectors, India is warned against departing from its minimalist notions of deterrence and adopting 'a destabilizing nuclear posture' (Center for Policy Research 2012: 32–4, 48). Menon, on his part, claimed that India sought nuclear weapons simply because of the 'strategic autonomy' they 'bestow' on the country, enabling it to 'pursue' its goal of socio-economic betterment at home without being bothered by external events. It is a testament to the Indian decision-makers' attempts to shrink the policy universe to manageable proportions that nuclear armaments are viewed as just another means of keeping the big bad world away from an India preoccupied with economically bettering itself and generally mending its broken-down internal system, rather than as means for a budding great power to assert itself on the world stage.

It is such fainthearted take on hard power and the armed might of the country that disconcerts the Indian military. 'I have yet to hear an Indian politician or diplomat or anybody [in position of authority in government] speaking even in the most innocuous manner about the nuclear deterrent, for instance. This conveys the message that we…are not leveraging the nuclear deterrent to compel, persuade, or even deter any country from doing something it shouldn't do', said Admiral Arun Prakash (Retd)), a member of several high-powered committees looking into problems of national defence and security.

'The great contradiction is that we work on two planes—one is that we have this great hubris about our past, our great cultural heritage—5,000 year old culture, etc., which propels the thinking that we are a great power, that we should be a great power,' he ventured. 'But practically, we do very little to show the world that we have the makings of a great power, or we act like a great power.'[60]

Great power cannot be conceived without hard power and the coercive wherewithal of the state. But there is official reluctance to do so. Menon, for example, defined national security as purely defence, 'not offense, unless offense is necessary for deterrence or to protect India's ability to continue its own transformation'. Whatever the reasons for this National Security Adviser's making the somewhat spurious distinction between offensive and defensive military strength, stance and posture, it indicates that New Delhi sees the country's military capabilities uni-dimensionally, providing a flawed template for the allround enhancement of the country's armed forces. In theory, at least, a stricture against acquiring offensive weaponry would limit the country's options, even though the purchase of some $50 billion worth of offence-capable new armaments, weapons platforms, and support systems in the period 2011–2015 belies any such restriction (Pandit 2012). Deliberately or otherwise, Indian government officials tend to mask the true intent of policy with verbiage about an India too stretched by its domestic problems to be proactive in regional and international arenas. The planned augmentation and modernization of the Indian military, the navy in particular, will endow the country with a substantial expeditionary capability to pursue an activist policy, if it wants to (Pubby 2012). It was natural, therefore, starting with the presidency of George W. Bush, for the U.S. government to 'look to India to assume,' as the 2008 National Defense Strategy noted, 'greater responsibility as a stakeholder in the international system, commensurate with its growing economic, military, and soft power.'[61] U.S. Deputy Secretary of State William Burns several months after Secretary of State Clinton's swing through India in 2011, spoke about 'India's strong presence across the Indian and Pacific Oceans' as a 'source of comfort and affirms its potential as a net security provider in the maritime domain.'[62] The Indian response to China, for example, has been belligerent and disingenuously tepid by turns. The foreign minister S.M. Krishna responded to Beijing's warning India not to collaborate with Vietnam in exploring for offshore oil with fighting words to the effect that the South China Sea is not China's sea, mirroring the challenge by a Chinese Admiral from an earlier decade that 'The Indian Ocean is not India's ocean'.[63] Menon, however, qualified that commitment, saying India would consider such a role in 'the Indian Ocean and our neighborhood' only if 'it contributes to India's own transformation'.[64] This left open the possibility, apart from joining other countries in safeguarding the global commons and freedom of navigation in the proximal waters, of India cooperating in a collective security endeavour and assuming responsibility for the wellbeing of smaller countries of South East Asia as it has done for island-nations in the Indian Ocean region (Maldives, Seychelles, Mauritius, and Sri Lanka). But because the policy principles enunciated so far are of essentially a tactical and defensive nature, one can't be too sure whether and how much India will put out in protecting the interests of other countries. Similarly, the priority Shivshankar Menon attached to obtaining 'a peaceful periphery' and 'sustained cooperative engagement' with countries of South East Asia, West Asia, Central Asia, and Africa was justified by him on the basis of enabling India's 'continued access' to natural resources and to its building 'strategic stockpiles and alternatives'. It hinted at military forces being tasked to safeguard natural resource assets (mining and oil and gas concessions and properties) secured by Indian public and private sector companies in far-off locales. But again, certainty of such military deployment cannot be gleaned from any public pronouncements. It is the ambivalence in defining a geographic ambit of responsibility, synonymous with the old world concept of 'sphere of influence', where India's national interests are inextricably involved, or in even identifying vital national interests materially in terms of protecting supply lines and sources of energy and other natural resources, that makes for policy ambiguity. It suggests not so much lack of plans but an infirm political will and a tendency to seek excuses for doing the minimum when it cannot get away with doing nothing at all. Employing the classic metric that if a country sounds and appears diffident about investing politically, economically, and militarily to keep the extended neighbourhood stable and orderly, and its distantly-sited economic interests protected, it cannot, by definition, be a great power, India is not a great power.

A more methodical view of India's prospects is provided by V.K. Saraswat, until June 2013 Science Adviser to the Defence Minister and head of the Defence Research and Development Organization (DRDO). 'India is emerging as a great power and this process of emergence has its own slope', he explained.

> If you divide the power into its different aspects—economic power, military power, cyber power, and so on, we are growing at a faster rate in some of these areas and slower in others. But if you integrate all these powers in the next 15–20 years, India will find its entitled place as a great power …with a say in the world community as a whole.[65]

This is a reasonable progress chart, but the tenor and substance of statements by high officials in the government, such as the National Security Advisers to-date, hint at a shriveled view of India's place in the sun and hesitation in owning up to the country's responsibilities. An inward-turned mindset means constricted Indian policy choices and priorities. Consequently, the Indian government projects an image of a country too caught up in its domestic developments to do other than the barest minimum in the external realm to keep its bona fides as a would-be great power afloat.

A limited vision for the country means India is unable to recapture the broad sweep of ambition that placed it, in Nehru's scheme of things, as mediator between the rival ideological blocs in the Cold War and, more significantly, as the pivotal power propping up an 'Asian Monroe Doctrine'. It is hard to see narrowly-based, short-ranged, and risk-averse policies, which seem to be the norm, doing much beyond reinforcing India's image as a country without the motor to make it really big in the world. The conclusion by George Perkovich of the Carnegie Endowment for International Peace, that based on the realist criterion of great power as the ability to both resist international pressure and influence other countries, India is only 'a middle rank power' that can resist pressure (as the success of its nuclear weapons and missile programmes in the face of severe technology denial regimes attest) but cannot influence countries, therefore, holds. The foreign policy principles espoused by top appa-ratchiks, moreover, depict India as a 'moralistic, contrarian loner', the reason why, Perkovich claims, India is not very popular and cannot muster the support in the United Nations General Assembly for a permanent seat in the Security Council. On the other hand, he believes, that were India, somehow 'to get it right', meet the aspirations of its billion plus population—which won't happen in the foreeable future—it would be a manifestation of global great power' (Perkovich 2003–04: 129–30, 140.). A manifestation, however, is not the same thing as actually being a great power and is something only votaries of India's soft power approach would welcome. Even when these Indians in leadership positions urge the country to 'think big' it is exclusively in terms of raising the economic growth rate.[66] High levels of growth may afford the country the resources of a great power but is not a substitute for great power. Then again, the former Prime Minister Manmohan Singh, echoing Indira Gandhi's line from the 1970s, made clear that India 'does not desire to be a global superpower'; it only wishes, he wrote, 'to live in peace and dignity' (Singh 2007: 19).

This was an unusually meager ambition for a country whose large economy and military, and growing political influence can serve grander aims. It's possible that this statement was made only for public consumption in line with the low-key official rhetoric and policy involving prudent engagement with the world. But it does manifest the institutional aversion to thinking big and chancing success, and denotes only limited regional and global ambition. Manmohan Singh's emphasizing the economic advancement of the country, moreover, ignored its connection with the military capabilities of the state because, as the Yale historian Paul Kennedy maintains, wealth is needed to underpin military power and military power is needed to acquire and protect wealth (Kennedy 1989). This is something China has learned well but India has yet to come to grips with. It indicates that even as India grows more powerful economically and more capable militarily, the muted and muddled national vision will be like the ball and chain around the country's ankles, preventing it from leaping ahead. Then again, may be, it mirrors the diffidence and sensitivity of a state that nearly seven decades after independence is unable to provide the bare necessities of life to a large part of its 1.2 billion population.[67]

The external affairs minister in the Vajpayee government, Jaswant Singh, who in the past talked of India's interests coinciding with its 'civilizational reach', blamed the 'timidity' of thought and of action 'born of the slavery India went through' and the fact that the Indian government is 'not yet free of [its] shadows and overhang', for the country's failure so far to make it as a great power.[68] It is a view seconded by many in the military. Former head of the Indian Air Force (IAF) and member of the National Security Advisory Board, Air Chief Marshal S. Krishnaswamy (Retd.) is trenchant in this regard. 'It is in our cultural DNA. We have been slaves who helped outsiders rule us for over fifteen hundred years.' [The elongated timeframe is a reference to the Muslim rulers of South Asia in the wake of the Arab invasion starting in the seventh century, the subsequent forays by adventurers from Persia and Central Asia, and finally the expansion of the power of the East India Company and the consolidation of the Crown colony following the first War of independence in 1857—all of which foreign entities, incidentally, co-opted native rulers and used local mercenary armies to extend and solidify their grip on the subcontinent].[69] 'So guarding someone else's interests, but not our own, comes naturally to us.'[70] The theme of foreign subjugation and the Indian people's central role in sustaining it hints at historical fears which contributed to India's nonalignment policy and its latter-day variant, strategic autonomy.

India's ego is fragile, and seeks international, especially Western, approval and validation of the country's standing and policies, and yet it is touchy about supposed slights, insults, and even unintended acts of 'condescension', impelling Indians and their government alike to show umbrage, and is part of the Indian persona and psychological baggage the people and the country carry.[71] The Indian armed forces, for instance, quietly bristled at a 2002 U.S. Department of Defense Report on 'Indo-U.S. Military Relationship', which seemed to confirm their worst fears of being fobbed off with 'low-end operations in Asia…[thereby] allow[ing] the U.S. military to concentrate its resources on high end fighting missions' against the Chinese threat common to both countries (MacDonald 2002). The low-end operations referred to Indian naval ships acting as armed escorts for U.S. naval flotillas transiting the Malacca Strait. But many fear that such secondary actions are all that India is capable of prosecuting, because it is culturally and politically disabled from thinking and acting big. 'Our culture is not an aggressive culture, it is not a far-seeing culture, we are satisfied by the meeting of immediate needs', said Dr. Saraswat, former DRDO head. 'We are not an ambitious people. Even if we want to become Number One in the world, the attitude is '*Haan, ho jayenge*' (Well, yes, we will become one in due time) we are not driven; that's the reason for our slow pace of progress.'[72] It marks India out as a country that isn't revisionist, won't rock the boat and, therefore, an ideal strategic partner for big powers such as the United States to help prop up the extant order in Asia they dominate (Clary 2011). New Delhi sees the country's ascent in terms of big powers voluntarily sharing 'the high table' (permanent membership in the U.N. Security Council, etc.) with India once it has persuaded them to get over their 'entrenched reluctance' to do so.[73] Implicit in all such official depictions of where India is headed is the basic belief that India will secure the great power position by goodwill and deft diplomacy unlike other states that obtained it by sheer will, strategic vision, and show of force. It is a desire to 'free-ride to great power status, which includes ducking hard decisions and avoiding shouldering a burden, [and] [not] bearing ...responsibility ' (Ladwig III 2010: 1171). It ignores Kautilya's advice to his emperor in 223 BC that *sama* (concessions, peace treaties and peaceful incentives of various kinds) and *dhan* (economic grants, financial credit and aid) are all very well, but it is *dand* (preponderant military power) that ultimately persuades unfriendly states to toe the line. Or, consider the advice by Europe's Kautilya come-lately, Machiavelli, to his Prince that for success to attend on his ventures he should have the cunning of a fox and the strength of a lion. In other words, guile works better when backed by the gun.

In contrast to China's grab-as-grab-can attitude to augmenting national power, India's less frenetically-run race to global presence, power and status is, perhaps, easier for the international community to digest. But New Delhi anticipates that this approach combined with the pull of demography—'the soft underbelly of geopolitics' will make the regional and international milieus receptive to its slow and steady rise as an Asian power.[74] With a young, vigorous, and aspiring demographic, however, India today is a very different country to the India of the past century—less forgiving and less patient. Saraswat believes the younger generation may be unwilling to wait too long for India to become a great power. 'They are not affected by [the current ruling generation's] cultural and historical background of morality, colonialism, religion, pacifism', he said. 'They are vibrant, ambitious for the country, willing to act, to take risk, and to take up challenges.'[75] The new BJP Prime Minister Narendra Modi reflected this restlessness of the young and the aspirational in the 'India First' doctrine he enunciated. 'Whatever we do, it must be for India', Modi told a youthful and enthusiastic audience in Spring 2013. 'We must never let India, her honour, the dreams of the people be adversely affected. India first it must be.'[76] Modi's 'India first' ideology and thinking could potentially alter how Indians see their own country and fire up policies to make India a great power.

Notes

1. Saini (2011). On the growth of the Indian software industry see a chapter by in a World Bank study, Bhatnagar (2006).

2. The conditions of extraordinary poverty, illiteracy, and religious superstition prevailing in India had changed little from its depiction some 20 years earlier by Mayo (1927) in her sensational book, *Mother India*. It was so stark in its portrayal of the country that an angry Mahatma Gandhi called it 'a drain inspector's report'.

3. Quote in Massie (1991: 54).

4. See Nehru's letters dated 19 July and 12 August, 1949 to his sister, Vijayalakshmi Pandit, whom he had appointed India's Ambassador to the United States, in Nehru (1991: 390–1).

5. Delegates from Burma, Indonesia and Vietnam, in particular, complained bitterly about the deployment of the Indian troops by the British against their freedom movements. Taken aback, Nehru explained these as colonial ventures and offered assurances that an independent India would have no truck with such activity and that his government was putting an end to all such military deployments. Refer the Round Table discussions on "National Movements for Freedom" at the Conference (Asian Relations Organization 1948: 71–89).

6. The conference secretariat in the 'Introductory' to the Report, noted that 'while [the defense and security questions] were undoubtedly important....the view prevailed that in an Asian Relations Conference we should avoid on the one hand controversial issues relating to particular states and, on the other, issues which have more than an Asian incidence and can be solved only at higher levels' (Asian Relations Organization 1948: 3–4).

7. 'A Note on the Strategic Implications of the inclusion of "Pakistan" in the British Commonwealth' by Field Marshal Sir C. Auchinleck, Top Secret, No. L/WS/1/1092: ff 51-6, General Headquarters, Delhi, reproduced as Appendix IX in Singh (2009: 563).

8. See 'Air Marshal Aspy Engineer's Recollections' at http://bharat-rakshak.com/IAF/History/1940s/Aspy01.html. Air Marshal Engineer was Chief of the Air Staff, 1960–3.

9. The Pentagon plans involved deployment of, among other forces, an Airborne Division, five Nuclear Demolition Teams, a Carrier Task Force, an Amphibious Force, an Underway Replenishment Group, a Marine Regimental Landing Team and a Marine Air Group detached from the U.S. Pacific Fleet; a Composite Air Strike Force, Airlift capability for one Airborne Battle Group, and a Medium Bomber Wing from the Strategic Air Command, Omaha, Nebraska, from U.S. Air Force assets, with still larger forces thought necessary to fight an 'internal communist revolution' in India requiring the posting additionally of two Fighter-Bomber Squadrons, a Composite Reconnaissance Squadron, and one Day Fighter Squadron by the U.S.A.F., a Corps Headquarters and an Infantry Division by U.S. Army, and the Third Marine Air-Ground Task Force (comprising a Marine Division and a Marine Air Wing) by the U.S. Navy. These American plans could not have been implemented without significant support from the Indian government and armed forces. See for more details and analysis of these Pentagon plans, see Karnad (2005: 132–46).

10. In an internal paper dated 21 September, 1945, authored by Nehru and his senior colleagues Vallabhbhai Patel, who became India's first Home Minister, and G.B. Pant, whooccupied Patel's cabinet post after the latter's death, the Congress Party's distrust of the Communist Party of India is manifest. For the text of this Paper, refer N. Singh (2010: Appendix II). For the specific quotes, see Nehru (1991a: 179–80). 'Armies are no doubt necessary to defend a nation but no army can fight unless there is adequate economic progress…which can bear the burden of war', he said at a public address in Kanpur on 28 August, 1949. 'Therefore, the economic question becomes very important. We cannot increase the strength of our army if we are unable to produce the necessary equipment.

11. www.friendsoftibet.org/main/sardar.html.

12. See his letter to his sister, Vijayalakshmi Pandit, appointed ambassador to the U.S. in Nehru (1991a: 356).

13. Because, Shashi Tharoor contends, it is 'still hard-wired into the consciousness of policymakers'. See Tharoor (2012: 15).

14. See Ambassador Bhatia (2014). It is a view current in U.S. policy circles as well. See Tellis (2005).

15. 'Remarks by President Obama and Prime Minister Singh of India during Arrival Ceremony', November 24, 2009 at www.whitehouse.gov/.

16. See Prime Minister Modi's National Security Adviser (NSA) Ajit Doval's views about having deterrence against Pakistani terrorism and about not compromising with China even a bit on territorial issues. See 'Will address problems with Pakistan, China through talks deterrence key to good relations: Ajit Doval', *Indian Express*, 22 October, 2014.

17. 'India shows concern to US over rejection of H1B, L1 visas', *Economic Times*, 27 March 2012; Rapoza (2012).

18. The skepticism about India making it at all, leave alone as a great power, is quite routinely voiced, but mostly privately, by senior political leaders and senior government officials.

19. See *India Vision 2020* (Planning Commission 2002: 86–9). Incidentally, 'vision' is only in the title. There is no elaboration anywhere else in the document!

20. Scindia (2011). Jyotiraditya Scindia is Minister of State for Commerce and Industry in Manmohan Singh's Congress Party government.

21. Personal communication from S.M Qureshi, former Chief Election Commissioner.

22. Humira Noorestani heading a U.S.-Afghan NGO, pleads for Bollywood to use its tremendous influence in Pakistan and Afghanistan to change bad social practices, such as discrimination against women and the girl-child, rather than reinforce them. See Noorestani (2013).

23. The Algerian Ambassador in Delhi, Echarif Mohammed-Hacere complained, for instance, that despite his protests, his country was either 'lumped' with Arab West Asia or considered part of Africa. Moreover, his pleas for years to the concerned regional desks in the MEA, not for financial aid which, he said, Algeria 'does not need', but for 'assistance to develop our human resources' via university-to-university ties, which he says 'we would appreciate', have fallen on deaf ears. Repeated representations to MEA during his tenure on this and other issues, he said, had made no difference. 'India,' he concludes, 'shows shortage of vision.' Author's interaction with Ambassador Mohammed-Hacere on the sidelines of a seminar on 'Cairo to Casablanca: The Jasmine Revolution', Center for Policy Research, New Delhi, May 17, 2011.

24. Quote in Karnad (2005: 83).

25. Malaysia's Foreign Minister and later Prime Minister Tunku Abdul Rahman, for instance, revealed how 'young aspiring politicians' in South East Asia in the 1930s and 1940s drew inspiration from the Indian freedom movement and regarded its leaders, particularly Nehru, 'as a most desirable pillar of strength'. See Institute of Diplomacy and Foreign Affairs, Malaysia (2008).

26. See his 'India's Grand Strategy', *Indian Express*, 3 February, 2012. The National Security Adviser, Shiv Shankar Menon, called him 'my guru' on the occasion to commemorate Subrahmanyam's life, India International Center, 19 January, 2012.

27. Shiv Shankar Menon, 'Asian Security Challenges', Speaking Notes, Seminar hosted by the Delhi Policy Group and the Massachusetts Institute of Technology Center for International Studies, New Delhi, 10 January, 2011. Emailed to the author by Menon.

28. First interview, 11 January, 2011.

29. On the failure of the Indian thermonuclear device, including the view of American seismologists, see Karnad (2005: 412–20).

30. Quote in Kennedy (1984: 132).

31. The chief promoter of this view was K. Subrahmanyam, a civilian strategist of renown. Refer his two articles published posthumously: 'India's Grand Strategy', *Indian Express*, 3 February, 2012 & 'India's Strategic Challenges', The *Indian Express*, 4 February, 2012. National Security Adviser, Shivshankar Menon, has publicly stated his intellectual debt of gratitude to Subrahmanyam. Refer his speech on 'K. Subrahmanyam and India's Strategic Culture', KS Forum Memorial Lecture, 19 January, 2012.

32. U.S. Defense Secretary Leon Panetta called India the 'lynchpin' of strategic security in Asia. See the text of his speech at the Institute for Defense Studies and Analyses, New Delhi, 6 June, 2012. (Copies of the Panetta speech were handed out at the venue by US Embassy staffers.) The George W Bush Administration's appreciation of India was that it is an 'emerging global power', see Condoleeza Rice, *No Higher Honor: A Memoir of My Years in Washington* [New York: Simon & Schuster, 2011], 127, 441.

33. Shivshankar Menon, 'India and the Global Scene', Prem Bhatia Memorial Lecture, New Delhi, 11 August, 2011. The text of the lecture was emailed the author by the NSA.

34. Quote in Fabian (2014: 100).

35. See the speech by Prime Minister Manmohan Singh at the 2010 Nuclear Security Summit in Washington, DC. For the text of the speech, see *Hindu*, 13 April, 2010.

36. '"India is a rising and responsible power"', PTI, *IBN Live*, 4 June, 2010 at http://mobi-ibn-in.com/news/.

37. S. Menon, 'India's Security Environment and Apparatus', National Defence College, 4 July, 2014; text emailed to the author by Menon. It was a speech made after he had demitted office as NSA.

38. Among the first foreign leaders to visit with the new Narendra Modi government was the Chinese Foreign Minister Wang Yi who reaffirmed the Chinese claims on Arunachal Pradesh and why Beijing would continue with its policy of stapled visas that New Delhi objects to. See by 'Stapled visas

to people of Arunachal "goodwill" gesture: China', PTI, *Times of India*, 10 June, 2014. United States has been warning about nuclear weapons/fissile material for radiation diffusion devices in the hand of terrorists. Henry Kissinger in mid-2006 wrote about the 'The world being faced with the nightmarish prospect that nuclear weapons will become a standard part of the national armament and wind up in terrorist hands.' (See his 'A Nuclear Test of Diplomacy', Washington Post, 16 May 2006) But it was during Kissinger's tenure as Secretary of State that the U.S. was complicit in creating this threat in the first place by permitting China to transfer nuclear weapon designs, materials, bomb-making expertise and missiles to Pakistan—the most likely source of fissile material leakage to, if not capture of whole weapons by, radical Islamists. See Pressler (1994). U.S. Senator Pressler is the author of the 1985 'Pressler Amendment' to the U.S. Foreign .Aid Act that banned aid to Pakistan except on annual certification by the U.S. President that 'Pakistan does not possess a nuclear explosive device and that the proposed United States assistance programme will reduce significantly the risk that Pakistan will possess a nuclear explosive device.' Besides a permanent nuclear proliferation threat, a nuclear-missile armed Pakistan is a perennial strategic problem for India.

39. See Modi's interview in *Economic Times* 22 April, 2014; BJP Manifesto at http://www.bjp.org/images/pdf_2014/full_manifesto_english_07.04.2014.pdf, 39. For a view opposing any N-doctrine revision, see Saran (2014).

40. Angell's famous tract was Angell (1913).

41. Quote in Ayaz Amir, 'A six-month timeline is all we have', *The News*, 8 November 2013.

42. Quote in Herring (2008: 600).

43. Second interview, 10 February, 2011.

44. Interview, 6 May, 2011.

45. Quote in R. K. Massie (1991: 54).

46. Narayanan's speech at a public function on February 29, 2012 to release a quasi-official strategy Paper—*Nonalignment 2.0: A Foreign and Strategic Policy for India in the Twenty-first Century* [New Delhi: Center for Policy Research, 2012], drafted by an eclectic group comprising a former diplomat, a military advisor to the National Security Council, two business leaders, and several academics; available at www.cprindia.org/sites/default/files/Nonalignmentper cent202.0_1.pdf .

47. Interview, 25 March, 2011.

48. Quote in L. Gandhi (2014). 'Mumbai's Forgotten Mutiny', *Indian Express*, 5 April, 2014.

49. For an analysis, for example, of Mahatma Gandhi's philosophy of nonviolence rooted, by his own admission, in fundamental Christian values, (Karnad 2005: 29–64). On Tagore's explication of India and Indian civilization's moral values, see Mishra (2012).

50. The novelist Arundhati Roy's vivid description of a post-nuclear attack scene—'Our cities and forests, our fields and villages, will burn for days. Rivers will turn to poison. The air will become fire. The wind will spread the flames. When everything there is to burn has burned and the fires die, smoke will rise and shut out the sun', was used by Sen to buttress his case against nuclear weapons. See his 'India and the Bomb' in Sen (2005: 257).

51. Interview, 25 March, 2011.

52. Brinda Karat at the *India Today Conclave*, New Delhi, 17–18 March, 2012.

53. The doyen of Indian civilian strategists, the late K. Subrahmanyam, related this in a discussion on 'International Studies in India' at the Institute of Defence Studies and Analyses, New Delhi, 16 February, 2010.

54. The draft of this undelivered speech by National Security Advisor, Shivshankar Menon, on 'India's Role in Global Politics' was emailed the author by the NSA with an accompanying light-hearted message that said: 'Here are some notes for a speech that was never delivered. I suppose you could say the speech bombed!' Quotes by the NSA, unless otherwise attributed, in the rest of this section, are taken from the emailed text of his speech.

55. The External Affairs Minister S.M. Krishna's hints at this in his statement: '[T]he..situation is rapidly changing and India, as a responsible power, must engage actively with the world'. See http://smkrishna.co.in .

56. 'A Conversation with Prime Minister Manmohan Singh', Council on Foreign Relations, 23 November, 2009 at www.cfr.org.

57. For an account of the strategic dialog and India–US relations during the Clinton Administration, see Talbott (2004).

58. Jaswant Singh, Member of Parliament, and External Affairs Minister in the BJP government; interview with author, 15 December 2011.

59. B. Mishra, 'Foreword' in Mishra (2012: 1).

60. Interview, 13 September 2011.

61. National Defense Strategy, June 2008, 14 at www.defense.gov/news/2008%20national%20defense%20strategy.pdf.

62. 'Deputy Secretary of State William J. Burns speaks on "U.S.-India partnership in an Asia-Pacific century"', U.S. Embassy, New Delhi, 16 December, 2011 at http://newdelhiembassy.gov/sr121611.html.

63. Minister Krishna said in Bangalore: 'India maintains that South China Sea is the property of the world. I think those trade ways must be free

from any national interference.' See 'India: Beijing doesn't own S. China Sea', *Times of India*, 7 April 2012.

64. G. Pyatt, US Principal Deputy Assistant Secretary of State, Bureau of South and Central Asian Affairs, 'New Steps on the Silk Road', talk in Chennai, 15 November, 2011, at www.state.gov/p/sca/rls/rmks/2011/177179.htm.

65. Interview, 11 March 2011.

66. 'Think big, work together to get growth ticking: PM', *Indian Express*, 16 August, 2012.

67. In this context, a former naval chief, Admiral A. Prakash (Retd.) said, that 'any talk of [India's] great power status seems like a mockery of their wretched existence.' See Prakash (2013).

68. Interview.

69. On Indian military labour, see Kolff (1990). For an interesting Victorian perspective on recruitment of natives in the armies of the British Raj, see Wheeler (2005 [1886]: chs II and III).

70. Interview.

71. A.K. Chaubey, 'From Mutiny to Mutinies: A Post-Colonial Study of Naipaul's India' at www.the-criterion.com/V2/n2/April 2011.pdf

72. Interview.

73. Puri (2013). Puri is a former Indian Permanent Representative at the U.N. in New York.

74. Owing to its one-child policy and the average number of children per woman at 1.6, and some 14 percent of its population already over 60 years of age, China will soon confront labour shortages in low-wage industries that are its economic bread and butter. Japan faces a higher order problem—a 'demographic catastrophe' with its population dropping in 2011 for the fifth consecutive year to some 126 million, and expected to tick down to 95 million by 2050. India, meanwhile, will overtake China's 1.35 billion-strong population and, in theory, at least, can rely on a large, young, and growing work force. See Sanders (2012).

75. Interview.

76. Bhattacharya (2013). For a balanced assessment of Modi, see Vaishnav (2013). The 'India First' concept was first coined and fleshed out by this author, pre-dating Modi's reference to it by over a decade, emphasizing an uncompromising attitude to national interest. It argued for jettisoning a the policy of national self-denial and self-abnegation because 'The mark of a great power is single-mindedly to pursue narrowly-defined national interest [not universal good] at the expense of every other principle, ideology, and value', and that great power status cannot be had on the cheap, nor is it

'a grant or a favour from powerful states in the international system'. See Karnad (2002).

References

Angell. N. 1913 [4th revised and enlarged edition]. *The Great Illusion: A Study of the Relation of Military Power to National Advantage.* New York: G.P. Putnam's Sons, Cornell University Library Digital Collections reprint.

Asian Relations Organization. 1948. *Asian Relations being Report of the Proceedings and Documentation of the First Asian Relations Conference, New Delhi, March-April, 1947.* Asian Relations Organization.

Baru, S. 2013. 'The Singh doctrine', *Indian Express,* 6 November.

———. 2014. *The Accidental Prime Minister: The Making and Unmaking of Manmohan Singh.* New Delhi: Penguin Books.

Bhatia, R. 2014. 'Challenges for India's Foreign Policy in the Next Decade', Distinguished Lectures, Ministry of External Affairs, Government of India, August 9, 2014 at www.mea.gov.in/distinguished-lectures-detail.htm?108

Bhatnagar, S. 2006. 'India's Software Industry' at http://www.iimahd.ernet. in/~subhash/pdfs/Indianper cent20softwarereper cent20industry.pdf.

Bhattacharya, D. P. 2013. 'My definition of secularism means India first, Narendra Modi tells overseas Indians', *Mail Today,* 10 March.

Blarel, N. 2011. 'India's Soft Power: From Potential to Reality?' in *India: The Next Super Power?* Special Report No. 10, London: London School of Economics at http://www2.lse.ac.uk/IDEAS/publications/reports/SRO10.aspx.

Center for Policy Research. 2012. *Nonalignment 2.0: A Foreign and Strategic Policy for India in the Twenty-first Century.* New Delhi: Center for Policy Research.

Clark, C. 2009. *Iron Kingdom: The Rise and Fall of Prussia, 1600-1947.* Boston: Belknap Press of Harvard University.

Clark, I. 1989. *The Hierarchy of States: Reform and Resistance in the International Order.* Cambridge, U.K.: Cambridge University Press.

Clary, C. 2011. *The United States and India: A Shared Strategic Future,* A Joint Study Group Report, Council on Foreign Relations and Aspen Institute India.

Clinton, H. 2011. 'Remarks on India and the United States: A Vision for the 21st Century', Secretary of State, Anna Centenary Library, Chennai, India, 20 July, at www.state.gov/secretary/rm/2011/07/168840.htm.

Debroy, B. 2008. 'India's Soft Power and Cultural Influence', Challenges of Economic Growth, Inequality, and Conflict in South Asia, Paper presented at the Proceedings of the 4th International Conference on South Asia, Singapore, 24 November, at http://eproceedings.worldscinet.com/9789814293341/toc.shtml.

Dietl, G. P. 2008. 'Selection, Security, and Evolutionary International Relations' in R. D. Sagarin and T. Taylor (eds), *Natural Security: A Darwinian Approach to a Dangerous World*. Berkeley & Los Angeles: University of California Press.

Gandhi, L. 2014. 'Mumbai's Forgotten Mutiny', *Indian Express*, 5 April.

Garver, J. W. 2001. *Protracted Contest: Sino-Indian Rivalry in the Twentieth Century*. Seattle: University of Washington Press.

Griffiths, Sir P. 1965. *The British Impact on India*. London: Frank Cass & Co.

Guha, R. 2011. 'Will India Become a Superpower?' in *India: The Next Super Power?* Special Report No. 10 [London: London School of Economics], pp. 15–16 at http://www2.lse.ac.uk/IDEAS/publications/reports/SRO10.aspx.

Herring, C.G. 2008. *From Colony to Superpower: U.S. Foreign Relations since 1776*. Oxford University Press.

Hiranandani, Vice Admiral (ret.) G.M. 2005. *Transition to Eminence: The Indian Navy 1976–1990*. New Delhi: Naval Headquarters and Lancer Publishers.

Integrated Headquarters. 2009. *Indian Maritime Doctrine, 2009*. New Delhi: Integrated Headquarters, Ministry of Defense (Navy).

Institute of Diplomacy and Foreign Affairs. 2008. *Tunku Abdul Rahman Putra al-Haj*, Diplomatic Profile Series—Profiles of Malaysia's Foreign Ministers. Kuala Lumpur, Ministry of Foreign Affairs, Malaysia.

Fabian, K. P. 2014. 'Bitter truths', *Frontline*, 19 September, p. 100.

Iyengar, P.K., A.N. Prasad, A. Gopalakrishnan, and B. Karnad. 2009. *Strategic Sellout: Indian-U.S. Nuclear Deal*. New Delhi: Pentagon Press.

Kagan, R. 2002. 'Power and Weakness', *Policy Review*, No. 113, June/July at www.mtholyoke.edu/acad/intrel/bush/kagan.htm.

Karnad, B. 1994. 'India's Weak Geopolitics and What To Do About It', in Bharat Karnad (ed.), *Future Imperiled: India's Security in the 1990s and Beyond*, pp. 30–1. New Delhi: Viking-Penguin.

———. 2005 [First Edition 2002]. *Nuclear Weapons and Indian Security: The Realist Foundations of Strategy*, Chs. 2 & 3. New Delhi: Macmillan India.

———. 2002. 'India First', *Seminar*, Issue No. 509, at http://www.india-seminar.com/2002/519/519%20bharat%20karnad.htm.

Karnad, B. 2008. *Indian Nuclear Policy*. Westport, CT: Praeger.

———. 2014. 'Giving our foes the advantage', *Hindustan Times*, 13 October.

Kennedy, P. 1984. *Strategy and Diplomacy, 1870-1945: Eight Studies*. London: Fontana Press.

———. 1989. *The Rise and Fall of the Great Powers*. New York: Vintage.

———. 2013. 'The Great Powers, Then and Now', *New York Times*, 13 August.

Kissinger, H. 2006. 'A Nuclear Test of Diplomacy', *Washington Post*, May 16.

Kolff, D. H. 1990. *Naukar, Rajput and Sepoy: The Ethnohistory of the Military Labor of Hindustan, 1450-1850*. Cambridge, UK: Cambridge University Press.

Ladwig III, W. C. 2010. 'India and Military Power Projection: Will the Land of Gandhi Become a Conventional Great Power?', *Asian Survey*, 50 (6) (November/December): 1171.

Lattimore, O. 1945. *Solution in Asia*. London: The Cresset Press.

MacDonald, J. A. 2002. *Indo-U.S. Relationship: Expectations and Perceptions*. Washington, D.C.: U.S. Department of Defense, Oct.

Maddison, A. 2007. *Contours of the World Economy, 1-2030 AD: Essays in Macroeconomic History*. Oxford, UK: Oxford University Press.

Malone, David. 2012. *Does the Elephant Dance: India's Contemporary Foreign Policy*. Oxford University Press.

Mandlebaum, M. 2010. *The Frugal Superpower: America's Global Leadership in a Cash-strapped Era* .New York: Public Affairs.

Massie, R. K. 1991. *Dreadnought: Britain, Germany, and the Coming of the Great War*. New York: Ballantine Books.

Mayo, K. 1927 [reprint, 1970]. *Mother India*. Westport, CN: Greenwood Press.

Mishra, B. 2012. 'Foreword' in *India-US Defence Trade Relations: Trends and Challenges*, compiled by Uma Purushottaman, ORF Seminar Series, 1 [April] (7): 1. New Delhi: Observer Research Foundation.

Mishra, P. *From the Ruins of Empire: The Revolt Against the West and the Remaking of Asia*. New York: Farrar, Straus & Giroux, 2012.

Morgenthau, H. J. 1967. *Politics Among Nations*, 4th ed. New York: Alfred A. Knopf.

Nehru, J. 1953. 'Nehru's 8 March 1948 speech in the Constituent Assembly', in *Jawaharlal Nehru's Speeches, 1946-1949*. New Delhi: Ministry of Information and Broadcasting, Government of India.

———. 1988. *Selected Works of Jawaharlal Nehru*, Second Series, Volume 7. New Delhi: Jawaharlal Nehru Memorial Fund.

Nehru, J. 1991a. *Selected Works of Jawaharlal Nehru*, Second Series, vol 11. New Delhi: Jawaharlal Nehru Memorial Fund.

———. 1991b. *Selected Works of Jawaharlal Nehru*, Second Series, Volume 12. New Delhi: Jawaharlal Nehru Memorial Fund.

———. 1992. *Selected Works of Jawaharlal Nehru*, Second Series, Vol 13. New Delhi: Jawaharlal Nehru Memorial Fund.

Noorestani, H. 2013.'The Bollywood Effect: Women and Film in South Asia', *Foreign Policy*, 11 April.

Nye, Jr., J. P. 2004. *Soft Power: The Means to Success in World Politics*. New York: Public Affairs Press.

Pandit, R. 2011. 'India world's No. 1 arms importer', *Times of India*, 14 March.

Parry, A. 2006. 'Why Bush is courting India', *Time*, 28 February.

Perkovich, G. 2003–04. 'Is India a Major Power?', *Washington Quarterly*, Winter 2003-04: 129–30, 140.

Planning Commission. 2002. *India Vision 2020*. New Delhi: Government of India.

Prakash, Admiral A. (Retd.) A. 2011. 'Is it time to send a destroyer?', *Indian Express*, 20 April.

———. 2013. 'India as a 21st Century Power: The Maritime Dimension', Admiral R.L. Periera Memorial Lecture, Bangalore, 25 May.

Pressler, L. 1994. 'The Restraint of Fury: US Non-Proliferation Policy and South Asia', in B. Karnad (ed.), *Future Imperilled: India's Security in the 1990s and Beyond*. New Delhi: Viking Penguin.

Priestland, D. 2012. *Merchant, Soldier, Sage: A New History of Power*. London: Allen Lane.

Pubby, M. 2012. '12th Defense Plan: Focus on Navy's "expeditionary" ops', *Indian Express*, May 4.

Puri, H. S. 2013. 'Forging a New Horse Shoe'. *Hindu*, 3 March.

Raja Mohan, C. 2010. 'India's strategic future', *Foreign Policy*, 4 November, at www.foreignpolicy.com/articles/2010/11/04/indias_strategic_future

Raja Mohan, C. 2014. 'Silk route to Beijing', *Hindu,* 15 September.

Rapoza, K. 2012. 'India Software Cos Not Happy With U.S. Visa Rule', *Forbes*, 1 April, www.Forbes.com

Rice, C. 2011. *No Higher Honor: A Memoir of My Years in Washington*. New York: Simon & Schuster.

Saini, A. 2011. 'India is an emerging geek super power', *Guardian*, 3 March, at http://www.theguardian.com/commentisfree/2011/mar/03/india-emerging-geek

Sanders, S. 2012. 'Demography as the soft underbelly of geopolitics', *Washington Times*, 12 August.

Saran, S. 2014. 'The dangers of nuclear revisionism', *Business Standard,* 22 April.

Scindia, J. 2011. 'India Engages the World: The View From New Delhi', *Global Asia,* March.

Sen, A. 2005. *The Argumentative Indian: Writings on Indian Culture, History and Identity.* New Delhi: Viking, Penguin India.

Sherman, W. 2012 . 'United States and India: An Indispensable Partnership for the 21st Century', Remarks, Under Secretary for Political Affairs, American Center, New Delhi, 2 April, at www.state.gov/p/us/rm/2012/187401.htm.

Showalter, Dennis. 2004. *The Wars of German Unification.* New York: Bloomsbury Press.

Singh, J. 1999. *Defending India.* Basingstoke, U.K.: Palgrave Macmillan.

———. 2009. *Jinnah-India-Pakistan-Independence.* New Delhi: Rupa & Co.

———. 2013. *India at Risk: Mistakes, Misconceptions and Misadventures of Security Policy.* New Delhi: Rainlight-Rupa.

Singh, Dr. M. 2007 . 'India—Opportunities & Challenges in the Twenty-first Century' in N. Shandare, (ed.), *India: The Next Superpower?* New Delhi: Roli Books.

Singh, N. (ed.). 2010. *Nehru-Patel: Agreement within Differences, Select Documents and Correspondences, 1933-1950 .* New Delhi: National Book Trust.

Tanham, G. 1992. *Indian Strategic Thought: An Interpretive Essay.* Santa Monica: RAND.

Talbott, S. 2004. *Engaging India: Diplomacy, Democracy and the Bomb.* Washington, D.C.: The Brookings Institution.

Tellis, A. J. 2005. *India as a New Global Power: American Action Agenda for the United States.* Washington, D.C.: Carnegie Endowment for International Peace.

Tellis, A. J., J. Bially, C. Layne, M. McPherson. 2000. *Measuring National Power in the Post-Industrial World.* Santa Monica: RAND.

Thapar, R. 1998 [revised ed.]. *Asoka and the Decline of the Mauryas.* New York: Oxford University Press.

Tharoor, S. 2012. *Pax Indica: India and the World in the 21st Century.* New Delhi: Allen Lane, The Penguin Group.

Vaishnav, M. 2013. 'The Modi Debate Worth Having in India', Carnegie Endowment for International Peace, 8 October, at http://carnegieendowment.org/2013/10/08/modi-debate-worth-having-in-india/gpfj.

Wainwright, A. M. 1994. *Inheritance of Empire: Britain, India and the Balance of Power in Asia, 1938–55.* Westport, CN, and London: Praeger.

Wheeler, J.S. 1999. *The Making of a World Power: War and the Military Revolution in Seventeenth Century England.* Gloucestershire, UK: Phoenix Mill.

Wheeler, J.T. 2005. [electronic facsimile reprint, original publication in 1886]. *India Under the British Rule from the Foundation of the East India Company.* London: Adamant Media Corp.

Williamson, J. 2006. 'The Rise of the Indian Economy', *American Diplomacy,* May 2006, at www.unc.edu/depts./diplomat/item/2006/0406/will/williamson_india.html.

Yong, T.T. 2005. *The Garrison State: Military, Government and Society in Colonial Punjab, 1849-1847.* New Delhi: Sage.

2

Rimland Coalitions and Indian Security

The Indo-Pacific region has six nuclear weapon states—the United States, Russia, China, India, Pakistan, North Korea; five chokepoints—Suez, Hormuz, Malacca, Lumbok, Sunda; four major players—India, U.S., China, Japan; three rogue, pariah, failed, or seriously troubled countries—North Korea, Iran, Pakistan; five disputed land and maritime borders—India–China, India–Pakistan (in Kashmir), China–ASEAN states in the South China Sea, China–Japan over the Senakaku/Diaoyu Islands, and the post–Second World War-related Russia-Japan tussle over the Kurile Islands; two hotly contested stretches of water—the South China Sea and the Senkaku Islands; an active theater of war—Afghanistan; and innumerable sources of sub-regional terrorist action triggering tumult and capable of escalating into military hostilities (India–Pakistan, Pakistan–Iran).

Heavily engaged with most countries in Asia, India is well-placed to control the five 'chokepoints' in the Indian Ocean, and competes with China for a foothold in natural resources-rich countries of Central Asia and, on the flanks of the Indian Ocean littoral in East Africa, South Africa and the African hinterland, and in South East Asia. The Indian Ocean is centered on India and constitutes the bulk of South Asia and, owing to its seaward territories in the Bay of Bengal—some 500 islands and over a third of the Indian Exclusive Economic Zone (EEZ) of 2,305,143 sq kms stretching southeastwards to just 90 miles off Sumatra, making it a Southeast Asian nation as well.[1] The Invitation to India to be a founder member of the ASEAN in 1967, however, went unanswered by an Indian government lacking the strategic wit to join. Grateful for the traditionally good relations and the gift of a bunch of corvettes along with stocks of spares and service support, Vietnam in 1992 offered India naval use of Cam Ranh Bay, which offer was also ignored. Indian leaders have clearly lacked an appreciation of geography as a strategic tool.[2] The Indian policy establishment and the strategic enclaves, taking their cue not from Nehru's outline of an 'Asian Monroe Doctrine', but from his damning the discipline of geopolitics for its association with Nazi excesses attributed by him to Hitler's geopolitical advisers, such as Karl Haushofer, likewise learned nothing from the success of the British geostrategic policy in the colonial age geared chiefly to safeguarding India by securing approaches to it on land and sea.[3] The disinterest in cultivating geopolitically important states is traditionally so deep that Prime Minister Manmohan Singh was reluctant (in 2004–06) to even meet with visiting Presidents of the Central Asian Republics and leaders of the ASEAN, and had to be prodded by the MEA into doing so.[4]

India cannot anymore afford to be geographically aloof and inattentive to geopolitical developments, particularly in the Indian Ocean, its own oceanic backyard, and on the landward side stretching to Central Asia. Maintaining effective control in the IOR does not in the twenty-first century mean the same thing it did two hundred years ago, when the Royal Navy disallowed entry into these waters by other European navies seeking trade and colonies. In the present day, it requires only that adversarial states are made aware that long sea distances from home base make hostile external naval forces vulnerable to actions by Indian naval ships, conventional and Akula-class nuclear-powered hunter-killer submarines (SSNs) and aircraft operating from carriers and peninsular bases. It is this geographic advantage in the nearly closed waters of the Indian Ocean, this chapter will argue, that is the foundation for the maritime end of an Indian Monroe Doctrine system, which can coexist with the two other similar Monroe Doctrine systems in the East Sea presided over by China, and in the Far East and the Western Pacific by Japan and the United States. It is a geostrategic system of inter-facing but clearly-defined systems that can oversee order and peace in seaward Asia, with the beneficial impulses of secure trade and commerce radiating outwards towards Eurasia and the oceans from these three Monroe Doctrine spheres, to facilitate amity and peace.

'Distant Defence' and its Prospects

The British concept of 'distant defence'—a phrase coined by Lord Minto, Governor-General of India in the early nineteenth century begat the policy of strengthening the 'Outer Ring' of India's defense. It led to the 'Great Game' of keeping Czarist Russia as far away as possible from Central Asia, controlling the court in Tehran and Persia's easterly ambitions, and securing the northwestern marches by dominating Afghanistan, and having the Arabian peninsula, the Trucial States, and the Gulf in a vice-like grip to protect the seaward approaches to the subcontinent and, later, the oil sea lanes. The Indian Ocean, moreover, was turned into 'an Indian lake' with the ships of the Royal Navy's Indian Ocean squadron performing constabulary duty assisted by coaling stations on the littoral in Simonstown, Mombassa, Aden, Karachi, Mumbai (Bombay) , Trincomalee, and Singapore, with Hong Kong tethering this system east of Malacca (Yapp 1980: 50–155). Complementing the 'Outer Ring' was the 'Inner Ring' of defence that Olaf Caroe, Foreign Secretary in the colonial Indian government of the late 1930s called, 'the Mongolian fringe' firmed up by treaties, military presence, and punitive expeditions. It created a Tibet distanced from the claims of Chinese suzerainty, a series of protectorates on India's Himalayan ramparts—Nepal, Sikkim, Bhutan, and Burma (Myanmar) functioning as virtual extensions of the British Indian territory. By administratively collapsing the tribal lands in the northeast—'the Naga Hills'—into the Indian colonial system, moreover, an elongated buffer was obtained separating India from the heartland behemoth, China (Brobst 2005: 60–97). The inner- and outer-ringed defence system bequeathed by the British and the strategic vision and goals driving it were, however, lost on a differently tuned Indian government post-1947 but, if revived could, with some obvious changes, work well in the twenty-first century, with the outer-ring encompassing the land-sea arc Central Asia-Vietnam-Australia.

Distant defence necessitates keeping close tabs on big and small changes in the near-abroad, and is predicated on a spatial understanding of evolving threats and the art of balancing power in the proximal areas and regions farther afield—something the British understood well but, historically, escaped Indian rulers. 'From the earliest times', said K.M. Panikkar, India's ambassador to China in the early 1950s and the only geopolitical-minded official close to Nehru, addressing the Indian School of International Studies on February 13, 1961, 'India lacked interest in the balance of power outside its own national frontiers. While China was continuously watchful of developments across the land frontiers and had developed a very efficient system of diplomatic relationship on a continental basis, the Indian idea of diplomacy was confined to states within the geographical limits of India....[S]o far as areas outside the physical boundaries of India were concerned, we were content to live with the attitude of complacent ignorance.' Repeated invasions from the northwest over a millennium did not reform the outlook of Indian rulers to try and assess the danger from that direction to get a drop on evolving threats over the horizon, and to take actions to preempt them. They waited as, Panikkar noted, for enemies to be at Delhi's doorstep before offering battle, proving that Indian regimes in those times were creatures of habit of mind, drawing no lessons from their own experience and history of military defeats.[5] The failure to convert his 'Asian' Monroe Doctrine idea into a more realizable Indian Monroe Doctrine system established much the same point about Nehru's lack of extended situational awareness.

The Nehruvian-origin insensitivity to geography and geopolitics, obediently absorbed by the Indian Ministry for External Affairs, has compounded the problem; its diplomacy, mistakenly emphasizing relations with big Western powers, missing out on the bigger, more lasting gains from cultivating lesser states in the region and in widening circles from the heartland. It is precisely because these ostensibly weak states were left unattended by New Delhi that they gradually got sucked into the orbit of a venturesome adversary, China. Unlike New Delhi, Beijing has diligently wooed the countries ringing India with financial aid, infrastructure assistance, trade concessions, and arms transfers. New Delhi may have kept its hand in, manipulating the internal affairs of adjoining states as and when necessary to persuade and pressure their governments to fall in line.[6] But it did not, and still does not have, the strategic foresight and policy to incentivize adjoining states to connect their economies to the Indian economy with generous aid and trade concessions and to strengthen them militarily so as to create a defensible line. The demonstration effect of such economic initiatives will have wider repercussions— engendering trust and, in more distant Asian states, confidence about New Delhi's intentions and ability to take on China. Indeed, the basic requirement of a great power that it have pacified neighbours is missing in the case of India, with most countries abutting it having strained relations with New Delhi. The Modi government having embarked on cultivating most of these states in the subcontinent, the outlook for India may change. But not if New Delhi is intolerant of their domestic politics and acts censoriously or meddles too overtly in their internal affairs. And yet, in the recent past, New Delhi aped the U.S. policy of pushing democratic values to the detriment of the national interest. Alienating the previously friendly military junta in Myanmar, for example, and driving it into China's embrace is nevertheless seen by many as 'smart' use of power (Menon 2014). In terms of the expected outcomes, it was as disastrous as the Indian government's deliberately ignoring over the years the main player in Pakistan, the Pakistan Army, and failing to cut a deal with it rather than entertaining the idea pitched by the likes of the late Pakistani leader Benazir Bhutto that dealing only with elected leaders and governments will help democracy flourish in that country. Democracy or lack thereof in other countries is no business of India's. In South Asia, its only concern should be how peacefully to recover the unitary economic and security space lost post 1947, and what it can do by way of politico-military inducements and economic incentives to bring this about. Converesely, the failure to mesh the subcontinental states in complex interconnectivity will permit extra-regional powers, such as China to fuse their interests with those of India's neighbours and turn them against New Delhi.

Nehru's conception of the 'Asian Monroe Doctrine' was fueled by his conviction that, based on the colonial geopolitics and the power of the Indian Army—both legacies of the British Raj, India's helming such a strategic architecture would have ready acceptability among other Asian states, and that New Delhi could thus advance its own interests, which were assumed to be convergent with Asia's, without attracting charges of 'big brother'. This was a fundamental mistake which Indian foreign policy still suffers from. Instead of using geography to map national interests and categorize them as core, vital, secondary, tertiary and short-term, medium-term, and long-term—an exercise that was not carried out by Nehru in his time nor by any Indian government since, the country's 'national interest' is a floating value that can be anything the prime minister of the day wants it to be and, absent such direction, anything any ministry or department of government decides it is (Karnad 2013). This is the reason for the inconstancy and incoherence in Indian foreign policy. When not conflating national interest with those of the unmanageable Third World group of nations in the Nonaligned bloc, Nehru mooted an Asia-wide security system or one tied to universal themes, such as 'general and complete disarmament'. Worse, being his own foreign minister and the fount also of ideas for the country's defence and, given deferential civil servants of the colonial era Indian Civil Service, manning the various ministries of government who feared reprisals against them after Independence and were relieved to find there were none and in gratitude and by force of habit looked up to the new political masters for policy guidance, there was no one to question Nehru's policy premises or the manner in which he made decisions. Hence, impromptu statements and pronouncements by the Prime Minister made quite literally on the run were treated as policy parameters by the Ministry of External Affairs and the Ministry of Defence and the Nehruvian ways of thinking, his outlook, approach, and policy lines got ingrained even as his nuances were missing.[7]

Thus, instead of prioritizing a careful tending of the immediate neighbourhood, Nehru sought to burnish his personal reputation and the country's stature by parlaying with the great powers to set the global agenda. It was the hey-day of Nehru's international activism based, as a Pakistani diplomat observed tartly, 'on global influence without military power.'[8] This tack quickly congealed into institutional prejudice in the Ministry, ironically, against the very developing states India hoped to lead. Thus, smaller countries—Burma (Myanmar), Sri Lanka, and even Pakistan—in the vicinity were perceived as weak entities having few options other than bend to New Delhi's decrees in the manner they had previously genuflected before the British Raj. Their security concerns of Communist China and suggestions for defence pact were airily dismissed.[9] This response to neighbours indicates Nehru did not foresee long term strategic gain from formal military ties with nearby states even as a means of firming up an Indian stake in the security of these countries and preempting outside powers from establishing a foothold in South Asia (Brobst 2005: 1).

Indeed, Nehru's skewed moral internationalism, which secretly acquiesced in a U.S.–U.K. military umbrella for India in the 1950s while seeking to deny it to other Asian states, perpetuated the official scorn for traditional alliances—what need for it if the same benefits could be reaped by maintaining the fiction of nonalignment and without undertaking any treaty obligations?[10] Nehru's daughter, Indira Gandhi, also adopted a moralistic posture but practiced a Moscow-leaning *realpolitik* during her tenure as Prime Minister (1966–1977, 1982–1984) (Tharoor 2012: 407). Unlike Nehru, who managed to benefit from sharpening the competitive instincts of both the United States and the Soviet Union, Mrs. Gandhi over-balanced towards Russia and could not fully exploit the superpower tensions during the middle years of the Cold War even as she retained Nehru's phraseology, and reinforced the Nehruvian rhetorical flourishes and socialist slant.[11]

Fifty years after Nehru's death, MEA still misses out on geopolitical imperatives, espousing nonalignment in the guise of 'strategic autonomy' as a prophylactic against having to make common cause with other nations against China.[12] It is the sort of thinking that has spawned 'a style of policy', writes Shashi Tharoor, a Congress party leader, that is 'long on rhetoric and short of hard-headed substance' and full of 'declaratory effulgences about nonalignment'. With a view, perhaps, to updating an old idea Tharoor, unhelpfully, coined another word synonymous with nonalignment—'multialignment' (Tharoor 2012: 406). To be multi-aligned, he claimed, is for India to 'belong to, and play a prominent role' in the UN and G-20, Nonaligned Movement and the Community of Democracies, G-77 and IORARC (Indian Ocean Rim Association for Regional Cooperation), SAARC (South Asian Association for Regional Cooperation) and the British Commonwealth, RIC (Russia, India, China), and BRICS (Brazil, RIC, and South Africa), and the

South-South alliances IBSA (India, Brazil, South Africa) and BASIC (Brazil, South Africa, India and China) (Tharoor 2012: 426). But to be aligned with every country or group of countries in sight amounts, in effect, to being aligned with nobody and, ironically, mirrors the sentiment of Nehru's confidante and Defence minister V.K. Krishna Menon. The 'essence of nonalignment', Krishna Menon explained, in 1955, 'is to be nonaligned! If all the impartial people gang up together they would become another block and aligned to each other, against the rest. The essence is…each country and government acts independently and not as part of group, or a block' (Karnad 2005: 91) To be nonaligned or multi-aligned segues into the 'friends with all'-mindset—a latter-day and still fuzzy update on the nonalignment/strategic autonomy idea, which leaves the country's foreign policy without a strong strategic undergirding.[13] Multi-alignment resembles the 'multipartner' world that Secretary of State Hillary Clinton in 2011 said the Obama Administration was striving to obtain, involving allies and peer-competitors joining the U.S. in upholding the extant global order (Drezner 2011: 64). Except, in the American scheme of things, partner-countries once identified and their willingness to partake of the shared mission ascertained, leads to follow-up steps, such as building up the partner state's capacity. In India's case, multialignment has the more limited purpose of preserving India's freedom of tactical maneouvre without expressly favouring any strategic partner.

In fact, as a big state with great power ambition, India shares with China some fundamental traits—functional autonomy, non-belief in alliance structures, and an independent foreign policy (Baker and Zhang 2012). But there are big differences. China believes in itself and in its rise and singlemindedly follows policies and engineers situations to further the goal of an Asia dominated by it. India perceives great power as a status other big powers will endow it with and hence tries and placates them, and it views 'strategic autonomy' as an expedient policy and, in tautological fashion, exercises it to be strategically autonomous! In the context of the 'strategic partnership' with the United States, it has the same relation—in practice that Nehru's nonalignment had with respect to Pentagon's plans for the 'Defence of India'—going overt with a military alliance with a big power only in time of extreme distress as occurred during the

1962 War with China. Indeed, Nehru made this clear in a parliament debate on Foreign Affairs on March 28, 1951. 'I do not understand why this wartime psychology of alignment should be imported into times of relative peace and why any country should be persuaded to line up with one group or another' (quote in Sehgal 2010: 62–3). Strategic autonomy that the Congress government of Manmohan Singh ballyhooed included the possibility that were the country to find itself in dire military straits, New Delhi would not hesitate to call friendly big powers for military help and diplomatic assistance. China's strategic autonomy, on the other hand, is an expression of self-confidence that it has arrived and has the wherewithal to fight its battles all by itself, dictate terms, and bend the global system to realize its ends (Jacques 2012a).

Strategizing requires, not demonization of any country, but a careful weighing of the balance of interests and capabilities, and recognition that if a conspicuous diplomatic, military and economic asymmetry occurs, it would spawn uncertainty and instability and, as between two comparable powers in Asia, lead to a situation in which China, feeling superior and sensing an opportunity, could initiate military hostilities, besides annexing disputed territory, to give a military glow to its standing in the world in the manner it did in 1962, when Nehru's running to Washington, for help burnished Beijing's image at the expense of India's reputation, which took a dive leeching in the process, all the self-confidence out of New Delhi. India and China are, however, only notionally in the same category, the latter having stolen a march and racing, as if possessed, to the First World ranks.[14] In the circumstances, the notion of an India able all by itself to protect its national interests vis-à-vis China by military means is problematic. Indian observers commenting on the growing disparity with China may well echo the Habsburg diplomat Ghiselin de Busbecq's rueful comparison in 1560 of the Austro-Hungarian Empire with its energetic Ottoman counterpart. 'On their side [is] endurance of toil, unity, order, discipline, frugality and watchfulness,' he wrote. 'On our side is public poverty, private luxury, impaired strength, broken spirit.' 'Can we', de Busbecq wondered, 'doubt what the result [of a war] would be?' (Quotes in Darwin 2008: 74, 77). How to stifle China's bellicosity is the principal problem facing India and the other states in the Indo-Pacific region. It is a concern evident in former Australian Prime Minister Paul Keating's asking 'why the U.S. never saw it coming; how did it not see the challenge to its primacy [from China] in the Pacific developing?' (Keating 2012).

Disruptive Behaviour as Dragon's Leverage

Obviously, America's Cold War strategy of building up China as a counterweight to the Soviet Union has backfired. It has only enabled China to rise some 40 years later as a militarily hefty and comprehensive great power, and as peer competitor to the U.S.[15] The hope the U.S., western Europe, and Japan had that their policies of economically boosting China, of helping it to become an industrial and trading powerhouse integrated into the existing international economic order, would persuade it to act as a 'responsible and con-structive stake-holder', has been belied. The heftier China grows, the more it seems inclined to throw its weight around, and the more the West tends to offer inducements to buy, or pay the price for, its good behaviour. Seeing it is all gain and no pain, Beijing's foreign policy has concentrated on creating global security problems to enhance its political and diplomatic leverages by deliberately nursing inter-national security threats—in the main, North Korea and Pakistan, whom it can manipulate to precipitate regional and international, usually nuclear, crises at will, because such crises raise the value of China's mediation that invariably follows.[16] Beijing has caused situa-tions to develop on the Korean Peninsula, by encouraging the North Korean dictator, Kim Jong-un, periodically to act up, create scares allowing Beijing to turn down the heat, defuse the situation, win accolades and gratitude all-round and strengthen the perception that no international issue of war or peace or concerning regional/interna-tional security can be resolved without its involvement. It is a means by which China renders itself indispensable to the smooth conduct of international affairs.[17] Neither New Delhi nor Washington seems to have caught on yet to this 'run with the hares, hunt with the hounds' Chinese strategy.[18] China's frisky foreign policy of slyly undermin-ing international norms of behaviour and multilateral institutions in practice is evidenced in its policy of calculatedly proliferating nuclear materials, technology, and expertise while formally sticking to diplo-matic niceties and swearing by nonproliferation strictures. It affords

Beijing power of mischief it does not hesitate to exercise, making China unique in its ability simultaneously to undermine the global system, strengthen its own relative position, and exploit the privileges and maneouvring room it creates for itself to at once source nuclear security/regional security problems and be an inalienable part of any solution.

With the international system apparently helpless, such unscrupulous Chinese behaviour justifies reciprocal overt or covert actions by states victimized by it, such as India. Thus, a belated response to China's nuclear missile-arming Pakistan would be India's assisting Vietnam and other countries on China's borders fearful of Chinese intentions and mindful of the attractions of the Bomb, to secure nuclear missiles to deter Beijing all by themselves (Karnad 2008: Ch 1, 30–1). This would right the situation tilted in China's favour and strategically discomfit the latter in the manner India has been discommoded by a Pakistan equipped with a force of Chinese-sourced nuclear weapons and delivery systems. It will compel China, as the Washington Post columnist Charles Krauthammer put it, to 'share the [nuclear] nightmare'.[19] In fact, such an action by India becomes growingly urgent with China offering a graver provocation—passing materials, design and technical assistance to Pakistan to acquire thermonuclear weapons.[20] Minus a harsh payback, China will persist with its untrammeled approach to nuclear proliferation.[21]

China is 'converting' its wealth to military power and acquiring interests (in energy and other raw materials) overseas in Africa and even Latin America, and consolidating its own distinct sphere of influence where it will brook no outside interference, in effect, an extended Chinese Monroe Doctrine.[22] That this development would centrally hurt the American profile in Asia is what tipped the U.S. to 'pivot' to the region China had marked out as its own and for President Obama to discover what his predecessor George W Bush had appreciated that, in the event, a power balance in Asia without India was infeasible.[23] Secretary of State Hillary Clinton sought to fill out the new security theme by voicing the need for enhanced 'coordination and engagement among the three giants of the Asia-Pacific, China, India, and the United States', and described India as the 'linchpin' of the U.S. government's 'new vision for a more economically integrated and politically stable South and Central Asia'. It was a description repeated by the visiting U.S. Secretary of Defense Leon Panetta in June 2012. While no doubt flattered to be accorded prominence in this new formulation, New Delhi reacted with its usual ambivalence. The often mercurial changes in the U.S. attitude and policies are legion and New Delhi has found it hard to keep up with the new policy foci and momentary enthusiasms of changing Administrations in Washington. The unpredictability so engendered is unsettling to Asian states which see policy flux as mirroring America's infirmity of will and of its security commitments, and uncertainty about what any retooled U.S. strategy may entail in a crisis (Alexander 2012; Zeng & Wang 2011). India's reserve is also because it has long been a free-rider on security provided by the U.S. military in Asia (Karnad 2009). As a rising power it feels no need, as the sinologist Mixin Pei noted, 'to shoulder a significant amount of the cost of maintaining the existing liberal order because [it has a] doubt about the added benefits [it] will receive for sharing part of the costs' (Pei 2012). New Delhi, however, sees positives accruing from the periodic trilateral meetings between India, China and the United States, in which India and the U.S. have mainly tried to address Beijing's suspicions of 'encirclement'.[24]

The fact of the international system being just too wild for the previously predominant power, the United States, to tame singly is by now a truism. In fact, Americans are reconciling to their country declining to the 'Number 2' position behind China.[25] What this means, the Singaporean diplomat, Kishore Mahbubani, pointed out is that 'When it is number one, it is in America's interests to see that the number one power has complete freedom to do whatever it wants to do. When it is number two, it is not in America's interests to see that the number one power has complete freedom to do whatever it wants to do.'[26] Indeed, keeping order may also be beyond the capacity of agglomerations of elite powers, such as G-8 or G-20, leave alone the America–China combine (G-2) or the India-Japan-United States (G-3) or any other combination of powers to handle resulting, Ian Bremmer opined, in a 'G-zero' world in which every country has to fend for itself (Bremmer 2012: 16). Such a world does not, however, preclude nations coming together and working collegially to put up a stiff front against a marauder state. The question is on what basis do they do so? Robert Kagan argues that 'a nation's form of government' and not its 'civilization' or its geographical location per se is the best predictor of its 'geopolitical alignment' (Kagan 2008). Actually, a far better predictor is national interest aligned with geography.[27] It explains America's 'rebalance to Asia' and shift of priorities and resources from the Atlantic littoral and Western Europe to Asia and the Pacific.[28] It also explains China's 'Move to the West', solidifying relations with European states, Russia, Iran, Central Asian countries, and Pakistan to breakout of what it conceives as U.S. containment pressures on her eastern and southeast Asian seaboards.[29] And Russia is trying to at once neutralize the U.S. by presenting itself to China as an alternative source of energy and other natural resources and as an alternative land route for the Chinese trade headed Europewards bypassing the Suez and Malacca Straits chokepoints, and otherwise to create a friendly periphery, including India.[30] The catch for Washington is that in its relatively weakened state it is confronted by a militarily revived Russia and an aggressive China ensconced at the two ends of the Eurasian continent.[31] With the diminution in American power grudgingly accepted in Washington, the regional cries of Asian 'Crimeas' and 'Sudentenlands' go unheeded, the U.S. is busy reaffirming, however unconvincingly, its military support for Asian countries.[32] The problem is Asian states see a U.S. bending over backwards to accommodate China.[33] It has flagged the issue of a diminished America not showing the requisite political humility needed to deal with Asian states who believe that a resources-strapped U.S. is a thin reed for them to lean on.[34] This is happening at a time when leading regional countries are rediscovering the benefits from forging links with each other and a more confident Moscow.[35] In the circumstances, getting even friendly countries to perceive threats in the same way as the U.S. does and to join it in tackling them on American terms is, as the Yale historian Paul Kennedy put it, to be oblivious to the decanting of power from America and the West to Asia. To, moreover, expect that Washington will or can always get its way now and in the future, when the cost of dealing with a belligerent Beijing in terms of the political, economic, and military fallout will likely be borne disproportionately by Asian states, he added, is to 'display a naïvete about power politics that is breathtaking' (Kennedy 2010).

If China is simply too imposing to be constrained by the United States alone, then a loose coalition of like-minded Indo-Pacific states with obvious geo-strategic compatibilities can be a countervailing force, helpful in maintaining a power equilibrium. Overlapping diplomatic exchanges and bilateral and multilateral free trade agreements (FTAs) in South Asia, South East Asia and the Far East, moreover, can firm up this arrangement, impact the Chinese strategic calculi, and restrain Beijing. But, for whatever reasons, the United States, is not playing ball. It could have eased India's entry into the premier economic grouping—the Asia-Pacific Economic Cooperation (APEC), but has been 'reluctant' to do so, just as it has not shown interest, since mid-2013, in holding the East Asia dialogue with New Delhi to discuss China-related issues, and has been tepid when it comes to the trilateral discussion forum involving India and Japan, lest Beijing find such meetings objectionable (Bagchi 2014). This even though, as former U.S. Ambassadors Teresita C. and Howard B. Schaffer observed, it would 'reinforce the strategic and economic interests that [India's] Look East policy has long recognized….as foundation stones for the new relationship with Washington.'[36] And, it insists India not resume nuclear testing even if this improves the quality of the Indian thermonuclear arsenal, achieves deterrence parity with China, and more credibly restrains Beijing strategically. Washington seems as concerned as China about not upsetting, what a Chinese strategic writer claims is, 'a delicate balance' obtained by the U.S. not testing its reliable replacement warhead lest it lead to China testing to improve and expand its nuclear armaments which, in turn, could blowback with 'a ripple effect on India and Pakistan'—'an outcome', he says, the United States doesn't want' (Shen 2007).

Contesting China's 'Peaceful Rise'

In history, there has been no such thing as 'peaceful rise' by any country because, however, peaceful the rise, it is still disruptive of the extant order, occasions shifts in power balances, and presages conflict (Kirshner 2008: 238). But it is convenient rhetoric China has wrapped its policies around. Its aggressive behaviour on the South China Sea disputes with weaker nations, and vis-à-vis Japan on the Senkaku/Diaoyu Islands, and its military incursions in April 2013 and again in September 2014 in the Ladakh region to test Indian resolve and the Indian Army's preparedness during President Xi Jinping's India visit, offer glimpses of its favouring the use of force. It suggests the jettisoning of what has been called the 'kindlier, gentler China' persona that Deng Xiaoping had cannily insisted his country cultivate until it reached a certain threshold of power (Tellis 2011: 24). Apparently, China's rulers believe they have now crossed that point, and the country can afford to be offensive.

But, how did matters come to this pass? Crucially, China's 'peaceful rise' has been facilitated by three Asia-Pacific countries—India, Japan and the United States. These states had the most to lose from such development and far from doing anything, singly or together, to hinder, or even slow down China's rise, in their separate ways and for different reasons, aided and abetted its ascent. Consider India's apathy: it neither blocked the Chinese economic, political and military inroads into southern Asia (Pakistan, Myanmar, Bangladesh, Nepal, and Sri Lanka) with deft diplomatic counter-moves, nor showed the gumption to respond in kind to a series of actions by Beijing strategically to undermine its interests by, as mentioned, tit-for-tat transfers of nuclear missiles to Vietnam, nuclear weapons collaboration with Taiwan, etc. Further, India's militarily fixating on Pakistan, which amounted to dealing with the cat's paw (Pakistan), not the cat (China), diverted the national focus and scarce resources from the China front, confirming Beijing's wisdom in beefing up Pakistan. New Delhi showed similar laxness in not siding with Japan, South Korea, Taiwan, and the ASEAN members to hamper China's advance. And it has not played the 'Tibet card' of assisting the Tibetan freedom movement by actively training and launching Tibetan guerillas against PLA targets in Tibet in response to China's help to rebel Movements in the Indian northeast (Sharma 2013). And by not pleading the cause of a 'Free Tibet' in multilateral forums failed to develop negotiating leverage on Arunachal Pradesh and the boundary dispute.[37]

Enabling Vietnam and other states of Southeast Asia to more effectively fence in China on their vulnerable land borders and sea territories by strengthening their military capacities is now recognized as the thing to do (Jimbo 2012). Better motivated states on the Chinese periphery with more at stake will more fiercely fight off

China than any outside powers if they are militarily empowered to do so. India's helping Vietnam out with strategic armaments and building up its fighting capabilities, and generally treating it as its military pivot in the South China Sea, will force China to concentrate on its security perimeter in Southeast Asia, thus loosening the Chinese pressure on the Sino-Indian land border. With a potentially hostile rear area to defend, the Chinese Navy in particular is likely to venture less deeply and in strength into the Indian Ocean. New Delhi's policy to help regional states become 'porcupines' to avoid being overwhelmed by the Chinese military is, however, only slowly gathering steam. Military assistance is beginning to be offered after gauging the requirements and the competence of friendly littoral countries.[38] For instance, the Vietnamese Navy in 2013 purchased six advanced Klub-S cruise missile-armed Kilo 636M diesel-electric submarines with improved stealth features from Russia (Kazianis 2013). By 2018 when all the submarines will be in service, Vietnam will have the largest sea-denial capability among Southeast Asian nations and this could be a 'game changer'. At any given time, four of these boats prowling the waters around Hainan Island will inhibit the outward movements of ships of the powerful Chinese South Sea Fleet and together with the shore-based Indian Brahmos cruise missiles in the Vietnamese armoury, squelch Chinese moves to grab more islands in the South China Sea (Collin 2012). Building up capacity by training Vietnamese submarine crews and air force pilots will be supportive measures.[39] Aware that such gang-ups will complicate its attempts at imposing a Chinese order in the local seas, Beijing has prevented the ASEAN forum from being used for dispute resolution and sought to dampen fears by offering a 'treaty of friendship and cooperation' the Southeast Asian states believing in hedging strategy have welcomed.[40] The Singapore Defence Minister Ng Eng Hen visiting Beijing agreed, for instance, to broaden the 2008 accord formalizing bilateral defence activities and to 'try to accommodate each other's security needs for mutual trust.' Apart from larger, more sophisticated joint military exercises, there was agreement to station a Chinese naval officer at the maritime security watch group, the Information Fusion Centre, in Singapore (Chow 2014). It is by such means that Beijing means to deal separately with the disputant states, believing it will help it extract bigger concessions from each of them and that interference by outside states can be minimized both because of the willing cooperation of the ASEAN members and because these external players will prize good relations with China more than the interests of the local states. It is all the more reason for India to ratchet up its military assistance programmes and proactively to forge close economic relations by signing the free trade agreement that's been hanging fire.[41]

The so-far moderate policies of India, Japan, and the United States have apparently led Beijing to assume that continuing with its approach of mixing aggressive action with talk of increased trade and economic tie-ups is the way to defang its foes, which logic these three countries have bought into. Many in the Manmohan Singh government were convinced that 'There are strategic advantages to offering a potential adversary a large market', which would persuade the Chinese to 'see Indians as consumers rather than as enemies' (Tharoor 2012: 138). The U.S. Secretary of State Clinton admitted similar accommodation, referring to it as a process of adjustment 'that has never been done in history…when an established power and a rising power meet' (Wan 2012). The hope of trade promoting amity has fueled the Chinese and Indian foreign policies since the mid-2000s, spawning the comforting belief that there is enough political and economic 'space' for both countries to rise peacefully together (Huang, Bajpai & Mahbubani 2012). It is a policy premise the United States too has accepted with Secretary of State Clinton saying in September 2012, that 'the Pacific is big enough for all of us'.[42] It may work at a declaratory level but cannot paper over fundamental differences and clashes of interest or obviate telltale friction-points.[43] Even so Shivshankar Menon in the waning days of the Congress party-led government dismissed 'divergences' of Indian and Chinese interests as 'mostly in bilateral issues and in the periphery' while highlighting 'strategic convergences' as leading the two states to anchor 'stability in the midst of turmoil'.[44] Japan's 'carrot and stick' China policy likewise errs on the side of rapprochement in relations.[45] India, Japan, and the United States are, however, now cautiously exploring the means of deflating the danger they helped create for themselves, for Asia and the world at-large by working together politically and militarily to rein in China's baser instincts. Their working premise being that the autocratic regime in Beijing will consider the benefits it derives from the global economy as outweighing the gains from confrontationist policies.

The fact is that China is a great power phenomenon; its rocketing rise similar in many respects to Japan's, post-Meiji Restoration. By 1941 Japan grew to challenge the United States for supremacy in the Pacific much as a dirt-poor China after the Communist takeover has done in the present day, transforming itself into the strongest power in Eurasia. After escaping feudal isolation, Japan took just 30 years to become a leading Asian nation, less than forty years to become a world power (by decimating the Russian Pacific Fleet in the Tsushima Straits in 1905), and fewer than 75 years to confront the U.S.—'the foremost industrial power in the world' (Evans & Peattie 1997: xx). Keeping to a like schedule, Communist China intervened in the Korean War in late 1950 and fought the United States, at the time the greatest military power, to a draw, 15 years to take on the Soviet Union, the most powerful military land power in the 1969 border conflict on the Ussuri River, and fewer than 25 years from its inception in 1949 to become a thermonuclear weapons state able to deter Washington and Moscow with ICBMs, and less than sixty years to become the leviathan in the Asia-Pacific and the equal of the United States.

An Indian Monroe Doctrine[46]

Halford Mackinder's insights into heartland powers with interior lines of communications and defence controlling Eurasia, commanding the world's resources, and dictating the course of history, offer a cautionary tale (Mackinder 1942). Alfred Thayer Mahan's exaltation of sea power as the means of global dominance was premised on an outward-looking economy and a thriving manufacturing base at home generating wealth through exports carried to distant shores on an expanding fleet of merchant ships over oceans kept free of peril by a huge navy of big ships armed with big guns whose roaming presence also opened up newer markets abroad for the home country's agricultural produce and industrial goods, and realized ever-widening spheres of interest and influence (Mahan 1957). In the late 1940s, Nicholas J. Spykman expounded a geopolitical scheme envisioning a host of independently motivated and militarily capable 'rimland' or littoral and offshore states making common cause against the potential heartland hegemon (Spykman 1951). If Mackinder's geographic determinism explains China's expansionism and consolidation landward in the relatively vast, open, and vacant spaces of Tibet and Xinjiang that it has forcibly annexed, and in the context of the Siberian steppes held by a weak Russia, and Mahan's thesis of seapower is supported by the historical examples of Britain and, in the twentieth century, of the United States, Spykman's riff on Mackinder and Mahan has particular salience in the new millennium with the center of gravity of land and sea power shifting inexorably to China. Mackinder's criterion of a nation's central location and size, Mahan's seapower imperatives, and the littoral coalition logic of Spykman, in fact, combine to suggest the primacy of large states with long coastlines, such as the United States, China, and India emerging as power centers around which smaller states arrange themselves (Pei 2012). The European Union (EU) could be the fourth such power were it to morph into a single political unit and with a role for itself as other than an American appendage. This will necessitate a militarily strengthened EU which, in a time of defence cost-cutting, seems unlikely (Goldfarb and DeYoung 2014; O'Donnell 2012).

International laws and institutions and 'rules of the road' drafted mostly by the United States shaped the liberal international order after the Second World War, protected the interests of the West, and encouraged rising states to benefit from subscribing to it, which India and China have done. The elasticity of the system prevented wars and serious dislocations that marred the previous epochs of power transition (Ikenberry 2008). Except, and this is the strange thing, India is the revisionist power seeking an overhaul of the rank-order of nations, a place in the highest rule-making forums—as permanent member of the U.N. Security Council, the Nuclear Suppliers Group, Missile Technology Control Regime, etc., but it acts like a state wedded to the status quo and intent on maintaining it (Schaffer 2009). In contrast, China is a beneficiary of, and with manifest stake in, the existing international system—a seat at the high table, enjoying all the rights and privileges, the recognition and the trappings of great power but is, nevertheless, dissatisfied, wants more, and means to get it using tactics and stratagems historically utilized by rising, revisionist, powers to upend the status quo. As the perennial malcontent and belligerent employing reckless methods—proliferating WMD and missile technologies, violating the United Nations Convention on the Law of the Seas (UNCLOS) principles in the South China Sea and the East Sea, and liberally exercising its veto in the UN Security Council and other multilateral forums—China, practices hard *realpolitik*, seeks to change in its favour what it considers an unsatisfactory 'correlation of forces' by any and all means available to it, including economic measures such as vast financial investment and infrastructure aid. It earns China fear and respect but not influence—among Asian states only Laos, Cambodia, North Korea and Pakistan feel close to China (Bremmer 2013). Even so strong policies are reinforced because they are seen by Beijing as paying dividends. In practical terms, China is inclined to undermine international norms, India to follow them (Szabo 2012). India's low key posture and show of restraint, New Delhi has always hoped, will not just burnish its image as a responsible state but win it respect, a wider circle of friends and influence, and recognition and a role in the top forums. India is easier to get along with, but with a fast-growing military clout and monies to dispense Beijing is confident it has the means of suasion India lacks.[47]

The demographics in India and China, however, presage volatility in the internal and external realms and, possibly, hostilities between them. With the pronounced preference for the male child, China already has 45–60 million 'excess' males who are prone, writes Sol Sanders, 'to aggressive policies, including those favoring foreign adventure' (Sanders 2012). The economic slowdown and the inability in the future to sustain a high growth trajectory may spur an ultra-nationalistic Chinese stance that can precipitate wars (Haass 2012). With the skewing of the sex ratio for similar social reasons in India, there is the natural bellicosity of an overwhelmingly young male population pushing India towards greater assertiveness in the external realm. Recent public opinion surveys carried out over 10 years reveal a distinct rightward lurch of the Indian population, with wider support for policies that are aggressive in advancing the national interest, standing up to China, and seeking to speed the country towards great power status while cooperating with a friendly Russia and the West when and where necessary. But the poll results also show that the people are not enamored by mere symbols of great power (as much as the Indian government seems to be), such as a permanent seat on the UN Security Council. The people would rather the country progress by dismantling the socialist state, installing a freewheeling economy, increasing economic opportunities, and by securing and using military power to safeguard national interests and improve the country's international ranking.[48]

Tibet Card

With China's exports-driven economy slowing down and India subsiding to a lower growth rate as well in the last years of the Manmohan Singh government, and the job markets in the two countries not growing at a pace to meet the aspirations of youthful populations, internal disturbances are set to increase in both countries.[49] As diversion, the Communist regime in Beijing could whip up nationalist sentiment and try and make a grab for Tawang in the Indian northeastern province of Arunachal Pradesh the Chinese call 'southern Tibet'. The capture of that area, containing the monastery most important to the Tibetan Lama-ist traditions, will symbolically, physically, and culturally sever Tibet's attachment to India. It is a plan the Indian army is prepared to thwart, which is the least a nationalistic upsurge will demand in case the PLA starts an affray.

International legal opinion is that 'China's continued presence in Tibet constitutes a serious violation of international law.'[50] The Dalai Lama, the spiritual core of the movement for Free Tibet, keeps reminding India that 'The Tibetan culture is actually India's culture [which] is facing destruction in Tibet. So our guru, India, should show concern [and] Tibetan culture 'will act as the first defense line of India.'[51] Beijing has employed its standard 'wait it out' tactics in negotiations with the Tibetan government in exile (TGE) based in India seeking genuine autonomy, which in another diplomatic form has also kept New Delhi hanging. More sinister is the Chinese advocacy for abrogating minority status [for Tibetans] as stipulated in the Chinese constitution thereby removing the basis of its autonomy.[52] Constitutional or not, this is a solution traceable to Sun Yatsen, the revolutionary President of the first Chinese republic in 1911 who for 'China's salvation' advocated forceful policies to rub out the ethnic minorities—Manchus, Tibetans, Uighur Muslims, and absorbing them into the Han mainstream because, he declared, 'In simple terms the race or nationality has developed through natural forces, while the State has developed through force of arms' (Karnad 1994: 21–2).

This leaves India with three options. It can continue to ignore the Tibetan issue in the hope that such a stance will lead to Chinese showing lenience in the negotiations on the border issue. It can do nothing, and keep the 'Tibet card' in abeyance, use it as negotiating leverage with Beijing or, it can play this card, revisiting this option last exercised in the late 1950s when it joined the U.S. in training Khampa warriors in guerilla warfare and launching them in operations inside Tibet.[53] 'Establishment 22' located in Dehradun in the Himalayan foothills is operational as the center for training the Special Frontier Force (SFF) manned by Tibetan exiles and officered by the Indian army.[54] The Chinese rule is under strain, and violent dissent is rising in both the far western regions of Tibet and Xinjiang since the 1990s, owing to identity politics and oppressive policies (Sarmiento 2014; Hastings 2014). Street protests and grisly self-immolations have kept the Tibetan cause alive even as the more violent Islamic militancy has taken hold in Xinjiang.[55] The militarized unrest involving the East Turkestan Islamic Movement is turning more violent with the al-Qaeda and the financially and resources-wise flush Islamic State with a 10,000 strong fighting cadre of whom as many as half are from outside Syria and Iraq intent on 'recovering' this province for Islam, it will soften up China (Miller 2014; Griffiths 2014)). The Chinese authorities blame Pakistan for radicalizing the native Uyghurs and seeding the problem in the first place, the beneficial side-effect of which, from India's perspective, is possible estrangement of the two 'all weather' friends (Pantucci 2011). The Islamic fighters taking on the Chinese state and with explosive violence, deaths, and dislocation in train, have achieved what years of peaceful Uyghur and Tibetan protest failed to do—impress the world community with the fact of restive ethnic minorities within China. To forestall any telling measures by the international community, Beijing has allowed the U.N. High Commissioner for Human Rights Zeid Ra'ad al Hussein to visit the less violence-prone Tibet.[56] These developments open up a strategic opportunity for the Indian policy to be rid of its standoffishness and lead the clamour in international circles for the restitution of genuine autonomy that Tibetans enjoyed prior to the annexation of their land by PLA in 1949 as Mao Zedong had promised. A global campaign for Tibet is gathering momentum and can catch fire, which Beijing will find hard to douse.[57] New Delhi has to get involved in canvassing for the Tibetan cause as it will provide cover for India's initiating low-key, plausibly deniable, guerilla strikes inside Tibet, as a belated response to Beijing's providing safe haven for rebels on the run and supporting over the years various tribal secessionist groups in the Indian northeast. It should be part of the political offensive to connect the status of the Shaksgam Valley in Pakistan-occupied Kashmir ceded by Ayub Khan to China in 1963 to buy peace and cultivate a counter against India with Beijing, the Aksai Chin area the Chinese annexed in the 1950s, and Arunachal Pradesh which China claims along with Tibet, Taiwan, and India's rethinking its support for 'One China'. Foreign Ministers S.M. Krishna in 2007 and Sushma Swaraj in 2014 have put Beijing on notice that India will not recognize 'One China' if Beijing doesn't align its policy and pronouncements to include Arunachal Pradesh in the 'One India' concept (Samanta 2014; Ramachandran 2011). The Indian government needs to follow up by actually showing Tibet in a different colour from the rest of China on official Indian maps to indicate its questionable status and New Delhi's seriousness in mirror-imaging Chinese policies so Beijing cannot continue to gain from a double-faced posture which has proved productive for Beijing only because India has stayed its hand, unilaterally accepting all Chinese territorial claims while China refuses acknowledging a constituent state, Arunachal Pradesh, as Indian. New Delhi's inaction on this front is due to MEA's belief that raising the Tibetan (or Uyghur) issue will give Beijing the handle on Kashmir. Except, Premier Zhouenlai, as long ago as February 1964 accepted Pakistan's claim on all of Kashmir, and so China has done its worst (Ramachandran 2011). It is time for India to get into the act and begin strategically discomfiting China, for a start, in Tibet and Vietnam. The Modi government's view that such foreign policy turn might severely curtail Chinese infrastructure investment, is baseless.

Beijing will try and use the release of such investment funds in drips not so much to improve India's dismal infrastructure but to influence its policies, evidenced in the less than $3 billion committed to Indian projects compared to the talk of $100 billion prior during President Xi's visit.[58] India's leadership of an international public campaign for a verifiably autonomous Tibet will also convince many states in Southeast Asia who doubt New Delhi has the guts to rile China, that it is in the game after all. The end-state of a substantively autonomous, demilitarized, Tibet, however this is attained will restore to an extent the buffer, and is any day preferable to having the PLA entrenched on India's doorstep.[59]

In this exercise, there's a diplomatic loophole that New Delhi has preserved for itself. It may have accepted Chinese 'sovereignty' but only over an 'autonomous' Tibet, and insofar as Tibetan autonomy is a sham India is free to reconsider its attitude to the Chinese-occupied Tibet. Actually, India is in a position to play the 'Tibet card' in the manner, the Chinese believe, the U.S. does the 'Taiwan card'.[60] In this context, doing nothing is a wasting option because China everyday tightens its grip on that outlying province, willfully reducing the native Tibetans to a minority inside Tibet with a programme of massive Han resettlement, cash incentives for inter-marriage, and co-opting of Tibetan youth leaders into the governing Communist Party structure, which measures are used in Xinjiang too.[61] Beijing seeks to preclude India's playing the 'Tibet card' by tempting New Delhi with economic deals and resolution of the border dispute.[62] With Xinjiang on the boil, India's pressing the button on 'free Tibet' and activating the sub-conventional and asymmetric option of guerilla operations by Tibetan exiles will hugely distend Chinese military and economic resources. With an eye on internal order, PLA will be less eager for the periodic aggression staged across the ceasefire line—Line of Actual Control, and serves India's purpose. Moreover, India has nothing to gain from aligning with China on the matter of 'terrorism' because in that country with peaceful dissent disallowed frustrated protestors taking to the gun in Xinjiang and potentially in Tibet are branded 'terrorists' and is actually subversive of any Indian intent to play the Tibet card. And New Delhi should stop talking about terrorism as a 'shared concern' as it has been doing for a while now.[63]

India Seaward

India bisects the Indian Ocean region, straddling the line dividing the economically exuberant eastern half from the relatively poorer, turbulent, unstable but oil-rich western half sourcing 80 per cent of the world's oil supply. Its dominating position in the oceanic swathe Simonstown-Sumatra empowers India, enabling it potentially to wield a tourniquet to the critical Gulf-East Asia energy and other-trade sea routes at the choke-points using its naval assets from the homeland, or from bases under the Indian military's integrated Andaman Command.

The western half of the Indian Ocean is an area of U.S. concern and American forces at sea in the Persian Gulf and on the littoral particularly in Saudi Arabia and Bahrain are a factor of stability and which presence conforms with Indian interests generally, if not in specifics such as with respect to Iran. It permits New Delhi to focus more on the eastern half where China is active. Even so India maintains a four point stance based on close security relationships with Israel, Iran, Afghanistan and Central Asia, and Saudi Arabia. While relations with the first three sets of states will be probed in a later chapter, it may be relevant to mention here the strategic benefit Israel derives from its strategic association with India and the emergence of Saudi Arabia as the locus of Indian interest in Arab lands. In the western Indian Ocean, Tel Aviv sees India as extending Israel's naval reach by affording its ships access to its ports and to help out with 'behind-the-scenes-assistance, in terms of intelligence and logistics' presumably with regard to the threat it perceives from Iran and Arab states bearing animosity.[64] The Indian Ocean Naval Symposium (IONS) is the Indian instrument to instill confidence and legitimate its role as security-provider in the Gulf region in the manner New Delhi has used the annual 'Milan' exercise to evoke camaraderie and inspire confidence with the navies of the littoral Southeast Asian countries on the Bay of Bengal, and for the naval commanders to strike up personal relationships and familiarize themselves with each other's standard operating procedures and understanding of 'rules of the road'. More materially, the Indian plans in the western Indian Ocean got a fillip with the 2010 'Riyadh Declaration' issued during Indian defence minister A.K. Antony's visit to Saudi Arabia, which called for military training of Saudi military personnel in Indian institutions, joint military exercises, 'defence cooperation', Saudi involvement in the Indian defense industrial sector, and active Saudi participation in IONS. The India-Saudi military strategic connection was cemented with a Defence Cooperation Pact in February 2014, extending the ambit of the Riyadh Declaration to allow 'exchange of defence-related information [and] cooperation in areas varying from hydrography and security to logistics', which hints at a contingent operational role for the Indian military.[65] It is a role that perhaps is reserved for when the U.S. departs the region or if it hugely diminishes its presence. Until then India can free-ride on the U.S. military's presence and can concentrate on its eastern sea approaches, where distances are daunting enough to deter sustained Chinese naval patrols.

Raja Menon, a former Assistant Chief of Naval Staff (Operations), observes that PLA Navy will have 'to do 3,500 miles just to step into the Bay of Bengal and [that] is a hell of a problem.'[66] But the effect of such distances are mitigated were China to have bases in the Indian Ocean region. This is why there was consternation in Indian naval and government circles when the first reports came in of a Chinese nuclear-powered fast attack submarine 'foraying' into the Indian Ocean in early 2014 and in September of the year a conventional submarine along with a submarine tender putting in at Colombo port.[67] There are apprehensions about the port facilities erected by the Chinese, such as at Humbantota in Sri Lanka, being used by the Chinese military.[68] The Sri Lanka Navy Chief Vice Admiral Jayantha Perera, however, reassured India, stating that 'We have very good cooperation with India [and] will never compromise India's national security', and dismissed Chinese military presence and interest in Sri Lanka as only 'commercial'.[69] This does not mean that the Sri Lankan government and the other regimes in South Asia will forsake moves, whenever feasible, to remind New Delhi of their strategic value to India vis a vis China in the game of extracting concessions and favourable terms on a host of issues.[70] The reality behind the Chinese modernization of ports and allied infrastructure is less worrisome. Sri Lanka had approached India in 1992 for help in developing the deep water port with the project costing some $750 million which New Delhi was not then in a position to ante up. Only after India professed its inability did Colombo accept the Chinese offer. The agreements China has with Sri Lanka and other Indian Ocean states (Maldives, Seychelles, Mauritius) for the use of their ports are pro forma accords littoral/island states routinely sign with friendly countries to allow ships to refuel, replenish, and put in for repairs in peace time. In war, there's no question of Chinese warships being allowed access to these ports, considering these small states rely on the Indian navy and armed forces for their ultimate protection and safety. The Indian Navy, for instance, patrolled the Palk Strait separating Sri Lanka and India to stop gun-running by Sri Lankan Tamil rebels during the civil war in that country, operates a radar and air surveillance grid around the Maldives, Mauritius, and Seychelles, and wards off pirates and adventurers (of the kind who staged a coup in 1988 against the Regime in Male, which ended with Indian air-borne action). It would not pay for any of these countries heedlessly to provoke India. In fact, India, Sri Lanka and the Maldives hold regular Trilateral Meetings on Maritime Security Cooperation with Mauritius and Seychelles invited to attend as observers to oversee the 'practical cooperation' between these countries on the ground.[71] Mahinda Rajapaksa of Sri Lanka, when he was president, voiced the view of other Indian Ocean island-nations when he said that Colombo 'has no reason to do anything that would hurt India's interests in the region.' Indeed, he revealed, for example, that other than Humbantota, India also passed up his offer to explore for oil and gas in the offshore Mannar basin, shared with India, whereupon Colombo contracted with Chinese oil companies to explore and drill.[72] Even so, the fact that New Delhi thus opened the door for China to saunter in and squat in India's backyard and even tap an energy source shows the extent to which New Delhi is devoid of a sense of strategic geography. Nevertheless India's role and presence is ample. As per the 1987 Accord with India Colombo, in order to allay the fears of the Rajiv Gandhi government about the U.S. military interest in Sri Lanka, agreed not to allow third countries to set up military bases anywhere in that country and set aside for exclusive Indian use Trincomalee, with its deep sea harbour and oil-tank farm, in northeastern Sri Lanka, and the nearby China Bay air base.[73]

But the mere fact of China trying to encroach India's maritime space, meaning the island-states that traditionally fall within the

Indian penumbra, has prompted New Delhi to alight on a supposedly effective 'theatre-switching' strategy in case of Chinese aggression in the Himalayas. It involves interdicting Chinese warships and merchantmen, and way-laying bulk energy containers ships in the Indian Ocean, and isolating and attriting the Chinese military presence in Tibet using air strikes to disrupt the civilian and troop movement and military supply chain to the mainland, and is a weak strategy. (Why this is so will be discussed in another chapter.) Achieving naval primacy among Indian Ocean states has nevertheless injected the Indian government with confidence, making it less reticent in wielding the country's sea power. It is something Southeast Asian nations have welcomed, some more vocally than others. For instance, Singapore, since its separation from Malaysia and independence in 1965, saw India in the immediate post-colonial period, rife with intra-regional conflicts, as filling the power vacuum created by Britain's departure 'east of Suez' and as a factor to steady the regional security situation (Brewster 2011: 106; Pham 2010). The state's founding Prime Minister Lee Kuan Yew offered the Indian navy the use of the city-state's ports, shipyards, and ship repair facilities. A strategically dim-witted Indian government ignored this plea. Five years later, in 1970, Lee once again, and with some asperity, asked the Indian Foreign Minister Swaran Singh if India intended to have a naval influence in Southeast Asia only to be told that the Indian naval forces were focused on the Arabian Sea (Brewster 2011: 106–7). After the announcement by New Delhi of its 'Look East' policy in 1992, Singapore and other AESAN members perceived the strengthened Indian naval presence and establishment of the integrated military command at Port Blair in the Andaman Sea as manifesting India's newly enunciated security commitment to the region, and as 'counter-balancing the other heavyweights'—China and the United States (Brewster 2011: 106–7). India's Southeast Asian naval and military thrust has since become more prominent, as is the belief in the importance of coordinating with Japan's powerful Maritime Self-Defense Forces (MSDF) active in the eastern seas.[74] With the Indian Navy west of Malacca and the Japanese Navy holding down the Far East, the Chinese People's Liberation Army Navy (PLAN) will be stretched on its two flanks.[75] Dividing PLAN's operational focus and forces thus is regarded by both the countries as the best way to compel an expanding PLAN to dilute its strength at both ends.[76]

The Indian Army's legacy forces, mainly armored and mechanized formations aside, India's military is increasingly tuning in to the Chinese threat. While Japan's problem with China—given the bad blood between them going back to the nineteenth century, is more complicated, Tokyo's willingness to shoulder responsibility for its own defence has increased with the uncertainty about whether and how much the United States will put out for Japan (Takahara 2008). Notwithstanding adverse official Japanese reactions to the Indian nuclear tests in 1998, Tokyo has since determined that an India pulling its weight in Asia is helpful. Indeed, Indian acquisition of nuclear weapons may have actually triggered a rethink about Japan's nuclear abstinence in Tokyo policy circles because nuclear weapons clearly help abate threats.[77] During his 2010 visit to New Delhi, Shinzo Abe likened Japan's situation vis a vis China to that of India's and advised New Delhi not to feel 'shy' in militarily cooperating with the United States and Japan. He suggested that India's colluding in such an effort would draw other Asian states, such as Vietnam, into a collective security enterprise and vouched for the compatibility of Indian and Japanese interests, saying 'India's success is in Japan's best interests and Japan's success is in the best interest of India.'[78] During his January 2014 visit to India Abe was still more ambitious. '[T]he bilateral relationship', he declared, 'is blessed with the largest potential for development of any bilateral relationship anywhere in the world.'[79] Tokyo is eager that the bilateral relations evolve such that India can be a 'defensive balancer against China', and as a 'partner in promoting multilateral political and economic institutions that allow for the inclusion of China in a way that is acceptable to the region.' The other role for India in Japan's strategic scheme is as a maritime security partner keeping the energy SLOCs in the Indian Ocean open 'in combination with, or potentially as a partial alternative to, Japan's reliance on the United States' (Brewster 2011: 80). These strategic desires of the Japanese government were voiced by Abe in 2007 in his address—'The Confluence of Two Seas'—to Indian Parliament. Admiral Kazuya Natsukawa, Chairman, Joint Staff Council, Japanese Self Defense Forces (SDF), was more direct. 'Only India has the capability and intention', he said, 'for security cooperation in this huge sea area, the west side of Malacca Strait.' Former Japanese ambassador to India, Yasukuni Enoki was still more emphatic. 'Japan's energy security is dependent on the Indian Navy...We have only the Indian Navy', he averred, 'which can be trusted. Other navies are not reliable.' And the Japanese National Institute of Defense Studies echoing similar views called India 'the sole dominant power' in the Indian Ocean. In September 2008, India accepted with alacrity the 'Security Declaration' proposed by the Taro Aso government and a year later the Japanese Vice Defense Minister Akhisa Nagoshima mooted a Japan-Taiwan-India maritime coalition as a hedge against China's seaward aggression—an arrangement Taipei endorsed.[80] New Delhi is receptive to such initiatives because New Delhi hopes to ride Japan's, Taiwan's, and ASEAN's keenness in having India as a counterpoise to China, to integrate into the political and economic institutions in Asia-Pacific, and to firm up its position in international councils such as the East Asia Summit (Brewster 2011: 81). India woke up to the positives from holding off China by cooperating with a remilitarizing Japan at a time when Sino-Japanese tensions have heightened and there's a fluctuating chill in their economic relations.[81] It was Singapore's Senior Minister Goh Chok Tong who in 2005 saw the rising importance of India to ASEAN and Asian geopolitics and security. 'With India's rise, it will be increasingly less tenable to regard South Asia and East Asia as distant strategic theatres interacting only at the margins', he stated, 'United States-China-Japan relations will still be important, but a new grand strategy triangle of United States-China-India relations will be superimposed upon it...Reconceptualizing East Asia is of strategic imperative....It would be shortsighted and self-defeating for ASEAN to choose a direction that cuts itself off from a dynamic India (Bergeman 2012: 21). It is another matter that it took the April 2013 armed intervention by PLA deep inside Ladakh for the Indian government to wake up to the value of strong military links with Japan.[82] Slightly differently, South Korea sees strong bonds with India as essential to a 'Middle Power' hedge both against U.S. and Chinese 'dominance'.[83]

Encouragement of an Indian military role by the U.S. and the littoral states has resulted in regular sailings by Indian Naval flotillas into the seas east of the Malacca Strait and joint naval exercises.

Earlier Japan sent only its Coast Guard vessels and was as unsure as New Delhi about such cooperation. India cancelled the first India-U.S.-Japan strategic 'trialogue' on the South China Sea scheduled for September 2011, for example, lest Beijing take umbrage.[84] The visit by the Indian Defense Minister A.K. Antony to Tokyo in November 2011, however, cleared misgivings on both sides and set security cooperation on a higher plane. An annual high-level defence dialogue between the top bureaucrats in the defence ministries is off the blocks, and the first of the annual Japan–India Military Exercises were conducted, significantly, near the disputed Senkaku Islands in June 2012 (JIMEX 12) involving Japanese warships and an Indian task force comprising a heavily-armed, multi-role, stealth frigate, a missile destroyer, a corvette and a tanker. Such flotillas annually exercise at different levels of operational complexity with the navies of Japan, South Korea, Vietnam and Singapore, making port calls along the way in Indonesia, and the Philippines. At Beijing's request, they also engage PLAN vessels in simple 'passing exercises' usually off Shanghai, on their way to or from the Far East. 'This', according to the Australian expert Rory Medcalf of the Lowy Institute in Melbourne, 'is part of a wider ambition to show flag regularly east of the Strait of Malacca, now that India is becoming an Indo-Pacific nation and not solely an Indian Ocean power.'[85]

Getting Australia into the Picture

India actually has to have a presence in the waters east of Malacca other than in Nha Trang in Vietnam on China's flank at a distance from the fraught situation in the South China Sea, and Australia's northern coast seems a viable location for an Indian naval presence to anchor the Indian Monroe Doctrine system at one end and Canberra seems more open now to regional approaches and, like many other offshore nations, views India as key to stabilizing the greater maritime Asian region.[86] Conflict between states, as a report by Lowy Institute, Australia's premier think-tank, says 'is more about constant competition and coercion than the prospect of all-out war' (Medcalf 2014). It is in this respect that the salience of Indo-Australian strategic cooperation should be seen. Considering its evolving view of India, bilateral relations with it are deemed important to Australia's security independent of the U.S.-Japan-India-Australia quadrilateral.[87] The former Labour Party regime of the Mandarin-speaking Prime Minister Kevin Rudd was influenced by the growingly beneficial exchange of Australian natural resources for cheap Chinese manufactured goods and investment, which trade today stands at $131 billion (compared to some $14 billion Indo-Australian trade).[88] What this means is that while Canberra will generally be in sync, policy-wise, with the U.S., India, and Japan, its anti-China pose will be finessed.[89] The new Prime Minister Tony Abbott has implemented the decision by his predecessor Julia Gillard of exporting uranium to India despite domestic opposition against fueling an India–Pakistan nuclear arms race. While mindful of links with China he, perhaps, hopes to replicate in time a similar relationship with India—exporting natural resources, and gaining from Indian light goods and investment. Canberra expects by these means to continue to extract economic benefits, balance the two coming powers in Asia and, along with India and Japan, also create a regional economic and security cushion should China turn rogue and an America, inhibited by its deep economic interlinks with that country, fail to take on Beijing.[90]

A tangible manifestation of Indo-Australian military cooperation, in light of the shared maritime concerns about China and Modi's desire for an expanded and deepened security cooperation not based on 'borrowed architecture of the past', may be for New Delhi to explore an extra-territorial 'home' basing arrangement in a northern Australian deep water port for the Arihant-class SSBNs.[91] It would be a spectacular upgrading of ties—an initiative that, other than bolstering Indian military presence in the extended region, would have a security multiplier effect, requiring the Indian and Australian navies to coordinate their submarine activity in a synergistic manner to cover a larger area and pose more complex problems of maritime offence and defence for China. Such a security gambit, moreover, meshes with official Australian military thinking about 'undersea warfare [being] a critical element in the strategic relationship with China'.[92] The basic rationale for such basing would be that while India and Australia individually lack the naval might to neutralize China, combining their sea denial assets with those of Japan will adequately blunt power projection by the Chinese Navy. It will be a strategic support for the Indian strategy of arming Vietnam, Philippines and other ASEAN members with the Brahmos supersonic anti-ship cruise missiles to ward off the Chinese nine-dash line threat in the South China Sea.

Such forward presence of Indian nuclear submarines in Australia will achieve several things: (1) inject enormous credibility into the Indian nuclear deterrent stance vis a vis China, (2) provide India more flexible strategic strike options, (3) hugely increase the maneuvering space for the SSBNs, (4) reduce transit times to patrolling areas and designated firing points off the Chinese coast, (5) markedly reduce the flight time of missiles fired from the Arihant-class boats to deep inland Chinese targets while concurrently lessening the reaction time of the Chinese Second Artillery Strategic Forces (SASF), thereby markedly increasing nuclear flexibility and options, (6) increase the time SSBNs spend on stations and loitering in the depths, with crews flown in and out of the nearest Australian city, (7) intimately link India militarily with Australia, (8) buff up Australia's security role in the larger Indo-Pacific setting, and (9) reinforce the common concerns about China shared by India and Australia, and the United States, and Japan, and seal the evolving entente of states offshore and on the Asian rim.

Alas, this basing option is unlikely to materialize for many reasons, chief among them Australia's closeness to the United States, which will expose the Indian SSBNs to U.S. intelligence scrutiny and probing that could compromise the most survivable and hence the most prized component of India's strategic triad. Such an Indo-Australian concert becomes plausible, however, if there's a sheer falloff in U.S.-Australian relations, which could happen for one of two reasons: Canberra decides, like other treaty allies that the U.S., owing to its economic stake in, and its eagerness to forge a new global order with, China, cannot be trusted to come to Australia's assistance, or if it believes that being part of an organic Asian security system, which may require Canberra to pull away from Washington, serves its long term national interests better. Because neither of these situations presently obtain, Indian submarine basing in Australia may not be politically and militarily feasible but it is an option worth exploring as there's much to commend it strategically and in the collective security sense. Then again, who knows what the initiation in 2015 of the joint Indo-Australian naval exercises will lead to?

A Proactive Japan

Tokyo is relying on India to provide security and safety for its energy and trade traffic transiting the Indian Ocean so that its own maritime forces can more effectively secure the sea lanes connecting the Malacca narrows to its home ports. It also seeks to preempt Chinese actions to establish physical presence on disputed territory and present a *fait accompli* as it did to the Philippines on the Mischief Reef and to Vietnam in the Paracel Islands by employing a strategy of slicing off a few disputed islands at a time in the belief that 'If sliced thinly enough, no one action will be dramatic enough to justify starting a war.'[93] The eviction of Chinese infiltrators from one of the disputed islands by the Japanese Navy prompted a hawkish PLA Major General Luo Yuan to demand that these islands be used as a target range. He also proposed fighting 'a guerilla war on the sea; …a people's war on the sea to keep the Japanese exhausted'. The Chinese animosity—equal amounts of fear and apprehension—with Japan is abiding; a placard at a recent anti-Japanese protest read 'All of China may become a graveyard but we will kill all Japanese'.[94] Such visceral and seemingly implacable Chinese hatred is among the reasons why a growing number of Japanese, particularly in the military, feel their country has no reason for complacency. They fear that a United States trapped in the logic of conciliation may buy peace with Beijing at the expense of Japan's security.[95]

A high-level Japanese delegation led by Lieutenant General Noboru Yamaguchi (Retd.), former head of Training and Doctrine-development Command of the SDF and now Director, Center for National Security & Crisis Management in the National Defense University, in an interaction in December 2011 at a military forum in New Delhi, surprised the Indians with his unvarnished take on the United States and China. Among the things General Yamaguchi said about the United States was that it swings between extremes, between being 'panda huggers' and 'dragon slayers' and one 'cannot', he said, 'put too much weight on current U.S. policy whatever it is.' On the other hand Japan, he added, 'does not trust' Beijing's nuclear 'no first use' promises, and hinted that Japan perceives a serious Chinese nuclear threat and, by implication, that in the context of the unreliability of U.S. nuclear protection, it could opt for an independent Japanese nuclear deterrent. The Japanese government may be awakening to the fact, Yamaguchi said, that 'good economic relations [with China] alone cannot guarantee peace', and that India and Japan should work together to 'influence' Beijing to move in a more pacific direction. One of the ways of dealing with Chinese assertiveness, he volunteered, was Indo-Japanese military cooperation and, in this context referred to the utilization of 'land-based air' by the Imperial Japanese Forces during the Second World War to sink two Royal Navy ships [HMS Hood and HMS Prince of Wales] 'near South China Sea'—the first instance in war of land-based aircraft destroying naval targets.[96]

Abe, who has always been a cheer leader for wider, more intense, Indo-Japanese military ties conceded that like India, Japan too had 'mixed feelings' about America—'They dropped the Bomb on us!', he said to a sympathetic audience in New Delhi. Nevertheless, mindful of the Indian government's tendency to do nothing to alienate Beijing he cautioned it against allowing a 'strategic void' to develop in Asia that China might fill and advised Indians 'not [to] be confused and jump into the wrong bandwagon and choose a wrong partner' because China is both 'an opportunity and a risk'. He desired 'maritime democracies [India, Japan, U.S. and Australia] to invest in building a robust, open, liberal, and safe and stable East Asia Summit-led Asian order.' He called this the 'realist-pragmatic' option that would end up reassuring the smaller Asian states.[97] Yamaguchi and Abe represent two streams in the realist thinking in Japan but, more generally, in non-Sinic Asia as well, the one tending towards beefing up one's own military muscle and finding effective partners, the other leaning on America to put a coalition together and to work it. The trouble with the latter option is that U.S.'s engagement in Asia is ultimately by choice, not necessity, which makes delivery on U.S. commitments uncertain and its security promises tenuous. A second reason is America's isolationist impulses.[98] Isolationism as ideology may be weak but, as Congressman Ron Paul's run in the Republican Party's 2012 presidential primaries showed, it is far from irrelevant, and the United States can decide at any time to draw in its talons, continue trading with Asian countries, but modulate its military ties. But this will weaken the extended deterrence afforded its Asian allies by the U.S. military and increase the risks for its friends, allies and strategic partners. To obviate such an eventuality may be why Shinzo Abe asked India to help shore up a mutual dependence system with America. '[I]n time of financial challenges', he said, 'the United States needs us as much as we need it.'[99] But, even an economically revived America, whose power is nevertheless in relative decline, can offer no guarantees of its direct intervention on the side of Asian states dragged into military hostilities by an overbearing China. India definitely does not expect help from the U.S. in any major way.[100] The U.S. reticence about getting embroiled in distant conflicts is of historic origins.[101] But it has not prevented America from entering into wars in Asia—Korea in the Fifties, Vietnam a decade later and, more recently, Iraq and Afghanistan—mostly with bad results, indicating the trouble it has had in Asia in picking fights, prosecuting land wars and, even more, in winning the peace that followed.[102] This record has engendered wariness in the U.S. about putting American boots on foreign soil, which grows in direct proportion to the possibility of tangling with China, something India experienced in 1962.[103]

The geostrategic trends favour India's going beyond rhetoric to actually building up structures for intense military cooperation with Asian states, in particular Japan. The Manmohan Singh government for most of its tenure remained resolutely aloof, leading to an uncharacteristic outburst by a frustrated Japanese Naval chief, Admiral Katsutoshi Kawano, against New Delhi's reluctance to enhance military, especially naval, ties, significantly, at the Chinese Fleet Review in Qingdao in late April 2014 to which the Indian Navy was invited to send its warships but Japan wasn't. 'We have been wanting very much to join the Malabar sea exercises with the United States and India', Kawano said. 'As I understand, the Indian Navy is keen and willing. But Indian politics is very complicated.' The reason for the Japanese Admiral's lament was the vacillating Indian government. It kept Japan out of the Malabar naval exercise in 2007 because China protested but seven years later renewed its invitation for Japanese naval participation for the 2014 version of this exercise. Kawano hoped the relations are on more solid ground now, the reason for military technology transfer programmes on the anvil, such as the contract with the Shinmeiwa Company for 15 US-2 flying boats. 'We are very interested', he said, 'in helping India develop its naval technology.'[104] Japan's exasperation with India's ambivalent and slow-footed policies is understandable. The fact, however, is that New Delhi is still not sure what role to play—as a 'strongman, constable, or free rider'?[105]

U.S. Intent and Disposition of American Forces

The United States has in the new millennium loomed large in India's policy radar with New Delhi striving to establish its strategic worth to Washington in Asia and hence adjusting to American sensitivities on Iran, nonproliferation, etc. The fact though is that India has more options and smaller countries offering lesser stakes to America may find the U.S. even less bankable in a crisis. This may be why countries of Indo-China, for instance, are averse to upsetting Beijing by getting too close to the United States. Questions about trusting the U.S. arise in Asian minds also because of Washington's strong instincts evident since the Bill Clinton presidency in the 1990s for concerting with China to manage the world.[106] Juxtaposed against the Clinton White House's leaking to the press—a clear violation of confidentiality—of the Indian Prime Minister Atal Bihari Vajpayee's personal letter in May 1998 justifying the nuclear tests as a response to the growing China threat, it reinforced deep down feelings of American untrustworthiness, especially as this leak was to win the goodwill of the Jiang Zemin regime at India's expense.[107] It suggested to New Delhi and, perhaps, other Asian capitals as well, that in its search for a *modus vivendi* with China, Washington finds the interests of friendly states expendable.[108] The third reason is the effect of austerity measures on the U.S. force structure and the Asia pivot. The University of Pennsylvania political scientist Michael Horowitz espies 'a tradeoff between providing relatively equal budget shares to the services—potentially reducing inter-service rivalries—and rebalancing toward the Asia-Pacific' which last would require, he contends, 'investments in the air force and the navy' to defeat China's A2/AD [Anti-Access/Area Denial] strategy based on its anti-ship ballistic missile system, at the expense of the U.S. Army and the U.S. Marines. However 'Washington's unwillingness to invest appropriately in relevant capabilities' would, he argues, 'undermine 'perceptions of U.S. resolve' in the region at large.[109] And the fourth reason is force attrition—the U.S. Navy, for instance, is reduced from some 600 bottoms in the 1980s to 285 ships today and the U.S. Army will shrink to its pre-World War II size of 440,000 troops.[110] It will both restrict the scale of deployment of the U.S. forces abroad, and compel it to be more parsimonious in their use. Thus, in the 'rebalance' of forces, the planned 60/40 split of the U.S. military assets between the Pacific and Atlantic regions would by 2020 lead to six of the 11 aircraft carriers (CVNs) and a 'majority of cruisers, destroyers, and littoral combat ships' to be assigned to the Indo-Pacific theatre.[111] After the Crimea crisis and the revival of military competition with Russia, however, the plan to thin out U.S. naval forces in the Atlantic is being reconsidered.[112] With budgetary restrictions in place, at a minimum U.S. forces would have to be balanced between the European and Asian theatres. In practice this will mean the inability of the United States to tackle either Russia or China very well. Sino-Russian security cooperation may be viewed as an 'Axis of Weak States'.[113] But together they can checkmate a weakening U.S. and its slack-willed NATO allies. In any case, what will accrue in the Indo-Pacific is the deployment of smaller forces than Obama's pivot policy originally envisaged. Worse, the force fraction detailed for the Indo-Pacific will be disposed in an unbalanced manner with the larger portion of the naval and air assets being tasked for the lesser threats in northwestern Indian Ocean—piracy, terrorism, Iran-related contingencies, and carrier-based aircraft and drone strikes on the Taliban in Afghanistan and ISIS in Syria and Iraq, compared to the insufficient strength arrayed against China to deter its Navy from adventurist actions and defeat its anti-access strategy that besides the anti-ship ballistic missile system also features a 'low visibility force multiplier—the accurate and lethal long range cruise missiles.[114] America's North Arabian Sea emphasis is reflected in the infrastructure buildup centered on the construction of the massive military base, port, oil refinery, and energy hub at Duqm on the Omani coast in answer to the Chinese control of the Pakistani port at Gwadar.[115] Further, in an eastern emergency, the carrier battle groups rushing thither from the Gulf area would have to face the perils of the narrows seas in the Malacca, Sunda, and Lumbock Straits, the limited space for maneuver providing an effective kill-zone for Chinese mines, land-based air, ballistic and cruise missiles and, at the eastern end of these straits, torpedoes. The difficulty of a long term Southeast Asian tilt to basing the U.S. Navy fleet (as an alternative to Bahrain) is because of two reasons. Singapore may not be viable owing to its waters not being deep enough to berth carriers and, while short stays may be welcomed by the city state, a permanent presence may be politically unacceptable, with the stationing of the four American littoral combat ships drawing political flak.[116] One of the finest deep water ports, Cam Ranh, refurbished by the Russians, is the obvious other choice, except Vietnam is unwilling likewise to have any foreign country turn it into a permanent military base.[117] Thus, with China as main worry, only the Indian Navy can fill the constabulary role and be the strategic tripwire in the Indian Ocean, a role first conceived for it in the 2008 *U.S. National Defense Strategy*.[118]

Organic Security and the Triple Monroe Doctrine System

India and China because of their population and territory, and strategic location on the Indian Ocean littoral and in the Asian heartland respectively, pack the most geopolitical weight. Size determines the economic, political, and military potential, and location decides the country's strategic utility as friend, and the liability in having it as foe. By these standards, India and China are predisposed to be adversaries, even if they had been ideologically in sync which they are not. History too is inimical to realizing genuine warmth between them with India (owing to the use by the British of the colonial Indian Army to reduce China in the Opium Wars of the 1840s and to quell the 1901 Boxer Rebellion) being held responsible, along with the West, for its 'century of humiliation' (Wang 2012; Lovell 2011). It led to Nehru trying to make amends by not resisting Chinese invasion of Tibet in 1950 and going overboard in envisioning a federation of Asian states, led by India and China to mark Asia's resurgence.[119] It may have motivated his 'Asian Monroe Doctrine' notion—Asian countries joining together in the post-Second World War years to thwart attempts by Western powers to re-establish empire, and to be accountable for their own security. Both the federation and the Asian Monroe Doctrine were idealistic formulations by Nehru even if the latter concept, as already discussed, reserved for India and the Indian military a central place in this architecture. With an aggressive and paranoid view of the world as staple, the Communist rulers of China were the more brusque practitioners of realpolitik, not shying away from the use of force.[120]

The Indian government's reflexive defensiveness when tackling China conjoined to developing close relations with a host of nations, especially Japan and the United States, has occasioned the belief that there's no great need energetically to project Indian military power in order to influence perceptions and help Indian diplomacy in the surrounding regions. A militarily outgoing India is a particularly valuable asset to countries of Southeast Asia, who are chary of getting too close to America, but will have few qualms about relying on India to ease a security pressure-cooker situation created by China, such as in the South China Sea, with Vietnam and the Philippines facing the brunt of Chinese maritime aggression.[121] Southeast Asia was described by Nehru as 'Farther India', a view restated in a slightly different vein by Prime Minister Manmohan Singh, who referred to countries in this region as 'civilizational neighbors'.[122] In this setting, 'unilateralism' is perceived as 'inadequate'. In the circumstances, a workable security schemata for the Indo-Pacific region was articulated in 2011 by the then Chief of the Integrated Defense Staff, Vice Admiral Shekhar Sinha. He talked of an 'open and inclusive [security system], allowing stakeholders, big or small, to "plug in and play", [and] to have the opportunity to have their "voice" heard and to work together to resolve issues of concern'. It fits in with the preferences of the ASEAN members, and jells with their outlook and politics of 'open, inclusive Asian security architecture'.[123] Except Congress government's National Security Adviser Shivshankar Menon introduced the possibility of involving Beijing, saying 'India and China will have key roles in forging' such a system.[124] This didn't travel far because the competing Chinese notion of 'integrative security' refers to 'many objects...put together in an organic unity'.[125] But 'integration' on Chinese terms is unacceptable to Asian states. With a proud history of standing up to China, Vietnam, for instance, would like to avoid trouble with Beijing but also to getting sucked into a Sino-centric system of periphery management.[126] Hanoi is wary as well about offering bases to foreign countries or being part of U.S. machinations because, as Defence Minister Phung Quang Thanh averred, even though it may seek cooperation with the U.S. his country is suspicious of American 'intentions'.[127] Vietnam's thinking fits in better with the Indian 'plug in and play' construct, with the naval port in Cam Ranh Bay, refurbished with foreign assistance, being offered to friendly out-of-area naval ships to extend their operational range and 'at-sea' time in the surrounding disputed waters that forward deployed Indian naval forces can avail of. The more the foreign navies frequent this waterway the more it is internationalized, and the more difficult it will be for China to turn the South China Sea de facto into a *mere clausum* or closed sea.[128] The Vietnam People's Army had complementary take on this evolving situation. Speaking at the same international conference in New Delhi where Vice Admiral Sinha had articulated the outlines of an Indian security architecture, Lieutenant General Tran Thai Binh asserted that in the face of 'the threat of use of force in international relations' the international community 'cannot act as bystanders', and praised the 'manifestation of the will to shoulder more responsibility by India as a major power in the region'. Maybe with the increased Indian naval activity in Vietnam's proximal seas, in mind, Senior Vietnamese army Colonel Tran Hau Hung described India's 'Look East Policy' as 'aiming at creating a stable foothold in Southeast Asia and gradually increasing engagement and influence in East Asia.'[129] The Indo-Vietnamese defence pact concluded during the visit of Prime Minister Nguyen Tan Dung in October 2014 cemented the Indian presence and role in the South China Sea to counter Chinese bullying and prospective annexation of disputed sea territory where India has oil interests.[130] The Modi government's decision to finally comply with the Vietnamese request for the Brahmos supersonic cruise missile, besides transferring patrol vessels, and expanding both the partner country capacity building exercise (with training programmes for Vietnamese submarine crews and Su-30 pilots and servicing personnel) and India's military-cum-energy stake by accepting Hanoi's offer of newer oil blocks falling within Vietnam's claim line in the face of Chinese protest, suggests New Delhi may finally be acquiring geopolitical common sense. It is an impression furthered by the proposal discussed by Prime Ministers Modi and Dung to form a regional sub-trilateral of India, Vietnam and Japan to coordinate policies and activities in the contested seas off China. A trilateral security relationship is always more stable than a bilateral one, providing the countries involved with more options and confronting the common adversary with trickier situations.[131]

Southeast Asian states may plug into the Chinese economy out of choice, economic necessity, or fear but Beijing sees them as potential dependencies, which can be lured by economic and trade concessions or militarily coerced to buy into Beijing's political and security agenda, a twenty-first century version of the wartime Japanese Asian 'co-prosperity sphere'. The dilemma for China and the states economically benefitting from plugging into its economy is, however, encapsulated in a Chinese aphorism—'same bed, different dreams'. Clashing dreams resulted in Beijing derailing the use of ASEAN forums by nations in the South China Sea dispute leading to these aggrieved countries 'turning to the U.S., Japan, Australia and India for balance against China'.[132] It has also prompted the less cowed down countries, such as Vietnam, to seek alternative economic patrons and markets for their goods. The visiting Vietnamese Prime Minister Dung sought 'economic, trade, and investment cooperation', and pitched for increase in the two way trade from the estimated $7 billion in 2015 to $15 billion by 2020.[133] The safety of numbers provided by overlapping security coverage from bilateral, trilateral and multilateral arrangements appears, in any case, to be the new norm. It reduces the effort of, and cost to, individual states and spreads the risk of conflict with China. Absent such schemes, many littoral states fear being swamped by Chinese economic and military power. In the event, a 'system of systems' may be surfacing as the sum of informal sub-regional security arrangements and formal pacts, partnerships and mutual understandings, such as the 'Five Power Defense Agreement' binding Britain, Australia, New Zealand, Malaysia, and Singapore, and in the ASEAN area the agreement involving Indonesia, Brunei, Vietnam, and the Philippines for coordinated patrolling of the waters around the archipelagic Natuna Islands, and the most recent India-Vietnam-Japan trilateral, backed by regional organizations (such as the ASEAN), with the still more prominent Indo-Pacific forums (like the Asia-Pacific Community, East Asia Summit) with the bigger, more powerful, players—the India-Japan-U.S. trilateral—taking the responsibility for balancing Chinese power in the extended region.[134] 'Wherever we go ... we are asked to become a net provider of security either as a neutral in local rivalries or as the only power within the region with the incipient capability do so', said the then National Security Adviser Shivshankar Menon.[135] These subsets of security formed owing to initiatives by countries in the region, could in the aggregate cover most of littoral Asia in the Indian Ocean and on China's periphery. 'Our condition and the state of the world', he asserted, in an address prepared for the Defense Services Staff College, 'require us to be...a bridging power, or a swing state'. India's inability alone to deal with China's rise has led, Menon averred to 'an approach [that's] a combination of engagement, of building our own strength, and of working with others, or, in academic jargon, of internal and external balancing.'[136]

The trouble is for the entire decade of the Congress party government 'internal and external balancing' was mostly talk. Former Foreign Secretary Shyam Saran and Chairman of the National Security Advisory Board, admitted as much, saying India 'responded... but not to the extent our partners want[ed] us to or what we [were] actually capable of in terms of the potential that we have'.[137] A former Deputy National Security Adviser, Leela Ponappa, attributed this hesitant approach to the government and MEA's traditional waffle when it comes to using military means to realize foreign policy goals. She recalled how in 2003–04, when she was ambassador to Thailand the Indian naval chief, Admiral Madhvendra Singh visited that country with a brief to get Bangkok interested in joint patrolling only to find the Thais upping the ante and proposing intensified navy-to-navy links, which enlargement of military ties into operational aspects, which took New Delhi by surprise. It took several years of inter-ministerial discussions, she said, to sort out and win cabinet approval for this proposal by when India had lost credibility with the Thai government. The cost to the national interest of lack of urgency in Indian government's decision-making has never been totted up nor remedial action ever considered. The Trans-Asian Highway project, which has security ramifications, was likewise delayed, Ponappa disclosed, this time because the Defense Ministry feared it would facilitate the movement of Chinese land forces. Even decisions to fulfill Thai requests for military equipment, ammunition, and anti-submarine warfare training similarly involved a lot of second guessing and needless prevarication within the Indian government. 'There's a huge area of ambivalence', Ponappa said, 'and it means we don't think politically, we don't think militarily.'[138] The government's aversion to the military tools of foreign policy has been India's failing, and constitutes the big hurdle and handicap in the country's quest for great power.

Even so Vietnam with its fighting qualities and traditional antipathy to China has surfaced as the obvious locus of Indian strategic interest in the South China Sea, and as the strategic analogue for Indian policy for Southeast Asia of Pakistan in the Chinese strategy for South Asia. Filling the Vietnamese armoury with lethal ballistic missiles with nuclear warheads and supersonic cruise missiles for its shore batteries, will instantly blunt China's small or even big stick diplomacy in the region.[139] It will restrict warships in China's South Seas Fleet to the Sanya base on Hainan Island and, in the Indo-Pacific context, have the same inhibiting effect on Chinese naval forces as the deployment of the Chinese long-range anti-ship ballistic missile (ASBM) could have on the U.S. Navy's aircraft carrier Task Groups in the western Pacific. Potentially raising the costs to, and putting military pressure on, China in this way may lead to Beijing relenting on its policy of keeping the border dispute with India unresolved in the belief that a more advantageous deal can be enforced in the future when China's power position, relative to India, further improves.[140]

If one were to pull back and view all these geopolitical developments, what is crystallizing is a grand scheme of three rimland security systems integral and organic to Asia—in the Indian Ocean, in the stretch of waters from east of Malacca Strait to the East Sea, and in the Far East-western Pacific, all orientating, in essence, towards barricading China and ensuring that its rise remains uneventful even if not always tension-free. Shared strategic interests revolving around a common threat perception is what's bringing India, Japan, the United States, and Australia together with the ASEAN members, who are immediately affected. Political and security cooperation between the three oceanic theaters is the glue. Looked at another way, the new Triple Entente of India, Japan, and the U.S. is a coupling of three near-autonomous 'Monroe Doctrine' spheres—the relatively uncontested Indian 'Monroe Doctrine' in the Indian Ocean with the U.S. Navy playing the helpful role of the Royal Navy during America's rise in the 19th Century, the highly contested Chinese 'Monroe Doctrine' in the seas off its coast, and the original U.S. Monroe Doctrine re-weighted from the Atlantic to the western Pacific, with Japan as the strategic touchstone, tripwire and, a 'unique bulwark to Chinese hegemony'.[141] With an Indian bulwark to bookend China at the other end, what is common to these three spheres is the American naval capabilities as backstop, except China will find the three big powers undermining its primacy along its own coastline. Whether or not the new entente powers act in informal lock-step, tensions and squabbles will continue to mar their separate relations with China, even as each of these countries will try and tamp down Beijing's worries about a concert working against it. Thus, India will keep talking of strategic autonomy, Japan about not raising its pitch, and the U.S. about balancing Chinese power not so much by 'containing' China's rise as 'managing' it (Tellis 2013). Considering the general wariness about Chinese aims and intentions and the growing understanding between New Delhi, Tokyo, and Washington (and secondarily Canberra), Beijing does not have the luxury of concentrating its resources in any one theater and is therefore impelled to thin out its military forces over wider expanses of land and sea. Nor can it expect Russia southwards from the Sea of Okhotsk to be less lenient in the defense of its offshore zone and in preserving its geostrategic imperatives in Siberia than Japan is in the Senkaku area, India in the Indian Ocean, and Vietnam and Indonesia in the Spratlys area, and the U.S.-assisted Philippines in the Paracel Islands zone.[142] And, it is the fact of its being reduced to 'masquerading' as a global power and risking 'becoming a raw materials appendage to China' that may induce Russia to moderate its tilt and act independently of Beijing.[143] Indeed, Indo-Russian military cooperation of late, is with China in mind, tending towards a joint show of force. The first ever series of joint air force exercises were conducted in 2014 off the Sakhalin Peninsula, around the same time as a scaled up Indo-Russian naval exercise got going in the Sea of Japan.[144] With its quarantining by the Western states, Russian instinctively lurched towards meeting China's military high-technology needs as a way of beefing up an anti-U.S.-NATO front in Eurasia.[145] Assuming Moscow's fears of China are not outpaced by its fears of what the U.S-led Atlantic Alliance may do, it doesn't prevent India from acting as the northern bridge, tying Russia to the Indian Monroe Doctrine sub-system propping up the 'triple Monroe Doctrines system' in Asia targeting China. China may thus find itself caught in several strategic pincers—between India and the U.S. at the Indian Ocean-end, India and Russia at the Central Asian-end, Japan and U.S. in the East Sea and the Far East, between India and ASEAN with Vietnam in the van in the South China Sea, and between Japan, U.S and Australia in the western Pacific with all the four powers cooperating, directly or indirectly, formally and informally, with each other and with its South China Sea ASEAN partners to keep the entire Chinese maritime and landward periphery under pressure.

These developments conform with what David Lampton of the Johns Hopkins School of Advanced International Studies said was 'the international politics version of Newton's Third Law'—'when one nation's policy goes out of kilter, it produces an equal and oppo-site reaction by others in the system.'[146] Distrust, rivalry, strategic competition drive the individual and collective strategies of the states arrayed against China.[147] The worst case would be if China succeeds in dividing this Indo-Pacific condominium by, for instance, buying off Russia and patching up with the United States, which would leave India and Japan at the geographic extremities and the ASEAN in the middle to handle China singly or together. In this scenario, Washington could accept a generalized agreement with China on the 'freedom of navigation' issue, say, but otherwise keep out of the green water disputes Southeast Asian states and Japan have with China.[148] Or, China satisfactorily resolves the border dispute with India, throwing in other sweeteners such as massive FDI in infrastructure projects, to get New Delhi to opt out of the balancing game, freeing Beijing to convert the South China Sea into a Chinese lake and to beef up its maritime presence in the Pacific that will stretch the U.S. military resources from Aden to Hawaii.[149] However, if the United States is seen as fork-tongued and diluting its commitments to make its intervention less automatic, Asian states will grow anxious about fights imposed on them by China. The more powerful among them (Japan, South Korea, and if sufficiently provoked, Taiwan) will then likely acquire nuclear weapons for self-protection.[150] China's secu-rity dilemma will, in any case, only grow because however the U.S. wields and manages its role, the Indian and Japanese militaries are muscular enough on their own and together can neutralize Chinese military initiatives in their respective areas.[151] They will, as discussed, continue equipping the Southeast Asian nations with progressively more lethal armaments to make life difficult for China.[152] In practical terms, Beijing will face the likelihood of being stalemated offshore and in more distant seas. As the China expert Cheng Li said 'Chinese leaders actually talk tough and act carefully, but sometimes it's out of your control.' For reasons of resurgent nationalism, Tokyo will not accept Chinese sovereignty over the Senkakus, even at the risk of imperiling bilateral trade worth $345 billion.[153] It underlines the Brookings analyst Richard C. Bush's view that owing to 'strategic mistrust, military operations, and points of friction' aided and abetted by 'proximity', there is 'finite danger' of a China–Japan clash.[154] These reasons for probable conflict hold for the India–China and Russia–China dyads as well.

China being both the proximal and distant threat on land and sea, India's main areas of proactive strategic activity, landward to stem Chinese influence, is Central Asia and, nearer home, the 'Mongolian fringe'—Nepal, Bhutan, and Burma (Myanmar), where China has made inroads but failed to turn the regimes against New Delhi. Caught between a domineering China and a softer India that is finding its strategic bearings, most of these countries have accepted Chinese largesse—infrastructure aid, military equipment, and in return supported 'One China' policy, but used the budding 'India-China rivalry', to get better trade and transit deals, lines of credit, and developmental and military aid from India.[155] These states are, however, aware that, while cultivating relations with Beijing is a good way to keep New Delhi interested, overdoing it could cost them dear (Pattnaik 2012; Vaughn 2010; Pande 2013). However, speedier economic integration of neighbouring countries with the Indian economy is precluded by New Delhi's exaggerated security-related fears. 'If India is to be a great power, it has to look at the world somewhat differently. The world is looking at India differently. I don't think we are looking at the world differently. We don't approach issues as a leader, as a confident, aspiring, great power. We still have the "follow the leader"-kind of passive-defensive attitude, and talk the language of us and them,' said Jairam Ramesh, Minister for Rural Development, who as Minister for Commerce in the Congress government took a number of unilateral initiatives in getting India close to the adjoining states, such as increasing textile imports from Sri Lanka and Bangladesh, and removing Bangladesh from the negative FDI list.[156] He was echoing the sentiments of the U.S. Deputy Secretary of State William Burns who said in June 2010 that 'India sometimes has a hard time realizing how far its influence and its interests have taken it beyond its immediate neighbourhood...that India doesn't see as clearly as others do how vital its own role in Asia is becoming.'[157] Indeed, Ramesh dilated some more on this subject, saying 'We have to redefine our relationship with our neighbours. We cannot be a great power until we do that. I am afraid there's a degree of patronizing condescension we adopt with them. We have legitimate security concerns, no questions about that. But our attitudinal big brother problem and lingering security distrust end up hurting our interests.' He sourced these problems to the foreign policy and security policy circles. 'The security establishment today is the biggest drag on any *modus vivendi* with our neighbours. When we try to do something different and creative with our neighbours, they always raise the security issue. Unless we say that we are large enough to take unilateral initiatives in trade, in investment, and will allow sub-regional arrangements, the situation is not going to progress', he said. Ramesh referred, moreover, to the need to allow India's Northeastern states to have closer economic relationships with Bangladesh and Myanmar, without losing 'overarching central control'. 'Why should everything be dictated from New Delhi?' he wondered. 'For Meghalaya, Assam, and Tripura cooperation with Bangladesh is a matter of life and death, it is not so for the civil servant sitting in Delhi. We cannot be a great power if we have *pangas* [discord] with all our neighbors.' But, he conceded that the attitude within the government and military to states in the near-abroad is changing.[158] It will be interesting to see the extent to which MEA's and MOD's traditionally petty and punitive attitude towards countries in the near-abroad will impact policy in the face of Prime Minister Modi's obvious interest in binding them to India, as his 'ambush diplomacy' in inviting the heads of government of SAARC countries to New Delhi for his inauguration and the initiatives taken since show.[159]

It is seawards, however, that India thinks it has an advantage relative to China, which it means to enlarge by collaborating with other maritime powers. Indian naval dominance of, and a strong air presence in, the Indian Ocean region; Southeast Asian nations militarily enabled by India and other powers and, therefore, less willing to take guff from China; a Japan unwilling anymore to be pushed around, and an America tilting to the Far East, have combined to keep China distracted and, it is reasonable to assume, disinclined to seriously test the mettle of any of the protagonists in the various rimland theaters, or of India across the undefined Himalayan land border.[160] With a convivial America as backdrop, India is in a position to enforce with a light hand an Indian 'Monroe Doctrine' in the Indian Ocean, owing to the fact that the United States has 'no core interests in India's Central and South Asia neighbors', which is 'unlike its interests in Japan, South Korea, Australia, and Southeast Asia' (Gilboy and Heginbotham 2012: 70). India's relations with Australia are simplified by Canberra's tendency to piggyback on American policy in Asia and, as a formal ally, to be part of the U.S. military plans for the region.[161] Thus, the India-Australia strategic partnership essentially is a sidecar, pulled along by the India–U.S. partnership.

China's imposing its Monroe Doctrine off its seaboard would be opposed by rival claimants to the continental shelf in the South China Sea and, off its east coast, by Japan. The 'freedom of navigation'-issue and energy investments by out-of-area states will, moreover, pull in outside powers intent on protecting their interests. It is not just the graduated increase in Indian military help and assistance to Vietnam and naval cooperation with other ASEAN members, but its programmes directed to make their navies effective and Vietnam, in particular, a formidable sea-denial and missile force, that will have a telling effect. Japan too is pitching in with advanced patrol craft for Hanoi, and America has armed the Philippines with a squadron of reconditioned F-16s and helicopters, and more armaments are in the pipeline. These measures coupled with the constant presence of Indian, Japanese, and U.S. naval ships transiting, exercising with littoral navies, or staging 'goodwill' visits and port calls in these seas, will make it difficult for Beijing easily to accomplish its tactical and strategic objectives.[162] If China is seen by the countries in its near-abroad as unable easily to have its way in this environment, its fear-inducing image and reputation will suffer, leading possibly to 'loss of face', diminished stature and standing, and local countries becoming more confident about resisting heavy-handed Chinese policies. Should Beijing, on the other hand, react violently, it will reinforce regional suspicions of China and further strain the current ties with countries on its periphery, and redouble their efforts to craft security arrangements with outside powers—a positive outcome in either case for the new Triple Entente of India-Japan-United States. Despite adverse developments, China cultivates the impression of a country coiling to strike.[163] It lends credence to the threat perceptions of the countries on its land and sea borders and cements the understanding between India, Japan, and the United States and the system of subsidiary but interlinked sub-regional security pacts and partnerships. In the analogy with the original triple entente of Britain, France, and Russia on the eve of the First World War, Wilhelmine Germany did then what China seems to be doing today—'deliberately frighten[ing] neighboring powers' which is 'self-defeating behavior of the first order.'[164]

There are those who wonder whether Washington has the 'will, and the wallet' to prosecute assertive policies in Asia, and whether Japan 'with rapidly rotating governments and a weakened economy will provide the resources for the significant levels of burden-sharing that the U.S. policy seemingly presupposes?'[165] But Japan is moving towards a stronger military posture and sturdy security cooperation with India whom Deputy Prime Minister Taro Aso described as 'natural-born partner' and an ally in all but name, a sentiment reciprocated by his Indian counterpart.[166] For this new age partnership to succeed it is 'imperative' for the three powers—India, Japan, and the U.S., to work 'around geography', 'array their forces wisely', and overcome 'operational, tactical, and hardware dimensions' owing to 'potential "interoperability" problems'.[167] Clearer delineation of operational boundaries and responsibilities will happen with greater interaction between the three 'Monroe Doctrine' systems—in the Indian Ocean where India predominates, and east of Malacca Strait where the U.S. and Japan hold sway. An effective deployment of forces would follow and, at a minimum, avoid needless duplication of effort—leaving proportionately larger responsibility to the air, land, and sea forces of the nodal powers in the three Monroe Doctrine theaters. For the Indian end of the Triple Monroe Doctrine system to work, besides refining relations with the adjoining countries in the subcontinent, Vietnam and other Southeast Asian states,

Australia, and Japan, which has been dealt with, Iran, the Central Asian Republics, Israel, the United States, and, tangentially South Africa and Brazil, are relevant. According to the historian Paul Kennedy, it is incumbent on a country paying attention to states it deems pivotal to its plans to 'anticipate the future rather than relying on the comfortable but outdated strategies and relationships'.[168] This is especially relevant to the Indian government whose policy constructs are stuck in the past. The most debilitating among these is the uni-dimensional belief that has plagued Indian foreign policy from the beginning and is still current in Indian diplomatic quarters, namely, that geopolitics and geopolitical schemes and an Indian Monroe Doctrine system in particular, rather than complimentary, are antithetical to the projection of India as an economic powerhouse that proximal nations can be incentivized to plug into for collective good.[169]

Notes

1. http://fisherymanagement.wikia.com/wiki/Exclusive_Economic_Zone.

2. For India's geopolitics that has endured from Nehru's time, see Karnad (1994). Source: Rajiv Sikri, former Indian Ambassador to Kazakhstan in the mid- to late-1990s, and Secretary (East) in the Ministry of External Affairs until 2006.

3. On Nehru's distaste for Geopolitics and geopolitical theories, see Karnad (1994: 31–3).

4. Personal communication from Rajiv Sikri, Indian Ambassador to Kazakhstan (mid- to late-1990s), and retired as Secretary (East) in the Ministry of External Affairs in 2006.

5. K. M. Panikkar on India's strategic omphaloskepsis, an extract from Panikkar's address at http://acorn.nationalinterest.in/ posted by Nitin Pai, 16 October, 2009.

6. A source at the senior-most levels of the Manmohan Singh government revealed several recent instances of when India worked behind the scenes to get what it wanted. For instance, it persuaded Maldives President Mohammad Nausheed, who lost his re-election bid in March 2014, to call off in 2013 a deal he had inked providing China an island for its use. In the November 2013 general elections in Nepal, with the Maoist leader, Prachanda, charging fraud and threatening to pull out (raising the spectre of a renewed civil war) , New Delhi informed the Chinese government that

the outcome of their man creating trouble could be that America—with former U.S. President Jimmy Carter in the international elections monitoring group, would establish itself in Kathmandu. The Yankee bogey worked. Within hours Beijing announced that it was satisfied with the fairness of the elections and Prachanda backed down.

7. An unpublished monograph by a former Foreign Secretary J. S. Mehta—'Panditji knows best'. Also Mehta (2010).

8. A. Z. Hilaly quoted in Bergeman (2012).

9. Karnad (2005: 71–2); Karnad (1994: 25–6).

10. Elaborate U.S. Department of Defense plans were, in fact, made in the mid-1950s for the 'Defense of India' in case of Communist revolution, or attack by Communist China that, depending on the scale of the contingency, involved deployment of substantial military assets, including an airborne division, five nuclear demolition teams, a carrier task force, an amphibious force, a Marine regimental landing team, a composite air strike force, airlift capability for one airborne battle group, and a medium bomber wing detached from the U.S. Strategic Air Command. For more details and analysis of these Pentagon plans, see Karnad (2005: 132–46).

11. So pronounced was the pro-Russian tilt that Soviet Defence Minister, Marshal Andrei Grechko, in 1972 even mooted a formal military alliance to the departing Indian Ambassador D.N. Dhar, a close adviser to Indira Gandhi. See 'Introduction' in Bhasin (2012: cxix–cxx).

12. A former Indian Foreign Secretary M.K. Rasgotra, during deliberations on the Strategic Review by the National Security Advisory Board (NSAB), for example, waved off consideration of any geopolitical scheme premised on coalitions against China, by proclaiming that India, 'wants to be friends with all'. Author's recollection from his time as Member of the National Security Advisory Board, Fall 1998.

13. *Nonalignment 2.0: A Foreign and Strategic Policy for India in the Twenty First Century* [New Delhi: Center for Policy Research, 2012] at www.cprindia.org/sites/default/files/Nonalignment%202.0_1.pdf. A semi-official document it has failed to gain traction.

14. China's per capita GDP rocketed to $5,432 from $1,135 inside of a decade (2002–2011) while India struggles in its familiar Third World bracket. See Jacques (2012b).

15. The Nixon-Kissinger entente with China, writes A. Tellis of the Carnegie Endowment, 'was shaped in part by the calculation that Chinese rivalry with the Soviet Union made it a suitable target for American support, while its deep…developmental challenges made bolstering its economic growth through enhanced access to international…but especially American, markets a relatively low-risk proposition.' See Tellis (2010) and Mori (2007).

16. 'Our engagement with China', writes G. Chang of the Gatestone Institute, 'has, unfortunately, reinforced the worst tendencies in Beijing by inadvertently creating a set of perverse incentives. With the best of intentions, we rewarded irresponsible conduct in the hope the Chinese would change. No matter how they continued in their ways, we failed to hold them to account.' See Chang (2013).

17. The U.S-China Economic and Review Commission scrutinizing 'China's Proliferation Practices' reported to the 109th Congress in March 2005 that China is a 'substantial source of WMD and missile related proliferation' to North Korea and Iran, voiced Pentagon's concern that 'improved [Chinese] technology and know-how will be proliferated' to these countries. It observed that while China has 'increased its public nonproliferation posture through its involvement in a number of multilateral nonproliferation commitments' such as membership in 2004 of the Nuclear Suppliers Group, and 'Despite Beijing's assertions that it is addressing the problem, the reality is that Chinese entities, many of which have close ties to the government, continue to provide nuclear, chemical, and missile-related technology to countries of concern.' The statement by the chairman of the Commission, Richard D'Amato, also hinted at Beijing's double-game, noting that 'It is possible that China wants to maintain the status quo, perhaps seeing that as desirable for its security interests.' The Commission, moreover, observed that the U.S. sanctions imposed on Chinese companies responsible for the proliferation activity had 'no teeth' and recommended that the U.S. Congress urge the George W. Bush Administration that if diplomatic efforts were 'unsuccessful in spurring' the Chinese government into taking 'effective actions' that it should use 'economic leverage' to hurt Chinese trade and commerce with America. See *China's Proliferation Practices and Role in the North Korean Crisis*, Hearing Before the U.S.–China Economic and Security Review Commission, 109th Congress, 1st session, March 10, 2005 at www.uscc.gov/hearings/2005hearings/transcripts/05_03_10.pdf.

18. Thus, when North Korea threatened to fire nuclear missiles at American targets in the region in April 2013, U.S. Senators, such as Kelly Ayotte, urged the Commander, U.S. Pacific Command, to reach out to China to resolve the trouble with Pyongyang. See *FP [Foreign Policy] Situation Report*, April 10, 2013. Chinese analysts have hinted that forward movement on North Korea might be possible if the U.S. reviews its policy of arms sales to Taiwan. See Beech (2010). As regards Iran, for instance, Beijing facilitates secret commerce in nuclear goods with Iran, which is passed off by Western Analysts as smuggling by Tehran. See Albright (2013). On China's sustained support of Iran's nuclear and missile programs, see Forden (2010).

19. Krauthammer suggested in 2003 that the best way to get Bejing to join Washington in preventing North Korea go nuclear was to encourage Japanese nuclear weaponization. 'If our nuclear nightmare is a nuclear North Korea, China's is a nuclear Japan' he wrote. 'It's time to share the nightmare.' See Krauthammer (2003).

20. Robert Kelley, who formerly worked at the U.S. nuclear weapons laboratory in Los Alamos and was a director at the International Atomic Energy Agency in Vienna has written that 'China is known to have given Pakistan a complete design for an implosion uranium device and may have also provided more advanced thermonuclear designs at some point. Given the information available today about thermonuclear design and modern computer codes, a simple [Pakistani] two-stage device may be possible without testing.' See Kelley and Cloughley (2014: 10). U.S. Federal Court documents indicate a direct Chinese hand in helping Pakistan acquire such technology. See 'In Court Papers, U.S. Openly Suggests Pakistan Interested in Thermonuclear Weapon', *National Journal*, July 19, 2011 at www.nationaljournal.com/. It is strongly suspected, moreover, that the 5.3–5.5 Richter scale seismic tremor picked up by the Russian ground station at Petropovlovsk, Kamchatka Peninsula, configured to detect tritium use, and to analyze the vented noble gas, Xenon, at the Punggye North Korean test site, for example, that the February 2, 2013 nuclear test was likely that of a Pakistani fusion-boosted fission (FBF) device, its design vetted by Chinese experts. The deal apparently was that in return for accepting the risks of testing, Pyongyang would bask in the glory of testing an 'enhanced' weapon. See http://bharatkarnad.com/2013/02/12/nokopak-h-bomb-test-superior-to-indian-s-1/. For a later confirmation in the West of North Korea 'going thermonuclear', see Lewis (2014).

21. It is argued, for instance, that the North Korean test in February 2013 helped China by reducing Japanese pressure as Tokyo now had something else to worry about, shifted U.S. attention away from China, and gave China and Russia 'a rare opportunity to jointly deal with their relationship with the United States and its allies.' See 'U.S. and Japan shocked: North Korea Nuclear explosion Brought China Three Major Benefits', Powerful Nation Forum, *People's Daily*, February 19, 2013 at http://chinascope.org/main/content/view/5258/103

22. See Walt (2012). For an earlier view of Southeast Asia as a Chinese Monroe Doctrine sphere, see Kurlantzick (2006).

23. It took brash rhetoric and behaviour to alert Washington to Beijing's policy tendencies and, as Harvard professor Stephen Walt said, 'against basing policy on wishful thinking' that 'a more powerful China will somehow act differently than other great powers have in the past…and accept

institutional arrangements that were "made-in-America" after World War II' and that 'Beijing will be content to let the United States maintain its current security posture on East Asia, and will not seek to undermine it over time.' See Walt (2011). Obama called India 'a leader in Asia and around the world...a rising power and a responsible global power...and indispensable to the future that we seek, a future of security and prosperity for all nations.' See '"India is a rising and responsible power"', PTI, *IBN Live*, January 4, 2010 at http://mobi-ibn.in.com/.

24. Shyam Saran, former Indian Foreign Secretary, faculty meeting, Center for Policy Research, June 18, 2012, related what happened in one such meeting in May 2012. The Chinese representatives, he said, aggressively questioned India's interest in the South China Sea while explaining their own country's presence in the Indian Ocean in benign terms of protecting its sea lines of communications (SLOC). They charged India with playing the role in Tibet they claimed China enacted during the war against the Soviet occupation in Afghanistan when Chinese government agencies bought arms for the mujahideen using monies funneled by the U.S. government, in other words, as an American proxy.

25. See, for example, Kenny (2014). For polling results by Pew Research Center reconciling to America's reduced status see, 'Public Sees U.S. Power Declining as Support for Global Engagement Slips: America's Place in the World 2013' December 3, 2013 at www.people-press.org/2-13/12/03/public-sees-u-s-power-declining-as-support-for-global-engagement-slips/.

26. See Mahbubani (2014).

27. 'Should American values trump American interests?', *Washington Post*, November 29, 2013. Blackwill is former U.S. Ambassador to India.

28. 'Remarks By President Obama to the Australian Parliament', November 17, 2011 at www.whitehouse.gov/.

29. 'Quishi: China Uses "Move to the West" Strategy to Break through U.S. Containment of China', *Chinascope*, April 22, 2014 at http://chinascope.org/main/conten/view/6286/104.

30. 'Russia and China can build new world order—political scientist', *Russia Times*, June 17, 2011 at http://rt.com/news/russian-chinese-relations-expert/; Keck (2013).

31. Russia has revived the Cold War practice of tasking its aircraft—now Tu-95 bombers, MiG-31 fighter aircraft, and Il-78 tankers to fly provocative sorties to test NATO air defences. See Michael Birnmaum, 'NATO said it intercepted Russian planes close to European airspace', *Washington Post*, October 29, 2014; Herszenhorn (2014); Klein (2009); Chivers and Herszenhorn (2014).

32. With regard to Chinese taking over Philippine islands President Benigno Acquino said: 'At what point do you say, "Enough is enough"? Well, the world has to say it—remember that the Sudentenland was given in an attempt to appease Hitler to prevent World War II.' See Bradsher (2014); Eilperin, (2014); Landler (2014).

33. Whence its advice to commercial airliners traversing the Asian skies, for instance, to respect the controversial Chinese Air Defence Identification Zone restrictions subsumed in Washington's policy of putting more store by diplomacy than military might to deal with China. Landler (2013).

34. Cha (2014); Duc and Tran (2014); 'Russia and Vietnam forge closer ties', AFP, Reuters, *Straits Times*, November 13, 2013.

35. 'Russia strengthens Ties With Vietnam', *Stratfor*, December 12, 2013 at www.stratfor.com/.

36. See their 'India and America, batting together in Asia', *Hindu*, March 27, 2013.

37. Karnad, *India's Nuclear Policy*, 30-1. On the strong opposition by the Tibetan people against Chinese occupation, see Woeser (2014).

38. Interview, Senior official.

39. Senior Naval officer.

40. This was offered by Chinese Premier Li Keqiang during the November 2014 East Asia Summit in Naypyitaw, the newly-built capital of Myanmar. See Ghosh (2014)

41. 'ASEAN block splinters over South China Sea', *AsiaNews.it*, August 30, 2013 at http://www.asianews.it/news-en/ASEAN-block-splinters-over-South-China-Sea-28875.html.

42. She said this at the Pacific Islands Forum attended by the Chinese Vice Foreign Minister Cui Tiankai. See '"Big enough for all of us": Clinton says US can work with China in Pacific.', NBC Newswire Services, *NBCNews.com*, 3 September, 2012.

43. The armed PLA military intrusion into Ladakh in April 2013 not much before the new Chinese Premier Li Keqiang visited New Delhi may be a pointer of things to come. See General (ret.) Deepak Kapoor, 'Chinese provocation: Is India prepared?', *Deccan Herald*, may 2, 2013 at www.deccanherald,com/content/329863/chinese-provocation-india-prepared.html . Said another ex-Army chief, General V.K. Singh 'If you give [the Chinese] the impression that you are flexible, they are ready to exploit it.' See '"China exploiting India's soft stance along the border" ', *Hindustan Times*, September 29, 2013.

44. S. Menon, 'The Significance of India-China Relations', Speaking Notes, Center for China Analysis and Strategy, April 11, 2014. Text emailed by the NSA.

45. Victoria Tuke, 'Japan's China Policy—Engagement but for How Long?', Policy Brief, The German Marshall Fund of the United States, May 2012 at http://www.gmfus.org/wp-content/blogs.dir/1/files_mf/1337625972Tuke_JapanChinaPolicy_May12.pdf.

46. An 'Indian Monroe Doctrine' was first fleshed out in Karnad (1994).

47. A mid-August 2012 commentary published in Huanqiu says that U.S.'s containment strategy will fail because it China will use 'economic means to break the weak link among [the American allies].' See 'Huanqiu: The United States Will Become Exhausted Trying to Contain China', August 16, 2012, *Chinascope* at http://chinascope.org/main/content/view/4780/103.

48. Some 36 percent of those polled in the 16-35 year age group in an August 2012 national survey conducted by the *Hindustan Times* and C-fore, when asked 'What is your idea of India? How do you want India to be in 10 years?' said they wanted the country to be 'An expansionist superpower like China'. A slight smaller, 33 percent of the youth said they preferred India to remain 'A pacifist regional power as at present' These divergent views neatly encapsulate the government's dilemma of being in tune with the thinking of the people—doing neither too little in the foreign and military policy fields, nor too much. Moreover, half of those surveyed and a clear majority (53 percent) in the younger age group, according to this poll wanted India to 'Follow independent policies even if it means losing the [UN Security Council] seat'. Like in the past, this survey too suggested that a majority (55 percent of the young, and 46 percent overall) consider the U.S. 'Friendly to India', which figures were exceeded only by the 58 percent and 60 percent approval ratings Russia racked up in the two age groups, with China perceived by 51 per cent of the young and by 48 percent of the those of all ages polled, as 'Inimical to India'. More interestingly, ideological-leanings-wise, 54 percent of the young, and 51 percent overall, acknowledge being 'Centrist-liberal', with 'Right of center' clocking the next highest percentages of 19 percent and 20 percent respectively, and 'Left of center/Left liberal' ideology being professed by just seven percent of the young and by 11 percent of the respondents overall. 'Majority of Indians are Liberal', A Hindustan Times-C fore Survey, *Hindustan Times*, August 15, 2012.

49. See the views on the Chinese and Indian economies of Ruchir Sharma, the Morgan Stanley analyst—his op/ed piece '10 reasons to believe in China slowdown story', *Economic Times*, July 9, 2012, and his interview. 'Pre 2003 growth rates to be new normal for Indian economy', *Economic Times*, June 11, 2012.

50. Praag (1987: 203). Walt van Praag is a Dutch legal expert.

51. 'Tibetan culture India's First Defense Line, says Dalai Lama', June 2, 2012, *Punjab Newsline Network* at www.punjabnewsline.com/.

52. After nine rounds of talks since 2002, during which every Tibetan memorandum and diplomatic Paper was rejected by the Chinese government, the two frustrated Tibetan representatives resigned, ending the dialogue with China. But Beijing may have a more sinister plan in mind as a TGE press release reveals. One of the Chinese negotiators reportedly advocated 'abrogation of minority status [for Tibetans] as stipulated in the Chinese constitution thereby removing the basis of autonomy.' 'Kalon Tripa Accepts Resignations of Special Envoy Lodi G. Gyari and Envoy Kelsang Gyaltsen', June 3, 2012 at http://tibet.net/.

53. For fascinating accounts of that operation overseen by CIA and Indian intelligence agencies, refer Knaus (1999), and Conboy and Morrison (2002).

54. See the blog by an Indian Army officer who served in 'Establishment 22' @Bhavanjagat at http://bharatkarnad.com/2013/05/03/tested-found-wanting/#comments.

55. 'China detains hundreds as immolations go on in Tibet', AP, *Times of India*, 1 June, 2012.

56. 'China does not rule out Tibet visit by the U.N. Rights Chief', *Reuters*, October 23, 2014, http://www.reuters.com/article/2014/10/23/us-china-un-rights-idUSKCN0IC1A220141023.

57. Elliot Abrams and Azizah al-Hibri, 'Challenge China to Free Tibetans', *Wall Street Journal*, April 18, 2013. Abrams and al-Hibri are members of the U.S. Commission on International Religious Freedom.

58. The $3 billion commitment is, moreover, to help Indian airlines lease Chinese-made commercial aircraft and in the telecommunications sector in which Chinese companies, such as Huawei and Xiaomi, have established a foothold in the Indian market. See 'China's Xi Jinping signs landmark deals on India visit', *BBC News*, http://www.bbc.com/news/world-asia-india-29249268. For a sceptical view prior to the Xi visit, see Gupta and Wang (2014).

59. This is precisely what the elected Prime Minister of the Tibetan Government in exile, Lobsang Sangay, an official invitee to Narendra Modi's inauguration ceremony on May 26, 2014—an invitation intended to signal greater Indian interest in the cause of genuine autonomy for Tibet. See Pesta (2014) .

60. Karnad (2008: 144–45); Dan Twining, 'Could China and India go to war over Tibet?', *Foreign Policy*, March 10, 2009 at www.foreignpolicy.com/.

61. Jonathan Kaiman, 'Chinese authorities offer cash to promote inter-ethnic marriages', *Guardian*, September 2, 2014, http://www.theguardian.com/world/2014/sep/02/chinese-authorties-cash-inter-ethnic-marriages-uighur-minority.

62. The most recent promise was held out on the eve of the new Chinese Premier Li Keqiang's state visit to India. See Sandeep Dikshit, 'Is India-China deal on border issue in the works?', *Hindu*, May 15, 2013. Dilasha Seth and Yogima Seth Sharma, 'India May Board Train to Chinese IT Market', *Economic Times*, March 19, 2014.

63. Sutirtho Patranobis, "'India, China have the same terror concerns'", *Hindustan Times*, November 1, 2014.

64. Magal, Zur, Kedem, 'The Growing Power of the Indian Navy', 113–14

65. Ankit Panda, 'India and Saudi Arabia Sign Defense Cooperation Plan', *The Diplomat*, February 27, 2014 at http://thediplomat.com/2014/02/india-and-saudi-arabia-sign-defense-cooperation-pact/.

66. Interview.

67. Toshi Yoshihara, 'Undersea Dragons in the Indian Ocean', *China-India Brief*, No. 37, October 14-28, 2014, Lee Kuan Yew School of Public Policy, National University Singapore, at http://lkyspp.nus.edu.sg/cag/publication/china-india-brief/china-india-brief-37?utm_source=China-India+Brief+subscribers&utm_campaign=29efa087a3-China_India_Brief_37_28_Oct_2014&utm_medium=email&utm_term=0_a8f8390d56-29efa087a3-96406833#guest.

68. James Holmes and Yori Toshihara, 'Is China Planning a String of Pearls?', *The Diplomat*, February 21, 2011, at http://the-diplomat.com/flashpoints-blog/2011/01/21/is-china-planning-string-of-pearls/.

69. 'Lankan navy chief plays down Chinese presence', *Hindustan Times*, October 29, 2014.

70. Colombo is playing up the port access afforded Chinese submarines, most recently an SSN, a conventional sub and submarine tender, for instance, in the face of Indian protests. See Chin Parashar, 'Sri Lanka snubs India, opens out to Chinese submarine again', *Sunday Times of India*, November 2, 2014.

71. 'Trilateral Indian Ocean Security Grouping Set to Expand', IANS, *New Indian Express*, March 6, 2014.

72. See his interview in *Times of India*, August 11, 2012.

73. Brewster (2014 : 48–49). 'Trinco' was deemed the finest deep sea harbour in the world by Admiral Lord Nelson, and by the British Prime Minister William Pitt the Younger in early 19th Century as 'the most

valuable colonial possession on the globe, as giving our Indian Empire a security which it had not enjoyed from its establishment.'

74. MSDF Vice Admiral (ret.) Hideaki Kaneda sees the intensification of maritime links with India and the U.S. as the two pillars of Japan's security policy under Prime Minister Abe. See his 'Japan Should Strengthen Naval Cooperation with India', *AJISS-ComWhile mentary*, No. 169, January 17, 2013 at http://www2.jiia.or.jp/en_commentary/201301/17-1.html.

75. This is what was hinted by Japanese Premier Shinzo Abe. 'I expect', he said, 'both Japan and India, as maritime states, to play a vital role together for the security of sea lanes and jointly carry out their responsibility in the region.' See his interview, *Times of India*, January 25, 2014.

76. This is the view of many senior Indian naval officers who have interacted with the MSDF.

77. In 2002 the Liberal Party president Ichiro Ozawa warned that Japan can, at any time, convert its vast holdings of reprocessed spent fuel from its numerous nuclear power plants into 'thousands of nuclear warheads'. 'If we get serious', he warned, 'we will never be beaten in terms of military power.' Other political leaders have been more cautious in their utterances, seeking to explore instead the extent to which India may be inveigled into joining Japan in hindering China's strategic abilities. Tokyo is, moreover, not averse to keeping China on tenterhooks about its nuclear intentions to convert its 44 tons of plutonium into armaments. See Gordon G. Chang, 'Japan's Gigantic Stockpile of Plutonium', *World Affairs Journal*, February 19, 2014 at http://www.worldaffairsjournal.org/blog/gordon-g-chang/japan%E2%80%99s-gigantic-stockpile-plutonium

78. Quotes in this paragraph in Bharat Karnad, 'Strategic and Nuclear Balancing of China in the Asia-Pacific' in *Peace and Stability in the Asia-Pacific Region: Assessment of the Security Architecture*, National Security Seminar 2011, edited by Major General (ret.) Y.K. Gera [New Delhi: United Service Institution and Vij Books India Pvt Ltd], 59, 61.

79. Interview, *Times of India*, January 25, 2014.

80. Karnad, 'Strategic and Nuclear Balancing', 56–60.

81. 'Sino-Japanese economic ties chill amid political disputes, hopes remain', *Xinhua*, September 17, 2013.

82. Kei Koga and Yogesh Joshi, 'Japan-India Security Cooperation', *The Diplomat*, July 17, 2013 at http://thediplomat.com/2013/017/17/japan-india-security-cooperation/.

83. Sukjoon Yoon, 'Middle-Power cooperation between South Korea and India: Hedging the Dominance of the Great Powers', *PacNet*, Number 19, Pacific Forum CSIS (Honolulu), January 28, 2014.

84. 'India develops cold feet on talks with Japan, US', *Times of India*, August 25, 2012.

85. Aarti Betigeri, 'As China Eyes Indian Ocean, Japan and India Pair Up on Defense', *New York Times*, July 27, 2012.

86. P. Vaidyanathan Iyer, 'Security, ties: Modi, Abbott play Bhai Bhai', *Indian Express*, November 19, 2014.

87. Rory Medcalf, James Brown, *Defence Challenges 2035: Securing Australia's Lifelines* [Sydney: Lowy Institute for International Policy, November 2014], 1, http://www.lowyinstitute.org/files/defence-challenges-2035.pdf.

88. Sandy Gordon, *Widening Horizons: Australia's new relationship with India*, Australian Strategic Policy Institute, 2007.

89. Keynote Address, S. Ganapathy, Secretary (West), MEA, Inaugural Dinner, India-Australia Roundtable 2012, arranged by the Lowy Institute and Observer Research Foundation, New Delhi, December 3, 2012.

90. A senior Australian diplomat.

91. Daniel Hurst 'Tonybbott expected to sign uranium deal with India on visit next month', *Guardian*, August 18, 2014.N.

92. The quote is from PM Modi's address to the joint session of Australian Parliament. Refer text of speech in *Hindu*, November 18, 2014.

93. See the interview of Michael Hayden, CIA and NSA chief in *Financial Review*, July 19, 2013. Also refer *Defending Australia in the Asia-Pacific Century: Force 2030* [Canberra: Department of Defense, Australian Government, 2009], 70–71, Chapter 8.

94. Robert Haddick, 'Salami Slicing in the South China Sea', *Foreign Policy*, August 3, 2012 at www.foreignpolicy.com/

95. 'Major General Luo Yuan: Make the Diaoyu Islands a Target Range and Launch People's War on the Sea', Huanqiu, August 21, 2012, *Chinascope* at http://chinascope.org/main/content/view/4792/150.

96. Shi Yinhong, a foreign policy adviser to the Chinese government, is quoted as saying 'Nationalism is the number one driving force complicating the problem' and that there was 'mutual hatred' between China and Japan. Refer 'Much at stake for US as tensions rise in troubled China Sea', *NBC News*, August 25, 2012 at http://worldnews.nbcnews.com/.

97. It was an interaction the author attended at the USI on December 2, 2011.

98. 'Ex-Japanese PM seeks security tie-up with India', *Times of India*, September 21, 2011.

99. The last time the U.S. followed isolationist policies was in the 1930s. For an analysis of this ideology as practiced in that period, see Ross

A. Kennedy, 'The Ideology of American Isolationism 1931–1939', *Cercles 5*, 2002 at www.cercles.com/n5/kennedy.pdf.

100. 'Ex-Japanese PM seeks security tie-up with India'.

101. Interestingly, on this subject see the views of a former Assistant Commander of the Israeli Navy, Admiral Yuval Zur (Retd.). He has written that, given American limitations and incompatibility of U.S. and Indian interests especially in the Indian Ocean, India does not believe the U.S. as reliable. See Yuval Zur, Tamir Magal, and Nadav Kedem, 'The Growing Power of the Indian Navy: Westward Bound', *Military and Strategic Affairs*, Volume 4/No.3/December 2012, 105.

102. President John Quincy Adams declared that America 'goes not abroad in search of monsters to destroy' and should not get involved beyond the power of extrication in all the wars of interest and intrigue ('John Quincy Adams Quotes' at HYPERLINK "http://www.presidential-power.org/quotes-by-presidents/john-quincy-adams/-quotes.htm".

103. Andrew J. Bacevich, 'The seductive allure of wars we're not winning', *Washington Post*, April 11, 2014. On America's recent wars see Shimko (2010) and McMahon (1999).

104. In his 2014 State of the Union Address, President Obama declared that he 'will not send our troops in harm's way unless it's truly necessary; nor will I allow our sons and daughters to be mired in open-ended conflicts.' The text at http://www.whitehouse.gov/the-press-office/2014/01/28/president-barack-obamas-state-union-address. Despite, albeit covert, plans hatched in the mid-1950s for military deployment of American troops and combat aircraft to fight alongside the Indian army and air force against the Chinese aggressors, when the PLA did attack in October 1962, U.S. restricted itself to airlifting war materiel. Karnad (2005: 92-153); Jeff Smith, 'A Forgotten War in the Himalayas', *YaleGlobal Online*, September 17, 2012.

105. Ananth Krishnan, 'Japan Navy Chief's message for new Indian govt.', *Hindu*, April 24, 2014.

106. James R. Holmes and Toshi Yoshihara, 'Strongman, Constable, or Free Rider? India's "Monroe Doctrine" and Indian Naval Strategy', *Comparative Strategy*, Vol. 28, 2009.

107. Clinton's National Security Adviser Anthony Lake talked about the U.S. helping the Chinese design a new global system of governance and, as evidence of American good faith President Clinton at the June 1998 Beijing summit with President Jiang Zemin acceded to the 'three No's', no support for—Taiwanese independence, the 'one China, one Taiwan' concept, and Taiwan's membership in international organizations that diluted the U.S. commitments to Taiwan. See Deborah Welch Larson and

Alexei Shevchenko, 'Status Seekers: Chinese and Russian Responses to U.S. Primacy', *International Security*, Spring 2010, 84–5.

108. This was the impression picked up by this writer in the months after the tests when the National Security Advisory Board was first formed as part of the National Security Council, Government of India, and I was appointed to serve on it. On the Beijing Meet, refer the relevant summit statements in Shirley (2012: 57–63).

109. Thus, in order not to rile China, in November 2013 India conducted its annual Malabar naval exercise in the Bay of Bengal at the same time as a joint Indian Army-PLA exercise, involving a small number of troops, was held in Chengdu. See Rajat Pandit, 'India strikes a balance with combat exercises with US, China', *Times of India*, November 5, 2013.

110. See Michael C. Horowitz, 'How Defense Austerity Will Test U.S. Strategy in Asia', *NBR Analysis Brief*, August 7, 2012. On China A2/AD strategy see Andrew S Erickson and David D. Yang, 'Using the Land to Control the Sea?: Chinese Analysts Consider the Antiship Ballistic Missile', Naval War College Review, Autumn 2009, vol. 62, No. 4 at http://www.usnwc.edu/getattachment/f5cd3bb5-a1d1-497d-ab70-257b9502d13e/Using-the-Land-to-Control-the-Sea--Chinese-Analyst.aspx.

111. James R. Holmes, 'Quality, Quantity and Mr. Miyagi', *The Diplomat*, February 10, 2012 at http://the-diplomat.com/flashppoints-blog/2012/02/10/quality-uantity-and-mr-mitagi/; Thom Shanker and Helene Cooper, 'Pentagon Plans to Shrink Army to Pre-World War II Level', *New York Times*, February 23, 2014.

112. 'Remarks by Secretary Panetta at the Shangri La Dialogue in Singapore', June 2, 2012 at www.defense.gov/

113. The U.S. Quadrennial Defense Review, for instance, released a short while before Russia annexed Crimea, accepted the risk of war with China, but not Russia. See Peter Croft and Adrian Croft, 'After Crimea, West plans for Russian military threat', Reuters, March 19, 2014 at http://www.reuters.com/article/2014/03/19/us-europe-russia-defence-idUSBREA2I2BZ20140319

114. Gordon G. Chang, 'China and Russia: An Axis of Weak States', *World Affairs Journal*, March/April 2014.

115. For an assessment of these Chinese technologies, see Gormley et al. (2014).

116. Robert Kaplan, 'The Indian Ocean World Order', Stratfor, April 10, 2014 published in www.realclearworld.com/articles/2014/04/10/the_indian_ocean_world_order.html.

117. James Holmes & Toshi Yoshihara, 'US Navy's Indian Ocean Folly?', *The Diplomat*, January 4, 2011 at http://the-diplomat.com/2011/01/04/

us-navy%e2%80%99s-indian-ocean-folly/. Hosting the four American littoral combat ships occasioned murmurs. See Evelyn Goh, 'U.S. "pivot" should not end up forcing Asia to chose sides', Singapore Institute of International Affairs, updated July 18, 2012 at www.siiaonline.org/.

118. 'Russia to build maintenance facility for ships in Vietnam's Cam Ranh', *Pravda*, September 30, 2013 at http://english.pravda.ru/world/asia/30-09-2013/125764-russia_vietnam_cam_rahn_bay-0/.

119. Excerpt in Holmes & Yoshihara, 'US Navy's Indian Ocean Folly?'

120. 'My own picture of the future', Nehru observed in his autobiography published in 1936, 'is a federation of which includes China and India, Burma and Ceylon, Afghanistan and possibly other countries.... We feel as Asiatics a common bond uniting us against the aggression of Europe (Mishra 2013: 249)'.

121. Said PLA Major General Peng Guangqian: 'When China's national core interests are violated, and when this cannot be stopped without military intervention, we have no choice but to use force to counterattack....We cannot beg for peace. Rather we can use force to obtain peace. If we give up the use of force, we can then only surrender and wait while others partition us at will.' See 'Peng Guangqian: Military Force is Always an Important Means to safeguard National Sovereignty', *People's Daily*, May 17, 2012—as carried by http://chinascope.org/. Alastair Iain Johnston, 'How New and Assertive is China's New Assertiveness?', *International Security*, Vol. 37, No. 4, Spring 2013. Michael Auslin, 'Beijing's Paranoid Worldview', *Wall Street Journal*, April 19, 2013.

122. Manila seems happy to give the U.S. Navy an 'access point', but does not care to overplay the potential benefits it may derive from intimacy with the U.S.. See William Wan, 'Defense Secretary Leon Panetta highlights U.S. ties to Vietnam during visit.', *Washington Post*, June 3, 2012.

123. Nehru, *Glimpses of World History*, 483; Admiral Nirmal Verma, Chief of the Naval Staff, Keynote Address in *Peace and Stability in Asia-Pacific Region*, ed., Gera, 9.

124. Vice Admiral Sinha, Welcome Address, in *Peace and Stability in Asia-Pacific Region*, 8.

125. Speech by Shivshankar Menon, 'Developments in India-China Relations'. 2012.

126. Su Hao in *Peace and Stability in Asia Pacific Region*, ed., Gera, 155–7.

127. Sino-Vietnamese enmity is of long standing and China has always had a hard time of forcing that Indo-Chinese country into its fold. In 1420–28, for example, the Ming Navy mounted several fruitless expeditions against the Annam Kingdom (Vietnam) and after numerous reverses the decision was made to abandon the campaign. In a missive to the Emperor

urging withdrawal, one of his ministers waxed eloquent about the futility of 'indulg[ing] in military pursuits [and] glorify[ing] the sending of expeditions to distant countries' (Macneill 1982: 46).

128. James Bellacqua, *The China Factor in U.S.-Vietnam Relations*, Center for Naval Analyses, March 2012 at www.cns.org/.

129. A Japanese analyst, Tetsuo Kotani, of the Okazaki Institute, has talked of China prosecuting 'lawfare'; as part of its anti-access strategy making 'a series of excessive maritime claims by requiring Chinese approval for innocent passage in the territorial seas by foreign warships'. See Gera, 2011. *Peace and Stability in Asia Pacific Region*, 42.

130. Presentation by Tetsuo Kotani, Ibid, p. 13, p. 70.

131. Brian Spegele and Vu Trong Khanh, 'Oil-Rig Dispute Marks Leap for China, *Wall Street Journal*, May 9-11, 2014; 'China-Vietnam face-off leaves India worried', *Times of India*, May 10, 2014; Jane Perlez, 'Beijing sends bold message with move in disputed sea', *New York Times*, May 10–11, 2014.

132. Modi also referred to defence cooperation with Vietnam as 'among our most important ones'. Indrani Bagchi, 'India ignores China frown, offers def [sic] boost to Vietnam', *Times of India*, October 31, 2014.

133. Shiraishi Takashi, 'China's Diplomatic Offensive: Consequences for Regional Relations', *Nippon.com*, August 7, 2012 at www.nippon.com/. 'When China was militarily weak, it supported the concept of putting aside sovereignty concerns and carrying out joint development [of the resources-rich South China Sea], aiming to reduce the potential conflicts from overlapping claims while buying time for its own naval development', notes a Stratfor essay. 'Meanwhile, to avoid dealing with a unified bloc of counterclaimants, Beijing adopted a one-to-one negotiation approach with individual countries on their own territorial claims, without the need to jeopardize [their own] nine-dash line claim [by the Koumintang government in 1947]. This allowed Beijing to remain the dominant partner in bilateral negotiations, something it feared it would lose in a more multilateral forum.' See Rodger Baker and Zhixing Zhang, 'The Paradox of China's Naval Strategy', *Stratfor*, July 17, 2012 at www.stratfor.com/.

134. See his interview in *Economic Times*, October 29, 2014.

135. On the least well-known Five Power agreement, see Carlyle A. Thayer, 'The Five Power Defense Arrangements: The Quiet Achiever', *Security Challenges*, Volume 3, Number 1 (February 2007); Takashi, 'China's diplomatic offensive'.

136. Menon, 'Our Changing External Environment: Challenges and Opportunities', 31 October 2011.

137. NSA, Shiv Shankar Menon, 'India's Role in Global Politics', July 15, 2011.

138. Interview, March 15, 2011.

139. Interview, June 24, 2011.

140. For an analysis of China's role in proliferating nuclear weapons and missile technologies to Pakistan, see Shirley A. Kan, *China and Proliferation of Weapon of Mass Destruction and Missiles: Policy Issues*, Congressional Research Service, Washington, DC. April 25. 2012 at www.fas.org/sgp/crs/nuke/RL31555.pdf. The strategy of nuclear missile arming Vietnam discussed in Karnad, *India's Nuclear Policy*, pp. 30–1, p. 144.

141. See Fravel (2008). For an Indian perspective, see Sudha Ramachandran, 'China plays the long game on border disputes', *Asia Times*, January 27, 2011 at www.atimes.com.

142. A professor at Pusan University Robert Kelly has described Japan as 'a unique bulwark to Chinese hegemony in Asia'. See his Asian Security blog, December 27, 2013 at http://asiansecurityblog.wordpress.com/201312/27/my-december-newsweek-japan-essay-japan-as-a-unique-bulwark-to chinese-hegemony-in-Asia/.

143. More in disappointment than anger, a commentary in *Huanqiu*, the official Chinese press outlet for chauvinism, called the Russian firing on Chinese fishing vessels and detention of its crew in the Sea of Japan on July 16, 2012 'reckless behavior' that 'not only harms Chinese confidence in fostering a long-term friendship with Russia, but also provides excuses for forces seeking to undermine Sino-Russia ties.' See 'Huanqiu; Russia Should Not Have Fired at Chinese Fishing Ships', July 18, 2012, *Chinascope* at http://opinion.huanqiu.com/1152/2012-07/2923188.html.

144. Stephen Blank, 'A (Multi) Polar Bear? Russia's Bid for Influence in Asia', *Global Asia*, June 2011.

145. 'India, Russia to hold first ever joint Air Force exercises', *Indian Express*, November 18, 2013.

146. 'Russia, China, to create new long range plane and helicopter—Rogozin', Ria-Novosti, *Eurasian Review*, June 8, 2-14 at http://www.eurasiareview.com/08062014-russia-china-create-new-long-range-plane-helicopter-rogozin/?utm_source=feedburner&utm_medium=email&utm_campaign=Feed%3A+eurasiareview%2FVsnE+%28Eurasia+Review%29.

147. See his 'China and the United States: Beyond Balance', Roundtable: Turning to the Pacific: U.S. Strategic Rebalancing toward Asia, *Asia Policy*, No. 14 (July 2012), 40 at http://asiapolicy.nbr.org/ .

148. Minxin Pei, 'China's trust problem', *Indian Express*, September 3, 2012.

149. Kristina Wong, 'Panetta tours Asia to advance "pivot" by Pentagon to Pacific region', *Washington Times*, September 15, 2012.

150. Especially worrisome to the U.S. would be the increasing numbers of Chinese warships and nuclear submarine deployments in the Pacific. See Demetri Sevastopulo and Jennifer Thompson, 'China nuclear subs "gallop to depths of ocean"', *Financial Times*, October 28, 2013.

151. Karnad, 'Strategic and Nuclear Balancing of China in the Asia-Pacific', 58-62'; 'Nuclear arms card for Japan', commentary, *Japan Times*, April 29, 2013; Mark Hibbs, 'Will South Korea go nuclear?', *Foreign Policy*, March 15, 2013.

152. Saibal Dasgupta, '"China sees growing India-Japan ties as move to counter it"', *Times of India*, September 20, 2012.

153. The Indian government is seriously considering transferring the Brahmos supersonic anti-ship cruise missile to Vietnam. Refer 'India to sell BrahMos Missile to Vietnam', *Asian Age*, September 20, 2011.

154. 'Tensions rise as China surveillance ships enter waters claimed by Japan', *NBCNews.com*, September 13, 2012.

155. Refer his *Perils of Proximity: China-Japan Security Relations* [Washington, DC" Brookings Institution, 2010], 86.

156. On India's policy to Myanmar, see Jo Johnson and Amy Kazmin, 'India under fire for military aid to Burma', *Financial Times*, December 8, 2006. 'India's Look East Policy and Ties with Asean', *Hindu*, May 29, 2012.

157. Interview, March 25, 2011.

158. Burn's remarks made on the eve of an inter-ministerial meeting between the Indian Minister for External Affairs S.M. Krishna and the U.S. Secretary of State Hillary Clinton. For the text, see http://www.state.gov/p/us/rm/2010/136718.htm

159. Interview, March 25, 2011.

160. Bharat Karnad, 'Uses of Ambush Diplomacy', *Open*, May 30, 2014 at http://www.openthemagazine.com/article/voices/uses-of-ambush-diplomacy.

161. Brad Glosserman, 'Evolutionary or Revolutionary? Japan's Defense Strategy', *The Diplomat*, August 11, 2012 at http://the-diplomat.com/2012/08/11/evolutionary-or-revolutionary-japans-defense-strategy; Martin Fackler, 'In Shark-Infested Waters, Resolve of Two Giants Is Tested', *New York Times*, September 22, 2012.

162. 'Australia-India Strategic Partnership in an Asian Century', Address by the Australian High Commissioner [Ambassador] to India, Peter Varghese, May 3, 2012, Observer Research Foundation, New Delhi, *ORF Discourse* at www.orfonline.org/.

163. Gabriel Kolko, 'Panetta's Pacific Vision', *Counterpunch*, June 8-10, 2012 at www.counterpunch.org/.

164. Baker and Zhang, 'The Paradox of China's Naval Strategy'. 'Analysis: China's "Small Stick" Approach to South China Sea', Reuters, *New York Times*, May 15, 2012.

165. James R. Holmes, 'Entente Growing Pains', *The Diplomat*, December 23, 2011 at http://the-diplomat.com/flashpoints-blog/2-11/12/23/entente-growing-pains/.

166. Thomas Fargo, 'The Military Side of Strategic Rebalancing' Roundtable: Turning to the Pacific: U.S. Strategic Rebalancing toward Asia, *Asia Policy*, No. 14 (July 2012), 35 at http://asiapolicy.nbr.org/; Lampton, 'China and the United States: Beyond Balance', 41.

167. Mindful of Indian sensitivities, Taro Aso, said 'We'll not call [India] an ally, but almost we are allies.' See Aso's Special Address on 'Japan's Revival and the Japan-India Global Strategic Partnership', May 4, 2013, New Delhi. Dr Singh, on a state visit in May 2012 called Japan 'a natural and indispensable partner'. See Jayanth Jacob, 'India, Japan vow to step up defense, bilateral relations', *Hindustan Times*, May 30, 2013.

168. Ibid.

169. See Shyam Saran, 'Grasp the nettle in Kathmandu', *Hindustan Times*, November 21, 2014.

References

Albright, D. 2013. *Ring Magnets for IR-1 Centrifuges*, ISIS Report, Institute for Science and International Security, 13 February, at http://isis.online.org/.

Alexander, D. 2012. 'Panetta: Majority of US warships moving to Asia', Reuters, June 2, at www.msnbc.msn.com/

Bagchi, I . 2014. 'US refuses to talk China with India', *Times of India*, 17 February.

Beech, H. 2010. 'What Will China's Next Move on North Korea Be?', *Time*, 24 November.

Bergeman, S.P. 2012. 'The United States-India Strategic Relationship', School of Advanced Military Studies, U.S. Army Command and General Staff College, Fort Leavenworth, Kansas, 20 June, 2012 at www.dtic.mil/get-tr-doc/pdf?AD=ADA566630, 9.

Baker, R. and Z. Zhang. 2012. 'The Paradox of China's Naval Strategy', *Stratfor*, 17 July, at www.stratfor.com/

Bhasin, A. S. (ed). 2012. *India-Pakistan Relations 1947-2007, A Documentary Study*, Vol-I-X: cxix–cxx. New Delhi: Public Diplomacy Division, MEA and Geetika Publishers.

Bradsher, K. 2014. 'Philippine Leader Sounds Alarm on China', *New York Times*, 4 February.

Bremmer, I. 2012. *Every Nation for Itself: Winners and Losers in a G-Zero World*. New York: Portfolio/Penguin.

———. 2013. 'China's Limited Influence', *New York Times*, 27 November.

Brewster, David. 2011. *India as an Asia-Pacific Power*. Abingdon, U.K.: Routledge.

———. 2014. *India's Ocean: The Story of India's Bid for Regional Leadership*. Abingdon, UK: Routledge.

Brobst, P. J. 2005. *The Future of the Great Game: Sir Olaf Caroe, India's Independence, and the Defense of Asia*. Akron, Ohio: University of Akron Press.

Cha, V. 2014. 'Avoiding a Crimea in Asia', *Korea Joongang Daily*, March 20, at http://koreajoongangdaily.joins.com/news/article/article.aspx?aid= 2986624.

Chang, G. 2013. 'China's Militant Nationalism', 29 April at www.gatestone institute.org/3687/china-militant-nationalism.

Darwin, J. 2008. *After Tamerlane: The Rise and Fall of Global Empires 1400-2000*. New York: Bloomsbury Press.

Conboy, K and J. Morrison. 2002. *The CIA's Secret War in Tibet*. Lawrence, KA: University of Kansas Press.

Duc, Khanh Vu and Duvien Tran. 2014. 'Less Money, less faith in US "pivot"', *Asia Times*, 6 March, at http://atimes/Southeast_Asia/SEA-02-060314.html.

Chase, Roberts, Emily Hill, and Paul Kennedy, *The Pivotal States: A New Framework for U.S. Policy in the Developing World* [New York: W.W. Norton & Company, 1999], 6.

Chivers, C.J. and Herszenhorn, D. M. 2014. 'In Crimea, Russia Showcases a Rebooted Army', *New York Times*, 2 April.

Chow, J. 2014. 'Concrete moves to make Sino-S'pore defence ties stronger', *Straits Times*, 15 November.

Collin, K. S. L. 2012 . 'Vietnam's New Kilo-class Submarines: Game-changer in Regional Naval Balance?', *RSIS Commentaries*, No. 162/2012, 28 August.

Drezner, D. W. 2011. 'Does Obama Have a Grand Strategy?', *Foreign Affairs*, July/August: 64.

Eilperin, J. 2014. 'U.S., Philippines to sign 10-year defense agreement amid rising tensions', *Washington Post*, 27 April.

Evans D. C. and M. R. Peattie. 1997. *Kaigun: Strategy, Tactics, and Technology in the Imperial Japanese Navy, 1887–1941*. Annapolis, MD: Naval Institute Press.

Forden, G. 2010. 'Master Proliferator or weapons Simple Front Company?' 2 May, at http://38North.org/2010/10/05/master-proliferator-or-simple-front-company/

Fravel, Taylor, M. 2008. 'China's Search for Military Power', *The Washington Quarterly*, Vol. 31, No. 3: 124–141.

Ghosh, N. 2014. 'Chinese PM's offer to Asean: Friendship pact, defence meeting', *Straits Times* (Singapore) 11 November.

Gilboy, George J. and Eric Heginbotham. 2012. *Chinese and Indian Strategic Behavior: Growing Power and Alarm.* New Delhi: Cambridge University Press.

Gordon, G. Chang, 'Japan's Gigantic Stockpile of Plutonium', *World Affairs Journal*, February 19, 2014 at http://www.worldaffairsjournal.org/blog/gordon-g-chang/japan%E2%80%99s-gigantic-stockpile-plutonium.

Goldfarb Z. A. and K. DeYoung. 2014. ' U.S. pledges $1B to boost military presence in E. Europe, urges NATO allies to boost funding', *Washington Post*, 3 June.

Griffiths, J. 2014. 'Al-Qaeda magazine calls for Xinjiang to be "recovered by the Islamic Caliphate"', *South China Morning Post*, October 21, http://www.scmp.com/news/china/article/1621190/new-al-qaeda-magazine-calls-xinjiang-be-recovered-islamic-caliphate?page=all.

Gupta A. K. and Wang, H. 2014. '$100bn from Xi's visit to India? Not likely', *Financial Times* blog, 15 September, see http://blogs.ft.com/beyondbrics/2014/09/15/guest-post-100bn-from-xis-visit-to-india-not-likely/.

Haass, R. N. 2012. 'What the Olympics medal count says about who runs the world', *Washington Post*, 18 Aug.

Hastings, J. V. 2011. 'Charting the Course of Uyghur Unrest', *China Quarterly*, volume 208, December; http://fpif.org/can-china-pacify-restive-minorities-peacefully/.

Herszenhorn, D. M. 2014. 'In Crimea, Russia Showcases a Rebooted Army', *New York Times*, 2 April.

Huang, J., K. Bajpai, and K. Mahbubani, 2012. 'Rising Peacefully Together', *Foreign Policy*, 1 August, at www.foreignpolicy.com/.

Ikenberry, G. J. 2008. 'The Rise of China and the Future of the West', *Foreign Affairs*, January/February.

Jacques, M. 2012a [2nd ed.]. *When China Rules the World: The End of the Western World and the Birth of a New Global Order.* New York: Penguin.

———. 2012b. 'China and Japan: Two nations locked in mutual loathing', *Daily Telegraph*, 20 August.

Jimbo, Ken. 2012 . 'Japan Should Build ASEAN's Security Capacity', AJISS Commentary, The Association of Japanese Institutes of

Strategic Studies, 30 May, at http://www2.jiia.or.jp/en_commentary/201205/30-1.html.

Kagan, R. 2008. 'The End of the End of History', *The New Republic*, 23 April, at http://www.tnr.com/print/article/environment-energy/the-end-the-end-history.

Karnad, B. 1994. 'India's Weak Geopolitics and What To Do About It', in B. Karnad (ed), *Future Imperilled: India's Security in the 1990s and Beyond*, New Delhi: Viking, Penguin India.

———. 2005 [First edition 2002]. *Nuclear Weapons and Indian Security: The Realist Foundations of Strategy*. Macmillan.

———. 2008. *India's Nuclear Policy*. Westport, CN, & London: Praeger Security International.

———. 2009. 'Habit of free-riding', *Seminar*, Issue No. 599, July.

———. 2013. 'Manmohan agenda to please the US', *New Indian Express*, 20 September.

Kazianis, H. 2013. 'Vietnam To Receive Advanced Russian Subs in 2013', *The Diplomat*, 2 April, at http://thediplomat.com/2013/04/vietnam-to-recieve-advanced-russian-sub-in-2013/.

Keating, P. 2012. 'The U.S. must share power with China', *Sydney Morning Herald*, 7 August, at www.smh.com.au/.

Keck, Z. 2013 'To Hedge Its Bets, Russia Is Encircling China', *Diplomat*, 5 November, 2013. http://thediplomat.com/2013/11/to-hedge-its-bets-russia-is-encircling-china/.

Kelley, R and B. Cloughley. 2014. 'Power Boost: Pakistan develops its thermonuclear weapons', p. 10. *Jane's Intelligence Review*, March.

Kenny, C. 2014. 'America is slipping to No. 2. Don't panic', *Washington Post*, 17 January.

Kennedy, P. 2010. 'Rise and Fall', *The World Today*, Aug/Sept at www.theworldtoday.org.

Kirshner, J. 2008. 'The Consequences of China's Rise for Sino-U.S. Relations' in R. S. Ross and Z. Feng (eds) *China's Ascent: Power, Security, and the Future*, p. 238. Ithaca, NY: Cornell University Press.

Klein, M. 2009. 'Russia's Military Capabilities: "Great Power" Ambitions and Reality', German Institute of International and Security Affairs, Berlin, October at http://www.swp-berlin.org/fileadmin/contents/products/research_papers/2009_RP12_kle_ks.pdf.

Krauthammer, C. 2003. 'The Japan Card', *Washington Post*, January 3, 2003.

Knaus, J. K. 1999. *Orphans of the Cold War: America and the Tibetan Struggle for Survival*. New York: Public Affairs.

Kurlantzick, J. 2006. 'China's Charm: Implications of Chinese Soft Power', Policy Brief 47, p. 4. June, Washington, D.C.: Carnegie Endowment for International Peace.

Lewis, J. 2014. 'Kim Jon Un's Thermonuclear Dreams', *Foreign Policy*, 10 April, at http://www.foreignpolicy.com/articles/2014/04/10/north_korea_new_nuclear_test_thermonuclear_multiple_detonation.

Landler, M. 2013. 'Obama Signals a Shift From Military Might to Diplomacy', *New York Times*, 25 November.

———. 2014. 'On a Trip That Avoids Beijing, Obama Keeps His Eye on China', *New York Times*, 26 April.

Lovell, Julia. 2011. *The Opium War: Drugs, Dreams, and the Making of China*. New York: Picador.

Mackinder, H. 1942 [reprint]. *Democratic Ideals and Reality*. New York: Henry Holt & Co.

Mahan, A. T. 1957. *The Influence of Seapower upon History 1560-1783*. New York: Hill & Wang.

Mahbubani, K. 2014. 'When America Becomes Number Two', *Huffington Post*, January 21, 2014 at http://www.huffingtonpost.com/kishore-mahbubani/when-america-becomes-numb_b_4603125.html

McMahon, Robert, J. 1996. *Cold War on the Periphery: The United States, India, and Pakistan*. New York: Columbia University Press.

Mehta, J.S. 2010. *Tryst Betrayed: Reflections on Diplomacy and Development*. New Delhi: Penguin India.

Menon, R. 2014. 'Concept and Application of Smart Power in Promoting India's National Interests and Strategic Objectives', 12th Major General Samir Sinha Memorial Lecture 2014, *Journal of the United Service Institution of India*, CXLIV (597).

Miller, G. 2014. 'ISIS rapidly accumulating cash, weapons, U.S. Intelligence officials say', *Washington Post*, 24 June.

Mishra, Pankaj. 2013. *From the Ruins of an Empire: The Revolt Against the West and the Remaking of Asia*. Picador.

Mori, A. 2007. 'Rich Country, Strong Armed Forces? The Sources of China's Comprehensive National Power', December 2007 at www.rchss.sinica.edu.tw/capas/publication/Newsletter/N38/38_01_02.pdf.

O'Donnell, C. M. (ed.). 2012. *The Implications of Military Spending Cuts for NATO's Largest Members*, Analysis Paper. Washington, D.C.: Center on the United States and Europe, Brookings Institution, July.

Pei, M. 2012. 'The Rise of the Rest and the Return of Spheres of Influence', *Global Trends 2030*, U.S. National Intelligence Council, May 28, at http://gt2030.com/2012/05/28/the-rise-of-the-rest-and-the-return-of-spheres-of-influence/.

Pesta, J. 2014. 'Government in Exile Seeks Tibetan Autonomy, Not Independence', *Wall Street Journal*, 5 June, at http://online.wsj.com/articles/tibet-seeks-end-to-chinese-repression-1401961197.

Pantucci, R. 2011. 'Uyghur Unrest in Xinjiang Shakes Sino-Pakistani Relations', Global Research and Analyses, Jamestown Foundation, August 19, at http://www.jamestown.org/single/?tx_ttnews%5Btt_news%5D=38346&no_cache=1#.VFM5PDTF8XV.

Pattanaik, Smruti S. 2012. (ed.), *India-Bangladesh Relations: Historical Imperatives and Future Direction.* New Delhi: Gyan Publishing House.

Pham, P.L. 2010. *Ending 'East of Suez': The British Decision to Withdraw from Malaysia and Singapore, 1964-1968.* Oxford, U.K.: Oxford University Press.

Pande, Jagannath. 2012. 'Bhutan eyes China, but bond with India stronger', *Global Times*, September 17.

Praag, M. C. van Walt van. 1987. *The Status of Tibet: History, Rights, and Prospects in International Law.* Boulder, CO: Westview Press.

Ramachandran, S. 2011. 'China ramps up pressure over Kashmir', *Asia Times*, 4 January, http://www.reuters.com/article/2014/10/23/us-china-un-rights-idUSKCN0IC1A220141023.

Sehgal, N. 2010. *Jawaharlal Nehru: Civilizing a Savage World.* New Delhi: Viking-Penguin.

Samanta, P. D. 2014. 'One China? What About One India policy: Sushma Swaraj to Wang Yi', *Indian Express*, 12 June.

Sanders, S. 2012. 'Demography as the soft underbelly of geopolitics', *Washington Times*, 12 August.

Sarmiento, P. 'Can China Pacify Its Restive Minorities Peacefully?', *Foreign Policy in Focus*, 8 October, 2014 at http://fpif.org/can-china-pacify-restive-minorities-peacefully/.

Schaffer, T. C. 2009. *India and the United States in the 21st Century: Reinventing Partnership.* Washington, D.C.: Center for Strategic and International Studies Press.

Sharma, M. S. 2013. 'Chinese arms fuelling NE Rebels' arsenal?', *Times of India*, 8 April.

Shen, D. 2007. 'Upsetting a delicate balance', *Bulletin of Atomic Scientists*, July/August.

Shirley A. Kan. 2012. *China and Proliferation of Weapon of Mass Destruction and Missiles: Policy Issues*, Congressional Research Service, Washington, DC. April 25. 2012 at www.fas.org/sgp/crs/nuke/RL31555.pdf.

Spykman, N. J. 1951 [2nd ed]. 'Eurasian Rimland in World Politics' in M. and H. Sprout (eds), *Foundations of National Power.* New York: D. Van Nostrand Company Inc.

Szabo, S. 2012. 'China's Challenge to the Liberal Order, India's Attraction to It, and the Possibilities for Western Revitalization in Light of the Global Embrace of Democratic Norms', Global Trends 2030, U.S. National Intelligence Council, 29 May, at http://gt2030.com/2012/05/29/

china-challenge-to-the-liberal-order-indias-attraction-to-it-and-the-possibilities for-western-revitalization-in-light-of-the-global-embrace of-western-norms/.

Takahara, Akio. 2008.'A Japanese Perspective on *China's Rise and the East Asian Order'* in *China's Ascent: Power. Security, and the Future of International Politics*. Ithaca, NY: Cornell University Press, edited by Robert S. Ross and Zhu Feng.

Tharoor, S. 2012. *Pax Indica: India and the World of the Twenty-First Century.* New Delhi: Penguin.

Tellis, A. 2010. 'Power Shift: How the West Can Adapt and Thrive in an Asian Century', Asia Paper Series, German Marshall Fund, 3 January, at www.gmfus.org/.

————. 2011. 'China's Grand Strategy', in Major General P.J.S. Sandhu (ed.), *China's Quest for Global Dominance: Reality or Myth?* p. 24. New Delhi: United Service Institution of India & Vij Books India Pvt. Ltd.

Vaughn, Bruce. 2010. *Bangladesh: Political and Strategic Developments and U.S. Interests*, Congressional Research Service, Washington, D.C. April 1.

Walt, S. 2011. 'Wishful Thinking', *Foreign Policy*, 29 April, 2011 at www.foreignpolicy.com/.

————. 2012. 'Dealing With a Chinese Monroe Doctrine', Room for Debate, *New York Times*, 2 May.

Wan, W. 2012. 'Hillary Clinton, top Chinese officials air some differences', *Washington Post*, 5 September.

Woeser, T. 2014. 'Tibet's Enduring Defiance', *New York Times*, 2 March.

Yapp, M.E. 1980. *Strategies of British India: Britain, Iran, and Afghanistan, 1798–1850*. Oxford: Clarendon Press.

Zeng, D. Z. and S. Wang. 2011. *China and the Knowledge Economy: Challenges and Opportunities*, Research Paper No. 4223, February 1, 2011, Washington, D.C.: World Bank.

3

Pivotal Relations

In India's idealistic worldview every state is a friend except a select few, like Pakistan, which are consigned to the small heap of countries considered irredeemably adversarial, a situation that stands Lord Palmerston's famous dictum that nations have no permanent friends or enemies, only permanent interests, on its head. This select category, however, leaves out China—the most obvious geopolitical and ideological rival, economic competitor, and military and strategic threat. Undue dread about tangling with China has led to New Delhi not retaliating in kind to Beijing's relentless minimizing of India's role, presence, and influence in its own South Asian region, and its drawing in Pakistan on its flank into the Chinese sphere, besides making inroads in Myanmar, Bangladesh, Nepal, and Sri Lanka. The need to recover the lost ground in southern Asia is an urgent prerequisite for India to make a success of its own Monroe Doctrine strategy and, on the larger stage, of the Triple Monroe Doctrine system. In any case, with the world conceived by New Delhi in mostly benign terms, New Delhi has not felt the need, as discussed in earlier chapters, to have a unique geopolitical vision backed by a strategic scheme (such as the Indian Monroe doctrine system) that Indian plans and policies can realize. Hence, there is no list of states considered pivotal to India's national security and interest that India needs to focus on and cultivate. This is, of course, a fundamentally flawed approach to international affairs. There is a hierarchy of states important to India, which need to be attended to. Some of these countries have already been identified. This chapter will deal with these states.

Co-opting South Asian States, Especially Pakistan

A glance at the map shows just why a Pakistan that can somehow be prevailed on to be, if not a friend, then not an adversary, is in India's strategic interest—it blocks India's land access to Iran, Afghanistan, and Central Asia. The alternative North–South route from Chahbahar-Zaranj to Kabul and points north and north-westwards is being developed. The overarching goal is to regain the pre-1947 unitary strategic and economic space of the subcontinent as the basic requirement for India to make good its great power ambitions. If the resources are harnessed well, such a naturally large South Asian marketplace can become an economic bloc and engine for much of Middle Asia and the Indian Ocean littoral. And with this bloc linking up with Southeast Asia and East Asia, the prospects for economic growth brighten immensely. The central problem with realizing such an outcome are not so much territorial issues such as Kashmir, Siachen, or Sir Creek, as the fact of the sheer disparity that exists between India and other states of the subcontinent, breeding apprehension of India in the states abutting it. India generates 80 per cent of the regional gross domestic product, so other states erect trade and tariff barriers to protect their economies; it is a situation vitiated by 'complex customs and transit procedures'. The result, notwithstanding a trade potential of $50 billion, is formal intra–South Asian trade of only 4 per cent valued at $5 billion (with India responsible for $3.8 billion or 76 per cent of it). It is miniscule compared to the intra–European Union trade of 67 per cent, and of 26 per cent within ASEAN. The resistance to free economic intercourse in South Asia has prompted India to open up economically to Southeast Asia and East Asia, when the other South Asian countries would have benefitted more from their interacting as a bloc with these flourishing eastern economies (Kher 2012).[1] Moreover, most of the legal mechanisms—such as SAARC, the South Asian Free Trade Association (SAFTA), and the SAARC Agreement on Trade in Services (SATIS)—for integrating the regional economies are in place, and require only the collective political will to be activated (Islam 2012).

The key to India's success in South Asia are good relations with Pakistan, which will get the other smaller and weaker countries to break out of their protective shells as well. Here, the asymmetry in military power has had telling consequences, with the India-centric infrastructure for war established in Pakistan pushing that country into difficult straits (Ahmed 2014). Islamabad sees the bind it is in, whence its occasional attempts to patch up relations by promising not to refer to the UN resolutions on Kashmir and by expressing readiness to provide India non-discriminatory market access (Ezdi 2014; Srivastava 2014). In fact, it is precisely the intermeshed socio-cultural and political milieu of the subcontinent and the organic ties between the peoples of the region which have dictated the extremely restrained warfighting that India and Pakistan have infrequently indulged in resembling not so much the usual wars to the death or to exhaustion, such as the ten-year Iran–Iraq War in the 1980s, as they do riots, a fact that Western and even South Asian analysts, for whatever reasons, simply neither acknowledge nor recognize as the truth. All the so-called India–Pakistan wars have been strictly counter-force engagements that are time-constrained (none has lasted more than a fortnight), with the hostilities severely limited in geographic space to a 60 kilometre belt on either side of the border accompanied by eschewal of counter-city bombardment. This is because of the shared sociocultural fabric and the history of the two militaries as part of the same colonial force. They share the same organizational norms and traditions and similar modes of warfare, leading to the famous jibe by the Israeli General Moshe Dayan that Indian and Pakistani armies 'fight by the book, the same book!'.

But these conflicts have in no way disturbed the ongoing kith and kinship relations between divided families and communities, more so now when the Muslim population in India has grown to be the second largest in the world after Indonesia, undermining the 'two nation theory' and the raison d'être for the founding of the state of Pakistan.[2] Another aspect is the evolving political map of India wherein in a third of the Lok Sabha constituencies Muslim voters—except in the 2014 general elections, when there was some degree of communal polarization of the electorate—wield the swing vote. It has, in any case, compelled even right-of-centre parties, such as the Bharatiya Janata Party (BJP), to moderate their anti-Muslim and anti-Pakistan rhetoric. In the event, Indian Muslims may countenance a little bloodying of Pakistan now and then in a scuffle usually started by the weaker state, but not its destruction.

All these unique factors have resulted in 'gentlemanly wars'— J. F. C. Fuller's description of the Boer War—where the superior Indian military is politically prevented from waging a 'war of annihilation' even as 'wars of manoeuvre' featuring clashes of armoured forces are tolerated. This is the military oeuvre of these two countries, reflected in their relatively meagre operational objectives and small war wastage reserve and war stock.[3] Indeed, the convention of prosecuting conventional conflicts of limited duration, scale, and with the utmost restraint has facilitated a nuclear *modus vivendi* as well (Karnad 2005a, 2005b: 563–78, 2008: Chapter 4). This is a far cry from the nuclear flashpoint theses Western analysts and South Asian 'experts' generally are fond of iterating based on the lack of understanding of the common socio-cultural milieu and continuing kith and kinship relations making for extraordinary restraint by both countries in their conflicts.[4] In this context, were India to display a bit of strategic foresight and unilaterally remove all forward-deployed nuclear short-range ballistic missiles from its western border and reduce and rationalize its exclusively Pakistan-centric armoured and mechanized strike forces (as analysed in a later chapter), which the Pakistan military fears, while bulking up militarily against China, it would have a positive effect of gradually eroding Pakistani suspicions and perceptions of the threat from India, without in any way weakening the security on the western frontier, nor the Indian military's ability to respond. This may lead in turn to a greater willingness on the part of the Pakistan Army to accept some face-saving diplomatic mechanism, such as the joint commission mooted by President Pervez Musharraf in 2007 to oversee affairs on both sides of the divide in Jammu and Kashmir. Had this proposal been accepted by Prime Minister Manmohan Singh, it would have resolved the dispute by semi-formalizing the Line of Control as the international boundary, and removed the barriers in Pakistan to economically link up with India, pushing the other South Asian states to plug in and benefit from the Indian economic system as well. This is still the way to pacify the neighbourhood—the basic prerequisite for establishing a loose Indian Monroe Doctrine system.

But Pakistan's unbridled animus towards India only highlights the fact that almost all of its other neighbours too have troubled relations with New Delhi, raising the question about why this is so. There is the historical aspect, of course, of Nehru expecting the states on India's borders to genuflect as if it were New Delhi's due, as the outlier regimes had done during the British Raj. The deeper reasons, however, can be traced back to the rather simplistic statecraft adumbrated in the Vedas and distilled by Kautilya in his *Arthashastra* circa 223 BC. The geopolitical paradigm of the *mandala* detailed therein enunciates some iron rules predetermining friend and foe premised on a sort of geometric determinism. Countries on the immediate border are invariably enemies, the states in the next outer circle are indubitably friendly, the tier beyond this is again adversarial, and the countries in the next outer circle are, well, benign, and so on. Hence, the heartland power is enjoined with to concert with the third-tier states to politically and militarily reduce the sovereign entity on its border as a prelude to absorbing it, whence the country that had helped the central state to eliminate the neighbour now instantly turns into its enemy by dint of now bordering the heartland power. It was statecraft that may have fit a mythical Bharat Varsha comprising a multitude of small states perennially at war with each other, with each state thinking of itself as the central power! But because this is a recipe for constant and interminable tumult, disorder, war, and destruction, this is what India suffered over the millennia.[5] It was only during periods when empire-builders—Chandragupta Maurya, Ashoka, the Moghuls, and the British—forcibly or by guile and other stratagems unified the warring kingdoms that India experienced peace. The mandala geopolitics is of limited relevance in the modern-day world. But, as is evident from the record post-1947 of the bad blood between India and each of its neighbours, there is no doubt about the logic of the concentric circles influencing, however much or little, the threat perceptions and policies of all the subcontinental countries.

Derived from such ancient Hindu geopolitics is the linearity of strategy reflected in the two-person game of *shatranj* (chess-type game) originating in the India of yore. It is a zero-sum game in which there is a winner and a loser, and the victory of the one necessarily means the defeat of the other. In the inter-state setting, this linearity lends itself easily to a Manichean worldview of good and bad states, responsible and rogue states, friendly and adversarial states, and to a simplifying of expectations about friend and foe and of policy-making. Thus, states deemed friendly are expected to always have benign policies, while malign intent is automatically attributed to or inferred into everything and anything rogue or adversarial states do. It has disabled India from coping with a China whose fundamental foreign policy principles are based contrarily on the equally ancient game of strategy, *wei qi*, where the aim is not frontal assault to take down the opponent's king piece or to kill off the queen piece, but on the play grid to occupy as many squares as possible by deliberate, long-sighted moves, and indirect approaches, ending in the enemy being left without space to manoeuvre and options.[6] By projecting the chess and wei qi tenets onto contemporary Indian and Chinese policies, one can clearly see why India (and the West) has found it difficult to cope with China's non-linear, multidimensional and intri-cate, parallel processor, moves that at once hold out military threats, seek improved trade and commerce, cooperate at climate and World Trade Organization meetings, and coopt by various means—arms aid, development aid, infrastructure investment—countries that are natural resource–rich or strategically placed in the IOR that can impede the adversary. And we can also see why Indian diplomats and the government, apparently mesmerized by the delicacy and deftness of Chinese diplomacy and strategizing, cannot see Beijing's simultaneously raising the military ante by a multiplicity of threaten-ing, proactive, and preemptive actions, and seeking enhanced trade and other cooperation, even as Chinese-assisted neighbouring states are encouraged to pin-prick India militarily and diplomatically to distraction. India seems stupefied—lulled one moment, alarmed the next—and, unable to respond in kind or even at all, ending up giving Beijing the benefit of doubt for any adverse development China may have, in fact, triggered. This is what happened for most of Manmohan Singh's tenure. Thus, the straightforward armed incur-sion in strength in April 2013 into the Depsang Bulge in Ladakh occasioned statements by the prime minister pooh-poohing this development as a 'local issue', at just the time when a PLA general was warning India against instigating 'new trouble'—which is how

Beijing saw the Indian Army's response. This is the way China keeps its enemies off balance. 'If Chess is about the decisive battle', writes Henry Kissinger, 'wei qi is about the protracted campaign' seeking 'relative advantage'; it is about 'the art of strategic encirclement', about moving into 'empty' spaces to gradually mitigate 'the strategic potential' of the opponent (Kissinger 2011: 23). Wei qi informed the thinking of the ancient Chinese strategist Suntzu and, in the modern day, influences *zhongnanhai* (the Chinese government complex) and the PLA. The outcomes of these differing forms of strategy and strategizing are there for all to see. The Indian government, unable to conceive of policies that can by slow degrees tame hostile states in proximity, such as Pakistan, with unilateral military measures that will cost little in terms of military advantage coupled to a raft of concessionary trade terms and investment and programmes to export IT skills, finds a poisonous South Asian environment with suspicious neighbours doubting India's bona fides, hindering India's advance at every turn. On the other hand, Beijing reserves its most potent military and economic capabilities to deal with the threat from the United States, routinely belabours weaker states, including Vietnam, on its periphery, while still managing to coopt them into its economic sphere with policies providing considerable benefits that also convert these states into economic dependencies, tempting them to gain more from binding themselves even tighter to China. This is the difference in a nutshell why China has by and large a pacified periphery and is a great power, and India, preoccupied with its neighbours, is not.

Courting Iran, Afghanistan, Central Asia

Regarding West Asia, India's policy of taking no sides, giving no offence, and tippy-toeing through the minefield of West Asian politics may be dictated by the domestic political need to keep Indian Muslims of various sects mollified. But it also frees New Delhi to transact with countries at the two ends of the Islamic sectarian rift—Saudi Arabia and Iran. The reluctance to spoil relations with Israel and the United States, or to break off ties with Iran, moreover, reveals the old Indian penchant for accommodating all the parties at the same time—the functional definition of strategic autonomy.

American badgering led to India reducing its offtake of Iranian oil, but dependence on Iranian energy sources never fell below 12–14 per cent level of the country's requirements.[7] It is not possible for many public sector refineries geared to process Iranian crude to go off-line, nor easily to switch to oil from other sources without expensive technological refitting, which the Indian government, facing huge fiscal deficits, is not eager to undertake. Realizing India's predicament, Tehran has tried to drive a wedge between India and the United States.[8] A powerful domestic political factor pushing friendship with Iran is the large Indian Muslim Shia community—the second largest outside of Iran. The Indian Shias are courted by Tehran, with the local clergy taking their cue from Qom, and opinion can be quickly mobilized against policies considered detrimental to close relations with Iran. It is influence that is deftly managed by the Iranian embassy in New Delhi to counter US and Israeli diplomatic pressure to cut off energy and other ties with Iran.[9] Indeed, with Western sanctions and trade embargoes isolating that country, India grabbed the opportunity to strengthen its trade with Tehran, which is expected to reach $24 billion in the mid-term future, up from the 2012 level of $14 billion (Gladstone 2012).[10] It did so while taking care to not rub Washington too much the wrong way (Dikshit 2014).[11]

Iran's importance to India cannot be overstated, as it is central to India's plans for gaining landward connectivity to Afghanistan, Central Asia, Europe, and Russia, which is unavailable more directly through Pakistan.[12] New Delhi is helping finance and build the North–South Corridor that, using Chahbahar as the entrepot, will have roads and railways thrusting northwards, linking up with Central Asia and with the existing networks in Russia, and thence to Europe via the Caspian Sea, Black Sea, and the Mediterranean, or the Baltic ports from St Petersburg. It will cut trans-shipment time for Indian container trade meant for European destinations by half compared to the sea route—5,245 kilometres, versus 16,129 kilometres via Suez—and save money (Fair 2007). The same corridor will enable Indian trade to flow to the Central Asian Republics via Kazakhstan, and oil and other natural resources in the reverse direction (Karnad 2012a).

There is, moreover, a growing Indian economic stake in Afghanistan that will only increase owing to the $1 trillion worth of unmined coal, rare earths, and minerals Indian business is attracted to. An Indian consortia has so far invested $2 billion to extract iron ore in the Hajigak region with estimated reserves worth $420 billion, producing $400 million as annual revenue for Kabul, and employing 30,000 Afghans. This presence competes with the Chinese concessions in copper mines and in reviving old oil and gas fields in the north (Hurst and Mathers 2014). Indian development aid, large infrastructure projects that are underway, including a new building to house the Afghan Parliament and a railway running parallel to the Zaranj–Delaram highway connecting to Chahbahar that India built, and extensive military and police training programmes are approved. The expanding Indian presence in Afghanistan will be serviced through the Iranian port that India is investing $100 million to develop. It was used for the first time in 2011 to transport 100,000 metric tons of grain as food aid to Kabul (Byerly 2012).[13] In April 2014, a Memorandum of Understanding on this transport network was signed by India, Iran, and Afghanistan, presaging a formal agreement on transit rights.[14] China's attempts to establish a strong presence in Afghanistan and, through the Shanghai Cooperation Organization, in the Central Asian Republics, has induced in New Delhi a certain urgency to operationalize the North–South Corridor, making Iran and Afghanistan the pillars of its 'Connect Central Asia' policy (Perlez 2012; M. S. Roy 2013).[15]

The Afghan regime of Hamid Karzai requested India for heavy weaponry, such as tanks, 105 mm field guns, and helicopter gunships, to fight the lighter-armed Taliban (Sawant 2013). New Delhi has met such Afghan needs in the past by arranging to buy these items from companies in the Ukraine and elsewhere in eastern Europe and transporting them via the land route to the Northern Alliance fighting the Taliban. The MEA in recent years has been tardy in approving this channel for facilitating arms aid, leading the newly elected Afghan President, Ashraf Ghani, to terminate discussions on this issue with Indian officials (Swami 2014). By such means does the MEA, with proven antipathy to military leverage of any kind, not just miss out on opportunities to solidify partnerships but actually ends up alienating neighbours, in this case, Afghanistan, India's 'gateway' to Central Asia, whose government only a few days earlier had called India 'an all-weather friend'.[16]

It may well be that Ghani seeks to increase his traction with India by closing in with China. In choosing Beijing as the first capital to visit after assuming the presidency, Ghani hopes to have China in the mix, promising support for 'Xinjiang, Tibet and other issues' in return for the opening of the Wakhan Pass and increased trade and connectivity to Central Asia, which Beijing has resisted for fear of facilitating an Afghan Taliban–Uyghur link-up. Even so, the Xi Jinping government stepped smartly into the space created for it by the new Kabul dispensation, with the idea of moderating the Sino-Pakistan relationship and the Pakistan-supported Taliban militancy (Khalilzad 2014). The Wakhan was not opened, but $327 million Chinese aid and a programme to train 3,000 Afghan professionals followed (Martina 2014). Like elsewhere in South Asia, New Delhi has to be smarter about dealing with nearby states alive to the potential gains from playing India off against China. It must stop prevaricating and renew the supply of armaments overland to Afghanistan via the Russian/Ukrainian pipeline, lest Beijing create yet another military dependency in the Afghan National Army.

India's Central Asia policy per se is four-legged, stressing soft power—Bollywood films and music that are a rage in these countries; education and technology; increased trade (up from $300 million to potentially $500 billion) and investment in the burgeoning energy sector; and security tie-ups (Joshi 2010).[17] It is a policy mix promising huge returns.[18] But the strategic advantage accruing to India is in the form of the wider military choices it is afforded. India's plate is pretty full, with refurbishing the Ainee-Farkhor air base in Tajikistan with a view to deploying Indian Su-30s there in crisis, buying off six IL-78 transport aircraft from Uzbekistan, servicing and upgrading MiG aircraft in the local Central Asian inventories, training Uzbek troops in counter-insurgency operations, agreeing on intelligence-sharing arrangements across the region, establishing electronic and other sensor posts to monitor Chinese nuclear and military activity and communications traffic, constructing the Military Training College in Dushanbe, dispatching Indian army teams to train Kazakh and Kyrgyz army units, securing a stockpile of spares for ex-Soviet thermal and electric torpedoes lying around with the landlocked Kazakhstan and Kyrgyzstan, and embarking on a collaborative naval R&D project with the Kazakhs at the premier Soviet-era naval testing facility on the Issykul Lake (Joshi 2010: 64–5).[19] Kazakhstan also looms large as a prime source of natural uranium to fuel an ambitious Indian nuclear energy programme (Rudenko 2014).

In the unlikely event of Afghanistan settling down peacefully and India's relations with Pakistan becoming normal, Turkmen gas would begin flowing to India, via the 1,680-kilometre-long TAPI (Turkmenistan-Afghanistan-Pakistan-India) pipeline costing $10 billion and passing through Herat and Kandahar in Afghanistan, and the civil strife–ridden province of Balochistan in Pakistan (Ebinger 2011: 148).[20] In its eagerness to throttle Iran's economy, which boasts of the second richest gas reserves in the world, Washington may have, for the nonce, diverted India from the politically and economically more viable Iran-Pakistan-India (IPI) pipeline (Mead 2012). Unless Islamabad backs out of its decision to proceed with the Iran-Pakistan part of the pipeline under US pressure and goes for Iranian gas liquefied in Oman—how this cuts Tehran out of the picture is not clear—New Delhi has the sensible alternative of completing the IPI project (Bhutta 2014). The resulting energy shortfall may be blamed on America's pressure tactics, which, in the past, produced that other great multi-billion-dollar energy boondoggle—the Dabhol-Enron power plant in Maharashtra. It will redouble doubts and suspicions that have long framed the Indian establishment's views of the United States.[21] It will be prudent for the Modi government to back the IPI pipeline as a prop for his larger policy of economically tying South Asia states to India. This is especially because multilateral pipelines involve permanent cross-border infrastructure and, willy-nilly create stakeholders and promote economic cooperation and energy stability. A profusion of such pipelines criss-crossing the map will accelerate regional economic integration, and tie up Pakistan in an energy embrace that New Delhi desires (Ebinger 2011: 12, 143). As an alternative to IPI, Tehran has proposed generating electricity from natural gas in Iran and transmitting it through Pakistan to India—a natural follow-up to India and Pakistan linking their power grids, a process that is under way (Sasi 2012).

Iran's indispensability to India was symbolized by the 2001 memorandum of understanding on defence cooperation that paved the way for Indian involvement in servicing and upgrading Russian military hardware ranging from submarines and T-72 tanks to MiG-29s combat aircraft in the Iranian inventory, sale of the Indian-built Dhruv Advanced Light Helicopter, and imparting specialized military training (Chansoria 2010; Fair 2007: 276–7). New Delhi also agreed to Indian Navy's joint exercises with its Iranian counterpart, significantly at the same time as US president George W. Bush was visiting New Delhi in March 2006. The added value of this military connection is the availability of airbases in eastern Iran to the IAF in crises involving Central Asia, Afghanistan, and Pakistan (Fair 2007: 277). These relations are set to grow with President Hassan Rouhani prioritizing warm relations with India (S. Roy 2013). New Delhi is walking the high wire, managing relationships with a variety of friends who do not get along with each other. Israel, for instance, has overlooked India's military ties to Iran and Arab states because of the profit it derives from the defence trade, and, more startlingly, because the geopolitical impact of its closeness with India may be moderating the attitude of the Arab world to the Jewish state (Inbar 2004: 104). Likewise, cultivating Arab states, Saudi Arabia in particular, and Iran affords India a handle on the Sunni–Shia schism that could combust at any time (Nasr 2006; Ullekh 2013). For a different set of reasons, the US, despite opposing the gas pipeline from Iran, determined in 2006 that India's relations with Tehran and the continued offtake of Iranian oil did not adversely affect major American interests (Fair 2007: 281–2). Elsewhere, at the level of the sectarian tussle in the Islamic world, Riyadh and Tehran may both frown on New Delhi's cultivating the other, but each country also sees gain from getting close to India with its large Muslim population, and the dangers of leaving the field entirely to the other.

The United States, Israel, and Iran are important in the Indian strategic calculus, for reasons of Asian geopolitics, and need for US capital and access to its market, military technology, and energy, and physical access to Central Asia, respectively. New Delhi, therefore, will not press Tehran on the nuclear issue, for instance, to the point of a breakdown in relations, any more than it will countenance Arab pressure to truncate its relations with Israel or take positions inimical to American interests to please Iran. Iran serves yet another purpose: calibrating relations with it provides New Delhi the means of counter-pressuring the wealthy Arab states (Saudi Arabia and the

Gulf Emirates)—the source of funding of Sunni charities in India that spread the harsh Wahabi Islam and radicalize Indian Muslim youth, causing hitherto peaceful provinces, such as the southern state of Kerala, to polarize along religious lines.

Dealing with countries to India's west is tedious business, where getting wrong-footed is easy and relations are eggshell-fragile, and the Indian government has always to worry about the domestic fallout. It breeds immense caution and explains why India's 'Look West' policy is not as dynamic as its 'Look East' policy, which deals with less complicated situations and is easier to conduct. The underlying problem however remains, of India putting itself, say, between the United States and Iran and getting squeezed at both ends to the detriment of its own national interest. The inability to satisfactorily explain its position and stand its ground is because the MEA neither thinks through policies nor pursues them in totality. Instead, segmented goals are sought to be achieved by the regional desks in the Foreign Office to resolve short-term problems that arise with make-do solutions. In the absence of an overarching strategic game plan, these solutions often collide with each other resulting, as in 2002–3, in New Delhi's ill-thought-out move that nearly dispatched an Indian Army infantry division to Kirkuk in Iraq. This move was apparently in gratitude for the George W. Bush administration according India importance in America's new geo-strategic thinking. India barely escaped getting mired in a particularly dirty war that would have irreparably damaged India's reputation and standing in Arab West Asia, and hurt India's energy and other trade with Iran. It made as much sense as India's coming to grief in the east by siding with the US in boycotting the authoritarian regime in Myanmar for human rights abuses, only to find its previously commanding presence in that country disappear and China filling the vacated space. Juggling contradictory policies is the stuff of visionary leaders. Nehru did it with panache in the 1950s, with some success—talking up disarmament while launching the country on the nuclear weapons course, spouting nonalignment whilst relying on American military muscle against China. With the complex fusion of clashing and collusive interests and relationships in the new century, New Delhi needs to show better strategic grasp and greater agility in its foreign policy.

African and Latin American Connections

Not many are convinced that the Indian government has done enough to cash in on opportunities and to capitalize on the half-chances to establish India's credentials as a coming power. Yashwant Sinha, minister for external affairs in the BJP government in the early 2000s, wondered why the Congress Party coalition government did not take up invitations to Indian farmers from Punjab by countries with surplus land and small populations, such as Mozambique and Angola in Africa, Paraguay and Uruguay in Latin America. 'If we want to be in the U.N. Security Council as permanent member, we'll need the votes of the Africans and the Latin Americans, and this is the manner in which to do it,' he said. He also felt that smaller alliance or partnership systems, such as IBSA, had been neglected with the Manmohan Singh regime sticking with 'large and unwieldy' groupings like the Nonaligned Movement, G-77, and G-15, or leaving 'things to one super power, which will call all the shots'.[22] While many of the Indian hopes for IBSA, for example, have not fructified, defence ties have taken a leap.[23] With Brazil inaugurating a project to produce nuclear attack submarines, nuclearized Indian and Brazilian navies could in the future emerge as significant players in the oceanic sweep connecting the southern Atlantic and Indian Oceans (Boadle 2013). Brazil and India, moreover, are discovering compatibilities, particularly now when the relations of both these countries with fellow BRICS member China are souring (Bremmer 2013).[24]

The fact, however, is that despite playing to its traditional strengths, fielding some imaginative programmes, and racking up considerable foreign policy successes in Africa and Central Asia, where Indian assistance programmes to build capacity have cemented an Indian presence in the local economies and in the extractive industrial sector, India has failed to convert the 'enormous goodwill' into what the Indian external affairs minister S. M. Krishna in July 2012 referred to, with respect to Central Asia, as 'a tangible economic and strategic advantage' (Jacob 2012a). This is because of the failure of the MEA to weave the various successful regional policy strands into a single fabric of grand strategy to serve the country's great power interests and ambition, a task that is not possible without a comprehensive national vision that the political leadership has not provided. This has not happened also because of the extreme compartmentalization or silo-based thinking and policy-making within and between the ministries in the Indian government (an aspect that will be dilated upon in Chapter 7). It leads to foreign policies in discrete streams that do not spring from the same fount and run separately, usually ending in uncoordinated, stand-alone, policies.[25]

The overarching reason for the less-than-expected returns from a potentially promising position in Africa, for instance, is the seeming disinterest of MEA to capitalize on the local goodwill for India, which is easily translatable into mining concessions and a major role in their security arrangements. Mozambique, for instance, sought India's help to train its military, establish and train a navy, and equip it with coastal policing vessels and surveillance gear. The MEA, locked into big power–centred foreign policy relating to the United States, Europe, and China, has not, however, found the time for African countries nor capitalized on the opportunities they provide. Some years back, both Mozambique and Tanzania offered India concessions to mine one of the richest veins of coal in East Africa on the condition that a 600-kilometre railway line be constructed from that site to the coast. The problem was that the senior MEA official responsible for the decision spurned the invitation conveyed to him by the Indian ambassador, saying that that region was 'not on our radar'.[26] Maputo's request to the Indian Navy to set up a Mozambiqan Navy was, likewise, not acted upon.[27] This is indicative of the superciliousness that many Indian diplomats affect with regard to African governments, notwithstanding disbursal of some $10 billion as government-to-government aid for infrastructure and development projects since 2008 by New Delhi. The private sector has been more successful in its forays in Africa. Relative to the 14 per cent decline in European trade with Africa, the India–Africa trade doubled to 6 per cent in 2000–13, with the two-way trade standing at $93 billion behind only China ($211 billion) and North America ($117 billion). Major investments by Indian companies are expected to soon capture 7 per cent of the IT, 5 per cent of the fast-moving consumer goods, 10 per cent of the power, and 2–5 per cent of the agricultural services sectors. A McKinsey report lists various reasons for this success, among them investing in local talent, partnering with local governments, involving local insiders as partners, and going 'granular—Understand[ing] local nuances and adapt[ing] business models accordingly, with 55 different countries, each with its own culture, customs and behaviours' (McKinsey & Company 2014). It has helped the Indian presence become part of the everyday African scene. In contrast, Chinese companies disinclined to bring their attitude in sync with African complexities, have remained insular, and have earned illwill. In fact, so voracious and single-minded have the Chinese been in extracting mineral resources, and so insensitive to environmental damage and local aspirations, that they are beginning to face local opposition and, sometimes, violent resistance (Heng 2013).[28] With Prime Minister Narendra Modi expressing the view that Indian diplomats should primarily be promoting India's economic interests abroad, Africa may in the years to come become a showpiece of his foreign policy (Bagchi 2014).

Russia in India's Plans

If IBSA is a promising coalition for the future, the 'eternal triangle' of India, China, and Russia—originally conceived by Nehru in the 1950s and revived in 1996 by the Russian foreign minister Yevgeny Primakov as a counterweight to the United States and the West, is distinctly of the past, and overtaken by the BRICS group of countries in the present. As practical geopolitics, moreover, such a grouping will not work owing to Chinese interests colliding with Indian and Russian economic and security concerns (Karnad 1994, 2010). India–Russia relations are 'enduring but non-exclusive' compared to China–Russia ties, which are 'complex and cautious', with Russian strategic interests consistent with strong India as its main armaments customer, offsetting the growing power of China (Mathieu 2008: 19–23). Strong trade relationships hint at a budding economic rationale for the Russia-China-India collective in Eurasia. Except, India and China share similar economic strengths and weaknesses and, in the long run, sharpened economic competition and military rivalry can be expected. Likewise, Russian vulnerabilities in the Far East to a Chinese demographic creep may precipitate military clashes.[29] The patterns of Russia's trade with the Asian giants were similar up until the fin de siècle, in that India and China accounted for over 60 per cent of Russia's arms exports, and, in particular, Russian oil and gas met 60–70 per cent of India's energy requirements (Mathieu 2008: 22). But while India continues to buy military hardware from Russia, the Chinese defence industry, having reverse-engineered Russian technology to near self-sufficiency, is producing cheap knockoffs that it markets to developing countries. Russia is therefore more wary and inhibited in exporting advanced systems to China, a cause for friction in relations (Kazim 2012). Moscow is also taking care to embed technical kinks to make reverse-engineering difficult, the reason why the Chinese have repeatedly failed to produce combat aircraft engines based on power plants outfitting the Su-27, sold in large numbers to China.[30] Moscow has no such problems with India and armaments still constitute the biggest component of Indo-Russian trade, touching $4.7 billion in bilateral trade valued at $6.94 billion in 2013 (MEA 2014).[31] It constitutes roughly a third of the arms exported by Russia worldwide.[32] In 2009, both sides set a target of US$20 billion bilateral trade by 2015. In comparison, the Sino-Russian trade hit the $100 billion mark in 2012 (Mathieu 2008: 23).[33] This latter surge is because of China's contiguity with Russia, which permits overland trade and movement of labour and resources.[34]

The overriding Russian concern, other than China, is with recovering its collapsed international status and sphere of influence in Europe and Central Asia. This it hopes to do by strengthening and modernizing its strategic forces and reasserting itself in Eurasia.[35] Its more muscular foreign policy, moreover, seeks to keep the energy and arms flowing to traditionally friendly states (Syria, Iran) in the face of American protests, to show that Russia matters and can stand up to the US (Sumsky and Kanaev 2012).[36] Part of the Russian policy to rejuvenate its standing is to also burnish its strategic ties with China and, inverting the Cold War US paradigm, to now play the 'China card' against the West and rough up American plans in Asia (Fisher 2012). With a consensus with New Delhi about a multipolar world, India is as much a means for Moscow to circumvent China as the United States. Moscow, moreover, is not above using the 'Pakistan card' to incentivize New Delhi to keep buying Russian military goods.[37]

It is in the context of Russia reclaiming for itself a measure of respect and standing lost in the aftermath of the Cold War that India has cannily increased its leverage in Moscow. New Delhi recognized

Russia's 'legitimate rights' in Crimea, and opposed the US-led sanctions, moving President Vladimir Putin to express appreciation for India's 'restraint and objectivity' (Radyuhin 2014). In fact, even before New Delhi's show of solidarity, the Russian ambassador in New Delhi, Alexander Kadakin, declared that relations with India 'are at the peak of their development [and entering] the stage of special and privileged strategic partnership, which Russia does not have with any other country of the world.' He added that 'as far as the prospects of the Russian-Indian cooperation, strategic partnership and friendship go, even the sky and the space are not limit for their development'.[38] It is the military technology end of this partnership that India prizes most, because Russia has been more open in sharing advanced technology than any other friendly state. It has moreover been generous, according to Ashok Parthasarathi, science and technology adviser to Prime Minister Indira Gandhi, in offering India 'enormous technical assistance to overcome our design and engineering problems' in the most highly valued programmes, including the *Arihant* SSBN and Agni missiles. 'Would the US be willing to even consider providing us such help?' he wondered (Parthasarathi 2014). Not surprising then that New Delhi extolled the 'special and privileged partnership' with Russia on the eve of Putin's visit to New Delhi in mid-December 2014 when Moscow showed ire about Western companies increasingly displacing Russia as the principal supplier of military goods to India, and pointedly offered a defence pact and arms to Pakistan (Karnad 2014).

Appreciating Taiwan's Importance

The Indian government and armed services are not voluble about cooperative security ventures the country is engaged in, are less tight-lipped when it comes to ventures with Taiwan. Both New Delhi and Taipei want to flaunt, albeit discreetly, their budding relationship in order to keep Beijing guessing, and to moderate China's attitude towards Arunachal Pradesh and Tibet in one case, and the PLA's hard line on forcible 'reunification' worrying Taiwan in the other. Bilateral relations are conducted under the cover of the India–Taipei Trade Council. Both share the view that their respective national interests are best served by intense cooperation in the security sphere, and by diverting larger Taiwanese investments to India as a way of diversifying risk and reducing dependence on the Chinese market and economy.[39] In fact, writes a Taiwanese scholar, there is a 'close correlation between Taiwan's interests in India and Taiwan's interests in China'; with the investment climate in China turning unfavourable in the mid-2000s, Taiwanese corporates began exploring other investment destinations, and India and Vietnam hove into sight. As a result, 70 per cent of all Taiwanese investment in India has been since 2009. In absolute terms, the investment of $66 million is only 0.03 per cent of the Taiwanese money invested abroad, but that is because of what a Taiwanese scholar refers to as 'lack of strong industrial foundations' and, more delicately, 'very complicated central and state level tax and legal systems' (*Hindu* 2013).

The economic partnership may afford the India–Taiwan partnership stamina over the long haul, but it is cooperation in the military-security field, both countries agree, that will cement it. President Ma Ying-jeou, during his first visit to India in 2007, met with the highest national security and foreign policy officials and, in April 2012, made a 'surprise stopover' in Mumbai on his way to Africa.[40] Exactly a year later, India upped the ante and allowed Taiwanese vice-president Wu Den-yih a layover, this time in New Delhi, which he spent consulting with senior Indian government and military officials while his plane refuelled for its onward journey (Parashar 2014). Yang Nieu-dzu, Taiwan's vice-minister of defence, describes promotion of 'Asia-Pacific long-term peace and stability' as a 'fundamental concept of Taiwan's defense policy', to further which aim, he says, his country's 'location' is a key factor. With this aim in mind, Taipei, he adds, 'looks for cooperation with other countries, including India, in the hope that regional security cooperation ... could be kept developing.' Interestingly, he quotes the Chinese defence minister Yuan Guanglie as saying that 'the center of gravity for China's military development is Taiwan's affairs'. It is precisely this slant India hopes to exploit by getting close to Taipei in the security field in order to dilute Beijing's focus on the border with India (Yang 2011). In fact, as New Delhi sees it, Taiwan and Vietnam are to China what Chinese-assisted Pakistan is to India—a constant source of strategic frustration and politico-military counter-leverage. India can be expected in the future to upgrade its relations with Taipei and its assistance to Hanoi to level the strategic playing field which, owing to lack of purposive thrust in New Delhi's policy in the past, has favoured China by default. Adding another arrow to the quiver is the forum for the India-Japan-Taiwan trialogue founded in 2006. It is gaining momentum with Singapore and the US keen to enter it, giving Beijing the jitters. China naturally sees the forum as a regional grouping to curb Chinese power, since it involves two of its most powerful challengers in Asia—India and Japan—getting together with a country claimed by China as its own, with America waiting in the wings to join. Taiwan sees these three countries, moreover, as being 'strategic allies' on the basis of their having the 'most developed scientific and technological industries' in the Asia-Pacific region.[41]

New Delhi is aiming to gain from Taiwan's unmatched penetration of the Chinese security system, and from its authoritative information and insights into the functioning of the Central Military Commission, PLA command circles, the Second Artillery Strategic Forces, the India-relevant Lanzhou and Chengdu Combat Zones, and Chinese cyber-operations and naval plans. To tempt India into more substantial joint ventures and more extensive and sustained security collaboration, Taipei has promised, for instance, to share its knowledge of the Chinese cyber grid that it has mapped out. To better use this information, the Indian Army has formed a nucleus of 100-odd officers with Mandarin proficiency honed in training courses held in Taipei by the Taiwanese military to man the China cells in the Indian Army's Military Operations and Military Intelligence Directorates, and in various theatre commands. These officers travel frequently to Taipei to liaise with their Taiwanese counterparts and military leadership. The army has also tied up for advanced and refresher language training for its specialist cadre of officers.[42] The Taiwan connection is regarded by the Indian armed services as a prized security asset, and by the government as one of the unacknowledged foreign policy irons in the fire to use against China.

The Israel Link

Israel is gradually becoming critical to India's security and defence industry. Tel Aviv's confidence in warm relations with India is premised on several factors. While it is reconciled to India's strong economic and cultural relations with the Arab and Islamic world generally, it is convinced this will not impair the growth of intimacy. India's West Asia policy is geared to protecting the oil supplies, Arab FDI, increased avenues of exports, and the interests of the Indian expatriate community which accounts for a large chunk of imported labour and hence for the huge remittances from the Gulf kingdoms and emirates.[43] But Israel sees its value to modern India as buttressed by strong political links dating back to the 1920s, and strengthened after independence by the friendship between the two fellow-socialists and prime ministers, Nehru and Ben Gurion (Kumaraswamy 2010). The bedrock of relations is the cultural affinity between the two old world-civilizational states struggling with newfound statehood, and warmed by the historical experience of Jews escaping persecution from as early as 2 BC and seeking refuge in India, where they have lived unmolested over the centuries mainly in port cities such as Kochi (Cochin), Mumbai (Bombay), and in the 'Baghdadi Jewish' enclaves of Kolkata without facing discrimination. This last has engendered enormous goodwill for India in Israeli society and a willingness on Tel Aviv's part to be helpful, with profit from defence and other transactions seen as a bonus.

In more recent times, the 'breakthrough in trust', according to Itemar Graff, principal deputy director of the Israeli Defense Export and Defense Cooperation Agency (SIBAT), Israeli Ministry of Defense, occurred during the 1999 Kargil border war with Pakistan, when Israel rushed the most advanced weapons such as advanced air-to-ground missiles and helped out with crucial signals intelligence. 'Now there's such great understanding between Israeli defence companies and the Indian armed services', Graff exulted, 'they deal directly with the Indian military chiefs of staff and don't anymore need SIBAT as intermediary.'[44] The intensification of military sales has led to a galloping trade—$80 million in 1991, jumping to $5 billion in 2010—vaulting India into the position of Israel's largest military trading partner after Russia. Barring Israeli arms supply to Pakistan—with news reports revealing Israeli export of components for the JF-17 fighter aircraft developed jointly by China and Pakistan, which could dampen New Delhi's enthusiasm for buying military equipment from Israel—this relationship is set to grow

(Ningthoujam 2013). The possibility, moreover, of a symbiotic relationship between India and Israel in the flourishing information technology sector is now matched by collaborative programmes in military high-technology R&D. In the civilian fields, Israel has found bestsellers in its desalination and drip irrigation technologies, the latter renowned for making the Israeli desert bloom (Feiler 2012: 37). Israeli experimental farms and agricultural extension service centres are conducting R&D, spreading modern technology, and gathering support and admiration for Israel in the Indian countryside (Mohan 2013; Sloman 2011).[45] This involvement complements Israel's resonance with the affluent Indian middle class.[46] 'Homeland security' is becoming a burgeoning area for cooperation, covering, as the former Israeli ambassador Alon Ushpiz says, 'a whole gamut of issues, from policing to counter-terrorism, including forensics, etc.', and including 'a joint working plan' and 'structure' to facilitate close links.[47]

Military technology is, however, the glue bonding the two countries together. Collaboration in the most sensitive technology areas of space, missiles, and avionics has resulted, for instance, in Israel equipping Indian military satellites (such as RISAT-2) with synthetic aperture radars capable of night and all-weather surveillance, the use of Indian polar satellite launch vehicles to inject Israeli TecSAR spy satellites into precise low-earth orbits, avionics retrofits and other technologies to upgrade and extend the life of vast numbers of Soviet-origin combat aircraft in service with the IAF, and the Barak-8 surface-to-air missile (SAM) that provides close-in protection to the Indian Navy's aircraft carriers and modern frigates and missile destroyers.[48] Indeed, the success of the Barak has led to a $2.5 billion joint development project to produce a longer (60–70 kilometre) range Barak-NG (Next Generation) SAM to arm warships and for land-based air defence. 'Such programs', observes an Israeli scholar,

> involve the most intimate sharing of each country's most advanced military technology secrets, that the failure of one party to successfully deliver its expected R&D contribution to the programme eliminates all of the investment and efforts of the other party; and the economic viability of the weapon produced by the program relies on the military establishment of each partner fulfilling its acquisition commitments. (Feiler 2012: 17)

Indeed, Israel is the preferred source for cutting-edge technology unavailable from any other source, like the jamming-resistant Active Electronically Scanned Array (AESA) radar for air-to-air and ground attack missions, touted as 4.5 generation and as good as any in the world, that will soon be on board the indigenous Tejas light combat aircraft.[49] Director of Policy and Political-Military Affairs, Israeli Ministry of Defense, Major General Amos Gilad (Retd) described his country's attitude to cooperating with India in military high technology as the Russians do: 'No limits, the sky is the limit.'[50] Encouraged by the quality and extent of armament sales totalling some $10 billion in the decade 2001–2011, Tel Aviv now seeks to co-develop weaponry in India, making use of the skilled manpower and industrial capacity available in the country, and to replicate, in effect, its successes in the Indian IT sector.[51] However, there is criticism that in collaborative projects such as long-range missiles, the Israeli tendency too often is for the mainly public sector Israeli defence majors to palm off the low-end portions of the work to Indian companies while retaining the more technologically challenging high-value jobs for themselves. But this is also very much the feature of joint ventures with Russia to produce, say, the Brahmos supersonic cruise missile (where India has no role in designing or manufacturing the ramjet engine, for instance). Many joint ventures with Indian private sector companies to produce military-use products for both the Indian and Israeli militaries and for export to third countries presuppose 'near total' technology transfer, including source codes, and are being retarded by differences over the extent of Israeli equity participation.[52] Twenty-six per cent share-holding by foreign firms in the nuclear, space, and military sectors was raised to 49 per cent, but Israel, the United States, and other Western countries would like the permissible equity level to be raised all the way up to 100 per cent.[53] Israel's success in India is drawing American attention, with analysts seeing Israel's *modus operandi* as something the US needs to emulate. American companies are not as 'keenly attuned to Indian user requirements and their need for customization' as the Israeli companies are, claim Amer Latif and former US assistant secretary of state for South Asia, Karl Inderfurth (Latif and Inderfurth 2012). 'Israeli companies are particularly adept in this area with officials spending time alongside Indian troops to understand the nature of their operating conditions. This familiarity, combined with Israeli willingness to adapt their equipment to meet Indian needs endears Israeli vendors to the Indian armed forces.' Technology transfers, co-production, and co-development, which the Indian government increasingly prefers as a way to build up the local defence industry, are also areas where Israel, Russia, and France have stolen a march over the US. The difference is that 'for the United States, technology', Latif and Inderfurth add, 'is a strategic commodity that must be transferred with great care. For most other foreign vendors, technology is largely a commercial commodity sold for economic gain' (Latif and Inderfurth 2012).

Notwithstanding the new warmth infused in the Indo-US relationship, and the American desire to sell India weapons systems, New Delhi has had to contend with the US impedances in Israeli technology transfers. Irked by India's uneven support for its Iraq intervention policy, the George W. Bush administration in 2003, for example, nearly ended the breakthrough sale to India of the Israeli Phalcon phased-array radar to equip the Indian Airborne Warning and Control System (AWACS).[54] But Washington's ability to run interference is being increasingly diluted by the fabled American Jewish lobby, which is helping to push an India-friendly agenda and assisting the Indian diaspora in the US to set up the US-India Political Action Committee along the lines of the powerful US-Israel Political Action Committee, to shape America's India policy.[55] In the context of the rock-solid US–Israel relationship, the concurrent positive trends in US–India and India–Israel relations have persuaded many Israeli analysts to believe that a 'strategic triad' of India, Israel, and the United States is in the offing (Inbar 2004: 102, 104). Then again, Washington does not always buckle under domestic political pressure. It pressured Tel Aviv against transferring the technology of the more powerful ELTA 2052 computer powering the AESA radar for the indigenous Tejas multi-role aircraft under joint Indo-Israeli development, permitting only the less capable ELTA 2032 computer to be used.[56]

The fallout of Israel's critical role in the Indian defence and security spheres is dramatic. It has led to secret understandings, perhaps, for intelligence sharing, contingency planning for joint special forces action against terrorist use of nuclear weapons by radical Islamist groups in Pakistan, or in case of internal tumult endangering the Pakistan Army's control of its nuclear arsenal.[57] In India's domestic politics, the Left parties aside, Israel's role in the security sphere is seen to be so beneficial, it has softened the attitude of even Muslim organizations and 'secular' political parties to a point where close ties with Israel are not an issue any more (Kahn 2008). Having unbundled its relations with Israel and the Arab states, the Indian government supports the formation of an independent Palestinian state even as it increases security cooperation with Israel.[58]

India–US Trust Deficit and the State of the 'Strategic Partnership'

'Trust is a central concept', writes Richard Ned Lebow (2013), who pioneered research into the psychological element in nuclear deterrence and political affairs generally, '[and] at the international level it almost invariably involves judgements about other actors: Will they prove faithful allies? Will they adhere to their treaty and other commitments? Do they have benign intentions?' There is uncertainty about America's intentions in official Indian circles, which has been one of the reasons for the hesitant progress in bilateral relations, leading to the impression doing the rounds that the Indo-US 'strategic partnership' has not delivered on its promise (Tellis 2014). This has not been for want of desire and motivation in New Delhi and Washington, or of inter-governmental accords and institutional mechanisms, or even of extensive engagement between government agencies and the militaries of the two countries. The US military, for example, has been involved in more joint exercises with the Indian armed forces than with any other country, some 50 exercises in all since 2001. The Defence Framework Agreement of 28 June 2005 preceded by about a week the Manmohan Singh-George W. Bush 'joint statement' that cleared the path for the 2008 India-US civilian nuclear cooperation deal. Subsequently, a number of new inter-governmental bodies, such as the apex Defence Policy Group involving the Indian defence minister and the US defence secretary, and the annual 'strategic dialogue' between the Indian minister for external affairs and the US secretary of state, have begun functioning.

It is the vigour with which Washington pursues its national interests without regard for Indian stakes in issues that not only emphasizes the absence of the requisite level of trust for a genuinely warm and intimate relationship, but actually increases distrust of the United States. Washington's relentless efforts to stall India's weapons programme and drag it into the nonproliferation net is well documented (Karnad 2005: 224–57). Both the BJP government of Atal Bihari Vajpayee and the successor Manmohan Singh government showed an incomprehensible desire to gain nuclear weapons state status by US and international acclamation rather than by actually testing, finessing, and fielding a proven nuclear and thermonuclear arsenal. That the nuclear deal would seek to strangle the country's nuclear and thermo-nuclear weapons programme and indigenous development of even civilian-use nuclear technologies was foreseen by persons advocating against the nuclear deal. They had warned that prompted by the strong nonproliferation lobby Washington would use it as a 'Trojan Horse' gradually to pull the Indian nuclear facilities left outside the ambit of international safeguards into the nonproliferation treaty regime (Iyengar *et al.* 2009).[59] Meanwhile, the spoiler value of Pakistan to the US, which has proliferated centrifuge technology to Iran and Libya, among other interested states, could not be higher, as attested by Secretary of State John Kerry's praise for the Pakistan Army as a 'truly binding force' in that country. The US also met Pakistan's request for eight fast 'global response cutters' with stealth features able to carry Harpoon and Exocet anti-ship missiles.[60] These boats can counter India's big ship navy, and the rigid inflatable vehicles they carry can be deployed in 26/11-type 'from the sea' terrorist strike missions. The fact is the US has stayed with its long-time policy of addressing Pakistan's fears of India by striving to maintain a rough conventional military balance (Feigenbaum 2010). Thus, India faces conventional Pakistani forces enhanced by US technology assistance—the payoff to Pakistan for being the perennial 'frontline state' in the Cold War against the Soviet Union, in the early 1980s against the Soviet military occupation of Afghanistan, and, in more recent times, against the Afghan Taliban and the terrorist outfits active in the Af-Pak region (Rudolph and Rudolph 2006). And, in the strategic field, it confronts a Pakistan armed by Chinese nuclear missiles. Such balancing to create a synthetic parity between the two grossly unequal South Asian states can hardly be expected to be perceived other than negatively by New Delhi, and colours the Indian view of US intentions. More so because it hints at a Sino-American consortium to restrict India's power.

The strategic suspicions and doubts about America's bona fides are strong enough even without other nettlesome subject areas concerning trade, intellectual property rights (IPR), especially in pharmaceuticals, IT, military-related technology, and climate, where the two countries differ markedly. These differences could hurt the relationship because they pit India's need for cheap medicines, its burgeoning IT industry, security interests, and the traditional 'smokestack' route to an industrialized economy against the interests of a post-industrial American society (Shanbhag 2014).[61]

Mistrust as 'a constant' can eat away at the foundations of good relations, and is not conducive to cooperative activity between nations (Kydd 2005: 5, 14, Chapter 8). The Indian strategic elite has always been suspicious of the US and this has been a stumbling block (S. Cohen 2001: 42–3). The US's technology denial policies too have left bitter memories.[62] The upside of being denied access to Western technologies was that, forced to do so, India developed most of the critical technologies for strategic use indigenously, including nuclear and thermonuclear weapons and missiles. This success has ended up mocking the American policy. The US's imposition of economic sanctions and technology denial regimes to punish India when it carried out nuclear tests, and ensuring that the US's European allies did so too, repeatedly hurt the Indian economy and, over the years, deepened doubts about the US in India. Should India in the future carry out nuclear tests needed to validate its thermonuclear weapons designs, nuclear trade with India may cease, economic and technology sanctions could be re-imposed, and the warming trend in relations with the US instantly reversed.

In response, a hard-nosed Indian government could conduct nuclear commerce outside the nuclear supplier guidelines. Nuisance has great disruptive value in foreign policy, and if properly utilized can further the national interest. This is something the squeamish MEA and Indian policy circles do not appreciate, being too consumed with meeting the Western standards for 'responsible' state behaviour to consider that actions disturbing of the extant order can go far in upping New Delhi's unpredictability quotient and increasing the fear and respect for it among the countries that count. It helped China to get to where it is now. In any case, this is a path New Delhi should have followed from the beginning to make India a first-rate nuclear vendor, the Indian nuclear industry profitable, and to use the country's position as a nuclear technology supplier of note as diplomatic lever. It would have rendered infructuous the entire West-dominated nonproliferation system and structures of trade and technology denial.

Such issues, however, leave the larger geo-strategic question unanswered: whether resumed thermonuclear testing will not make the Indian thermonuclear deterrent at once more reliable and credible and help the country reach deterrence parity with China, and whether this will not better serve the long-term security and balancing interests of the US and countries in Asia. The political and military price the US may have to pay for an unproven Indian fusion weapons arsenal could be huge. It would allow China to flex its thermonuclear muscle without care and to grow to hegemonic proportions, with no Asian state remotely in a position to contest its dominance. In a crisis, the United States would be pushed to the forefront, compelled to take on China rather than have a comparably endowed India, whose interests are immediately impinged, stand up against the rogue hegemon. A nonproliferation-blinkered Washington may, on the other hand, view the untested Indian thermonuclear weapons as firming up India's dependence on the US in a crisis with China and, by extension, India's acceptance of a Sino-US duopoly—the G-2 emphasized in President Barack Obama's early foreign policy pronouncements.[63] Close military-to-military links with China are sought by the US as a means of building up mutual trust (Hille 2013). But those who conceive of a Sino-American condominium seem oblivious of Beijing's policy of seeking to displace the United States as the lone superpower, not work with it to run the world, assuming that between them, they could do so (Castle and Crowther 2006; Friedberg 2011; Jacques 2009).

With China investing and upgrading its strategic missile forces on a priority basis, the dilemma facing India regarding its unproven thermonuclear weapons inventory, and hence the need to resume testing, becomes starker still.[64] The influential strategic analyst, the late K.

Subrahmanyam, had a myopic solution, which many in the Indian policy establishment surprisingly support. It is to bide time, facilitate an accelerated increase in American FDI and other economic and strategic stakes in India to a level where the US simply cannot afford to disengage, whereupon Delhi can restart an open-ended nuclear testing programme with complete impunity and confidence that there will be no negative repercussions.[65] Many highly placed Americans second the view that, should bilateral relations become sufficiently intimate and dense, India's testing would elicit a tame US response.[66] But such a denouement presumes a tight India–US economic and strategic hug, which may be precluded by domestic politics on both sides. Moreover, the expectation that India will act as America's 'eyes and ears' in the region suggests a subordinate relationship, and will be even less tolerable.[67] An overtly 'junior partner' role for India is a domestic political liability for any Indian government inclined to accept it, as it hurts the country's *amor propre* and perceptions of great power, and circumscribes its options.[68] Consequently, a time may be approaching—what with the regional and international security situation hurtling downwards—when India will be left with no alternative but to test to validate its hydrogen weapons designs to match the proven calibre of its delivery systems—accurate missiles and bomber aircraft.[69] Disenchantment in the United States would be risked to achieve the greater good of preventing the strategic situation from tilting even more dangerously in China's favour. That issues can even be framed in this way suggests just how much India–US relations are hostage to fundamental policy differences and strategic compulsions. Evidence of Washington's tone-deafness on sensitive issues is available in Washington's brusque insistence that India scrap provisions in its law—the Civil Liability for Nuclear Damage Act 2010—that hold nuclear suppliers liable for damages in excess of the $300 million cap suggested by the Convention on Supplementary Compensation for Nuclear Damage, which supposedly represents international best practice. This would then help expedite purchases of reactors as a payoff to Washington for shepherding the nuclear deal through the international maze (Jacob 2012b). The US did not consider that this was the equivalent of New Delhi demanding that Washington overturn the Henry J. Hyde United States–India Peaceful Atomic Energy Cooperation Act of 2006 enabling the nuclear deal at the American end, which is politically impossible for any US administration to do. This attitude is all the more galling to the Indian government because it had indicated its readiness to do business by tweaking the interpretation of a certain provision in the Indian liability law (Rule 24), which Washington rejected, leaving New Delhi with an all or nothing proposition destined to bury any possibility of compromise (Sengupta 2011). 'While India is taking on legally irrevocable obligations that tie the hands of future generations',' writes A. N. Prasad, former director of BARC, 'America's own obligations under the deal are unequivocally anchored in the primacy of its domestic law and thus mutable' (Sengupta 2011).

A potentially more significant aspect of the Indian mistrust is the deeply held belief among the Indian armed services that the United States is an unreliable military supplier, and that it means to use 'the short reins' policy to influence Indian foreign policy. The historical record reinforces this perception.[70] Many in the Indian military fear that with more and more US and other Western weapons and platforms in Indian inventories, the Indian armed services may be jumping into the familiar dependency predicament, except now, Washington, Paris, and London will join Moscow in manipulating spares availability to get the Indian government to relent on some foreign policy issue or the other. This situation arises at precisely a time, ironically, when Russia has realized the dangers of alienating the Indian military by such means, and is trying to spruce up its servicing and spares support system.[71]

Then there is the controversial end-use memorandum (EUM), required by the US Arms Export Control Act and the US Foreign Assistance Act—a source of Indian angst. The EUM mandates periodic inspections by US representatives to physically verify and certify that the American-sourced military equipment is not being put to improper use. It is the sort of intrusive activity by a supplier country India has never permitted, and the Indian military is unused to and does not care for. The apprehension is that the American inspectors would thereby be in a position to pick up operationally valuable information. Further compounding the unreliability issue is the uncertainty attending on contracts signed with American companies and backed by the US government. Often recalled by senior Indian officials in this respect is the agreement for the supply of enriched uranium fuel for the lifetime of the General Electric reactors that began operating in 1967 at Tarapur. When India conducted its first nuclear explosion in 1974, this contract was abrogated by the US Congress, which rewrote the law with retrospective effect. There is no guarantee that any aircraft, ship, or artillery obtained from the US today will not suffer similar treatment tomorrow, with these systems being grounded by spares cutoff mandated by a retroactive amendment of existing US laws barring military trade and commerce with India. Many US military professionals appreciate the Indian concerns and acknowledge that the Congressional power to rewrite US laws, combined with the cumbersome and illiberal US export licensing regime, will limit the defence trade with India, and generally prevent an energetic relationship. A US Army War College study observes the need for American laws and procedures to keep in mind that the Indo-US partnership 'will be a unique relationship [and] given the interests of both countries, [it] will not be a traditional alliance', adding that India will be 'an equal partner [not] a subordinate client state to the United States'. Without the current export licence regime being 'tailored with an India-specific set of rules', the United States, the report concludes, is unlikely to 'become a major defense supplier' (Denney 2007).

The trust problem, however, goes beyond amending licensing procedures and schemata, and has to do with the impermanency of contractual undertakings in a context in which the US Congress can retroactively void treaty obligations. This may be a systemic virtue in terms of internal checks and balances in the American system. But it inhibits strategic cooperation and close military supply ties with an already suspicious India. With the US Congressional power to fiddle with sovereign agreements as background, the only way ostensibly for a country to guarantee steady, uninterrupted supply of spares and service support for weapons systems it buys from the US and, courtesy the nuclear deal, of enriched uranium fuel for American nuclear reactors it may import, should that happen, is by ensuring its foreign policy is majorly convergent with that of the US (Iyengar et al. 2009, 35). To believe that India, prickly about the infringement of its sovereign rights and strategic autonomy and proud of its independent foreign policy, will tailor its foreign policy to Washington's onerous preconditions is to expect too much.

The Manmohan Singh government nevertheless procured in the last decade capital military systems (C-130J and C-17 airlifters) to show good faith, incurring, in the process, the risk of a spares cutoff for any of a host of reasons, and not restricted to the renewal of nuclear testing. These platforms were procured even though, owing to the lack of the Communications Interoperability Security Memorandum of Agreement (CISMOA), which New Delhi is unwilling to sign, they were shorn of the most advanced sensors and support equipment. In effect, India paid big money for suboptimally equipped transporters.[72] Punitive legislative measures by the US Congress could well disable whole sections of Indian fighting capability and create a political firestorm in India, bringing all previous defence deals and even the wisdom of the rapprochement with America into question. A rupture of relations with the United States would then become inevitable, and the political, diplomatic, and financial cross-investments made by both sides over the years will be negated. If doing military business and cementing a strategic partnership with the US requires India to assume all the political, financial, and national security risks, the attractiveness of such a partnership will necessarily be low and would prevent the accumulation of trust. By way of abundant caution, therefore, what 'off-the-shelf' purchases New Delhi has so far made concern military hardware and platforms in support or secondary roles—airlift, maritime surveillance (MR) aircraft like the P-8I, a variant of the Poseidon P-8A serving the US Navy. The decision to procure the Apache Longbow attack helicopters has been the exception. This aspect is a major reason why the aircraft the US entered in the IAF's medium multi-role combat aircraft (MMRCA) sweepstakes were handicapped from the start. After all, it is one thing to have the air force's transport fleet grounded owing to cutoff of spares, quite another thing to have frontline squadrons meet the same fate. Despite its bad experience with the Sea King helicopter owing to US components in it, the Indian Navy, with a longer track record of engaging with its US counterpart, has been more risk-acceptant, ordering 24 P-8Is and evincing interest in as many as 22 Sikorsky Seahawk SH-70B helicopters for tactical operations.

These latter two acquisitions are tricky exercises and test cases in accommodating each other's sensitivities, negotiating procedural barriers in both countries, and building mutual trust. The Indian government insists on offsets to the tune of 30–50 per cent of the value of major contracts, in terms of project-related goods, technologies, and materials sourced from India. This condition has forced American companies, prime contractors and sub-contractors alike, into a unique modus operandi. Indian private sector companies and public sector partners have to be selected, basic technologies transferred to them for the Indian partners to work on in terms of reconfiguring them for Indian end-use, adding value in terms of technology changes and enhancements, and shipping these back to the US prime contractor to integrate into the weapons platform for use by the Indian military. The monetary value of the Indian enhanced and manufactured items is notched up against the offsets obligations. More generally, the Indian government's desire to use the offsets provisions to genuinely increase the country's technological capabilities has run smack into US resistance. The US Trade Representative Michael Froman has sought dilution, for instance, of the offsets obligations by pleading a weak IPR protection regime in India.[73] And, while doubting India's ability to absorb military high technology, he played on the Modi government's pet 'Make in India' theme by indirectly asking for the conversion of the offsets requirement, undoubtedly perceived by him as 'localization of [trade] barriers', into permission to US companies to set up 100 per cent owned firms to assemble military equipment in India to meet the offsets requirement.[74] The record of US companies in offsets does not inspire confidence, with MOD officials dismissing it as 'mockery'. Thus, Lockheed Martin, with a $962 million (Rs 3,855 crore) contract for C-130J in the bag, wrote off the cost of importing and installing simulators and trainer systems for this aircraft and other extraneous charges against the offsets account (Shukla 2010). Nevertheless, the assault on the Indian offsets requirement, combined with the US policy of getting companies to 're-shore' American industries to America to create jobs by using tax regimes punitively, could hurt India's IT and IT-enabled services sectors and its 'frugal engineering' edge, and India's economic advancement generally.[75] Beyond a point, it will become a political issue and could derail relations.

Military IPR Complexities

Intellectual property rights (IPR) issues are hardly ever clear-cut. To get an idea of just how complex they are, consider the $2.1 billion deal for the first set of eight P-8Is. India cannot be sold this MR aircraft with its original suite of electronics and sensors, in part because India has not signed the GSOMIA. So, Boeing as main contractor and the various sub-contractors constituting 'the Team'—Northrop Grumman, General Electric, Raytheon, Spirit Aerosystems, BAE Systems, and CFM—transferred certain basic 'avionics and aerostructures' to their Indian partners (Upadhyay and Chandra 2010: 42).[76] But regarding the most critical and sensitive systems, in particular, 'Data Link-II' and the radar fingerprinting systems—these were entirely Indian-developed. Data Link-II is an Indian counterpart of the US Link-16 system connecting all space, airborne, seaborne, and land-based sensors and cyber warfare sources with military command and control centres and deployed fighting assets, enabling them to 'talk' to each other, pass data, and imagery, thus enhance their situation awareness; few things merit higher classification status.

The Indian DPSU Bharat Electronics Ltd (BEL) produced the Data Link-II cryptographic protocol, as also the radar fingerprinting system. A senior Indian government official in the highest echelon voiced confidence that the Indian systems passed on to Boeing for integration into the MR platform were secure, but expert critics are not so sure.[77] They point out that however well protected it was internally, with software to detect intrusion, to be properly integrated into the platform, Data Link-II needed the power fraction to run each of the system functions to be disclosed to Boeing. From this information, it is feared, Boeing and the US government would deduce the system architecture and software details, fatally compromising the entire Data Link-II system.[78] Similar is the anxiety regarding the radar fingerprinting system. The official Indian view that American companies and intelligence agencies cannot reverse-look into the Indian bank of radar signatures, including those of all Indian military fighting platforms, may be a little optimistic. Indeed, the DRDO chief Avinash Chander perhaps had such joint projects in mind when he said at the 2014 DefenceExpo that, unless India is involved in a weapons systems or sensor platforms programme from 'the design stage', it will be difficult to assess the threat from malware injected in the imported military systems, because foreign suppliers do not part with source codes (Bhatnagar 2014). The official Indian view is that the cryptographic protocol in the Data Link-II can be rewritten in case US access and penetration is suspected, but that will require downing the platform for almost a year. Considering, moreover, that all the sensors and other major systems are of Indian origin, critics are beginning to wonder if the country paid too much—twice the price of a Boeing 747 Jumbo jet for the shells of two Boeing 737 aircraft as P-8I platforms.[79] There is also the question of the IPR ownership of such systems if the Indian partners have added huge value to the capability of a bare-bones configuration that may have been passed on to them. Technology transfer and cooperation aspects aside, these ventures involve issues as disparate as supplier reliability, the ability of the US vendor to protect Indian and third-party-developed technology and related IPRs, and, with US companies as prime integrators on such projects, a verifiable guarantee that the integrity of India-produced sensors and systems is not violated.

Still greater complications will surface with the Indian Navy seeking integration of the versatile supersonic Brahmos cruise missile—a product of Indo-Russian collaboration—as the main armament on the *Seahawk*. Two things will need to happen. Washington will have to give permission for this fitment; more problematically, New Delhi would have to approve, and get Moscow's nod, for handing over this missile—the only one of its kind in the world—to the Sikorsky Company for integration purposes. The Russian government–owned company, NPO Mashinostroyenia, in the joint Indo-Russian company Brahmos Aerospace producing this missile will be especially protective of the innovative technologies in the ramjet engine powering the missile. This technology is in the process of being transferred to India, and the Indian DRDO has specifically developed the avionics and software for controlling its flight and guidance. Both the Russian and Indian partners are distraught at the prospect of having to disclose technology secrets to American defence firms with respect to the 2.8 Mach-capable cruise missile, and the even more lethal hypersonic 6-7 Mach Brahmos-II scheduled for prototype testing by 2017.[80]

The Indian MOD has in the past reorganized military maintenance schemes to allay Washington's anxieties about US high technology being even accidentally accessed by Russian personnel servicing ex-Russian equipment on Indian bases and ships, whence the servicing streams were physically separated. This is so with regard, for instance, to the Barak-8 missile system with some American components, on board Indian warships built in Russian shipyards, such as the *Talwar*-class stealth missile frigate (modified *Krivak*-III design) and its newest aircraft carrier, *Vikramaditya* (ex-Russian *Gorshkov*). The Indian and Russian concerns on the Brahmos exactly mirror US worries of proprietary technology and secrets being filched, especially as Boeing is in the process of developing a hypersonic cruise missile (X-51 Wave-rider) for the US Air Force. India and Russia will probably demand similar airtight measures and other assurances, and may insist on physical oversight at American plants. It will be interesting to see how such sensitive technology issues are sorted out, and may become a model for protecting Indian and third-party technology and IPR when dealing with the US defence industry. Even if all other aspects of India's arms deals with America are sorted out, many in the armed services warn that hardware bought from the US could be compromised by the installation of 'bugs' to provide real-time electronic intelligence to the US, and satellite-activated 'kill switches' to deactivate these systems (Aroor 2010). The trouble is fair-weather spares supplying is not the same thing as maintaining supplies in a crisis when, if so ordered by Washington US companies would shut shop. This fundamental problem became starker with the 'Strategic Guidance' issued by the US Department of Defense in January 2012. 'We will expand our networks of cooperation with emerging partners throughout the Asia-Pacific to ensure collective capacity for securing common interests,' the document states. 'The United States is also investing in a long-term strategic partnership with India to support its ability to serve as a regional economic anchor and provider of security in the broader Indian Ocean region' (US DOD 2012). But how is India to satisfactorily perform the regional security anchor and security provider roles if its US-origin military systems can be so easily crippled?

Deriving from America's technology denial approach was the equally cussed US policy that attempted over time to undermine strategic and indigenous Indian high-technology military projects. For instance, India in good faith sent its design for the light combat aircraft (LCA) for wind tunnel testing at supersonic speeds, and certain other technologies related to the LCA developed in India, for validation in the US facilities at the Wright-Patterson air force base in Ohio. The news of the Indian nuclear tests in May 1998 not only led to instant termination of the testing and validation regimes, but to confiscation of the Indian designs, technologies under testing, and the related painstakingly compiled documentation, and also to the barring of Indian engineers from the facility. Another example: the failure of the first test-firing in June 2001 of the Brahmos supersonic missile is authoritatively attributed to the fact that the American global positioning system (GPS) it was using 'blinked' at a critical point in its flight path.[81] The cumulative effect of such experiences is to aggravate doubts and keep the embers of grievance from the past glowing, nursing suspicion of US intentions, seeding wariness about US plans, and hardening the apprehensions in the Indian political, military, and bureaucratic psyche, which could hurt forward progress in the Indo-US partnership.

Memories also linger about Washington blotting its copybook in other policy areas, for instance, Afghanistan. 'My experience in the Foreign Office was that the American advice always was please allow Pakistan to do a little bit of terrorism in your territory, otherwise how will Musharraf survive? In plain English, this is what [American importuning] amounted to', recalled the foreign minister in the first BJP government, Yashwant Sinha.

> Why do you mind a few losses here and there? We are in Afghanistan, so the [Pakistan militants] are not allowed to go west, so they go east! The US priority is US interests. Our priority should be Indian interests. And that's where we should draw the line. And wherever they are crossing the line we should be able to tell them.[82]

Two other historical examples of the US pushing its perceived interests of the moment while gutting its own and India's larger strategic interests: Indira Gandhi had moved towards liberalizing the Indian economy in 1966–7, but the Lyndon Johnson administration, with a view to punishing New Delhi for its opposition to US policies in Vietnam, defaulted on a promised grant of $980 million to bridge the effects of devaluing the Indian currency. It led Mrs Gandhi to revert with a vengeance to a worse form of socialism than her father, Nehru, ever practised, pushing back free market reforms by 30 years. In an alternative universe, India's taking to the free market norms then would have strengthened the Indian model of democratic development at the height of the Cold War, something Washington had ardently desired, and not handed China the economic edge that followed the US opening to that country (Williamson 2006). The other example pertains to the even more extraordinary lapse in American calculations of deliberately ignoring proliferation of nuclear weapons and missiles to Pakistan conducted in plain sight by China in the late 1970s and early 1980s. The justification that ignoring the surreptitious nuclear missile-arming of Pakistan by China was a price worth paying for Islamabad's participation in unsettling the Soviet occupation of Afghanistan seems in hindsight to be incredibly shortsighted.[83] The wonder is that with such a record of bad faith and scheming, India still retains equanimity in its relations with the United States!

It is revealing of the American policy mindset that, while the US frustration with the slow pace of defence relations is manifest, none of the trust-related issues that are holding back more fruitful relations have merited scrutiny by the US government or American analysts and think-tanks. When the absence of trust does come up, it is in the context of India having to do more, sign bigger procurement contracts before Washington and the US defence industry can trust India with advanced military technology.[84] When juxtaposed against New Delhi's leap of faith in letting American companies integrate highly classified Indian-developed technology and systems in the US, the American attitude appears small-minded. India could well have insisted, for instance, that all indigenously produced items be integrated in India by an Indian system integrator as the condition for the sale of the P-8I to proceed, leaving American companies little leeway. It indicates the extent to which New Delhi has accommodated the US without any signs of reciprocation by America. The Indian attitude of openness in contrast to Washington's approach that India should buy more to earn US trust before the technology gates are eventually opened in the indeterminate future is an unviable strategy with a distinctly transactional slant to it. It becomes conspicuous when set against other countries with equally advanced defence industrial capabilities, such as Germany, which is coming into India in a big way, and is prepared to use the Indian manufacturing base to export to third countries (Kazim 2012).

But mutual trust issues exacerbated by differences over the legal requirements (GSOMIA, CISMOA) Washington insists on have dogged India–US security relations since the 1980s, when President Ronald Reagan sent his defence secretary Caspar Weinberger to India to forge a new military supply relationship.[85] This is the case despite a GSOMIA already on the books, signed between the Acquisitions, Technology, and Logistics cell attached to the Office of the US Under-Secretary of Defense and the Indian DRDO in 2001 as an icebreaker and a precedent. It confirms Indian suspicions of Washington's interest being motivated less by grand strategy than a potential $100 billion Indian market for defence goods, with deals totalling some $10 billion already signed, and another $8 billion worth of contracts in the pipeline (Raghuvanshi 2012). Indian purchases become especially important at a time when the US government is cutting back on military acquisitions as per the new deficit reduction plan.[86] In the circumstances, it is curious that the Indian prime minister or foreign minister did not, over the last decade of the Congress Party coalition rule, do some plain talking of the kind Sartaj Aziz, the Pakistani foreign policy adviser to Prime Minister Nawaz Sharif, did with the visiting secretary of state John Kerry. 'At what stage,' Aziz asked Kerry, 'does a normal transactional relationship become strategic?' He went on to list the 'prerequisites' for a strategic partnership as 'mutual trust at all levels and among all key institutions [and] the expectation [that] legitimate US concerns ... must be balanced by ... Pakistan's own security concerns.... If these important prerequisites are met,' Aziz concluded, 'then the contribution of other elements of this important relationship, such as expanded trade, high level of private investment, long-term partnership on some major projects, will become far more significant and mutually reinforcing' (quoted in Haider 2014). These are suitable metrics to judge the India–US strategic partnership as well.

Two additional agreements the US wants India to endorse in order to cement India's stature as a military ally in all but name, and for it to enjoy blanket exemption in accessing American military high technology, are even more problematical. These are the Logistics Support Agreement (LSA) that will allow ships and aircraft of the two countries to repair, refuel their weapons platforms, and replenish their stores at each other's bases and supply depots, and the Basic Exchange and Cooperation Agreement (BECA) with the US National Geospatial Intelligence Agency in the Pentagon enabling the sharing, in the main, of micro-digitized maps. These are precursor documents legitimating India's standing in the American scheme of things, permitting each country's forces to plug into, and benefit from, the defence and security infrastructure of the other. In 2006, Obama's deputy secretary of defence Ashton B. Carter, then at Harvard trying to sell the US Congress on the nuclear deal with India, described in testimony to the US Senate Foreign Relations Committee how, with such agreements, the US–India 'security partnership' would evolve. Anticipating that joint action 'can lead first to joint military planning, then progressively to joint exercises, intelligence sharing and forging of a common threat assessment, and finally to joint capabilities', he went on to add that

> there could be occasions when access for and, if needed, basing of US military forces on Indian territory would be desirable. At first this might be limited to port access for US naval vessels transiting the Indian Ocean and over-flight rights for US military aircraft, but in time it could lead to such steps as use of Indian training facilities for US forces deploying to locations with similar climate. Ultimately, India could provide US forces with 'over the horizon' basing for Middle East contingencies of the sort preferred by Saudi Arabia and other Gulf states.[87]

But it is precisely the inflated expectations in responsible US circles that damage the prospects of the strategic partnership. It is why such talk spooks New Delhi, which at once resents the notion that India can so easily be rolled over, like another Saudi Arabia or a Gulf emirate, and why both the mechanics and the conferment of the ally status are what the Indian government wishes to avoid, notwithstanding the fact that many of the things mentioned by Carter—overflights, refuelling of aircraft, access to Indian ports, and joint exercises, are agreed to on a case-by-case basis, without publicity or ceremony. The Indian government will always fear the damage to the country's image and reputation for strategic autonomy and, even more, the domestic political fallout, with the opposition parties criticizing it for turning India into an American client state. A former chief of the air staff explained just why the Indian government and armed services are opposed to LSA and CISMOA. The LSA, he said, was 'no go' because the 'question is asked: how often would Indian ships and aircraft refuel and replenish at US bases, while US forces doing so at India facilities would be round the year for operations in the areas from West Asia to Malacca.' This, he added, 'will create perceptions of India as an American ally, which the Indian government does not want'. Further, CISMOA, he asserted, mandates 'communications integration right to the farthest backend to the national command network and individual service networks, which will compromise Indian security'. He is for relying on the arrangement used in joint military exercises. 'A one-point communications setup', he said, 'can be established at any time such a thing is needed—a flotilla engaging with US Navy ships, a flight of IAF aircraft with their opposite numbers.' According to him, 'the still larger political problem' with CISMOA 'is that it would integrate India into the communications net of US's NATO allies'. All such schemes are redundant, he claimed, because 'there's never any likelihood that Indian military units would serve under US military control or command. The only collective or joint military operations contemplated are under the U.N. flag.'[88]

The unequal benefits of LSA, the perceived threat of CISMOA to the integrity of the Indian government and the military's communications networks, and the potential of these agreements to initiate political disquiet at home and harm India's reputation abroad as an independent power are, from New Delhi's point of view, too high a price to pay for the perceived meagre benefits the country may derive from them. This view may, however, be changing. While saying that not signing these accords will not hurt, a former IAF chief, Air Chief Marshal N. A. K. Browne (Retd), contended that these agreements 'could be negotiated to suit Indian sensitivities'. For instance, CISMOA can be negotiated, he said, for 'the desired level of interoperability' and the US Defense Department, he claimed, 'is quite prepared for such a thing'. The LSA, he suggested, was more problematic because it involves designating air bases, ports, berthing piers, and so on, where the US would set up its logistics presence and infrastructure. This agreement, he said, is opposed by MEA for obvious reasons of violating Indian sovereignty. The MOD, he added, is caught between the MEA and the military, with the navy in particular maintaining that these agreements, because they will provide access to over 400 US overseas bases, would be useful in terms of extending the range of Indian ships and aircraft and the sustainability of distant operations conducted by the Indian military in the future. It would also allow access to the latest communications technology as original equipment in such hardware and platforms as the C-17 and C-130J airlifters, that India has bought. But Browne did foresee a real problem with the end-user verification provision in CISMOA that requires American personnel to periodically certify that the communications technology has not been tampered with.[89]

Reservations on the Indian side will compel the Indian and US armed forces to do what they have done in the past—resort to quick-fixes whenever they engage in any cooperative activity. Such as, for example, joint naval exercises in which the Centrix interface is plugged into Indian warships and operated by American sailors to enable them to communicate with US vessels. This sort of thing is routine, with the two sides using filters and layers to prevent the other side 'penetrating' one's own communications and command and control systems.[90] It emphasizes the absence of a high degree of trust, and, pending its accrual over time, the Indo-US strategic partnership may have to make do with these looser, informal, less elaborate, and less encumbered arrangements for military coopera-tion and defence industrial collaboration.[91] This is so despite a sin-gular policy advantage enjoyed by the United States. Jairam Ramesh, minister in the Congress Party coalition government, described the advantage thus: 'There's a great deal of empathy for the USA, no question. Why? Among other reasons and, I don't want to trivialize this, because 99.99 per cent of the policy elite have their children or grand children studying in the US or settled there. That's a very important factor.'[92]

The lack of trust bedevilling India–US relations may be a function of the limited personal experience over time of dealing with people and agencies in the other country, but it will begin to hamper and hurt collective effort, especially now with New Delhi, Washington, and Tokyo striving to obtain 'compound containment' of China.[93] The backdrop to the new Great Game that is unfolding has to do with the economic difficulties these entente powers are having with China (McIntyre and Weigley 2012). It could trigger a trade war engulfing much of Asia.[94] None of the three powers, however, wants to irreparably hurt its economic relations with Beijing or, even less, slip into military hostilities with China. They rather hope that seeing so many Indo-Pacific states arrayed against it will be perceived by Beijing as the sort of 'nightmare of coalitions' that the Prussian chancellor Otto von Bismarck in the nineteenth century found a little daunting (Helwig 2006: 111).

Relations between India and the United States, according to Admiral Samuel J. Locklear, commander, US Pacific Command, 'remain on an upward trajectory', but 'process issues in the Indian bureaucracy' keep the two countries 'on parallel, if independent paths'.[95] What does this mean in terms of the assistance that India, a non-treaty partner, can expect from the United States in a crisis with China? A military planner with the US Department of Defense confessed Washington's unwillingness to fight the Chinese to safeguard third-country interests in Asia, but hinted that America could provide the Indian military with invaluable high-technology support in operations. American sensors may be able to intimate on a real-time basis electronic and other intelligence, such as high-resolution photo imagery showing the disposition of Chinese forces, support Indian missiles and precision-guided weapons with target coordinates, help with keeping missiles and aircraft on target over long distances, and share with the Indian military the techniques, skills, and methodologies developed by the US armed forces over the years to neutralize short- and medium-range ballistic missile attacks (of the kind that can be expected from massed Chinese short-range ballistic missiles (SRBMs) and medium-range ballistic missiles (MRBMs) in Tibet and from short-range Pakistani missiles).[96] With its lead role and operational responsibility in the Indian Ocean theatre, the Indian military can expect to obtain, through intensive interaction and cooperation with its US counterpart, the practical knowledge to operationally use advanced weapons systems and data feeds from multiple sources for maximal effect in an information-networked battlefield. New Delhi's shying away from the three foundational accords—LSA, CISMOA, and BECA—may not, therefore, affect military cooperation all that much, in part because interoperability norms may be established through a more circuitous path with the increased induction of US-sourced military hardware and support systems into the Indian order-of-battle.

The US assistant secretary of state, Bureau of Political-Military Affairs, Andrew J. Shapiro, explained just how such a situation would come to pass. 'When a country buys an advanced US defense system through our Foreign Military Sales (FMS), Defense Commercial Sales (DCS), or Foreign Military Financing programmes, they aren't simply buying a product, they are buying into a relationship,' he told a US Defense Trade Advisory Group,

> These programmes both reinforce our diplomatic relations and establish a long-term security relationship. What is generally underappreciated is that the complex and technical nature of advanced defence systems frequently requires constant collaboration and interaction between countries over the life of that system.... . This may include training and support in the use of the system, assistance in maintenance, and help to update and modernize the system throughout its life-cycle. This cooperation therefore helps build bilateral ties and creates strong incentives for recipient countries to maintain good relations with the United States. (Shapiro 2011a, 2011b)

Speaking at the Carnegie Endowment, Shapiro elaborated some more on this aspect, affirming that India and America 'are building a robust relationship based on shared security interests', and that 'since the signing of the bilateral defense framework agreement in 2005, our defense relationship has become a major pillar of the strategic partnership.' To address the reliability aspects bothering the Indian government and military, Washington, he said, was strongly pushing FMS overseen by the Pentagon and not the DCS route, which was problematic due to its 'transactional nature'. Because 'the US-India defense and trade relationship would benefit by linking defense sales with broader strategic goals ... we specifically articulated', Shapiro said, 'the technical and political advantages that FMS offers. This entails political buy-in and support from Congress. The full faith and backing of the US government, transparency, support throughout the system's lifecycle, as well as expanded interoperability between our forces ...' (Shapiro 2012). The US military too favours the FMS route because, as Vice-Admiral Jeffrey A. Wieringa, then director, Defense Security Cooperation Agency, explained in 2008, the 'first order effect ... is building relationships, and that's the key part as opposed to just selling equipment', and the second order effect is 'interoperability'—'critically important to work[ing] together'.[97] With several major defence systems entering Indian military service, and many more arms contracts in the offing, the need to familiarize Indian operators with the technology and its nuances will mean American military and defence industry personnel becoming part of the Indian security scene, and thus becoming familiar with Indian procedures and ways of working.[98] New technology-operator interfaces thus created will enable multi-sourced systems, including from the US, in the Indian military inventory, to 'talk' and interact operationally with each other and their counterparts in the US and NATO militaries. Soon enough there will transpire a workable communications and operations grid even without the LSA, CISMOA, and BECA.

This is an indirect strategy for capacity building in a partner country and promoting interoperability while skirting political and procedural potholes, and it will be no less effective because of the roundabout way in which it is achieved. Lack of formal agreements, moreover, may lead to some bumps in the relationship, but will draw less political attention to the substantive military cooperation structures already in place, and avoid exciting Leftist political parties and creating a political ruckus. The International Military Education and Training (IMET) programme also helps in generating mutual trust. According to Shapiro (2012), 'The linkages established through IMET also help build personal relationships between officer corps, which helps bolster our relationship over long term, as well as helps professionalize partner militaries.' Some 1,700 Indian military officers have attended courses in America over 40 years as part of the IMET scheme. But it is the 50-odd joint military exercises that have helped in advancing 'interoperability' at the personal and unit levels, and to a reassuring discovery by American servicemen of the competence of their Indian counterparts.[99] The Indian Navy is 'rated NATO quality', and the IAF's performances to date in the Red Flag and other exercises have passed muster with the US Air Force. Such exercises have also prompted calls for more complex service-to-service and more real-life mixed-services (Indian Navy with US Air Force, and so on) exercises to validate 'air-sea' battle concepts and prepare for more realistic conflict scenarios of the future (Neuman 2012).

Technology cooperation may be the key to germinating and growing trust. A good example of this is the P-8I maritime reconnaissance aircraft being configured by Boeing as per Indian naval specifications, requiring, among other things, a 360-degree coverage-capable radar and a magnetic anomaly detector for hunting submarines to be added to its equipment suite. Significantly, this necessitated that Indian defence industrial companies, public and private, to develop extremely secret and sensitive technologies and then hand them over to Boeing, the prime integrator, for fitment onto the basic Boeing 737-800 platform. As discussed earlier, such items as the Data Link-II tactical data exchange system, the radar fingerprinting system, and a 'speech secrecy system', were shipped to the US in the expectation that secrecy and IPR norms would be respected. A well-received return gesture was the US Navy acceding to its Indian counterpart's request to have its officers on board American P-8As when out on missions in order for them to learn how best to use the on-board sensors and technologies for maximum results.[100] The US military's incomparable operational experience and high-tech savvy is being tapped by the Indian armed services in other ways as well. The first of such pioneering cooperative ventures involved the naval variant of the Tejas light combat aircraft under development. Facing difficulties, the Indian Navy project team had considered consulting EADS or Dassault in areas such as determining the location of the arrester hook-landing system, ways to test this system, 'aerodynamic fixes' to improve carrier take-off and landing, optimizing landing gear design to handle larger operating weight, integrating operational payload, reduction of aircraft weight, selecting a different engine for better power-to-weight ratio, and so on. It finally decided on seeking technical advice from the US Navy, with the most carrier aviation experience. The Indian letter of request occasioned a brief but intense debate in the Office of the US Chief of Naval Operations, before a decision was made to help. A letter of agreement and a consultancy contract were soon drawn up, and veteran American naval aviators deputed for the job began working with the Indian Navy's LCA team in 2011. The reason this scheme succeeded, according to a Pentagon officer, was because it avoided the red-tape-minded Indian defence ministry, with all relevant decisions on the Indian side—from initial contact, drafting the consultancy contract, to payments and arrangements for hosting the American naval officers—being made by a single-point authority, the Indian naval officer heading the project. The second of the prototype carrier-operable LCAs, incorporating American technical advice, underwent flight trials a year later, and could be the forerunner of more such direct, hands-on, military-to-military schemes, wherein no technology is transferred, but the Indian services benefit from the skills sets and practical insights of American military personnel to iron out kinks in hardware and in the melding of hardware and software (Karnad 2012b).

The P-8I and naval LCA are the kind of successful collaborative projects that could increase mutual trust and fuel serious Indian interest in 'joint development' of major weaponry, which many US military analysts see Indo-US defence cooperation graduating to (Neuman 2012: 133). While the trust is growing, it did not reach a level at least during the Congress Party rule for India to work with the United States on cyber operations against China.[101] Indo-US partnership can grow openly or by stealth. Stealth seems the more likely route in the main, because anti-Americanism remains a political reflex in New Delhi. Despite the joint exercises, deepening military exchanges, purchases of US military hardware, the Indian government's avowed interest, and the large Indian middle class's love for everything American, there will always be powerful political sections that believe it is best to keep the United States 'at arm's length'.[102]

With India militarily reorientating and strengthening its stance with the acquisition of high-performance armaments, and embarking on strategic cooperation in a big way with the United States and Japan, the last thing anybody wants is Pakistan as a distraction. But that is precisely the fly that is sought to be inserted into the ointment of warming bilateral relations by the US's partiality for Cold War–vintage offshore balancing. Questions are raised about whether helping India to beef up militarily, and otherwise enabling it to compete with China, will not lead to ignoring the 'nested security dilemmas' at the sub-regional level and upset the 'South Asian military balance' (Gilboy and Heginbotham 2012: 274). Should such views influence American policy, it will be seen by New Delhi as an egregious move by the US to make common cause with China to prop up a dysfunctional Pakistani state. It would also send out the wrong signals to rimland Asia of a US, maladjusted to the millennial reality, thinking nothing of weakening its Asian partners. Moreover, Washington's return to re-hyphenating US relations in South Asia, former Pakistan foreign secretary Shamshad Ahmad (2012) feels, will reinforce the Islamic radicalization of Pakistani society, fan ill-will in India, and unravel the Indo-US military cooperation so painstakingly stitched together. The other counsel, that the US should help strengthen India militarily but 'avoid providing offensive weapons and training', show 'restraint in the transfer of weapons and defense technologies', and use 'geopolitical, nuclear, military, and technological cooperation [as] America's trump cards' in dealing with Indian leaders who 'prize status-related achievements even more than many other US partners', will also get up New Delhi's nose (Gilboy and Heginbotham 2012: 277–90).

Arms Supply, Technology Transfer, and Influence

The Indian Navy is at the forefront of efforts to forge a strong security partnership with the United States. It is instructive, therefore, to consider its views which, on balance, are almost equally divided between those who are wary about getting too close to the United States and others who welcome it. This is surprising because the bulk of the Indian Navy's officer corps has served on ex-Soviet/Russian ships and submarines, with a minority cutting their teeth on the British *Leander*-class frigates manufactured under licence in a government-owned dockyard in the late 1960s and 1970s. Naval aviators on the two carriers—the (first) *Vikrant* (ex-*HMS Hercules*), now decommissioned, and *Viraat* (ex-*HMS Hermes*) on life extension, have bought into the US Navy's aircraft carrier philosophy. 'The biggest reservations one has are about the reliability of the US as a partner. It goes against all historical evidence to adhere to the view that we have a strategic convergence of interests,' said Vice-Admiral Ravi N. Ganesh (Retd), the only officer in the Indian Navy to have commanded a nuclear submarine (the *Charlie*-I class boat leased from the Russians in the 1980s) and the carrier, *Viraat*. 'The US has aided Pakistan against India, sought to egg China to attack India' (a reference to US Secretary of State Henry Kissinger encouraging Beijing to try and distract the Indian military involved in prosecuting operations against the Pakistan Army in the Bangladesh liberation war in 1971, by mounting a diversionary attack against Indian forces in the Himalayas), 'and pressured third countries such as Britain to apply embargoes on [*Sea King*] aircraft parts at critical times.' In the event, 'the current "strategic partner" phase with India', he ventures, 'is part economic opportunism and part alliance-building against China, of which the US is extremely wary.' Ganesh, who after retirement headed the project to build the *Arihant*-class SSBN, also thinks the importance of joint naval exercises is overstated. 'Despite all the hyperbole', he asserts, 'nearly two decades of the annual Malabar exercises [involving the Indian, US, and, occasionally, other regional navies] are still not at tactical level but focus mainly on inter-operability.' Referring to the unfulfilled promises in the 2005 Framework Agreement, Ganesh dismisses the Indo-US partnership as 'largely observed in political rhetoric but as being less noticeable in terms of real benefit to India'[103]

Those partial to warming relations with the US speak of the US as a potential source of advanced technology and FDI, and refer to the shortcomings of Russian technology and deficiencies in the Russian supply chain, and of having to rely on the US in a confrontation with China. 'Let's put the horse before the cart', declared Admiral Arun Prakash (Retd), former chief of naval staff, naval aviator, and an alumnus of the US Naval War College.

> We have certain needs. We need technology, foreign investment, we could at some point of time even need military assistance if there's a face-off with China. Those are our needs. Where do we get it from? We could get it from one or two other sources. But America is a good source for technology, FDI and some military assistance, directly or indirectly. So to the extent it meets our needs, let's deal with them on that basis.[104]

With other sources now available, some senior serving and retired officers frown upon the idea of continuing with a close relationship with Russia, and are scathing about the Russian connection. 'There's no doubt that the Russkies have ripped us off, and made complete monkeys out of us in the past 20 years. But my guess is', said a senior naval person, speaking candidly and on a non-attributable basis, it's the DRDO and possibly the DAE [Department of Atomic Energy] who are the reason that we remain tied to [Russian] coattails. DRDO is definitely beholden to the Russkies for borrowing technologies which [DRDO] later claim as their own. I suspect that [*Arihant*] submarine [highly-enriched uranium-fuelled, pressurized] reactors plus fuel as well as underwater [missile] launch and rocket propellant technologies come from them [Russians]. They [DRDO] have direct access to the PM [Prime Minister] and there is no one to challenge their claims. So the apex is convinced that if they ditch or upset the Russians the bottom will fall out of 'strategic autonomy".

As an 'equal opportunity critic', this officer then rounded on the United States, seconding what Ganesh had stated. 'For all their big talk', he said, 'they [Americans] haven't parted with any useful technology to us.'[105]

Technology is the decisive issue shaping the Indian government's attitude to supplier states. Countries that transfer sophisticated weaponry and help India build up its defence science and technology base enjoy special warmth in relations. However, when India has been forced by circumstance and international technology denial regimes to rely on itself, it has spurred local ingenuity and effort and a defiant attitude, resulting in the country acquiring the prized capability. This attitude is typified by the statement of the former rocket engineer and head of DRDO, Dr A. P. J. Abdul Kalam, in the mid-1990s when, referring to the Missile Technology Control Regime, he exhorted missile designers and engineers thus: 'When the developed world says don't do that, we will do that' (quoted in Karnad 2005: 611). So, when the Boris Yeltsin government under American pressure stopped the transfer of the Russian cryogenic rocket in the mid-1990s, the Indian Space Research Organization (ISRO) redoubled its efforts and developed a cryogenic engine on its own. In instances where the US is supposed to have ensured the failure of certain high-value strategic weapons, it led inadvertently to higher-order Indian achievements. The 'blinking of the American GPS' episode during the first Brahmos missile test, for instance, strengthened the Indian resolve to have its own GPS—the Indian Regional Navigational Satellite System or the 'Gagan' system that is likely to be fully operational by 2016, with three of its satellites in geo-stationary orbits already up, and covering an area 2,000 kilometres in radius around India, generating 20-metre (but some insiders maintain sub-metre) accuracy (Yadav 2011). To augment its footprint, the system plugs into the Russian Glonass GPS, with India developing software for the Indian military and civilian user interface with it, but turning down a Russian proposal to co-develop advances in its 31-satellite system (Kashin 2012).

Russia has been the military supplier of choice because it has been less restrictive in its exports and in assisting India in many of its most sensitive military projects. In the heyday of the bloc rivalry, Moscow cemented the friendship with offers of frontline equipment, such as the Tu-22 Backfire strategic bomber in 1971, which the IAF foolishly declined, thereby early forsaking the capacity to strike deep Chinese targets (Karnad 2005b: 663–8). Except for the foreign ministerial tenure of Andrei Kozyrev, when Moscow, siding with Washington, adopted a less friendly posture, Russian policy has backed Indian interests and accommodated New Delhi's concerns. With the geo-politics-minded Yevgeny Primakov taking over as foreign minister in the 2000s, the once-powerful Soviet Union now reduced to an incomparably weaker Russia desperately needed a friendly India to keep purchasing its defence wares—some 800 Russian defence production facilities depended on the Indian lifeline (Conley 2001). Since then, Russia has increased its courting of India, taking a tack opposite to the one adopted by Washington. When the US was pressuring the Indian government to sign the Comprehensive Test Ban Treaty, Russia signed a contract for the supply of two 1,000 MW nuclear power plants to be erected at Koodankulum, 'grandfathered' by a reactor supply agreement from the 1980s. More impressively, from the Indian point of view, in the aftermath of the 1998 series of Indian nuclear tests, formally heralding weaponization that saw the Clinton administration throwing fits, conspiring with China, imposing sanctions, and seeking futilely to 'freeze, cap, and rollback' the Indian nuclear weapons programme, Moscow was reviving its offer of the latest version of the Tu-22 strategic bomber, leasing an Akula-II SSN, and signing a new 10-year treaty on military and technological cooperation that realized military sales worth $15 billion for Russia in the first decade of the new century (Conley 2001). And Moscow throughout retained the policy of behind-the-scenes involvement without fuss or publicity in prestigious, cutting-edge Indian technology projects. The Soviet Union/Russia from the start appreciated the basic axiom of international relations in the modern age, that a major military supply relationship 'pre-determines' the foreign policy of the recipient country.[106] But what it instinctively also knew was that with India and its many sensitivities, it is best to wield the silk glove, not the iron fist. Surprisingly, the US government still finds it hard to accept this bit of practical foreign policy wisdom. Using the MiG-21 gambit in the mid-1960s, Russia edged open the Indian arms market, shoved aside the British and French armament companies that had until then monopolized the trade, provided advanced weaponry to the Indian military services, and, in the process, lifted them up professionally, massaged their service egos, and created captive lobbies, with the armaments provided at affordable prices and on easy credit. By 1991, Russia had reached its apogee as military supplier, meeting 85 per cent of the IAF's hardware requirements, 80 per cent of the Indian Navy's, and 70 per cent of the Army's, with total sales amounting to as much as $16 billion over the previous 30 years (Conley 2001). Such over-reliance on Russia may have declined somewhat in recent years, as New Delhi unveiled a policy of diversification to avoid being caught in a military supply crunch. But Russia's position as the prime supplier of high-value weaponry remains, with the sale to the Indian Navy of the carrier *Gorshkov*, and the IAF's commitment to the fifth-generation fighter aircraft (FGFA).

The real reason for the high trust and comfort levels that Russia enjoys in the Indian national security establishment is its willingness to go beyond selling hardware to assisting India, in meaningful ways, to become genuinely self-reliant in the military high-technology and allied fields. It has helped Indian scientists and engineers get over and around technological humps in the many indigenous, prestige programmes the government has invested its political and financial capital in. In the project to design and produce the *Arihant*-class SSBNs, for instance, Russian consultants first helped refine the design by the Bhabha Atomic Research Centre, Trombay, for the 80 MW highly enriched uranium-run pressurized water reactor, and then helped Indian engineers implement the design. Elsewhere, the Russians are passing on to Indian designers and engineers extremely sophisticated and futuristic pump-jet technology for submarine propulsion, featured currently in the latest generation of submersibles that make the Russian *Borey*-class and its equivalents elsewhere faster, and more silent and manoeuvrable. This technology is to be incorporated in the successor SSBN, designated S-5, as well as in the indigenous nuclear-powered attack submarine (SSN) in the final design stage.

Keen to replicate the Russian success in India and become a long-term military supplier in a close and sustained relationship, France is using the $4.5 billion *Scorpene* submarine deal to firm up its credentials as a source of advanced technology. France has joined with the private sector Pipavav shipyards to produce, in the future, the top-of-the-line *Mistral*-class assault ship/landing platform dock, the FREMM multi-mission frigate, and the *Gowind* corvette.[107] Importantly, France has seen the light in another respect as well. It has become aware, as Russia has been for many decades, that traction in Delhi is secured by cooperating with India especially in the nuclear military field and the most advanced conventional weapons systems. Thus, as inducement for India to buy the *Rafale* combat aircraft, Paris dangled access for Indian nuclear scientists to the Megajoule inertial confinement fusion (ICF) facility near Bordeaux (Lamont and Boxell 2012).[108]

It is now a buyer's market as far as military hardware is concerned. With New Delhi apparently getting serious about building up a local defence industry with its insistence on 'Make in India' weaponry, the threshold for suppliers peddling military wares has been raised. The US as last mover has the advantage of avoiding making the mistakes the other suppliers did, except that Washington's policy of over-protecting US-origin technologies is a drawback. The transfer of technology clauses in current deals require going beyond the 'know-how' stage to 'know-why', which, in the case of combat aircraft, requires the vendor to transfer source codes (millions of lines of software about every aspect of the aircraft design) of the aircraft, comprehensive flight control laws, and the algorithms driving them. It is a standard Russia has contracted to meet for the first time in the $35 billion deal for the FGFA from the Sukhoi stable—the Su-50 PAK/FA.[109] India will develop the software and the mission control computer for both versions of the aircraft, which will also see Russian expertise in titanium structures (for the leading edges) marrying up with the Indian expertise in carbon-carbon composite material (for use in the fuselage section). The two countries will share '50-50' in

IPR, with India being free to market its own version.[110] In contrast, the French have been lot more hesitant in transferring *Rafale* technology, with the Dassault company reserving the more high-value on-board systems relating to avionics and data fusion, for instance, in the category of technologies to be supplied by French companies as 'black boxes' technologies for the duration of the production run in India, which constitutes some 30 per cent of the contract value of $26 billion, for the lifetime of the *Rafale* programme. This did not go down well in India (Karnad 2013a, 2013b).[111]

The United States has had a real problem parting with high technology. During his July 2012 visit to Delhi, US Secretary of Defense Leon E. Panetta acknowledged that issues relating to military technology transfer were crimping bilateral relations. US Deputy Secretary of Defense Ashton Carter, asked by Panetta to untangle issues, was bluntly told about the barriers to defence cooperation. Indian officials at the highest level identified four problem areas. First, India's placement in the category of 'other friendly states' with respect to defence commerce because it has not signed the foundational agreements means that it does not enjoy the kind of blanket exemption on technology sales and transfers that countries in the first two categories—NATO and Japan and South Korea, do. Second, the details of total transfer of technology—in terms of source codes, flight control laws, and driver algorithms are spelled out when the Indian Ministry of Defence issues the Request for Information—the very first stage in the Indian procurement process. If the United States, for whatever reasons, feels unable to fulfil this condition, it should not enter the competition in the first place. To get in half-way, that is, to make a bid but hold back on total technology transfer, only breeds misunderstanding. Third, the changes in the arms export laws President Barack Obama promised during his November 2010 visit to India have not materialized, leaving the main Washington bureaucracies not on the same page when it comes to approving the sale of military technology. The US Department of Defense and armed forces are enthusiastic about close security and defence industrial links with India; less so is the State Department, whose approach is dictated by the restrictive Munitions List; and the most reluctant is the US Department of Commerce which, ironically, was less stringent than the Pentagon during the Cold War years in deciding on the sensitive technologies American industry could sell or transfer to members of the Soviet Union–led Warsaw Pact countries under the Coordinating Committee for Multilateral Export Controls (COCOM) regime established in 1949.[112] And, last, the end-use memorandum requirements will have to be modified and US military inspectors satisfied with perusing the paper records pertaining to the disposition and use of American equipment and technology without having physical access to them. To speedily resolve these and other problems and remove institutional barriers, Carter and Menon decided on each side forming an inter-agency team, with Indians making a priority list of technologies and preferred co-development programmes they desired, and the Americans a definitive list of technology ceilings in different areas to remove uncertainty and confusion in New Delhi and, in a sense, exactly define the levels of technology that may be sold and/or commercially transferred by US companies to India without let or bureaucratic hindrance.[113] At an interaction hosted by the Confederation of Indian Industry in July 2012, Carter conceded that speed bumps had slowed down the strategic partnership, but reaffirmed US eagerness to find 'concrete areas to step up our defense cooperation, so that only our imagination and strategic logic, and not administrative barriers, set the pace.' 'We want [to] strip away the impediments' such as 'an export control system' that 'can be confusing, rigid, and controls too many items for the wrong reasons', he added. Carter, like other Pentagon officials before him, spoke of FMS mediated by the US Department of Defense as compared to DCS as the route Washington hoped India would prefer in acquiring 'exceptional' military technology with 'a high degree of transparency, and no corruption'. But he also conceded that this might not always work with the lowest tender system subscribed to by the Indian Defence Ministry, which, he implied, favoured price more than quality or military value. He urged the Indian government to raise 'its Foreign Direct Investment ceiling to international standards to increase commercial incentives to invest', and cautioned New Delhi that an offsets policy—the Indian government's tool to germinate a local defence industry—can be 'tremendously helpful to growing industrial capabilities' but only if it is 'calibrated' and mindful of the 'absorptive capacity' of Indian companies. He mentioned the 'great first step in co-production' as the unleashing of 'the potential of our private industries' (Carter 2012).

The main reason for the low equity ceiling, former head of the DRDO (the main government agency to approve such collaborations) Dr V. K. Saraswat explained, is the worry that 'Indian industry will become totally subservient and more like a dealer of foreign technologies than developers of technology. We don't want that. We want synergy, we want [technology] incubation and, we want growth.' But, with the Indian government moving forcefully for full transfer of technology on arms deals, including source codes and so on—the 'know-why' element in designing weapons—Dr Saraswat expressed confidence that supplier countries will see the benefits to them from establishing comprehensive military hardware design and production presence in India.[114] In this regard, New Delhi may not be able to resist for long the push by the Israeli, US, and British governments to increase foreign equity as a means of incentivizing foreign defence companies to set up shop in India and become part of the Indian defence industrial and military procurement scene.[115] Higher foreign equity could be allowed on condition that the companies incubate technologies in India rather than simply act as purveyors of slightly dated foreign technology. The administration has also accepted the need to involve the Indian private sector more centrally in the defence industry. Important new projects, for instance, to build, in-country, a new class of minesweepers, frigates, and the Project 75i conventional submarine for the navy and a medium transport aircraft for the air force, are being channelled to the private sector (Sidhartha and Gupta 2014). It is enticing large Indian corporations to enter the defence industrial business.[116]

With India transitioning from a consumer of military goods to co-developer, and the competition getting keener, Russia has decided to switch foci and concentrate mainly on joint projects with 'immense political value', in the words of the Russian deputy prime minister Dmitry Rogozin.[117] Compared to the co-development of the high-end Brahmos missile and the FGFA Su-50 PAK/FA, US Deputy Secretary of Defense Ashton Carter's suggestion that the two countries 'co-develop' 'batteries and micro-UAVs' as 'good, initial steps' seem trivial. His pitching America as 'India's highest-quality and most trusted long-term supplier of technology, in such fields as maritime domain awareness, counter-terrorism, and many others', moreover, sends out the wrong message (Carter 2012). At a time when other traditional suppliers are moving determinedly from selling military goods and technology to offering co-development that the Indian political and policy establishments have set their sights on, it reveals that Washington is behind the curve, and its 'vision' for US–India defence cooperation is stilted. It may be in the right to plead for the defence industrial milieu to be made foreign investment–friendly, but for the US to use that as an excuse to push only military sales—even as the other supplier states, such as Russia, Israel, and France, are adjusting faster to Modi's 'Make in India' policy to boost the Indian manufacturing sector and defence industry—may result in the US once again missing the bus.[118] Contemplating 'America's new partner', Ashton Carter (2006), not then in government, had insightfully observed in a 2006 article in *Foreign Affairs* that 'no government in New Delhi can turn on a dime in regard to a broad set of actions that support US interests; only a profound and probably slow evolution in the views of India's elites could produce such change.' It may have dawned on Washington that such change in views is best effected by high-end collaborative defence projects.[119] There is, however, no sign yet that this change has taken effect.[120] One other thing—the attitude of the US government—could derail the relations. Nicholas Burns (2014), former US under-secretary of state, explained the problem thus:

> The United States is accustomed to calling the shots with its allies in Europe and East Asia. That won't work with India, which will insist on equal standing with the United States. To be effective in dealing with New Delhi, American diplomats must therefore pay special attention to Indian sensitivities, maintaining a realistic sense of what is and what is not possible with modern India.

It is advice that will be helpful in dealing with a strong-minded Indian government.

Notes

1. Addressing the conference of BIMSTEC states (Bangladesh, Bhutan, India, Myanmar, Sri Lanka, and Thailand) in Phuket in early March 2014,

where a framework agreement for free trade was signed, Prime Minister Manmohan Singh said: 'In coming together, we are not only stepping out of narrow, traditional definitions of regions such as South Asia or Southeast Asia, but we are also building a bridge across Asia's most promising and dynamic arc' (see Sinha 2014).

2. There is no end to the continuing public debate in the Pakistani media about the merits of partitioning India. As to how the Partition pathologies and neuroses have affected Pakistan's domestic politics and foreign policy, see Haqqani (2013).

3. For more detailed analysis of India–Pakistan conflicts along these lines, see Karnad (1996).

4. Publications sourced to the Henry L. Stimson Center in Washington, specializing in South Asian deterrence schemas, are typical of such Western writings (which South Asian academics have long imitated); it is another matter that the Center's focus on the nuclear flashpoint in Kashmir, for instance, is with a view to pushing its other agenda—nonproliferation.

5. The mandala geopolitics is analysed in Karnad (2005b: 3–14).

6. Henry Kissinger (2011), typifying something resembling awe of China in the US policy establishment, is swept away by both the game of wei qi and the sophisticated Chinese diplomacy it has spawned.

7. 'India may get US waiver for Iran oil', *Times of India*, 25 May 2013.

8. The new Iranian government of Hassan Rouhani has talked of increasing energy exports to, and establishing defence linkages with, India. At the same time, Tehran is rejecting payment for oil imports in Indian rupees, which allowed New Delhi to skirt the American ban on financial transactions with Iran. This creates problems for India and compels it to break on this issue with the US (see Aneja 2013; Ranjan 2013). See also 'Iran seeks enhanced defense ties with India', *Times of India*, 22 July 2013.

9. Referring to differences with the US over Iran, National Security Adviser Shivshankar Menon (2013) said that these were 'inevitable between countries in different circumstances, at different levels of development, and in dissimilar geopolitical situations'.

10. 'Trade with India to touch $24 billion in medium-term, says Tehran Chamber', *Economic Times*, 9 May 2012.

11. 'India to slash Iran oil imports to meet nuclear deal parameters', *Indian Express*, 12 March 2014.

12. Addressing a meeting of Indian ambassadors to Central Asian states, the Indian foreign minister S. M. Krishna said: 'To overcome the connectivity problems, be it land or sea, efforts are underway to re-energize alternate sea and land routes through Iran.' A saving of $100 million accrued to Indian trade using Chahbahar in 2012 (Jacob 2012).

13. 'Khurshid leaves for Iran, Chahbahar port on agenda', *Indian Express*, 3 May 2013.

14. 'Iran-India transit corridor: Iran Daily', Islamic Republic News Agency, 19 April 2014, available at http://www.irna.ir/en/News/2673042/Economic/Iran-India_transit_corridor___Iran_Daily.

15. 'China, Afghanistan to build strategic partnership', *China Daily*, 8 June 2012.

16. 'Afghanistan calls India an "all-weather friend"', *Express Tribune*, Islamabad, 22 October 2014.

17. India has taken a 15 per cent stake in the Alibekmola oilfield costing $1.5 billion in the Caspian basin, and a 25 per cent stake in the Satpaev oil bloc in Kazakhstan. The possibility of importing hydroelectricity from Tajikistan and Kyrgyzstan through Afghanistan and Pakistan is also being explored (see Schaffer and Hate 2007).

18. 'Indian policy', writes Frank Starr (2010: viii) of the Johns Hopkins School of Advanced International Studies, 'leads with trade, education, health, technology and transport', not anti-terrorism as emphasized by the US, or 'large scale exploitation' of natural resources as evidenced in the Russian and Chinese approaches. 'India's expanded presence, while still limited', he adds, 'is in areas that are directly relevant to ordinary people', and therefore likely to have a deeper and more lasting impact.

19. Major General (Retd) B. N. Sharma, former military attaché in Kazakhstan, personal communication, 4 April 2013.

20. The delivered cost estimated at $13 per unit is three times the price New Delhi pays its own domestic producers of offshore gas. India's assumption of 'indirect responsibility' for its safe transit and delivery is problematic. See 'India to pay $13 per unit for natural gas from TAPI pipeline', *Economic Times*, 28 May 2012.

21. Former US assistant secretary of commerce in the Bill Clinton administration, Raymond E. Vickery (2011: 149–52), blames the Dabhol fiasco on 'the perils of fast-tracking' energy projects.

22. Yashwant Sinha, interview.

23. India joined the Brazilian and South African navies in maritime exercises. The most recent of these exercises in late 2012 practised an elaborate air-sea assault on inland targets using ships, aircraft, and special forces. Personal communication.

24. This has led to Brazil siding with India to keep China from investing in a rich oil find. See 'ONGC Videsh blocks China bid to buy stake in Brazilian oilfield', *Indian Express*, 18 September 2013. This may be seen as Indian retaliation for China blocking India from acquiring a stake in an oilfield in Kazakhstan (see Gordevyava 2013).

25. Such failure in the case of Central Asia, for instance, has been noted. 'For India, Central Asia has been a squandered opportunity for twenty years', wrote Illan Greenberg (2013), a scholar at the Woodrow Wilson Center. 'There is still time for India to play a significant and mutually positive role in Central Asian affairs, but it will require a much more muscular and coordinated effort from India's foreign policy establishment, business leaders, and military strategists.' New Delhi's unwillingness to play a more prominent role may be due to calculations about piggybacking on a Russia that it hopes will make a comeback in the region. Between waiting for a desirable outcome it can capitalize on and doing nothing to further Indian interests, lie missed chances. India has failed, for example, to deploy the 'burgeoning diaspora of globalized professional talent'.

26. K. V. Bhagirath, former Indian ambassador, personal communication.

27. Commodore Sujeet Samaddar (Retd), personal communication. Samaddar, as principal director, Naval Plans, headed the Indian Navy team to Mozambique in the early 2000s.

28. A report on Chinese mining operations in Gabon and the Democratic Republic of Congo, in the executive summary, says that compared to companies from other countries, 'discernable differences ... pertain to factors such as company size and culture. The research shows that language barriers, cultural differences and misunderstandings arising from these are impediments to communication and interaction between Chinese, African and Western stakeholders in Africa ... [and] should not be understated' (Jansson *et al.* 2009).

29. When a Russian coast guard vessel captured a Chinese fishing boat found fishing illegally, a Chinese commentary, for instance, warned that 'the reckless behavior of the Russians at the grassroots level not only harms Chinese confidence in fostering long-term friendship with Russia, but also provides excuses for forces seeking to undermine Sino-Russian ties.' See 'Huanqiu: Russia should not have fired at Chinese fishing ships', Chinascope, 18 July 2012.

30. Based on an Indian source familiar with Russian defence industry.

31. 'Russia sold $4.7 bln in arms to India in 2013', *Sputnik*, 16 February 2012, available at http://en.ria.ru/trend/russian_arms_export/.

32. 'Russian arms exporter sold $13.3 Bln in 2013', *Sputnik*, 27 January 2014, available at http://en.ria.ru/military_news/20140127/186951155/Russian-Arms-Exporter-Sold-132Bln-in-2013.html.

33. 'China-Russia trade close to hitting targets', Xinhua, 15 June 2012, available at http://news.xinhuanet.com/english/business/2012-06/15/c_131655138.htm.

34. Russian Siberia contains 85 per cent of Russia's natural gas, 80 per cent of its oil and coal, 40 per cent of its timber, and huge deposits of nickel,

zinc, copper, aluminum, and mercury. The region is a natural target for a Chinese 'land grab' either by conventional military means or, more likely, through legal migration but mostly illegal demographic seepage of Chinese people seeking land and opportunities across the border (Stakelbeck 2005; Trenin 2012: 34–6).

35. 'Putin pledges 400 ICBMs for Russia in ten years', RIA Novosti, 20 February 2012; 'Whither goes Russia in the post-Soviet space?', International Relations and Security Network, 18 May 2012, available at www.isn.ethz. ch/isn/. Russian Strategic Forces at http://russianforces.org/.

36. Russia is supporting the Bashar al-Assad government to the hilt (Kramer 2012; Landler 2012; Lynch and Sly 2012); see also 'Russia accuses US of arming Syrian rebels', *Telegraph*, London, 13 June 2012.

37. Russia has loosened its arms ban on Pakistan with an attack helicopter as initial offering. See 'Russia lifts arms embargo to Pakistan: Report', *Express-Tribune*, 3 June 2014.

38. 'Russia-India ties at their peak—Alexander Kadakin', *Russia & India Report*, 11 February 2014, available at http://in.rbth.com/economics/2014/02/11/russia-india_ties_at_their_peak_alexander_kadakin_32981.html.

39. Currently, only 0.4 per cent of outgoing Taiwanese capital heads for India, and bilateral trade is at a low $5.47 billion level, but the bid to attract Taiwanese investors has by and large failed, despite Taipei's push for collaborative ventures in software, high-technology R&D, and automobile spare parts and ancillaries (Batabyal 2012; Chang 2011).

40. 'Tsai calls for Taiwan to speed up efforts to strengthen India ties', *Focus Taiwan*, 20 September 2012; 'Taiwan president makes surprise India transit', AFP, 7 April 2012.

41. 'India-Japan-Taiwan Trialogue: Prospects for Democratic Cooperation', Thinktank, n.d., available at http://www.taiwanthinktank.org/english/page/7/32/57/263.

42. Personal communication, senior officer, Army Headquarters, September 2012.

43. West Asia generated most of the remittances totalling $7.18 billion in 2013, which was a tenth of the global remittances. See 'NRI remittances surge to $7.18 bn in 2013', *Business Standard*, 30 March 2014. Further, fully 44 per cent of the population of Bahrain, 37 per cent in the UAE, 35 per cent in Qatar, and lesser but significant proportions in Oman, Kuwait, and Saudi Arabia are of Indian origin. Combined trade with all Arab countries is in excess of $62 billion (compared with some $63 billion with China and nearly $46 billion with the United States) (Feiler 2012: 20–1, 27).

44. Meeting with the author in Tel Aviv, 30 May 2012.

45. '"Spicing" up Israeli agriculture', *Jerusalem Post*, 15 May 2012. Also see the interview of the Israeli ambassador in India, Mark Sofer, *Outlook*, 21 August 2008. According to Israeli ambassador to India Alon Ushpiz, Israeli agricultural services centres and demonstration farms are transferring technologies and techniques for water management and hydroponic farming to Indian agriculturists and improving the lives of people in the countryside, particularly in arid and semi-arid provinces such as Rajasthan where Israeli programmes have helped establish olive and pomegranate orchards. Personal communication.

46. Israel's country page on Facebook is the third most popular in India (after the US and UK). See 'India Likes Israel', Press Release, Embassy of Israel, New Delhi, 14 June 2012.

47. See the interview of Ambassador Ushpiz, *Times of India*, 13 June 2014. Besides technology areas 'ranging from nanotechnology to mega-infrastructure', a former adviser to the Israeli government, Martin Sherman (2014), also singled out 'intelligence and counter-intelligence collaboration; naval cooperation in the Indian Ocean theatre; development of rural India; and sidestepping of EU sanctions' as the areas the two countries can fruitfully engage in.

48. While Israel has used its 'Shavit' rockets to launch TecSAR satellites in sun synchronous orbits, use of the Indian PSLV rocket and launch facilities at Sriharikota in southern India avoids payload and placement limitations (because by launching a satellite from Israel westwards against the rotation of the earth, it is more difficult to reach and place the satellite in its precise orbital space). See 'India launches $200M TECSAR Spy Satellite', *Defense Industry Daily*, 20 April 2009.

49. Personal communication, senior Indian Embassy official, Tel Aviv.

50. Meeting with the author in Tel Aviv, 30 May 2011.

51. Personal communication, senior Indian Embassy official, Tel Aviv. Efraim Inbar and Avilith Singh Nanigthaujam, 'Indo-Israeli Defense Cooperation in the Twenty-First Century', IDC Herzliya, Global Research in International Affairs Center, December 22, 2011; Yiftah S. Shapir, 'Israel's Arms Sales to India', *Strategic Assessment*, November 2009, Volume 12, No. 3, Institute of National Security Studies, Tel Aviv University, Tel Aviv.

52. Itemar Graff, meeting with the author, summer 2011.

53. 'US companies ask for higher FDI cap in defence, insurance', *Indian Express*, 27 June 2014.

54. 'Collateral damage: US asks Israel to cancel Awacs deal with India', *Financial Express*, 1 April 2003.

55. On the power of the American Jewish lobby, see Mearsheimer and Walt (2007).

56. Personal communication, senior Indian official.

57. This was hinted at by Israeli Ambassador to India Mark Sofer in 2008. 'We do have a defense relationship with India, which is no secret,' he said. 'On the other hand, what is a secret is what is the defense relationship [but] the secret part of it will remain secret.' See Mark Sofer's interview, *Outlook*, 21 August 2008.

58. Should there be deterioration in Arab–Israeli relations, a recent study by the Begin-Sadat Center at the Bar-Ilan University concludes, 'India will probably maintain its balancing act between the Arabs and the Israelis' (Feiler 2012: 37).

59. A Washington-based think-tank has demanded that the uranium centrifuge enrichment plant—the Special Material Enrichment Facility—coming up in Chitradurga in Karnataka state to service the expanding *Arihant*-class SSBN fleet be brought under International Atomic Energy Agency safeguards. See Albright and Kelieher-Vergantini (2014).

60. 'Kerry praises Pakistan Army as "a binding force"', *Express Tribune*, 2 December 2014, available at http://tribune.com.pk/story/800543/kerry-praises-pakistan-army-as-a-binding-force/. 'US DSCA Approves Sale of GRC43M Global Response Cutters for $350 Million to Pakistan', *DefenseWorld.net*, 31 October 2014, available at http://www.defenseworld.net/news/11418/US_DSCA_Approves_Sale_Of_GRC43M_Global_Response_Cutters_For__350_Million_To_Pakistan#.VH6vdtLF9iM. These cutters are like the aluminium-hulled Cochin-class fast patrol craft with the Indian Navy, except their range of 4,500 nautical miles is three times that of the Indian vessel (1,500 nautical miles) but more versatile in terms of its armament and capabilities.

61. According to the IPR lawyer and UN Rapporteur on the Right to Health Anand Grover, 'There is no evidence [that higher investment] will happen'. Indeed, he warns that 'if we change our laws to suit external interests [in IT and pharmaceuticals], we could end up destroying our domestic industry.' '"Make in India"', he says, 'should be made in India by Indians for Indians and for the whole of humanity. It should not become Make in India by foreigners, where they take over our industries.' See his interview in *Sunday Times of India*, 30 November 2014. For the US view, see 'US urges India to toughen patent laws to draw investors', *Economic Times*, 25 November 2014.

62. In the mid-1990s, for example, under US pressure, the Boris Yeltsin government cancelled technology transfer of the Glavkomos KVD-1 cryogenic rocket engine that India meant to use for space probes and to hoist satellites into high-earth geosynchronous orbits. Kazakhstan was caused to renege on exporting 'yellow cake' (milled natural uranium) to the Indian

nuclear energy programme. Personal communication, Rajiv Sikri, former ambassador to Kazakhstan.

63. On the occasion of the first Strategic and Economic Dialogue with Beijing, Obama said, 'The relationship between the US and China will shape the 21st century, which makes it as important as any bilateral relationship in the world.... . If we advance [our mutual] interests through cooperation, our people will benefit and the world will be better off—because our ability to partner with each other is a prerequisite for progress on many of the most pressing global challenges.' Quoted in Bush (2011).

64. See Richard D. Fisher, Jr's testimony before the US House Armed Services Subcommittee on Strategic Forces regarding 'China's Future Strategic Nuclear Capabilities', 14 October 2011.

65. Personal communication from the late K. Subrahmanyam, a former civil servant specializing in security and strategic affairs, who was influential in official circles.

66. Personal communication from a senior official involved in pushing the nuclear deal in the George W. Bush administration.

67. This is a role a US diplomat has sketched out for India (see Avery 2012).

68. See *Nonalignment 2.0* and Ashley Tellis's critique of it. A former adviser to the US ambassador in India, Robert Blackwill, who pushed the nuclear deal at both the Washington and Delhi ends, concludes about the semi-official Indian strategy paper that 'the strategic solution to India's predicament cannot consist of resurrecting nonalignment in some new numerical iteration, but rather of India's decision to solder a deeper and closer engagement with the world in general, and with its most capable friends and allies in particular. The alternative [of a nonalignment policy] fails to provide a rational solution to the problems of security competition and economic interdependence' (see Blackwill 2012: 29).

69. Regarding the Indian deterrent having thermonuclear weapons/warheads of questionable quality but highly tested and accurate missiles, see Karnad (2008: Chapter 3).

70. Other than the airlift of small arms and ammunition, there was little other US aid and assistance during the 1962 war with China. In more recent times, according to a personal communication from Brigadier (Retd) Arun Sahgal, former head of Net Assessment, Headquarters, Integrated Defence Staff, the US sanctions in the wake of the 1998 tests grounded the Indian Navy's fleet of Sea King helicopters bought from Britain, because their engines contained some American components. More recently, a dozen or so artillery-spotting Raytheon An/TPQ-37 'Firefinder' radar units procured by the Indian army post-sanctions and after the 1999 Kargil border conflict

with Pakistan through the US Foreign Military Sales route have been non-operational for want of spares, and boast of less than 20 per cent serviceability rate. American government officials, per Sahgal, blame the acquisition cycles not being in sync and fault the Indians for failing to detail in the contract the extent of spares stocks and service support required to keep these radars on-line.

71. Russian president Putin addressing a meeting of the Commission for Military Technology Cooperation with Foreign States in July 2012 stated: 'We also need to make big improvements to our after-sales and maintenance services. This is a very profitable market that we cannot afford to ignore. I am referring to supplies of spare parts and assistance in repairing and upgrading equipment. In this respect, I note the general systemic problem of work with potential customers.' See 'Meeting of the Commission for Military Technology Cooperation with Foreign States', 2 July 2012, available at http://eng.kremlin.ru/news/4121.

72. For a list of advanced technologies not fitted on the Indian C-130J short take-off and landing transport aircraft, for example, see 'No CISMOA? Here's what they're pulling from the Indian C-130J', Livefistdefence.com, 6 October 2010, available at www.livefistdefence.com/2010/10/exclusive-no-cismoa-heres-what-theyre.html.

73. See Michael Froman's interview in *Business Standard*, 15 July 2013.

74. Refer to Froman's testimony to the US Senate Committee on Finance, 1 May 2014, available at http://www.finance.senate.gov/imo/media/doc/Ambassador%20Froman%20-%20Trade%20Agenda%20Hearing%20Testimony%20-%2005012014.pdf. See also Jacob (2014).

75. According to Froman, every billion dollars of export creates 5,400–5,900 jobs in the US. See Froman's Congressional testimony cited in note 59.

76. For a list of systems Indian companies have developed for P-8I, refer to the Brief dated 10 February 2011 by Boeing P-8I Program Manager Leland Wright, who was available at the Indian Air Show, Aero India 2011.

77. Unattributable discussion with the official.

78. Official sources.

79. See reactions to the main blog on P-8I, on 'Without CISMOA, the Indian Navy works the P-8I', Livefistdefence.com, 26 July 2012, available at http://livefist.blogspot.in/2012/07/without-cismoa-indian-navy-works-p-8i.html.

80. 'Hypersonic Brahmos cruise missile to be ready by 2017', *Indian Express*, 28 June 2012. The hypersonic Brahmos will hit with 36 times more kinetic energy than a missile hitting the target at Mach 1 speeds, which even hardened targets will be unable to resist. The US Tomahawk flies at 0.8

Mach. See 'Brahmos Hypersonic Cruise Missile', Brahmos Aerospace, www.brahmos.com/content.php?id=27.

81. DRDO sources.

82. Interview, 6 May 2011.

83. See the record of the hearing on the Pressler Amendment and Pakistan's Nuclear Weapons Program, US Senate Foreign Relations Committee, 31 July 1992, available at www.fas.org/news/pakistan/1992/920731.htm. For Senator Pressler's take on the US government's complicity in nuclearizing Pakistan, see Pressler (1994). Pressler was the US senator after whom the amendment to the US Foreign Aid.

84. Center for Strategic and International Studies, 'Audio: US-India Defense Trade—Opportunities for Deepening the Partnership', Discussion between Amer Latif and Karl Inderfurth, 12 July 2012, available at http://csis.org/multimedia/audio-us-india-defense-trade-opportunities-deepening-partnership-0.

85. Personal communication from Michael Pillsbury Indian Market', *Defense News*, April 2, 2012. Denney (2007) on the staff of Secretary Weinberger.

86. 'Defense industries face $100B less orders', UPI, 13 June 2012, available at http://www.upi.com/Business_News/Security-Industry/2012/06/13/Defense-industries-face-100B-less-orders/45411339619355/.

87. Ashton Carter testifies before the US Senate Foreign Relations Committee on the recent nuclear agreement between the United States and India, 26 April 2006, available at http://www.hks.harvard.edu/news-events/news/testimonies/ashton-carter-testifies-before-the-u.s.-senate-foreign-relations-committee-on-the-recent-nuclear-agreement-between-the-united-states-and-india.

88. Interview, 23 September 2011.

89. Air Chief Marshal Browne, meeting with the author, 24 October 2011.

90. Personal communication from an Indian naval officer who has participated in the annual Indo-US 'Malabar' naval exercises.

91. The US government is reconciled to this problem. Deputy Secretary of Defense Ashton B. Carter said as much during his July 2012 Delhi visit. 'On both sides we need to change, reform, and push ourselves to get to a place where US-India defense relations are limited only by our thinking, not our capacity to cooperate.' See Carter (2012).

92. Interview, 25 March 2011.

93. Robert J. Art (2008: 263) writes that 'compound containment' of China would require 'stalemating' it militarily and 'waging economic denial against it'.

94. The Republican Party is inclined to bring China to book on trade-related issues (see Eldridge 2012; Krishnan 2012; Lal 2011). See also 'Panasonic, Canon shutter China factories amid violent anti-Japan protests', NBC News, 17 September 2012.

95. Testimony before the US House Armed Services Committee, 5 March 2013.

96. At a seminar in Washington, D.C., in November 2011.

97. Wieringa was testifying before the US House Foreign Affairs Sub-committee on the Middle East and South Asia on 16 September 2008, on the sale of the advanced version of the F-16 (Block 52) to Pakistan. Hearing on 'Defeating Al-Qaeda's Air Force: Pakistan's F-16 Program in the Fight against Terrorism', available at http://www.foreignaffairs.house.gov/.

98. 'Defense Ministry clears Rs 3,000 cr deal to acquire 145 Howitzers from US', IANS, *India Today*, 11 May 2012.

99. Major Brian Brobeck, operations officer of the 2nd Engineer Brigade of the US Army Pacific, after a 14-day joint exercise code-named 'Yudh Abhyas' (War Study) held in India in April 2012, said: 'We have much in common, from structure to warfighting ethic, and I wouldn't have thought that before I came here.' See Cowles (2012).

100. Senior naval and other sources.

101. When such cooperation was mooted by a visiting senior US official, the Indian government showed no interest, according to a senior official engaged in the country's cyberwar effort.

102. The left-leaning defence minister A. K. Antony and minister for external affairs S. M. Krishna were the senior ministers in Manmohan Singh's cabinet who opposed closer relations with the US, as told to the author by several senior military officers.

103. Email interview, 4 February 2012.

104. Interview, 13 September 2011.

105. Email correspondence.

106. I thank Sunjoy Joshi, director, Observer Research Foundation, New Delhi, for this insight.

107. 'Pipavav shipyard ties up with French shipbuilder DCNS for technology transfer', *Businessline*, 11 June 2012.

108. As regards the thermonuclear device that fizzled out in 1998, see Karnad (2005b: 412–20).

109. Interview with Dr V. K. Saraswat, head of DRDO.

110. 'India, Russia still brothers in arms', *Asia Times*, 27 October 2007; 'India to develop 25% of fifth generation fighter', *Business Standard*, 16 December 2010; 'India, Russia close to pact on next generation fighter', *Business Standard*, 16 December 2010.

111. See also other writings posted on the author's blog at www.bharat-karnad.com.

112. On COCOM, see Lewis (1990).

113. Senior Indian government official.

114. Interview with Dr V. K. Saraswat.

115. Referring to the British defence firm BAE's push for 49 per cent equity, the British ambassador in India Sir James Bevan said, 'The main benefit [from increased foreign equity in Indian defence ventures] will be to the Indian people because extra investment helps create jobs, greater growth and greater wealth for the country.' See interview with Sir James Bevan, *Sunday Express*, 22 July 2012.

116. Reputed Indian business houses such as Tata and Larsen & Toubro are already well established and increasing their military design and manufacturing capabilities. But there are also new entrants, such as Reliance Industries Ltd, amongst the richest corporations, which is investing over a billion dollars to start up an aerospace division headed by a former Boeing official. See 'RIL lines up billion-$ plans in aerospace biz', *Economic Times*, 27 July 2012b.

117. 'India pitches for Brahmos induction in Russian naval fleet', *Indian Express*, 17 July 2012.

118. '"Make in India" drive to boost mfg [sic]', *Times of India*, 30 August 2014.

119. 'India, US to move beyond buyer-seller ties in defense: PM', *Indian Express*, 2 October 2013.

120. Washington tried to talk up the joint development of the next generation of the Javelin anti-tank missile system as a flagship enterprise, with the extent of the technology transfer element still undecided. The Defence Ministry chose the surer thing, the Israeli Spike missile with total tech transfer in a $525 million deal (Cohen and Reuters 2014).

References

Ahmad, Shamshad. 2012. 'The perversity of extremism', *News*, Islamabad, 25 September.

Ahmed, Khaled. 2014. 'When reality outruns strategy', *Indian Express*, 3 March.

Albright, David, and Serena Kelieher-Vergantini. 2014. 'India's New Uranium Enrichment Plant in Karnataka', Institute for Science and Security, 1 July. Available at http://isis-online.org/isis-reports/detail/indias-new-uranium-enrichment-plant-in-karnataka1/.

Aneja, Atul. 2013. 'Deepening of India-Iran energy ties, a win-win outcome', *Hindu*, 21 August.

Aroor, Shiv. 2010. 'US strips IAF plane', *Mail Today*, 28 October. Available at http://indiatoday.intoday.in/story/us-strips-iaf-plane/1/118036.html.

Art, Robert J. 2008. 'The United States and the Rise of China: Implications for the Long Haul', in *China's Ascent: Power, Security, and the Future of International Politics*, edited by Robert S. Ross and Zhu Feng. Ithaca, NY: Cornell University Press.

Avery, William H. 2012. *China's Nightmare, America's Dream: India as the Next Global Power*. New Delhi: Amaryllis.

Bagchi, Indrani. 2014. 'Perestroika for foreign office: Modi promises to transform how Indian diplomats do their job', *Times of India*, 4 May. Available at http://liveblogs.indiatimes.com/Globespotting/perestroika-for-foreign-office-modi-promises-to-transform-how-indian-diplomats-do-their-job/.

Batabyal, Anindya. 2012. 'Speaking Frankly: India Renews Taiwan Embrace', *Asia Times*, 5 October. Available at http://www.atimes.com/atimes/South_Asia/NJ05Df01.html.

Bhatnagar, Gaurav Vivek. 2014. 'DRDO chief: Cyber threat possible from imported defence systems', *Hindu*, 8 February.

Bhutta, Zafar. 2014. 'Crucial talks on IP project in Tehran today', *Express Tribune*, 28 October.

Blackwill, Robert. 2012. *Nonalignment Redux: The Perils of Old Wine in New Skins*. Washington, D.C.: Carnegie Endowment for International Peace, July.

Boadle, Anthony. 2013. 'Update 1: Brazil launches program to build nuclear submarine in a decade', Reuters, 1 March.

Bremmer, Ian. 2013. 'The under-appreciated tension between China and Brazil', Reuters, 28 May. Available at http://in.reuters.com/article/2013/05/28/column-bremmer-india-china-brazil-idINDEE94R0GT20130528.

Burns, Nicholas. 2014. 'Passage to India', *Foreign Affairs*, September–October.

Bush, Richard, III. 2011. 'The United States and China: A G-2 in the Making?', 11 October. Available at http://www.brookings.edu/research/articles/2011/10/11-china-us-g2-bush.

Byerly, Rebecca. 2012. 'Why India is trying to expand trade with Iran', *Christian Science Monitor*, 29 March. Available at: www.csmonitor.com/World/Asia-South-Central/2012/0329/why-India-is-trying-to-expand-trade-with-Iran.

Carter, Ashton B. 2006. 'America's New Strategic Partner?', *Foreign Affairs*, July/August.

Carter, Ashton B. 2012. 'Towards a Joint Vision for US-India Defense Cooperation', Confederation of Indian Industry, New Delhi, 23 July.

Castle, Colonel Douglas A., and Colonel G. Alexander Crowther. 2006. *Shaping China's Rise through Strategic Friction*. Carlisle Barracks, PA: US Army War College.

Chang, Meg. 2011. 'Taiwan-India relations scale new heights', *Taiwan Today*, 13 October. Available at http://taiwantoday.tw/ct.asp?xItem=17 7919&ctNode=1734.

Chansoria, Monika. 2010. 'India-Iran Defense Cooperation', *Indian Defense Review*, vol. 25, no. 1, 17 February.

Cohen, Gill, and Reuters. 2014. 'India buys $525 m worth of missile from Israel, rejecting the rival US offer', *Haaretz*, 25 October. Available at http://www.haaretz.com/news/diplomacy-defense/1.622677.

Cohen, Stephen P. 2001. *India: Emerging Power*. Washington, D.C.: Brookings Institution.

Conley, Jerome. 2001. *Indo-Russian Military and Nuclear Cooperation: Lessons and Options for U.S. Policy in South Asia*. Lanham, Maryland: Lexington Books.

Cowles, Army Captain Bonnie. 2012. 'Exercise Yudh Abhyas bridges US, Indian army engineers', *US Army Pacific*. Available at http://www.usar-pac.army.mil/ya/112/fullstory.asp?files20120412&id=0.

Denney, Colonel D. Scott. 2007. *US-India Military Relationship: Matching Expectations*. Carlisle Barracks, PA: US Army War College, 14 May.

Dikshit, Sandeep. 2014. 'With sanctions on Iran eased, India to hold dry run in transport corridor', *Hindu*, 26 February.

Ebinger, Charles K. 2011. *Energy and Security in South Asia: Cooperation or Conflict*. Washington, D.C.: The Brookings Institution.

Eldridge, David. 2012. 'Romney rips Obama on China', *Washington Times*, 15 September.

Ezdi, Asif. 2014. 'Course correction', *The News* (Islamabad), 3 March.

Fair, C. Christine. 2007. 'India-Iran Security Ties: Thicker than Oil', *Middle East Review of International Affairs*, vol. 11, no. 1, March.

Feigenbaum, Evan A. 2010. 'India's Rise, America's Interest: The Fate of the US-Indian Partnership', *Foreign Affairs*, March–April. Available at http://www.foreignaffairs.com/articles/65995/evan-a-feigenbaum/indias-rise-americas-interest.

Feiler, Gil. 2012. 'India's Economic Relations with Israel and the Arabs', Mideast Security and Policy Studies no. 96, Begin-Sadat Center for Strategic Studies, Bar-Ilan University, Ramat Gan, July.

Fisher, Richard, Jr. 2012. 'China Counters US Tilt toward Asia', *Aviation Week & Space Technology*, 2 July.

Friedberg, Aaron L. 2011. *A Contest for Supremacy: China, America, and the Struggle for Asia*. New York: W.W. Norton.

Gilboy, George J., and Eric Heginbotham. 2012. *Chinese and Indian Strategic Behavior: Growing Power and Alarm*. New Delhi: Cambridge University Press.

Gladstone, Rick. 2012. 'India explores economic opportunities in Iran, denting Western sanctions plan', *New York Times*, 9 February.

Gordevyava, Mariya. 2013. 'China buys into giant Kazakh oilfield for $6 billion', Reuters, 7 September.

Greenberg, Illan. 2013. 'India and the silk road not taken', *National Interest*, 14 January.

Gupta, Surojit, and Sidhartha. 2014. 'Airbus may partner Tata for manufacturing defence transport aircraft', *Times of India*, 26 October.

Haider, Ejaz. 2014. 'Time for niceties is over', *The News*, Islamabad, 29 January.

Haqqani, Husain. 2013. *Magnificent Delusions: Pakistan, the United States and an Epic History of Misunderstanding*. New York: Public Affairs Books.

Helwig, Holger H. 2006. 'Command Decision Making: Imperial Germany, 1871–1914', in *The Fog of Peace and War Planning: Military and Strategic Planning under Uncertainty*, edited by Talbott C. Imlay and Monica Duffy Toft. Abingdon: Routledge.

Heng He. 2013. 'Ghana gold mines suggest larger crisis for China', GhanaWeb, 12 June. Available at http://www.ghanaweb.com/Ghana HomePage/NewsArchive/artikel.php?ID=276946.

Hille, Kathryn. 2013. 'Beijing and Washington all at sea on naval power', *Financial Times*, 3 June.

Hurst, Cindy A., and Robert Mathers. 2014. 'Strategic Implications of the Afghan Mother Lode and China's Emerging Role', *JFQ (Joint Force Quarterly)*, no. 72, first quarter.

Inbar, Efraim. 2004. 'Indian-Israeli Entente', *Orbis*, Winter.

Islam, Md Rizwanul. 2012. *Economic Integration in South Asia: Charting a Legal Roadmap*. Leiden: Brill.

Iyengar, P. K., A. N. Prasad, A. Gopalakrishnan, and Bharat Karnad. 2009. *Strategic Sellout: Indian-US Nuclear Deal*. New Delhi: Pentagon Press.

Jacob, Jayanth. 2012a. 'India seeks better physical links with Central Asia', *Hindustan Times*, 4 July.

———. 2012b. 'Hard bargain on N-liability clause', *Hindustan Times*, 4 December.

———. 2014. 'America pushes for overhaul in India's offset policy for defence', *Hindustan Times*, 5 December.

Jacques, Martin. 2009. *When China Rules the World*. New York: Penguin.

Jansson, Johanna, Christopher Burke, and Wenran Jiang. 2009. 'Chinese Companies in the Extractive Industries of Gabon and DRC: Perception of Transparency', Center for Chinese Studies, University of Stellenbosch, August. Available at http://www.congomines.org/wp-content/uploads/2011/10/JohannaJansson-CCS-2010-ChineseCompaniesExtractiveIndustriesGabonAndDRC.pdf.

Joshi, Nirmala, ed. 2010. *Reconnecting India and Central Asia: Emerging Security and Economic Dimensions*. Washington, D.C.: Central Asia Caucasus & Silk Road Program, SAIS, Johns Hopkins University.

Kahn, Jeremy. 2008. 'Critics slam India-Israel arms trade', *JTA Jewish News Service*, 25 February.

Karnad, Bharat. 1994. 'India's Weak Geopolitics and What To Do About It', in *Future Imperiled: India's Security in the 1990s and Beyond*, edited by Bharat Karnad. New Delhi: Viking, Penguin India, pp. 34–41.

———. 1996. 'Key to Peace in South Asia: Fostering "Social Links" between the Armies of India and Pakistan', *The Round Table: The Commonwealth Journal of International Affairs*, no. 338, April.

———. 2005a. 'South Asia: The Irrelevance of Classical Nuclear Deterrence Theory', *India Review*, vol. 4, no. 2, April.

———. 2005b [First Edition 2002]. *Nuclear Weapons and Indian Security: The Realist Foundations of Strategy*, 2nd edition. New Delhi: Macmillan India.

———. 2008. *India's Nuclear Policy*. Westport, CN, and London: Praeger Security International.

———. 2010. 'The "Eternal Triangle"—India, Russia, China: A Brief History of the Origins of the Concept and Its Irrelevance in the 21st Century', *Synergy: Journal of the Center for Joint Warfare Studies*, July.

———. 2012a. 'US wrong on India's Iran policy', *Diplomat*, 19 March. Available at http://the-diplomat.com/2012/03/19/u-s-wrong-on-india%E280%99s-iran-policy/.

———. 2012b. 'Art of deal-making', *Asian Age*, 2 February. Available at www.asianage.com/columnists/art-deal-making-480.

———. 2013a. 'Stop wasteful military deals', *New Indian Express*, 1 November.

———. 2013b. 'Scrap Rafale, Viva Tejas!', *Asian Age*, 11 April.

———. 2014. 'Indo-Russian ties at inflection point', *New Indian Express*, 11 December.

Kashin, Vasily. 2012. 'All systems go for exports', 29 February. Available at http://rbth.asia/articles/2012/02/29/all_systems_go_for_exports_15585.html.

Kazim, Hasnain. 2012. 'German arms firms seek cooperation with India', *Spiegel Online*, 18 July.

Khalilzad, Zalmay. 2014. 'Why Afghanistan courts China', *New York Times*, 3 November.

Kher, Priyanka. 2012. 'Political Economy of Regional Integration in South Asia', UNCTAD, October. Available at http://unctad.org/en/PublicationsLibrary/ecidc2013misc1_bp5.pdf.

Kissinger, Henry. 2011. *On China*. London: Allen Lane.

Kramer, Andrew E. 2012. 'Russia sending missile systems to shield Syria', *New York Times*, 16 June.

Krishnan, Ananth. 2012. 'Amid strains, India, China push trade ties', *Hindu*, 27 May.

Kumaraswamy, P. R. 2010. *India's Israel Policy*. New York: Columbia University Press.

Kydd, Andrew H. 2005. *Trust and Mistrust in International Relations*. Princeton, NJ: Princeton University Press.

Lal, Neeta. 2011. 'India's trade balance problem with China', *Asia Sentinel*, 6 September.

Lamont, James, and James Boxell. 2012. 'A dogfight over Delhi', *Financial Times*, 7 February.

Landler, Mark. 2012. 'Influx of heavy arms pushes Syria toward civil war', *New York Times*, 13 June.

Latif, S. Amer, and Ambassador Karl F. Inderfurth. 2012. 'US-India Defense Trade: Opportunities for Deepening the Partnership', *US-India Insight*, vol. 2, no. 7, July, Center for Strategic and International Studies, Washington, D.C.

Lebow, Richard Ned. 2013. 'The Role of Trust in International Relations', *Global Asia*, vol. 8, no. 3. Available at www.globalasia.org/Issue/ArticleDetail/460/The-Role-of-Trust-in-International-Relations.html.

Lewis, Major Rand C. 1990. 'COCOM: An International Attempt to Control Technology', 26 June. Available at www.dtic.mil/cgi-bin/GetTRdoc?AD=ADA497085.

Lynch, Colum, and Liz Sly. 2012. 'Clinton accuses Russia of selling attack helicopters to Syria', *Washington Post*, 12 June.

Martina, Michael. 2014. 'China says Afghanistan president vows to help China fight militants', *Reuters*, 29 October. Available at: http://www.reuters.com/article/2014/10/29/us-china-afghanistan-idUSKBN0IH1D420141029.

Mathieu, Charlotte. 2008. *Assessing Russia's Space Cooperation with China and India: Opportunities and Challenges for Europe*. Vienna: European Space Policy Institute, 12 June.

McIntyre, Douglas A., and Samuel Weigley. 2012. 'States that have lost the most jobs to China', NBC News, 17 September.

McKinsey & Company. 2014. 'Joining Hands to Unlock Africa's Potential: A New Indian Industry-Led Approach to Africa', McKinsey Asia Center, March.

MEA (Ministry of External Affairs). 2014. 'India-Russia Relations', MEA, Government of India, January. Available at http://www.mea.gov.in/Portal/ForeignRelation/Russia_January_2014.pdf.

Mead, Walter. 2012. 'TAPI pipeline adds to Iran's economic woes', 17 May. Available at http://blogs.the-american-interest.com/.

Mearsheimer, John J., and Stephen M. Walt. 2007. *Israel Lobby and US Foreign Policy*. London: Penguin Books.

Menon, Shivshankar. 2013. 'India and the USA', Speech delivered at Aspen Institute India, New Delhi, 20 September.

Mohan, Vishwa. 2013. 'Israel to expand agri footprint in India by '15', *Times of India*, 10 October.

Nasr, Vali. 2006. 'When the Shiites Rise', *Foreign Affairs*, July–August.

Neuman, Craig H., II. 2012. 'Forging an Indian Partnership', *Strategic Studies Quarterly*, Summer, pp. 129–32.

Ningthoujam, Alvite Singh. 2013. 'Return of Israel's arms sales diplomacy?', *Jerusalem Post*, 24 June. Available at http://www.jpost.com/Opinion/Op-Ed-Contributors/Return-of-Israels-arms-sales-diplomacy-317587.

Panetta, Leon E. 2012. 'Partners in the 21st Century', Speech delivered at the Institute for Defense Studies and Analyses, New Delhi, 6 June.

Parashar, Sachin. 2014. 'Taiwan vice-president to land in Delhi, China likely to bristle', *Times of India*, 27 April.

Parthasarathi, Ashok. 2014. 'Some myths about the Indian military-industrial complex', *Business Standard*, 27 February.

Perlez, Jane. 2012. 'China shows interest in Afghan security, fearing Taliban would help separatists', *New York Times*, 8 June.

Pressler, Larry. 1994. 'The Restraint of Fury: US Non-Proliferation', in *Future Imperiled: India's Security in the 1990s and Beyond*, edited by Bharat Karnad. New Delhi: Viking Penguin India.

Radyuhin, Vladimir. 2014. 'Putin thanks India for its stand on Ukraine', *Hindu*, 18 March.

Ranjan, Amitav. 2013. 'New Tehran regime scraps oil, gas concessions to India', *Indian Express*, 18 September.

Roy, Meena Singh. 2013. 'India's "Connect Central Asia" Policy: Building Cooperative Partnership', *Indian Foreign Affairs Journal*, vol. 8, no. 3, July–September.

Roy, Shubhajit. 2013. 'India a foreign policy priority, says Rouhani', *Indian Express*, 11 July.

Rudenko, Yelena I. 2014. 'India, Kazakhstan, and the Uranium: The Issues of Nuclear Cooperation', *Dialogue Quarterly*, vol. 15, no. 3, January–March.

Rudolph, Lloyd I., and Susanne Hoeber Rudolph. 2006. 'The Making of US Foreign Policy for South Asia: Offshore Balancing in Historical Perspective', *Economic and Political Weekly*, 25 February. Available at http://political-science.uchicago.edu/faculty/rudolphs/us-asia.pdf.

Sasi, Anil. 2012. 'Iran keen to step up India engagement beyond oil', *Indian Express*, 25 June.

Sawant, Gaurav C. 2013. 'Afghanistan seeks tanks, field artillery and attack helicopters from India', *India Today*, 20 November. Available at http://indiatoday.intoday.in/articlePrint.jsp?aid=325670.

Schaffer, Teresita C., and Vibhuti Hate. 2007. 'India's "Look West" Policy: Why Central Asia Matters', *South Asia Monitor*, no. 110, Center for Strategic and International Studies, 3 September.

Sengupta, Arghya. 2011. 'Liability rules leaves very little recourse', *Hindu*, 1 December.

Shanbhag, Raju. n.d. 'Drug Patents—India, US on collision course', *Aseema*. www.aseema.net.in/drug-patents-india-us-on-collision-course/.

Shapiro, Andrew J. 2011a. 'Remarks to the Defense Trade Advisory Group', US Department of State, Washington, D.C., 9 November. Available at www.state.gov/t/pm/rls/rm/176925.htm.

———. 2011b. 'Essential Role of US Security Assistance in Addressing Today's Challenges and Building New Partnerships', Remarks at the Center for New American Security, Washington, D.C., 27 September. Available at at www.state.gov/t/pm/rls/rm/174122.htm.

———. 2012. 'Talks with India and Bangladesh', Carnegie Endowment Roundtable, 24 April. Available at: www.state.gov/t/pm/rls/rm/188522.htm.

Sherman, Martin. 2014. 'From the world's largest democracy to its most beleaguered', *Indian Express*, 13 June 2014.

Shukla, Ajai. 2010. 'Lockheed offsets mock MoD norms', *Business Standard*, 9 December.

Sinha, Rakesh. 2014. 'Let us seal free trade pact, Manmohan tells regional club', *Indian Express*, 5 March.

Sloman, Mark. 2011. 'Israel-India Cooperation in Agriculture and Water', *The Israel Project*. Available at www.theisraelproject.org/.

Srivastava, Shruti. 2014. 'Pakistan asks India for sweetener before it grants NDMA', *Indian Express*, 20 February.

Stakelbeck, Frederick W., Jr. 2005. 'China's Manifest Destiny', *American Thinker*, 1 June. Available at http://www.americanthinker.com/articles/2005/06/chinas_manifest_destiny.html.

Starr, Frank. Preface, in Joshi, Nirmala (Ed). 2010. *Reconnecting India and Central Asia: Emerging Security and Economic Dimensions* http://www.silkroadstudies.org/resources/pdf/Monographs/2010_03_MONO_Joshi_India-Central-Asia.pdf.

Sumsky, Victor, and Evgeny Kanaev. 2012. 'Russia's Arms Boom and Changing Priorities: Where Does Asia Stand?', *Global Asia*, vol. 7, no. 2, Summer.

Swami, Praveen. 2014. 'Upset with delay, Kabul shelves request for arms aid from Delhi', *Indian Express*, 30 October.

Tellis, Ashley J. 2014. 'Getting India-US ties back on track', *India Today*, 21 April.

Trenin, Dmitri. 2012. *True Partners? How Russia and China See Each Other*. London: Center for European Reform.

Ullekh, N. P. 2013. 'Gulf money fueling Muslim extremism in Kerala', *Economic Times*, 3 July.

Upadhyay, Vidhi, and Atul Chandra. 2010. 'Defense on the Platter', *Force*, November.

US DOD (Department of Defense). 2012. 'Sustaining US Global Leadership: Priorities for 21st Century Defense', January. Available at www.defense.gov/news/Defense_Strategic_Guidance.pdf.

Vickery, Raymond E. 2011. *The Eagle and the Elephant: Strategic Aspects of US-India Economic Relations*. New Delhi: Oxford University Press.

Williamson, John. 2006. 'The Rise of the Indian Economy', *American Diplomacy*, May. Available at http://www.unc.edu/depts/diplomat/item/2006/0406/will/williamson_india.html.

Yadav, Manmohan. 2011. 'Indian GPS: Indian Regional Navigational Satellite System (IRNSS)', 24 September. Available at www.indiandefence.com.

Yang Nieu-dzu. 2011. 'Taiwan's Defense and Strategy', *India Strategic*, January. Available at http://www.indiastrategic.in/topstories867.htm.

4

Hard Power and the Deficit of Strategic Imagination

The jacket cover of a recent book on Chinese and Indian strategic behaviour featured two photographs. The top panel showed fierce-looking, heftily moustachioed Indian troops in turbaned finery with assault rifles at the hip sitting astride colourfully caparisoned camels, and the bottom panel a line of marching Chinese sailors in smart naval whites framed by red flags. The impression created was of an exotic, somewhat antique Indian military and modern, professional Chinese armed forces; the subliminal message was: pomp and pageantry are no match for cool proficiency (See the jacket of Gilboy and Heginbotham 2012).

Two things are wrong with this impression. First, the camel-mounted troops are part of the Home Ministry–controlled paramilitary Border Security Force, not so identified in the photograph. Its members are not as nattily accoutred when patrolling the international boundary separating India and Pakistan in the Thar Desert. And second, the Indian armed forces are possibly the most battle-hardened and operationally tested of all the militaries (including the PLA) in Asia. No Asian army has been as continuously blooded in live-fire situations for as long. Engaged in virtually non-stop counter-insurgency operations in the forested hills of the Indian north-east from 1948, a year after independence, and in the contested Kashmir province in a similar role since 1989, it has also acquired unparalleled competence in jungle warfare, anti-guerrilla missions, and in regular warfare at very high altitudes (with Indian Army encampments at altitudes of 18,000–21,000 feet on the Siachen Glacier). Moreover, a nearly 5,000-kilometre-long ceasefire line separates India and China in the Himalayas, and India and Pakistan in the disputed Jammu and Kashmir, 45 per cent of which province is controlled by India, 35 per cent by Pakistan, and 20 per cent by China, owing to the Chinese forcefully annexing part of Indian Aksai Chin in the 1950s, and to Pakistan ceding the Shaksgam Valley to China as per the 1963 agreement. Hence, while India sees the ceasefire line with China as being 3,488 kilometres long, Beijing thinks it is only around 2,000 kilometres (Ramachandran 2011). The entire ceasefire line is a live border rife with artillery duels, exchange of small arms fire, intimidatory moves and counter-moves, and infiltration of hostile jihadi fighters from the Pakistan side, and with incursions by armed PLA units, requiring the Indian Army to be in operational readiness at all times. With four controlled fights with Pakistan under its belt—in 1947–1948 (Kashmir), 1965, 1971 (Bangladesh), and 1991, the last a conflict in the Kargil sector of Kashmir—and notwithstanding the political and milieu-related constraints (outlined in the previous chapter, and to be elucidated further later in this chapter) that permit only limited counter-force engagements in sparsely inhabited areas, the army has considerable experience in plains and desert warfare, and, as proved in Bangladesh, in riverine territory as well.[1] The one military failure in the short conflict with China in 1962—when just one-and-a-half divisions actually went into action—was, in the size of the forces committed, even less of a 'war' than the hostilities with Pakistan, except that it left a bitter residue, and fired up an enduring animus. In its wake, the army beefed up to a point where, 50 years later, a repeat of the earlier fiasco in the mountains is unthinkable.[2] Indeed, in a recent ranking of military capabilities of nations, involving complex variables, the Indian military was rated the fourth most powerful in the world after the US, Russian, and Chinese armed services, and ahead of its British, French, and German counterparts (Jones 2013).

But, to return to the book jacket, in a deeper sense, the implied differential between the two militaries is more apt as regards their transformative ability and the state's appreciation and use of its hard power capability. The Indian armed forces no longer suffer from resource constraints.[3] As former NSA Shivshankar Menon clarified in another context, the problem is 'not resources; resource scarcity is gone. It's the will.' But political will is part of the software package along with vision, policy, strategy, plans, posture, and generally the thinking about military power animating national security and foreign policies, where India is grossly deficient. But because political will can be bent to serve any policy thrust, when the Congress Party returned to power in 2004, rather than militarily beefing up against the country's chief adversary, it sought to contest the shared periphery with China by finding 'a new equilibrium', 'building mutual stakes', and avoiding 'zero-sum outcomes that traditional geopolitics foresee'.[4] Except, New Delhi seemed not to care that there never is a power equilibrium or balance that the more powerful state does not try and twist in its favour.[5] In relation to the resource-rich and amply strategic-minded China, India will always find itself at a disadvantage unless it counters with imaginative visioning and an asymmetric strategy, which last is China's forte (Horta 2013). For instance, an Indian asymmetric strategy featuring light offensive mountain forces able to take an attack to PLA units on the high-altitude Tibetan Plateau, coupled with the emplacement of Atomic Demolition Munitions (ADMs) along likely ingress routes through valleys in the Himalayan Range, will, on the one hand, confront the PLA entrenched in strength in Tibet with a mobile attacking force capable of mayhem and, on the other hand, kill off the Chinese urge for a quick land grab beyond the watershed (more on the ADM option in the next chapter). The Manmohan Singh government's 'don't rock the boat' attitude to China, however, translated into a security policy overdosed with caution, which the NSA elaborated as being purely defensive. 'Defense becomes just that, defense not offense', he declared, 'unless offense is necessary for deterrence or to protect India's ability to continue its own [economic] transformation.' He did not say what the tipping point might be for the country to go on the offensive, in which case could the necessary fighting assets and capability be obtained and plans changed overnight? If not, then obviously it is a contingency the country needs to gear up for. Failure to do so will mean another debacle occasioned by a Chinese military gambit being met by a predictably defensive Indian reaction which, because it has been anticipated by the PLA, will be countered by overwhelming force. The Indian Army's long-standing defensive stance seems geared to avoiding war at all costs, rather than advancing India's security interests. It took the 1962 conflict with China to show up India's complete lack of military preparedness. It was only thereafter that the mountain divisions were raised on a war footing, which took 15 years to equip, train, and field. In a milieu of competitive-cum-cooperative relationships in the twenty-first century, however, Shivshankar Menon was convinced that a carefully crafted defensive strategy, minus any offensive mountain warfare capability, will succeed in not creating 'self-fulfilling prophesies of conflict with powerful neighbours, like China'.[6] Apparently, the Manmohan Singh government failed to take Nehru's observation that the 1962 military defeat was 'a permanent piece of education' to heart (quoted in Raghavan 2014). This chapter deals with the lack of strategic imagination to tackle the main threat posed by China, which, it is argued, has hampered India's exercise of power and influence even within the limited geographic ambit of the IOR.

Wrongly Weighted Military Orientation

The 2010 Strategic Directive issued by the government to the Indian armed forces outlined a dissuasive capability against China, while the army's sword arm—the three strike corps (comprising armoured and mechanized forces)—were poised for use in the desert and semi-desert areas against the far smaller, much weaker, Pakistan. This was justified by Menon as 'the force strength to deal at the tactical and operational levels to maintain our dominance. I am not going to throw this away for some future long-term issue,' he said, and added:

> There's [an] issue here about … spending all [our] monies against the larger, long-term threat. The fundamental issue here is that the balance is relatively stable with China at the strategic level. It doesn't look like [we] are going to have immediate trouble with the Chinese… . We can't afford to end up in the situation where very great powers have before, where they prepare for one thing, but they are so rich and so powerful they can cope with other things. We don't have that luxury.

Perhaps worried that his justification for the Pakistan-weighted posture was sending the wrong signals about insufficient attention being paid to the danger from China, Menon urged that the country's strategy not be inferred from the pattern of force deployments. 'Deployment', he asserted, 'is just deployment, it is what happens on the ground.... Do not confuse deployment with strategy.' So, what is India's strategy? 'Why should we articulate it, tell our adversaries what we think, what's the advantage, what's the point of it?'[7] This is specious reasoning. First, because with the rapid growth of the Pakistani nuclear arsenal, the strategic situation with Pakistan too has become meta-stable; and second, because the government's reluctance to sketch out the strategy may hide the fact, if not of its absence in terms of being well thought out, then of its being ad hoc to match the ad hoc manner in which the rest of the Indian governmental system operates. Justifications are alighted on *ex post facto*, with decisions made as situations unfold. 'The lack of vision or strategy document [to get everybody on the same page] means that we do not know what we want and no one knows what's right,' said former Indian Air Force chief, Air Chief Marshal S. Krishnaswamy (Retd). 'So, on the same subject, different official delegations visiting foreign countries have different messages, say different things. Moreover, because of the sheer indiscipline in government, the [bureaucratic] underlings have the tendency to talk of the [political] boss as an idiot, an ass, and to push their own agendas, rather than a single official line.'[8]

In this environment, it is natural for each armed service to self-servingly define its own goals, priorities, and requirements and to act as per its own preferences. Without the will to change the existing system, and the non-articulation by the government of a strategic vision or of national interests, strategy often amounts to sticking with past policies and the unchanging and apparently unchangeable processes of policy-making rather than being concerned about outcomes. It also confirms what is sought to be conveyed in this book—the absence of any real conviction of those at the helm that India can make it as a great power. Policy-making is thus reduced to doing just enough to obviate an immediate crisis or system breakdown, and, should things go wrong, to resort to *jugaad* (improvisation). 'We [in the military] have learned', Krishnaswamy said, 'to live in this jugaad world but it is an expensive way of looking after the country's interests.'[9]

Reduced to its working principles, the prevailing national security non-strategy seemingly requires of India—constituting 72 per cent

244 | *Why India is Not a Great Power (Yet)*

of South Asia's land mass, 76 per cent of the population, and 76 per cent of the national income of the region—to militarily dominate Pakistan, and merely hold off China (Karnad 2005: 563). At the same time, the widening strategic nuclear and conventional military gaps with the PLA are downplayed, notwithstanding the Chinese economy being three times as large as the Indian, its defence spending thrice as large, and its pace of military transformation into fourth- and fifth-generation warfare such as to worry even the US.[10] Making a decent effort of taking on China is an expensive proposition, which the Indian government believes will entail diversion of funds from programmes for social welfare and economic growth. 'We need at least 15 more years of 9–10 per cent growth if we are to abolish the mass poverty which still afflicts us,' explained Shivshankar Menon.[11] 'So, while India is already a major economy in terms of mass and ability to influence prices and supply and demand in certain markets, it [is] still a country of poor people with overwhelming domestic priorities for an extended period of time.' By way of fiscal prudence, any heightened threat from China was sought to be dealt with by the Congress regime by relying on a concert of major powers and regional states. However, Menon also explained why such a policy would not work. 'Where the balance of power between [the US and China] is more even than it has been in a long time, local powers can … make a difference at the margin, short of creating outcomes themselves. The Indian difficulty is that we are in the midst of the most crowded balances where changes are the greatest and most rapid.'[12] What he probably meant to say was that the system of complex balancing could break down at any time, leaving India to fend for itself. What he did not say is that India would have been able to impose unacceptable costs on China in case of hostilities, had the existing policy been configured specifically to neutralize China which, *en passant*, would have brushed off any conceivable threat from Pakistan. Instead, India, after a decade of doing little that was new, has military capabilities to restrain Pakistan but not hold off China in a scaled-up conflict the PLA might prosecute. Perhaps mindful of this capability deficit, New Delhi has sought to compensate with appropriate diplomacy to keep Beijing mollified. In the event, securing the military means for counter-attacking the PLA is considered as overreach, and as unreasonably stretching Indian ambition and resources.[13] Such thinking represents an India that is unwilling to come out of its shell. Other than conceding Chinese military superiority and India's unwillingness to contest it, such a policy has other costs. Not rejecting outright Chinese proposals such as the 'maritime silk route' that could eventuate in an encirclement of India, and trying too hard to appear conciliatory or avoid provoking China, signals strategic diffidence that may lead potential partners in the IOR and the extended Asian littoral to believe that India is not up to the job of 'net security provider'.[14] The reluctance to tangle with its main rival, however, meshes with New Delhi's strategic slant of lying low and achieving little that has long made India a classic underachiever among potential great powers (Karnad 2005).

For a country India's size and potential, it is surprising that its long history of subjugation has not been connected in political circles to the absence of a muscular armed services, or driven the nation to acquire what Jaswant Singh, minister for external affairs and, for a time, defence minister in the first BJP government, called 'surplus military power'. This shortage has led, he said, to the reduction of the Indian 'philosophy of national security to being merely an episodic, reactive military function' (J. Singh 2013). Remarkably, many of the policy-makers who held sway during Manmohan Singh's decade in power suspected that the hullaballoo about 'India as a great power' was a ruse by motivated Western powers to nudge New Delhi into becoming more active in pushing their agenda, which would create trouble for India. 'Today we hear much loose talk about India as a potential superpower', said Shivshankar Menon, 'and are encouraged by international partners to be a responsible power, whatever that may be. What it seems to mean to each of them is that we should do what they would like us to do! Objectively speaking, ... India ... [will] increasingly integrate into the world ... [and] the world [will move] towards a more even distribution of power'.[15] In other words, the fact that the United States, Japan, ASEAN, and other states have urged India to play a larger, more active military role in Asia ought, by this reckoning, to be doubted because such a role would also benefit these other countries. Apparently this was good enough reason to shy away from that role altogether, even though it would primarily help Indian security and allow the country go up in the world. Implicit in such thinking are the questionable beliefs that:

(*a*) nations can be divorced from their self-interest; and (*b*) in order not to collaterally serve the interests of any foreign countries, it is better for India to do nothing that other countries would like India to do, and to wait for power to devolve to it as a result of a general diffusion of international power under way in an emerging multipolar system.

A less exacting policy mindset is hard to conceive, especially as such thinking has held India back, representing as it does a lazy nation's path to a semblance of power, one that requires no real effort except to keep out of trouble. It is another version of great power as entitlement (discussed in the first chapter) shared by the policy elite, a status that will come to India which needs only to stand and wait. Such a route to great power is the proverbial fool's gold, chimerical stuff, and does not account for the fundamental facts of international affairs, namely, that in a system of sovereign states, power differentials especially in terms of economic and military power matter; that hard power rates higher than soft power, which is to say that the military card trumps the economic card every time; and that these differentials cannot be wished away. In any case, were a world to obtain that is flat in terms of power distribution, then one may find that because every country is as powerful as every other country, no country is a great power.

India's Relative Military Standing

The Indian Army, second largest in the world, is deployed in the most diverse terrains. The widely varying operational milieus have shaped versatile land forces that also include an army marine brigade for expeditionary duties with the Army's Southern Command, an amphibious brigade with the Integrated Andaman Command for littoral warfare, an airborne paratroops brigade, some nine battalions of Special Forces useable in distant operations, the Siachen Brigade on the glacier in the Karakoram Range—perhaps the most dangerous and physically demanding battlefield site with manned posts at altitudes as high as 21,000 feet—and on the Kargil peaks at up to 18,000 feet, and some 11-odd army divisions stationed on the Himalayan ridges and watershed along the undemarcated border with Tibet facing two PLA group-armies billeted on the plateau. The Indian Army's aptitude in mountain and high-altitude warfare, in the event, is unparalleled. But owing to its mainly territorial defence orientation, and hence its smaller operational compass post-1947 and its relatively low-technology profile, the history of the Indian Army in its colonial avatar as the force that secured the Raj, the Asiatic empire that made Britain great, kept peace, and maintained international order—the Pax Britannica of the nineteenth and early twentieth centuries—is rarely remembered.[16] The much diminished present-day Indian Army has been judged by US Army stalwarts, on the basis of numerous professional interactions, as 'not yet ready for complex joint exercises or for exploring, new strategic roles' (quoted in Neuman 2012).

The IAF is the fourth largest in the world, with a growing inventory of advanced aircraft—the upgraded Anglo-French Jaguar for low-level strike, MiG-29 for offensive air defence, the multi-role French Mirage 2000H (being upgraded with avionics, structural retrofitments, and weapons load to Mirage 2000-5 standard), the Russian Su-30 MKI, and four squadrons of the souped-up variant, the 'super Sukhois'. Under possible acquisition are the French Rafale to meet IAF's MMRCA needs, the Russian FGFA—the modified Su-50 PAK AF—and the bulk air defence aircraft undergoing test trials, the indigenous Tejas light combat aircraft (LCA) outfitted with 4.5 generation avionics, including an AESA radar under development, replacing the MiG-21 in the short-range air defence role. Besides the 'force extenders'—aerial tankers and AWACS, the IAF also operates long-range heavy-lift aircraft, and is hailed as 'a full spectrum combat air arm with a precision conventional strike capability' by Benjamin S. Lambeth (2012: 3), an American combat aviation expert. The Indian Navy, the seventh largest and rated NATO standard, is the only Asian maritime force with extensive experience of operating aircraft carriers in blue water and, other than PLAN, is the only one to operate a nuclear-powered ballistic missile-firing submarine (SSBN). The indigenous Arihant-class is undergoing sea trials and is expected to enter fleet service by 2015–16. The navy also possesses, since its induction into service in April 2012, the Akula-II class-nuclear-powered hunter-killer submarine (SSN) *INS* Chakra, and a second SSN (the Iribis) upgraded to Akula-III standard soon to be procured on lease from Russia. The Indian military may be unimaginatively used by the Indian government (as this chapter will show), but it is not a force to be trifled with.

A thumbnail comparison: the 2012 Annual US Department of Defense report on Chinese military power noted that the PLA, which last fought a (land) war in 1979 against Vietnam and then did not fare too well, 'remains challenged by a lack of combat experience'.[17] The Chinese navy (PLAN) is still only a green-water force with aircraft carrier pretensions; its fleet of strategic nuclear submarines is only just beginning to venture far from home ports.[18] And the PLA Air Force (PLAAF) is a mostly unknown commodity unveiling ever newer aircraft (such as the J-21), but new aircraft do not alone an effective air force make (Hardy 2012). This is not to underestimate the Chinese armed services, but to inject some perspective on the quality and operational effectiveness of the forces China can, in fact, field. However, its successful perception management has guaranteed that China will be taken at its word and be seen as a great, big, thrusting military power intent on recovering land and sea territories based on remote historical claims and hazy notions about an imperial Chinese expanse. Thus, if the Indian military appears less than what it can do, the imposing but largely untested contemporary Chinese armed forces are blown up—by dint of self-advertisement and alarmist Western commentaries—to be, perhaps, more than what they probably can achieve in war.

Inflated or not, the China threat looms in the calculations of Asian countries because of the iron will propelling the implementation of expansive geo-strategic designs, laced with the traditional Chinese stratagem of projecting menace to cow down smaller, weaker states in contiguous areas, and induce caution in powerful adversaries (Sawyer 2006: 1, 33–4). A reputation for ruthlessness is carefully cultivated to shield military weakness.[19] The violent annexation of Tibet in 1949 and the sustained oppression of the Tibetan people since then; the occupation of Mischief Reef and Sansha Island in the Paracel archipelago under Philippine control, and of islands in the Spratly chain in the South China Sea claimed by Vietnam; the violent squelching of unrest in Xinjiang, of religious sects (Falun Gong), the 1989 political unrest in Tiananmen Square, innumerable labour demonstrations in the wealthy eastern coastal belt, and farmer protests in the hinterland over the years of the country's 'peaceful rise'; the aggressive installing of oil rigs in disputed waters in the South China Sea; and the provocative actions in the waters off the

Senkaku/Diaoyu Islands—these reinforce the scary views of China (Triplett 2012). Growing discontent at home and differences with adjoining states over sea and land borders have, however, led to an 'overstretching' of its armed strength (Scobell and Nathan 2012).

India's main problem is not so much the availability of resources or military wherewithal, and even less the quality and competence of its armed forces. Rather, it is the absence of a grand strategic design and an infirm political will of the government, coupled with an apparent inability to think straight and strategic, even less to imagine an alternate strategic universe where Indian national interests that the country can work to realize are paramount. This is the consequence of a lack of interest of the political class in foreign and military affairs. 'Politicians are too concerned with constituency matters and internal-party and intra-government politicking to be interested in the external world, or want to learn about military and national security issues,' confessed M. M. Pallam Raju, until October 2012 the junior minister for defence in the Congress Party government and among the more conscientious political leaders. 'I had to learn about the ministerial domain only after becoming a minister, when earlier I had no inkling about anything related to defence and military related stuff. This is truer of younger ministers. The older stalwarts don't care if they don't know.'[20] With little political interest, no one minds that a document stating a strategic vision for the country is missing, or that there are no formal documents to detail strategy that all agencies and arms of government can access and conform to when implementing policies and actions. The main reason for this state of affairs is the fear of not being able to obtain a consensus. It has led, for instance, to national interests remaining undefined and uncategorized, leave alone graded. As a result, policy aims and objectives are vague and hence able to fit any policy.

With a disinterested government issuing generalized directives, the three armed services and the coast guard are left to carry on, on their own, each of them prioritizing threats, deciding on strategies, and securing the forces and the means in the way they believe best serves the national interest. According to Admiral Arun Prakash (Retd), the services thus end up 'extemporiz[ing] in order to undertake planning in a strategic void.'[21] It resembles the way foreign policy has so far been made.[22] Immediate requirements therefore dominate; strategic, long-term needs such as overseas bases and an expansive Indian sphere of influence and responsibility are only unclearly discerned. In practice, the Indian government's time is monopolized, former foreign secretary Shyam Saran revealed to a tri-service audience in Port Blair, at the Headquarters of the Integrated Andaman Command, in maintaining equipoise in its relations with the United States and China, taking care not to tilt to one or the other side, but beavering away, as inconspicuously as possible, at expanding 'our own strategic space', which pertains, he helpfully explained, less to geography than increasing 'India's strategic autonomy' and the multiplicity of 'options' for the 'national leadership'. Generating options would, however, preclude, he said, 'the worst situation one could face' of being 'left with a binary choice—either capitulation or a recourse to arms'. He further explained that

> having options is as important in dealing with countries we consider friends, as with countries whom we consider not so friendly. In dealing with either type of country having fewer options may mean that the former takes you for granted and squeezes you, confident that you have no or few alternatives; the latter, to take the worst case, may consider a hostile act, military or otherwise, a low risk, low-cost means of adding to its own strategic space at your cost.

But, Saran qualified that this accretion in the country's 'strategic space' is sought without offering provocation for fear that 'nervous articulations of a threat can trigger mirror-image and hostile perceptions on the other side'.[23] One wonders what the military officers made of this overly nuanced view of Indian strategy that in, plain-speak, amounts to justifying India's policy of doing the minimum that it can get away with to stay relevant. In effect, Saran only encapsulated the passive-reactive-defensive policies that have long been an Indian staple. China, for good reason, applauded this timid strategy.[24]

The trouble is that trying to secure advantage by maintaining a power balance and furthering strategic autonomy is not to articulate a great power vision; even less is it to map out a strategy or work out a game plan. The traditional dull, risk-averse China policy that the influential MEA mandarins side with was subscribed to by the Congress coalition government. It seemed to mirror the grey, procedure-bound personality of Manmohan Singh, a career bureaucrat hoisted as prime minister, and is counterpointed not just by the confident, outgoing approach of his successor Narendra Modi, but also by the brashly confident India of the 1950s when Nehru was in his prime, and New Delhi, without boasting of any of the accoutrements of power, inserted itself unbidden into the high-stakes Cold War politics. Now that India has the resources and many of the prerequisites of a great power, it is found floundering in the shallows. Bereft of forward-looking policies bent on making big national gains, and hobbled by confusion about how strategically to use the country's improved visibility in the world and its modern and muscular armed forces to best effect, India seems all drift and very little direction. The policy of calculated inaction affected the military, which took to playing safe, in the process becoming as allergic to risk-taking as the Indian government when challenged strategically. It is a habit of mind that lingers, translated in real terms into concentrating on the smaller foe, the lesser threat. Planning predicates and preparedness regimes, consequently, emphasize Pakistan, even though China is the primary source of danger to national security, the main economic competitor, and the only credible geopolitical and ideological rival in Asia. For an India hankering for great power recognition, this is a grievous flaw, projecting an image of a state content with playing big in the small leagues, and playing small in the big leagues. It indicates a want of strategic imagination that Nehru's India, whatever its other shortfalls, was never short of.

Forward Presence in the Quadrant

The historical quadrant in which British India implemented its 'distant defence' *qua* virtual 'Monroe Doctrine' is the area encompassed by the Indian Ocean, its littoral, and landwards from the Gulf to the Caspian Sea to Central Asia, that India naturally dominates.[25] It is geographic space India's strategic policy should try and dominate. Peninsular India, jutting out, as it is said, like the prow of an aircraft carrier into the Indian Ocean, moreover, enables land-based air, carrier aviation, and naval forces to sweep, sanitize, and shut down the crucial energy and trade-bearing oceanic traffic.[26] It is a region that has seen movements of peoples, cultures, militaries, and traders over several millennia in all directions to and from the Indian subcontinent—the centrally positioned fulcrum of this vast region—and, since the European discovery of the sea route to India and the east in the age of Vasco da Gama, the movement of the Indian army, Indian traders, and Indian labour that firmed up the British Empire. It is a wide swathe of land and sea that, according to the Harvard historian Sugata Bose, embodies organic unity (Bose 2006; Panikkar 1953). India and Indian culture, values, and diasporic communities are part of the weave of societies along the littoral and inland. Hence, New Delhi's contemporary interest and concern for the security and well-being of these countries are neither looked at askance by the local governments nor resisted by the people. India is thus advantaged in pursuing cooperative strategies in landward Asia, the Indian Ocean rim, and Southeast Asia, as suspicions are not aroused, and motives and intentions not questioned—the sort of thing that greets a China with a history of bellicosity. This last is evidenced in the wariness with which countries on its periphery regard Beijing's every political and military move, notwithstanding the desire to latch on to its fast-growing economy (Nye 2012).[27] It may also be that unlike India that is comfortable in its multicultural ambience, and able, therefore, to adjust to regional and global cross-currents, China thinks of culture, knowledge, and values as flowing outward from its heartland, civilizing the 'barbarian' peoples in these outer realms.[28]

A country's geography suggests its strategic potential and possibilities (Kaplan 2012). China's domination of the east Asian seaboard and the Asian heartland, Japan and the United States enjoying stellar status in the Far East and the Western Pacific, and India sitting astride the Indian Ocean—these are the three main powers in the Indo-Pacific region, afforded degrees of separation by geography, constituting, as discussed in the previous chapter, the triple Monroe Doctrines system. India's centrality in the ocean bearing its name and featuring the most important energy trade routes dictates its maritime strategy, of course. But the terrain that historically funnelled invasions from the Central Asian steppes into the Indo-Gangetic plains through the narrow defiles in the Hindukush range provides, in the present day, a channel for the reverse flow of Indian influence to the northern portions of the quadrant—Afghanistan and Central Asia—and for strengthening its politico-military posture in the arc—the Arabian Peninsula-Iran-Afghanistan-Central Asia. If, as Robert Kaplan avers, 'geography is commonsense', the desirability for India of setting up a layered defence is self-evident, with concentric defensive tiers, each acting as tripwire to activate the next inner line of defence, and so on, with a number of these tiers buffering the homeland. The United States followed this architectural principle when establishing NATO across the Atlantic by arming countries of West Europe, having them host land- and air-based tactical nuclear weapons, and covering them strategically by extended deterrence operated by and from the United States. In the Pacific theatre, the US had a similar structure with treaty allies in Japan, South Korea, Taiwan, the Philippines, New Zealand, and Australia, except in Asia this configuration acts as a barrier against China.

Finding itself surrounded by nations subscribing to a cooperative push-back strategy, Beijing aggressively brandishes its newest weapon, such as anti-ship ballistic missiles (ASBM) and cruise missiles in order to vacate the sea of American presence starting with the first island chain running from Japan's Kyushu and Ryukyu Islands to Taiwan and the Philippines in the first phase of its anti-access, area denial (A2AD) strategy. Beijing hopes that ASBM and an expanding submarine fleet will, in time, push the US forces away from the second island chain—the east-central coast of Japan through mid-Pacific Guam to Papua New Guinea, and finally out to the third island chain, the middle of the Pacific to Hawaii (Bush 2010: 53). This last, if achieved, would extend China's A2AD strategy to America's doorstep and divest most of the Pacific Ocean of US influence. The presumed attraction of this strategy is that even if such an objective is too big to be easily attained, the fact of China straining to realize it alone will unsteady the United States and make its Asian allies doubt America's ability to protect them, and the island nations in the western and South Pacific concerned about getting caught in the crossfire, to affect a neutral posture.[29] The Chinese ASBM system also endangers Indian aircraft carriers, for which the Indian Navy has no counter. Should nuclear-powered carriers (CVNs), driven by scaled-up reactors from the Arihant-class SSBNs, enter Indian service as contemplated by the Indian naval brass, China will try and negate them with fast cruise missiles and ASBMs, and erecting a bank of target-spotting over-the-horizon radars looking south-westwards towards the Bay of Bengal.[30]

In the Indian Ocean littoral, China has succeeded in softening up countries with easy credit, arms sales on easy terms, and offers of new and revamped infrastructure projects, without, however, winning their hearts and minds, something particularly evident in Myanmar (Biswas 2012; Tuan 2012). While New Delhi, *sans* the necessary strategic wit, failed to prevent the Chinese from coming into this region with preemptive policies mixing economic generosity with security assistance, it is now seeking to capitalize on the resentment and unease China has generated among the local populations with its intrusive presence. India has thus managed to recover some of the lost ground in Myanmar, made it a point to stand with the beleaguered Southeast Asian nations in their disputes with China in the South China Sea, reaffirmed its oil stake in the area within the Vietnamese claim line, and even dispatched warships to safeguard its interests (Williams 2011). It is, however, the comprehensiveness of Beijing's vision and plans and their speedy implementation that New Delhi, because of the shortcomings of its own vision, strategy, and political will, has found hard to match. In the face of a relentlessly expansive Chinese geo-strategic policy, the importance of an aggressive stance featuring extra-territorial presence and forward military bases as building blocks of a long-term strategy to enlarge the country's footprint are things the Indian government and armed services seem not fully to understand.

Desperate Necessity for Foreign Military Bases

India's layered littoral/oceanic defence of the quadrant in the east would have to rely on Japan-Taiwan as the outermost defensive perimeter, which can take care of itself and requires only an amenable Indian attitude to bolster it. Vietnam-Philippines-Indonesia constitute the second defensive tier that requires a proactive policy to keep the ramparts strong. The innermost tier consists of Thailand and Singapore backed by India's Andaman Command. Capacity-building for the second-tier states with nuclear missiles and other strategic-impact weapons, such as the Brahmos supersonic anti-ship cruise missile, and training crews for submarines, surface combatants, and fighter pilots, would deny the Chinese navy unobstructed freedom in the South China Sea and, in crises, bottle up China's powerful

South Sea Fleet in its base on Hainan Island.[31] Such a line of lethally armed states would be able to prosecute what Maozedong called 'self-defence counter-attack' against an overbearing Chinese navy. At the very least, having no assurance that these smaller states will not react adversely will compel Chinese war planners to be cagey. Combined, moreover, with Indian naval flotillas frequently traversing these waters, putting in at Nha Trang, Da Nang, and Subic Bay, and the US Navy's carrier battle groups constantly plying the Asian waters, it would maintain the status of the South China Sea as an internationally navigable waterway, not sovereign Chinese territory, and reassure the local states. But Vietnam, for instance, is no brash belligerent. While prepared to fight any comer in defence of its claims and interests, it is mindful of its military weakness with respect to China, one of which is its seaward flank. Hanoi has, therefore, viewed a meaty presence particularly of out-of-area friendly naval powers, such as India, with outstanding territorial disputes of their own with China, as insurance to ward off dangers. A Vietnamese military delegation headed by its naval chief, Vice-Admiral Ngyuyen Van Hien, visiting New Delhi in late June 2011 offered the port of Nha Trang on the South China Sea with line-of-sight on Hainan Island for the Indian Navy's exclusive use—the only foreign navy so favoured—besides agreeing to accord docking rights to Indian naval ships in Cam Ranh Bay, 60 miles down the coast.[32] In October 2014, Prime Minister Nguyen Tan Dung renewed the offer, first made a year earlier, of extensive new offshore oil and gas blocks to up the Indian energy stake in the South China Sea (Ranjan 2013). Indian naval ships voyage frequently between India's eastern coast and the Andaman Command, often proceeding to the Gulf of Tonkin. Their sailings are sustained by a provisioning arrangement with Vietnam on the central coast, an Indian forward position that can seriously impair Chinese naval and strategic activity. It is an analogue of the access the Chinese navy enjoys to the Pakistani port of Gwadar, and can aggravate China's offshore situation already roiled by the US Navy's loitering in this area, contested, other than by Vietnam and China, by Malaysia, Philippines, and Brunei. The common aim of Indo-Vietnamese security cooperation was symbolized in 2011 when the captain of INS Airavat, an Indian amphibious assault ship docking at Nha Trang, was taken ceremoniously to lay a wreath at the statue of a thirteenth century Annamese general who had defeated the Chinese in battle. India has also stationed its naval personnel in Cam Ranh Bay to man a signals intercept/electronic intelligence station monitoring Chinese naval activity and communications traffic ex-Hainan Island, which hosts both the Chinese South Sea Fleet headquarters and the PLA's Cyber Command (Datta 2011).

In the western Indian Ocean, there was a long-standing offer to India from the Mauritius government of the two-island set of the Agalegas, nearest to the Indian mainland, to anchor Indian military presence. In July 2012, the visiting Mauritius defence and trade minister Arvin Boollel for the first time publicly dangled these two islands before New Delhi in return for retaining the 1983 Double Taxation Accordance Agreement in its current form, which is beneficial to Mauritius.[33] The agreement has long been suspected by New Delhi as a channel for laundering unaccounted Indian money as foreign investment into India.[34] The Indian Navy has already hydrographically surveyed the island nation's extensive sea territories, and the strategic attractions of the islands are obvious enough. The 12.5-kilometre-long North Agalega Island has an air strip that can be lengthened and widened to take heavy lifters like C-17s and C-130Js, and to embark P-8Is and fighter aircraft, and the South Agalega Island provides deep-water anchorage. Building up these islands as military bases would enable Indian forces to sandwich any hostile Chinese naval actions out of Sri Lanka, assuming Colombo can survive being treated as 'belligerent' by India.[35] The navy's enthusiasm for the Agalegas, however, was not reciprocated by the Manmohan Singh government, primarily because of Defence Minister A. K. Antony's misguided Leftist ideological view that foreign bases are 'imperialistic' in nature. It dulled the service's strategic ambitions.[36] New Delhi's interest has so far been limited to securing the Indian Ocean, providing security to Seychelles, Mauritius, the Maldives, and Sri Lanka, without any permanent foreign bases. The navy has sought reconsideration of the Agalegas offer, arguing that it would extend air and sea surveillance area and increase manifold the sustainability of Indian naval operations and the sea-time warship groups can pull in the antipiracy mission and sea order patrols. Another self-imposed limitation that has cramped the Indian military's interest in the Agalegas is the MEA's attitude of approving military-related ventures only when there is no opposition in the region, or only after regional resistance is overcome by an elongated process of consensus-seeking. With European powers in the Indian Ocean opposing Indian bases India's in Mauritius, New Delhi, in effect, handed a virtual veto to France and the UK with their Indian Ocean territories, centred respectively on Reunion Island, and the Chagos chain, a part of which, Diego Garcia, claimed by Mauritius, was transferred in the 1960s by the British to the United States.[37] Prime Minister Modi signed an accord for developing defence infrastructure during his official visit in March 2015, permitting Indian military use of the Agalegas.

The Indian Navy also runs naval aerial surveillance out of Gan, a former British air force base, in the Maldives. A berthing-basing option ashore in Mozambique on the African littoral is available for the asking, with Maputo keen to have a major Indian naval shore installation to add to the Indian electronic intelligence post established some years back on its northern coast. The Indian radar systems in Mozambique, networked with similar facilities in the Seychelles, Mauritius, and the Maldives, monitor the south-western Indian Ocean, with overlapping and extended 24/7 real-time surveillance (Ramachandran 2007). An Indian naval team dispatched to Mozambique during Atal Bihari Vajpayee's BJP government in the early 2000s even identified the 300-foot-deep Madagascar Channel as a possible intermediate-range ballistic missile (IRBM) launch point for the *Arihant*-class SSBNs.[38]

The telling reason why New Delhi has eschewed foreign basing is the MEA's view, seconded by the Defence Ministry cell dealing with Planning and International Cooperation, that it is redundant. With reference to the east, it is argued, for instance, that the Nha Trang option should be held in abeyance because, with the South China Sea disputes in the international limelight and the US Navy engaged, India can free-ride without incurring any of the costs of such deployment or the risks of rubbing up against China. The Agalegas have been neglected for similar reasons of free security being afforded by the US military ex-Diego Garcia in the southern Indian Ocean. In the event, the Indian Navy is restricted to unobtrusively showing interest in the security of the member states of the Indian Ocean Naval Symposium (IONS) involving the littoral states, Australia, and

the Southeast Asian countries participating in the annual Milan multilateral naval exercise, and to communicating Indian readiness to
cooperate in joint security enterprises. It has utilized these forums to
show respect for the littoral navies and their concerns, and to expose
them to its own professionalism in onshore events, supported by regular naval exercises on a bilateral basis, such as those conducted regularly with Singapore since the mid-1990s, Indonesia and Thailand
since 2004, and, more recently, in the Gulf with Oman and Iran.
It pumps up the navy's reputation and India's image as a concerned,
helpful, and friendly power.[39] With interaction in these forums sup-
plemented by gifts to island nations of fast attack craft, patrol boats,
aerial surveillance aircraft, helicopters, and radar stations, India has
sought to tighten its grip on the IOR. The good feelings spawned
by such gestures led, for instance, to Mozambique requesting the
Indian Navy for perimeter security for the 2003 African Union summit staged in Maputo and the 2010 World Economic Summit. It
eventuated in the 2006 comprehensive accord with Mozambique for
Indian military assistance to train that country's military personnel,
and transfer military equipment and technical know-how for repairing and servicing military vehicles, patrol boats, and small aircraft.[40]
Such military cooperation is all very well but is simply not the equal
of foreign basing for the Indian military.

The MEA's skittishness to date about overseas bases is also because
an influential section of the military seems unsure about their utility. 'What do you mean by bases? Do you need to set up colonies?
We have basing rights in Oman, Seychelles, and Sri Lanka, we have
agreements with these countries that any Indian ship can put in any
of their ports at 24 hour notice to pick up fuel, water, or whatever
you need. These are as good as bases', says Admiral Prakash, who,
much like the Congress Party defence minister Antony, conflated
foreign bases with colonialism. 'All you need are way-stations to turn
around in. A good navy should be able to sustain itself at sea... .
If you have good, hardy sailors and officers, who don't mind a bit
of deprivation, you don't need bases.' Indeed, he considers foreign
bases a liability. 'Why go all the way to create a base and go under
obligation to somebody? If you have friends you don't need bases.'
Besides, he noted,

By convention, we can put into any friendly port. We have agreements with 25 states to say that if we send you a telegram, the next morning our ships will come in, our aircraft too can land in these port areas. As long as we can have usage of physical facilities, we don't have to have a physical presence. No upkeep costs, no diplomatic hassles.[41]

These are widely held views.[42] With experience of taking a Western Fleet task force to evacuate the Indian Army's Somalia Brigade in December 1994, and operating for three weeks off Kismayu and Mogadishu 'with nothing but old INS Shakti [a tanker] to sustain us', Vice-Admiral R. N. Ganesh too was sceptical. Bases, he felt, would 'antagonize the local populace'. 'This is happening in Mauritius with the Creoles objecting violently to the proposed 'gift' [of the Agalega Islands]. What we should value most in Mauritius [with a majority Indian-origin population] is the affinity which we share.' While port visits with 'basic facilities like cranes, a berth at a jetty, and logistics like water and oil' are required for lengthy stay in distant locations, a task group, he explained, 'would have integral logistics with workshop facilities and a tanker (which would itself need topping up). An airfield is a distinct advantage for flying personnel and stores in and out. So today's naval task force does not require that kind of shore-based technical support.' He, however, drew a distinction between global powers, such as the United States, needing far-flung bases, and single-ocean powers, such as India, that can do without them. 'We need milk, but don't have to own the cow,' he concluded.[43] But Rear Admiral K. R. 'Raja' Menon argues otherwise. 'If we are at all serious about projecting power with distant operations, we'd have done something about Agalega Islands. [The navy] says we regularly go to southern Africa. Going is one thing but operating there is something else. The [foreign] bases are required', he contends, 'because in hostilities access will not be available. We have to have Agalegas in the east [to complement] the Andamans in the west.' He blamed the Congress Party defence minister Antony for non-movement on Agalega, his fellow service officers for toeing the minister's line and 'behaving like *babus* [bureaucrats]', and Manmohan Singh's NSA Shivshankar Menon for not 'doing a thing'. The lack of bases abroad, he asserted, only increases the value of signing the Logistics Support Agreement with the United States, which is also not being done.

'Logistics are a big down step and we are not getting it,' he said. 'The Americans are everywhere. And if you haven't got any facilities you can use the US facilities, such as in Diego Garcia.'[44]

The IAF's perception of bases abroad runs along two lines. The first is in terms of the viability of an expeditionary policy, and the other as regards the returns from such investment. Air Marshal A. K. Singh (Retd), former commander, Western Air Command, while conceding that the air force and navy can airlift and sealift forces and equipment to any point in the Indian Ocean arc fairly rapidly, wondered if India has

> the financial ability to sustain such an operation for 10 days, 30 days, 50 days, how many days would the government want us to be out there? Or do we deploy indefinitely? In that case, I'm afraid the cost of running a base abroad, which is ten times that of running a base in India would have to be factored into an explicit policy document so instructing the military forces.[45]

The concern about the economic viability of foreign basing seems to be the main reason for New Delhi's not cashing in on opportunities. 'We are', Shivshankar Menon said, 'economical in our foreign entanglements but not engagements,' alluding to the costs of an Indian extra-territorial presence as entanglement.[46] The IAF's second line is with regard to long-range platforms in its inventory that make foreign bases superfluous. Air Chief Marshal N. A. K. Browne, as chief of the air staff, mentioned in this respect the long-distance, unrefuelled sorties carried out in mid-2012 by the newly acquired C-130J airlifters, in the one case to Ainee-Farkhor in Tajikistan, overflying the northern Arabian Sea and Iran, and another sortie all the way to South Africa.[47] The implication is that if IAF can marshal advanced military transport and aerial tankers to ensure lift and range to permit establishment of a military presence on a need-to basis and in an expeditionary role whenever and wherever required in the quadrant, why get saddled with static facilities in foreign countries that will be a drain on resources, which can be better spent for other purposes? Former foreign secretary Shyam Saran, voicing the MEA viewpoint, supported the view that foreign basing is impracticable owing to the paucity of funds. The stationing of ships, aircraft, and troops, he said, needs a huge logistical and infrastructural build-up. So, there is a certain prudence and caution which is all to the good. Rather than think of hard power as ability to place bases around the world, or put a detachment here or there, the first order of business is to address the weaknesses that we have such as the military infrastructure [roads, etc.] on the border [with China].[48]

However, with senior military leaders and MEA making their case in 'hot-button' terms of 'colonies', redundancy, and drain of financial resources, potential political and diplomatic troubles, and trade-offs with in-country expenditures on security infrastructure, a political leadership, even one convinced about the virtues of distant defence, can be forgiven for backing off. There was, perhaps, yet another reason for the Congress government's hesitation on this issue—the fear that China would follow suit, starting a pell-mell rush for military bases in the Indian Ocean, which it feared it may lose owing to Beijing's larger purse and successful record of cashbook diplomacy.[49] Whatever the immediate nature of its presence, the steady augmentation of China's military strength in the IOR ought to worry New Delhi.[50] 'A Chinese fable tells of how a frog in a pot of lukewarm water feels quite comfortable and safe,' writes John Garver, a leading American expert on Sino-Indian relations, likening India to the frog in the pot. He continues

> [It] does not notice as the water temperature slowly rises until, at last, the frog dies and is thoroughly cooked. This homily, *wen shui zhu gingwa* in Chinese, describes fairly well, China's strategy for progressing its influence in South Asia in the face of a deeply suspicious India: move forward slowly and carefully, arouse minimal suspicion, and give no cause to New Delhi to react forcefully or to attempt an escape from its predicament. (Garver 2012)

As Garver observes, India, like the frog in the warming vessel of water, has been complacent, showing no awareness of the dangers of allowing China to settle in the region. Thus, New Delhi woke up late to China's offer to build and launch satellites for a string of countries in the proximal areas—Bangladesh, Sri Lanka, Maldives, and Nepal—which was followed by the usual scrambling around by New Delhi to recoup at least a bit of the lost ground (Philip and Sruthijith 2013). New Delhi was approached to upgrade the Humbantota port by Colombo but declined, whereupon China rushed in. Maldives has asked for Indian assistance in constructing a military base off Malé on the Uthuru Thila Falhu Island for the Maldivian National Defence Forces, besides seeking the *Dhruv* advanced light helicopters and additional berths for its personnel in Indian military training institutions. The Indian foreign secretary who inspected the site of the proposed base in May 2014 is also aware that China has offered to build the base infrastructure (Pubby 2014). It is hoped that the BJP government will not repeat the Humbantota mistake in Sri Lanka, and will expeditiously agree to bankroll (to the tune of Rs 3,000 crore) and build the military base in the Maldives in return for its use of the facilities by Indian naval, air force, and army elements at all times.

The official apprehension of China reacting to India's first moves is a bit misplaced, considering that Beijing is shedding its reserve about bases abroad, coming around to the view that the country's political, economic, and cultural influence would be augmented by piggybacking on a spread-out military presence that a string of overseas bases provides (Yung *et al.* 2014). China may once again beat India to the draw, with the opponents of overseas military basing apparently insufficiently appreciative of the fact that such presence is, as a report on the US overseas facilities mentioned, 'designed to deter and, if necessary, to fight major battles. Having forces abroad also provides … multiple options for using military power for limited political purposes, [and] to send messages or reaffirm resolve' (O'Hanlon 2008: 48). Even without any distant military engagements on the horizon, the fact is that bases in island nations and on the littoral and deep in Asia, such as in Tajikistan, will grow the impression of India as a power that matters, and, if India moves quickly, preclude the possibility of China in the future occupying these strategic spaces. If New Delhi tarries, it will come out second best, something it seems to be getting used to.

India is rarely proactive, seems always on the back foot, reacting furiously once China has got its foot in the door, with the MEA and MOD preoccupied with the here and now. With the sights not set on preemptive or preventive diplomacy, no effort is made to divine what wind is blowing which way, and where, and then quickly interceding to divert possibly hurtful situations and tendencies in countries in the region or actions by adversary states, or to support positive trends advantageous to the national interest. It is almost as if the Indian frog is by now so well cooked it has become helpless, its brain affected, nerves deadened, and the motor mechanism beginning to slow down. Of course, the Indian frog can still jump out of the vessel, but it will require major effort. The trouble is that by the time the heat finally registers and it decides to try and make the jump, the water may begin to boil and it will be too late. Still, certain agencies of the state soldier on, with the Indian Navy in particular being assertive, seeking to enable Southeast Asian nations in particular to become porcupines with sharp quills, so as to prevent China from taking liberties in its own backyard.[51] It has been especially vigilant about Chinese developments, with senior Indian Navy officers responsible in 2013, for example, for talking Tehran out of permitting China to buy into the Chahbahar port expansion project—which is central to India's plans for accessing Afghanistan and Central Asia, and pressuring the Maldives government against leasing one of its southernmost islands close to the Indian mainland as a site for a Chinese 'Green Pines'–type radar station, a mere 19 kilometres from India's Minicoy Islands.[52]

In the sphere of big power politics, the Congress Party regime mostly finessed its policy of cultivating Beijing by not overtly siding with the United States or Japan, but doing just enough to make Beijing hesitate about acting egregiously against Indian interests. In these aspects, India has many elements in common with Japan's approach of balancing the United States and China (Samuels 2013), and, with respect to Southeast Asia, strengthening the capabilities of the littoral navies in order to divide the Chinese naval focus and forces between the South China Sea and the East Sea.[53] But such delicate actions cannot be sustained for long, in part because of the relatively faster accretion in China's comprehensive strength. In the event, India has bought into Japanese prime minister Shinzo Abe's concept of the 'democratic security diamond'—an updating of his 2007 security quadrilateral idea (Bagchi 2013a; Hornung 2013). Together, Japan, India, the United States, and Australia, he said, could prevent the South China Sea from being transformed into 'Lake Beijing', and committed to investing 'to the greatest possible extent [of] Japan's capabilities' in this area (Abe 2102). But New

Delhi has yet to work the 'security diamond' into Indian policy in a major way. Part of the strengthened ties Abe seeks with India and Australia are in the commonality of military hardware and seamless interoperability.[54] These goals are helped by talk in Australian security circles about procuring and adapting a Japanese submarine, and in Indian naval quarters about locally manufacturing the Japanese Shinmeiwa US-2 short take-off and landing flying boat for surveillance and defence of island territories and for Special Forces maritime missions. For a while, interest was even evinced in the *Soryu*-class conventional submarine as a possible choice for the Indian Navy's Project 75i (Kazianis 2012; A. K. Singh 2013). India's elevation of its relations with ASEAN to strategic partnership has hastened this process (Roy 2012). What is gradually taking shape is an elastic *cordon sanitaire* around seaward China that may bend but will not break. To maintain profitable economic relations with Beijing, many countries of the Indo-Pacific would, however, like to be discreet about it. Whence there is appreciation of India's role as a 'soft balancer' that does not preclude hard cooperative actions (Noi 2013). However, on this subject, the Manmohan Singh regime took its usual slow style of decision-making a little too far. While recalling the interest of states in Southeast Asia and the Gulf region in India's provision of security, Shivshankar Menon confessed that the real reason behind New Delhi's being non-committal was that, 'We are yet to think this issue through for ourselves.'[55] By then, the dispensation was nearly a decade old in office!

Absent any sense of urgency at the Indian end, potential friends and security partners find it difficult to plan ahead. The time involved in taking decisions masks a fundamental problem—New Delhi's inability in the period 2004–14 to reconcile the country's traditional emphasis on landward defence with Washington's demand that India focus on maritime security.[56] India's ambivalence, while frustrating to the regional states, has not been taken amiss so far, because most of the states seeking security assurances from India have gained from China's economic largesse and trade concessions, which they cannot do without. These gains would be endangered were New Delhi to go public with its commitments or about the extent of its strategic intimacy with these states, which is where the trust factor kicks in. While grudging and denying India nothing by way of physical access or whatever else is needed in military terms, the friendly regional countries expect India to be sensitive and discreet, and not disclose the details of the ongoing and underway strategic collaboration programmes and projects, just so they can preserve the facade of equidistance and the beneficial economic relationship with China.[57]

Capacity-Building in Partner States

Military capacity-building in partner states in the Indian Ocean basin, Southeast Asia, and Central Asia does several things. It strengthens the concentric tiers of India's defence, enables the friendly countries in these tiers to resist Chinese pressure, and distances India from the frontlines of possible conflicts in the extended region while keeping the Indian hand in. The basic premise being that the partner countries will be far better motivated than an outside power to safeguard their own and joint interests with the outside power on their territories by any and all means. Whence the commitment of Indian military and naval forces at the first hint of trouble with China is rendered unnecessary and, in real terms, constitutes a fire-break in the conflict spectrum with that country. It may involve prioritizing the requirements of partner countries over those of the Indian armed forces, but the payoffs in terms of firming up distant ramparts will be greater. Not appreciating this aspect led, for example, to New Delhi's ignoring for a long time Vietnam's and Indonesia's request for the Brahmos supersonic cruise missile on the plea of limited production and the priority to equip Indian forces. The other equally unconvincing reason offered was that the Russian company in the joint venture producing the Brahmos missile, NPO Maschinostroeyenia, forbade its sale or transfer, when the fact really was that the Manmohan Singh government did not want to upset the Chinese government by pushing hard for the sale or transfer of this weapon. It led to Indonesia directly approaching Moscow and procuring the slightly derated version of the Brahmos, losing India traction in Jakarta.[58] That there was no good reason to deny Hanoi this missile became evident when the Narendra Modi regime, less intimidated by China, promptly agreed to pass it on to Vietnam, which should be the model to arm the Philippines and other states on the Chinese maritime border desiring protection.

A fuller and more formal partner capacity–building programme as part of security cooperation is what the Indian military wishes the Indian government would put in place, because of its potentially big impact and influence in Africa, IOR, and in the areas east of Malacca. However, the armed services also fear that such expenditure, if it is not separately funded, would be gouged out of their own budgets and they would face harsh trade-offs resulting in the cooling off of the military's ardour for such outreach. The navy, for example, confronted the choise of funding an onshore facility in Mozambique—a jetty able to berth two frigates complete with a breakwater Maputo was eager for or spend the Rs 2,000 crore ($400 million)—the cost of this project—to enhance the capacity of the new major naval base in Karwar down the coast from Mumbai housing the Western Fleet.[59] Faced with such choices, the armed services naturally look at the service interest first and fall in with the MEA's less venturesome attitude, limiting themselves to military diplomacy stressing humanitarian assistance and disaster relief.[60]

The hesitation in availing of such opportunities, of course, has cost the country plenty strategically. The Philippines, for instance, offered the former US naval port at Subic Bay and Clark air force base for onshore use and military positioning. This was because Manila sees an overt Indian military role based on its territory and offshore in the neighbouring seas, much as it views the defence treaty with the United States, as added protection against China.[61] Unlike other proximal states, the Philippines would rather the world come to know about its military overtures and responses by out-of-the-area powers. New Delhi has not responded formally, but Indian naval ships in the South China Sea have taken to routinely pulling into Manila and Subic Bay on impromptu port calls and 'goodwill visits'. While this may not fully erase the view of India as a country whose talk impresses more than its actions, MEA's thinking is that because the strategic circumstances are unlikely radically to change for the Philippines, Subic and Clarke will always be available to India whenever required and whether or not there is a prior agreement.[62] Manila, like other capitals in the littoral and offshore Southeast Asia, is trying to cement its military links by procuring its threat-relevant military hardware from India.[63] New Delhi seems to have finally learned from Beijing, if still only partially, the benefits of politico-military activism in the rival's backyard. While the Indian prime minister was in Beijing in October 2013, the second meeting of the Philippines–India Joint Commission on Bilateral Cooperation concluded in Manila with a joint statement expressing support for 'freedom of navigation' and 'rule of law' in the 'West Philippine Sea' also known as the South China Sea (Roy 2013). Not much later, for the first time, an Indian ambassador was appointed to ASEAN (Bagchi 2013b). This was followed from Fall 2013 onwards by New Delhi upping the optics by scheduling a series of high-level visits to New Delhi by notables from rimland Asian countries—General Secretary of the Communist Party of Vietnam Nguyen Phu Trong, Emperor Akihito and Empress Michiko of Japan, President of South Korea Park Geun-hye, and, to emphasize Japan's importance in India's strategic scheme of things, by Premier Shinzo Abe of Japan as the chief guest at the Republic Day parade and celebrations in January 2014. This is foreign policy conducted with a lining of military muscle.

Military Diplomacy

What has hurt military diplomacy is the institutional-bureaucratic impulse of MEA officials to preserve turf and show the military its place. The armed services are actively discouraged from straying into the foreign policy field, with national security strategy papers drafted by the Integrated Defence Staff, for instance, being politely dismissed by the foreign secretary as falling outside the domain of the Defence Ministry and the military. Nor are the armed forces brass consulted by MEA before crafting foreign policy choices that could fare better with military inputs and show of steel.[64] Such factors have contrived over the years to reinforce the inward-turned, self-absorbed, and reactive-passive-defensive posture and attitude of the armed services, until now when it has become second nature. This, for self-serving reasons, is reinforced by the MEA acting with speed to put out even a flicker of activism by the military. Thus, it has consistently ruled against the navy's instinct to rescue Indian victims of piracy and shelved the showing of force to prevent excesses against Indian diasporas in the Indian Ocean rim and beyond. In 2003, for example, there was a virtual pogrom against Fijians of Indian descent by the then government in Suva. It triggered talk in official corridors about dispatching an Indian warship to anchor off the Fijian capital, an action that might have 'stretched' the navy's resources had it lasted more than a month. 'But a month is enough', noted a retired senior naval officer risibly, 'for a destroyer to sort out a few grass-skirted natives.' Such old-style gunboat diplomacy is, however, frowned upon by the Foreign Office.[65] Had such action been ordered, it would have outlined India's sphere of responsibility, defined a threshold for future Indian military interventions, and signalled the governments of countries with significant Indian-origin populations to be civil to all their peoples. In the process, it would have marked out an extended Indian influence zone stretching from Fiji in the Western Pacific to the Gulf and the East African littoral.

The military blames the lack of 'synergy' to the turf war between MEA and MOD. It also contests the view by a former diplomat, K. Shankar Bajpai, that even though the country's strategic interests stretch from 'the Suez to Shanghai', India has 'neither the manpower nor the strategic thinking to handle these challenges'. The void in the strategic thinking field is plain enough, but the paucity of manpower can be easily made up, it is argued, by the cross-posting of military officers in the MEA. Such a move, like that of the entry of outside domain specialists at the middle levels to give Indian diplomacy a technical edge, is opposed by the Indian Foreign Service leadership, which is fearful of diluting the importance of its own cadre (Katoch 2013: 393–5).

The annual allocation for foreign military cooperation programmes, such as IONS and Milan, inclusive of certain partner capacity–building schemes in 2012, was Rs 150–200 crore ($40 million), which MEA funds and is, therefore, determined to dictate its contents. It has often led to serious differences with the military over when and what to sell, gift, or transfer by way of armaments, sensors, and weapons platforms, and to which countries. The armed services charge MEA with an 'obstructionist' bent of mind when it comes to military transfers and sales, implying that its financial control inhibits their initiatives.[66] The Foreign Service stalwart Shyam Saran, however, retorted angrily to such charges. The MEA, he asserted 'will not support Ministry of Defence or the armed forces going off and running their own foreign policy.' Without 'proper assessment as to where [these transactions and security cooperation programmes] fit into the larger picture, they are not advisable', he said, more soberly. Complications inherent in foreign arms sales, such as 'commissions' and bribes, he believes, are things that the public sector ordnance factories, shipyards, and aircraft production plants are simply not institutionally geared to handle, given the rigours of the accounting system. He admitted that such rigidities in the Indian system are counterproductive. Having served the BJP prime minister Atal Bihari Vajpayee and his Congress Party successor, Manmohan Singh, as Foreign Secretary, Saran is of the view that, as regards foreign bases, arms transfers, and projecting power military, 'the policy oscillation is much smaller than the rhetorical oscillation.' He described Indian policy as hewing to principles of *realpolitik*. Saran explained: 'It is *realpolitik* in the sense that there's a more comprehensive assessment of where our strengths lie, what the weaknesses are, and how to neutralize them. So it is not *realpolitik* in the sense that we need hard power and that's it, and that's what will determine where we are going to be,' he stated. 'Hard power is essential but hard power in the larger diplomatic context. The Indian *realpolitik* is more nuanced. For successful diplomacy it is important', he added, that 'we should have hard power as well. But it is not necessary that unless we have hard power we cannot promote our interests.'[67] This is an unexceptional statement evocative of Nehru's belief in the power of diplomacy, even as there is only a halting recognition in it of the diplomacy of power, of military capability as a policy tool useful in advancing national interest and realizing national ambition.

The Indian government has been bit more receptive, however, when it comes to helping out island states in the Indian Ocean facing trouble. In 1983, a possible coup by the Creole challenger, Paul Berenger, against the Aneroodh Jugnauth government in Mauritius was averted merely by New Delhi intimating its intent to embark an expeditionary force on a flotilla of six destroyers (Operation Lal Dora). A frigate, INS Vindhyagiri, was sailed in 1986, aborting a coup in Seychelles (Operation Flowers Are Blooming), and, two years later, an airborne unit ended a coup d'état attempted by a bunch of Sri Lankan adventurers against the government of President Abdul Gayoom in the Maldives—Operation Cactus (Brewster and Rai 2013; Dikshit 2013). More recently, the regime of President Mohammad Waheed was brought to heel in the Maldives when a big naval exercise, Tropex 2013 involving some 50 ships, that was originally to be conducted in the Bay of Bengal, was shifted to somewhere off Malé, the main island. Waheed had moved to discard a political compromise in February 2013, painstakingly put together by Indian diplomats with his opponent, the more India-friendly former president Mohammad Nasheed, who had taken refuge in the Indian embassy (Gupta 2013).

MEA's Bent of Mind on China

The military by and large is unconvinced that the government either appreciates hard power or understands its nature. A senior uniformed officer in the National Security Council secretariat during the Congress government expressed doubt, saying India has the hard power, but gives the impression of being a 'pushover state' because there was no will in the government to take a stand on any foreign policy issue. According to him, Prime Minister Manmohan Singh's view was that hard power is good to have, but it was not for show or for actual use, except in extreme circumstances. Such thinking has percolated into the thinking of the armed services, leaving them unprepared in crisis to launch a hard response even when the government contemplates it. Thus, after the 26/11 attack on Mumbai, the air force chief Air Chief Marshal Fali Major told the prime minister he did not possess (and neither did the intelligence services) the exact coordinates for the Lashkar-e-Taiba and Pakistan Taliban training and logistics centres in Pakistan-occupied Kashmir as targets for a punitive strike. The army chief General Deepak Kapoor too expressed doubts about successfully mounting Special Forces action against terrorist concentrations within Pakistan. None of the military chiefs of staff assured Manmohan Singh that, in the wake of such Indian operations, military escalation would not occur, which last was the clinching argument ensuring there would be no punitive retaliation whatsoever (Swami 2014).

One may argue that an instant retaliation by pin-point bombing of terrorist targets combined with a massive information campaign to explain it as a limited punitive action with a promise to strongly meet any Pakistani escalation in kind would have mobilized international opinion and world capitals, and stayed the hand of those in Islamabad seeking to escalate hostilities (Karnad 2009). Instead, a military unwilling to risk a fight covered up its loss of nerve by pleading absence of information and capability. The IAF, it may be recalled, had—again for fear of escalation—declined to go into action in the 1999 Kargil conflict when the army first asked for air support against the infiltrated Pakistan Northern Light Infantry troopers occupying mountain redoubts (Malik 2006: 121). Such apprehensions on the part of the military fed into Dr Singh's inherent disinclination for military tension and conflict, his larger position being that Pakistan can be rendered amenable by means of trade and economic linkages alone and that China, assuming it does not resort to military force, would likewise react well to a judicious Indian approach minus unnecessary chest-thumping.[68] New Delhi has been over-mindful of the ramifications of military hostilities especially with China, apparently taking to heart the Singaporean savant Lee Kuan Yew's warning that 'if relations between India and China were to become hostile, … tension and instability would deter trade and investment, slowing the region's growth. It is in everyone's best interest for these two behemoths to maintain a stable and amicable relationship' and engage 'in friendly competition to win over the neighbors' (Yew 2011).

This is a line that Shivshankar Menon subscribed to. He posited 'hard/traditional security'—'largely a zero sum game'—as pulling in the opposite direction to 'economic security', entailing 'trade and economic cooperation', with the latter offering not 'win or lose choices' but 'simultaneous gains for multiple actors' (Menon 2013). Menon, in fact, had on several occasions deemed military rivalry with China as not 'inevitable'.[69] The trouble is that such an institutional outlook has bred a posture- and policy-bending lassitude in India with respect to a revanchist China, especially as New Delhi is well known for its failure to apprehend hazard until it is too late to do anything about it, and ends up paying the price (Lee 2013). 'MEA's wishful thinking and smart-arseism, its belief that Beijing can be induced into a deal with delicate verbiage and fancy diplomatic footwork is going to land India into trouble,' said a former diplomat and member of a government task force set up to review national security in Manmohan Singh's second term. This diplomat was alarmed by the Congress government's tendency to shape foreign policy on the basis of watered-down perceptions of the China threat.[70] Intentions of countries, however, can change quickly, are unpredictable, and do create 'radical uncertainty'.[71] The MEA is, however, convinced that conveying by word and deed India's peaceful intentions to Beijing would kindle like Chinese feelings and is redolent of Nehru's thinking pre-1962 War.

Yet Nehru was realistic about China and played a double game, even if he lacked decisiveness (as when he did not pursue weaponization when the nuclear programme reached the weapons threshold in 1964). On the eve of taking up his post in Beijing, the Indian ambassador-designate G. Parthasarathi in March 1958 was instructed by Prime Minister Nehru, who was his own foreign minister, thus: 'So, ... what has the Foreign Office told you? *Hindi-Chini bhai-bhai?* [Indians–Chinese are brothers?] Don't you believe it! I don't trust the Chinese one bit. They are a deceitful, opinionated, arrogant, and hegemonistic lot. Eternal vigilance should be your watchword.' Further, fearing that MEA officials would distort the communications Parthasarathi would send from Beijing, or keep certain correspondence from him, Nehru ordered the ambassador-designate to 'send all your telegrams only to me—not to the Foreign Office. Also, do not mention a word of this instruction of mine to Krishna [the defence minister V. K. Krishna Menon, Nehru's close friend]. You and I share a common world view and ideological approach. However, Krishna', Nehru cautioned, 'believes erroneously that no Communist country can have bad relations with any Non-Aligned country like ours.'[72] Remarkably, Nehru was warning against what was generally perceived even by him as the terminally conciliatory 'Nehruvian' attitude to China internalized by the MEA. Nevertheless, such thinking persists, legitimated by Nehru's contrary and more numerous public pronouncements avowing friendship for China rather than his basic distrust of that country.

A latter-day manifestation of such an attitude can be found in Shivshankar Menon's explication of the Congress Party regime's China policy in its waning days. He said that the government put greater store by the 'congruences between our views and assessments of the shifting balance of forces in the international situation' than on 'our differences', owing to the disputed border and problems in our respective peripheries (Pakistan, Tibet, South China Sea, Myanmar). He also downgraded the idea of containing China 'by any third power or group of countries'. He favoured a concert with China to achieve a multipolar global order, not so much to undermine the effort by the US and the West as 'to set new standards for trade and investment flows among preferred partners' by arrangements such as the Trans-Pacific Partnership, which, he said, 'would only dangerously fragment world trade and abet the rise of protectionism in developed countries', and to keep open the possibility of an arrangement with China promising like benefits.[73] This seems to not just place such common interests as may exist with China above India's national security concerns, but also to underestimate the value of a string of strategic partnerships with states adjoining China, geared to denying Beijing's foreign and military policy the room to manoeuvre. The fount of such views was the China Study Group (CSG), comprising Mandarin-speaking former and serving diplomats and intelligence officials headed by Shivshankar Menon. It stressed the efficacy of what is believed was finely calibrated diplomacy, combining soft talk in public with keeping the sword sheathed whatever the Chinese provocation.[74] It about equalled the tolerance showed by Nehru who, despite correctly reading the threat from China in the 1950s, 'had been remarkably lax in preparing to defend that not-quite-so-impregnable [Himalayan] rampart, ... or even countenance his own military doing so.'[75] Nehru could plead meagre resources and competing development demands on the government rupee; it is not an excuse available any more to the Indian government.

How effective is this policy approach against a muscle-flexing China that grows militarily more powerful by the day, with the ability to project power into 'distant seas', considering that President Xi Jinping has unambiguously linked his 'dream of a strong nation' to a 'strong military' that uses 'battle-ready standards in undertaking combat preparations [and insists on] rigorous military training based on the needs of actual combat'? In similar vein, PLA Major General Luo Yuan turned mystical, calling on the Chinese nation to revive 'the militaristic spirits worshipped by our ancestors, as well as the promotion of the revolutionary heroism of the Red Army' (quoted in E. Wong 2012; see also Perlez and Buckley 2014). There is a real danger of the more belligerent brand of Chinese nationalism having freer play in the future, and of hostilities breaking out on the land border, or a maritime incident, precipitating war that India, in the absence of an appropriate military build-up, may find hard to wage.[76] In 1962,

Mao initiated war (in response to Nehru's hop-scotching 'forward policy' of setting up outposts) 'to teach India a lesson' with the goal of pulling India down politically a peg or two in the Afro-Asian world, an aim which he realized. In the second decade of the twenty-first century, India cannot afford to lose even a skirmish, because it might mean losing its future as a great power. To be beaten a second time in a military clash with China, besides the irrecoverable loss of face, would make palpable India's inability to defend itself, let alone shield other countries in the region. India's loss of credibility and standing in Asia will then be absolute.

Dangers of the Sino-US Nexus

The perils of the more manageable 'Sino-Pakistani nexus' is the stuff of strategic contemplation and military planning, but not so the more probable and potentially more alarming Sino-US connection. In a previous chapter, it has been discussed why it would be imprudent for India, a would-be great power, to expect serious military help and assistance (of the kind treaty allies such as Japan and the Philippines can expect, if push comes to shove) from a friendly United States, in a crisis with China. We have also seen why the proposed geopolitical triptych of the three interlinked Monroe Doctrine spheres in Asia manifests a distribution of power and resources that makes the evolving Indo-Pacific security system workable. The possible glitches here are two trends involving America and India: The United States trying to do too much by itself and, with the underway fiscal austerity measures and close economic relations and 'mutual [military] vulnerability' vis-à-vis China, growingly unable to do so.[77] And India not doing enough despite conducive regional and international milieus and its ability to fill, to an extent, the breach. For example, China's 'cost-effective' strategy of using Pakistan to 'counterbalance' India in South Asia is underwritten by US financial aid and assistance to Islamabad. But with an imploding Pakistani society enfeebling an already weakened Pakistani state, and the US pulling out of the Afghanistan-Pakistan (Af-Pak) region, the situation can quickly get out of hand unless India steps in to cement good relations with Islamabad. The democratic government of Prime Minister Nawaz Sharif desperately wants amicable relations to shore itself up politically and by and by, to reduce the Pakistan Army's role and relevance.[78] China cannot help to internally stabilize Pakistan in a way that India can. Beijing, moreover, is worried about the restiveness of the native peoples, its position being 'fragile' in Xinjiang and Tibet, its six decade old programme of inducements and coercion failing to overcome the alienation of the ethnic minority populations there lest the discontented youth take up arms. The Dalai Lama has counselled peaceful methods, but warned that if Beijing does not relent in granting genuine autonomy to Tibet, there are no guarantees that Tibetans won't pick up the gun.[79] A similar warning is implicit in the statements of Ilham Tohti, the moderate campaigner for Uyghur rights, who has been imprisoned for life (Johnson 2010). On the other hand, for an America on the verge of 'strategic insolvency', to turn things around will require it to revive its economy, amend its military deportment, and change the existing 'paradigm' of global system management by inviting 'a set of emerging powers into the shared leadership of norm- and institution-bound world politics' (Mazaar 2012: 18–19). The 'Asia pivot' makes it clear that India is one such emerging power, but the danger is that the economic nexus between the United States and China, as has been repeatedly mentioned, is so crucial to both these countries and to the health of the global economy at large, and the consequent mutual interdependence has developed to such an extent, that the temptation in Washington will always be to widen areas of cooperation, avoid military confrontation, and cut separate deals with Beijing at the expense of its Indo-Pacific partners. The Obama administration has displayed just such a bent of mind.[80] Many American experts see China as helping to further the US nuclear nonproliferation agenda by acting as an intermediary between nuclear weapons states and non–nuclear weapons states to push for universal adherence to the Additional Protocol to the International Atomic Energy Agency safe-guards regime, encourage implementation of UN Resolution 1540, and ensure the success of the 2015 Non-Proliferation Treaty Review Conference, in return for Washington keeping in mind China's regional interests (Cossa *et al.* 2013). The likely outcome of the mutual accommodation by the United States and China could lead to the dilution of America's security commitments to Asian states. On the Senkaku Islands, for instance, there is already some consternation expressed in US circles that Article 5 in the 1960 Treaty of Mutual

Cooperation and Security may drag America into an unwanted military tangle with China (Keating 2012). The failure of the visiting Japanese prime minister Abe to get President Obama's support on the disputed islands confirmed Japanese fears of American abandonment (Ng 2013). The point is that resource constraints will limit the extent and quality of the US rebalance to Asia, and incline it always to mollify China.[81] There could, therefore, be a grand exchange—in return for less American support to Japan on the Senkakus than Tokyo believes prudent, China could agree, say, to turn the screws on Pyongyang or on Islamabad on issues dear to Washington, such as the North Korean and Pakistani nuclear and missile programmes, reining in the Haqqani network active in Afghanistan, and/or reeling in the radical Islamists patronized by the Pakistani Army.[82] The point is not that the US-Chinese pressure on Pakistan on some of these issues will not serve Indian interests, but rather that with the 'major power relationship' offered by President Xi on the anvil as the grand prize, Washington could similarly press India to desist from militarily enabling Southeast Asian nations more forcefully to resist China, or stay its options on Tibet. Further, as with Japan on the Senkakus, in a direct India–China territorial conflict, the US may keep its own counsel. Weakening American resolve and security commitment to Asian states were always going to heighten the fear and anxiety about China in Asia, leading to the 'hyperbolicization of security' and the gravitation towards the nuclear bomb by the more powerful regional countries (Karnad 2005: Chapter 1). This is now happening. The perceived unreliability of US defence commitment and North Korea's nuclear shenanigans, combined with China's assertiveness, are resulting in, conservative sections in Japan aside, influential South Koreans calling for rethinking the nuclear weapons option, and Abe amending the pacifist constitution imposed by the US such as to permit a comprehensive upgrade of its military capability and the use of force for 'collective defence' (Fackler and Sang-Hun 2013).[83] Should relations with China deteriorate, both Tokyo and Seoul may seek succour in the bomb.

The need, therefore, is for India to develop a uniquely effective military capability conjoined to an agile foreign policy that forges strong security relations with countries bordering China, transfers strategic armaments and offers military training and technical expertise, and launches targeted intelligence and cyber operations in league with states, such as Taiwan, to check Beijing. Such capability will compensate for the declining power and interest of America in Asia and a possible 'hands-off' US policy, including in the trans-Himalayan region and in the areas east and west of Malacca. India cannot allow itself to become hostage to third-party foreign policy interests and strategic foci which can change with every new administration in Washington, without deeply and irreparably hurting its own position. Security self-sufficiency, moreover, will mark it out as a strong and independent actor, burnishing India's role and reputation and winning it respect. India should, moreover, be no part of any global power arrangement that requires it to compromise its economic interests, like carbon emissions and unrestricted trade in agricultural goods at the Doha Round of the General Agreement on Trade and Tariffs. On these issues, New Delhi would do well to take cover behind positions taken by China, rather than allow China to use India's opposition as a shield to safeguard its own interests. As the Chinese vice foreign minister Song Tao said at the 2013 Munich *Wehrkundtagung* (Defence Conference), 'To ask emerging economies to assume the same international responsibilities as developed economies is to ask a passenger who boards a train at Frankfurt to pay the full fare for the journey from London to Munich.' Except unlike Beijing, New Delhi during Manmohan Singh's tenure seemed unable to resist US pressure and ante up the full fare (quoted in Nayar 2013). Sympathizing and maintaining solidarity with China in select economic sectors (such as climate and IPR) is, in any case, not to assume an overlap of interests in security and geo-strategic areas, which does not exist. New Delhi should even more strenuously decline siding with any US-led politico-strategic initiatives, such as signing the Comprehensive Test Ban Treaty, for instance, which will mean forswearing thermonuclear testing in exchange for a seat in the UN Security Council, among other things—the sort of transaction New Delhi has shown susceptibility to.

India should selectively build up a mix of military capabilities able effectively to dissuade and deter China from threatening the use of force, or turning up the pressure for any reason, within the Indian quadrant and outside of it. This will require New Delhi to shift its tactical focus and military obsession with Pakistan to concentrating strategically on China. Ironically, the unwarranted military attention to Pakistan only grew after the 1971 Bangladesh War, when that country was halved, its religion-based 'two-nation theory' foundation was wrecked, and it was rid of its pretence of parity with India. So egregiously skewed is this threat perception, particularly with a dangerous China getting a free pass from New Delhi, that even friendly extra-regional powers have long been bewildered. Speaking to the Indian ambassador D. N. Dhar in Moscow in 1972, Soviet defence minister Andrei Grechko, for instance, accused the Indian government of 'overstating the Pakistan threat' but missing out on 'the ominous source from where the real threat to India emanates namely China.' For emphasis, the decorated Soviet war hero added that 'China was the real danger and India would be well advised to constantly remind herself of this fact. She could ignore this only at her own peril' (Bhasin 2010: cxix). Grechko's advice was disregarded. After that comprehensive military victory, the Indian government and armed services failed to do proper stocktaking or settle on more realistic threat bearings, until now, when the Indian military, by and large, is stuck in a legacy scenario, unable to transform itself to keep pace with the advances in technology and changes in the threat and conflict milieus and mode of warfare.

Fixating on Pakistan

Since independence, India has faced a 'two-front war' situation, which was off-centre from the beginning owing to Nehru's powerful defence minister and Leftist ideologue, V. K. Krishna Menon. Nehru's experience of taking the Kashmir dispute to the United Nations at Britain's urging only to see the issue become a plaything of great power politics, soured him on the West but made him receptive to Krishna Menon's anti-Western outlook. Consequently the latter propagated and institutionalized the view in the MOD of Pakistan as an American/Western pawn and an ideological affront to socialist India, and its military reduction as an anti-imperialist responsibility. By the same token, Communist China was viewed by Krishna Menon as ideologically compatible and diplomatically *simpatico*.[84] Nehru did not, however, allow the animus against Pakistan to boil over into all-out war even after the 1947–8 conflict in Kashmir, because of the personal relations he and his cabinet colleagues had with the Pakistani leaders and former comrades in the freedom struggle. Hence, very civil relations obtained between the two countries until the 1965 conflict. On the northern front, however, Nehru was alive to the danger from China, and prudently acquiesced in the US military plans for the 'Defence of India' in case of Chinese attack, which was central to Nehru's double game (Karnad 2005: 132–46). The American plans, promising protection in dire contingencies, reassured Nehru, but Krishna Menon's blustery anti-Western rhetoric and anti-Westernism was tolerated because it was popular with the developing countries and eased India's assumption of leadership of the Third World (Karnad 2002: Chapter 2). Nehru did not foresee that the end-state of Pakistan-as-Yankee-stooge mindset, combined with the traditional Hindu–Muslim tensions in society, would end up embedding an entirely twisted threat perception and worldview, and that this would take deep root, making nonsense of realistic threat perception and rational military planning. The strategic myopia is, therefore, a legacy issue that both the Indian government and the military struggle with, and is a cross they continue to bear.

The two-front war notion has been stretched in the current situation into a 'two-and-a-half war' concept, with the half-war being the ongoing counter-insurgency operations in Kashmir, the north-east, and, should the armed forces be ordered to provide 'aid to the civil' in the 'red corridor', in fighting the indigenous Maoist (or Naxal) revolutionaries (Kanwal 2012).[85] With respect to the two main fronts, what is crucial is which country—Pakistan or China—merits consideration as the principal adversary, and here, for the reasons adduced (in this and previous chapters), the Indian security system has been motivated by the wrong country—Pakistan. This has only dissipated national resources and the country's regional and international credibility and potential impact and influence.

Shivshankar Menon, in his time as NSA, strangely invoked the Tamil poet and sage Thiruvalluvar (who is supposed to have lived between 2 BC and 8 AD) to explain this anomalous situation. 'You have no allies. You are faced with two enemies,' he quoted from the philosopher's oeuvre. 'Make it up with one of them and make of him a good ally... . Which one you choose [to make up with] is up to you.'[86] Thiruvalluvar apparently referred to two nearly equal enemies. Yet the then NSA used this historically revered figure to accord parity to Pakistan and China, and worse, he presumed that China could become a 'good ally' and help in the collaring of Pakistan. Thus, the process of designating national security threats and allocating funds to build capabilities to counter them, as we shall see, tilted conspicuously away from China and towards Pakistan. This process is revealed by the erstwhile NSA's statement to be less a function of a realistic estimation of the strengths, capabilities, and strategic facts than a subjective, jaundiced view of a particular state as posing mortal danger, a view that is grounded in Partition pathologies and segues with the Hindu majority's cultural and social bias against Muslims. This manifestly wrong military orientation, ironically of a Congress Party–led government, is so entrenched that notwithstanding China's rocketing rise, massive gains in its military strength, and a record of keeping the disputed border disturbed by hostile tactical moves and pinpricking military actions, governments in New Delhi have underreacted to the significant and comprehensive military danger posed by China while making much of the relatively slight threat (of terrorism) posed by Pakistan. As the 'general mobilization for war' (Operation Parakram) ordered by the BJP government in 2002 proved, the threat posed by Pakistan can be better tackled with targeted intelligence operations, in the words of the ancient Indian strategist Kautilya, *kutayuddha* (covert war), than with vast field armies (Kilcullen 2011; K. Roy 2012: Chapter 3).[87]

The probable cause for focusing on Pakistan is its seemingly successful use of Islamist jihadi terrorism as an asymmetric tool of warfare as the preferred option of a weak state (Arreguin-Toft 2001; Stepanova 2008). Under the protective overhang of its nuclear weapons, the Pakistan Army has utilized these means effectively to agitate India—a country that inspires 'neuralgic fears' among Pakistanis but is seen by them to be unstoppably on the rise, which in fact only strengthens their resolve to hang on to the one means of pressure they do have—terrorism (Fair 2011).[88] In turn, it solidifies also the institutional habit of mind of the Indian Army—a carry-over from the days of the native armies facing north-westwards to deal with Afghan and Central Asian invaders and, during the colonial age, of focusing on the possibility of Czarist Russia seeking the warm water ports of the Arabian Sea, having its army stream across the Amu Darya and the Bolan and Khyber Passes into India and the Arabian Sea. After 1947, the Indian Army remained west-facing, except now it confronted the smaller, other part of itself—the Pakistan Army—which together had formed the old British Indian Army. It has eventuated, as discussed earlier, in the two South Asian militaries being at loggerheads, engaged in occasional conflicts as a form of blood sport—'communal riots with tanks' that, remarkably, leave the Indian and Pakistani states and societies, other than the loss of war materiel and bruised egos, largely unaffected.[89] With the conflicts limited by the governments to manoeuvre and counter-force (tank-on-tank, infantry units against each other) battles on the plains and the unpopulated sectors of the Thar and Cholistan Deserts, total war was never on the cards.

How ingrained is the Indian military's focus on plains warfare with Pakistan was evidenced in the 1999 conflict on the Kargil heights. The IAF, for instance, discovered to its chagrin when called up for action that it had not developed air tactics to drop bombs and fire missiles on enemy targets in rocky defiles and on steep mountainsides, even though Indian forces had been arrayed against the Pakistani army in Kashmir for the previous 52-odd years, and against the PLA in the Himalayas for just as long (Lambeth 2012). India's military effort against Pakistan to keep an upstart rump-state in its place and, in more recent times, to chastise it for its sponsorship of anti-India terrorist outfits, is particularly stark when compared to its conciliation-flecked policy towards China and the lack of desire on the part of the Indian military to build up comprehensively against the PLA. It represents the 'shallow realism' of a Neville Chamberlain (Kaplan 2003: 18). The threat of limited war by the conventionally superior Indian Army does not easily intimidate Islamabad, both because it is now reassured psychologically by its nuclear arsenal, and, as a more pliable state, by its indispensability to the United States and China, in contingencies relating to the Gulf, Afghanistan, Iran, Central Asia, India, and South Asia generally. The failure of massed armies to deter terrorism in the wake of the 2002 Operation Parakram did not, however, prompt a rethink in New Delhi of India's strategy. It is a problem that turns on itself and was described by a former service chief thus: in the absence of a great power vision paper or document clearly stating the long-term strategic objective or goal for the military to work towards, the government issues 'tactical directives' to the three armed services, who implement them in the light of their own plans, mostly originating in the past.[90] In fact, it was the norm till the 1990s for the army's Operations Directorate to be tasked with outlining the threats and drafting operational plans, which the MOD then formally reissued as a 'political directive' to the military (Nayar 2013: 181–2). This job has since been taken over by the Headquarters Integrated Defence Staff, which last updated the 2006 directive in 2010.[91] Unfortunately, the armed services seem loath to restructure and reorganize to fight wars in a high-technology milieu lest they be required, in the process, to diminish the legacy combat arms. Hence the great profusion of old cavalry regiments transmuted into armoured and mechanized units, whose continued existence is justified only by perpetuating the notion of Pakistan as a substantive threat. So the armoured and mechanized forces comprising the army's three 'strike corps' are periodically 'modernized' not in terms of system transformation to acquire new kinds of warfighting capability, but in terms of older weapon systems being replaced by newer versions of the same weapon tasked for the same old role to be utilized in the same old way. To the extent that the need for new or novel capability is accepted, the services conceive of it as additional to the existing forces and capabilities, and requiring new raisings and extra financial subventions which end up enlarging the service's size and operational turf without greatly improving the army's fighting abilities and effectiveness. Should some of these newer missions involve more than one service, the exercise quickly gets bogged down in inter-service tussling, bureaucratic one-upmanship, and empire-building competitions (such as the fight over the army's helicopter aviation corps, which the air force opposed and eventually lost).

The government is usually a mute spectator up to the point when a cabinet decision has to be made. Even then, it neither contests the threat orientation, force structure and disposition, or force augmentation or force modernization proposals, nor directs the services to retire or substantially reduce this or that capability that has become redundant or irrelevant in the changing context. It almost never instructs the military to refocus on emerging threats and to shift funds and operational foci with a view to enhancing new, more relevant capabilities. There is, in fact, very little political direction given to the armed forces—the result of the 1962 military defeat against China that cured the political leadership of even legitimate and reasonable intervention in the 'professional' conduct of the military's affairs (Raghavan 2009: 172–4). As during the British Raj, the military stays isolated from the national mainstream, located in spiffy 'cantonments' and in built-up areas and well-kept compounds, left to carry on with their professional duties without much oversight by politicians and distanced from the hurly-burly of normal civilian life. It also means that decisions by the armed services headquarters about procurement and expenditure priorities, force structures and deployments, and other security-related issues are rarely questioned by the government, as long as these hew to the generalized 'operational directive' that the military has a role in crafting.

Much in the national security sphere, in other words, happens by rote, with the various agencies of government doing what they have always been doing and in the way they have always been doing it, with very little new or innovative thinking coming into play, least of all by the political leadership and the democratically elected rulers. In more advanced countries, the legislatures scrutinize every aspect of the defence policy and the military's functioning. When threats change, so do the emphases on capabilities, and instructions are issued by the government to the armed services to jettison this arm, demobilize that capability, and build up a singularly different force structure for the emerging environment. This constant monitoring of the external milieu by the political leadership and agreement on military priorities is what keeps the armed forces relevant. In India, however, none of this happens. In a democracy, which states are regarded as primary, secondary, and tertiary threats is a political decision for the political rulers of the day to make, not something for the military and careerists in the MEA and the MOD to decide. But this is precisely what does not happen. Had threats been periodically reassessed by newly elected prime ministers, it would have convinced them that in the new millennium, while the Pakistan threat, which never amounted to much if ever it amounted to anything at all, was declining fast, China loomed ever larger, and the reasonable thing to do was to begin aligning, reorienting, and restructuring the armed forces for the conflicts of tomorrow with China—a complex, growingly powerful, and diplomatically inventive adversary that will test the military's strength, strategy, stamina, and every sinew of the Indian state, and countering which needed new solutions and capabilities. But this requires the mechanisms for new ideas and novel analyses to be generated first, and debated and discussed later, within cabinet circles. For this, the incoming prime minister has to have a policy ideas cell in his or her office, such as the policy unit with Prime Minister Margaret Thatcher which seeded most of the extraordinary changes wrought during her time as head of the British government, or President Ronald Reagan's appointment of Harvard professor Richard Pipes to head a 'ginger group' to produce policy ideas to defeat the Soviet Union that the White House could run with. In the event, Thatcher's unit generated policies that wrought social revolution in the UK, and Reagan seeded the demise of Soviet Russia. That kind of self-confidence and the desire to radically change policies and their outcomes have not been evident in New Delhi. All that newly elected governments do is embroider at the edges the threats and military solutions the armed forces and MOD and MEA bureaucrats are habituated to.

Take the case of offensive warfare capability in the mountains. A need for such capability was first envisioned in the 1970s, but the authorization for two divisions both prospectively stationed in Assam came through only in 2009, with these formations expected to take the field by 2015–17. A formal approval for an MTC for offensive operations was also cleared, but only after the Chinese PLA intruded deep inside Ladakh in April 2013, creating a public furore. What has been authorized is a strike corps establishment of 80,000 troops with two independent brigades each of infantry and armour.[92] The MTC envisages each of these brigades as operating with integral airlift and logistics and capable of independent action, or, in concert with other brigades, of converging at certain points for attack or ingress into Tibet. The brigades include a provision of T-90 tanks to debouch onto the Tibetan plateau from the northern Sikkim plains in the east and the Demchok area from the western end in Ladakh. Close air support for the land forces has always been a lesser consideration for the IAF, which nevertheless opposed the army having its 'own little air force'. It was the usual turf war, which Defence Minister A. K. Antony passed off as 'family problems'.[93]

A typical 'please all' compromise followed with the army getting its aviation arm with a sanctioned strength of 400–500 aircraft, with 80 attack helicopters and 114 utility helicopters to be available to the army by 2022, in addition to the 250 indigenous *Dhruv* armed helicopters (designed and produced in Bangalore with assistance from the German firm Messerschmitt-Bolkow-Blohm (MBH) replacing the *Cheetah* (licence-produced *Aerospatiale Alouette* II) and *Chetak* (*Alouette* III) helicopters it already employs as 'air observations posts' for battlefield surveillance and for anti-tank encounters. The IAF bought 22 AH-64D *Apache Longbow* attack helicopters equipped with the anti-armour Hellfire missiles for $1.4 billion.[94] But this deal was linked to a larger scheme, with the aviation corps being seen as the Indian government's way of compensating the Indian Army for agreeing to deprioritize the MTC in line with a controversial Finance Ministry assessment that China did not constitute a threat in the foreseeable future, and that the initial cost of raising such a corps of Rs 64,000 crore ($13 billion) was prohibitive (Karnad 2012b). However, after the Chinese armed intrusions into Ladakh in spring 2013, the money was found and the MTC restored to the army. Luckily for the army, it gained its own aviation arm and the MTC!

In the event, a capability, including infrastructure for helicopter pilot training and servicing, has been duplicated in the two services, with a capital-intensive combat aviation arm, which has been on the cards since the mid-1980s when the then army chief General K. Sundarji, an alumnus of the US Army's Command and General Staff College, Fort Leavenworth, oversaw the mechanization of the land forces and reorganized them in accordance with his version of the air-land battle doctrine based on a fleet of 360 attack helicopters and over 600 mobile and towed artillery pieces. This plan was only partially funded, ensuring a modicum of mobile warfare capability, but ere long the air-land concepts that justified such purchases in the first place obsolesced, not least owing to the nuclearization of South Asia, even as the requirement for the urgently needed mountain offensive forces to keep the PLA in Tibet honest was formally voiced for the first time after 1979. The army's desire to retain its massive armoured and mechanized formations, add offensive mountain fighting forces to complement its defensive mountain divisions, and start up an air combat arm reflects the bureaucratic instinct and tendency of individual military services everywhere to secure the wherewithal to fight wars, as much as possible, by themselves. In India's case, where military capability decisions are always made in the context of a careful husbanding of resources, continuing weight accorded to improving mobile plains warfare capability with induction of new tanks, self-propelled guns, and mobile air defence artillery keeps the army's order-of-battle unbalanced. It suggests that the army is more serious about retaining a plains warfare capability, even when there is no big adversary to merit such forces and compel huge investments in them, than in snuffing out the danger from China (Pandit 2013b). Worse, continuing with the plains warfare–relevant force structure decants allocations from the urgently needed construction of military-use infrastructure on the China border, rendering impossible the funding of an additional two MTCs for a total of three offensive MTCs needed for the army to react flexibly and forcefully to Chinese aggression, and credibly to mount operations inside Tibet. The government is unwilling to make the hard choices of: (*a*) rationalizing and reconstituting the armoured/mechanized forces into a single composite corps with a number of independent armoured brigades under command to meet with any Pakistan-related contingency while transferring the manpower, establishment, and materiel from the two redundant strike corps to make up the two additional MTCs for offensive operations (instead of funding an MTC as an 'additionality'); and (*b*) denying the army its aviation arm but meeting its objections of an absent aerial ground support role by ordering IAF to put its helicopter wings fully under the army's operational control. This reluctance points up the lack of an institutional mechanism for *inter se* prioritization, and the inevitability of the government ultimately choosing the most expensive option available. It ensures that India never obtains a unified and cost-effective military and the proportionate bang for the buck.

Pakistan as the Indian government's and military's *idée fixe* means that the grand strategic aim of drawing Pakistan, in slow stages, into a subcontinental security system has been lost sight of. The opportunity cost to India and Pakistan of their forswearing normal trade and commercial relations, which could quickly jump to $40 billion annually from the present over-modest level (of around $3 billion), is especially hurtful to the prospects of the latter to fight its way out of the morass of terrorism and misgovernance it has contrived over the years to get mired in, and share economic opportunities and prosperity with India and the other subcontinental states (Nawaz and Guruswamy 2014). It is not that reorganizing the Indian land forces—by creating a single composite corps for the western front out of the three existing strike corps for plains warfare, and shifting the surplus resources to two additional mountain offensive corps—will instantly dissolve mistrust. But it will make Pakistan's apprehensions of India more difficult to sustain in the face of contrary and substantive evidence of an Indian army turning seriously China-wards, and gradually erode the Pakistan Army's unbridled hostility, and aid in the gradual normalization of India–Pakistan relations, starting with trade and economic cooperation.[95] It will shake the Indian armed forces out of the rut they are in, used as they have been for the last nearly seven decades to dealing with a Pakistan they knew could be beaten any time, to now having to prepare for the far sturdier military challenge posed by China, where the outcome is less predictable. Islamabad may still depend on China for its armaments and use its 'all-weather friendship' with Beijing as political leverage against India, but this will, as time goes on, matter less and less because an Indian military capability shaped to deal with China will be more than capable of tackling Pakistan, while the reverse is not true as is evidenced with the prevailing order-of-battle—the reason why India is militarily disadvantaged against China. Inducements offered to Islamabad in terms of unbeatable terms and preferential access to the Indian market, moreover, will progressively distance Pakistan from China, because Beijing cannot match the comprehensive benefits that could accrue to Pakistan from capitalizing on its geo-cultural nearness, and the natural affinity and connectivity between the South Asian peoples and economies at large. Befriending and coopting Pakistan in order more boldly to take on the bigger, more potent rival China, is the realist twist to the sage Thiruvalluvar's precepts. And, incidentally, it resonates with the advice proffered to his emperor by the still more ancient strategist from 223 BC, Kautilya (Chanakya) (Karnad 2005: 10–13) of collecting small neighbouring states to take on the behemoth. It has the virtue of trumping any variation of the current policy of non-provocative foreign policy coupled with passive-reactive defence against China, and attempts to overawe Pakistan by keeping the armoured strike forces cocked. It only exacerbates Islamabad's fears, persuading it to enlarge its nuclear weapons inventory, get closer to Beijing, ignore the possibility of a rapproachment with India, and provide Beijing the edge.

India's military growth is inevitable, but New Delhi cannot afford to spook smaller neighbours, a mistake made by Wilhelmine Germany, which persuaded a whole lot of adjoining states to seek security in a coalition that spelt its doom in the First World War. Indeed, pre–First World War Germany and the rising Japan of that era seem to be on the minds of Indian security managers. 'History is replete with examples of rising powers', said Shivshankar Menon, 'who prematurely thought that their time had come, who mistook their influence and weight for real power. Their rise, as that of Wilhelmine Germany or militarist Japan, was cut short prematurely.'[96] This is as surprising a takeaway by the former NSA as his slant on Thiruvalluvar, unless it is the case that he espied India doing a Germany or Japan, which, considering New Delhi's so far bumbling record in power politics, seems far-fetched. Moreover, like the mandala paradigm for geopolitics, this too represents a wrongly deterministic view. The fall of Wilhelmine Germany was no more inevitable than that of imperial Japan, had both these countries, having risen to the top, instead of territorial self-aggrandizement and throwing their weight around, opted to stay peaceful and become rich and powerful into the future. Bellicosity is not necessarily an adjunct of national power, which is what New Delhi believes and so shies away from. But the end-point of such logic is that because India forswears bellicosity, it should not strive for great power. The underlying premise, moreover, of such thinking by Menon and others of his ilk, that rising powers invariably become belligerent and militaristic, is both factually wrong and wrong-headed, in that it seems designed in the Indian context, where the political leadership, post-Nehru, has been unimaginative when not retiring and unobtrusive in the external realm, and only too willing to do less when more is required in big power politics. It is to circumscribe national ambition, set Indian policy in a declinist mode before the country has in any sense peaked, and to ensure that a whale-sized India continues to have the impact of a minnow. In such a milieu where political visioning and direction is missing but not petty politiking by politicians, India was bound to get a lot wrong in the foreign and military policy fields for very long. In practical terms, the reason for this state of affairs is attributed by the former BJP external affairs minister Jaswant Singh to the 'schism' between the foreign policy and military establishments. It has led, he writes, to 'lack of planning [which has] rendered our foreign and defense policy functions as two separate, often disjointed activities rather than as a functional whole. Consequently, our defense efforts are rendered inefficient, with unacceptable time and cost overruns, needless political interference, and counterproductive inter-service rivalries' (J. Singh 2013: 165).

Notes

1. The 1965 operations witnessed the biggest tank battles since the Allied Eighth Army clashed in the North African Desert with Rommel's Korps in the Second World War (see Keegan and Wheatcroft 1986: 55–6).

2. Army Chief General Bikram Singh said that a new Mountain Offensive Corps and a bunch of armoured brigades will be posted to the China border, and the strengthened stance can also deal with the 'China–Pakistan nexus'. See 'There will not be repeat of 1962 war, says Army chief General Bikram Singh', *India Today*, 20 September 2012, available at http://indiatoday.intoday.in/story/general-bikram-singh-sino-indian-war-indin-borders.1/217981.htm.

3. In one fell swoop, the BJP defence minister Arun Jaitley cleared Rs 70,000 crore worth of procurement deals for the armed services, ranging from submarines and guided munitions to missiles (Pandit 2014).

4. Shivshankar Menon, 'Asian Security Challenges', 10 January 2011.

5. On this issue, American geo-strategist Nicholas Spykman wrote: 'The truth of the matter is that states are interested only in a balance which is in their favor. Not an equilibrium, but a generous margin is their objective…. there is security only in being a little stronger…. . The balance desired is the one which neutralizes other states, leaving the home state free to be the deciding force and the deciding voice.' Quoted in Levy (2004: 44).

6. Shivshankar Menon, 'India's Role in Global Politics', 15 July 2011.

7. Interview, 10 February 2011.

8. Interview, 7 May 2012.

9. Interview, 7 May 2012.

10. On the decreasing military gap between China and America, Andrew S. Erickson of the US Naval War College says: 'Beijing has started far behind, but is closing the gap rapidly.' See 'An Interview with Andrew S.

Erickson', 19 September 2012, available at www.nbr.org/research/activity. aspx?id=272. Also see Philipp (2013).

11. Shivshankar Menon, 'India's Role in Global Politics', 15 July 2011.

12. Shivshankar Menon, 'Our Changing External Environment: Challenges and Opportunities', K. Subrahmanyam Forum, 31 October 2011.

13. Shivshankar Menon, 'India's Role in Global Politics', 15 July 2011.

14. David Scott, 'China's "Maritime Silk Route" Proposal—An Uncertain Chalice for India?', China–India, Brief #29, Centre for Asia and Globalization, National University of Singapore, 19 June 2014, available at http://lkyspp.nus.edu.sg/cag/publication/china-india-brief/china-india-brief-29?utm_source=China-India+Brief+subscribers&utm_campaign=81d9e435f1-China_India_Brief_29_10_June_2014&utm_medium=email&utm_term=0_a8f8390d56-81d9e435f1-96406833#guest.

15. Shivshankar Menon, 'India's Role in Global Politics', 15 July 2011.

16. The British Indian Army was the main force in the 'opium wars' of the 1840s that reduced China; it defeated the 'Mahdi' (the Osama bin Laden of the 1880s in the Sudan), pacified Egypt around the same time, lifted the siege of Beijing, contained the Boxer Rebellion in China in 1901, fought German forces in East Africa, and ousted the Ottoman Empire from its strongholds in Palestine and Mesopotamia in the First World War, besides sending units to the killing fields in Europe. It formed the bulk force in the Allied Eight Army that defeated Rommels' Afrika Korps in the North African deserts, and in the Fourteenth Army that destroyed the imperial Japanese land forces in Southeast Asia.

17. See *Annual Report to Congress: Military and Security Developments Involving the People's Republic of China 2012*, Office of the Secretary of Defense, May 2012, p. 8.

18. Andrew Scobell, lately of the US Army War College, is of the view that China 'is an ambitious power with weak naval capabilities'. See his 'China's Geostrategic Calculus and Southeast Asia—The Dragon's Backyard Laboratory', Testimony before the US-China Economic and Security Review Commission, 4 February 2010, available at http://uscc.gov/. See also Perlez (2012). However, PLA subs are active—22 contacts were reported in early 2013 (see Cole 2013).

19. Illustrating this aspect is the former Chinese defence minister Chi Haotian's statement that 'the ruthless have always won and the benevolent have always failed.' See Sawyer (2006: 33).

20. Meeting with the author, 18 October 2011.

21. Admiral Arun Prakash (Retd), 'India as a 21st Century Power: The Maritime Dimension', Admiral R. L. Pereira Memorial Lecture, Bengaluru, 25 May 2013.

22. The former NSA Shivshankar Menon said that, with 'India's interests abroad' expanding, it 'will no longer be possible to improvise and extemporize with what little we have.' See Menon, 'GP and the World', G. Parthasarathi Birth Centenary Lecture, 18 November 2013.

23. Shyam Saran, Special Envoy of PM, 'India's Foreign Policy and the Andaman & Nicobar Islands', Address to officers of the Integrated Andaman Command, edited version, Port Blair, 5 September 2009.

24. A former Chinese ambassador to India, Chen Ruisheng, for instance, extolled the importance of 'balance', which he believes India, China, and the US have achieved in their triangular relationship. 'Balance is very important; if one country can have good relations with the other two, then this country will have a very advantageous position', he said in an interview to an American academic journal. 'If one country has good relations with one country and not the other, then it will be disadvantageous, if one country has a bad relationship with both countries, then it will suffer from a very disadvantageous position.' See 'Reflections from China: An Interview with Cheng Ruisheng', *Journal of International Affairs*, vol. 64, no. 2, Spring/Summer 2011, p. 215.

25. In 2007, the IAF chief, Air Chief Marshal Fali Major (2007: 5), sketched 'the redrawn strategic boundaries of a resurgent India' as extending from 'the Persian Gulf to the Straits of Malacca and from Central Asian Republics to the Indian Ocean'. It requires, he said, 'radical change in our strategic thinking'.

26. The IAF recently reactivated its base at Thanjavur (previously Tanjore) on the south-eastern coast for maritime operations by Su-30s. See 'A. K. Antony dedicates IAF base at Thanjavur to nation', *Times of India*, 28 May 2013. The Thanjavur base was used during the Second World War to launch Lockheed Hudsons, P-47 Thunderbolts, and Hawker Hurricanes in the Southeast Asia theatre.

27. See also Joshua Kurlantzick, 'China's Charm: Implications of Chinese Soft Power', Policy Brief 47, Carnegie Endowment for International Peace, June 2006, pp. 4–8.

28. In a Chinese book on 'cultural flow', for instance, less than three pages out of 397 are devoted to Buddhism travelling from India to China and converting the Han ruler—incidentally, the only thing that is acknowledged as an Indian cultural import (see Fuwei 1996).

29. Proactive Chinese diplomacy in Micronesia and in the small island nations in the Pacific could loosen some of the US alliances and modify the attitude of a few countries. It is an exceedingly grand strategic design, but Beijing is not flinching from it. In fact, in furtherance of this objective, it has in recent years virtually colonized the island states in the Pacific with

migrants, methodical usurpation of economic space, and generous 'checkbook diplomacy'. See Bertil Linter's 'China's Third Wave' series, especially Linter (2007a, 2007b).

30. The Indian naval plans conceive of two 65,000-ton CVNs in service (Pandit 2013a).

31. On Vietnam's specific request for the Brahmos missile, see Roy Chaudhury (2013).

32. 'Vietnamese naval chief visits India to foster defense ties', *Defence Now*, available at www.defencenow.com/news/223/vietnam-naval-chief-visits-india-to-foster-defence-ties.html.

33. 'Mauritius offers India 2 islands in effort to preserve tax treaty', *Economic Times*, 3 July 2012.

34. Because of nil capital gains tax, Mauritius earns revenues from processing and routing fees for amounts constituting 40 per cent of foreign investment into India (Ramdas 2012).

35. Personal communication from a former naval chief.

36. Personal communication from a senior naval person. Also see Karnad (2012a).

37. Personal communication, February 2014, from K. V. Bhagirath, a retired Indian diplomat who served as the high commissioner to Mauritius in the early 2000s.

38. Personal communication from a retired senior Indian Navy officer.

39. Impressionistic evidence often cited for the success of this strategy is how regional naval chiefs gravitate towards the head of the Indian Navy not just at the IONS and Milan forums, but even at meetings in the West, such as the conference of naval chiefs called every alternate year by the chief of naval operations, US Navy. Communicated to me by a senior Indian naval officer.

40. A former foreign secretary was adamant that such cooperative military activity should not be advertised, because the recipient states had rather it not be made public.

41. Interview, 13 September 2011.

42. Communicated to the author by a former assistant chief of the naval staff (foreign cooperation and intelligence).

43. Email correspondence, 1 October 2012.

44. Interview, 21 October 2011.

45. Interview, 3 May 2012.

46. Shivshankar Menon, 'GP and the World', G. Parthasarathi Birth Centenary Lecture, 18 November 2013.

47. Personal communication, 12 September 2012.

48. Interview, 15 March 2011.

49. During his Indian tour in September 2012, Chinese defence minister General Liang Guanglie stated that 'the PLA has never established a military base overseas. The PLA Navy ships, while conducting long distance voyages, often went to close ports of littoral countries for logistic supply.... . Such logistic supply activities do not have any connection with establishing military bases overseas.' See his interview in the *Hindu*, 4 September 2012.

50. The assessment of the US Department of Defense, for instance, is that PLAN's goal is to 'extend its operational reach beyond the western Pacific and into ... the "far seas"', among them the Indian Ocean. See the *Annual Report to Congress: Military and Security Developments Involving the People's Republic of China 2014*, p. 37, available at http://www.defense.gov/pubs/2014_DoD_China_Report.pdf.

51. The Indian navy chief Admiral D. K. Joshi revealed that Indian warships were ready to thwart any attempts by the Chinese to hinder free passage in the South China Sea, prompting the Philippines to welcome the Indian stand (Bagchi 2012).

52. Personal communication from a senior naval officer. The Maldivian president Mohammad Nasheed, deposed in February 2012, revealed that a week before he was ousted, he had been under pressure from the Maldivian military to sign a defence pact with China. See Pubby (2014).

53. Tokyo has gifted patrol boats to Vietnam, and the Philippines is now the largest investor in Vietnam. See Trajano (2013). See also 'Japan, Vietnam vow to cooperate on regional challenges', *Nation*, 17 January 2013.

54. Tokyo is exploring arms sales as a means of security cooperation. See Zhigang (2014).

55. Shivshankar Menon, 'Our Changing External Environment: Challenges and Opportunities', K. Subrahmanyam Forum, New Delhi, 31 October 2011.

56. 'India-U.S. Relations: Progress amidst Limited Convergence', *CSS Analysis in Security Policy*, no. 117, July 2012, Center for Security Studies, ETH Zurich, available at www.css.ethz.ch/publications/pdfs/css_analysen_nr117_e.pdf. There is an argument being made that, for reasons of keeping China distracted on its land frontier, Washington ought to help India beef up its land forces, not the Indian maritime capability, as a way of easing military pressure on the US in the Western Pacific (Montgomery 2013).

57. Interview, Shyam Saran.

58. 'Vietnam India's pivot', *New Indian Express*, 31 October 2014.

59. Interview with a former naval chief, 5 October 2012.

60. C. Raja Mohan, 'Indian Military Diplomacy: Humanitarian Assistance and Disaster Relief', ISAS Working Paper, no. 184, National University of Singapore, 26 March 2014.

61. Personal communication from a former naval chief.

62. Personal communication from a former service chief.

63. Manila has evinced interest in buying two *Shivalik*-class stealth frigates. See 'Phl eyes frigates from India', *Philippine Star*, 23 October 2013, available at www.philstar.com/headlines/2013/10/23/1248390/phl-eyes-frigates-india.

64. Personal communication from Senior Integrated Defence Staff officers.

65. Email correspondence, 5 November 2012.

66. 'While IONS has great potential', avers Admiral Prakash, 'it has so far received only lukewarm support from the MEA.' See Admiral Arun Prakash (Retd), 'India as 21st Century Power: The Maritime Dimension', Admiral R. L. Periera Memorial Lecture, Bengaluru, 25 May 2013.

67. Interview with the author.

68. Personal communication, February 2012.

69. Most recently, see Shivshankar Menon, 'Samudra Manthan', 4 March 2013.

70. Personal communication, 8 October 2012.

71. John Mearsheimer, 'The Gathering Storm: China's Challenge to U.S. Power in Asia', Fourth Annual Michael Hintze Lecture in International Security, University of Sydney, 4 August 2011.

72. This anecdote is retailed in B. G. Verghese, '50 Years After 1962: A Personal Memoir', Subrahmanyam Forum, Round Table, New Delhi, 6 September 2012. Verghese, a veteran journalist, was information adviser to Prime Minister Indira Gandhi in the 1960s.

73. Shivshankar Menon, 'The Significance of India-China Relations', Speaking Notes, Centre for China Analysis and Strategy, 11 April 2014; text emailed to the author.

74. The MEA has always had a China-leaning group, as Nehru himself was aware. It is interesting to see what the take of the US Embassy in New Delhi was prior to the 1962 India–China conflict. Alan Carlin of the embassy, in his memo dated 17 July 1962 to the State Department, writes: 'The China section of the Ministry of External Affairs is dominated by a pro-Chinese group of which R. K. Nehru is a leading member. The Indian policy regarding China is based on a continuing belief that China does not want war (since Communism, according to Nehru, does not imply violence or expansionism), the pacifist fear that even if she does, such a war might develop into a major one, and the hope that the Russians would come to the rescue if worse came to worse. Until such time as this pro-Chinese group may be removed from the Ministry, no serious policy planning is likely to take place. The main obsession continues to be Pakistan, especially on the part of Menon.' This memo is available at www.rand.org/about/history/wohlstetter/DL10703/DL10703.html.

75. B.G. Verghese, '50 Years After 1962: A Personal Memoir', Subrahmanyam Forum, Round Table, New Delhi, 6 September 2012.

76. Closed session on 'China', Brookings-Federation of Indian Chambers of Commerce and Industry Dialogue on the India–US Strategic Partnership, New Delhi, 9 October 2012.

77. See the report *China-US Cooperation: Key to the Global Future*, by a China–US Joint Working Group, 17 September 2013, available at www. atlanticcouncil.org/.

78. 'Indian opposition welcomes Nawaz's India outreach', *Pakistan Today*, 15 May 2013, available at http://pakistantoday.pk.com/2013/05/15. indian-opposition-welcomes-nawazs-india-outreach/; and David Karl, 'India Should Not Leave Nawaz Sharif Hanging', Foreign Policy Association, 21 August 2013, available at http://foreignpolicyblogs.com/2013/08.21/ india-should-not-leavenawaz-hanging/.

79. See Karl, 'India Should Not Leave Nawaz Sharif Hanging'. For an analysis of the progressive radicalization of the Tibetan youth and society, see Arpi (2009).

80. 'I'm not convinced that increased military ramp-up is critical yet', said US Secretary of State John Kerry during his confirmation hearings. 'We have a lot more bases out there than [China]. We have a lot more forces out there than any other nation in the world, including China today... . You know the Chinese take a look at that and say, what's the United States doing? They trying to encircle us? ... every action has its reaction.... it's not just the law of physics; it's the law of politics and diplomacy. I think we have to be thoughtful about ... how we go forward.' Quoted in Economy (2013).

81. Deputy Secretary of Defense Ashton Carter admitted at a Congressional hearing in February 2013 that 'one of the ways our strategy would need to change is we couldn't do what we want to do in the rebalance in the Asia-Pacific theater.' He said the US would be unable to maintain its 'pivotal role', and US strategy 'is put in doubt and put in jeopardy if these further budgets cuts go on' (quoted in K. Wong 2013).

82. One of the senior staff members who prepared the US government report *Global Trends 2030* mentioned such an exchange in a personal communication to the author.

83. See also 'Hawkish Abe wants to change Constitution', *Japan Times*, 17 December 2013.

84. B.G. Verghese, '50 Years After 1962: A Personal Memoir', Subrahmanyam Forum, Round Table, New Delhi, 6 September 2012.

85. The Maoist guerrillas are active in a swathe of land stretching from the peninsular province of Andhra Pradesh, north through parts of central and eastern India, to the Nepal border, covering some 223 of the 603 administrative districts in the country. See Bedi (2011).

86. Shivshankar Menon, 'Our Changing External Environment: Challenges and Opportunities'.

87. For the then Indian army chief General S. Padmanabhan's views on why Operation Parakram failed, see Swami (2004).

88. The Pakistani analyst Ayesha Siddiqa (2014) argues that India has, in fact, turned Pakistan's asymmetric strategy against Pakistan, and is now using the cover of its nuclear weapons for aggressive action on the Line of Control in Kashmir.

89. Sporting, especially, boxing, metaphors revealingly abound in writings about India–Pakistan conflicts. See Khan (1979). Air Marshal Khan was chief of the Pakistan Air Force. See also Rikhye (1984).

90. Interview with the author.

91. Personal communication, former CINC, Integrated Defence Staff.

92. 'Army gets final nod to raise strike corps along LAC', *Times of India*, 20 November 2013.

93. 'Antony downplays IAF-Army turf war', *Times of India*, 19 October 2012.

94. Personal communication from an additional director-general in a directorate at Army Headquarters, 23 September 2012.

95. The normalization under way in India–Pakistan relations is palpable. The Indian Home Ministry, always very suspicious of allowing Pakistanis to enter India freely, has relented—approving not only a resumption of cricketing ties, with the Pakistan team undertaking a short tour in December 2012, but entry visas for Pakistani cricket enthusiasts to attend the matches. India, on an urgent request, has agreed to the export on a priority basis of 65 refurbished heavy duty diesel locomotives to the Pakistan railways. Pakistani films have, for the first time, been selected for the Mumbai Film Festival, and Islamabad sent its top official to negotiate the purchase of petroleum products from Indian refineries. On any given day, Pakistani dailies carry a mix of such stories. For example, see the e-version of the *Express Tribune* (Islamabad), 17 October 2012, available at www.tribune.com.pk. See also Hussain (2013).

96. Shivshankar Menon, 'India's Role in Global Politics'.

References

Abe, Shinzo. 2012. 'Asia's Democratic Security Diamond', *Project Syndicate*, 27 December. Available at http://project-syndicate.org/.

Arpi, Claude. 2009. 'How the Dalai Lama forsakes Independence', *Dialogue*, vol. 10, no. 4, April–June.

Arreguin-Toft, Ivan. 2001. *How the Weak Win Wars: A Theory of Asymmetric Conflict*. Cambridge: Cambridge University Press.

Bagchi, Indrani. 2012. 'Manila hails navy chief's stand', *Times of India*, 12 December.

———. 2013a. 'Abe's win augurs well for India's Japan-centric Look East policy', *Times of India*, 23 July.

———. 2013b. 'Suresh Reddy to be first envoy to Asean', *Times of India*, 29 October.

Bedi, Rahul. 2011. 'State told to disband militia fighting Maoist guerillas', *New Zealand Herald*, 13 July.

Bhasin, Avtar Singh, ed. 2012. *India-Pakistan Relations 1947-2007: A Documentary Study*. New Delhi: Public Diplomacy Division, MEA and Geetika Publishers.

Biswas, Ashis. 2012. 'Fresh tensions between China and Myanmar', *Echo of India* (Kolkata), 23 August. Available at http://epaper.echoofindia.com/sites/defauklt/files/P5_125.pdf.

Bose, Sugata. 2006. *A Hundred Horizons: The Indian Ocean in the Age of Global Empire*. Boston, MA: Harvard University Press.

Brewster, David, and Ranjit Rai. 2013. 'Operation Lal Dora: India's Aborted Military Intervention in Mauritius', *Asian Security*, vol. 9, no. 1.

Bush, Richard C. 2010. *Perils of Proximity: China-Japan Security Relations*. Washington, D.C.: Brookings Institution.

Cole, J. Michael. 2013. 'Red Star over the Indian Ocean?', *Diplomat*, 9 April. Available at http://thediplomat.com/flashpoints-blog/.

Cossa, Ralph A., Brad Glosserman, Lewis A. Dunn, and Li Hong. 2013. 'Building toward a Stable and Cooperative Long Term U.S.-China Strategic Partnership', *Issues & Insights*, vol. 13, no. 2, Center for Strategic and International Studies, 21 February. Available at http://csis.org/.

Datta, Sujan. 2011. 'China in mind, salute & port plea to Vietnam', *Telegraph* (Kolkata), 17 September.

Dikshit, Sandeep. 2013. 'When India drew top secret "red line" in Mauritius', *Hindu*, 10 March.

Economy, Elizabeth C. 2013. 'John Kerry on China', *Asia Unbound*, 27 February.

Fackler, Martin, and Choe Sang-Hun. 2013. 'Threats have South Korea flirting with nuclear talk', *International Herald Tribune*, 12 March.

Fair, C. Christine. 2011. 'The Militant Challenge in Pakistan', *Asia Policy*, no. 11, January. Available at http://asiapolicy.nbr.org/.

Fuwei, Shen. 1996. *Cultural Flow between China and Outside World through-out History*. Beijing: Foreign Languages Press.

Garver, John W. 2012. 'The Diplomacy of a Rising China in South Asia', *Orbis*, vol. 56, no. 3, Summer.

Gilboy, George J. and Eric Heginbotham. 2012. *Chinese and Indian Strategic Behavior: Growing Power and Alarm*. New Delhi: Cambridge University Press, First South Asian edition.

Gupta, Shishir. 2013. 'Indian warships closed in as crisis played out in Maldives', *Hindustan Times*, 11 March.

Hardy, James. 2012. 'China's new stealth fighter gambit', *Diplomat*, 21 September. Available at http://thediplomat.com/2012/09/21/china-new-stealth-fighter-gambit/.

Hornung, Jeffrey. 2013. 'Japan and India's growing embrace', *Diplomat*, 12 January. Available at: http://thediplomat.com/2013/01/12/japan-and-indias-growing-embrace/.

Horta, Lora. 2013. 'Dragon's Spear: China's Asymmetric Strategy', *YaleGlobal Online*, 17 October. Available at http://yaleglobal.yale.edu/content/dragon's=spear-asymmetric-strategy.

Hussain, Masood. 2013. 'LOC trade: goodwill hunting', *Economic Times Magazine*, 24–30 March.

Johnson, Ian. 2010. '"They Don't Want Moderate Uighurs"', *New York Review of Books*, 12 June. Available at: http://www.nybooks.com/blogs/nyrblog/2014/sep/22/trial-ilham-tohti-they-dont-want-moderate-uighurs/.

Jones, Brian. 2013. 'The 10 most powerful militaries in the world', *Business Insider*, 12 June 2013. Available at http://www.businessinsider.com/10-most-powerful-militaries-in-the-world-2013-6?op=1#ixzz2hU34dGF5.

Kanwal, Gurmeet. 2012. 'India's Military Modernization: Plans and Strategic Underpinnings', *National Bureau of Asian Research*, 24 September. Available at http://www.nbr.org/research/activity.aspx?id-275.

Kaplan, Robert D. 2003. *Warrior Politics: Why Leadership Demands a Pagan Ethos*. New York: Vintage Books.

———. 2012. 'Geography Strikes Back', *Wall Street Journal*, 7 September.

Karnad, Bharat. 2005. 'Aim Low, Hit Lower', *Seminar*, January. Available at www.india-seminar.com/.

———. 2009. 'Little room for manoeuvre', *Mint*, 21 January. Available at http://www.livemint.com/Opinion/QpmwEhapRefMYKgm6E1K9M/Little-room-for-manoeuvre.html.

———. 2012a. 'Defense tutorial', *Asian Age*, 25 October.

———. 2012b. 'Delhi is in a China daze, again. Beware!', *Asian Age*, 30 August 2012. Available at: www.asianage.com/.

Katoch, P.C., Lt Gen. (Retd). 2013. 'Military Diplomacy and National Security', *USI Journal*, July–September.

Kazianis, Harry. 2012. 'Australia's Japanese sub play', *Diplomat*, 12 July. Available at http://thediplomat.com/flashpoints/.

Keating, Joshua. 2012. 'Why the Japan-China island dispute is an American problem', *Foreign Policy*, 12 September. Available at http://blog.foreign-policy.com/.

Keegan, John, and Andrew Wheatcroft. 1986. *Zones of Conflict: An Atlas of Future Wars*. New York: Simon & Schuster.

Khan, Mohammad Asghar, Air Marshal. 1979. *First Round: Indo-Pakistan War, 1965*, 1st Indian edn. New Delhi: Vikas.

Kilcullen, David. 2011. *The Accidental Guerilla: Fighting Small Wars in the Midst of a Big One*. New York: Oxford University Press.

Lambeth, Benjamin S. 2012. *Airpower at 18,000': The Indian Air Force in the Kargil War*. Washington, D.C.: Carnegie Endowment for International Peace.

Lee, John. 2013. 'Revanchist China', *Project Syndicate*, 25 February.

Levy, Jack S. 2004. 'What Do Great Powers Balance Against and When', in *Balance of Power: Theory and Practice in the 21st Century*, edited by T. V. Paul, James J. Wirtz, and Michel Fortmann. Stanford: Stanford University Press.

Linter, Bertil. 2007a. 'A new breed of migrants fans out', *Asia Times*, 16 April.
———. 2007b. 'The Sinicizing of the South Pacific', *Asia Times*, 17 April.

Major, F. H. 2007. 'Aerospace Power in a Changed National Security Environment', *Air Power Journal*, vol. 2, no. 3, Monsoon.

Malik, V. P., General. 2006. *Kargil: From Surprise to Victory*. New Delhi: HarperCollins India.

Mazaar, Michael J. 2012. 'The Risks of Ignoring Strategic Insolvency', *Washington Quarterly*, Fall.

Menon, Shivshankar. 2013. 'National and Economic Security', *Growth Net*, 11 March.

Montgomery, Evan Brandon. 2013. 'Competitive Strategies against Continental Powers: The Geopolitics of Sino-Indian-American Relations', *Journal of Strategic Studies*, vol. 36, no. 1.

Nawaz, Shuja, and Mohan Guruswamy. 2014. *India and Pakistan: The Opportunity Cost of Conflict*. South Asia Center, Atlantic Council, Washington, D.C., April. Available at www.atlanticcouncil.org/publications/reports/india-and-pakistan-the-opportunity-cost-of-conflict.

Nayar, K. P. 2013. 'The national security adviser's speech in Munich', *Telegraph* (Kolkata), 13 February.

Nayar, V. K., Lieutenant General (Retd). 2013. *From Fatigues to Civvies: Memoirs of a Paratrooper*. New Delhi: Manohar.

Neuman, Craig H. 2012. 'Forging an Indian Partnership', *Strategic Studies Quarterly*, Summer.

Ng, Teddy. 2013. 'Japan's PM Shinzo Abe fails to win Obama's support in Diaoyus Row', *South China Morning Post*, 24 February.

Noi, Goh Sui. 2013. 'Asean eyes India as "soft balancer"', *Straits Times* (Singapore), 11 March.

Nye Jr, Joseph S. 2012. 'China's Soft Power Deficit', *Wall Street Journal*, 8 May.

O'Hanlon, Michael. 2008. *Unfinished Business: U.S. Overseas Military Presence in the 21st Century*. Washington, D.C.: Center for New American Security, June.

Pandit, Rajat. 2013a. 'Eye on future, India mulls option for nuclear-powered aircraft carrier', *Times of India*, 1 August.

———. 2013b. 'Army weapons upgrade plan yet to gather steam', *Times of India*, 23 October.

———. 2014. 'Govt to take call on key def deals worth Rs 70,000 cr', *Times of India*, 23 October 2014.

Panikkar, K. M. 1953. *Asia and Western Dominance: A Survey of the Vasco Da Gama Epoch of Asian History, 1498–1945*. London: Allen & Unwin.

Perlez, Jane. 2012. 'China launches carrier, but experts doubt its worth', *New York Times*, 25 September.

Perlez, Jane, and Chris Buckley. 2014. 'China's leader, seeking to build its muscle, pushes overhaul of the military', *New York Times*, 24 May.

Philip, Jojithomas, and Sruthijith K. K. 2013. 'As China takes space, India looks for room', *Economic Times*, 18 March.

Philipp, Joshua. 2013. 'China expands space warfare capabilities', *Epoch Times*, 24 September. Available at www.theepochtimes.com/.

Pubby, Manu. 2014. 'Maldives seeks India's help for new naval base', *Indian Express*, 19 May.

Raghavan, Srinath. 2009. 'Civil-Military Relations in India: The China Crisis and After', *Journal of Strategic Studies*, vol. 32, no. 1.

———. 2014. 'The Henderson Brooks morality play', *Indian Express*, 20 March.

Ramachandran, Sudha. 2007. 'India's quiet sea power', *Asia Times*, 7 August. Available at www.atimes.com/.

———. 2011. 'China ramps up pressure on Kashmir', *Asia Times*, 4 January. Available at http://www.atimes.com/atimes/South_Asia/MA04Df01.html.

Ramdas, A.K. 2012. 'Agalega or Andaman Islands? Develop both as strategically important', *Moneylife*, 1 October. Available at www.moneylife.in/.

Ranjan, Amitav. 2013. 'Countering China: Vietnam offers five blocks to India on nomination basis', *Indian Express*, 21 November.

Rikhye, Ravi. 1984. *The Fourth Round: The War That Never Was*. New Delhi: ABC Publishing House.

Roy, Kaushik. 2012. *Hinduism and the Ethics of Warfare in South Asia: From Antiquity to the Present*. Cambridge: Cambridge University Press.

Roy, Shubhajit. 2012. 'India, ASEAN elevate ties to strategic partnership', *Indian Express*, 21 December.

———. 2013. 'India signs "West Philippine Sea" statement', *Indian Express*, 23 October.

Roy Chaudhury, Dipanjan. 2013. 'Vietnam leader's visit key to rebalancing in SE Asia', *Economic Times*, 20 November.

Samuels, Richard. 2013. 'Evolution of Japan's Grand Strategy', *East Asia Forum*, 4 June. Available at: www.eastasiaforum.org/2013/06/04/evolution-of-japan's-grand-strategy/.

Sawyer, Ralph D. 2006. 'Chinese Strategic Power: Myths, Intent, and Projections', *Journal of Military and Strategic Studies*, vol. 8, no. 4, Summer.

Scobell, Andrew, and Andrew J. Nathan. 2012. 'China's Overstretched Military', *Washington Quarterly*, Fall.

Siddiqa, Ayesha. 2014. 'Logic of deterrence', *Express Tribune*, 30 October.

Singh, A.K. 2013. 'Japan as partner in the East', *Asian Age*, 17 January.

Singh, Jaswant. 2013. *India at Risk: Mistakes, Misconceptions, and Misadventures of Security Policy*. New Delhi: Rainlight-Rupa.

Stepanova, Ekaterina. 2008. *Terrorism as Asymmetrical Conflict: Ideological and Structural Aspects*, SIPRI Research Report No. 23. Oxford: Stockholm International Peace Research Institute and Oxford University Press. Available at: http://books.sipri.org/files/RR/SIPRIRR23.pdf.

Swami, Praveen. 2004. 'Gen. Padmanabhan mulls over lessons of Operation Parakram', *Hindu*, 6 February. Available at: http://www.hindu.com/2004/02/06/stories/2004020604461200.htm.

———. 2014. 'Talking to Pakistan in its language', *Hindu*, 11 June.

Trajano, Julius Cesar I. 2013. 'Japan-Philippine Relations: New Dynamics in Strategic Partnership', *RSIS Commentaries*, no. 037/2013, 28 February.

Triplett, William C., III. 2012. 'On China's many atrocities', *Washington Times*, 28 September.

Tuan, Hoang Anh. 2012. 'Chinese Strategic Miscalculations in the South China Sea', *Asia Pacific Bulletin*, no. 181, 27 September. Available at: http://eastwestcenter.org/sitea/default/files/private/apb_181.pdf.

Williams, Matthias. 2011. 'India courts Myanmar, Vietnam amid China tension', Reuters, 10 October.

Wong, Edward. 2012. 'China's communist party chief acts to bolster military', *New York Times*, 14 December.

Wong, Kristina. 2013. 'Gen. Martin Dempsey: Pentagon reassessing defense strategy under sequestration', *Washington Times*, 14 March.

Yew, Lee Kuan. 2011. 'China's growing might and the consequences', Forbes.com, 28 March.

Yung, Christopher D., and Ross Rustici, with Scott Devary and Jenny Lin. 2014. *'Not an Idea We Have to Shun': Chinese Overseas Basing Requirements in the 21st Century*. Washington, D.C.: National Defense University Press.

Zhigang, Da. 2014. 'Japan's new arms export riles offer many loopholes to nationalists', *Global Times*, 19 March. Available at: www.globaltimes.cn/.

5

Military Infirmities and Strengths

India's military is not strategic except in parts. Its sense of operational space is limited to the subcontinent and its aversion to foreign basing to enlarge its presence, shows that it lacks the will, if not the aptitude or the wherewithal, for expeditionary, actions. There is, however, now desire, as the then air force chief-designate, Air Marshal Arup Raha wrote, 'to provide the desired strategic footprint' described by him as 'the capability to influence the environment from the Suez to Malacca/Shanghai'.[1] As armed forces of a would-be great power they ought to have an institutional role in national security policy-making, which they do not, compelling them to deal with the government through the agency of the Ministry of Defence manned by generalist civil servants with little domain expertise or technical competence. Ideally, the armed forces would have to be familiar with modern technology and its ramifications, keep updating their knowledge base with regard to operational circumstances in modern warfare, and have to be open to the transformative effects of technology organizationally and in terms of the inter- and intra-service communications and command and control structures. It is in this respect that the Indian armed services, with the army in the van have, by and large, remained immune to technology-induced transformation and, hence, haven't implemented systemic changes to make them capable of obtaining decisive results fast, with minimum loss of life and expenditure of resources. In short, the Indian military is years away from having its disparate capabilities integrated operationally and command-wise, becoming network-centric, and experiencing the so-called Revolution in Military Affairs (RMA). It is presumably by such metrics as also the more traditional ones that the 'combat power' of the Indian military suffers in comparison to China in the ratio of 1:3, according to an official document. By 2027 is when that the 'desirable ratio' of 1: 1.5 is expected to be reached, with the deployment of the newly raised offensive mountain corps reducing the imbalance to 1:2.1 by 2022.[2]

India's military, despite boasting of a fine operational record and being battle-hardened with enormous live-fire experience is, nevertheless, mostly industrial age, with only limited skills in a contemporary high-technology battlefield. Being unreceptive to technology-dictated organizational transformation has costs: The most it will be capable of in the future is what it has done well in the past—mostly fight the old style conventional wars with Pakistan, or in close quarter fighting take on insurgents and terrorists in the sub-conventional context. This is not to say that Indian armed forces are not impressive and cannot hold their own against a modern military as this chapter will show. But rather that had they been more intellectually alive, organizationally elastic, and open to the change-inducing aspects of technology, while retaining its strengths, such as the army's fabled regimental spirit, the Indian military would be a more useful instrument in boosting the country's stock as a coming power.

This chapter will discuss the weaknesses and strengths of the three armed services less with reference to their weapons inventories than the political restraint on them, their operational capability, reaction to new technology, receptivity to organizational change, and their antipathy to home-made military goods.

Technological Deficiency

The Indian armed forces have always been technology-deficient for several reasons, some of them historical. In the colonial era, British units had better weapons than their Indian counterparts, who were kept studiously away from acquiring expertise in handling long range guns, for example, because the British feared they would be turned against them. In the precursor colonial forces, moreover, Indians entering officer ranks starting in the 1920s (with the underway programme of 'Indianisation' of the officer cadre) in the British Indian

Army, the Royal Indian Air Force, and the Royal Indian Navy, were kept busy with regimental/fighting unit-level duties and sharpening their tactical skills and rarely posted to the General Staff to acquire skills in strategizing, and in assessing international developments, trends in military technology and changes in warfare, and in drafting war plans, and planning force structures for future conflicts. After independence and the fairly abrupt departure of the British officers, these Indian officers, lacking experience in higher military planning and strategic thinking, won accelerated promotions to senior ranks where they institutionalized their own professional limitations and severely tactical mindset. With tactical proficiency as the main consideration for promotion, a service culture and reward system evolved such that use of intellect for strategic visioning and for generating insights into threat and outcomes-based force planning were not at a premium, but being with the troops out in the field was.[3] In the event, technological advances propel transformative change, which has to be envisioned and prepared for and leads to periodic upheavals in military organizations (Adamsky 2010: 2). But change is not what the Indian armed services are good at.

The Indian Air Force, having started as a tactical adjunct to the Royal Air Force, is the worst off in this respect, its leadership's experience of small actions, when not sitting out numerous small wars the country has engaged in since 1947, merely reinforced the view the service had of itself as a sub-strategic force. 'What happened was that when we inherited from the RAF the Spitfire and the Tempest aircraft, and whatever else was available to us, the mindset remained of the Second World War...So...talking of what is our thought process, even today we are still mired in World War Two, whereas things have moved far ahead,' confessed Air Marshal A.K. Singh (Retd.), former Commander of the Western Air Command. 'Until and unless the government suggests that we need to direct our power outward, how will we plan?'[4] One of the effects of the overly-tactical approach is the emphasis on the newest fighter plane and making ad hoc acquisition of whichever aircraft were available. Instead of planning on the basis of long-term, medium-term, and immediate requirements, 'What we have been doing,' he explained, 'is making Hobson's choices' of the aircraft on offer, even as the IAF has 'projected an image that [it] will be in a position to counter any attack from Pakistan, and maybe—that's a huge question mark—to do something against China.[5] This has been enough to reassure the Indian government, which too rarely thinks beyond Pakistan. Whence purchases of mainly tactical jets have been approved with huge price tags without reference to indigenous aircraft under development whenever the IAF made noises—which was all the time—about falling combat aircraft squadron strength. With new fighter planes obtained virtually at its will, the air force has felt no compulsion, for example, to consider economical alternatives, such as retrofitting the latest avionics and integrating the most advanced weapons into slightly older but adequate platforms.[6] Nor does it feel the need to commit to indigenous aircraft design and development projects that in the long run would make it independent of foreign suppliers and, therefore, a more effective force capable of sustained warfighting instead of, as is the case now, being at the mercy of supplier states for spares and service support procuring which, in war time, can quickly become an expensive and tricky diplomatic business and reduce force effectiveness. To the extent it countenances locally made products at all it is mostly licensed production of proven foreign aircraft.[7]

The navy is different. Its oceanic medium has endowed it with a strategic perspective reflected, for instance, in an in-house warship and submarine design and development directorate, emphasizing self-reliance. This attitude is attributed by naval stalwarts to the fact that Royal Navy officers commanded the service into the late 1950s, instilling the habit of planning long, thinking distant, and securing appropriate long-haul ships, like the first aircraft carrier (ex-HMS Hercules, renamed Vikrant) in the 1960s—the first Asian navy to secure one.[8] The correlation between British commanders into the 1950s and the service becoming strategic in its perspective cannot, however, explain why, despite the IAF being headed by a British Chief as late as 1954, it did not benefit in the same way as the navy did.[9]

But the most telling reason for the short-range, short-term, mindset of the military was the advice offered by the British physicist, Lord Blackett, who had considerable influence on Nehru's thinking on defence. As regards the type of military India should have, Blackett argued at the time of independence that India, given its economic limitations, ought realistically to prepare to fight only, what he called, 'marginal wars'. His contention was that were India to take on a world-class power, it would lose no matter how well it planned operations and its troops performed on the battlefield. On the other hand it would win without undue effort were it to tangle with smaller adjoining states and, therefore, that the Indian armed forces ought to optimize their capabilities to take on a like military power. In the aftermath of the indecisive 1947–1948 conflict over Kashmir, Pakistan fell into that slot of a country to fight 'marginal wars' with even though it was not then, and is even less today a power on par, leave alone a credible military threat. With the disparity generally between the two countries growing fast, India's military concerns about Pakistan are simply not maintainable (Karnad 2005: 127–30). Further, 'marginal war' by definition cannot be annihilatory or decisive in nature, which fits in with the domestic political constraints (discussed in earlier chapters) owing to the organic socio-cultural links with Pakistan. It has tied the Indian government's hand, as it were, permitting the prosecution of only heavily curtailed conflicts which pass for 'wars'. But Blackett's advice of the late 1940s related to an impecunious India with limited military capacity. The trouble is Nehru took it too much to heart, and pruned the wartime Indian Army of nearly 2.4 million to a force of 400,000 at Partition and to 280,000 by September 1947. This was around the time, writes Major General (Retd) P.J.S. Sandhu, 'when the Chinese had made their intentions of liberating Tibet quite clear and their forces actually advanced into Tibet in January 1950 [even as] the Government of India continued with its "economy" exercise in relation to defence expenditure' with the defence spend plummeting to 0.52 per cent of GDP in 1960. It is hardly to be wondered, adds Sandhu, that the Commander-in-Chief, India, General K.C. Cariappa when asked by Nehru in 1949 if the Indian forces could intervene to block the PLA said they could not.[10] Nevertheless, the Pakistan orientation of the Indian military got entrenched in the following decade with the defence minister, Krishna Menon, giving the anti-Pakistan tilt a Cold War ideological hue as putting the boot into a US client and, by extension, an imperialist America. It has since become an institutionalized posture of the three services with the land, air, and naval deployments heavily skewed towards the western border and the northwestern Arabian Sea with no thought given to whether Pakistan in fact poses any real danger as to warrant such singular attention. Nor have the political and strategic costs incurred in terms of India being unprepared and incapable of taking on the larger, more potent adversary ever been calculated. The attitude of the armed services to pick on a smaller adjoining state, keep this enmity stoked, and reap the benefit of justifying a force structure heavily weighted, as earlier mentioned, with legacy assets—vast fleets of tanks and armoured personnel carriers (APCs) in the three Strike Corps (I, II, and XXI) constituting the sharp edge and the pride of the army, never mind the excessive cost of keeping them in fighting trim. Three such corps are deemed necessary, ironically, because of a 1962 China War-related Resolution of Parliament still on the books, to defend 'every inch of territory'. This political injunction has been literally interpreted, instilling in the military the fear of losing even miniscule amounts of land to adversary states resulting in a rigorously defended border and an intensely defensive approach, requiring very large forces to hold ground. The army brass, as a consequence, has grown as risk-averse as the government, contemplating offensive action only if the situation holds not the slightest possibility of a reverse involving loss of territory. In practical military terms, it has psychologically disabled the Indian land forces from carrying out offensive actions and against preparing for straight-out offensives and the Indian military, generally, from thinking strategic and out-of-area because most of their resources are inward-turned, focused on keeping the border intact![11] Curiously, the 'not an inch of land to be lost' mentality also apparently motivates the PLA, except in contrast to the situation in India the Chinese leadership sanctions an aggressive, proactive, and pre-emptive approach to protecting territory by defending national interests at distance from the heartland.[12]

The air force because of its aforementioned ingrained tactical attitude is, likewise, more comfortable tackling a predictable foe, Pakistan, than tangling with its Chinese counterpart. The exception again is the Indian Navy, which perhaps because of its sea power traditions escaped the narrow interpretation of this stricture, and today has more credibility with the government as a versatile, over-the-horizon, force capable of realizing a 'theatre-switching' response to Chinese aggression across the mountainous border (more on this later). Worse, the limited war notions ingrained in the army and air force means they prepare only for short, sharp, encounters restricted to the disputed border areas, with matching levels of stocks and replenishment of the war wastage reserve (spares and POL—petroleum, oil, lubricants) and war stock (ammunition, artillery shells, missiles) without very elaborate logistics infrastructure. Adhering to these basic parameters of armed campaigns, the Indian military ends up waging precisely the sort of 'marginal wars' with Pakistan conceived by Blackett; that in 1965, for instance, ended in an impasse because both sides exhausted their ammunition. The longer duration, more decisive, wars China can impose on India is something the Indian armed services have simply not contemplated, are unprepared to fight, and realistically cannot cope with. This situation is compounded by the fact of an under-developed indigenous defence industry unsupported by the military, that is capable of only license-manuscfacture of foreign armaments from imported semi- and completely-knocked down kits, and lacks both the capacity for technology innovation and for surge production to meet heightened requirements in war time.[13]

Laggards in Transformation

Tradition-bound militaries are rarely able to affect speedy transformations. Organizational overhaul and attitudinal change are resorted to only when it is unavoidable and then the changes are rung in at a deliberate speed over a long period of time. Because technology and changes in the regional and international security milieus do not wait upon unreceptive militaries, the Indian armed services invariably find themselves behind the curve.

As the senior service, the army, has shown little interest in or talent for continually absorbing new technologies and adapting itself to them, having undergone this process precisely twice in the last six plus decades. The first was after the cathartic defeat in the short war with China in 1962 that brought in mountain warfare divisions. And the second time was in the mid to late 1980s when a headstrong chief, General K. Sundarji, rammed his concept of air-land battle down the army's throat. The fighting forces fronting on Pakistan were reconstituted, for this purpose, into Reorganized Army Plains Infantry Divisions (RAPIDS), including armoured and mechanized units for offensive and defensive operations in the Punjab and desert sectors.[14] This last makeover was, however, only partial because the up-tempo, mobile, operations he envisaged requiring a force of vastly augmented surveillance systems, attack helicopters, and self-propelled artillery operating in unison with masses of tanks and APCs, and involved huge initial capital investment and recurring expenditure which the government did not commit to.

Wholesale military re-organization and reconstitution to unify the forces and the higher command has not happened because the armed services brass are comfortable with the individual service turfs and autonomy in decision-making. As the senior service, the army sets the tone for the Defence Ministry and the government because it takes up half the defence budget and, unlike the air force and navy, is closest to the ground and on a permanently active mode. Owing to the permeable and contested border in Kashmir, which Pakistan-based jihadi terrorist guerrillas surreptitiously try and cross, and trigger artillery duels and exchanges of small arms across the Ceasefire Line (called the Line of Control or LoC) on an ongoing basis with the Pakistan Army. To the north and east is the disputed and undemarcated border with China called the Line of Actual Control (LAC), hostile actions by PLA keeps the army vigilantly busy, as do counter-insurgency operations against rebel movements in the northeastern provinces. Politicians are especially sensitive to the army's concerns also because as a large employment generator, military remittances upkeep local economies, and service families together with the politically mobilized community of ex-Servicemen comprise a vote bank that cannot be ignored. Within the army, the tussle to influence the army brass and, by extension, the government is between the Military Operations (MO) Directorate at the Army Headquarters, in-charge of the day-to-day operational issues, and the Perspective Planning (PP) Directorate tasked with drawing up long-term force planning and qualitative force upgrade schemes to fight tomorrow's wars. With the government defining national security narrowly as strictly border defence, and the concerns about loss of territory and untoward happenings on a daily basis along the two disputed borders, the MO Directorate's emphases and outlook end up taking precedence over the PP Directorate's plans when it comes to procurement priorities.

Thus, much of the military ends up engaged in filling the chinks revealed by the latest conflagration on the border and the last crisis. The result is an army-induced pull in the Indian military's thinking, attitude, effort, and disposition towards a status quo that fits in with the government's policy, of dealing forthrightly with Pakistan and, pussyfooting around China's provocations.

'Getting into a fight with China,' declared Manmohan Singh's NSA Shivshankar Menon, 'is the worst possible scenario' and is to be avoided.[15] Such a weak-kneed stance vis-à-vis the graver threat reflects only too well the circumspection when dealing with armed Chinese intrusions and ends up side-tracking plans to shape forces for more testing contingencies. Thus, a 2009 Indian Army study on force transformation listed the weaknesses against China—unfavourable combat ratios, poor border infrastructure hindering rapid mobilization and deployment of additional forces within short timelines, and large 'gaps' especially in space-based systems and, in particular, intelligence–surveillance–reconnaissance and cyber warfare capabilities. These gaps persist because the immediate needs of deployed forces consume the bulk of the army's budgetary allocation for the China sectors (Sahgal 2012: 293). This deficit can be made up by de-rating the Pakistan threat, and diverting funds from the armoured/mechanized forces-related programmes and other expenditures on the Pakistan front.[16] But this is not done—the reason why the China front-specific capabilities, such as mountain corps for offensive warfare on the Tibetan plateau, took long to materialize, why only two of the three authorized regiments of the specialized mountain-use Brahmos supersonic cruise missile able to pop up over the ridgeline, speed vertically down to ground level before homing in on targets, have been fielded when the original deployment timeframe for three regiments was 2015, with another three regiments by 2027, and why the conversion of the Agra-based airborne unit into a heliborne Air Assault Brigade is incomplete.[17]

Cooperation, Not Integration

There's much talk and any number of seminars in military training forums on the need for integration and joint operations by the three armed services, but there's almost no movement on the ground to achieve these goals. Moreover, inter-service clashes of interest have derailed the reforms aiming for unified armed services under a Chief of Defence Staff (CDS). The IAF's long-time resistance to CDS, because of the fear of the army as senior service monopolizing that post, is now buttressed, ironically, by the army's newfound opposition to it because of its apprehension that the IAF and navy having, by its light, captured the government's imagination in the new Century with the authorization of a number of combat aircraft procurement schemes (Su-30s, 'Super Sukhois', and the MMRCA) and of the naval plans to obtain a 50 capital ship-navy by 2030, that it fears officers from these services, may be preferred as CDS. The mutual suspicions of the army and IAF, in the main, even killed off a compromise proposal recommended by the Task Force on National Security chaired by a former Defence Secretary, Naresh Chandra, of a fourth four-star rank officer as permanent Chairman, Chiefs of Staff Committee (CCOS), as a quasi-CDS.[18] The jaundiced reaction of the army and air force to the CDS system is echoed among the political class and the civilian permanent secretariat (the bureaucracy), who equate such a post with the increased possibility of a *coup d'état*. The existing antiquated system of the three autonomous military services with their integration proceeding on a need-to basis thus gets a lease on life. It has exasperated the more enlightened military brass.[19] The lowest common denominator solution, in the event, is inter-service 'cooperation' as a tried and tested system which worked in the past and is expected to deliver the goods in the future. But such cooperation is the bottom step in a 'four-rung ladder' with the next higher rungs progressively being 'coordination', 'jointness', and finally 'integration', with the integrated forces, in the last stage, carrying out missions/roles in seamless fashion under a comprehensively unified command and unified structures down to the lowest levels of fighting, communications, and logistics units.[20] With the military functioning as tardily as the over-bureaucratized Indian state it deals with, absent CDS or even a permanent CCOS, means that in crisis, as in peace time, the existing ramshackle system of fitful, sometimes even grudging, inter-service cooperation is what the country has to make do with. Indeed, the single service attitude is so pronounced that while the idea of three additional unified or 'integrated commands' has been accepted as jointly manned outfits, it has gone down easier only because each service has been allotted one of these new commands to lead permanently—the prospective Aerospace Command as the air force's bailiwick, Cyber Command the navy's, and Special Forces Command the army's.[21] This arrangement is unlike in the two existing 'integrated' commands—Strategic Forces Command (SFC) controlling the nuclear forces and the Andaman Command—where integrated functioning is undermined by rotational leadership. In addition, there are 17 other operational (or theatre) commands run separately by the three services, none of them, however, co-located, ensuring distance will lead inevitably to communications and operational snafus. A former service chief disclosed why the present system is favoured by the military: It allows the CCOS of the day, he said, to use the marginal advantage his perch allows him to push his own service's programmes with the Defence Ministry. That left him, he said, with just '15–20 per cent' of his time for devoting to jointness-integration issues and the demands of the other two services. A CDS, supported by the Headquarters Integrated Defence Staff as his secretariat, and deciding on inter se prioritization of plans and procurement programmes, because they'll be unable to control the decision process, is something the services oppose.[22]

Autonomous functioning by the services is, however, taken to extremes, For example, not only do the three services have separate communications platforms and protocols, which makes them difficult to be on the same line real-time, they absolutely avoid cooperating jointly to procure the same genus of hardware, often from the same supplier, which because of larger volumes would fetch the country better financial terms and the services better unit price. Instead, to justify the separate roles, the suppliers are asked to tweak the systems just enough, to conform to the slightly differing requirements, just so they are not inter-operable, necessitating separate operating norms, protocols, and units and larger over-all expenditures for duplicated or triplicated fighting, surveillance, and servicing capacities.[23] The competitive conditions created by individual service-based decision-making, planning, and acquisitions processes have belatedly been recognized as a liability, but the solutions mooted are not holistic. Emblematic of this problem is the project spearheaded, for instance, by and at the initiative of the Indian IT major, Tata Consultancy

Services (TCS). Working with the army's signals directorate, TCS activated a secure communications platform in end-2012 that for the first time linked 22 'strategic' points and command posts with each other in the country and MOD (including nine army corps commands, six air force theatre commands, Andaman Command, Strategic Forces Command, and two naval fleet commands). However, the efficacy of this system is weakened because all communications below this level are still channelled through individual service communications grids.[24] This is an improvement on what existed before but preserves the downstream ills of an adversary being able to exploit the disjunctions in the digitized battle space. The autonomous service mentality is encouraged and fortified by the absence of a single comprehensive strategic vision/ends-and-objectives document from government that the services can refer to as joint planning mandate. Thus, on the battlefield success is dependent, as in the past, on happenstance and personal relations between commanders (fostered, for instance, by being batch mates in the graduating class from the tri-service National Defence Academy) than because the outcomes were planned. Invariably, capabilities that are sanctioned will suffer from having lacked for enough strategic inputs and jointness attributes, and acquisitions will continue to be ad hoc and single service-oriented, leading to wastefully redundant capabilities, and of downstream institutions and effort. In fact, so conspicuously spendthrift, unbalanced, and mid-twentieth century vintage is the Indian military system that visiting foreign military officers are taken aback. Recalling his meetings with the Indian Chiefs of Staff, a visiting Vice Chief of the U.K. Defence Staff, for example, professed surprise at their 'resource constraints-free' thinking and attitude and how 'conservative' (meaning traditional, non-innovative) their thinking tended to be. He also pointed out the lack of a 'strategic' sense and method in the acquisitions plans of the three services with the Indian government allowing each service to buy what it wants without reference to the hardware procured by the other two services, and the overall strategic goals and objectives set by government. This he contrasted with Britain where the three military services facing reduced budgets, plan procurement on solely joint basis and with full knowledge that, owing to budgetary cuts enjoined by Whitehall, even the most prized weapons platforms or traditional organizational artifice (such as army regiments with hallowed histories) that individual services prize, are on the chopping block.[25] But organizational rigidities are setting up the Indian military to experience functional breakdown in the wars of tomorrow considering how China is reorganizing and modernizing its higher defence reorganization.[26] The integrated theatre command concept is being introduced with the four inland Military Regions—Shenyang, Beijing, Chengdu, and Lanzhou (the latter two MRs responsible for India-related contingencies) being folded into the massive Chengdu and Lanzhou 'combat zones' under unified command, each of which will have units of PLA navy, air force and the second artillery strategic forces under its command. These reforms have been affected to 'recover' territories, such as Arunachal Pradesh, claimed by China.[27] A PLA driven by the desire to be the equal of the U.S. military is transitioning from basic strategies of self-defence to an 'outgoing strategy', which as a journal of the Communist Party School of the Central Committee, said involves 'stopping any country that is against our vital interests abroad...and stopping any neighbouring countries that play with fire and intensify conflicts.'.[28] The PLA means business and, despite assurances offered in various forums as part of the Border Defence Cooperation Agreement signed between India and China, continues deliberately and periodically to violate the Line of Actual Control seen by the Chinese as asserting their dominant claim on the disputed land.[29] This to say that China has its political-military act together while India is struggling with fundamental problems of an archaic military system.

Formal evidence of the prevailing single service mentality is available, for instance, in the IAF's 'basic doctrine' document. After making the obligatory bows to 'jointness' as 'a principle of war', it enunciates its basic belief that 'true synergy only obtains if each part is strong, competent, and adaptable in its own right', and that 'the challenges facing joint operations' are those related to 'interoperability and the shedding of dogmatic approaches [meaning those that vouch for jointness in] war fighting', before taking a huge step back and concluding that 'Single service approaches to war fighting cannot be wished away immediately' and that genuine jointness would have to await 'a visionary leadership' which last, of course, the service does not want to offer.[30] It, moreover, confirms that 'control of the air' is

IAF's primary objective in war.[31] This is so, notwithstanding the fact that, other than in the skies over Dhaka during the 1971 Bangladesh War, in all the major conflicts with the minor foe Pakistan and in the 1962 war with China, the IAF failed to establish air superiority or to seize control of the air and, owing to its wrong emphasis, failed to provide the 'counter-surface' or close air support to land forces, which would have assisted army formations to carry out their objectives more effectively. Thus, the IAF fleet of sophisticated aircraft suddenly discovered when called into action in the 1999 Kargil War in the mountains of north-western Kashmir that it hadn't the requisite skills. Andrew Lambeth, in his study on the use of Indian airpower in that conflict, observes that 'it was a sobering wake-up call for the IAF, which evidently had not given much thought to such a scenario and had not trained routinely at such elevations until it was forced to do so by operational necessity.'[32] The IAF did not know, leave alone train, on how effectively to use the technology it had against targets at high altitude and in craggy mountain terrain, and paid the price of inappropriate conventional bombing techniques. It lost three aircraft—a MiG-27, MiG-21, and a Mi-17 helicopter without a flare dispenser, in that order in the first three days of the border war—an astonishingly high attrition rate—to man-portable ground-to-air Stinger missiles fired by Pakistani troops. Moreover, it revealed, as Lambeth notes, 'A major interservice shortcoming' in the initial phase of the conflict 'highlighted...by the near-total lack of transparency and open communication between the Indian Army and IAF' regarding the nature and extent of infiltration across the Line of Control (LOC) by Pakistani troops who, undetected by the periodic aerial surveillance sorties carried out by IAF in the months prior to the conflict, were ensconced in the high mountains overlooking the strategic Leh–Kargil Highway—the sole supply route sustaining Indian Army formations facing the Chinese PLA in Ladakh and the Pakistani forces on the Siachen Glacier.[33] Constrained further by the Indian government's prohibition against Indian combat aircraft crossing the LOC, the IAF was discommoded for the first month of the war by its senior commanders not approving unusual technical solutions worked out in the field by pilots, ground personnel, and technical personnel from the Aircraft and Systems Testing Establishment (ASTE), Bangalore. Among these solutions were:

(1) using the electro-optical LITENING infrared imaging/targeting pod on the Mirage 2000H aircraft to do high-speed reconnaissance runs, (2) using the continuously computed release point (CCRP) technology on board the Mirage fighter aircraft for precision dropping 250 kg 'dumb bombs' of 1970s vintage on hard-to-visually-acquire targets, and (3) cohering bazaar-bought hand-held GPS sets with stop watches that pilots in the older MiG-21/23s/27s utilized to release weapons on target coordinates communicated by army designators in night time, and to strike impact points on mountains to create landslides and avalanches that buried the supply nodes in the Pakistani logistics chain rendering the occupation of the Kargil heights by Pakistan Army's Northern Light Infantry troops difficult. It took weeks of unproductive flying and needless aircraft losses and high infantry casualties exceeding 1,000 troops before these innovative solutions were approved by senior IAF commanders, whose unfamiliarity with the newest technology made them hesitate to use them.[34] 'Such improved development of solutions to major problems under the pressure of immediate operational need, more often than not by exceptionally clever and creative junior officers,' writes Lambeth echoing the views of a former fighter ace, Air Marshal V.K. Bhatia (Retd.), 'is a distinctive cultural trait of professional airmen the world over known in Indian parlance as *jugaad*, sometimes translated loosely as "frugal engineering".'[35]

The new aerial tactics devised on the run and as an outcome of *jugaad* is not unusual in Indian military settings. *Jugaad* is essentially improvisation to cover up for dated technology, lack of systemic solutions, intra- and inter-service feuds and turf battles, and to solve communications and other problems by creating jerry-rigged technical interfaces to get over problems of differing communications paraphernalia and protocols. A former Congress government minister Kamal Nath a trifle grandly called *jugaad*, 'a kind of scientific innovation' (Nath 2008: 8).[36] But scientific innovation or not, jugaad cannot make up for the missing interoperability not only between the three Indian armed services but, in fact, even between combat arms within single services! Thus, the army's infantry units and armour, for instance, cannot 'talk' to each other due to different communications systems and operating standards and fall back on improvised solutions stitched together quite literally on the run in war exercises as much as in the battlefield. But *jugaad* is not just the military, but how the entire Indian system, works.[37] The products of *jugaad* are utilitarian within the scope and context of specific situations, and geared mainly to getting the job done, not to optimizing resource use or achieving high levels of efficiency. Ironically, it's a standard often used in the Indian system to judge an individual's resourcefulness, initiative, and merit as well as collective unit success. But implicit in this improvisation concept and its working is the recognition that the normal is flawed and that bending rules, resorting to unconventional methods to get around laid-down procedures and problems endemic to the extant system, is what works. Despite no lack of evidence of how these shortcomings hurt the military's (and, in the larger setting, the government's) functioning, there is no impulse to reform the system crippled by firewalls at every turn, dense bureaucratism and insistence on the correct procedure, and a Gordian knot of contradictory rules and regulations, ensuring that the non-standardisable *jugaad* is the only way to sort out even routine problems.

Improvisation in operations is all very well when it works, but it is not a corrective for wrong threat perceptions centring on Pakistan that fuel skewed policies or a flawed strategy featuring lopsided military priorities and wrongheaded procurement programmes. The reason the IAF did not prepare for tactical missions in the mountains in Kargil is because IAF Chiefs up until and during that border war were unfamiliar with sophisticated technology on board newer aircraft, their own experience having levelled out at the MiG-21/MiG-23/MiG-27 threshold. Proving that limited knowledge can be a dangerous thing, the IAF leaders at the time with limited understanding of advanced technology and its possibilities, self-servingly propagated within the service, in inter-service circles, and in interactions with the government its reasons justifying its preferred policy of inaction. Any use of airpower in the mountains, it argued, might be escalatory and dangerous and, therefore, given the unlikelihood of the government approving potentially dangerous actions, there was no need for its combat pilots to hone their mountain target bombing techniques or for the service to emphasize it in training.[38] The Kargil episode revealed that because for the Indian military brass advanced technology is something of a black hole, technological options are ignored and operations are conducted on the basis of risk-avoidance. This factor, in turn, firms up the play-safe attitude of political leaders and government in using the military in any crises short of all-out war initiated by the enemy. The fact is democratically elected governments anywhere in the world will avoid hard options when the armed services chiefs warn about escalation uncertainties and shy away from even legitimate use of force. It explains why the threat of use of force and use of force as instrument of Indian foreign policy is mostly absent.

In the Indian military context, moreover, innovation in operational thinking and in devising and practicing new tactics is not hugely prized at the senior levels. Rather, it is approved only when the tried and tested methods fail, backs are to the wall, and sheer necessity overcomes the institutionally inbred suspicion of new and novel ways of using technology. The IAF's prioritizing the 'strategic air campaign' it's unlikely ever to implement at the expense of the more likely operational scenarios requiring 'counter surface' tactical operations in the plains and in the mountains potentially against China (and secondarily, Pakistan), which it will have to execute in cooperation with land forces, is symptomatic of the larger malady afflicting the armed forces and government. In trying to get the big things right they fail to do the small things well, and end up short on both counts.

Military bureaucracies become 'ossified' due to sticking with expertise in older methods of war (Horowitz 2010: 210). In India's case, moreover, what is militarily sufficient to deal with Pakistan may prove inappropriate and inadequate against China, which is fast transforming into a comprehensively modern military power. But transformation, as was alluded to earlier, does not come easily to the Indian armed forces. The Indian Army resists change in part because it is a conservative, hide-bound, service that having long ago been set on a certain path and grown comfortable in its organizational and operational skin finds it difficult to change, and up-shift into, the realm of twenty-first century warfare. Dragging an industrial-age Indian military into the digital era is not easy because it means leap-frogging the stage of 'fourth generation warfare' to fifth generation warfighting mechanics, which will require incorporating genetics, nanotechnology, and robotics into its conventional order-of-battle and methods of war (Singer 2009: 10). In fact, drones infused with artificial intelligence and able to discriminate and choose targets on their own was tested for the first time in the United States in October 2014.[39] But Indian armed forces are far, far away from such technology and the change it compels in warfighting and organizational behaviour, because it seems too big a leap for the Indian armed forces to make. In the event, the most the Indian Army can do is begin internalizing some basic tenets of the Revolution in Military Affairs. The process of assimilating new technology and making organizational adjustments to maximize its effects is, however, undercut by the fundamental conviction of the Indian Army generals that, keeping in mind the low quality of recruits from the countryside, a fighting force is made effective when the skill-sets required to be implanted do not tax the intellect of the lowliest trooper too much and, in the event, that the new technology is simple to handle. So, instead of introducing a technology-familiarization regimen, the training is dumbed down to a series of simple, interminably iterated, drills. But a soldier, however well-drilled and even competent in the old ways of war, cannot compete against sophisticated technology slaved to brain and brawn that fetches disproportionate results. In this respect, interacting and exercising with high-tech militaries helps, but the Indian Army has not been as fortunate as its sister services. Unlike IAF and the Indian Navy, who have observed and learned new techniques and ways of using weapons platforms and systems and sharpened their tactical skills in exercises with the more advanced militaries, the numerous joint exercises the army has held with its US counterpart have not motivated the Indian Army to acquire sophisticated technology nor train its forces in the best ways of using it. The joint exercises have, however, benefitted the American units in terms of picking up 'tricks' gained from the Indian Army's counter insurgency, jungle warfare, and high-altitude survival and fighting skills.[40] It proves an observation by the American strategist Edward Luttwak that 'inferior armed forces that in theory could learn the most from the best practices of others typically learn little or nothing and apply even less, while it is the better armed forces that keep learning from others'.[41] Advanced technology is increasingly at the core of conventional military success. The Indian Army's negative attitude to novel technology that could give the soldier an edge, is given the short shrift. The evidence is available in what happened to an innovative project conceived in the first year of the new millennium to improve the battlefield situation awareness of troops in counter-insurgency operations, which despite being developed in-house, tested and seen to work with near illiterate troops nevertheless met an untimely end, owing to the caution and disinterest shown by the higher army leadership. A brief case study of one such project to illustrate this point follows.

The Travails of SATHI and Its Larger Implications[42]

The technology and transformation resistant attitude of the army is best exemplified by briefly examining the fiasco attending on the SATHI (Situational Awareness To be Handled by Infantry) device, successfully developed and tested by an army team, which was prematurely discarded. As originally conceived in 2001 the device was to incorporate three or four state-of-the-art technologies where India has competence, including nanotechnology and the small, cheap, 'simputer' designed and developed by the Indian Institute of Science, Bangalore. A middle level officer—Colonel K.C.M. Das of the Signals Regiment was chosen to head the project, given the freedom to pick his team, and instructed to develop a compact, handheld, system to be carried by soldiers in the field against guerrilla insurgents. With the device linked with remote sensors and other sources of information useful on the battlefield, including a moving map, soldiers so equipped would, it was hoped, be able to locate their peers and their unit commander, and the enemy, all in real time. It would help them efficiently to eliminate the enemy, and avoid ambushes as well as 'friendly fire' incidents. 'What we actually did—and the future of innovation lies there—is in picking up solutions which are nearly there,' revealed Col. Das. 'It involved progressing technologies that had reached 60–70 per cent of potential but required heavy funding to bridge that remaining 30 per cent.' The army stepped in with $2 million in R&D funds, empowering a relatively junior officer (Das) with, as he put it, 'freedom with deliverables [and] no oversight except a review committee.'

The first set of prototypes of system SATHI, which acronym conveniently means 'companion' in Hindi, was ready inside of two years, by 2003. This device had to win the confidence of the army leadership, and this is where its troubles began. The senior command-ers were divided between the yea- and naysayers and a third group that doubted the Indian soldier could handle SATHI, a prejudice traceable to the colonial British belief in the poor technology handling capac-ity of the native peasant soldiery. To prove otherwise, the team took the device to the Gorkha Regiment—a unit of the Indian Army with the lowest entry-level educational qualification. These troops from the hills around the Pokhara region of Nepal, are barely literate, but have earned worldwide renown as doughty fighters. It was around the time that mobile telephony was coming into vogue, and which the Gorkha soldiers had learned to use, as they did the SATHI device after initial training. They found it helpful in operations and in carrying out their missions, in avoiding casualties, and in keeping their morale high. 'And then,' said Das, '[the project] just died'.

The colonel attributed the abrupt termination of the project to the 'significant amount of differential in innovation capacity between junior leaders in the army and the army leadership—not so much in terms of the technology issue, but in terms of the ability to handle change-issue'. This was slightly different from the IAF brass' suspi-cions of innovatively using modern technology during the Kargil air operations (analysed earlier), but was generally in the same genre of problems to do with the unfamiliarity of the senior officers with innovative technology. 'What was required when the SATHI was suc-cessfully tested,' he said, 'was for it to have an operational owner, the Director-General (DG), Infantry or the DG, Information Systems, at the Army Headquarters or an army theatre commander or two to own up to the device, bring it into the operational scale of delivery, and declare it as the platform for the next 15–20 years.' That didn't happen. 'Part of the reason,' Col. Das ventured, 'was the ingrained belief that our system is not ready to accept even the SATHI level of technology. And partly it was a marketing issue,' he revealed. It 'drew extremely high visibility cutting across hierarchies—from the army chief to the theatre commanders, everybody wanted to know where it had reached. We had given a demonstration to Arun Singh [adviser to the then BJP defence minister Jaswant Singh]. He reviewed it, but instead of green signalling its rapid development to final product and induction at any of these levels, he along with the higher-ups in the army hierarchy adopted a "wait and see how it develops" attitude instead, and in effect, killed the project'. 'Had SATHI entered service on a fast tracked schedule, the common soldier would have become familiar with this high-technology platform, which could have been continually updated with advances in technology every two years, and would have been as good as any system available in the world,' Das maintains. It would, moreover, have been incorporated as one of the core technologies in the Future Infantry Soldier as System (FINSAS) with wearable computers, and so on that the Indian Army is evaluating. 'But we didn't do it,' said the talented Col. Das, who subsequently resigned from service and joined Cisco Systems India as its Vice President. Das, however, cited an example of innovation successfully driving change only because a senior officer assumed stewardship. The then Additional Director-General, Military Operations, Major General Shami Mehta, marshalled the assets of the meteorological service, collating the incoming weather data streaming in from defence and non-defence sources in order to create a system of weather forecasts specific to operational areas in 48-hour time slots. This information is transmitted to units particularly in the northern and eastern mountain sectors to help plan their daily activities. The common element in both the air force's Kargil and the army's SATHI experiences is the technological awareness of the younger lot of officers as compared to the technology allergy of seniors in the services who are less plugged in but nevertheless decide on technological matters. It resulted in the first case in not deploying technology until it was almost too late, and in the latter case, even when presented with evidence of the increased operational efficacy of the SATHI device, showing insufficient interest in it, which led to project termination.

That in the twenty-first century, the air force still relies on the fighter jock's skills to subdue ground targets and the army on the foot soldier to take out an insurgent around the corner rather than both the services using innovative indigenous technology suggests basic institutional defects and flawed mode of technology-distanced operations. It reveals an ecosystem that incubates military leaders who are neither attentive to technological progress nor appreciative of junior officers using locally produced technology imaginatively, and whose instincts when it comes to modern technology is not to trust indigenously developed military goods but import technology and solutions.

This presumption of inferiority by the military brass of the locally conceived, designed, and manufactured military products is one of the main reasons why indigenous defence industry has failed to take off. It is another matter that the foreign-sourced goods usually fail to meet specified standards owing to the supplier countries' reluctance to part with state-of-the-art technology, which compels the Indian armed services to settle for less while paying immensely more for items that do not meet the prescribed performance standards, when the same locally produced product could be had at a fraction of the cost of the foreign item. The cost to the country of such institutionalized bias against home-grown military goods and technology innovation and financial profligacy involved in buying foreign hardware is illustrated by the epilogue to the SATHI project. Having allowed its own successfully tested and proven project to wither away, the army approached a foreign vendor, the Swedish firm Ericsson, for a similar product. Das authoritatively speculates that the chosen foreign company will 'bring in some small system, develop a prototype, see how it works, learn from that, and then ask some Indian Company to build it on a large scale.' And make a lot of money.

Because the government does not question the choices made by the armed services nor insists that imports be considered only as extreme resort, importing foreign weapons and platforms and support systems is the first recourse for the military. It has dimmed the prospects of the public sector-dominated local defence industry which, in any case, had no incentive to become technology creators and innovators, and for the private sector defence industry to actively seek foreign technology to win the Indian military's approbation. In the circumstances, defence public sector units (DPSUs) prudently opt to limit their activity to licensed production, which earns them custom from the military. In recent years, this over-reliance on foreign military equipment has alarmed the government, which belatedly introduced Defence Production Policy (DPP) guidelines incentivizing private sector involvement, and equity participation by foreign defence industrial firms, requiring substantial offsets in terms of technology transfer, establishment of R&D centres, to germinate a high-end aero-space industrial sector in the country. These offsets are pegged at 30–50 per cent of the total value of any major deal. Nevertheless, DPP has been slow to get off the ground in part because, as the ex-NSA Shivshankar Menon admitted, there is not enough mature defence industrial capacity and trained manpower pool in India to absorb the sophisticated technologies transferred by the vendors, no large institutions to ingest source codes, flight control laws, and armies of algorithm-writers to convert even such 'know why' as is transferred into a high-value technology base in the country.[43]

So, given his CISCO background, what is Das's expert prognosis about the Indian military's capabilities in his field of work—network-centric and cyber warfare? 'There's the hardware component, there's the doctrinal part of it, and then you have the leadership and strategy,' he explained. 'In hardware terms, we are surplus against the doctrine and strategy. We are equipped ahead of what we have delivered... To elaborate a little further, the innovation and changes that were to happen in operational work flows, in operational doctrine, at the level of the formation headquarters, in keeping with the hardware that's been coming in, those innovations have not materialized.' What that means is that the army has some first rate sensors, such as the long-range optical sensors 'at the edge' for surveillance, which give a 'phenomenal view on the horizon, in the plains and in semi-mountainous areas, for example. These are integrated to UAVs (Unmanned Aerial Vehicles). But the operational formations are able to leverage it only to the extent of 50–60 per cent of its capacity. 'This differential in leveraging,' said Das, 'is due to the lack of command agility to collaborate on the battlefield, i.e., between units and between formations, coordination and the whole practice of working together. This technology was supposed to fill in the time and space gaps, so while in some areas the time gaps were filled and you have 24/7 view from the operations room, in terms of space gap [of unit and formations commands coordinating actions], they are still adrift.' He likened the weaknesses in the coverage to the extant Air Defence Ground Environment System (ADGES) on the western border, which has advanced aerial surveillance technology in some places interspersed with obsolete troposcatter systems susceptible to weather fluctuations. This is at a time when all regiments of the PLA besides being comprehensively networked are GPS-enabled.[44] As a system corrective, Das believes that the senior army leaders 'need significant amount of training about what actually is available on the ground.' Then there are technical problems. For instance, data is created in such vast quantities by the forward-based sensors that 'beyond a point first degree correlations and things like that' are needed, said Das. The army has demanded software to do this which is in the pipeline. In the meantime suboptimal leveraging continues. It is a situation that can be corrected if the operational commanders are empowered to seek solutions. But because the entire network is part of a big, grand, system envisaged by the Long Range Integrated Perspective Plan, it is realized in dribs and drabs, with those systems that were inducted early being over 18 years old, while other systems, such as the Air Defence Controlling and Reporting System (ADCRS) being only about eight years old. 'Everybody knows they are going to be part of the bigger information reporting–decision-making system, but they are all under separate functional directorates, which are developing different parts of that system, with each having its own pace for fielding their products. As yet they haven't come together to connect into that bigger system. In the lab the system works perfectly, but at the Divisional headquarters, where the all-arms battle is fought, they don't have it all together, that's one level at which you can gauge operational progress,' Col. Das elaborated. This problem prevails due to differences at the inter-service level because of rivalries and service egos, he said, translating into serried and separated levels of functioning. At the tactical level 'our battle procedures and drills are fine. But when you move into the operational and strategic levels where you have senior military leaders in one operations room, the difficulties become visible.' Why? 'Because while at the tactical levels you can call in air strikes, the operational capability at the joint services level has not been networked yet. Regarding joint net-enabled operations, there are some plans in the early state of testing and development.' How long will it be before all the military points in the country are covered? 'That's more of a capacity exercise. It depends if there's strategic disruption, in which case, the networking will be speeded up, otherwise it's business as usual. I don't see it happening before 2022–27,' Colonel Das said. In other words, the systemic faults are corrected on a war-footing only when there's a war, especially a war, with the pace of change accelerating if the war is lost or similar large-scale disruption occurs. 'When disruption happens, ad hoc solutions [are] pulled in at high cost to meet the immediate contingency. But an ad hoc solution cannot be scaled up, that's the challenge,' he warned. The problem of the armed services being insufficiently communications networked within and with each other and with the government at the highest levels, is compounded by the related falloff in cyber warfare capability, which is even less of a joint activity with each service having its own platform and protocol and, at the national level, a separate organization—the National Technical Research Organization (NTRO) being installed as the apex authority. It is everybody trying to do everything by themselves and the enormous 'hacker' resources of the country mobilized from among the highly motivated youth being utilized in a slapdash manner when not wasted in turf feuds.[45] Efforts are afoot to have the disparate efforts and institutions, and hardware and software, private sector, government, and the military cohere.[46] The government as always woke up late to discover the mess and has instituted measures such as appointing a National Cyber Security Coordinator and tasking the NTRO for cyber offence and the National Intelligence Agency (NIA) for cyber defence, which arrangement may or may not work.[47] China meanwhile has developed cyber warfare capability the United States is worried about and India is vulnerable to.[48]

With technology fuelling military proficiency elsewhere in the world, one would have expected the Indian armed services to be on the ball, ensuring that technologically competent officers rise up to naturally command them, which has rarely happened. There is recognition within the services' community that this bodes ill for the future of the Indian military.[49] Most of those making it to the top rungs of command are unimaginative time-servers with a strictly tactical outlook. This is particularly so with the army. Indeed, since the uptick in counter-insurgency operations in 1989, officers involved in these actions in Kashmir and the northeast are routinely allotted extra points when determining promotions. So, there's a paradox—the more India and its military step into the world of twenty-first century advanced technology-assisted warfare, the less technology-savvy are military leaders, who win promotions as reward for getting after insurgents in close encounters. Thus, counter-insurgency specialists distanced from higher strategy and technological developments hog the top army posts. It is unclear how a military led by foresight-challenged officers can be competitive against the Chinese PLA that has transitioned into an RMA-savvy force.[50]

IAF: Flying Short

'Technological blindness' is conspicuous in the case of IAF even though the service is supposedly 'technology intensive'. Because, unlike most major air forces, it does not incentivize officers to keep up with technological advances nor reward them for doing so with promotions and plum postings, which are monopolized by the elite fighter pilot stream. And as in the rest of the military, it is strictly seniority, not merit, that counts. Thus, the air force did not even contemplate force multipliers, such as aerial tankers and AWACS, for example, until George Tanham pointed out the potential benefits in his 1995 RAND study on the IAF (Tanham 1995: 77–90). Even then it took three years, Air Chief Marshal Krishnaswamy recalled, to persuade the then service chief, Swaroop Kaul, to approve the acquisition of these systems. Krishnaswamy, the then Assistant Chief of the Air Staff (Plans), was repeatedly badgered, he said, by questions from MEA, such as 'Why do you need the tankers when your task is territorial defence? Who is asking you to go expeditionary?' and from his boss, Kaul: 'How much will it cost? Aren't there better uses for that kind of money?' and, more technical questions, such as 'Will we be able to maintain them? Who will deal with the engineering problems?' and so on. Only after receiving a certificate from the Air-Officer in-charge of Maintenance of IAF did Kaul relent. It took the air force several years of intra-service wrangling to come to a decision, but only six months to integrate the tankers into fleet operations after the original order for eight tankers was met.[51] It underscores the fact that military advancement is usually affected by 'change-oriented personalities…who help make the changes they foresee actually come true' (Singer 2009: 206).

The IAF says it is 'transforming' itself into a strategic air force and flaunts its 'expeditionary' capability courtesy the newly inducted C-130J and C-17 airlifters and the flying time they log (2,30,000 hours in 2013) as signalling its intent. However, this message is undercut by its main concern with bolstering its tactical component—fighter squadron strength.[52] Whether a military force is expeditionary in nature depends on how well it can pull off distant missions, which is also a matter of political calculus, will, and desire of the government. Military operations have been mounted in the past (such as Operation Cactus to nullify the 1988 coup d'état in the Maldives) with An-12s and An-32s, and major airlifts executed with these aircraft. The 'strategic' character of an air force is determined more by dedicated stealth strategic bombers, which are missing from the IAF inventory.[53] Fighter aircraft, such as the medium-range Su-30, with its range extended by aerial tankers cannot pass muster as long range bombers. Moreover, its combat aircraft squadrons are divided between the west against Pakistan and facing China in the same 60:40 ratio as the army's and navy's main forces, as per the 2010 political directive, which has no specific instruction from the government to reorient China-wards. The escalatory potential of instantaneous retaliatory attacks in response to some terrorist incident, no matter that in a pinch the IAF has always shied away from such missions, is the reason often cited for weighting the forces on the western border. Also, the case is made that in time of need, whole squadrons can be moved in short order to the northern and eastern fronts, with the main bases and satellite airfields prepared to receive the sudden influx with prepositioned stores and aviation fuel stocks.[54] By 2022–25, IAF hopes to have a fleet of 45 squadrons with roughly 300 each of the Fifth Generation Fighter Aircraft (FGFA)—the Su-50 PAK AF possibly modified to Indian specifications with two pilot configuration, one to fly, the other to man the weapons fire control system, and more advanced avionics, Su-30 MKIs, and a Multi-role Medium Range Combat Aircraft and, for air defence, some 100 odd MiG-29s and 200 plus advanced version of the locally-designed and built Tejas Light Combat Aircraft. For sustained operations, 18 aerial tankers (mostly Il-78s, with the last 6–7 units sought to be sourced from the west, either the EADS Airbus A330 MRTT (multi-role tanker transport) or the Boeing KC-46A, and 10 AWACS (Bariev A-50 Phalcon) and 3–4 indigenously-developed limited aerial battle management systems mounted on the Argentine Embraer platform, with 350 mile all-round surveillance and multiple tracking capability of the Phalcon AWACS compared to the 250 mile range with look-see restricted to either side of the plane, with locally designed sensors and software on Embraer aircraft.[55] Except the Israeli Phalcon phased array radar on the Indian AWACS is 30 per cent less powerful compared to a similar item with the Chinese Air Force, and, owing to the newness of the system in Indian service and the limitation of spares, its 'down time' is 50 per cent higher.[56]

Plans for military conflict initiated by PLA to take Tawang or intrude well inside Indian territory involves an escalatory counter-strategy of offensive air actions. According to retired IAF chief, Krishnaswamy, the escalation up the conventional ladder will be slow and deliberate, but should the Chinese try to do a '62, there'll be no hesitation on the part of the government this time, he asserts, to order meaningful use of air power, with 2,000 km deep strikes at logistics hubs and supply lines, especially the Qinghai-Lhasa railway. Among the immediate actions IAF is contemplating is targeting the fragile high altitude desert ecology of Tibet. Su-30 bombing sorties with '20–30 gravity bombs' will be ordered to destroy the permafrost along the LAC so that the entire Chinese line and border infrastructure collapses and isolates the aggressor PLA units. The IAF has a slate of graded responses to provide fire-breaks for possible termination of conflict. Should matters turn serious, and based on whether China initiates conventional missile attacks on targets within India, Indian counter-reaction will beget concerted air attacks on Chinese SAM sites in Tibet. In the subsequent stages, depending on the Chinese response, attacks will be launched against logistics depots deep inside Tibet up to its borders with the adjoining Gansu, Yunnan, and Sichuan provinces and other areas. If Indian cities and/or mainland infrastructure and industrial centres are struck by Chinese missiles and planes, then Indian reaction will be to widen the scope of conventional counter-attacks on Chinese cities in widening circles, not excluding conventional cruise missile and conventional missile attacks from air and seaborne platforms, of course, but also to sever all transport links to Tibet, in particular the Qinghai-Lhasa railway and the Xinjiang Highway skirting the border and the various parallel 'shunts' (alternate east-west roads) in Tibet. These strikes will directly target, Krishnaswamy said, the permafrost in the interior to cave in the rail bed on which the arterial Qinghai-Lhasa railway line runs. Together with strikes on the road networks within Tibet, it is expected to devastate the entire PLA supply chain and possibly make the Chinese military and civilian presence in Tibet untenable.[57] The devastating IAF strategy of hitting the permafrost by conventional ordnance is hinted at in the Manmohan Singh regime-facilitated national security document *Nonalignment 2.0*.[58] When thinking of war Beijing will, moreover, have to consider the near catastrophic ecological consequences of such an Indian air offensive, even if exclusively with conventional weapons, such as the release of the greenhouse methane gas trapped within the frozen soil. As it is, global warming may soon reduce the permafrost to puddle, leading to the sagging and sinking of the Qinghai-Lhasa railway line which, as the *Scientific American* reported, 'crosses about 550 kilometres of some of the most delicate and treacherous frozen soil region on Earth.'[59] The rate of melt of the permafrost, incidentally, already exceeds what the Chinese engineers had factored into the construction of the rail-bed. Besides, there is the fact of rapidly disappearing glaciers in Tibet pointing to a delicate high-altitude desert environment under strain.[60] Combined with launching Tibetan guerrilla teams recruited from among the exile community in India and disillusioned local youth inside Tibet to operate behind Chinese lines along with local sympathizers, inside Han-populated Tibetan cities, and Tibetan-majority areas in the surrounding provinces of Sichuan and Gansu incorporated from the eastern Kham region of Tibet, the majority Han population, civilian authorities, and the PLA will find itself islanded on the plateau. The value of a 'Tibet card' in such circumstances is finally being recognized by New Delhi as part of an Indian response toolkit. A pleased Dalai Lama, who has been fighting for genuine autonomy for Tibet for the last sixty-odd years, stated that India had finally shed its 'over-cautiousness'.[61] The clearest sign of a rethink on the Tibet issue was the formal invitation to Lobsang Sangay, the elected prime Minister of the Tibetan Government in Exile to attend Narendra Modi's investiture ceremony.

In such an escalatory conflict situation, Beijing is expected to be deterred from ramping up the proceedings to the nuclear level by the triad of the 5,000–8,000 km Agni-V and 2,000 km-range Agni-II IRBMs, and 750 km-range Agni-I MRBMs against targets in Tibet and the surrounding Chinese provinces, the Arihant SSBN (and follow-on boats of the same class) on station possibly offshore of the Chinese coast, with the option that will have to be explored with littoral and island countries of operating out of forward bases in the region, and which submersibles Indian naval persons believe are more silent than the newest Chinese counterpart, the Jin-class SSBNs sheltered in the Sanya base on Hainan Island. The air force will also have the FGFAs and MMRCAs available in the conventional bombing role and, should it become necessary to drop nuclear ordnance, and to fire nuclear cruise missiles from standoff range. The Indian SSBNs, packing the K-15 cruise missile and the intermediate range K-4 SLBM, would reach inland targets or take out prized wealth-producing centres and cities in China's coastal belt.

IAF and naval strategists, moreover, are of that view that India has the upper hand in a potential escalation spiral in the conventional military sphere even in a limited war scenario owing to the nature of targets in China. After all, like countries that have grown prosperous, China too is expected to become more sedate as it grows richer because it will have far more to lose in an all-out struggle with India that's allowed to spiral to the nuclear level. India being farther behind in the economic-development scale will have, in that sense, less at stake. Other than the vulnerable permafrost and logistics infrastructure, the escalation dynamic disfavours China also because of the obvious massive infrastructure that offer themselves as attractive targets to air-launched ordnance. Particularly vulnerable is the gigantic 1.4 km long and 607 feet high Three Gorges Dam on the Yangtze River with an annual hydroelectric generation capacity of 84.7 billion kilowatts.[62] 'Intelligent targeting requires that the Three Gorges Dam [and the Gezhouba Dam and the Zhi River railway bridge] not be attacked at the first instance,' said Krishnaswamy.[63] This dam has been supposedly engineered to withstand both conventional and nuclear strikes on the basis of data from ten nuclear explosions conducted in the 1960s on four dams in Xinjiang. But that nuclear and conventional explosive testing is not regarded as having realistically replicated actual attacks. Indeed, General Zhang Aiping, deputy director, PLA General Staff, asked by Premier Zhou Enlai in 1958 to study the vulnerability of such a dam then at the pre-design stage, concluded that while a conventional air attack could be thwarted with air defence measures, 'a nuclear attack would be something completely different. If the dam were bombed in a nuclear attack, the water would rush all the way down to the city of Nanjing, which would suffer enormous damage, as would the Dongting and Poyang lakes.' He added that the 'the only defence is release of water from the reservoir ahead of time.' This is the passive defensive measure the Chinese expect to rely on—with a discharge capacity of 110,000 cubic meters of water per second, to empty out the 600 km long reservoir in 4–5 days. The big 'if' here is the availability of adequate warning time of an impending attack. If the reservoir is destroyed or prematurely emptied owing to false warning, there will still be hell to pay for the Chinese because of the havoc caused by heavy flooding downstream, and is an unbearable prospect. Taking an ostrich-like view, a Chinese government official's assessment in 1987 simply assumed that war would not threaten the dam. More objective Chinese analysts, however, believe the dam would be struck, and the consequences of the destruction of the Three Gorges Dam 'for the military, and for the entire nation, would be disastrous' (Bing 1998: 171–2, 175). The dire consequences for the Chinese communist regime and the PLA from such an enemy strike, or even from a false warning of attack that may empty out the dam's vast reservoir area is precisely why Taipei has this dam in its crosshairs. Taipei is convinced that posing a credible threat to this dam will 'deter Chinese coercion'.[64] New Delhi may be thinking along similar lines.

Four additional squadrons of the 'super Sukhoi'—a souped-up variant of the Su-30 MKI, are being procured for the China front. In the interim, four of the 12 squadrons of this aircraft in service are currently stationed for exclusive use in the eastern theatre, which force can be quickly expanded.[65] A Su-30 squadron supported by a tanker or two, and transport aircraft, and support elements may be deployed in Central Asia, and placed in Ainee to 'generate pressure' on China's western flank (and secondarily Pakistan). Used by the Soviet air force as a satellite air field, the Farkhor air base 'has fantastic facilities but was in bad shape,' said former vice chief of IAF, Air Marshal Satish Inamdar (Retd.), regarding the base which the IAF has refurbished, including resurfacing its long landing strip. 'It is coming up to scratch now,' he volunteered. Ainee may not be the lone Indian presence in that area, however. 'Other Central Asian Republics too are amenable to our initiatives,' Inamdar stated.[66] In a nuclear crisis, the Tajik base puts the Chinese nuclear weapons facilities in Lop Nor in the sight of IAF Su-30s. Lop Nor is a very valuable potential target to hold hostage in a tough situation with China.

Starting sometime in 2003-2004, IAF's operational plans began focusing on the China-Pakistan nexus in war and it was decided, in Air Marshal Inamdar's words, to have a 'holding operation on one side, and going whole hog on the other side. We are building up capability for that—the 45 squadrons ought to suffice. Lethality of ordnance has undergone a quantum change and accuracy has changed a hell of a lot, with accuracy now being a force multiplier.'[67] The plan is also for the range of Su-30s to be extended by using 6-8 aircraft in a squadron of some 16 aircraft as 'buddy refuelers' as alternative to the vulnerability of tankers in missions requiring loitering by a strike/air superiority force over a target area.[68] But, like the army and navy, IAF too seems to have got its threat bearings wrong—a holding action against Pakistan while fighting China hard is the more sensible strategy, if India is not to make itself entirely irrelevant to the larger game underway in Asia in the new century.

This begs the question—does the IAF have a strategic vision? 'No, the IAF has never had a strategic view,' declared Air Marshal A.K. Singh. 'Of course, we'll do interdiction, counter air, and we'll do air defence, which does not form a strategic view. It is just fire-fighting.' He went on to explain that 'The root of the problem is that the Indian government had no strategic view until 2009 when the Prime Minister said India's strategic interests lie from the Spratleys, later he corrected that to the Malacca Strait, right down to the Indian Ocean region, and then to the Gulf of Hormuz'. Air Marshal Singh confessed, however, that it was difficult to take such statements seriously. 'It is easy to say these are our areas of interest [but] we have never had any out-of-area contingency plans—not any of the three services, even though the air force can be used for instantaneous power projection—for precise attacks on targets without fear of escalation or abusing anyone's territorial integrity, and hardly any collateral damage, with PGMs (precision guided munitions) that have maximum error of 20–30 meters, but usually we are within 3–7 meters.' Not having a strategic policy direction meant, he said, that 'we are always Pakistan-centric...It is only now that China has come on the threat radar, that we need to be ready to thwart it.' But can IAF tackle the Chinese air threat? Given their radii of action, Chinese aircraft cannot reach any important Indian targets and, in any case, will be intercepted by Indian Su-30s, MiG-29s, and Mirage 2000s. 'But this will be very short-lived,' he admitted. 'In 1999 in Kargil, within 10 days, we started running out of rockets and bombs. So when we talk of a two-front war, have we planned for it? Yes, we have plans...but have we actually planned that every three years we'll need to replenish the depleted holding because most of the modern rockets, missiles, and bombs run out of shelf-life, so we perforce go into situations where our dynamic load of explosives has to be reassessed and found fit to be used.'[69] Singh reinforced what has been iterated by officers from the other services—that lacking a local defence industry able to produce weaponry and quickly replenish military consumables, switching speedily from peacetime mode to accelerated wartime requirements becomes an infinitely complex business. In such a milieu, a former Deputy Chief of the Army Staff indicated, the system is prone to error. For India, which expects to get involved in conflict only occasionally, minus the defence industrial capacity to back up the war effort, it has to rely on outside suppliers to make up the shortages in a hurry. This is when, he said, 'calculations go wrong in a hurry' and will adversely affect the conduct of war.

The IAF seems unmindful of the strategic gap developing in the Indian air order of battle owing to the missing long range bomber in its fleet even as most major air forces, including the Chinese air force (with the Xian-8 and the purchase of the Tu-22M3M production line from Russia), have such aircraft in their inventory and are replacing them with more powerful planes.[70] The Indian air force, in fact, allowed an existing bomber capability to waste away after the British-made Canberra medium-bombers were phased out in the Seventies. The service's short-legged aspirations of besting its Pakistan counterpart even led to its spurning the Tu-22 'Backfire' bomber as far back as 1971 when the Soviet Union had earmarked a squadron of this aircraft for transfer (Karnad 2005: 663–8). The IAF never expressed any requirement for a specialized aircraft because in the 1970s the Mach 2-capable Su-7, optimized for ground attack, was rigged to carry nuclear bombs and, thereafter, avionics-wise more advanced fighter-bombers able to fly farther with a bigger bomb-load, entering service were thought adequate.[71] In the last decade it considered the 'C' version of the Backfire a number of times, and even considered securing a squadron of the Tu-160 'Blackjack' that Russia was prepared to lease, but backed out each time. Investing in and running a squadron of Tu-22s or Tu-160s was dismissed as 'a waste of resources'. The price tag of some $400 million, for instance, for a Backfire squadron, the then IAF Chief Browne agreed, was bearable but said the service blanched at the annual upkeep costs of

Rs 800–1,000 crores ($160–200 million), which he claimed were a third more than that for a Su-30 squadron.[72] Thus unsupported by the air force, the Strategic Forces Command (SFC) controlling nuclear weapons has, however, time and again voiced apprehension about the unavailability of a recallable manned strategic bomber option that would be useful to manage escalation dynamics. In the teeth of IAF's opposition, SFC failed to push through the acquisition of the Su-35 as a second-best option, after the Tu-160 or Tu-22M3. The Chinese Navy, which has acquired large numbers of this aircraft—boast of the Su-35 having 'speed and ample tanks'.[73]

The trouble with the Su-30MKI as a make-do alternative to a genuine strategic bomber is that it will need mid-course refuelling to reach distant Chinese targets. This, in turn, will require placement of aerial tankers somewhere out at sea off China and outside its air defence and detection zones. But with the Chinese satellites and prowling airborne early warning systems networked with ground radar, the chances of the Su-30s on nuclear attack missions flying undetected even with complex tactical routing, and of the tankers staying undetected and unmolested on station for the strike aircraft to rendezvous with them, before making the final run to their assigned targets, are slim. The IAF's lack of interest is one thing; but its dog in the manger attitude denied the navy the Tu-22Ms as an ostensible maritime reconnaissance platform. NHQ had hoped that, in time, it would result in its snatching the strategic bombing role.[74] Such over-zealous protection of the missions has undermined India's strategic security by denying the country military flexibility, in this case, in distant-strike In both instances the strategically myopic government sided with the air force.

The Indian strategic triad with a vulnerable Su-30 as a recallable option masquerading as a strategic bomber is unconvincing. Many in the IAF contend that the Russian Tu-22M3M or the supersonic Tu-160 with 13,200 km range are old platforms and cannot match the anti-aircraft technologies and, therefore, are simply not worth leasing from Russia, except they are being upgraded with superior avionics and weapons suites.[75] Even so the Tu-160 platform is from the 1970s. A better, long term, option in the event, which has been offered New Delhi, is to partner Russia in designing, developing, and manufacturing a fifth generation long range supersonic stealth bomber—the PAK DA, with advanced sensors and hypersonic standoff weapons on board, which Moscow approved in 2012 and which is being rushed through to induction by 2020.[76] India decided to commit some Rs 35,000 crores to the development of the Russian FGFA. Transferring the bulk of these monies to the PAK DA programme instead is something Russia would agree to, and will fetch a bigger strategic dividend in terms of a strategic capability upgrade of the IAF fleet, a credible manned option into the future, the strengthening of the strategic triad ensuring India co-owns the intellectual property rights on sophisticated technologies developed for this aircraft, including metallurgical innovations such as the special sensor-embedded 'skin' of this aircraft, etc. Such access to the most advanced aviation technologies will raise the technology levels of the Indian defence industry. This makes sense considering the differential in fighting attributes between the souped up Su-30MKI, which can be inducted in greater numbers in IAF and at much lower cost, and the FGFA is not all that much.

In the larger context of evolving air power as component of India's comprehensive military strength, the IAF's conceptualization of it as merely 'air dominance' and that too as something only air force can provide, is at fault, believes Admiral Prakash, a naval aviator who won a gallantry award flying IAF Hunter aircraft in 1971 operations.'[S] hould the attainment of air dominance become an end in itself [and replace] military and maritime strategies? Or should air power be seen as a powerful instrumentality to gain operational objectives on land, sea and air by the three Services?' he wonders.[77]

The IAF's most serious weakness, however, is the mind-boggling diversity of aircraft—combat planes from Russia, France, and United Kingdom, airlifters from Russia and the United States, and trainer aircraft—the Super Hawk from Britain, Pilatus PC-7 turboprop from Switzerland, and the indigenous HPT-32 (propeller) and HJT-16 (jet). It is faced with a hellish logistics problem even in peacetime. According to Air Marshal Inamdar, it has resulted in perennial spares shortages, preventing the operational readiness of the force from exceeding 60–70 per cent, with this number falling to as low as 30 per cent during crises. 'The multiplicity of aircraft is not a problem, it is a logistics nightmare,' he said, recalling his own experience. 'We survived because of luck and cannibalization [of parts owing to commonalities in Russian-sourced aircraft]. Luck was we didn't have breakdowns as often as we could have had them. [And] there was no war attrition of the order in which it would have made it impossible for us to sustain ourselves as a fighting force.' But luck is not a factor that can be called up whenever needed, and does not address the tendency of vendor countries to use the flow of military spares to pressure the Indian government on policy issues. Inamdar, however, clarified that with respect to the Soviet/Russian supply chain 'We didn't do a lot of things by way of homework to do the ordering correctly.... There's a protocol for every aircraft [about changing parts after certain number of hours, etc.]. We kept on learning about the nuances of indenting for Russian aircraft, and still do so...There was a different list of spares we needed on priority...for our terrain, climate conditions... such as actuators, stabilizers, fuses. There was our way of doing things and then there was their way of doing things. By the time we realized to fill the gap, we reached the end of the life of the aircraft!' But Western suppliers too follow a short reins policy on spares and service support. To avoid the perils of over-dependence on any single supplier country, and prompted by the at times severe discomfiture faced by the Indian military, the government alighted on the diversification policy since the end of the Cold War. It has landed the country with a different kind of logistics conundrum—how to operate in conditions of spares uncertainty, not knowing what aircraft in the fleet will be grounded when and for how long. And it has allowed this problem to become more complicated by letting the IAF shortlist the French Rafale as MMRCA. To escape the fire India may have climbed into the pan, without escaping the dependency cycle now involving many more supplier countries, any of whom can disable important parts of the Indian Air Force and the military at-large as it suits their interests. This is the main reason for self-sufficiency in arms that Nehru understood well but subsequent Indian leaders have not.

Naval Confidence

Distanced from the close-in tactical engagements of the kind the army is involved in, the air force and navy in their globe-spanning mediums of air and sea would be expected to be more strategic in assessing threats and deploying their assets. But are they? The sheer size of the army, as compared to the other two services, and the weight of its effort emphasizing Pakistan, which the government endorses, has affected the operational leanings of the other two services as well. The manner, for instance, in which the Indian Navy has arrayed its forces towards the North Arabian Sea, belies its doctrine of 'power projection' clubbed under three distinct categories of operations— 'amphibious', 'expeditionary', and 'distant'.[78] Seventy per cent of its major surface combatants (carrier, missile destroyers, frigates, and corvettes) and 66 per cent of its submarines are with the Western Fleet and orientated thus. The unequal distribution of the naval assets as between the Eastern and the Western Fleets is, however, attributed by Vice Admiral R.N. Ganesh, former commander of the Western Fleet, to the 'non-synchronous evolution of the Western and Eastern Naval Commands' with the Western Command being strong in Western naval technology, including naval aviation, and the fact that the Mumbai port-city and hinterland area, were more developed industrially, and offered better support. The Eastern Naval Command hosts mostly ex-Soviet and Russian ships and submersibles including the SSBNs and the Akula SSNs, and the amphibious assets. He justified the westward look of the navy to 'short term threats' emanating from that quarter and to the fact that ships from the Western Fleet, were these needed to back up the Eastern Fleet, are a mere three sailing days away from the Bay of Bengal.[79] The Pakistan tilt was magnified when the Western Naval Command, elbowing aside the Coast Guard, took charge of coastal security as well in the wake of the 26/11 seaborne terrorist assault on Mumbai in 2008.[80] With naval ships being saddled with this additional duty nearer shore there is a reduced force-fraction available for traditional blue water roles. From this viewpoint it seems a grievous strategic error on the part of the Indian Navy comparable to its picking a host of Petya corvettes in the Seventies when it could, just as well, have acquired a fleet of big warships from the Soviet Union on easy terms. What it does is pull the navy landward, turning it, in effect, into an extension of the army in the brown water. A contrary push deep sea-ward will begin to work once the Western Fleet is shifted majorly in the 2017–19 timeframe to its designated home-port in Karwar, down the coast—'only twenty hours steaming at economical speed', from Mumbai. The carrier, Vikramaditya (ex-Gorshkov), inducted in November 2013 is berthed there along with its escort ships with an alternative home-base being created for it in the east at Rambilli on the Andhra coast, which will also feature the Chinese Sanya naval base-like facilities, such as allowing nuclear submarines to steal into or egress without detection from their pens excavated in the cliff below the waterline.[81] The shifting of the Western Fleet will decongest Mumbai, with just a few ships being retained there for seaward defence. 'With deep water at the doorstep and the naval aviation base [at Dabolim in Goa] within hailing distance, the shift to Karwar will improve the Fleet's response time for operational deployment,' asserted Ganesh. The Dabolim naval air base, incidentally, is where a static deck was built to familiarize and prepare pilots for MiG-29K operations off Vikramaditya and the second indigenous carrier, under construction by the Hindustan Shipyard Ltd. in Kochi. But because of the location of the premier Mazgaon naval dockyard in Mumbai, it may lead, Ganesh said, to the 'seemingly paradoxical situation of the operational edge of the Navy being in the "rear" while the logistics and maintenance are nearer to the perceived threat [Pakistan].' However, he was quick to add that 'Future strategic tasks will be in more remote areas such as the southern Indian Ocean trade routes and in our Eastern areas of interest' with 'the operational focus... then [being] the interdiction of hostile fleet units at long range, the defence and control of SLOCs, and sea denial ... to inimical powers for specific periods.'[82]

The Indian Navy, the most forward-looking of the services, is expected by 2030 to field as many as nine SSNs, six SSBNs, some 30 SSKs, three aircraft carriers, including two locally built vessels and Vikramaditya, in all 50 major surface combatants—multi-purpose stealth frigates and missile destroyers in the 4,000 ton to 9,000 ton class, 16-18 P-8Is for armed maritime reconnaissance, a squadron of upgraded navalised Jaguar strike aircraft out of the Car Nicobar Island base, any number of Brahmos supersonic cruise missile batteries, and a fleet of amphibious warfare vessels—Landing Ships Dock, Landing Ships Utility, and Landing Ships Tank that will make possible 'from the sea'-type of amphibious actions in the Indian Ocean basin.[83] The second carrier from the Kochi shipyard will, incidentally, be equipped with a steam catapult, enabling the acquisition of the E2C Hawkeye Aerial Early Warning (AEW) System.[84] Such an Indian presence, Rear Admiral Raja Menon claims, will obtain the 'proper maritime density', rendering any Chinese naval presence in the Indian Ocean region 'grossly inferior'.[85] In fact, the strategy is for a maritime response to a Chinese attack on land, which has been evolving for some time now (Karnad 2005: 141–42).

The 2012 document *Nonalignment 2.0* mentions the asymmetric use of Indian naval superiority in the Indian Ocean as part of a counter-attack strategy in case of a major land offensive begun by PLA.[86] 'We tried to push the idea,' said Rear Admiral Menon, who is a leading advocate of this strategy, 'that India should be able to counter-threaten China in the Indian Ocean, counter-threaten their entire transiting trade [in the event of the Chinese] fingering us in the mountains…If escalation happens in the mountains, we should escalate in the Indian Ocean'.[87]

The Indian Navy successfully sold this naval riposte idea to the Manmohan Singh government, and there is little doubt about its ability to implement the promised manoeuvres. But, there are numerous demerits attending on such retaliatory action if this is to be the sole response to the PLA initiating hostilities in the mountains. The most probabilistic scenario is for the Chinese to start the proceedings with a tactically provocative action across the LAC that escalates quickly into a 'limited war of high intensity' or remains 'a short punitive campaign'; in either case, short duration hostilities are assumed (Sahgal 2012: 290–1). In this setting, time being of the essence if retaliation is to be causally linked to conflict initiation hundreds of miles away on land, other than redirecting warships and submarines already at sea, it will take time for a consequential force of sea-borne combatants to be constituted into battle groups, to get them ready and get going in search of appropriate targets in the Indian Ocean. Secondly, the targets would be Chinese naval vessels, assuming a few of them can be found loitering in easy reach of Indian ships. If the hunting packs cannot find Chinese warships and submarines to sink, would they torpedo Chinese merchantmen instead, assuming these are properly identified as Chinese owned? Will ships carrying Chinese trade, under other flags, be spared? Would such targeting be seen by Beijing as escalatory action, and then what? It will require

Indian intelligence to gear up and real time satellite-derived information to maintain a 24/7/365 register of Chinese commercial ships in
the Indian Ocean and their designated routes as ready-to-use target
list.[88] Thirdly, and more importantly, the Chinese may not withdraw
from Tawang or other captured Indian territory as happened in 1962.
Would the sinking or capture of a few Chinese ships or temporary
disruption of Chinese trade and energy traffic in the Indian Ocean
compensate for the permanent loss of strategic areas, such as Tawang,
say, housing the most famous monastery of the Gelugpa school of
Mahayana Buddhism founded by the Fifth Dalai Lama in the seventeenth century and central to the Lama-ist traditions of Tibet, which
keeps alive India's cultural links to Tibet and New Delhi's 'Tibet
card', and to the disputed border being pushed southward to a less
defensible line? And finally, a 50 ship-strong Indian Navy is nowhere
large enough to impose a Total Exclusion Zone in the Indian Ocean;
even much larger naval forces will find it difficult to do so.[89] And
finally, is the sinking of a few Chinese warships and the apprehension
of several merchantmen the equal of, and enough recompense for,
the loss of valuable territory to China for good? While conceding
that such a 'theatre switching' response to counter a Chinese move
in the mountains may not work, Rear Admiral Raja Menon, the
principal author of this strategy, more reasonably maintained that a
navy disposed to disrupt China's energy and trade traffic through the
Indian Ocean and hence its economy dependent on African minerals
and Gulf oil, can breed 'insecurity' for Beijing, which is a good thing,
and the more the insecurity the better it is for India.[90] The Congress
government's approval of the two offensive mountain Divisions and
a mountain corps was because of the possibility that the maritime
response might not work. 'Theater-switching is what we are suggesting,' he said also because. '[there's] relatively little Indian trade that
can be so jeopardized by the Chinese navy in the South China Sea.'[91]
But it is not clear why the Congress Party Singh government linked
the naval 'theatre-switching' strategy to land operations. The need for
according priority to several army offensive mountain corps (MTC)
capable of instantaneous strikes in Tibet along several axes of their
choosing and to seal the escape route of, and box in, the attacking
PLA units well inside Indian territory for destruction in detail once

the deployed Atomic Demolition Munitions (ADMs) come into play, are a different priority (more on ADMs in a later section).

Naval Muscle[92]

To return to the more prosaic issues relating to hard power, the Indian government has confidence in the country's naval prowess and sees it as a winning card against China. So, how does it actually measure up as a fighting force capable of sustained distant operations? Rear Admiral Raja Menon, an accomplished naval analyst and Russian-speaking and trained submariner, in fact, points out many weaknesses in the Indian Navy's force structure and capabilities. Among the metrics one can use to evaluate Indian naval power is how many of the ships in the fleet are long legged, meaning those that are 'refuelled in about 5-6 day intervals'. The navy, he claimed, has barely crawled out of an era when Soviet ships, such as missile boats, Petya-class corvettes, and minesweepers were chosen on the basis of 'weapons density... [to] take care of any threat'. These were inducted in the 1970s without reference to their short range, high specific fuel consumption, very high power-to-weight ratio, and short engine-life. These factors, he said, 'really brought our sea-going capability down to very low levels' and did not compensate for the fact that the Soviets were usually first off the blocks in terms of introducing new technology—such as CODOG (combined diesel or gas) gas turbine (on Petyas), a 'non-reversible' CODOG, meaning the gas turbine could only be 'used as boost' with the diesel engine providing the main propulsion. So the Indian Navy of those years had punch but no range or stamina. This changed in the Eighties with the entry into service of the gas turbine-driven Kashin-II class guided missile destroyers (DDGs). The Ukrainian gas turbines powered five of these 1980s vintage Kashins (Rajput-class modified to Indian specifications in electronics and combat systems with Brahmos supersonic cruise missile in vertical launchers as part of their newest weapons suite) and the subsequent three Delhi-class (indigenously designed and produced in mid-'90s) guided missile destroyers, and the six Russian built Talwar-class (modified Krivak-III stealth frigates (FFGs), with a completely Indian communications suite and ASW sensors). Compared to the Petyas, the Ukrainian gas turbines afforded 'tremendous amount of sea time' said, Menon, but 'unrefuelled they were not as good as the CODOGs which we discovered after we switched over to the General Electric LM 2500 gas turbine engine for the Shivalik-class stealth frigate'. The Shivalik-class boat is Indian produced, three of which have been delivered with seven more on order. The Delhi-class ship can go without refuelling for 5–6 days, the Shivaliks, 10–12 days. Moreover with the LM 2500, ships can 'average 450 miles per day at 20 knots; if you go flat out, you'd have to refuel every three days.'

The next metric to consider is the tanker-to-warship ratio. 'The more short-legged the ships or the more flotillas you send out, the greater the need for tankers, so total tankage doesn't help in the latter instance of flotillas off in different directions, you'll need tankers with each of them. So you need …lots of little tankers to accompany ships.' Here, he charged, the navy had fouled up. 'It has accepted the idea that the tanker to ship ratio is a matrix but has not implemented that decision.' So, the navy has bought one large tanker for the two it could have procured for the same price, and three large tankers at present, when it could have had six and improved its sea presence proportionately. By 2030, it could have had 10 smaller tankers for the 50 capital ships in its fleet, instead of the five larger fuellers it may actually end up with. The next criterion to judge a navy is its situational awareness. Russian ships like the Petyas were entirely devoid of it, he said. The first of the Godavari-class (follow-on to the Leander) frigates had an Italian-made IPN-10 communications system which allowed them to talk to others of its class but not to other ships. The Talwar and Shivalik-class FFGs, on the other hand, are able to communicate with the maritime reconnaissance (MR) aircraft and 'you can get pictures transmitted by MR aircraft 500 miles away', which is far more important, Menon said, than data linking ships that make them situationally aware only to the extent of 200 miles away. But in this realm, he disclosed, there are two or three *jugaad*s underway to bring the Delhi-class DDGs up to pace, and a couple of formal projects 'that are fleet oriented and navy-oriented, i.e., all the pictures that are available to the fleet command in, say, Mumbai, are interlinked with the Naval headquarters in New Delhi, as are air force pictures, which can also feed UAVs, so there's an all-India link. Then there's the fleet link, which runs on communications that have to be longer than visual range. But running on low power High Frequency was indiscreet; anybody can tap onto it'. Navy's own satellite to remove this vulnerability finally went up in early 2012; in a geostationary orbit over the Indian Ocean, it has a footprint from the East African littoral to the South China Sea, and is part of the ultimately 7–13 satellite constellation in high and low orbits in the commercial GAGAN (GPS-Aided Geo Augmented Navigation) architecture. It will do double duty of surveillance in peace time and, in war, link up with the Russian Glonass system for extended sub-meter resolution targeting capability.[93] This being the first of the dedicated military satellites, the navy sought IAF's participation in the 'broad band' coverage with a view to sharing cost and usage time, but was rebuffed. IAF's disinterest in the naval satellite was perhaps because it apprehended that establishing a precedent of sharing a naval surveillance and communications platform may lead to the Navy wanting rotational leadership of the separate Space Command that IAF expects to head, or worse, that the government may decide on the basis of the naval satellite experience, that IAF does not really need dedicated satellites of its own and even less a separate Space Command. But Rear Admiral Menon admitted that just having the satellite up in space will not solve the navy's problems because, he said 'It isn't as though everything else is ready. We are unready as far as the maritime domain is concerned. Technically, we are putting everything on to this one set, and that could be a problem.' The integrated communications arrangement of ship-to-ship, ship-to-shore, ship-to-aircraft, and shore/ship-to-submarine links were comprehensively tested in a major sea exercise in the Bay of Bengal in January–February 2012. Menon also mentioned 'maritime surveillance density' normally of one long-range MR aircraft (Il-38, Il-76, or P-8I) to one major warship. 'Here we don't match up,' he said. 'We have one aircraft for every four to five ships.'

Yet another metric this time to gauge Indian naval operational orientation is the main armament. In the Indian Navy, he said, it is surface-to-surface missiles (SSMs) rather than land attack missiles—the Brahmos cruise variety and the (ex-Russian) Klub, the latter available in two versions—Ship-to-ship missile and cruise—that 'haven't come in that amount of numbers yet.' The situation is 'you'll find you have as many SSMs in small combatants—the Veer-class Tarantula corvettes—13 of them—as you have them in large combatants.' However, the 'preponderance' of SSMs is shifting from the short-range, small combatants to the Delhi, Talwar, and Shivalik-class DDGs and FFGs. 'It means,' he averred, 'that our main armament is now out in the open ocean, in the blue water,' in the ratio 7 to 5 favouring the capital ships. But the Tarantula 'is fulfilling the role of, what the Americans call, littoral combat ship. This is not because,' Menon confided, 'we have been clever and thought about it but because it happened by accident,' winning ex-post facto validation, 'in the sense that we have got a strategic problem, which is that we have got this monkey [Pakistan] on our backs which won't go away, and which the Tarantulas can handle in the littoral warfare kind of scenarios. And so a large number of these small combatants with SSMs who present small targets can go over there and mix it up with the Pakis, But it won't stop us from going blue water, take on China, go to Durban, even stop Chinese SLOCs in the Atlantic, and all that.'

He, however, fears that while the Indian Navy talks of having plans for 'distant water operations…they don't understand it [namely, the demands of sustained power projection].' Dilating on this subject some more, he said: 'There's a big difference between operating at 1,000-1,500 miles and operating at 4,000 miles (Durban). It's 1,750 miles to Malacca Straits and another 1,300 miles to South China Sea, about 3,500 miles in all. It's all a question of time and space, which is completely different in that when you are talking about two refuellings to reach there and normally ships are kitted out for 45 days at sea; you'd have to do that for 100 days. You'd have to carry double the amount of stuff you are carrying now. There'll be space enough within the bigger ships to manage that. At the moment, we have tankers but no provision ships. Tankers can be made to carry provisions, but they haven't actually done so. [The navy] is bullshitting when they say we have this capability, we haven't ever done it.' This is where, he implied, the utility of overseas bases such as Nha Trang in the central Vietnamese coast, Subic Bay, or the Agalegas in Mauritius would manifest itself. In lieu of ships and foreign bases, the present policy of training Vietnamese crews to operate the Russian Kilo SSKs Hanoi has procured, providing 'shore support', and passing on to the Vietnamese Navy SSM-armed small combatants for these to 'rush out and rush back home' and, along with the Kilo submarines, to keep the Chinese Navy busy, will have to do as a short term solution. 'By 2022, we'll have the capability,' he confided, 'and would be able to spare some six-odd large warships' for permanent flotilla duty in the South China Sea.

It is a strategy of distant sea balancing involving, other than Vietnam, Indonesia, and Philippines, and has got the Indian government's nod. There are two prongs to this policy; one is to increase Indian military presence in strength in the immediate vicinity of South China Sea. The Indian island possessions in the Nicobar chain serve this non-intrusive strategy. A naval air station, INS Baaz, commissioned in mid-2012 in Campbell Bay with an airstrip that's expected to be lengthened to 3,000 meters to permit operation of both Su-30s and the C-130Js for possible Special Forces actions, will help dominate the six-degree channel and the Malacca Strait, as also the Lumbock and Sunda Straits that Chinese naval vessels have to cross to get to the Indian Ocean. Forward naval operating bases at Kamorta in the Nicobars and Diglipur in the Andamans too have been activated, as part of a plan drawn up two decades earlier. More air bases and naval installations on other islands to facilitate 24/7 surveillance of the extensive island territories and quick turnaround are coming up, extending the range of Indian warships and maritime reconnaissance and combat aircraft.[94] The other prong, as discussed in earlier chapters, is to assist the Vietnamese and Indonesian armed forces beef up their military capabilities. Jakarta is keen for a comprehensive security tie-up with India, including pilot training and aircraft maintenance for its fleet of Su-27s and Su-30s. Significantly, the IAF has taken over these duties from the Chinese Air Force (PLA Air Force). India is also helping Indonesia with co-production of ammunition and weapons systems, and sharpening its military's skills in joint exercises. Indian Defence Minister A.K. Antony in Indonesia in October 2012 talked up defence cooperation and offered a rationale for it by referring to the 'power rivalries' in the South China Sea that are adversely impacting the wider region.[95] The Indian Navy is confident about having a drop on its Chinese rival. 'For a long time, we should be so much superior with four of the 16 P-8Is in the air at any given time—able adequately to cover the Indian Ocean. For the next 20 years we have the SSNs, the SSKs and the Brahmos cruise missile. PLAN can't do all that much,' opined Raja Menon. 'They are grossly inferior to us in this Ocean, and will remain so for the next 30 years even with their carriers. Once their carrier becomes operational, then the navalised Jaguars that are being upgraded to carry advanced anti-ship missiles will make a huge difference. And that's why Agalega in Mauritius and the Andamans in the west are both needed.'[96]

'As for sustaining a fleet' in the Andaman region Vice Admiral Ganesh said that 'as big a task force as is required [can be up-kept] there indefinitely. We have a logistical chain from the mainland [to the integrated Andaman Command]'.[97] Further, this Command's littoral intervention capability, besides the air cover provided by carrier aviation, mainland-based air, and combat aircraft squadrons embarked from Car Nicobar, will by 2030 be powered by 4 Landing Ships Dock (LSDs) probably of the Mistral-class (at 32,000 tons displacement with ballast), apart from the Jalashwa (ex-USS Trenton) in service, along with some 22 other vessels of the Landing Ship Tank and Landing Ship Utility-variety for amphibious missions. An army brigade under the Andaman Command constitutes the land-force element that can be speedily augmented with forces from peninsular stations. The army, according to its former chief, General Deepak Kapoor is, in fact, equipping an entire infantry Division with lighter weapons to make it deployable abroad on short notice. 'If an air field is available at the other end, we can transport forces starting with an infantry brigade,' he stated and recalled that the fleet of An-32s, the main IAF transport workhorse, was funded out of the army budget with the aim of airlifting army troops.[98] This airlift fleet can, he added, easily transport an infantry Division to distant locations in three days, as its operation to move some 47,000 Kashmiris from the earthquake-affected areas in 2003 proved.[99]

The Indian armed forces growingly have the wherewithal to carry out expeditionary operations but the label—'expeditionary' is deemed politically sensitive and is generally avoided by the military and government to describe capabilities associated with it, owing to its 'negative connotations'. In any case, the armed services 'do not think expeditionary because,' as Air Chief Marshal Krishnaswamy observed, 'there's no articulation of expeditionary missions [by the government].'[100] A former Chief of the Air Staff, Air Chief Marshal N.A.K. Browne, whilst in office, went so far as to flatly declare in autumn 2011 that IAF was 'not an expeditionary force'. This phrase, he explained has a 'hegemonic or quasi-imperial' sound to it and that it is not so much actual operations but 'a matter of [using] the right semantics.' Whether it is Ainee (in Tajikistan) or anywhere else 'we need to protect our mineral-oil assets, it would be natural for IAF to go in,' Krishnaswamy explained, and admitted that the government was funding the air force and the navy for expansive missions and roles which, do not, however, involve 'fighting other people's wars'.[101] As far as China is concerned, in the context of the limited forces it can bring to bear west of the Malacca Strait, there's not a conceivable contingency New Delhi believes the Indian military cannot handle. The Navy-driven military acquisitions and build-up plans over the last decade, prioritizing procurement of hardware for maritime and aerial-strike, and distant actions, besides the Arihant SSBN and the Akula-II SSN for serious sea-denial—with two-and-half crews trained in the Russian naval base at Archangel, and another one-and-half crews in the nuclear submarine training base in Vishakhapatnam, together with land-based IRBMs for strategic deterrence, reflect this goal of achieving shutdown dominance in India's oceanic compound in the decades ahead.[102] It helps that 52 per cent of the warships are less than 15 years old—a rough measure of modernity of a naval force.[103] It will be an even more modern fleet in the years to come with 46 warships under construction and another 49 in the underway naval building plan worth $ 54.6 billion (Rs 2.73 lakh crores).[104]

China's 'string of pearls' strategy of cultivating Indian Ocean states and countries in this littoral with aid and infrastructure projects amounts to little in military terms because in war-time none of these small countries would risk the stick in India's 'carrot and stick' policy that Yashwant Sinha articulated for them in the early 2000s. 'I made it clear to all our neighbours,' Sinha revealed, 'that we'll go to a totally asymmetrical relationship with them, loaded against India, in the economic, trade and investment fields. But there's one thing we'll insist on and that is don't mess around with us. If that happens we'll feel free to take whatever steps to ensure national security for India.'[105] This is no empty threat. In the 1980s India, for example, informally sealed its borders over serious differences, bringing life in Nepal to a halt, abetted secessionism in northern Sri Lanka by training the cadres of secessionist LTTE (Liberation Tigers of Tamil Eelam) after disapproving of the harsh measures taken against the Tamil community in that country, and obtained an India-friendly dispensation of Abdulla Yameen Gayoom in the Maldives.

The trouble with the Indian naval order-of-battle in the second decade of the 21st century is the reverse of what obtained in the 1970s when the Petya-class corvettes dominated the fleet—it is consumed by gigantism, emphasizing big capital ships rather than the more numerous multi-purpose frigates and corvettes to buttress the strength of fast attack craft and patrol vessels needed to constantly monitor the 572 islands in the Andaman Sea, for instance, of which only 234 are inhabited. It is a telling imbalance of forces and the absence of appropriate vessels that the Andaman Integrated Command as against the requirement of at least 18–20 offshore patrol vessels (OPVs) to carry out its sea order and surveillance missions had in December 2014 not a single such boat under command. The lone OPV available with it was pulled for anti-piracy duties off the Gulf of Aden in early 2014. It has therefore to make do inefficiently with LSTs (landing ship tanks) to police the extensive territorial waters.[106] The craving for aircraft carriers of the Indian Navy seems more a desire to make an impression than maintain visibility in the seas. Two aircraft carriers are to be built at the Kochi shipyard—the first of these is under construction and will be ready for fleet duty by 2018-2019, to be followed by a still more modern boat featuring the electro-magnetic aircraft launch system (EMALS) technology the U.S. has offered.[107] Able to launch the E2C Hawkeye kind of airborne early warning system of the latter's deck, it is expected to increase the carrier's radius of operations and provide better management of its air arm for extended fleet air defence and littoral strikes. But carriers raise several questions about their utility at a time when supersonic cruise missiles, such as the Chinese CX-1—the Chinese counterpart of the Indian Brahmos, are coming on the scene and in time could be passed on to Pakistan. Carriers are very large, can't-miss, targets for such missiles, and highlight their immense vulnerability. They will also require more ships and submarines to be attached to them as protective escorts in a task group, which protection is, in any case, useless against a CX-1, there being no defensive technology even on the horizon to neutralize such missiles, leave alone hypersonic missiles that are in the development phase. Further, with so many capital ships providing cover for carriers, the navy's presence in the 73,556,000 sq. km expanse of the Indian Ocean will be much diminished, unless the numbers of missile destroyers and frigates are much increased. In the meanwhile, the trade-off between quality and quantity and the 'high-low' mix of weapons platforms will compel the navy to have fewer flotillas dotting the seascape cumulatively to cover a greater maritime area. It is plain that in the context of the Indian Ocean replacing the Atlantic as an oceanic highway with the densest traffic, smaller ships make more sense for the same reasons that Rear Admiral Menon advocates smaller tankers permitting more task groups led by destroyers and frigates. Of course, carriers are impressive in the flag-showing role in peacetime; in war, however, their size and their symbolic value will render them prime targets and liability for the navy, which cannot afford to use them or lose them. In effect, in conflict they will be holed up in well-defended bases, as the original Vikrant was in the Vishakhapatnam port for the duration of the 1971 India–Pakistan War. In the event, are INS Vikramaditya, costing around $5 billion with its aircraft complement, along with its sister carriers with only slightly smaller price tags, worth the money, considering the sums expended on the three carriers would have bought the country 12 Kolkata-class guided-missile destroyers and numerous lesser ships, or five SSNs, or a mix of nuclear attack submarines and conventional destroyers/frigates to afford the country more spread out and sustained 'maritime density' and punch?

Army's Legacy Burden

The fundamental problem for the military is the twisted threat perception distorting India's military posture, which problem is evidenced in defence spending. Analysis of defence budgets over 40 years and a rough breakdown of expenditures according to broad missions/roles reveals a certain pattern—21–23 per cent of the total defence budget is usually consumed by armoured and mechanized forces; 14–16 per cent by plains warfare formations (including the so-called 'pivot corps' forming part of the initial armoured drive conceived in Cold Start-type punitive actions against Pakistan), and 10–12 per cent by mountain divisions. Out of the remaining 54 per cent of the budget,

20 per cent is allotted to strategic/counter air inclusive of AWACS and aerial tankers, 8–10 per cent to air defence aircraft and surface-to-air missiles, 2–3 per cent on air lift/transport, 11 per cent to sea control missions (surface combatants) and 8–9 per cent to submarine assets in sea denial role, and 5–6 per cent to Defence R&D.[108] The force deployments fit the expenditure trends in that they suggest that both the bulk and the sharp edge of the Indian military are fielded against Pakistan. The Indian Army's armoured and mechanized units in the three strike corps are usable in mass only on the western front. So much public money, military manpower and material, and effort invested over the years in vast capital-intensive forces for such small returns—to affect 'shallow penetration', capture Pakistani territory, and use it as card to negotiate a compromise on Kashmir or to end Pakistani-sponsored terrorism! That India is able to inflict pain on Pakistan is not in question. But it has so far failed to deter Islamabad from wielding terrorism—its asymmetric means of warfare or holding back from aggressive actions on the LOC. The conspicuously small returns highlights the disproportionately big investment in a wrong force structure and a waste of precious resources.

In any case, India's operational plans bank on the first prompt retaliatory action to a sizeable Pakistani provocation inside of three days by battle-ready armoured and mechanized units in the 'pivot corps' (whose main task otherwise is as holding or defensive formations), which will attempt instant breakthroughs across a broad front. The breaches in the Pakistani defences are supposed to be exploited by eight independent battle groups (IBGs) with integral logistics as spearheads reconstituted on the move to the front from armoured and mechanized forces in the three strike corps headquartered rear-wards.[109] Except, sustained and rapid breakthroughs by the IBGs would require these units to be fully mechanized which, because they are not, make these so-called 'Cold Start' plans non-executable.[110] Previously, these plans contemplated an advance along the Rahim Yar Khan axis in the semi-desert sector, which bereft of built-up areas, permitted relatively fast progress by mobile forces. Except, the sparsely habited tracts are also attractive venues for the Pakistan Army to do what it credibly threatens to do in that situation—target advancing Indian armour inside its territory with tactical nuclear weapons.[111] To divest Pakistan of the temptation of early nuclear weapon use and to lengthen the nuclear fuse, the old Indian strategy has been dispensed with. The new strategy is for the IBGs to rush headlong towards a few Pakistani cities in the 'strategic corridor' running north to south near the Indian border and to quickly close in on these industrial and population centres. Investing these large urban nodes in strength, and advancing in lockstep with any Pakistani attempts at military and civilian withdrawal deeper into their own territory, at once presents the Pakistani nuclear planners with a severe dilemma. Initiating first use of nuclear weapons in these circumstances immediately outside their own cities may take out bits of Indian armour without appreciably slowing down the concentration of armoured/mechanized units operating in sealed, hatch-down, mode (T-72 and T-90 tanks in the Indian inventory being operable in an irradiated environment) around Pakistani cities. The thermal flash, kinetic death-blows, and radiation from the Pakistani nuclear device use will severely impact the unprotected Pakistani military units and population in the surrounded cities as much as they will do the Indian forces. The Pakistan nuclear strategists may in the event decide on striking Indian military targets within India and, as per the Indian nuclear doctrine, trigger 'massive retaliation' or, on a lesser escalatory scale, a chain of uncontrollable nuclear strike and counter strike in action-reaction sequence. In either case, the hostilities will spiral into total war, which Pakistan cannot survive, because of an over-adverse 'exchange ratio' (the ratio of destruction suffered to destruction imposed on the adversary).[112] It is this ultimately prohibitive price of a nuclear exchange that's likely to dissuade the Pakistan Army from violating the nuclear taboo in the first place.[113] The IBGs would have 180 pieces of self-propelled artillery and the air support of 72 helicopters (of the total 150-175 helicopters with the army, the rest going to the two offensive mountain Divisions), with two squadrons of 24 armed helicopters assigned to each strike corps. General V.K. Singh during his tenure as Chief of the Army Staff (2010-12) presented an 'integrated battle plan' to the Defence Minister Antony in 2010 that essentially brought the IBGs under a separate theatre-level 'Strike Command', with the head of this Command left free to devolve operational authority as he saw fit and the circumstances permitted. However, MOD rejected such re-organization without, however, rejecting the planned force disposition.[114]

The irony in this Pakistan conflict scenario is two-fold. Firstly, as already stated, massive armoured and mechanized capability, representing nested capital, is tasked for the relatively minor job of restraining Pakistan and suggests wrong military priorities and misuse of financial resources. In the early 1970s, Soviet Defence Minister Andrei Grechko, plainly perplexed by the lopsided nature of India's military preparations, castigated it for chasing 'little phantoms like Pakistan' while ignoring 'the unpredictable enemy from the North' and 'ominous source from where the real threat to India emanates namely China'.[115] And secondly, short of the concept of 'limited war' using armoured forces in a nuclearized milieu being reworked for the China front, such large armoured and mechanized strength seems a thinly-veiled excuse to retain at any cost the existing forces led by the money-guzzling strike corps. According to a former army chief, the justification for retaining the massive armour component is to be 'so far ahead' of the Pakistan Army as to make it futile for it to even start an affray.[116] But as the record of Pakistan initiating the Kargil conflict and not backing down in 2002 in the face of a mobilized Indian field army indicates, the Pakistan Army while wary of the Indian strike forces is insufficiently dissuaded.

Indian armoured and mechanized units can be deployed against the PLA on the high altitude flatland, but the units will have to be down-sized, and outfitted ideally with lighter tanks accompanied by BMP-2 armoured combat vehicles, both with engines able to ignite quickly and more reliably in high-altitude conditions, permitting them to skitter about in harassing operations on the Tibetan plateau, with the attack helicopter component for air envelopment in a strategy to isolate and destroy PLA aggresssor concentrations. In fact, such helicopters could be perfect also for surveillance along the LAC. The limitations of armoured forces is that they can debouch to high-altitude plateau only from two staging areas—the 'Demchok Triangle' in the western sector and the northern Sikkim plains at the other end. An economical and effective land war strategy involving the entire armoured and mechanized component of the army requires the three strike corps to be restructured into a single composite strike corps plus a number of independent armoured brigades equipped with mostly the indigenous Arjun main battle tank that, in field trials, has bested the vaunted Russian T-90 tank in every respect.

Together with the armoured and mechanized element in the pivot corps, it will more than adequately deal with any Pakistan-related contingency. The manpower and materiel freed-up from the strike corps could be switched to constitute two additional offensive mountain corps featuring T-90 and T-72 tanks. Thousands of antique and mothballed ex-Soviet T-55 and ex-British Vijayanta tanks still on the rolls of the strike corps can be safely junked, leaving a smaller, more manageable tank inventory. More importantly, such restructuring will not incur huge additional costs and actually manifests more responsible and efficacious use of the nation's hard-earned financial resources. The offensive mountain corps would complement the 12 mountain infantry divisions currently arrayed along the border with China—nine in the Northeastern sector and one-and-a-half divisions each in the Central and Western sectors, with two new divisions tasked for offensive operations and deployed by 2015–17. The fact is just one offensive mountain corps of the kind the army seems satisfied cannot muster the critical mass of armour/mechanized units necessary to generate momentum or impact the entrenched PLA. Hence, the two new offensive divisions will end up supporting the defensive mountain divisions deployed to conduct positional warfare in the mountains. On the other hand, were three mountain corps complete with integral armour, attack helicopters, airlift, and logistics, to materialize they could be moved—disaggregated into fighting brigades—to converge on a single point or several points after being funnelled onto the Tibetan plateau, owing to ease of ingress access, through mostly Demchok and, secondarily, Sikkim.[117] The IAF's Apache AH-64D squadron would be the air-attack spearhead. The logistics support for forward deployment in the mountains has all along been hampered by nearly non-existent border roads. Concerns for national security did not persuade the Environment Ministry during Manmohan Singh's rule to lift its ban on road construction. All the projects hanging fire—6,000 kilometres of roads mostly in the eastern and western Himalayas, and a naval radar station on Narcondam in the Andaman Sea with an extinct volcano rising to over 700 meters, placing a radar atop which will provide a wide and sweeping coverage coverage Malacca wards—were cleared on priority basis within a fortnight of the successor Modi government taking charge. Disregarding Chinese protest, the 1,800 km long highway skirting the entire ceasefire line with China and linking all the 12 border districts in Arunachal Pradesh has been sanctioned as also a new airfield in Tawang.[118] This is to increase seamless connectivity with the heartland and employment growth by attracting investment in industrial parks. In the decade 2004-2014 while 2,400 kilometres of mostly interior roads were approved, only 230 kilometres were completed. A law ensuring environmental concerns don't undermine military projects is on the cards.[119]

The strategic utility of the MTCs to distract and unsettle the PLA with aggression in kind, notwithstanding, the residual resistance within the army and government to such offensive corps is because of the conviction that elements of such corps, once launched on the high-altitude Tibetan desert, would become easy prey for the PLA. And that a more effective strategy is, therefore, to exploit the mountainous terrain advantaging the defender.[120] Except, a strategy of positional defence adopted in the 1962 War failed in the main because the PLA units simply flowed round these Indian strong points. In any case, the army's traditional defensive-mindedness underestimates the immeasurable psychological effect on the PLA and the shock value of three Indian mountain corps worth of offensive forces able, with attack helicopters, instantly to deploy on the Chinese side of the LAC inside Tibet, and create mayhem and uncertainty that defensively-disposed Indian forces cannot do. Three such corps make sense also from a practical viewpoint. A commander of an army Corps in the northeast mentioned the difficulty of debouching armoured and mechanized elements especially from the northern Sikkim plains at an altitude of 17,000 feet, where the performance of machines degrades by some 40 per cent. 'We will be happy if these tanks can even start up!' he said, while pointing to the Demochok Triangle in the north-western Ladakh as better suited for operations by tanks, except there are more PLA built-up areas in the east to target than in the west.[121] The point however is that it is better to have a bigger mass of even performance-wise degraded armour and mechanized units than a smaller one, to guarantee at least some impact in terms of the ability to radiate outwards from these staging areas along a number of axes, and thus complicate the PLA's response calculus than have nothing at all by way of an offensive option.

National security aspects aside, the thrust of reorganizing the army to better tackle the China threat will have positive spill over effects in South Asia, only if there's a concurrent thinning of forces on India's western border. If the Indian strike corps are persevered with because they supposedly strike fear in the Pakistan Army, less expensive options are available that operationally will have greater impact. One such option is to induct the highly lethal and accurate Prahar short-range ballistic missile (SRBM) in large numbers as area-weapons, and the even more lethal Pragati tactical missile system under development. A salvo of six Prahar SRBMs can, for instance, crater 2,000 square meters. Had the Prahar firepower been available in Kargil, the occupation by the Pakistan army unit would have ended inside of a few days, instead of the months it actually took for the infantry conjointly with pinpoint aerial strikes—that the IAF took a while to mount—and artillery barrages to clear the heights of enemy soldiers, and would have spared the country the losses in terms of casualties, time, and money.[122]

A rationalization of the Indian armoured and mechanized forces on the western front and the transposing of surplus units from the west to form offensive mountain corps will amount, moreover, to a substantive and credible confidence and security-building measure with Pakistan. The disbandment of two strike corps opposing it will gradually erode the Pakistan military's and, by extension, the Pakistan government's and people's simmering distrust of India.[123] Besides unilaterally trimming its armour holdings, India can also safely and unconditionally remove the nuclear-warheaded Prithvi SRBMs deployed on the border with Pakistan as a good faith gesture, especially as the longer-range Agni missiles fired from hinterland points can take out any targets within Pakistan. This valuable nuclear signal will further defuse the situation, compelling the Pakistan Army to take note. It may provide the Pakistani generals the confidence to, on the one hand, wage a forceful campaign to eliminate militant Islamic groups, such as the Tehreek-e-Taliban Pakistan, waging a vicious war against the Pakistani state and, on the other hand, approve the dissolution of terrorist groups, such as Lashkar-e-Tayyaba, it deploys against India, and support the civilian government's attempts to restore normal relations. The conspicuous pivoting of the Indian air and land forces to the north and northeast against China, in any case, requires to be done to gain credibility for India as a counterweight to China in the rest of Asia as well. Coupled with measures to ease trade and commerce, and the visa regime, it will reassure even the die-hard sceptics in the Pakistan government and society, and enlarge the constituency for permanent peace and conciliation with India (Karnad 2005: 572–7). In the negotiation track, the break-up of the three strike corps can be presented as meaningful response to the proposal by the former Pakistan President General Parvez Musharraf for 'proportional reductions' of forces. Musharraf had hoped that were India to agree to this it would show 'that it is a big country with a big heart rather than a big country with a small heart.'[124] It is in India's interest to pursue such force reductions on its western border by unilateral or negotiated means, because it will enable it to more effectively husband its military resources in its more enduring confrontation with China, and help the two dominant militaries of the subcontinent to turn outwards, rather than inwards to fight each other.

Such security cooperation may find support in Pakistan, because that's how its founder, Mohammad Ali Jinnah, envisaged a security condominium for South Asia, in which Pakistan would be the guardian of the western marches, and India would be responsible for the defence of the maritime domain and the northern and eastern approaches.[125] A modified Jinnah scheme for the defence of the subcontinent, with India concentrating on China, can serve as a distant goal for all the countries of South Asia to work towards. With the democratically elected government of Nawaz Sharif in Islamabad and the smooth transition from General Ashfaq Kayani to General Raheel Sharif as Pakistan Army chief chosen by the civilian government, Pakistan is preoccupied with quelling the internal security threats.[126] The gains from India and Pakistan working together to mesh their economies and trading systems for mutual benefit— permitting Indian goods to transit through Pakistan to Afghanistan and Central Asia, and laying energy grids, constructing transportation corridors within the subcontinent, forging connectivity to Iran and Central Asia and, simultaneously, drawing Afghanistan and the Central Asian Republics into the larger South Asian market, will be immense, in line with Prime Minister Modi's transnational economic policy focus.[127] For India such a development is an imperative

because without a peaceful subcontinent and a pacified neighbourhood plugging into the Indian economy and growth engine, the
Indian Monroe Doctrine system will remain unfulfilled as will India's
great power ambitions.

In this regard, a new 'second track' effort—'India-Pakistan Soldiers'
Peace Initiative'—got underway in end-2012 to get the militaries of
the two countries to talk directly to each other, something the Indian
government was previously leery of. It indicates the direction in which
the breeze should blow.[128] A policy of fostering social and cultural links
between the Indian and Pakistani armies, starting with 'partitioned'
regiments getting together in sports meets, exchange of officers to
regimental centres, and similar ventures will go a long way in seeding
mutual confidence and trust presently missing between the two parts
of the once British Indian Army.[129] The Bharatiya Janata Party is,
however, wary of such peace-building actions involving any unilateral
measures, believing they'll prove futile and, ultimately, 'deleterious to
national security.'[130] Such a position, unfortunately, entrenches the
present force structure, mindset, and the associated problems. The
2010 Directive to the armed services from the Defence Minister
stressed the looming China threat without expressly instructing the
armed services to rebalance away from Pakistan to China, which
Indian government seems wary of ordering. Barring such change
though, a smart military build-up to buttress India's great power ambition is precluded. The armed services then will continue on the basis
that China needs building up against while retaining the legacy forces
for any untoward Pakistan-related event. But because India cannot
afford large scale military augmentation on both fronts, the country
will likely end up staying on the present course and spending more
on conventionally deterring Pakistan than on sufficiently and strategically neutralizing China. The fact is India cannot have two live fronts
as the military is certain it cannot effectively handle a Pakistan-China
nexus in war.[131] It will spare MoD the financial juggling as regards the
allocations for the Pakistan and China theatres.[132]

Army's Warfighting Stamina and Inescapable 'Voids'

The Indian Army's dominant Pakistan orientation is anomalous and
marks it out as a sub-strategic, tactically-minded, force. Of the 14

corps in the Indian Army, eight are dedicated to the western front, including 85–90 per cent of armour and mechanized units. The remaining six corps are meant for China-related contingencies.[133] To deconstruct the deployment picture some more—of the total 350 infantry regiments and 250 regiments of artillery in the Indian army, two-thirds are posted on the (3,323 km) border with Pakistan, and the remaining third on the longer (4,057 km) front with China; 90 per cent of the 60 plus armoured regiments and 40 mechanized regiments are tasked for operations against Pakistan. A former Deputy Chief of Army Staff explained away the imbalance this way: 'What we are looking at on the two fronts is punitive deterrence against Pakistan, and dissuasion versus China, and wanting to build up to a conventional deterrence from the present position of low-end deterrence existing where China is concerned.' This situation will hold, he added, only if the air force is factored into the equation and the border infrastructure is fully built up.[134] If elsewhere in the country the quality of infrastructure (road, bridges, railways, airports) is atrocious, on the border with China it is nearly absent. According to an ex-army chief, of the 1,000-odd miles of border roads that are supposed to be completed by 2015, only 30 per cent of them are ready and usable. The estimated date for completion of the entire road network has been pushed to 2025, the delays caused by the Congress government of Manmohan Singh having paid greater attention to ecological concerns than to national security, and the more practical problem of transporting the heavy road-building machinery to mountain locations. In fact, some of these regions are so remote and undefended, especially some valleys east of the Kameng administrative Division (where the Tawang Monastery is sited) the PLA can, he claimed, 'simply walk in'.[135] The government's tardiness in border road building after the 1962 conflict is blamed on the defeatist outlook of the political leadership, which felt it was prudent to not have roads than to build them and see the PLA utilize them to invade India.[136] The fear of Chinese troops using Indian rolling stock and railway infrastructure not destroyed in a scorched earth policy to penetrate deep inside India, perhaps, also explains why nine of the 14 strategic railway projects to link the northern and northeastern areas bordering China to the heartland have not materialized. The Railway Ministry has complained in the past about its being cash-strapped, and unending discussions about which ministry—defence or railways, is to be billed for what railway construction, has delayed implementation.[137] The railway ministry is also adamant that it won't do a second survey of the terrain on the other side of the Teesta River for laying a railway line to Sikkim, insisting that the project proceed along the same alignment as an existing road on one side of the river.[138] Seeking to perpetuate the border infrastructure imbalance advantaging the PLA, Beijing has authorized a survey for a second loop-line of the Qinghai-Lhasa railway to Nyingchi close to Tawang to complement the 253 km railway line to Xigatze on the Nepal border, which opened recently, even as New Delhi was warned against building 54 new military posts on the Arunachal border.[139] Rather than an infrastructure construction race, Defence Minister Liang Guanglie called for 'unilaterally expand[ing] area of activities and military deployment along the Line of Actual Control, so as to jointly maintain a stable situation in the border areas.'[140] Beijing apparently views any attempt by India to build border roads and airfields within its claim-line which includes all of Arunachal Pradesh and stretches all the way to the north side of the Brahmaputra River, as destabilizing, and is too self-serving a Chinese proposition for India to pay heed.

As for trouble, it will come, says the former deputy chief of the Indian Army, were the PLA to 'advance in a layered offense—informationalised warfare, rapid reaction forces, air drops, followed by the advance of the main force, and exceed 30 per cent of its current capability by bringing in 30 Group Armies (or Divisions) on to the plateau inside of 28 days.' That, he said, 'will be bad for us' if the huge voids [in the War Wastage Reserve and War Stock] remain unfilled, and 'if we haven't modernized our forces' or procured long-range artillery. India, he added, continues to lack 24/7 sustainable surveillance and intelligence systems to 'look deep into [the PLA forces arrayed in Tibet in] tiered offense', and even a limited offensive capability of the two offensive mountain divisions 'to open another front'.[141] Other than airlift, the Qinghai-Lhasa railway enables rapid mobilization of resources and forces. On an average, the Chinese run 11 trains a day into Lhasa from the mainland, each with 20 wagons, each wagon carrying a 20 ton load.[142] The comparable picture, from the Indian perspective is dismal. Mountain-fighting capabilities-wise the Indian Army, the retired deputy army chief ventured, will have to do 'some 80 per cent more' in terms of acquisitions and force augmentation with in-built redundancies, which the budgetary allocations at the current 2.2 per cent of the GDP level don't permit. The recommendation of the 12th Finance Commission (a Constitutional body established every five years to prospectively divide the projected pool of revenues between the centre and the provinces and, at the federal level, between the various ministries of Government of India) in 2005 pegged defence spending at the three per cent of GDP-level, hasn't yet been effected.

The seemingly laid-back attitude of the government and the military to the Chinese build-up and the threat it poses, may be sourced to a 2007 paper put up by the then Chief of the Integrated Defence Staff, Lieutenant General H.S. Lidder to the army chief, General J.J. Singh. It pointed out that the topography in much of the 'central sector' with rows of very high Himalayan mountain ranges will be difficult for the PLA to cross, and that this will funnel the Chinese forces into attacking at the two ends of the border where the terrain is less daunting, simplifying India's war response calculus. And secondly, that as per a basic mountain warfare predicate, Chinese troops even when fighting downhill from their staging areas in the high-altitude (oxygen-deprived) Tibetan plateau, will be able to carry little by way of arms, ammo and rations, necessitating the deployment of some 60 PLA Group Armies to overwhelm the ten Indian Divisions in defence—a logistically difficult—exercise for China at any time. The basis for this comforting prognosis was backed by the assurances by the external intelligence agency—Research and Analysis Wing (RAW), that it will be able to generate a 60-day-warning of attack, which the armed services believe is enough notice to gear up for hostilities.[143] But India can ill-afford such a relaxed approach considering that the operational flexibility provided by a single offensive mountain corps is insufficient to impel the PLA to retain substantial forces on the plateau for defence. Moreover, certain Chinese ingress routes haven't been considered, such as from east of the Kameng sector in Arunachal Pradesh, and the equally lightly defended stretch of the border with northern Myanmar through which PLA can advance on the old 'Stilwell Road', a route if taken would surprise the Indian military units facing in the wrong direction. But the army claims that the use of the Stilwell Road will require the PLA to cross some 500 kilometres of Myanmarese territory, a logistically difficult task, even with a friendly Kachin Army assisting its forward movement, and the 18 airfields the Chinese have built in that area receiving air-transported supplies, two whole Indian Army Divisions facing north-western Myanmar will still need to be overcome.[144]

The more serious problem for the army as well as the other two services is their endurance or war-fighting stamina: How long can they engage in operations, with what intensity, and how fast can the conflict be terminated on favourable terms without completely exhausting the holdings of spares and petroleum products (war reserve) and of ammunitions, shells, and chemical explosives (war stock)? Complicated calculations are involved for every weapon system and its share of ammunition/shells and spares, and the extent of usage, spoilage, and expenditure in training over its lifetime and the choice, given a limited budget, between building up the stocks of spares, ammunition, etc. and force modernization. The history of short duration India-Pakistan wars that are politically and socially convenient to both countries in fact allows the armed services to set aside a bigger quantum from their budgets for force modernization programmes. But this tendency does not account for longer duration conflict that China may inflict, which will find the Indian military exhausting its reserves of essential war materiel. A solution for this grave problem has not been found. The army, especially, 'cannot go by the book' in stocking spares, ammo, etc. for all its armaments, the former deputy army chief cautioned, because then the costs involved—some three times the initial cost of the weapon system—would leave just enough money to buy only very limited force modernization, and not enough spares and servicing support for all the items in the arsenal. This is the reason he said, why 'voids' of spares get created with monies set aside to fill these only to the extent of two-times the capital cost of weapons. Invariably then, there are shortages in time of war when the consumption rises sharply with rapidly depleting stocks of ammunition and spares. It is this costing and inventory management, he said, 'that's not been done very well by us'.

Whatever shortages occur in wartime are, however, speedily addressed when New Delhi finds the monies for the usual frenzied purchases abroad, paying top-dollar for critically needed war materiel to make up the shortfalls that have been permitted to grow in peacetime. Such gaps have not so far hurt the country or affected the outcomes of the conflicts the country has been involved in. But that was because of their short duration involving an adversary, Pakistan, that like India, is hampered by a similar policy of small spares stockpiles. Reconciling the demands of a long war with the government's unwillingness to fund an orderly and routine build-up more economically to enable the military to be better prepared to ride out such contingencies is harder.

The problem is exacerbated by the nonexistence of a comprehensively capable local defence industry able to replenish with surge production of the items consumed at high rates. The deputy army chief counsels a new metric for stockpiling spares—moving the Indian armed forces, from capabilities-based planning (replacing the previous threats-based planning) to priorities-based planning, which he says the armed services are resisting, perhaps, because the priorities have not been established by the government. What it comes down to is the need for an Operational Directive ordering the military to align majorly against China and secondarily against Pakistan. It will guide the shaping of land forces accordingly, and compel the military brass to make difficult choices in terms of force structures and procurement. If this is not done, then the armed services will continue in the manner they have been doing all these years—fund a little of everything under the rubric of a 'balanced force' (inclusive of the very large legacy combat arm—armour and mechanized forces) and thus rob the country of a potent military capability against the heftier foe.

The disparities between the Indian military and the PLA are significant in terms of numbers of major weapons systems (see Table 5.1), but not necessarily in terms of quality.[145] China, moreover, is bordered mostly by states that are allergic to its growing power, requiring the PLA to prepare for more varied contingencies on its land and sea borders. It cannot, for instance, afford to thin out its forces opposite Taiwan to strengthen, say, the Lanzhou and Chengdu 'command zones' adjacent to India, which in any case are also kept busy by the Tibetan unrest and the Uyghur troubles in Xinjiang. India needs to enlarge these force asymmetries, besides the mountain offensive corps, by quickly deploying more regiments of the specially designed mountain-use Brahmos cruise missile than the total of four regiments

TABLE 5.1   Weapons platforms

	India	China	Pakistan
ARMY			
Main Battle Tanks	3,274	7,430	2,411
AIFVs	1,455	2,150	–
APCs	366	2,900	1,390
Artillery	9,682	12.367	4,607
AIR FORCE			
Bombers	–	82	–
Fighter aircraft	63	842	200
Fighter/Ground attack	736	543	174
AWACS	3	8	4
Tankers + transport	6+238	10+326	4+34
NAVY			
Aircraft carriers	1(+1)	1	–
SSBN	1	4	–
SSN	1	5	–
Conv submarines	15	61	8
Frigates	12	62	10
Destroyers	11	14	–
Anti-Sub Warfare	9	93	–
Amphib ships	24	85	–
Tankers+logistics	3+50	3+205	0+4
NAVAL AVIATION			
Bombers	–	30	–
Combat-capable ac	34	341	–
Fighter ac	15	72	–
Fighter/Ground attack	10	200	–

Source: *Military Balance 2013*, IISS, London, 2013.

that are planned. Batteries of the Prahar area-destruction missile to deliver hard punches too should be inducted in a hurry and in daunting numbers. Force transformation decisions take a decade to have effect, warned the ex-Deputy Chief of the army. 'So, whatever it is we want [by way of forces to deal with China], the government better take a decision now. Or, the government has to say we'll leave it to diplomacy and to various other factors.'[146] Considering that the last time the country relied on diplomacy or other countries (the U.S. and U.K.) during Nehru's time, India came to sorrow and paid for it with military defeat, it is an option that does not inspire confidence.

State of the Strategic Deterrent—Accurate Missiles, Iffy Thermonuclear Weapons

As the world grows more insecure and security threats and uncertainty multiply, and the old Cold War-type tensions resurface, major powers are rediscovering the value of nuclear weapons as both political and military instrument.[147] It is in this context of the new nuclearized global milieu that the Indian strategic deterrent must be analysed.

India is advantaged by its oceanic and Asian continental location offering an unusually large menu of deterrence options and strategic military solutions both against China and Pakistan. The Indian Ocean region includes narrow seas (Malacca, Lumbok, and Sunda Straits), an expansive littoral, and the Indian peninsula jutting out, offering India the use of conventional, strategic, or dual-use wherewithal to eliminate all manner of threats and dangers. Thus, other than the SSBNs, the prospective Project 75i conventional submarine with nuclear weapon and conventional warheaded 1,000 km Nirbhay subsonic cruise missile, for instance, can take out targets within range on shore and at sea from air-launched, land-based and seaborne platforms, and conventional submarines. Akula SSNs operating in the submarine-to submarine mode can hunt down enemy nuclear and conventional submersibles and the peninsular air bases can embark Jaguar and Su-30 sorties against Chinese warships in the Indian Ocean, and extend their range eastwards from the Port Blair and the Car Nicobar air strips. And, corvettes from the mainland or Andaman Sea bases can launch torpedoes against capital surface combatants, and the larger Indian naval ships the conventional and nuclear Brahmos supersonic cruise missiles. In most such situations, the country's strategic arsenal is vastly augmented by conventional and strategic platforms bearing nuclear and conventional missiles. Missiles is what will matter the most. It is precisely the variety of strike options, that'll enable 'interval attacks' as a strategic crisis involving nuclear weapons use unfolds, and will 'allow for conflict resolution between each attack'.[148]

Many analysts, especially in the South Asia-centred Henry L. Stimson Center in Washington, DC American, worry about the so-called 'stability-instability paradox' to make the point that nuclearized India and Pakistan constitute a nuclear flashpoint requiring outside mediation. The argument goes something like this: India's conventional military superiority is balanced by Pakistani nuclear weapons and results in stability. But the use by Pakistan of the nuclear overhang to fight unsymmetric warfare using terrorists creates instability because India cannot retaliate conventionally without risking Pakistani use of nuclear weapons.[149] The basic flaw in this argument is the presumption of India as a passive-defensive entity, which sees use of massive conventional forces as the only reply to terrorist and other provocation by Pakistan. What would happen if India replied to Pakistani provocations in kind thereby passing the onus for escalation to the other side? India would always be advantaged in any military face-off no matter what means or wherewithal was involved, ranging from asymmetric sub-conventional to nuclear. Thus, India can opt to counter Pakistani aid to secessionists in Kashmir by helping out the Baluch insurgency, the Pakistani use of jihadis by funding certain sections of Pakistani and Afghan Taliban in their war against the Pakistani state and, on a lower scale, direct more serious and sustained artillery fire at longer ranges in response to similar fire by the Pakistan army along the Line of Control in Jammu & Kashmir. So there's no possibility of instability and escalatory spiral tripping the nuclear wire because India can re-stabilize the situation anytime Pakistan destabilizes it by responding to it in tit-for-tat fashion. The issue then becomes one of the resource base and endurance, which Pakistan cannot win, whence the 'paradox' is actually nullified (Karnad 2007). The hardnosed Indian government of Modi proved the point. When India responded with harsh artillery fire in response to Pakistan's initiating an artillery barrage the Pakistan Army Chief, instead of ordering escalatory action, complained to the U.S. government and Pakistani commentators began talking about India using the lee of nuclear weapons to terrorize the Pakistani civilian population residing on the border with sustained long range gun fire.[150] The fact is Pakistan is a weak state as compared to India just as India is a weak state relative to China, except India can achieve a modicum of balance of power with China that Pakistan simply cannot with India. In the event, China should be the principal focus of India's strategic policies and arsenal.

On September 16, 2013, the Agni-5 IRBM in its second test-launch took off from the Wheeler Island missile launch site on India's east coast, and splashed down 5,500 km downrange in the southern Indian Ocean with the dummy nuclear warhead exploding on target with extreme accuracy due to the combination of the Russian Glonass GPS, and the on-board inertial navigation system and laser ringed gyro. Russia and China labelled it an inter-continental ballistic missile (ICBM) after its first test-launch in April 2012. The head of DRDO and Science Adviser to Defence Minister, Avinash Chander, endorsed this view. 'I have no hesitation in saying that we have ICBM capability. Range is not a problem. We can go up to 10,000 kilometres'.[151] With the Arihant SSBN joining the fleet by 2015-2016, the strategic triad conceived in the 1998 draft doctrine (and formally accepted by the government in January 2003) will become operational.

The nuclear arsenal is disposed such that 50 per cent of the weapons are sea-borne, assigned to the most invulnerable and survivable leg of the triad—the SSBNs, 40 per cent are mostly road-mobile Agni medium-range and intermediate range ballistic missiles, with two active rail-mobile systems, and a growing number of IRBMs/ICBMs housed for invulnerability in horizontal mountain-tunnel complexes increasing numbers of which will be built to store ICBMs in the future. The remaining 10 per cent of the nuclear ordnance inventory is set aside for delivery by manned bomber—the most flexible response option.[152] The weight assigned to submarine basing, mobile land-based missiles, and mountain-staging is, in line with the doctrine, to enhance the survivability of the nuclear arsenal and guarantee retaliatory strike, assuming the 'No First Use' principle is adhered to in wartime. The strategic bombing option nurses the realistic possibility that, as already discussed, absent a dedicated high-altitude supersonic strategic stealth bomber, Su-30 MKI medium range aircraft tasked with nuclear delivery may not survive an increasingly dense and sophisticated Chinese air defence network, leave alone get to anywhere near the target areas considering the unlikelihood that the aerial tankers will be permitted by Chinese interdiction assets peacefully to refuel the attacking aircraft en route to their targets. This truncated bomber option, however unsatisfactory, is nevertheless good enough for signalling intent in strategically tight situations, which submarines and land-based missiles cannot do as well. In any case, the long-range strike component presently comprises ten Su-30 MKIs, each of them accompanied by ten air superiority fighters—Mirage 2000s and, after 2019, the FGFAs—Su-50 PAK Fas, as escort and to fly combat air patrols over target zones to thwart Chinese attempts at interference, for a total force of some 110 aircraft controlled by SFC in a nuclear exchange situation. For the nuclear bombing missions, moreover, there will be several tankers attached and the nuclear air armada will rely on 'strenuous' tactical routing to escape detection for as long and as deep into the sorties as is possible.[153] Force sizing-wise, a former commander Strategic Forces Command, Lt Gen. B.S. Nagal mentioned three basic principles: (1) requirements for 'massive retaliation', (2) the size of Chinese and Pakistani nuclear weapons inventories, plus an additional number for 'unforeseen contingencies', and (3) a 1:3 target-to-weapon ratio—deploying three weapons per target. Thus, the arsenal size could work out, he declared, to a stockpile of as many as 600 strategic nuclear weapons, including 60–120 weapons as contingent reserve. He also mentioned a separate holding of 300 tactical nuclear weapons. The growing momentum of the Indian strategic build-up is raising questions about the 'minimum' aspects of India's nuclear deterrence.[154] This is because most Western (and Indian) analysts have not paid heed to the 'elastic' nature of India's 'credible minimum deterrence' concept in the nuclear doctrine (Karnad 2008: 63–106). Indeed, the NSA in the new BJP government, Ajit Doval, has talked about 'credible' and 'effective deterrence', leaving out the qualifier 'minimum' his predecessors had sworn by.[155]

Perhaps, this revised view involves a more substantial force, which is merited, other than by the adversary inventories, because, as Nagal added, due to (i) the 'No First Use' principle requiring India to absorb losses of its nuclear weapons in enemy counter-force first strikes, and (ii) compensate for the untested weapons at the two ends of the spectrum—high yield thermonuclear weapons and miniaturized tactical nuclear warheads sported by China and Pakistan in their respective arsenals. He particularly emphasized the untested aspects of the Indian thermonuclear and low-kiloton weapons and, by implication, the need for resumption of nuclear testing by pointedly referring to the penchant of Indian weapons designers 'to overstate the [performance] and for the weapons to under-perform'.[156] So there's no certitude in military circles about the yields of, other than the 20 KT simple fission weapon, the thermonuclear payloads and miniaturized tactical nuclear warheads. Unless these weapons are physically tested and seen to deliver the results as advertised, the yields of the 125 KT and 175 KT fusion warheads/weapons atop the Agni MRBMs and IRBMs/ICBMs, in particular, will remain the stuff of speculation, their performance a matter of faith. On the other hand, there's quiet confidence about the various missiles to deliver payloads accurately. The performance anxiety is sought to be alleviated by two factors: the 3:1 missile to target ratio, which promises three Hiroshima-yield weapons slamming into a single high-value target by initially three but eventually 6–8 multiple independently targetable vehicles (MIRVs) each mounting a 20 KT weapon on Indian IRBMs, with Agni-5 being specially designed for a MIRV-ed configuration.[157] The military's doubts regarding the nuclear warheads are sought to be addressed by means other than renewed underground testing, such as complex and realistic simulation. But the discomfiture with the fizzled fusion device tested in 1998 (deduced from the questionable yield and explanations, such as 'partial thermonuclear burn) persists with the authoritative 2009 revelation by the director of the 1998 field tests, K. Santhanam, that the fusion device had produced a far lower yield than it was designed for, which fact, he said had been formally communicated to the government in November 1998 along with his recommendation for more tests.[158] Some Indian defence scientists, however, maintain not very convincingly that the hydrogen device was deliberately tailored to produce small yield because of the intrusive verification provision in the Threshold Test Ban Treaty that India has signed. This treaty allows signatory countries to challenge and inspect the test site if the stated yield is above 50 KT, and it was feared that Pakistan or the U.S. may ask for such inspection, which would give away design secrets.[159] Even so the confidence of the Indian weaponeers is probably because of the use in the thermonuclear design of metastable nuclear isomers, which are lighter, produce more bang for the given weight of fissile material, and make for more effective weapons—as suggested by the late P.K. Iyengar, who as chairman of the Indian atomic energy commission in the mid-Eighties, initiated the thermonuclear weapons project.[160] Whatever the quality of the complex software and computer simulation the claims about the weapons by the nuclear scientists, without actual testing of thermonuclear and tactical designs in weaponised mode, and without an advanced in-house inertial confinement fusion chamber (the access to the Russian ICF in Troitsk outside Moscow being infrequent) and a dual-axis radiographic hydrodynamic testing facility, do not bear scrutiny (Karnad 2002: 71–7). Testing may, in any case, become necessary for other reasons. It is not clear whether the proven 20KT fission weapon, and the untested 125KT and 175KT fusion weapons in the Indian arsenal have been designed for safety and yield-to-weight ratios or for long life.[161] Apparently, these weapons were not designed with longevity in mind because R. Chidambaram, chairman, atomic energy commission and long-time science and technology adviser to the Prime Minister Manmohan Singh, confessed not long after the 1998 tests that his claim that further tests were unnecessary was valid only for ten years (Karnad 2008: 69). Hence, validation of the extant fission and fusion weapons by new tests is long overdue.

Central to beefing up a credible, effective, deterrent is open-ended nuclear tests both to verify weapons designs and to build up a data-bank on the explosive physics involved in fusion, kiloton, and sub-kiloton fission tests to write better software for future simulation, which last is also a function of the available computing speeds. Testing of fusion designs by India is also required for more effectively miniaturizing the warheads. Absent tests the nosecone geometry and other aspects of missiles are designed on the basis of certain estimations of weapon size. If the estimates are wrong, the missile performance will suffer.[162]

The other ostensible weakness that has been widely discussed is the command and control setup which heretofore consisted of the cumbersome 'troika' of political authority, scientific technician in the firing loop to prime and fuse the weapon in the penultimate stage of alert, and the military deliverer (SSBN commander, land-based missile battery commander, or pilot in aircraft on a nuclear bomb-drop mission), which reduced both accountability and effectiveness

(Koithara 2012). Recent technological innovations have, however, eliminated the complexity. According to Avinash Chander of DRDO, beginning with Agni-5, all missiles will be hermetically sealed and 'canisterised', for 'ready deployability'.[163] This will make for instantly useable weapons, which Nagal implied, was prompted by India's 'weak signalling' in the wake of the 26/11 terrorist attack on Mumbai in 2008 that did not 'reassure the [Indian] people'. But concerns that could arise from ready-to-fire nuclear weapons enabling a 'launch on warning' strategy have sought to be doused by what Nagal said was a system of 'short reins' on the weapons and 'tight control', rather than 'delegated control'.[164] In the event, what obtains is a system in which both the technician and platform commander are absent from the firing loop. The most difficult-to-communicate-with nuclear delivery platform—submarines are the test-bed for this newly installed command and control communications technology—the secure Strategic Communications Network (SCN). In place of the usual two-key firing system involving the SSBN commander and his executive officer, is the SCN facilitating centralized direct control by the Prime Minister—the final triggering authority—over the seaborne nuclear weapons and, by extension, over every single ready-to-launch nuclear weapon deployed anywhere. It is a holistic communications solution containing the Permissive Enabling Links and Permissive Action Links to arm, fuse, and ready the weapons for launch, which in the first phase will be tested on SSBNs. Even the launch-point coordinates to which the SSBN (or any other platform) is to proceed will be electronically communicated via SCN to the commander of the nuclear submarine, with the mission control computers in the SLBMs and SLCMs in these missiles directly interfacing with the firing authority, and the final order for launching the nuclear ordnance also being conveyed directly to the missile after the boat reaches the designated firing station.[165] The SCN actually emulates the Soviet-era Russian system in which signals were directly communicated to the weapons/warheads in the submersibles through multiple, redundant, channels, such as ship, aircraft, and shore-based VLF (very low frequency) and ULF (ultralow frequency) transmitters, and satellites.[166] This presumably is the schemata for direct control adopted by the Indian government as well and is to be extended to nuclear glide bombs on aircraft, and

Agni MRBMs and IRBMs emplaced on missile trains, road-mobile multi-axle Tatra platforms, and IRBMs/ICBMs trundled out of mountain tunnels. Such a communications-command-control system is a match for the most advanced C3 systems in the world in terms of minimizing the dangers of accidental, unintended, and rogue launches and retaining political control to the last moment.

As with all technologies, the SCN system has weaknesses. What happens, say, if the shore-based and air- and ship-borne transmitters are pre-emptively destroyed and/or the satellites electronically relaying the orders knocked out? The SLBMs/SLCMs and the Agni missiles, will be inerted, and the nuclear deterrent rendered useless. There is thus a necessity for the SCN technology to be tweaked to provide a fall-back system of manual over-ride or an alternate activation/deactivation link operable by the platform commander. The SCN becomes even more problematical with the battlefield tactical nuclear armoury. The unintended consequence of a system, *sans* a fall-back scheme, could be that in case of a decapitating first strike and follow-on attacks that takes out the Prime Minister and the extended National Nuclear Command Authority and successor levels of authority, coupled with the destruction of individual SCN components, the Indian nuclear strategic forces would stand disabled even in a total war, which will be an ironic counterpoint to the 'massive retaliation' the official Indian nuclear doctrine professes.

There are other weaknesses in the over-all nuclear system as well. There's still no integration of the nuclear armaments into the larger conventional military set-up other than through the agency of SFC, and no formal war-planning as such in the overlap areas between conventional military operations and the use of tactical nuclear ordnance. In the Indian government's view, a conflict is expected to have clear lines demarcating the spheres of nuclear and conventional operations, with the nuclear exchange, once that Rubicon is crossed, to be managed according to the war plans drawn up by SFC but directed exclusively by the Prime Minister from his invulnerable underground command post. This latter stream will be operable at a distance from the conventional warfighting prosecuted by the theatre commands under the supervision of the chiefs of the three armed services. Once nuclear weapons, including the tactical variety, are brought into play by the adversary, SFC enters the picture—at once deploying and controlling the lone brigade-sized formation with the army, equipped with anti-radiation suits and mobile decontamination booths in the radioactive battle areas. Outside the immediate radiation-affected units, the armour and mechanized formations are expected to continue advancing and fighting in a 'Sialkot Grab' kind of mission of investing border Pakistani cities, with follow-on mobile units skirting the radiation zones created by tactical nuclear strikes. These plans can be suitably adapted for operations against PLA in Tibet as well. In that sense, there is no fire-break between nuclear and conventional warfighting (Karnad 2005: 670–73). Whatever the plans, beyond the point of nuclear first use though, the conduct of parallel fighting of nuclear and conventional wars is likely to be reduced to 'playing it by the ear', a process that will be aided by a specialist nuclear cadre of officers were this to be created by the army and air force emulating the navy.[167]

Missile Power

Well into the second decade as a formal nuclear weapons state, what is most significant is India's emergence as a formidable missile power. In its quiver are the 150 km short-range Prithvi, the medium range 700 km Agni-1, and the 1,200-1500 km Agni-2 and the 2500–3000 km Agni-3 (also known as Agni-2 Prime–A2P, which was the 'technology demonstration' test-bed for most of the new and innovative missile technologies featured in the Agni systems, the 3000–3500 km Agni-4, the very advanced 8,000 km Agni-5 IRBM/ICBM, and the 2,000 km range K-4 SLBM in the final stages of development and the underway programme of the 6,000-8000 km range K-5 SLBM, and a set of cruise missiles—the 700 km-range seaborne K-15 hypersonic cruise missile (SLCM), the 1,000 km turbo-fan driven Nirbhaya cruise missile, and the Brahmos supersonic cruise missile, which last has been tested for 'S manoeuvres' at sea-level, armed with conventional high-explosive warheads and the 20 KT fission warhead.

Among the technological innovations proven on A2P and incorporated in the Agni missiles, on some missiles as retrofitments, are the Kevlar and carbon-carbon all-composite missile casing and rocket motors of diameters ranging from 1 meter to 2 meters and, experimentally, 2.5–3 meters, canisterization, and an electronics upgrade to reduce launch times to minutes. The Agni-5 has the most advanced features of any missile anywhere, which will be progressively incorporated in missiles with lesser range and in the 10,000 km Agni-6 ICBM able to carry a 3 ton payload.[168] The land-based Agni missile systems will, moreover, be enhanced with a TEL (transporter, erector, launcher) carriage set reduced from six Tatra all-terrain, multi-axle, vehicles to just two—one carrying the erector-launcher and the other the command and control (C&C) unit. To make it extremely difficult for an adversary to get a satellite fix, the two vehicles can be de-coupled, enabling them to travel separately by road and unpaved track to pre-designated points for 'marry and launch'. But such decoupling also increases the danger of the weapon system being neutralized by enemy action aimed at taking out one or the other of the Tatra carriers. Even so, considering its advantages, this mobility system will be the preferred mode for deploying all canisterized land-mobile missiles hereafter, especially as the rail-borne Agni-2 missile system, patterned on the Russian SS-18 Satan ICBM, has been found, over the last several years to be relatively more detectible and, given the dense traffic on the vast Indian railway network, its near continuous movement difficult to arrange. It is unlikely, in the event that the number of rail-mobile nuclear missile systems will increase beyond the two missile trains currently doing duty. Barring a direct, high-yield, thermonuclear hit on the fortified entrance of the mountain tunnel complexes, the long range land missiles emplaced within them will enjoy virtually the same level of invulnerability as the SSBN (Karnad 2005: 633–34). Two such complexes are already commissioned; many more are planned and being built, each able to store and house a number of active and inactive nuclear missiles.

It is Agni-5 IRBM, however, that will be India's strategic calling-card. Other than the advanced chip-embedded guidance system on this 'fly by wire' missile, an expert elaborated on its other technological attributes. The A-5, he said, 'has digitally connected multi-channel communications built within its body for the control system', thereby reducing a lot of the weight and cabling complexities that would have otherwise gone into this missile. This reduces the risk of missile system failure and increases dependability and user-confidence. The embedded guidance system on chip (SOC) in the A-5, according to project director, Tessy Thomas, has 'pin-point, single digit accuracy'.[169] The on-board computer, driving the A-5 system, is more powerful than any used in previous vehicles, weighs just 200 grams but possesses 7–10 times greater processing power. The embedded SOC concept, in any case, requires very little power, takes up less space, requires far less cooling, and is not only more reliable and efficient, but allows for far greater flexibility in the payload mix. The versatile SOC, in fact, has been tested for its MIRV capability in the Polar Satellite Launch Vehicle (PSLV-C20) which on 25 February 2013 precision-ejected seven small satellites into predetermined orbits.[170] The DRDO chief, Chander, promised that an upcoming test-firing of Agni-5 will fully test the MIRV technology under development since 2002.[171]

Further, the all-steel second-stage in the A-5 will be replaced with the composite material first stage and at 2 meter diameter ensure both a larger, lighter missile able to carry more fuel and armed with MIRVed warheads reach intercontinental distances. The K-4 and K-5 Sea-launched ballistic missiles with SOC guidance will boast of the other Agni-5 innovations as well.[172] Until now, Indian missiles were all MARV-ed (Manoeuvring Re-entry Vehicle) to defeat ballistic missile defences.[173] By 2020–25, Indian nuclear strike forces will feature a mix of MARV and MIRV missiles.[174] Initially, there are likely to be three warheads in a MIRV-ed configuration able to hit targets 150 miles apart, which capacity will increase in phases to seven to eight warheads per missile.[175] Figure 5.1 shows the reach of the various Agni missiles.

SFC has a different take on the MIRV aspect, however, with Nagal worrying that MIRVing missiles would be 'dangerous' if the total strength of missiles in the forces are kept 'low'. Because then the possibility would arise, he believes, of counter-force attacks taking out a larger fraction of the nuclear warheads/weapons, leaving fewer assets for retaliatory purposes.[176] This view may be why the Congress government held off approval for testing of MIRV technology, which has been on the shelf since the mid-2000s (Karnad 2008: 80–1). But inherent in Nagal's fears about the government capping the missile forces at low numbers was the Congress coalition regime's insistence on defining deterrence minimally. This involved the Strategic Forces Command deliberately not being told about the actual numbers of nuclear weapons/warheads in the inventory lest the diffusion of this piece of information within the Command lead to its being

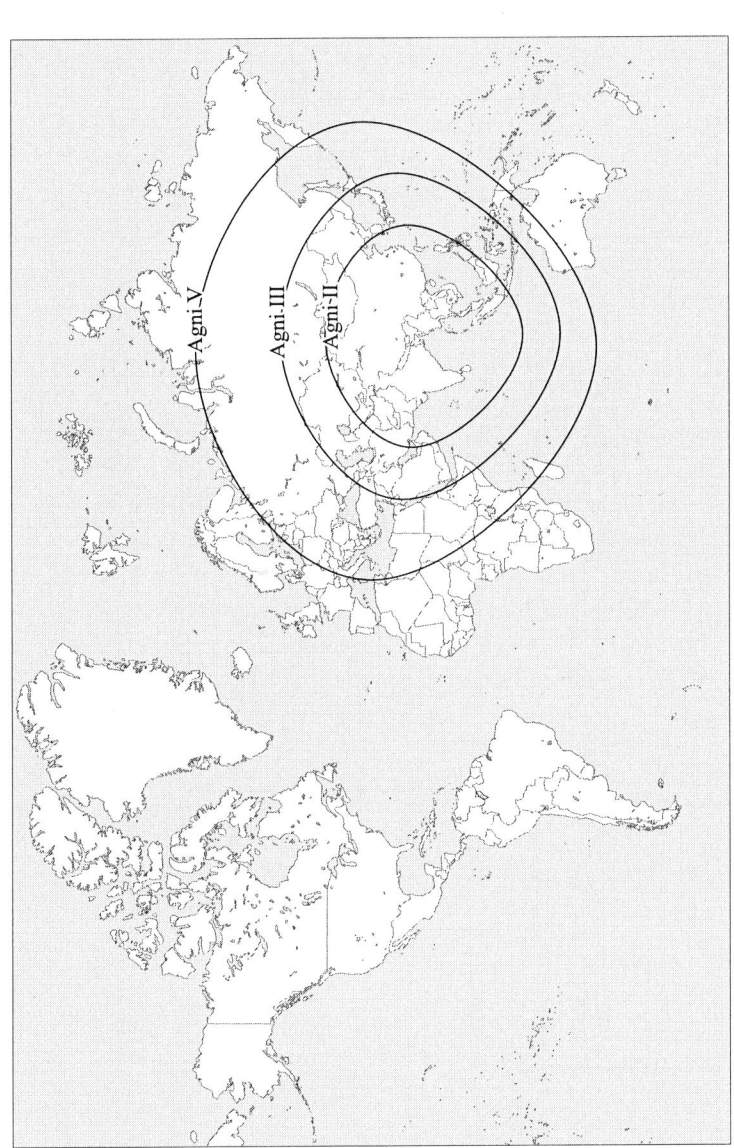

FIGURE 5.1   Agni Missile Range

Source: https://commons.wikimedia.org/wiki/File:Agni_missile_range.svg

leaked.[177] This suggests that during the Manmohan Singh period the operational planning for nuclear war was based on speculative numbers—a dangerous situation but typical of a civil servant-dominated system where the military is considered almost extraneous to the business of national security. It points up how civil servants monopolize 'sensitive' information in the belief that information is power except, as in this case, it could have turned into unimaginable tragedy because the SFC, denied information about the actual number, planned incorrectly for the worst case scenario. After M.K. Narayanan demitted office in 2004, the flow of information to the SFC resumed. Juxtaposed against the fast growing and modernizing Chinese nuclear arsenal estimated at 1,600–1,800 warheads by a former commander of the Russian Strategic Forces, Colonel-General Viktor Yesin, and with growing numbers of MIRV-ed missiles with the Chinese forces, limiting the size of the Indian missile force and preventing its accelerated MIRV-ization seems imprudent.[178] But delays in fielding advanced technologies, such as MIRV-ing are attributed by missile engineers to the government's requirement that approval be sought for every new phase in technology development, rather than approving the whole programme on a one-time basis. This is resented by the Agni missile designers and developers at the Advanced Systems Laboratory in Hyderabad, who blame it for the torpid pace of missile technology development and the languid pace of induction into service of the Agni missiles, and for the programme generally progressing in fits and starts, rather than at an even speed.[179]

Nuclear Banding of India and Pakistan

The banding by the U.S. and the West of India and Pakistan in the nuclear sphere is done notwithstanding the recognition that the latter 'is competing far above its weight in this competition'.[180] This has happened mainly because of New Delhi's constantly harping on the so called 'Pakistan threat', which has reduced India, in the eyes of the world, to Pakistan's size, endowing the neighbouring country with the parity it craves but in no way merits. The parity notion is reinforced by India, despite its nuclear infrastructure and resource base being many times larger, failing to maintain a qualitative and quantitative gap in nuclear forces with Pakistan of the kind it has opened up in the conventional military arena (see Table 5.1). Stuck for too long in the rhetorical mud of nuclear minimalism, it didnot think it needed to. A clear nuclear edge would have helped convey to Islamabad the message that the alignment of the Indian strategic forces is with regard to the China threat. It is a message that could still get across to the Pakistan Army and government if India, as discussed previously, reduced its armoured forces exclusively meant for use against Pakistan combined with unilaterally withdrawing the short-range ballistic missiles from the western border. Indeed, New Delhi's insistence on subterraneanizing the nuclear side of national security by keeping all its aspects secret is in line with its ideological discomfiture with India as a nuclear weapons state, and was part of the official attitude during the Congress coalition rule, of holding India to a higher moral standard. It turned out to be a self-inflicted liability. Prime Minister Manmohan Singh's apologetic tone on nuclear weapons was primarily to blame. India's nuclear weaponization, he said, was necessitated only by 'the harsh security environment'. His oft-expressed hope was also that the world would one day follow India's lead with a global convention on No First Use which accord, he claimed 'can open the ways to gradual reduction and finally elimination' of nuclear weapons.[181] It suggested that New Delhi is only reluctantly into nuclear security, an impression strengthened by the government being content with a single 100 MW military-dedicated plutonium reactor with a second such unit authorized in 1996 still to see the light of day. In comparison, in the last five years Pakistan commissioned three 50 MW reactors, and is bringing the fourth on stream, in record time at Khushab, all these units together producing some 54 kg of weapon-grade plutonium good for 10–12 weapons/ warheads annually.[182]

Confusion over Nuclear Deterrence in the Manmohan Singh Decade

The Manmohan Singh regime so strongly professed minimal deterrence and No First Use that the mere possibility of revising and updating the nuclear doctrine mentioned in the 2014 BJP general election manifesto touched off alarms and a storm of mostly uninformed protest at home and abroad.[183] Seeking to sidestep foreign pressures, Modi intervened to say that the doctrine won't be revised.[184] But that was 'public' diplomacy. Nothing prevents the BJP Prime Minister from having a small cell revise certain elements in the doctrine and issue it to the SFC and other concerned agencies, and announce at a later date that a new nuclear doctrine is in force and, no, India will not make it public. After all, nuclear doctrines are routinely revised by major nuclear weapons states to account for changes in the milieu, none of whom has made its doctrine public.[185] Nuclear testing, to the extent necessary, will indicate India's resolve to obtain the same level of certitude about their weapons as major nuclear powers enjoy, and pulling the doctrine into opacity will ensure that the activity in the nuclear security field is not an open book, and its various aspects cannot easily be deduced by friends or adversaries. Unless these sorts of action are taken, adversary states will not be moved to think about India as other than a malleable nuclear player—cagey, reluctant, and unresponsive to strategic provocation. It advantages China, whose all-purpose strategy of prolific use of conventional and nuclear missiles controlled by the same agency—PLA Second Artillery Strategic Forces (SASF), is to create 'daunting uncertainties' in order to deter both conventional war by a conventionally superior enemy, such as the United States, and a nuclear war by a conventionally inferior foe, such as India.[186] By injecting opacity into the doctrine—by rewriting parts of it and not making the changes public as the original draft version was ill-advisedly done in 1998 by the Vajpayee government without much forethought about the ramifications of such action, New Delhi can create counter-uncertainties to hold China strategically in check.

In force-structuring terms, it will require massive enlargement of the inventory of nuclear MRBMs, IRBMs/ICBMs, and cruise missiles and their forward deployment in protected shelters, to prevent Indian conventional forces from being stunned by Chinese strikes by short-range missiles massed in Tibet. As part of this comprehensive strategy, and to reiterate, India needs quickly to nuclear missile arm and strategically empower countries on China's borders, Vietnam for starters, by covertly on-passing nuclear warheads to equip the Brahmos supersonic cruise missiles, as a slow-evolving realpolitik counterpunch and, as advocated elsewhere in this book, engage intensively in strategic military collaborative activity east of Malacca with the ASEAN states, Japan, Taiwan, Australia, and the United States. It will be a culmination of Suntzu's strategy of overwhelming the enemy without fighting. An 'attack equilibria' is supposed to occur 'when the balance of credibility' favours the 'hard challenger' against a 'soft defender' (Kugler 1996: 261). On the basis of past record, India is the soft defender, lacking the strategic mindset and will to generate appropriate policies, secure the necessary means, and to carry out actions injecting credibility into its posture in any confrontation with China. In other words, the attack equilibria will always favour China—a hard challenger and a hard defender. China means to supplant Pax Americana with Pax Sinica, at least in Asia, and without certifiable and formidable high-yield Indian thermonuclear weapons, India's ambitions and security interests will be the first casualty.[187] New Delhi's strategic build-up and dynamic balancing of China can proceed alongside increasing trade and commercial relations, and infrastructure investment in India.[188] This will be a clever Indian policy exactly mirroring the multi-pronged Chinese policy which simultaneously emphasizes economic engagement but seeks to undermine the adversary militarily and by diplomatic means. It is the danger of India's fostering a common front that Beijing seeks to head off lest it emerge as a major strategic hurdle for China. Whence President Xi Jinping's publicly tempting New Delhi with talk of massive Chinese investment in Indian infrastructure build-up.[189] Beijing's new 'look west' policy, Wang Jisi of the Chinese government's powerful Foreign Policy Advisory Committee elaborated, would entail cultivating India and, with Islamic terrorism in Xinjiang on the rise, also resetting ties with its 'all-weather friend', Pakistan.[190] Prime Minister Manmohan Singh reassured the Chinese leadership during his October 2013 state visit that India would not be used as a tool to contain China.[191] However, the new BJP government of Narendra Modi signalled a contrary intent by labelling China an 'expansionist' power. Sushma Swaraj, the External Affairs Minister, demanded that Beijing commit to a 'one India (inclusive of Arunachal Pradesh)' if it wants the BJP government to back the 'one China' policy.[192] And, to drive home the point, that relations will not anymore be one-sided in terms of PLA offering provocation and New Delhi seeking ways to de-escalate the situation, Home Minister Rajnath Singh warned that roads constructed by China on the Indian side of the claim line would be destroyed.[193] Strong and self-sufficient conventional military and strategic nuclear forces, besides keeping China respectful, will obviate India having to rely on the United States in a military crisis or war, because it is never a good idea for a would-be great power to dilute its stature by trusting its security to another country's safekeeping. In the circumstances, no Indian government can believe that the test moratorium can be maintained for very long what with a Chinese Defence White Paper boasting that the PLASAF are improving their capability for 'rapid reaction, penetration, precision strike, damage infliction, protection, and survivability'.[194] The days when India passed off its lack of strategic sense as responsible restraint are gone.[195] But residual incoherence in policy remains.

Mitchell Reiss speculated as far back as 1988 that Indian restraint was due to incoherent thinking about nuclear weapons (Reiss 1988). That incoherence still persists, hampering a clearer charting of the nuclear course. Much of this recently precipitated confusion is attributable to Shyam Saran, former chairman of the NSAB and holdover from the Manmohan Singh regime, who apparently is convinced that adversaries will be so over-awed by the 'mass destruction' connotation of nuclear weapons that retaining 'massive retaliation' as retaliatory response should continue to be the country's doctrinal centre-piece. His view is that a massive response, rather than an articulated proportionate response, to even a small tactical nuclear attack initiated by Pakistan inside its own territory on advancing Indian armour is fine because Pakistan would have initiated first use, no matter that, other than a few tanks, there was no 'mass' destruction![196] Saran seems unmindful of the principle of proportionality of response being an established principle in the military sphere or that massive retaliatory response combined with 'minimum deterrence' he supports will quickly empty out the arsenal and that in a fundamental sense 'massive retaliation' cannot coexist with 'minimum deterrence'.[197] It reveals lack of knowledge and deep understanding of deterrence compounded by a muddled view of the utility of nuclear weapons—all of which factors are widespread in the Indian policy establishment. While vouching for the benefits to India from possession of nuclear weapons, such as deterring threats and attempts at 'nuclear coercion', Shivshankar Menon, for example, stressed 'that our nuclear weapons [are] weapons of deterrence and not, I repeat not, war-fighting weapons.' This justifies, he claimed, the No First Use principle embedded in the nuclear doctrine. 'These weapons are for use against a nuclear attack on India….and not meant to redress a military balance, or to compensate for some perceived inferiority in conventional military terms, or to serve some tactical or operational military need on the battlefield.' Menon thus missed out on the basic truth about nuclear deterrence, namely, that extensive and visible preparations for fighting a nuclear war, such as civil defence measures and regular, well-publicized nuclear war games and exercises are crucial to convincing an adversary that its first use of nuclear weapons would, in fact, lead to total war and that it is better to avoid going down that path or, in any other way, testing India's resolve. Considering how quickly it loses its nerve and how badly New Delhi handles crises generally, Menon's view is almost an invitation for a risk-acceptant state—China and even Pakistan—to call out India.

In the Congress party's view, the Indian nuclear arsenal was meant to prod and push the major nuclear weapons states towards a nuclear weapons-free world outlined in the 1988 Rajiv Gandhi Action Plan to be achieved within a time-bound framework.[198] This is one of those Indian conceits against which there is no defence! Indeed, Prime Minister Manmohan Singh's enthusiasm for President Obama's 2010 Prague Initiative and his presence at subsequent 'nuclear summits' in Washington and Seoul surely put paid to the Action Plan, which the Congress Party, whether in or out of power, will continue for sentimental reasons to swear by, reinforcing the official view of nuclear weapons as 'political' weapons.[199]

Qualifying any weapon as 'political' in the context of disarmament is, however, to fudge its essentially military character and purpose and render it a negotiable instrument in arms control parleys, participation in which is not in India's interest. It matters that the Indian thermonuclear weapons work as advertised and are seen to do so and hence it is necessary to expend political capital on testing. But it is the theme of an existential nuclear weapon to deal with an existential, somewhat abstract, nuclear threat around which a corpus of thought about its non-use has evolved that has really hobbled the

Indian strategic deterrent. Thus, countries that believe nuclear weapons are for warfighting, such as China from Mao's days and Pakistan, will always have the upper hand in any confrontation with an India that believes otherwise.

As in the conventional military sphere, in the nuclear realm too Pakistan is sought to be deterred and China dissuaded through differential schemes. The general strategy of deterring Pakistan by having armoured and mechanized forces speedily converge on Pakistan cities has been previously analysed. The more difficult situation involves responding to an act of nuclear terrorism—a radiation diffusion device (RDD) or 'dirty bomb' exploded by a Pakistan-backed terrorist outfit in an Indian city, considering how easy it is for terrorists to cross the permeable land border in the desert or come in from the sea as happened in the 2008 attack on Mumbai.[200] With the National Technical Research Organization (NTRO) developing the forensics capability and data-base, the source of the fissile material would be traced (Karnad 2009). Indeed, it is precisely the certain identification of Pakistan-sourced fissile material in the RDD and the unpredictability of the consequences that will likely inhibit the Pakistan Army's nuclear managers from ordering such a high-risk mission, because terrorists are inherently uncontrollable—as Pakistan's present fight with Islamic militant groups shows; terrorists armed with a 'dirty bomb' could be as dangerous to their handlers as their intended targets.[201] Should there be an RDD attack, the nuclear taboo would be violated and, depending on the severity of attack and the extent of damage, the popular pressure to respond with nuclear weapons, as the doctrine mandates, will be intense. If such terrorist use in peacetime is judged to be first use, and there's no reason to believe it wouldn't be, then the logic of 'massive retaliation' as advised by the Indian nuclear doctrine, would kick in. This is another danger of an institutional belief in massive retaliation, reason why the drafters of the doctrine in 1998–99 underlined the 'retaliation only' concept as 'dynamic… related to the strategic environment, technological imperatives and the needs of national security' and particularly stressed that retaliation would be with 'sufficient weapons' and in a 'rapid punitive response' mode.[202] Saran, muddied the Indian deterrence waters by making much of the 'minimum' nature of the deterrent—which has been disavowed by Prime Minister Modi's NSA, Ajit Doval who has talked of a 'credible' and 'realistic' nuclear arsenal. It is also interesting that Saran asked for an annual and public accounting of the country's nuclear weapons assets, without appreciating that the essence of deterrence as a 'mind game' is not just in preserving the ambiguity of intention and response but also in masking the strength of the strategic forces.[203]

Moreover, given the unbridgeable gap in strategic forces that China has opened up with India, it is suicidal for New Delhi to expect that the threat from a small force of small-yield weapons would either deter or be dissuasive. A Beijing determined to push its conventional military advantage may encounter a New Delhi (1) sticking by its No First Use pledge, and if it doesn't (2) trumping the Indian threat of first use by a counter-threat of massive counter-retaliation with megaton weapons that India cannot match. In either case, the Indian government is bound to be self-deterred and pre-disposed to desist from tripping the nuclear wire for any reason. If India too had megaton weapons, the Chinese would hesitate more about raising the ante. It is the wages of 'muddled deterrence' that India may end up paying dearly for.[204]

It is obvious the Manmohan Singh government was seriously conflicted between the ideals of a nuclear weapons-free world and the imperatives of nuclear security. The result was that Indian nuclear strategy precariously straddled these two stools. New Delhi remains unconvinced about taking the necessary corrective measures to negate the widening advantage accruing to China, inclusive of the Chinese use of two breeder reactors for weapon grade plutonium production, and to neutralize the minor threat, Pakistan, which is ramping up its production of tactical nuclear warheads and missiles.[205] Pakistan, on the other hand, knows whom it has to deter—India, and how—by threatening first use of tactical nuclear weapons against the superior Indian conventional military strength, knowing fully-well that any actual nuclear use could well spell its end.[206] Even so Islamabad's conviction that India is easily deterrable explains its pell-mell rush to speedily augment its nuclear arsenal. India, in contrast, has acted dazed, decommissioning its 40 MW CIRUS reactor in Trombay as part of the nuclear deal with the United States, for example, well before the second military-dedicated 100 MW plutonium reactor was ready.

Utility of India's Ballistic Missile Defence

Pakistan, it may be argued, was prompted to enlarge its nuclear missile forces because of India's developing a ballistic missile defence (BMD). There could be other reasons for Pakistan's nuclear missile build-up being on over-drive: The fear that 60–70 per cent of its nuclear arsenal would be destroyed by collusive Special Forces actions by the U.S., India and Israel and other more direct means of pre-emption.[207] Such apprehension is increased by influential American think-tank studies referring to 'the risk of nuclear weapons getting into wrong hands' and, hence, 'the need to occupy at least a part of [Pakistan].'[208] The nuclear authority—the Special Plans Division located at Chaklala (outside Rawalpindi), Pakistan is, therefore, determined on expanding its force fraction able to survive such pre-emptive attacks and efforts to capture or destroy its arsenal. However, Western commentaries justifying Pakistan's nuclear build-up to redress conventional inferiority can loop back to encourage Pakistani adventurism.[209] The existential problem for Pakistan is that while it survived risky conventional military actions in the past owing to India's forbearance, it will not a nuclear conflict fuelled by its misconceived bravado because then none of the socio-cultural constraints on New Delhi that limited conventional conflicts to-date, will apply.

The Indian military on its part scoffs at the BMD that is based on two shots per kill-principle—if the first missile fired at an incoming missile in its downward ballistic trajectory in the exo-atmospheric stage doesn't get it, the second missile fired in the endo-atmospheric phase will.[210] The nine tests conducted (up until April 2014) of separate exo- and endo-atmospheric interceptors were rigged, say senior military officers, in that the flight coordinates of the exact path of the target missile were fed into the tracking computer.[211] Ex-DRDO chief, Saraswat, who headed the BMD project, does not contest this charge and admits that the system cannot handle saturation attacks. In that case, he said, 'the cost-effectiveness of the ballistic missile defence is not good.' Then again no BMD technology has so far been developed anywhere in the world which can deal with saturation attacks.[212] The physics seems to be against it. Saraswat nevertheless maintained the BMD 'will be a factor of deterrence. It's going to make the enemy think four times before he initiates anything. Nuclear deterrence associated with a potent BMD, particularly with an NFU policy, makes for a tough deterrent.'[213] Because an adversary at marginal cost can build more missiles to overwhelm an overly-expensive and, therefore, necessarily thin-on-the-ground BMD, missile defence cannot be effective and the investment in it appears to be dead waste because a serviceable missile defence to hold off attacks by large batches of incoming missiles, at the present stage of technology, is unachievable.[214] India is thus stuck familiarly with the worst possible worlds—no ballistic missile defence worth the name but the Indian BMD spurring Pakistan and China to multiply their stocks of weapons/warheads and missiles preparing for saturation attacks to overcome the BMD, even as the Indian nuclear weapons and missile inventories grow at a leisurely rate.

By this reckoning BMD appears to be a prestige project in the same category as the aspirational Chandrayan Moon Mission and the exploratory Mangalayan probe to Mars criticized for their misplaced priorities.[215] Except the space missions have showcased the country's competence in space technology, establishing India as an attractive partner in extra-terrestrial ventures and as a provider of economical, reliable, and commercially viable satellite launch services.[216] Similarly, substantive reasons are adduced for the Indian BMD that DRDO and the Indian government have not publicized but which could fetch the already deployed system credibility and the military's support. Because the system is capable of stopping single or a brace of nuclear missiles fired from Pakistan getting through, that's the scenario justifying BMD. The Indian thinking involves terrorists in Pakistan, who, with or without official connivance, get their hands on a nuclear missile or two, or a few radicalized Pakistan Army artillery handlers of a nuclear missile battery turn rogue, and in either case a sudden surprise attack is unleashed on Delhi. A very small number of enemy missiles so fired will be destroyed mid-flight, even with the flight times to the national capital region from anywhere in Pakistan being in the 8–10 minute range. This is enough time, it is averred, for the proven 'Green Pines' radar (acquired originally from Israel) and its Indian derivative, Swordfish radar, slaved to the BMD missiles, to pick up the launch, relay this information along with the coordinates of the impact point to the missile unit, and pass real time information about the incoming missiles for the BMD interceptors continuously to realign and reorient for the 2-shot 'kill'. The other gains from the BMD are that this the most network-centric military system in the country is plugged into the air defence ground environment system (ADGES), and is a demonstration model for the rest of the armed services to emulate. Further, the BMD can be used as an anti-satellite weapon to eliminate enemy satellites in low-earth orbits over the Indian Ocean as part of the Chinese Beidou GPS system in any drag out fight with China, for example. More importantly, the BMD missiles are ready platforms for weapons of the future that are under development, such as the 10 KW laser and the EMP (electro-magnetic pulse) weapons economically to disable incoming nuclear warheads over a wide area.[217] There is a strategic deterrence angle to the BMD, which makes it useful in another respect as well. If the BMD is, in fact, able successfully to interdict a 'rogue' nuclear missile in war, then it would constitute a fire-break, postponing a retaliatory launch on warning of Indian missiles, affording the Pakistan Army time to rethink its strategy of following up this 'probing attack' with a saturation salvo, or permitting it to draw back from the nuclear abyss in time. These are good reasons to persist with the BMD.

Atomic Demolition Munitions as Peace-Keeper

The strategic dilemma India faces is of a different kind altogether. In a nuclear crisis with China, India's still modest nuclear forces will confront an enemy with nearly unlimited initiatory and response options while obligating India to be discriminate and careful in the use of its nuclear weapons in the retaliatory mode for fear of emptying the weapons stockpile quickly. Going up against a China not constrained quantity-wise, will entail certain defeat because the larger the weapons holdings the more calculatedly weapons can be expended to outlast the enemy, something the Indian government seems not to appreciate. Worse, the lack of proven high yield, especially megaton warheads and bombs on the Indian side, means that the destruction India can threaten with its 20 KT weapons may not be frightening enough to stay Beijing from 'pushing the envelope' in terms of provocation and, in case of total war when all bets are off, to quickly establish escalation dominance. Because deterrence is a game of psychological one-upmanship, the usual fecklessness of the Indian government in time of crisis would ensure that the mere threat of incoming megaton thermonuclear ordnance will persuade New Delhi to capitulate, and seek termination of hostilities on Chinese terms. This is the situation when the need will be hard felt for much larger numbers of advanced thermonuclear missiles with very high yields, and for MIRVed warheads with variable or dialled yield for wide-area destruction.

It is argued that the Indian thermonuclear armaments even without the benefit of additional tests will deter because the adversary will have to assume the risk of these proving to be duds. But the risk calculus begins skewing in favour of the risk-taker when the ability and the credibility of Indian weapons designers—already handicapped by the government's testing moratorium decision—is under a cloud owing to doubts heatedly voiced by stalwarts of the Indian nuclear programme (Karnad 2005: 412–30). Moreover, in international strategic circles, and at home in SFC, Indian weapons scientists are perceived as 'drivers' of India's deterrence policy, who routinely exaggerate their ability to design advanced weapons without iterative testing and solely on the basis of simulation and computational speeds.[218] The conclusion is the same as that of many Indian sceptics that the weapons in the Indian arsenal are unreliable, whose credibility cannot simply be talked up by the nuclear weapons designers and the government. Ironically, it is precisely the 'massive retaliation' the Indian doctrine promises that the 20 KT weapons-armed Indian strategic forces cannot deliver, no matter what government officials facilely assert.[219] If the massiveness of promised destruction is the measure to judge the deterrent quality of weapons, then the 20 KT-yield armament won't do, it'll not be destructive enough compared to the 3 megaton (or even the lesser 500 KT or even 300 KT) weapons/warheads in Chinese employ. To secure the level of credibility of weapon yields the PLASASF can summon, India will have to grit its teeth and resume open-ended testing or accept the possibility of losing a conflict laced with nuclear threats without a single nuclear weapon being fired.

India's nuclear forces are victimized by arguments about the deterrent needing to be more minimum than credible, and about even small numbers of low yield weapons sufficing for deterrence purposes.[220] It is a line the Indian armed forces too mindlessly voice.[221] The case is made thus: with the Agni-5 accuracy at extreme range, the possibility of a host of 20 KT weapons carried by single and MIRVed Agni IRBMs homing in on Shanghai will give Beijing pause for thought, because it is loss that cannot be compensated by political gains from whatever strategic victory China may be able to rack up against India. This was the Congress party government's point of view. It sought to make the best of a bad situation in terms of thermonuclear weapons of questionable quality by motivating missile designers and terminal guidance engineers to strive for ever smaller Circular Error Probable. Delivery accuracy is supposed to make up for the small (20 KT) yield of proven warheads, and timed Indian salvoes to avoid 'fratricidal kills' are to be utilized to reduce large, high-value, enemy target areas to rubble. Such a deterrence strategy is considered credible against China.

However, this is to misread the larger strategic game afoot. China's goal seems to be to strategically over-awe India and keep it nuclearly preoccupied with Pakistan, and to pre-empt New Delhi's contemplating harsh military measures in response to even significant provocations, such as the diversion of the Yarlung-Tsangpu River at the Great Bend in Tibet (when it enters the Indian border province of Arunachal Pradesh as the Brahmaputra, which under international law is *casus belli* or cause for war). [222] It is an aim China has succeeded in achieving. Thus, confrontational Chinese claims on Arunachal Pradesh and repeated violations of the LAC, even after the advent of the BJP government, has begot little beyond dissimulation by New Delhi. In theory, this is a manageable escalatory sequence if the destruction is restricted to counterforce targets with minimum collateral damage, and there is decent interval between such strikes, affording a deliberate ratcheting up of the force used. The side with the smaller arsenal and, hence, ipso facto with the lower tolerance threshold will, however, eventually fold before the exchange moves to cities and other counter-value targets (industrial complexes, atomic power plants) and the imperative shifts to massive retaliation.

The trouble with controlling a limited escalatory exchange is that India does not, as iterated, have a big enough stock of weapons at the two ends—tactical nuclear weapons in the 2KT-5KT-10KT range and, especially of the 125 KT-175 KT class, leave alone megaton-yield, strategic weapons. Were the low KT weapons to be available in large numbers, the 20 KT weapon in the Indian inventory with Hiroshima-size effects would have been a firebreak between tactical nuclear weapons and 20 KT area weapons on the one hand and the 20 KT and the still larger yield area weapons, on the other hand. But Indian use of 20 KT weapons are unsuitable in a tactical exchange because their use would signal the intent to move the war to a strategic level. Moreover, an exchange of 20 KT weapon strikes may not greatly deplete China's counter-punching capability because it will have immeasurably more weapons in store. A small weapons stockpile will also mean that sustaining tactical strikes with 20 KT weapons would dangerously thin out armaments reserved for the strategic strike role.

The likely strategic scenario may witness Indian defensive forces on an interior line of pre-positioned stores experiencing difficulty in tackling PLA units fighting massively downhill from their elevated plateau jumping off points, despite being disadvantaged by the high altitude limiting what can be carried into battle, and especially if the Chinese advance is fast and skirts Indian strong points as is likely to happen.[223] India's threatening to trip the nuclear wire in this situation or if this line is hugely breached will hold few terrors for a PLASASF that will have assessed the scenario in which its threat to launch the short and medium range nuclear warheaded ballistic missiles from Tibet, and the DF-21 mod 2 IRBMs deployed in Chengdu and Xining as backup, will likely squelch any Indian desire for escalation.

The only credible nuclear deterrent in the circumstances are atomic demolition munitions (ADMs) placed just behind the prepared defensive line along the likely ingress routes of the PLA in the mountains, a line beyond which Chinese intrusion is deemed unacceptable. It may be a very long border but there are surprisingly few valleys providing easy routes for the PLA to intrude in strength across the Himalayan watershed, and these are restricted to the western and the eastern ends of the disputed border. The public announcement of placement of ADMs without disclosing their locations would transfer the onus and risk of breaching the LAC and tripping the nuclear wire to China. The compactness of ADMs, their portability and placement, and the ambiguity about where and when these might be remotely triggered, will engender enormous uncertainties for the

PLA of a kind it has not to-date encountered. Normally, ADMs would come into play only after PLA units have penetrated deeply and massively into Indian territory, which will automatically legitimate the Indian ADM use. The possibility of whole mountainsides coming down and burying its forces, and of units that escape being either destroyed in detail or, taken prisoners of war, affording India political and negotiating leverage, is not a prospect Beijing will take lightly. Were China to disregard the warnings of ADMs, its case that these constitute first use of nuclear weapons will not carry weight either, and the responsibility for crossing the nuclear threshold too will lie with Beijing (Karnad 2005: 671–72, 690). The easy-to-design and produce ADMs, moreover, fit in with India's traditional non-provocative, passive-defensive, approach to both conventional and nuclear security.[224] ADMs can thus play a stellar role in deterring the PLA from launching a major land offensive against India and, hence, even preventing conventional hostilities if the Indian army also has the offensive mountain corps to deploy on the Tibetan plateau to match any force the PLA can assemble.

In the larger context, New Delhi's apparent lack of concern about the strategic disparity compared to the PLASASF may, perhaps, be explained by the ex-NSA Shivshankar Menon's description of Indian policy as displaying 'tactical caution and strategic initiative, sometimes [implemented] simultaneously'.[225] By this reckoning, reconciling to inferiority in the conventional military and nuclear security fields, rather than arms racing with China, is a matter of 'tactical caution'. At the same time, the effort to stabilize relations with Beijing is the strategic initiative to try and see if Beijing's urge to upset the status quo can be contained through diplomatic means. The pursuit of this steady-state is apparently supposed to produce leverage for India with Beijing with New Delhi bolstering its strategic ties with the ASEAN members and other rimland states, such as South Korea, immediate offshore nations, like Japan and Taiwan, and the more distant entities such as the United States and Australia, to produce a bedrock scheme for 'congaging' China.[226] In an intermeshed global system, the chances are this scheme may work. There's, however, an iffy-ness to it because it relies on too many external actors for its success, each of whom has a separate political-strategic dynamic working with Beijing. Even if it succeeds on occasion, it will not enable India to carve out a place for itself in a world where hard power and felicitous use of it still marks out countries as great powers that are 'indispensable' to carrying out bigger regional and international security roles and responsibilities.[227] 'In strategic tensions with China short of war, the balance of credibility,' concludes an Australian think-tank report, 'will become as important as the balance of hard power.'[228] Except the balance of credibility tilts against India because it is minus the conventional military punch the three offensive mountain corps could have delivered inside Tibet, and because Indian leaders, unlike their counterparts in other countries, have never regarded versatile and robust thermonuclear forces as the decisive element of great power in war and peace, as Lord Nelson once did 'A line of British ships of war'—as 'the best negotiators... they always speak to be understood, and generally gain the point'.[229]

Notes

1. See his 'National Security and Aerospace Power', *Air Power: Journal of Air Power & Space Studies*, vol 8, no. 4, Winter 2013, 21–22.

2. Singh, R. 'India far behind China's combat power', *Hindustan Times*, 12 December 2013.

3. Rear Admiral (Retd) Raja Menon, 'Great power ambition sans the attitude', *Hindu*, 16 April 2013.

4. Interview, May 3, 2012.

5. Ibid.

6. Karnad, B. 'Scope for Meeting National Security by Effective Management of Available Funds' in *Impact of Decreased Defense Spending on the Indian Armed Forces*, Proceedings of a Seminar, 28–9 November 1996, USI—Seminar, Number Eighteen, USI, New Delhi.

7. A senior serving IAF officer.

8. Personal communication, Vice Admiral (Retd.) K.K. Nayyar, former Vice Chief, who in the early years of service was the 'Flags' (junior naval assistant) to the last British Chief of the Indian Navy, Vice Admiral Stephen H. Carlill, who demitted office in 1958.

9. Air Marshal Gibbs of the Royal Air Force was the last British head of the Indian Air Force, 1951–1954, and was succeeded by the first Indian Chief of the Air Staff, Air Marshal Subroto Mukherji.

10. Sandhu's letter to editor, in response to Manoj Joshi, 'Nehru, the pragmatist', *Mail Today*, 20 November 2014. (Text of Sandhu's letter emailed to author by retired Lt. Gen. P.K. Singh.)

11. Karnad, B. 'Defense Tutorial', *Asian Age*, 25 October 2012.

12. Chinese Foreign Minister Wang Yi on the sidelines of the National People's Congress in Beijing said: 'We will not take anything that is not ours, but we will defend every inch of territory that belongs to us.' He added: 'On the two issues of principle—history and territory, there is no room for compromise.' See 'Will defend every inch of territory, China minister warns', *Sunday Express*, 9 April 2014.

13. A former Deputy Chief of the Army Staff.

14. 'Indian Army Divisions', GlobalSecurity.Org, 7 September 2011 available at www.globalsecurity.org/military/world/india/divisions.htm and Mandeep Bajwa and Ravi Rikhye, 'Indian Army RAPIDS Divisions', 11 February 2001 available at http://orbat.com/site/toe/toe/india/rapids.html.

15. Shivshankar Menon at the Annual Seapower Conference, National Maritime Foundation, New Delhi, 27 February 2012.

16. Kanwal, G 'India's Military Modernization: Plans and Strategic Underpinnings', *National Bureau of Research*, 24 September 2012 available at www.nbr.org/research/activity.aspx?id=275.

17. Military sources.

18. Pandit, 'Civil-military ties worsening?' *Times of India*, 7 October 2013.

19. A former naval chief Admiral Arun Prakash blames 'the irrational suspicion of the military' for the nonintegration of the military services. See his 'Muddy Waters, Navy Blues', *Times of India*, 6 March 2014.

20. Karnad, B. 'National Security Management: The Prospect for Military Jointness in a Disjointed Government System', *Jointness in the Defense Forces: Challenges and the Way Ahead*, Annual Seminar 2006, College of Defense Management.

21. Pandit, R. 'Forces mulling 3 joint commands', *Times of India*, 24 September 2012.

22. Interview.

23. This is true especially for Unmanned Aerial Vehicles (UAVs) obtained from the same Israeli company. The three services cannot operate each other's drones. Personal communication, two star rank officer.

24. Personal communication, Lieutenant General S.P. Kochar, Signals Officer-in-Chief, Indian Army. 9 October 2012.

25. Personal communication.

26. A Pentagon report on the Chinese military says that 'the PLA is investing heavily in its ground force, emphasizing the ability to deploy campaign-level forces across long distances quickly' with 'improved [command and control] networks providing real-time data sharing within and between units'. See *Annual Report to Congress*, 2014, 10.

27. Jayadeva Ranade, 'Aim of China's Military Reforms', *New Indian Express*, 21 January 2014. Ranade is a former senior China specialist with RAW.

28. 'Study Times: China's Dream Includes a Stronger Army and an Outgoing Military Strategy', *Chinascope*, 27 January 2014, available at http://chinascope.org/main/content/view/6104/105.

29. Tiwary, D 'Chinese troops enter Ladakh every 14 days', *Times of India*, 8 January 2014.

30. *Indian Basic Doctrine of the Air Force, 2012*; 114–15, 146, available at http://indianairforce.nic.in/Basic%20Doctrine20%of20%the20%India n20%Air%20Force.pdf.

31. Ibid. If the length at which mission/roles are described is any guide, air superiority— strategic air campaign, offensive and defensive counter air— take up 24 pages (39–56, 69–74) of the total 146 pages versus 12 pages for counter-surface, air-land (plus two pages for maritime land-based air strikes).

32. Lambeth, *Airpower at 18000 feet*, 38.

33. Ibid, 36.

34. Three star rank officer, Integrated Defense Staff. Lambeth, *Airpower at 18,000'*, 29–30.

35. Quote in Ibid, end-note # 107, 52.

36. Nath, K. 2008. *India's Century*. New York: McGraw Hill, p. 8.

37. In the north Indian countryside, for example, one often finds diesel engines designed to pump water out of the ground being mounted on platforms rigged up to drive a rear wheel-axled vehicle and, voila!, the country-folk have a no-frills motorized transport that is noisy, belches fumes, but carries people and farm produce to towns more speedily than bullock carts.

38. Discussion in 1999–2000 with many senior serving and retired IAF officers.

39. Markoff, J. 'Weapons that choose own targets cause alarm', *International New York Times*, 13 November 2014.

40. A senior Indian Army officer.

41. Luttwak, Edward N. 'Affordable Defense: Cross-Country Experiences' in *International Seminar on Defense Finance and Economics, New Delhi, 13-15 November, 2006*, Ministry of Defense, Government of India, 26.

42. This section based on an interview of Col. K.C.P. Das (Retd).

43. Interview.

44. 'CRN: Chinese Army's Regimental Combat Troops Armed with Beidou Positioning System', *China Review News*, 9 November 2013, *Chinascope* available at http://chinascope.org/main/content/view/5922/105

45. Karnad, B. 'Cyber Neanderthals', *Asian Age*, 5 July 2012 and available at www.bharatkarnad.com

46. For a review of the state of cyber security, see *India's Cyber Security Challenges, IDSA Task Force Report*, (2012), New Delhi: Institute of Defense Studies and Analyses.

47. Joseph, J. 'Gulshan Rai tipped to be first coordinator of national cyber security agency', *Times of India*, 4 November 2012. Jain, B. 'E-security network ready', *Times of India*, 7 November 2012.

48. Raman, B. 'Why India is at risk from China's cyberwar ability', *First Post*, 10 January 2012, available at http://www.firstpost.com/world/why-india-is-at-risk-from-chinas-cyberwar-ability-177567.html.

49. Writes Air Marshal R.K. Nehra (Retd.): 'The Indian Armed Forces are capable of taking on any world class military machine, provided we can get our mental act together; some 90% of our problems is in our mind.' See his 'India's China Syndrome', *Indian Defence Review*, 30 November 2013.

50. *India's Cyber Security Challenges*, 2012, 245–246.

51. Air Chief Marshal (Retd.) Krishnaswamy, interview.

52. Pandit, R. 'Dwindling number of fighters biggest challenge for new IAF chief', *Times of India*, 1 January 2014 available at http://articles.timesofindia.indiatimes.com/

53. Karnad, B. 'Strategic bomber for IAF', *New Indian Express*, 7 February 2014, available at http://www.newindianexpress.com/opinion/Strategic-Bomber-for-IAF/2014/02/07/article2042008.ece#.UvQulWKSw7s and on my blog http://bharatkarnad.com/2014/02/07/strategic-bomber-for-iaf/

54. A three star-rank officer in the Integrated Defense Staff.

55. Discussion with Air Chief Marshal Browne when he was the IAF chief.

56. Official sources.

57. Interview, 7 May 2012.

58. It mentions the development of a 'capability to interdict China's logistics and operational infrastructure in Tibet.' See *Nonalignment 2.0*, 35.

59. Lustgarten, A. 'Will Global Warming Melt the Permafrost Supporting the China-Tibet Railway?', *Scientific American*, 23 November 2009.

60. 'Glaciers in Tibetan Plateau shrinking rapidly: Report', *Times of India*, 22 May 2014.

61. Gupta, S. 'India now firmer with China on Tibet issue: Dalai Lama', *Hindustan Times*, 3 November 2012.

62. Wertz, R. R. 'Three Gorges Dam: Special Report' available at www.ibibo.org/chinesehistory/contents/07spec/specrep0.1.html, last updated 22 March 2011.

63. Interview.

64. Wertz, R. R. 'Three Gorges Dam'.

65. Senior IAF officer.

66. Interview.

67. Ibid.

68. Air Chief Marshal Browne; personal communication.

69. Interview.

70. 'China Tests Stealth Bomber: Neighboring States on High Alert' (undated) accessed November 2, 2012, Taiwan Ministry of National Defense website www.nmd.gov/tw/english/ . On China buying the Tu-22M3M, see 'Tu-22M3M line for China, Admiral Joshi, General Bikram', 11 December 2012 available at http://bharatkarnad.com/2012/12/11/tu-22-m3m-line-for-china-admiral-joshi-general-bikram/ . 'New U.S. Strategic Bomber May be Axed if Costs Exceed Limits', March 1, 2012, *Global Security Newswire* avalaible at www.nti.org/ and 'Putin says Russia needs new strategic bomber', AP, 14 June 2012 available at www.businessweek.com/ap/.

71. Interview, Air Marshal (Retd.) Satish Inamdar.

72. Air Chief Marshal Browne, discussion.

73. Senior official. About the Chinese interest in Su-35, see Peter Wood, 'Why China Wants the Su-35', *China Brief*, 13(30), 10 October 2013 available at www.jamestown.org/

74. Karnad, B. 2002. *Nuclear Weapons and Indian Security*, pp. 667–8. On IAF's resisting the Su-35 buy, an official source.

75. 'Russia to Upgrade Over 10 Tu-160 Bombers by 2020', Ria-*Novosti*, 7 February 2012 available at http://en.ria.ru/military_news/20120207/171200584.html

76. 'Russia Speeds Up Development of New Strategic Bomber', *Ria-Novosti*, November 28, 2013 at http://en.ria.ru/military_news/20131128/185110769/Russia-Speeds-Up-Development-of-New-Strategic-Bomber.html. As regards the offer to India: an informed source.

77. Admiral Arun Prakash (Retd.), 'Sharing the Pie in the Sky: Define Roles and Missions', *Indian Defense Review*, November 2012.

78. *Indian Maritime Doctrine*, 2009. New Delhi: Integrated Headquarters, Ministry of Defense (Navy), pp. 82–5.

79. Vice Admiral (Retd.) R.N. Ganesh, former commander, Western Fleet; e-communication, Oct 2012.

80. A former CINC, Western Naval Command, justified the move thus: 'One needs to bear in mind that the Indian Navy is charged with safeguarding the Maritime Security of India. Coastal security is but a subset of the overall Maritime security responsibility. It is therefore not possible to bifurcate this responsibility. What the Government of India proposed after 26/11 was to designate Director-General, Coast Guard, as the C-in-C of the Coastal Command. This was a hair-brained idea which goes against the well-established norms of military command and control. You just CAN NOT have two C-in-Cs in the same geographical location doing what

actually is a seamless job between the coastal police, the Coast Guard and the Navy.' Email correspondence, 11 October 2011.

81. Pandit, R. 'India readies hi-tech naval base to keep eye on China', *Times of India*, 26 March 2013.

82. Vice Admiral (Retd.) R.N. Ganesh, e-mail correspondence, 4 February 2012.

83. Interview, Admiral (Retd.) Arun Prakash.

84. Author's meeting with the Chief of the Air Staff and Chairman, Chiefs of Staff Committee, Air Chief Marshal N.A.K. Browne, 24 October 2011.

85. Interview, 21 October 2011.

86. *Nonalignment 2.0*, 35.

87. Interview, 21 October 2011.

88. A beginning has been made. Able to track 30,000–40,000 ships in the Indian Ocean daily, the National Command Control Communication Intelligence (NC3I) network has been established, with threat and contingency analysis to be provided by the Gurgaon-based Information Management and Analysis Centre with real-time data feeds from several terrestrial and extra-terrestrial platforms. This is to be part of the more comprehensive underway National Maritime Domain Awareness project. Rajat Pandit, 'Naval intel network launch tomorrow', *Times of India*, 22 November 2014.

89. Karnad, B. 'Failure-bound maritime strategy', *New Indian Express*, 9 August 2013 available at http://newindianexpress.com/Failure-bound-maritime-strategy/2013/08/09/article1725052.ece and in the author's blog—www.bharatkarnad.com

90. USI-IISS Second Nuclear Workshop, 'Defence, Deterrence and Stability in Southern Asia', New Delhi, 11 November 2014.

91. Interview, 10 February 2011.

92. Much of this section owes to an interview-discussion with Rear Admiral K.R. 'Raja' Menon (Retd.), 21 October 2011.

93. Senior naval officer. On the commercial aspects of GAGAN, see Anindya Upadhyay, 'When Flights of Fancy Touch Down: As GAGAN Takes Off, Fuel Costs Plummet', *Economic Times*, 8 October 2012.

94. Sharma, R. 'The Garuda, Asean Need Not Fear the Indian Navy's Strategic Eagle', *Jakarta Globe*, 17 September 2012, available at www.thejakartaglobe.com/

95. Pubby, M. 'India to train, support Indonesian Sukhoi fleet', *Indian Express*, 17 October 2012.

96. Interview.

97. Email communication, 14 August 2012.

98. Interview, 22 August 2011.

99. Air Marshal A.K. Singh (Retd.), interview.

100. Interview.

101. Personal communication by the IAF Chief, 24 October 2012.

102. Senior naval person.

103. Vice Admiral (Retd.) R.N. Ganesh.

104. Pandit, R. 'India's elusive nuclear triad will soon be in place, say Navy chief', *Times of India*, 8 August 2012.

105. Interview, 6 May 2011.

106. Former Commander, Andaman Integrated Command; personal communication.

107. 'US offers help for next generation aircraft carrier', *Indian Express*, 19 September 2013.

108. Karnad, B. 'Scope for Meeting National Security by Effective Management of Available Funds', 1996.

109. Ladwig, Walter C., III 'A Cold Start for Hot Wars? The Indian Army's New Limited War Doctrine', *International Security*, 32 (3), Winter 2007/08.

110. Ravi Rikhye, (2012) *Complete World Armies*. Takoma Park, MD: General Data LLC, p. 371.

111. David O. Smith, 'The U.S. Experience with Tactical Nuclear Weapons: Lessons for South Asia', Stimson Center, [undated, probably 2012] available at www.stimson.org/images/uploads/research-pdfs/David_Smith_Tactical_Nuclear_Weapons.pdf

112. This outcome has been extensively gamed by the Indian military and the Strategic Forces Command.

113. A former Indian Army Chief; personal communication. Such a strategy was advocated by the author. For further explication and analysis of such strategy, see Karnad, Karnad *Nuclear Weapons and Indian Security*, pp. 677–683, and '"Sialkot Grab" and Capturing the "Corridor": Objectives and Tactics in a Nuclear Battlefield', *Army War College Journal*, 34, (2) Autumn 2005.

114. Discussion with General V.K. Singh, 22 November 2012.

115. Bhasin, *India-Pakistan Relations 1947-2007*, cxvii, xix-cxx.

116. Discussion with an ex-COAS.

117. Discussions with a former Army Chief and three star-rank officers from Army Hqrs and Integrated Defense Staff.

118. Singh, V. 'India to build 1800 km highway along China border in Arunachal', *Indian Express*, 15 October 2014. General V.K. Singh (Retd.),

Minister of State in MEA, responsible for the Northeastern states, showing chutzpah, announced the construction of the Tawang air field while visiting Beijing. See Saibal Dasgupta, 'India may build airport in Tawang, near China border', *Times of India*, 1 November 2014.

119. Pubby, Manu and Anubhuti Vishnoi 'Defence projects near China border in fast lane', *Indian Express*, 13 June 2014.

120. Personal communication, senior NSC staff member. Indian.

121. Personal communication.

122. A source familiar with the Prahar missile programme.

123. The former Pakistani ambassador in the U.S., Husain Haqqani, delves into a bit of the post-Partition history and Nehru's thinking to argue that Pakistan's abiding and mortal dreads of India is not merited by reality or its past experiences. See his 'Reworking the idea of Pakistan', *Indian Express*, 12 June 2014.

124. Interview, NDTV, 18 November 2012.

125. In 1940, Jinnah proposed a division of military labour: 'Muslim India will guard so far as the [North West] frontier is concerned' he said and hoped 'the Hindus will guard so far as the South and Western India is concerned. We join as good friends and neighbours and say to the world, "Hands-off India!"'. As Governor-General of Pakistan, Jinnah in August 1947 reiterated 'the vital importance to Pakistan and India as independent sovereign States to collaborate in a friendly way jointly to defend their frontiers both on land and sea against aggression.' The quotation is Karnad (1995: 25).

126. Speaking at a ceremony to induct the first batch of five F-16s from the Jordanian Air Force into the Pakistan Air force at the Sargodha base, Air Chief Marshal Tahir Rafique Butt, significantly, emphasized the use of these aircraft against Islamic militants, not India. See 'Pakistan Air Force receives F-16 fighter jets from Jordan', *Express Tribune* (Islamabad), 27 April 2014.

127. 'The better it gets between India and Pakistan in all aspects of life,' said Afghan President Hamid Karzai, in Mumbai to drum up Indian investment in his country, 'the better Afghanistan's chances are of a better economy, a more prosperous country, more peace and stability for all of us.' See his interview, *Indian Express*, 12 November 2012.

128. Nandi, J. 'Once enemies, now peace messengers', *Times of India*, 11 November 2012.

129. Bharat Karnad, 'Key to Peace in South Asia: fostering "social" links between the armies of India and Pakistan', *The Round Table: The Commonwealth Journal of International Affairs*, Number 338, April 1996.

130. 'I am not convinced. I personally feel,' said Yashwant Sinha, former BJP foreign minister, 'that the kind of hatred that's been imbued in the

Pakistan population against India will take generations for that poison to wash out of their minds. It's not as if Pakistan Army or government will issue a fiat one day and the enmity towards India will vanish. Ultimately in the final analysis, it's hatred.' Elaborating on the theme some more, he observed that 'The basic problem of Pakistan is a crisis of identity, which automatically, naturally, pits them against India—army or no army. Secondly, what would we do with [the province of] Jammu & Kashmir? Say we give Pakistan a deal it cannot refuse. But Pakistan will not accept trade or money, what they want is for us to hand over J&K.' Interview.

131. Pubby, M. 'Will be tough to tackle collusive threat from Pak, China: IAF', *Indian Express*, 19 February 2014.

132. Facing a cut of Rs 10,000 crore in the budget for 'modernization', Defense Minister A.K. Antony confessed that he was 'struggling to get the budgetary amount.' See 'MoD braces for spending cuts', *Indian Express*, 9 November 2012.

133. Rikhye, *Complete World Armies*, p. 355.

134. Interview.

135. Interview.

136. Discussion with a former army chief.

137. Siddhanta, P. 'MoD sounds alarm as Rlys fails (sic) to build 14 vital links', *Indian Express*, 8 November 2012.

138. Personal communication, an army Corps commander.

139. 'China to construct a new railway line near Arunachal Pradesh', *Times of India*, 31 October 2014.

140. Interview, *Hindu*, 4 September 2012.

141. Interview, 10 April 2012.

142. Rikhye, *Complete World Armies*, p. 301.

143. Interview, Lieutenant General (Retd.) H.S. Lidder, 13 June 2011.

144. Personal communication, an army Corps commander.

145. For a rough comparison of Indian and Chinese military strength, see 'India: Military strength', *Global Firepower*, available at www.globalfirepower.com/country-military-strength-detail.asp?country_id=India and 'China: Military Strength', *Global Firepower*, 29 October 2012 available at www.globalfirepower.com/country-military-strength-detail.asp?country_id=China

146. Interview.

147. Moscow has decided to end cooperation in nuclear weapons area with the U.S. and NATO. See 'Russia to limit role in nuke security', New York Times, *Straits Times* (Singapore) 15 November 2014; Meanwhile, the U.S. is finding weaknesses in its nuclear arsenal and in the nuclear weapons infrastructure at-large that needs rectification. See David E. Sanger and

William J, Broad, 'U.S. nuclear arms hampered by flaws', *International New York Times*, 15–16 November 2014. Of course, any attempts by the U.S. to rectify shortfalls in its weaponry will likely set-off a strategic arms race with both Russia and China.

148. Forman, D. S. 'Deterrence With China: Avoiding Nuclear Miscalculation-Analysis', *Eurasia Review*, available at http://www.eurasiareview.com/13112014-deterrence-china-avoiding-nuclear-miscalculation-analysis/?utm_source=feedburner&utm_medium=email&utm_campaign=Feed%3A+eurasiareview%2FVsnE+%28Eurasia+Review%29.

149. Michael Krepon, 'The Stability-Instability Paradox, Misperception, and Escalation Control', available at http://www.stimson.org/images/uploads/research-pdfs/ESCCONTROLCHAPTER1.pdf.

150. 'Army chief relays concerns about Indian ceasefire violations to US: report', *Express Tribune* (Islamabad), 19 November 2014; Ayesha Siddiqa, 'The logic of deterrence', *Express Tribune*, 30 October 2014.

151. See 'Agni stretches Indian reach', *Telegraph* (Kolkata), 17 September 2013.

152. Lt. Gen. (Retd.) B. S. Nagal, 'India's Deterrence and Dissuasive Posture with Focus on Desired Nuclear Capability, including Tactical Nuclear Weapons and The Command and Control Structure' at a surprisingly thinly-attended panel discussion on 'India's Nuclear Deterrence: An Appraisal' at the United Services Institution, New Delhi, 4 October 2013. As a public presentation, the talk by Nagal, a former commander of the Strategic Forces Command, who was re-hired, after his retirement in 2011, to streamline the apex level of the nuclear command authority within the Prime Minister's Office and the nuclear command and control system generally, was unprecedented in its candor and revelations. It, perhaps, reflects increasing confidence in the country's nuclear deterrent. See 'Agni stretches Indian reach', *Telegraph* (Kolkata), 17 September 2013.

153. Ex-CINC, Strategic Forces Command.

154. Hans M. Kristensen, 'India's Missile Modernization Beyond Minimum Deterrence', *FAS.org*, October 4, 2013 at http://blogs.fas.org/security/2013/10indianmirv/.

155. 'All problems with Pakistan can be resolved through talks', *DNA (Daily News & Analyses)*, October 21, 2014.

156. Nagal, B.S. 'India's Deterrence and Dissuasive Posture'.

157. Mallikarjun, Y. 'Agni-V to be modified to attack multiple targets', *Hindu*, 28 May 2013.

158. On various theories about how and why the thermonuclear device failed, see Karnad, *Nuclear Weapons and Indian Security*, 403-430. For

Santhanam's revelation, see his interview, *Outlook*, Oct 5, 2009. Available at www.outlookindia.com/article.aspx?262027.

159. Dr V. Siddhartha, a former adviser on technology in MOD; personal communication.

160. Iyengar, P.K. 'Non-proliferation and advances in nuclear science', *Current Science*, 68(3) 10 February 1995.

161. A distinction made by Michaela Bendikova in her lecture on 'The Future of the U.S. Nuclear Weapons Program', The Heritage Foundation, Washington, D.C., 8 August 2012 available at www.heritage.org/.

162. Senior missile scientist.

163. Interview, *Geopolitics*, vol III, Issue X, 2013, 50–51. Post-second test firing of Agni-5, DRDO chief Chander, moreover, promised a test-launch of a canisterized Agni-5 within 'a few months'. See 'Ajai Shukla, 'Agni-5 on target, despite glitches', *Business Standard*, 16 September 2013.

164. Nagal, 'India's Deterrence and Dissuasive Posture'.

165. Senior naval officers.

166. A mid-level military officer, early 2013.

167. The first batch of nuclear-trained officers graduated in 2013 from the Naval Academy in Ezemalai. Senior naval officer. Also refer Bharat Karnad, 'INS: Indian Nuclear Service', *Asian Age*, 16 August 2012 available at www.asianage.com/columnists/ins-indian-nuclear-service-094.

168. Shukla, A 'Agni-5 on target, despite glitches', *Business Standard*, 16 September 2013.

169. 'Agni-V vital: Tessy Thomas', *Hindu*, 1 October 2013 available at www.thehindu.com/todays-paper/tp-national/agniv-vital-tessy-thomas/article5191824.ece.

170. Informed Source.

171. Senior DRDO official.

172. See 'Agni-V— guidance-on-chip' 26 April 2012 available at www.bharatkarnad.com.

173. Kristensen, H.M. 'India's Missile Modernization Beyond Minimum Deterrence', *FAS.org*, 4 October 2013 available at http://blogs.fas.org/security/2013/10indianmirv/.

174. Most of the information on the Indian missiles conveyed separately by several senior missile engineers and outside experts.

175. Source: senior missile program engineers.

176. Nagal, op. cit.

177. M.K. Narayanan, NSA, 2005–2010, as a throwaway line said to a former SFC commander: 'Not sure you are quite aware' of the number of

weapons. USI-IISS Second Nuclear Workshop, 'Defence, Deterrence and Stability in Southern Asia', New Delhi, 11 November 2014.

178. Further, Yesin faulted the U.S. estimates of the Chinese warhead strength as 240–400 for not accounting for the warheads atop Chinese tactical, short-range ballistic and cruise missiles, MRBMs, and the stock of some 320 B-5 nuclear bombs for loading on the 300 Q-5 bombers. See Bill Gertz, 'Number the Nukes', *The Washington Free Beacon*, 14 December 2012. Another estimate of Chinese N-warheads/weapons is 50-1,800, including 440 B-4/B-5 nuclear bombs on for the bomber fleet. See John J. Tkacik Jr., 'China builds nuclear arsenal while rest of the world disarms', *Washington Times*, 28 September 2012. For the investigative study on the extensive network of tunnels that hugely increases the Chinese arsenal size estimates, see Philip A. Karber, *Strategic Implications of China's Underground Great Wall*, Georgetown University, 26 September 2011available at www.fas.org/ nuke/guide/china/Karber_UndergroundFacilities-Full_2011_reduced.pdf. On MIRVing, see Nicolas Giacometti, 'China's Nuclear Modernization and the End of Nuclear opacity', *The Diplomat*,10 April 2014.

179. Senior missile engineers.

180. Krepon, M.'Pakistan's Red Carpet Treatment', *Armscontrolwonk. com*, 27 October 2013. Available at http://krepon.armscontrolwonk.com/ archive/3930/pakistans-red-carpet-treatment#more-4019

181. 'PM proposes no first use of nuclear weapons', PTI, *Hindu*, 2 April 2014.

182. The four 50 MW reactors will annually produce 24–48 kg of weapon-grade plutonium at the Khushab Complex with an on-site plant producing 100 kg of Heavy Water. See 'Khushab Complex', *NTI (Nuclear Threat Initiative)*, 13 December 2013, available at http://www.nti.org/facilities/940/

183. Saran, S. 'The dangers of nuclear revisionism', *Business Standard*, 22 April 2014. The New York Times editorialized that revising the doctrine amounted to taking 'a more provocative stance toward Pakistan and China' and abandoning NFU to a regional disequilibrium. See 'Risk to India's Nuclear Doctrine', *New York Times*, 9 April 2014.

184. 'India not revisiting N-doctrine: PM to Japan', *Times of India*, 30 August 2014.

185. Thus the United States, for example, which last revised its nuclear strategy/doctrine in 2006, is doing so again to take into account the growing threat from hostile states and non-state actors. See Dianne Barnes, 'The Pentagon Is Revising Its WMD Strategy', *Defense One*, 10 April 2014 available at www.defenseone.com.

186. John W. Lewis, Xue Litai, 'Making China's nuclear war plan', *Bulletin of Atomic Scientists*, September/October 2012. At http://bos.sage-pub.com/content/68/5/45.

187. Tkacik, 'China builds nuclear arsenal'.

188. Vice Admiral A.K. Singh, a former commander of the Eastern Naval Command, recommends attracting Chinese capital reaching some $2 Trillion. See his 'At Sea, Sino-India ties need propulsion', *Asian Age*, 11 April 2014.

189. Patranobis, S. 'Striking alliance with India is my historic mission: Xi Jinping', *Hindustan Times*, 21 March 2014.

190. 'China's new "Look West" policy to give primacy to ties with India, says expert', *Economic Times*, 1 November 2012.

191. 'India can be balancing power in triangular ties" Chinese Daily', *Zee News*, 23 October 2013. Available at http://zeenews.india.com/news/nation/india=can-be-balancing-power-in-triangular-ties-chinese-dail_885238.html.

192. Samanta, P.D. 'One China? What about One India policy: Shushma to Wang', *Indian Express*, 12 June 2014.

193. 'Will "break" any Chinese construction on Indian territory, Rajnath warns', PTI, *Times of India*, 17 November 2014.

194. China's National Defense in 2010: Full Text available at http://news.xinhuanet.com.

195. Thus, Prime Minister Manmohan Singh said: 'We are the only country that demonstrated its capacity in 1974 but maintained a quarter century of restraint...'. See 'PM proposes no-first use of nuclear weapons'.

196. Saran, S. 'The dangers of nuclear revisionism'.

197. Karnad, B. 'India's nuclear amateurism', *New Indian Express*, 28 June 2013. Available at http://newindianexpress.com/opinion/indias-nuclear-amateurism/2013/06/28/article1655987.ece.

198. Menon, S. 'Why Do We Need Nuclear Weapons?', Conference on Global Nuclear Disarmament Indian Council of World Affairs, August 21, 2012. For a revamped and updated version of the Rajiv Gandhi Action Plan, See *Informal Group on Prime Minister Rajiv Gandhi's Action Plan for a Nuclear-weapons-Free and Nonviolent World Order 1988*. Report of the Informal Group, New Delhi, 20 August 2011.

199. Menon, S. 'K. Subrahmanyam and India's Strategic Culture', KS Forum Memorial Lecture, New Delhi, 19 January 2012.

200. Sharma, A. 'Most Ports Vulnerable to Smuggling of "Dirty Bombs"', *Economic Times*, 4 December 2013.

201. For an analysis of this attributability factor as the key factor against fissile material diffusion, see Keir A. Lieber and Daryl G. Press, 'Why States Won't Give Nuclear Weapons to Terrorists', *International Security*, Summer 2013, 38(1).

202. 'Draft Report of the National Security Advisory Board on Indian Nuclear Doctrine', Ministry of External Affairs, Government of India, 17

August 1999. Available at http://mea.gov.in/in-focus-article.htm?18916/
Draft+Report+of+National+Security+Advisory+Board+on+Indian+Nuclear+
Doctrine.

203. Saran, S. 'The dangers of nuclear revisionism'. For an analysis
of the credible minimum deterrence concept, see Karnad, *India's Nuclear
Policy*, 84–86, 88–89.

204. On 'muddled deterrence', see Richard K. Betts, 'The Lost Logic of
Deterrence', *Foreign Affairs*, March/April 2013.

205. Jeffery Lewis, available at www.armscontrolwonk.com.

206. Senior Pakistan army officers in-charge of nuclear weapons and
decision-making admit to their country suffering a disproportionate 'disaster' and 'massive holocaust'. See David O. Smith, *The U.S. Experience with
Tactical Nuclear Weapons: Lessons for South Asia* (Undated, but probably late
2012), Stimson Center, 44 available at www.stimson.org/images/uploads/
research-pdfs/David_Smith_Tactical_Nuclear_Weapons.pdf.

207. Major General Ausaf Ali, Head of Strategy and Plans in Pakistan
Army's Strategic Plans Division, offered the 60–70 percent figure as the
force fraction SPD believes will be lost to collusive Special Forces actions
by the U.S., India, and Israel and other means, in his presentation at the
International Conference on the Nuclearization of South Asia, Islamiya
University, Bahawalpur, March 12–14, 2007. Also see Bharat Karnad,
"Nuclear mind-games"—'Security Wise' column, *The Asian Age*, 16 Feb
2011. Available at www.bharatkarnad.com.

208. Johnson, Blickstein, *et al*, *A Strategy-Based Framework*, 11.

209. Michael Krepon of the Stimson Center, for instance, writes: 'The
next crisis in South Asia will play out in the context of a greater disparity
in conventional capability in India's favor and a greater disparity in nuclear
capability in Pakistan's favour—hardly a good equation for deterrence
and crisis stability.' See his 'Learning from South Asia's Many Crises' at
www.stimson.org. Lodi, M. 'Pakistan's nuclear compulsions', *The News*, 6
November 2012.

210. The government has no great hope of the BMD actually being
operationalized, said a senior uniformed member of the National Security
Council staff, but is kept alive as 'technology demonstrator' and as a
test-bed for missile defense technologies in the offing, to avoid buying
these systems from abroad once these technologies mature. Personal
communication.

211. A senior officer in the HQ Integrated Defence Staff.

212. In fact, the former commander of the Russian strategic forces
Colonel-General Viktor Yesin estimates that 5-7 ground based interceptors
will be required to take out a single Topol ICBM. See 'US Needs 5-7 GBIs

to Intercept One Topol ICBM— Expert', 2 April 2013, *RIA-Novosti*, available at http://en.rian.ru/military_news/.

213. Interview.

214. For a skeptical military view calling for realistic tests of the BMD, see Air Marshal Arjun Subramaniam P, 'India's ballistic missile defence', *Air Power: Journal of Air Power & Space Studies*, l8, (4) Winter 2013, 59.

215. Fenner, J. 'India Mars Mission to Launch Amidst Overwhelming Poverty', *Guardian Liberty Voice*, 3 November 2013, available at http://guardianlv.com/2013/11/india-mars-mission-to-launch-amidst-overwhelming-poverty/.

216. Rogers, J. 'Experts: Cheap Mars mission could prove lucrative for India', *Fox News*, 26 September 2014, available at http://www.foxnews.com/science/2014/09/26/experts-cheap-mars-mission-could-prove-lucrative-for-india/.

217. Discussion with a senior DRDO scientist.

218. See Graham, T.W. 'Nuclear Weapons Stability or Anarchy in the 21st Century: China, India, Pakistan' at http://www.npolicy.org/.

219. Menon, S. 'India's National Security: Challenges and Issues', P.C. Lal Memorial Lecture, Air Force Association, New Delhi, 2 April 2012.

220. Subrahmanyam, K. & V.S. Arunachalam, 'Deterrence and Explosive yield', *The Hindu*, 20 September 2009.

221. For instance, former Director-General Artillery, Lieutenant General (Retd.) Vinay Shankar's remarks at the October 4, 2013 USI panel discussion on 'India's Nuclear Deterrence: An Appraisal'.

222. For possible nuclear conflict scenarios with China including the diversion of the Yarlung Tsangpu, See Karnad, *India's Nuclear Policy*, pp. 133–149.

223. This is what the Indian Army expects will happen. See Rahul Singh, 'India far behind China's combat power'. Op. cit.

224. John W. Gilbert, former British Minister of State for Defense and now a member of the House of Lords, has argued for a border belt planted with ADMs and Enhanced Radiation and Reduced Blast weapons in Waziristan to stop the infiltration across the Durand Line by the Taliban. See 'Lords Discussion on China and Multilateral Nuclear Disarmament, November 2012' available at http://acronym.org.uk/parliament-records/201211/lords-discussion-china-multilateral-nuclear-disarmament-november-2012?page=show.

225. Menon, 'India's Role in Global Politics'.

226. Congagement—combination of containment and engagement was conceived by Zalmay Khalilzad. Khalilzad wrote that it would 'enhance economic, political, military-to-military relations and cultural ties at all

levels.' See his 'Congage China', Issue Paper, 2006, p. 6 at http://www.rand.
org/content/dam/rand/pubs/issue_papers/2006/IP187.pdf.

227. Former U.S. Secretary of State Madeleine Albright said of the
U.S. armed intervention in Iraq: 'If we have to use force, it is because we
are America; we are the indispensable nation.' This quote in Steven Mufson,
'China, the new indispensable nation?', *Washington Post*, 12 November 2014.

228. Medcalf, Rory, James Brown, *Defence Challenges 2035: Securing
Australia's Lifelines* [Sydney: Lowy Institute for International Policy,
November 2014], p. 7, http://www.lowyinstitute.org/publications/defence-
challenges-2035-securing-australias-lifelines.

229. Nelson wrote this in a letter to his lover, Emma Hamilton. The
quote is from Adkins and Atkins (2006 : 62).

References

Adamsky, Dima. 2010. *The Culture of Military Innovation: The Impact of
Cultural Factors on the Revolution in Military Affairs in Russia, the US, and
Israel.* Stanford, CA: Stanford University Press.

Adkins, Roy and Lesley Adkins. 2006. *The War for All the Oceans: From
Napoleon at the Nile to Napoleon at Waterloo.* London: Abacus.

Bing, D. 1998. 'Military Perspectives on the Three Gorges Dam', in Dai
Bing, John Thibodeau, Philip B. Williams, eds., *The River Dragon Has
Come!: The Three Gorges Dam and the Fate of China's Yangtze River and Its
People.* New York: M.E. Sharpe.

Horowitz, Michael C. 2010. *The Diffusion of Military Power: Causes and
Consequences for International Politics.* Princeton: Princeton University
Press.

Karnad, B. 1995. 'India's Weak Geopolitics and What To Do About It' in
Bharat Karnad, ed. *Future Imperilled: India's Security in the 1990s and
Beyond.* New Delhi: Penguin.Viking .

———. 2005 [First Edition 2002]. *Nuclear Weapons and Indian Security:
The Realist Foundations of Strategy.* New Delhi: Macmillan India.

———. 2007. 'South Asia: The Irrelevance of Classical Deterrence Theory',
India Review, 4(2). Also published in E. Sridharan, ed., *The India-
Pakistan Nuclear Relationship: Theories of Deterrence and International
Relations* Abingdon, U.K. and New Delhi: Routledge.

Koithara, Verghese. 2012. *Managing India's Nuclear Forces.* Washington,
D.C.: Brookings Institution Press.

Kugler, J. 1996. 'Beyond Deterrence: Structural Conditions for a Lasting
Peace' in Jacek Kugler and Douglas Lemke eds *Parity and War: Evaluations
and Extensions of the War Ledger*, Ann Arbor: University of Michigan.

Nath, K. 2008. *India's Century.* New York: McGraw Hill.

Reiss, M. 1988. *Without the Bomb: The Politics of Nuclear Non-Proliferation* New York: Columbia University Press.

Sahgal, A. 2012. 'China's Military Modernization: Responses from India', in Ashley J. Tellis and Travis Tanner eds., *Strategic Asia 2012-13: China's Military Challenge*, Seattle: National Bureau of Asian Research.

Singer, P.W. 2009. *Wired for War: The Robotics Revolution and Conflict in the 21st Century.* New York: Penguin Press.

Tanham, G. 1995. *Indian Air Force: Trends and Prospects.* Santa Monica, CA: RAND, pp. 77–90.

6

Indian Defence Industry
The Weak Link

Comic books in the 1950s and 1960s featured, usually in the inside pages of the cover, an advertisement for a body-building regimen devised by Charles Atlas, a former Mr Universe, who was featured with the mandatory rippling muscles. An accompanying cartoon strip showed a thin youngster on the beach getting sand kicked in his face by a beefier man who also steals his girlfriend. The touted solution was for the '100 pound weakling' to take the Atlas course, work up his body, become a match for the bully, and avoid such humiliation in the future. The Atlas-type programme was predicated on interested folks having strong will and desire, and high motivation levels to improve their physique. There are no such schemes to build up nation-states, no easy way to acquire real military muscle (different from merely procuring military hardware), but if there were one it would have discovered that while India has the desire to become a great power there is no commensurate will and motivation to mobilize the national resources or put in the necessary effort. The ability of a country to make its own armaments is a precondition for great power. It is not met because the capillaries in the system to achieve self-sufficiency in arms requiring comprehensive defence industrial build-up are sickly and, minus a radical structural/systemic rejig, will keep India a marginal power.

Previous chapters have shown how and why the unimaginative and cautious Indian diplomats in the MEA backed by a risk-averse political class pursued a feeble foreign policy, and proved a major obstacle to India's achieving great power. Comprising mostly tactics and very little strategy, Indian foreign policy, it is said, is only helping 'a would-be great power' resist 'its own rise' (Chatterjee 2013). Similarly generalist IAS officers controlling the workings of the Indian state, professionally ill-equipped to run technical and specialist ministries, such as the Ministry of Defence (MOD), have obtained indifferent military capabilities for the country and perpetual bickering and bad blood between them and the armed services.[1] Gaining an understanding of military issues to make informed judgments is in any case beyond the ken, uniformed officers believe, of the average civil servant who flits about from ministry to ministry and has no incentive to acquire domain knowledge. The ministry, writes former naval chief Admiral Arun Prakash, 'consists of wandering generalists who can barely begin to grasp intricate military issues before they move on to another ministry. So we are landed with a toxic combination of decision makers in MOD, politicians who are hard pressed for time and bureaucrats who lack adequate comprehension'.[2] In the event, IAS officers occupying the top posts in the MOD concern themselves not with the meat of policy but with the processes of decision-making without concern for the outcomes.[3] But, far from owning up to their lack of understanding, they often act contrary to military advice and make their decisions stick under the rubric of civilian primacy. Moreover, the IAS has prevented the 'knowledge void' in MOD from being filled by means of 'cross-staffing' of military officers in the Ministry, exacerbating civil-military tensions.[4] Unable to grasp the intricacies of military arguments or comprehend the technical content of presentations made to them, MOD bureaucrats often rely on precedent and past file-notings to reach non-controversial conclusions, and in case controversy is apprehended pass the buck so the next man in the job bears the onus. It leads to unending delays on even simple matters and often, when decisions are taken, they reveal the bureaucrat's inability to distinguish grain from chaff.[5] Thus, the revival of the Indian Air Force's aerobatic squadron was approved at a time when using these funds for the enlargement of the Su-30 fleet also sought by the IAF, or the raising of an army offensive mountain corps for the China front, would have made more sense and meant better use of scarce resources.[6] Jaswant Singh, who was defence minister for a while in the Vajpayee government, blames this state of affairs on what he calls 'psychological disarming' of the Indian people in general and those within the Indian government in particular as a result of Mahatma Gandhi's stress on nonviolence combining with 'a militarily illiterate and untrusting civilian control of the armed forces'.[7]

The Indian military is further agitated by what a former army chief General V.K. Singh, and a junior minister in the Modi cabinet, called the 'greatest con job' annually pulled off by MOD staffers. It refers to the impressive allocations for defence acquisitions announced by the Finance Minister during presentation of the budget in February every year that are routinely prevented from being spent by the armed services by a variety of procedural means and contrivances. This is done, apparently on express instructions of the Finance Ministry, because the unspent monies revert to the general pool and are usually utilized to fund politically popular schemes for food and energy subsidies. MOD bureaucrats may be following orders to gum up the works but this ruse is central to projecting the impression of a richly funded military that permits blame for the allotted funds lying fallow to be shifted to the armed services. In 2011–12, for instance, only eight of the 106 military procurement proposals won approval, with fully 70 per cent of the original capital budget diverted for other uses (Singh 2013: 314–15). In this way the government has it both ways. It cannot be accused of denying the armed services the necessary funding and is yet able to find the resources for expenditure programmes that are a financial drain and increase the fiscal deficit but fetch votes.

IAS officers in MOD also oversee the Department of Defence Production and, as will be shown, are a significant barrier to India's emerging as a country self-sufficient in armaments with a comprehensively capable defence industry. Despite the public rhetoric of the government, the existing wasteful system actively undermines any movement towards self-reliance. This is because private sector defence industrial capacities are not recognized as national resources by the ministry, and actively discouraged from bidding for weapons production contracts, notwithstanding a stream of constantly revised Defence Procurement Procedure norms that, in theory, promote indigenization. The private sector companies survive on sub-contracts and spillover business from the contracts monopolized by defence public sector units (DPSUs). Set up during the heyday of the socialist Indian state in the 1960s and 1970s, many of the DPSUs and numerous ordnance factories trace their origins to the colonial era. Without strong government direction the public and private sectors are unlikely to merge their capacities and strengths and help the Indian defence industry become world class with the ability to produce technologically up-to-date weaponry.

This chapter will examine the weaknesses of the existing defence industrial set-up and the virtual absence of the Indian private sector from the procurement cycle. It will look at certain projects to emphasize how the Defence Ministry bureaucracy, DPSUs, and the armed services join in slowing down and killing off indigenous projects, and outline a scheme for founding two competing defence industrial combines to rapidly grow the local defence industry.

Starting Out Right

Instinctively understanding the perils of arms dependency, Nehru began on a high note in the 1950s by building on the foundations of an industry built up during the Second World War when India was the 'eastern arsenal' supplying war materiel of every kind—from artillery to bomber aircraft (B-24 Liberators), from clothing to food, for the Allied Southeast Asia and the Middle East Commands. Imaginatively, he started at the top-end, initiating the most technologically challenging project outside of making the atomic bomb—a supersonic combat jet aircraft, and imported skilled talent from erstwhile Nazi Germany to form its nucleus. Nehru's successors, lacking his foresight, fell in with the IAF's short-term palliative and imported whole aircraft instead, rooting in the process the institutional habit of mind of trusting in and buying foreign military hardware. The fact that the armed capability thus obtained looks good on paper but is thin in terms of operational sustainability, because it is military strength secured at the supplier countries' sufferance, does not apparently bother the government or the military much. The fact that India's wars have been mainly of short duration has prevented the problem from becoming a full-blown crisis. Over time and in the context of India's growing requirements, the supplier countries gained a whip-hand in their dealings with the Indian state because they are in a position to bring critical portions of the Indian military to a standstill by merely slowing down the flow of spares and technical support. They can do this at will or as dictated by their foreign policy interests of the moment. The reverse leverage afforded India is that now defence industries in several countries—in particular Russia, Israel, France, Britain, and growingly the United States rely on Indian sales to boost their bottom line. Just how big is the Indian market? A 2013 McKinsey Report estimated it at $150 billion by 2017 with a potential defence spend of $71.6 billion for naval platforms—submarines, surface combatants, and supports ships, $51.2 billion for military aviation—combat and trainer aircraft, support aircraft, and helicopters, and $24.5 billion for land warfare systems—fighting vehicles, artillery, missiles and infantry systems (Chibber 2013).

The disturbing flipside of this reality is that the vast defence industrial assets in the public sector are involved in very little technology creation and innovation and survive mostly on licenced manufacture of foreign equipment to meet the immediate needs of the armed services. It nullifies any acquisitions planning based on long-gestating indigenous research & development projects to produce armaments. This sort of short-termism which seems like it is here to stay materialized after the shock of military defeat in the 1962 War with China when the Indian government compensated for its previous lack of concern for preparedness with a focus narrowly on meeting the military's immediate requirements. Over decades, it transmuted into the present 'buy and make' policy—buying a certain number of weapons systems/platforms off-the-shelf and assembling the rest from imported semi-knocked down (SKD) kits and completely knocked-down (CKD) kits and, if the order is large enough, for the DPSUs to produce a growing portion of it in-country according to manufacturing blueprints from the supplier that require only 'screwdriver' level technology skills. It often leads to misrepresentation of Indian defence industrial attainments with the warships built in the public sector Mazgaon Dockyard Ltd (MDL) in Mumbai and the Garden Reach Shipyard in Kolkata, and with combat aircraft at HAL, for example, boasting of as much as 70–80 per cent indigenous content, except such high local content is by weight, not value, and the most advanced sensors and other electronics, and components in the vessels and in the communications, fire-control and weapons suites are imported for the entire production run.[8] The reason for this state of affairs is that the production contracts are monopolized by DPSUs with the Department of Defence Production (DDP) acting as facilitators. This system is sustained by calcified procurement rules and procedures that fly in the face of economic best practices and the national interest, expressly discourage and disincentivize the potential Indian vendors and private sector companies from entering the game. Thus, rules mandate production in small tranches with no guarantee that the local private sector company which invests in R&D, innovates, produces a component or sub-system, meets rigorous military specifications, and wins the initial contract to supply a product, will get the succeeding contracts for the same item when the subsequent tranches of production come due, because it cannot be sure of being the lowest bidder again. Further, while foreign vendors are allowed to factor foreign currency fluctuations into their final costing after winning the bids, Indian private sector firms are permitted no such grace which, considering they too import components and subsystems, makes it uneconomical for them to vie for contracts. It prompts foreign suppliers to quote low prices at the time of tendering and win contracts while Indian firms are forced to build in cost escalation into their more realistic estimates, which loses them bids. By such contrivances, the Indian private sector is prevented from competing fairly with foreign companies, even as the screwdriver-level technology-proficient DPSUs are allowed to corner the actual production contracts in major defence deals. Hence, the principle of competitive tendering and the lowest bidder winning the production contract–the so called 'L1' process–is turned by MOD defence production department into an insurmountable obstacle to the advancement of the local defence industry.[9] The DPSUs working on 'cost plus' basis are thus predetermined to win custom because the remit of DPP bureaucrats is to ensure the financial health of these public sector entities. This is an insidious process perpetuating the country's status as an arms dependency. The arbitrariness of the L1 process makes it difficult for small, private companies that in Germany and France, are the prime high-technology innovators (mittelstand), in India cannot even amortize their investment in R&D and production facilities and prefer, therefore, to pursue small-time sub-contracts from DPSUs. Hence, no matter how much better the private sector defence industry is in ingesting and innovating foreign technology, how much more efficient and effective it is in its manufacturing methods and labour productivity, how much more skilled and productive its workforce is as compared to their public sector counterpart, and how much of the capacity is under-utilized and lying fallow, it gets very little of the defence business while foreign suppliers are the greatest beneficiaries.[10] It describes India's defence industrial problems in a nutshell. An example to illustrate just how shabbily even private sector leviathans are treated, consider the case of Larsen & Toubro (L&T), one of the country's largest and most versatile corporations that has partaken of some of the most sensitive projects (such as the Arihant-class SSBNs) and over the years has built up its wherewithal, capabilities, and reputation for high-quality work. It has sunk in excess of Rs 4,000 crores into creating a new ship-building complex at Kattupalli near Chennai with a 2.2 km waterfront, 16 metres channel depth, a ship-lift capacity of 21,050 tonnes, and the ability to manufacture two submarines, frigates, and corvettes annually.[11] This entire capacity is largely going waste because the MOD not only did not divert any business its way, but actually favoured the French company, DCNS, at L&T's expense. This relates to the production of the nose sections of the four Scorpene diesel submarines. Owing to the complexities involved in making them because of torpedo tubes and placement of sensors, such as sonar, etc., the DPSU–Mazgaon Dockyard Ltd. begged off, whence L&T offered to do it; after all, it had built the titanium double hull, including the nose section of the Arihant and perfected the necessary plasma welding techniques. It argued that this work was not coming out of MDL's work share but DCNS' and would save the country large dollops of hard currency, fire up idle capacity, and strengthen indigenous submarine building skills. None of these arguments budged the MOD even a bit, and DCNS won the day.[12] Little wonder international arms companies consider India as a prime market. The Indian arms bazaar, in fact, is so indulgent towards foreign peddlers that not only does the Indian government not believe in leveraging its bargaining power to extract technologies it most needs, but also routinely permits them to 'bait and switch', lay down unacceptable conditions, 'string along' critical indigenous projects with hollow promises of collaboration and technology transfer, and create rifts between DRDO and the military services. In the case of the French company, SNECMA, and the indigenous Kaveri power plant originally meant to equip the Tejas, SNECMA, for instance, 'prolong[ed] the negotiations for several years ...[making] India's engine development programme [with single crystal blade technology and tap-thrust] lose precious time' before bailing out once the Rafale powered by a SNECMA engine won the MMRCA race, when a separate deal for assisting India develop its own aero-engine with similar characteristics made no sense (Soman 2013).

The building blocks of a strong defence industry in terms of manufacturing plants, R&D centres, testing facilities, and trained manpower are available within India, their non-use, under-use, or misuse being a stark reminder of the potential that exists. All that is needed is an Indian government with a long-term view and iron will to push reforms in procurement policy to advantage fully indigenous weapons systems production and, by way of facilitating this goal, to treat all built-up capacities, whether in the public or private sector, as national resources for symbiotic and integrated use. It follows therefore that there is not a single conventional weapon system in the Indian military's employ that is of purely Indian make–from design to finished product. Hundred per cent level of indigenization, a senior DRDO official stated, is uneconomical and does not always make sense. What is important he said is that the design is entirely homemade as are the basic technologies. Except designs configured in-country are deemed unsatisfactory by the military with the army, for example, disapproving designs relating to even simple pieces of hardware such as the next-generation infantry rifle, carbine, and pistol.[13] In the event, most locally produced military goods have unacceptable levels of foreign components, sub-systems, systems, sub-assemblies, and assemblies, rendering their production as vulnerable to a cutoff of material as any imported weaponry are to denial of spares. Thus, 75 per cent of all long-range surface-to-air missiles produced in the country, for instance, are of foreign origin, as is 64 per cent of the Arjun main battle tank, 47 per cent of the Advanced Light Helicopter, and 40 per cent of the Tejas LCA. DPSU majors, such Bharat Electronic Ltd, HAL, and MDL, however, assert the imported content of the systems/platforms they produce has remained static at around 38 per cent.[14] But the Indian content of the Su-30 MKI, the Russian air defence fighter capable of ground attack manufactured by HAL is 62 per cent by weight not value. It is, however, claimed that with large 'technical' design inputs by IAF engineers and DRDO, the Indian-made version of this combat aircraft under production has 75 per cent indigenous content that is expected to increase to 85 per cent by 2016 (Parthasarathi 2014).[15] Then again, despite the DPSUs manufacturing over 1800 T-72 tanks and in excess of 600 MiG aircraft and thousands of jet engines in the last fifty years under license, there is no accumulated knowledge in the Avadi Heavy Vehicles (tank) factory and in the Hindustan Aerospace Ltd (HAL)–the DPSUs producing tanks and aircraft respectively. HAL, for instance, has not maintained a comprehensive manufacturing database for all the products it has outputted to date. Hence the indigenous Tejas light combat aircraft programme, entering production stage, is not benefitting much in terms of specific tooling, jigs and production wherewithal from HAL's experience.[16] Further, the cost-plus basis on which DPSUs operate means they are not inclined to bring in any project on time or within the stipulated cost-range, nor are they penalized for late delivery. Thus, the license-manufactured French Scorpene diesel submarine is lagging a decade behind schedule, and the indigenous Tejas Light Combat Aircraft, likewise, is overdue by 15–20 years with its costs rising 15-fold over the original estimates.[17]

On the rare occasion when a concerned service shows solicitude, the indigenous project is successful. For example, the aircraft carrier variant of the Tejas nursed by the navy climbed the development curve faster than the air force version, because navy took ownership of it, with naval officers overseeing and driving the project, while the IAF, in contrast, waited, as in the past, for DRDO to deliver an acceptable aircraft while doing everything possible to hinder its fast-paced growth, like insisting on production of two prototypes and then an additional eight, before permitting the aircraft to undergo the certification process, and finally ordering a miniscule number—just 20 LCAs with the promise of another 20 aircraft should the first lot pass muster. Such procedures cause avoidable delays, preclude economies of scale, and are followed, many believe, to scuttle the LCA project and buttress the service's demands for imported multi-role combat aircraft such as the French Rafale, and to put off consideration of the DRDO's Advanced Medium Combat Aircraft (AMCA) programme–a 6th generation stealth warplane.[18] It confronts the Modi government with hard choices: Whether to spend $30 billion (Rs 1,80,000 crores) for 126 Rafales or a slightly smaller sum for fewer aircraft and help keep the French major, Dassault, afloat, or to fast-forward the Tejas LCA programme and finance AMCA development, putting the Indian aerospace sector on a strong footing to meet future IAF needs, and terminate the import option once and for all.[19] The IAF's resistance to the Tejas is puzzling considering that (1) the Tejas Mk II is an equivalent of the Gripen NG that was entered by Sweden into the MMRCA race, (2) Rafale is an aircraft from the 1980s, straddling the 3rd and 4th generation fighter aircraft, and (3) the modernization of the old fleet of Mirage 2000s is contracted out to Dassault for unit price that can fetch the country three Tejas aircraft. A single Tejas may not be able to take on the Rafale but three Indian LCAs can easily take down a single Rafale and in operations a swarm of cheaper aircraft are more effective than a smaller force of more capable combat aircraft. It is a quality-quantity argument that was played out in the United States in the 1970s, and was won hands down by the F-16 which represented low cost and quantity (Fallows 1981). From this angle the procurement of many more lower cost Tejas makes more sense than fewer of the high-cost French Rafales. The IAF's dislike of the Tejas is reflected in its studiously avoiding the principle of 'concurrency' that most advanced air forces follow with respect to underway combat aircraft programmes in their own countries. This principle allows technological and design fine-tuning of aircraft to proceed alongside induction into service.[20] Unlike the navy, with a warship design directorate producing designs for and managing production of all manner of warships—from corvettes, frigates, missile destroyers, aircraft carriers to submarines, the army and the air force have developed no comparable in-house capabilities, used as they are to indenting for whatever available imported equipment.[21]

And yet, paradoxically, the most high-end, high-technology, and decisive strategic armaments are all indigenously designed, developed, and produced in the country, ranging from the Agni series of ballistic missiles and the 'K' series of sea-borne ballistic and cruise missiles (K-4 and K-5, and the K-1 hypersonic cruise), the Arihant-class SSBNs, the ability to inject satellites into precise earth orbits–an *in situ* MIRV capability, a dual-use constellation of some seven satellites that by 2017–2018 will provide an indigenous Global Positioning System (GPS) for over-the-horizon targeting and other military uses, and nuclear and thermonuclear payloads to fit the nosecone geometries of various missiles. In a similarly unconstrained environment DRDO has developed niche technologies such as the carbon-carbon composite material for air frames and missile casing and nosecone and, in a field it excels in, software, it has 'customized' avionics for the fifth generation fighter Su-50 PAK FA to be procured from Russia, and an Indian avionics package (centered on the Flight Control System[FCS]) that the Malaysian, Indonesian, and Algerian air forces have preferred over the Russian original in the Su-30s they have purchased. So much so, Russia has gone in for the Indian FCS for part of its own Su-30 fleet and for export to third parties.[22] Such competence, with its analogous success in the civilian IT field, is so marked that the U.S. F-16s equipped with flight Control Laws (CLAWS) generated for the Indian Tejas Light Combat Aircraft actually flew better.[23] And the still more significant achievement of writing the guidance software that has transformed the Brahmos anti-ship supersonic cruise missile system into a ground-to-ground attack system capable of difficult 'S-maneuvers' before striking the target dead-centre.[24]

The situation of self-sufficiency in sophisticated strategic armaments but dependence on imported conventional weaponry is because most of the items in the former category were indigenously designed and developed in projects in 'mission-mode', where human and material resources were mobilized outside the rules and regulations-bound system of production and procurement, and were not dragged down by L1 pressures. It permitted local capacity building and technology innovation in which Indian industries and entrepreneurs were encouraged to conduct R&D and create modern manufacturing units–along 'mittelstand' lines, and guarantees of long term custom to make such ventures profitable. There is so no dearth of local ingenuity to innovate high-technology products. For instance, a small manufacturer of ceramic tiles in Andhra

Pradesh who approached the SSBN project on his own, was given a single anechoic tile of Russian origin to study, which he did. He 'reverse-engineered' it, perfected the technology to mass produce such tiles that are made of rubberized synthetic polymers and as outer skin of submarines makes detection by sonar difficult. Each such tile with thousands of voids to absorb and distort sound waves makes detection by sonar difficult. It fulfills all specifications, is available at a tenth of the Russian cost of over $800 per tile, and the supplier meets the requirements of the SSBN programme.[25] Likewise, the Integrated Guided Missile Development programme, responsible for all missiles in the Indian inventory including the Agni series, and the Indian Space Research Organization, together technically assisted several small companies manufacturing methyl alcohol and chemicals for industrial use to produce first liquid and later solid rocket propellants with critical characteristics, such as high specific impulse, controlled burn, etc., until now when the county is fully self-reliant in rockets and propellants for even deep space probes.[26]

The mission-mode research, development, and production was initiated in the 1950s by Dr Homi J. Bhabha, better known as the founder of India's nuclear programme, who also seeded the missile and space programmes. He called it 'growing' science'. It was based in the early years on talented scientists and engineers being sent abroad for fast-tracked training in cutting-edge nuclear and rocket disciplines, returning to drive high-technology projects where the accent was on trial and error, and experimentation, and learning from doing with minimal technical and material inputs from abroad.[27] The self-help attitude in the strategic technology development areas was in the subsequent decades compelled by the international technology-denial regimes strictly enforced by the United States, especially after the 1974 nuclear test. No expense or effort was therefore spared, nor were any systemic hurdles tolerated by the Indian government. The highly motivated Department of Atomic Energy, Department of Space, Integrated Guided Missile Development Project, and the SSBN called the ATV (advanced technology vehicle) project, flourished, successfully creating the infrastructure, the design and development capabilities, and nursing the talent, all outside the normal stultifying MOD system.[28]

No such urgency, technological challenge, or sense of purpose, however, informed projects to develop conventional military armaments. The competing approach to Bhabha's had taken root in other sectors of the government, however, with ministries buying whole steel plants, oil refineries, power plants on a turn-key basis, and was adopted by MOD on the pretext, after the 1962 War with China, of meeting urgent military needs. In time, not just immediate requirements but all needs were sought to be met by purchases from abroad leading, as Admiral Prakash said, to India 'spending colossal amounts of money without a clue as to what we are spending it on'.[29] This system was cemented because importing military hardware offered corrupt politicians, bureaucrats, and military officers an avenue to enrich themselves illegally with monies the foreign suppliers freely dispensed in return for help in elbowing out competition and winning contracts.[30] Had certain seminal projects initiated in the late 1950s been propelled by iron will and stern messaging to the military that imports would not be allowed except as rarity and then only in extreme cases, it may have by now resulted in a versatile, advanced, and flourishing defence industrial sector envisaged by Nehru, who laid its foundations. The most remarkable of these projects was the one that built a supersonic fighter aircraft in record time, which if it had been properly followed up, would have eventuated in a world-class Indian aviation and aero-space industry.

The United States and Russia raided the German military-industrial complex at the end of the Second World War for talent, which catalyzed the long-range American and Russian missile programs. India did much the same thing, except it was in the field of aviation.[31] In 1957, Nehru hired Dr. Kurt Tank, the legendary designer of Focke-Wulfe Fw190 fighter and other planes for the wartime Nazi Luftwaffe, to design and develop a Mach 1-plus capable multi-role jet plane at HAL, Bangalore. Four years later, the first prototype of the Marut HF-24 fighter-bomber rolled out for test-flight, the first such warplane produced outside the United States and Europe. However, Nehru's decision to produce a 'nonaligned aircraft' by marrying Tank's superlative aero-frame to a power-plant built by a team of Messerschmitt engineers (that Tank, at Nehru's behest, arranged to work in Gamal Abdul Nasser's Egypt) never fructified as the L 600 power plant which the latter were supposed to produce failed to reach the production stage.[32] The Marut was thence outfitted with the weak Orpheus 703 engine powering the smaller agile short-range fighter, Folland Gnat, being license manufactured at HAL. A powerful jet engine—the BOR 12, originally engineered by the British firm Bristol-Siddeley for competition to equip the NATO fighter, was offered for adaptation for HF-24 for Rs 7 crores. This proposal was vetoed by the leftist Defense Minister Krishna Menon which decision led to the IAF limiting its intake , and pushing the underpowered HF-24 into oblivion. Even so, in 1967 when Tank returned to Berlin as consultant to Messerschmitt-Bolkow-Blohm (MBB) company the West German government evinced interest in manufacturing the HF-24 under license in Germany and for further joint development of the aircraft. Berlin no doubt planned to build and equip the plane with a more powerful engine and thus restart a full-fledged combat aircraft industry. But Nehru died in 1964 and there was no one in the Indian government with the strategic foresight to approve such a collaborative venture.[33]

This episode had an even more tragic postscript from the point of view of attaining self-sufficiency. With IAF in the market for a low-level strike aircraft and aware that the Kurt Tank-trained team of HAL designers was working on a Mk-II version of the Marut, the Bristol-Siddeley Company this time offered an appropriate up-rated engine for the more advanced HF-24 platform. But the IAF chose to buy the Anglo-French Sepecat Jaguar instead for low-level 'deep penetration and strike' mission at the expense of the Indian product on the anvil. It killed off the HF-24 Marut Mk-II combat aircraft programme for good and ended all indigenous combat aircraft design and development in the country. Indeed, so keen was the IAF to terminate the design and development capacity created by Kurt Tank at HAL in Bangalore and prevent it from thereafter producing warplanes that it feared it would be compelled to fly, it scrupled to nothing to achieve this aim. Thus, a British-made NAVWASS (NAVigation Attack Weapon Aiming Sub-System) from Marconi-Elliot and a Head-Up display (HUD) from Smiths equipping the Marut HF-24 was rejected by the IAF-controlled Aircraft & Systems Testing Establishment (ASTE) Bangalore in 1979, but the same NAVWASS was found acceptable on the Jaguar later procured from British Aerospace.[34] The IAF's fear ostensibly was that accepting the NAVWASS on the Marut would extend its service in IAF and consolidate an aircraft design and development capability at home. After a 15-year-break and the loss of the Tank-trained generation of gifted aircraft designers, such a capability was revived with the Tejas Light Combat Aircraft programme.[35] In the context of IAF's dislike for indigenous aircraft, the Science Adviser to the Defence Minister, V. S. Arunachalam, in the 1980s decided he'd brook no IAF role or participation in the design and development of the LCA until the prototype stage. A thus alienated air force found another reason now to swear off the Tejas, reinforcing the services' and the military's antagonism generally to locally produced military goods.[36]

In any case, the Marut Mk-II was the last time a foreign company offered an aero-engine for an Indian designed air frame because such couplings would have encouraged a low cost Indian competitor to take wing in the international aviation bazaar. Foreign military suppliers quickly learned that it was more profitable to sell combat aircraft to IAF with HAL as licensed manufacturer than to assist India make its own fighter planes. Hence, a 'what if' of history: If New Delhi had decided in the early 1970s to go with Marut MK-II and/ or taken up on the Tank-inspired German government offer, there might have emerged a formidable Indo-German military industrial combine and, at a minimum, a truly sophisticated Indian aviation industry that would have imbibed the German work ethic, modern production techniques, and realized the 'mittelstand' (emphasizing small tech-innovation firms) for generating new defence technologies. S.R. Valluri, a Caltech-trained aeronautical engineer, who retired as head of the National Aeronautical Laboratory, observed laconically about the deliberately stalled Marut Mk-II project and the eviction of its talented design leader, Dr Raj Mahindra, that

> The Air Force was not unhappy with this situation, as they were able to obtain the aircraft required by them by outright purchase from abroad or production under license. ...The HAL was not unhappy either as they were having enough business through production under license. The South Block [where important ministries of the government, including Defense, reside] administrators were not unhappy ..., as they did not have to answer any embarrassing questions from the Parliament. The research organizations were busy, such as they were, by taking up R&D conceived by them [rather than because of

project demand pull, with the result that] we were nowhere near to the objective of obtaining even a modicum of self-reliance. (Valluri 2007)

It aptly describes the reasons why the LCA has made lapidary progress.[37] A post-script to the German interest in co-developing the HF-24 was the inquiry in more recent times from Berlin which, impressed by the Tejas as a low weight, low cost, air defence fighter to complement the more advanced but inordinately expensive Eurofighter in a high-low mix of aircraft for the Luftwaffe, asked about jointly producing the LCA. Astonishingly, New Delhi again showing no foresight, did not react at all.[38]

Post-HF-24, the pattern is for an initial buy of certain number of aircraft off-the-shelf from the foreign vendor, followed by the aircraft being manufactured under license by HAL with minimal transfer of technology (TOT), even though what is paid for is comprehensive technology transfer. This happens even though it is as well known in international aerospace industrial circles as it is to the IAF and MOD that stuff like flight control laws, source codes (millions of lines software) for each of the major systems in a modern aircraft, and the algorithms driving them, are never transferred.

HAL, as a DPSU, mindful of the IAF's penchant for foreign aircraft, has specialized only in assembling aircraft and, therefore, in process engineering, and has no capacity to ingest foreign technology or even innovate such technologies as have been transferred by foreign aircraft companies, leave alone demanding the advance technology that has been paid for. Thus, HAL and other DPSUs have been content sticking with the no-risk end of the business of cobbling weapons and weapons platforms together from SKD and CKD kits, and if the requirement is large enough, graduating to manufacturing the desired weapons and weapons platforms–aircraft, tanks, guns, and ships, under license, while sourcing high-end items such as avionics, fire-control systems, special steels, and 'black box' fitments from the original foreign vendor for the duration of the production contract. 'You can', as Air Marshal A.L. Matheswaran (Retd) said at an air power seminar in June 2014, 'keep buying, keep spending money, but that's not going to give you real strength, or make you a great power'.[39] For the foreign supplier, however, this is a perpetually paying proposition–reason why more and more foreign countries are eager to sell to India, and why the competition to meet the requirements of the Indian military is so fierce as in the recent case with the Multi-role Medium Range Combat Aircraft competition won by the Rafale aircraft produced by the French company Dassault Avions (Tellis 2011). In servicing the captive Indian military market, moreover, DPSUs do not canvas for change in the government policy banning arms sales abroad, which would, in theory, improve their profit margins and economies of scale, and reduce the unit-cost to the Indian armed services. But because generating exports involves too much trouble of actually having to produce quality goods and hard sell these products to foreign customers, they are happy to stay with the 'cost plus' regime they have grown accustomed to.

The armed services identify their requirements and draw up the Staff Requirements detailing the specifications of performance for any weapons platform or armament system. When the technologies involved are considered too steep technologically for DRDO and DPSUs to produce at home, it is tendered abroad. But foreign suppliers, hampered by restrictions on the level of technology they can sell or transfer to foreign countries, end up offering products that don't meet Indian military's specifications but are bought anyway because the Indian military would take an inferior foreign product to an item engineered at home to their specifications because of the sheer 'mistrust' between the armed services and DRDO.[40] The DPSUs also rely on their guardian in the government—the Department of Defence Production in MOD to take care of their interests by ensuring there is a license manufacture component for them, and that TOT too are channeled to them even though they are unable to benefit from technology transfer, which private sector firms are better motivated and able to do with an eye on eventual commercial spinoffs. It results in what is described by a former technology adviser in MOD, Dr. V. Siddhartha, as the 'triple trap' system the country is victimized by: 'What is developed abroad will not suit our new requirements; what is suitable will be denied; what is not denied will be unaffordable.'[41] In this situation, licensed production is mistakenly seen as a great leap into self-reliance.

Consider the problems the Tejas Light Combat Aircraft (LCA) Mk-I, geared for short-range air defence, is facing. After the elaborate certification process, it is going into the Limited Series Production phase (for 40 odd aircraft) as prelude to full production. Its bigger Mark-II variant is under development to fill the MMRCA bill, making the import of Rafale redundant, as already discussed. But the induction of the Tejas was slowed down by IAF's insistence that all the operational clearances after the first one obtained in 2012 also be obtained at HAL rather than in squadron service as is the concurrency norm with combat aircraft produced in other countries. Also, the aircraft is purchased by IAF not in bulk orders but in small numbers at a time, which makes economies of scale impossible to achieve and raises the unit cost which, in turn, is held against the aircraft by IAF. This even though the LCA, like the Marut, has the makings of an international best-seller if only HAL and IAF got their act together, and part of the production chores were shared with private sector companies.[42] At the heart of this aircraft is the 4.5 generation avionics suite–the equal of the unit on board the Rafale, featuring the powerful Active Electronically Scanned Array (AESA) radar (enabling a combat aircraft to switch from air-to-air to air-to-ground surveillance, tracking, and targeting mode) based on the Israeli ELTA 2032 radar, instead of the more powerful ELTA 2052 that Washington pressured Tel Aviv into withdrawing. It will be tested on a Dornier turboprop test bed soon.[43] Alternatively, the DRDO programme can reorient the locally produced receiver-transmitter nodules for the early warning system configured to be carried on the Brazilian Embraer platform, to an AESA configuration. All it requires is changing the nodules from L-band to X-band. The performance level of the Indian product is comparable to the Thales RBE2 AESA radar that, when fully developed, will be standard equipment on the Rafale. The development of the larger, longer-range, Tejas Mk-II as MMRCA, equipped with the Indian AESA, could be accelerated but isn't because the Indian government and IAF, while aware of the progress the Tejas Mk-II is making, went ahead with negotiating for the Rafale as MMRCA. This even though the whole notion of a 'medium' aircraft is an IAF concoction, circa 2004–2005, designed to befuddle the bureaucrats in MOD and politicians in government by conceiving a new category of aircraft and then demanding the government meet this urgent need.[44] Except the IAF's light, medium, and heavy categories for combat aircraft are entirely arbitrary distinctions in operational terms. The indigenous 'light' combat aircraft Tejas, for instance, with 4.5 generation avionics–is exactly of the same quality and performance level as that onboard the so-called 'medium' weight Rafale combat aircraft, or the Mirage 2000 with the IAF, except the LCA has a 4 ton weapon load capacity compared to the latter's 5 tons. Then again, the Mirage was originally purchased as an air defence replacement for the MiG-21, which is able to carry just 1.8 tons of ordnance, but whose radius of action of only 50 kms is one-fifth that of the LCA. Likewise, the Su-30 is dubbed a 'heavy' warplane for no good reason. 'New phraseology', said Vice Admiral Raman Puri and former head of the Integrated Defence Staff, creates new equipment 'voids', which the government is then frightened into filling with scare tactics about force imbalance relative to the adversary's strengths. 'How many countries have five types of combat aircraft in their inventory?' he wonders.[45] In reality, these are redundant weapons platforms with overlapping performance envelopes, which MOD and the Indian government, run by civil servants without specialist knowledge, cannot question. It is a lexical means the military has invented to get around political and bureaucratic hurdles. To fuel a sense of urgency about the MMRCA, the IAF even junked a deal negotiated with Qatar in 2004–2005 for 11 Mirage 2000–2005 combat aircraft with 85 per cent of life intact and a stock of 500 air-to-air and air-to-ground missiles. IAF's insistence on paying only $347 million for this transaction and not $600 million as agreed upon, ended in Qatar pulling out.[46] So there is no real urgency to fill the depleting fighter squadron strength, nothing in any case that cannot be sacrificed to push the IAF's case for desired new aircraft. It is by such means that the pitch for acquiring the Rafale took hold. The Rafale deal, initially pegged at some $10 billion will, however, balloon to over $30–$40 billion entailing the import of expensive avionics and sensor packages for the lifetime of the production contract. It will not only amortize the French government's investment in this aircraft but keep the French aviation industry in the clover for the next few decades.[47] The pattern of the British Jaguar aircraft being procured at the expense of the Marut Mk-II is thus being repeated with the Rafale MMRCA displacing the Tejas Mk-II. Self-reliance in arms, it seems, is only the stuff of public speeches and posturing by Indian politicians.[48] The entrenched vested interests together with a skewed procurement system defeat attempts at holistic reforms. Indeed, sizeable sections of the military, Defence Ministry, and the government believe the system is beyond repair. As a result, foreign suppliers demand extortionate prices for even dated technology. Dassault, for example, is to upgrade the IAF fleet of 51 Mirage 2000H fighter-bomber to Mirage 2000-5 standard for some $3 billion at a unit cost that could buy the country a new advanced aircraft, such as the Su-30MKI with full weapons load.[49]

The defence industrial system would have got a boost had another egregious mistake, in a series of such mistakes, not been made by the government in the mid-1990s, harking back to what Nehru did with Kurt Tank but Prime Minister Narasimha Rao didn't do with Russian experts on offer. The services of top-rated Russian nuclear and missile scientists, and skilled designers and production engineers of conventional armaments from the Russian defence industry were offered to India because Moscow was unable to afford their salaries and to upkeep the projects they were working on. This offer by an apparently desperate regime of President Boris Yeltsin was rejected for the pettiest of reasons, because the emoluments sought for the Russian personnel (which were a pittance—involving at that time, free boarding and lodging and a monthly stipend of $200 for each of the imported personnel) surpassed the pay-scale of top civil servants. The effect these Russian scientists and technologists would have had in revving up and fast-forwarding ongoing projects in all fields related to strategic and conventional military hardware, and to get the Indian defence industry humming, cannot be exaggerated. At a minimum, integrating the Russian expertise into indigenous programmes would have jump-started the dormant ship, submarine, aircraft, tank, and artillery design bureaus and development, and production capacities in the country. The result would have been a leap in the quality of Indian-made armaments of all types, in the transmission of esoteric technology development skills, and of the diffusion of these skills and capabilities to the Indian industry at large.[50] India's loss was China's gain, as Beijing grabbed the Russians, which may explain the surge in the last decade in the quality and variety of weapons programmes under development by the Chinese defence companies.

The core problem are the armed services, owing to whose usually wrong procurement priorities and choices the allotted funds are not used smartly. Lacking a long-term strategic master-plan from the government, the guiding principle for expenditure is the Defence Minister's current operational directive. But this directive, as has been iterated, being a generalized statement, not specific instruction to change course, or redirect effort, or focus on a new threat, the services feel free to continue funding the prevailing force structure and disposition and fill the 'voids' in War Wastage Reserve and War Stock in 4–5 year time slots. Thus, it is instructive that the biggest increase in weapons-platform inventories in the period 2000–2011 was 21 per cent in the army's Pakistan-specific fleet of tanks with the navy's surface combatants coming next with 10 per cent increase (Chibber 2013). However, as Vice Admiral Puri, who also pulled time as member of the Defence Acquisition Council chaired by the Defence Minister, points out 'Force structuring and strategic planning requires a 15–20 year timeframe. The two are very different and, clearly, we'll always be preparing for yesterday's wars.' If a breakthrough technology is at the fundamental research stage, a weapon to be produced will take 25–30 years, if it is at the stage of technology development 10–15 years, if it is at the stage of production engineering 5–8 years. But with the acquisition planning time horizon in the present system of 2–5 years, it is hardly surprising,' says Puri, that DRDO ends up 'only tweaking the available technology at best'. And, pressed for time, 'we [end up] running after [foreign] technologies that will become obsolete by the time they come into [Indian] service' or, he states, systems are 'reverse-engineered, which requires developing technology that somebody else developed 20 years ago'. Then if the services do get the indigenous technology product, because of the time it took to develop it, the 'staff requirements' will have changed and the item is deemed obsolete. Given the nature and the speed with which military technology is advancing, even if the Indian defence-industrial combine runs hard to remain in place, it will find itself falling behind in delivering products desired by the armed services. 'As there's no long-term planning, we have no programme budgeting, and we have no outcome budgeting. The result is we are making acquisitions', Puri avers, 'without knowing what our liabilities will be' in terms of the costs of spares, service support, etc. It is a problem worse confounded by the fact that no life-cycle costing of anything is done and that's because the defense ministry does 'not retain the data bases for anything'. Indeed, so entrenched is this monumentally flawed procurement system that even the reasonable change mandating life-cycle costing of weapon systems is regarded by politicians as detrimental.[51] According to Puri, the situation is actually a lot worse. 'Every year there's a procurement policy. There's a defence production policy. But this policy will not talk about how the required technologies will be acquired. If you do not know what technologies to acquire, you can only buy. We go in for "buy and make" and will continue to do that—a good phrase for licensed production. There's thus copious use of technologies labeled as indigenous,' he says. It results, he contends, in anarchical acquisitions that do not hew to any plan parameters, except in a vague sort of way, and beget the armed services capabilities they desire, not what the country needs. The result is a multiplicity of weaponry from diverse sources, which doesn't worry the military much because it plans for short wars and so the possibility of the spares-spigot being turned off to hurt military operations is discounted.

With the emphasis on having an up to-date order-of-battle with showy weapons platforms rather than on relying on home-grown products without fear of spares cutoff and firming up of warfighting stamina by building up spares stockpiles to enable prosecution of longer decisive, wars, the armed services have devised various ways to bamboozle the civilian bureaucracy in the MOD and to force the government to give into their demands. Thus, novel nomenclature is often invented, as previously discussed, to push for newer combat aircraft and the like. 'Given designated force levels, the services don't care how they bring their forces up to those levels. Because indigenization is prevented by the military as much as the defence bureaucracy habituated to importing armaments, the 'voids' [in terms of force levels and capabilities] are increasing. Once the voids increase', explains Brigadier Arun Sahgal (Retd.), former Director, Net Assessment, Headquarters Integrated Defence Staff, 'the services begin howling to the government saying we are falling below sanctioned force levels… No holistic appraisal is done when hundreds of billions of dollars *are* to be spent…in the next 10 or 15 years.' From a foreign vendor's point of view, however, this system of functional anarchy–that permits separating the fool from his money—couldn't be more profitable.[52]

Such a spendthrift procurement approach is, of course, inherently leaky and corruption-prone. It is aided by the Defense Ministry, for example, not collating the information about technologies being developed in the country nor insisting on the armed services using them once these technologies are developed. The outcome is farcical. 'The government says it wants to retain the country's strategic autonomy', says a frustrated Puri. 'How the hell do you retain strategic autonomy when you are 80 percent bought out?'[53] The supreme irony, he suggests, is that

> At the technological level we are perhaps ahead of the Chinese in many areas, such as avionics and system integration....But we will lose the edge if we continue to buy foreign. Look at the Arihant now; because it is strategic everything's done here–Russians have helped us no doubt, but by and large, we have understood the technologies that go in. Combat system engineering is known to us. Most of it was designed at home. What's the difference between the combat system in the SSBN and the one going into the French Scorpene diesel submarine [bought by the Navy]? By going in for platform management and the combat system in a new conventional submarine imported from France, the government', he charged, 'has disregarded the capability built up in the country [in both the public and private sectors for the SSBN project].

Such weighty arguments almost convinced the Vajpayee government in the early 2000s to rethink the Scorpene deal with France, which was resumed, Admiral Prakash claims, only because the rupees one crore per day penalty clause in the contract began kicking in.[54]

The examples of the AESA radar and the Arihant submarine technologies being elbowed out of the picture highlight the Indian military's lack of confidence and institutional distrust of home-made technologies and goods, and the government's disinterest in enforcing indigenous equipment choices on the military. If this continues, Puri fears, the human resources will atrophy, DRDO will lose its best people because technological challenge is what young talent likes to overcome.[55] A recent example of this invidious system at work was the Manmohan Singh government's approval for the navy globally to tender for yet another diesel-electric submarine except with air-independent propulsion (AIP)—Project 75i. This project was originally conceived as amalgamating the best ideas from the Russian (SSBN) and the Western conventional (German HDW 209, French Scorpene) submarine design philosophies for a totally indigenous programme worth $10 billion.[56] But the import culture rooted in the innards of the military and defence establishment affected the navy too—the most progressive of the services. It created confusion about the best east-west submarine design compromises, and fueled uncertainty. Thus, importing of yet another Western submarine for Project 75i was put on the table because, according to Vice Admiral K.N. Sushil (Retd.), a distinguished submariner and former Commander, Southern Naval Command, the navy's Directorate of Naval Design Submarine Design Group (DNDSDG) was 'not clear about its design philosophy'. Decisions about design features—double hull or single hull, and standardizing the diving depths, the factor of safety, operating pressures, and other technical criteria, the steel to be used—Russian, HY series (used in the German HDW 209) or the HLES (in the French Scorpene), etc., have not been made. 'The crucial issue is that the DNDSDG is not sure of building any hull without help. Since the Russians prefer double hull they think and justify double hull. They are surprisingly unwilling to accept that double hull or single hull, the structural normatives have to be same to ensure structural safety since both hulls will be subject to same pressures.'[57] The possibility of importing a new foreign submersible, Sushil implied, only increased procrastination. Admiral Prakash contrarily believed that the submarine design group, despite its engineers spending a lot of time attached to design bureaus abroad (Rubin design bureau in St. Petersburg and the German HDW design facility in Kiel) lack broad confidence. He recalled that despite being specifically tasked by him in 2004, this group was unable to even design and develop a 'chariot'—a small one-man submarine for near-shore and special operations.[58] But such doubts were doused and the Modi government made the decision pending from 1999 to build 24 submarines in 30 years, and that the six Project 75i submarines would be built entirely in-country by the selected DPSU (MDL or Hindustan Shipyard Ltd) or private company (L&T or Pipavav with the second largest dry dock in the world on the Gujarat coast but no experience of building submarines) per the chosen foreign design (from the French DCNS, German HDW, Swedish Saab, or the Russian Rubin design bureau) (Nayak 2014). Reflecting the private sector-led 'Make in India' thinking of the Modi government, the sometime Defence Minister Arun Jaitley prevented the Department of Defence

Production from favouring MDL by imposing a techno-economic condition on L&T to move its production base to Hazira, the company's secondary base.[59] The foreign partner aspect was approved because of the navy's diffident submarine design directorate, which still needs some hand-holding by a foreign firm. Even so, the Indian Project 75i will be a composite boat outfitted with the DRDO developed Air Independent Propulsion system, and with a weapons mix featuring K-15, K-4, and K-5 land-attack, cruise and ballistic missiles and the Nirbhay 1,000 km subsonic cruise missile with conventional/ nuclear warheads fired from vertical launch systems and torpedo tubes.[60] Nirbhay was successfully tested in late October 2014.[61] The 75i model may be the forerunner of other 'Make in India' projects, including AMCA, some 50+ medium turbo-prop transport planes, 197 light helicopters and all sorts of artillery for the army.[62]

Colonel Das of Cisco Systems India and veteran of the army's SATHI fiasco agrees with Vice Admiral Puri's assessment of institutionalized disregard for indigenous production of armaments and high-value weapons platforms despite having in-country design-to-delivery capability. Das is of the view that the ecosystem for producing strategic systems should be replicated for conventional arms as well. He cites the example of the communications interface between the Strategic Forces Command and the conventional military command structure, which is much better than the one existing between command units within the conventional military. Besides the fact that it has been modeled well, has limited turf, is so bounded that it gets premium attention and, 'in our geography, it's a point problem to solve, and if we could apply those administrative and logistics models from the strategic sphere to conventional military procurement, we'd do a lot better. In the strategic field, the streamlined decision norms, acquisition procedures, the various protocols, are all handled by the Prime Minister's Office, and that allows', he said, 'the things to converge a lot faster'.[63]

The malaise in the defence industrial-cum-procurement system as is apparent can be attributed to many factors. Among these is the 'two year window'—the minimum tenure of appointees to senior posts within the military, civilian bureaucracy, and DRDO. Thus, those filling the posts are motivated to show stellar achievements during their time at the top and latch on to short-term palliatives, such as imports to improve the orders-of-battle.[64] Another crucial factor, according to a flag-rank officer who didn't wish to be identified, is the fact that senior military leadership posts, in particular, responsible for acquisitions decisions, are often held by persons clueless about technological advances and their military applications, about systems analysis, research and development or anything remotely connected with engineering and technology, their background being only that of users of technology. Their interest is not in the technology itself or in the country producing it but in having the most advanced weapons systems however that is managed. Moreover, it does not seem to be so much the quality of military hardware as its foreign origin that apparently convinces the military services of its quality, notwithstanding the fact that derated or second-grade armaments are purchased as the vendor states do not part with cutting-edge technology. Because foreign-origin weapons inspire confidence in the service brass, these are preferred to indigenous ones and get license-produced in DPSUs. Hence such leaning of HAL was institutionalized by IAF officers helming it in the past, among them two former chiefs, P.C. Lal and L.M. Katre.

Then there's the mismatch in plans and their timelines. 'Acquisitions take place as per the annual acquisitions plan,' Das says, 'which has nothing to do with the 5-year defense plan, which has nothing to do with the 2-year plan the services follow. So, of course, things will be delayed, because no acquisitions process [involving a foreign supplier] will deliver anything in less than 8–10 years'.[65] But, because of the military's antipathy to DRDO, procedural firewalls are erected to frustrate indigenous effort. Thus, very elaborate General Staff Qualitative Requirements (GSQRs) with hundreds of clauses to take care of every possible contingency are drawn up by the armed services for the warfighting systems they desire. But these GSQRs apply only to indigenous items and not to foreign-sourced equipment. Hence, the Indian armed services, which carp about home-grown technology as not top-notch, happily accept whatever foreign hardware is on offer.[66] 'Everything's designed so that our foreign buying spree does not end', observes Vice Admiral Puri. Higher defence R&D mechanisms built over the years—the Integrated Guided Missile Development Project had produced the Agni series and sea-borne missiles, the Aeronautical Development Agency that designed and developed the LCA, the Advanced Technology Vehicle project that produced the Arihant-class of SSBN, could step into the conventional armaments sphere, but are not tasked to do so. 'When a Fifth-generation combat aircraft is to be designed, we go off to Russia. Why wasn't ADA cleared to develop the two-engine variant of LCA instead, which would have met the FGFA specifications, and which proposal was forwarded to the government in 2005?' asks Puri. The LCA is a much delayed project that has progressed from zero-base because of attrition of most of the designing and production skills acquired in the HF-24 programme. It has experienced time and cost over-runs that have plagued most combat aircraft development programmes the world over. Defensive about its perceived disinterest in the LCA, Air Chief Marshal Browne, when he headed the air force, blamed the manufacturing agency—Hindustan Aeronautics Ltd., for its troubles. 'The Tejas is facing problems notwithstanding the fact that all the technologies are developed, and approved by IAF, and it is ready for production, except HAL has not readied its production engineering processes,' said Browne. 'HAL's disinterest is because of its hurt feelings that it had no role in its R&D and, therefore, that it has no stake in the LCA. And that's where the whole matter has come to a stop. And the Defence Minister and the Prime Minister are unwilling to do anything more than exhort everybody to produce this indigenous aircraft'.[67] But Browne was being disingenuous, considering IAF's inglorious record with the HF-24 Mk-II and now Tejas and its reluctance to subscribe to the 'concurrency' principle of fine-tuning technology and removing technological and design kinks after an aircraft has entered squadron service, which is followed by all major air forces. Air Headquarters cannot explain why, if it was so keen on locally-designed and made aircraft, it has not spearheaded projects in the manner the navy has done its warship and SSBN projects, and speeded up the navalized Tejas programme. Unhappy with the functioning of DPSUs, and their proven inability to bring projects such as LCA in on time and within cost, New Delhi has decided gradually to corporatize and privatize them, to begin with, by offloading 10 per cent of HAL shares, 24 per cent of shares of Bharat Electronics Ltd.—the defense electronics major, and 34 per cent of the equity in Bharat Earth Movers Ltd. manufacturing Tatra trucks, and heavy military vehicles, on the market.[68]

Dr V.K. Saraswat, former head of DRDO, readily acknowledged the drawbacks of the existing public sector-dominated defense industry in India and the licensed manufacture level at which it has stagnated, but attributed it to the unwillingness of foreign suppliers to part with 'know why'. It does not, however, explain why considering how crucial Indian sales are to the future of foreign defence industries, MOD does not make all deals contingent on absolutely full transfer of technology, with hefty penalty clauses for any falloff in this respect, and why it doesn't insist on valuable, collateral, even if unrelated technology to be transferred as part of the 50 per cent offsets policy. But DRDO is no part of the deal negotiating process, it is not asked to draw up a list of topdrawer technologies to build up a high-technology base, and which technologies can be extorted from the vendors as price for a contract. Thus, MOD failed to extract the French Neuron drone technology or the ceramic blade technology for jet turbine engines to benefit the next generation Kaveri power plant as pre-condition for the Rafale deal, something a desperate France would have agreed to keep its combat aviation sector alive.[69] Unwilling to take advantage of a buyer's market, India suffers owing to the inadequacies in the procurement system and the cupidity of the political class, MOD bureaucrats, and the the military services running it.[70] So Saraswat's contention of 'know why' doesn't hold if MOD makes no effort to pressure the supplier for the most advanced technologies and doesn't impose stringent conditions on the supply of the contracted technologies. Such opportunities to squeeze advanced technologies out of foreign vendors in order to improve the indigenous technological and industrial competences are routinely ignored by MOD. Saraswat acknowledged a 'disconnect between the user services and the R&D department' primarily because DRDO conducted R&D on the basis of its own agenda and the military procured weapons systems as per its needs. The twain don't often meet but can, he maintained. He referred to the DRDO bringing some 400 companies from the private sector into the defense industrial business, and realized natural synergies. But the government, he admitted, still discriminates in giving loans, opening credit lines, and generally treating private and public sector companies on par. The government, he also volunteered, has the bad habit of setting up new production lines for critical technologies even when existing modern capacities in the private sector remain unutilized. He tried, he said, to reverse this trend by persuading the government to invest in public and private sectors in the ratio 1:4 favouring the latter. 'The [Manmohan Singh] government thinking [was] why should private sector be benefitted from such investment?' Saraswat said. He identified three ministries during the Congress party regime— Energy, Heavy Industry, and Defence, which own 60–70 per cent of the heavy industrial infrastructure controlled by the government as the tortoises who will never win any race but effectively prevent the private sector hares from even entering the race. They cannot, he said, stomach a seamless private-public partnership in defence and cutting-edge technology sectors. He, however, felt that the notion of licensed manufacture has undergone a revision and will, in fact, lay the foundations for a strong defense R&D and production base. 'There are no pure licensed manufacture agreements anymore', he clarified, and mentioned the agreement with Israel to produce an AESA radar and long-range and medium range SAMs. Israel, according to Saraswat, 'will keep nothing to themselves, whether it is software or hardware, drawings, designs, know-why, documentation, including technology for making TR (transmitter-receiver) nodules for AESA and other radars—which is the latest technology'. The collaboration with Israel on the AESA radar has helped DRDO to locally produce TR nodules; it is the optimum geometry for placing the nodules that is now sought to be perfected, and will be showcased when it is tested.[71] As part of the 70 km long range surface-to-air missile being developed jointly with Israel, DRDO has designed and tested a two-pulse motor, first flown in May 2010, that will make the missile very manouevrable in the terminal phase to destroy 'juking' targets (Unnithan 2010).

Saraswat said India is in a position to export military goods, such as the LCA and there was foreign interest too, but for that, he said, India needed to 'change gears', set up assembly lines. India can quickly increase its defence sales from 1–2 per cent level of the country's total exports, but will require the government to change its mindset which, he said, was not visible during most of the Congress party government's tenure. But there is a perceptible softening of attitude towards export of military goods by the private sector.[72] Saraswat's successor, Avinash Chander, who formerly was the boss of the missile programme, forthrightly asked the Modi government for a 'policy mechanism' and 'single window [time bound] clearance' for arms sales to friendly countries and said the country was in a position to export as many as 500–1000 Tejas LCA, and all kinds of missiles from the 290 km Brahmos supersonic cruise missile to the 150 km area destruction missile like Prahar, if the production wherewithal is ramped up. He added that India can even export strategic long range missiles as China had done [the 'Silkworm' CSSC-2 missile] to Saudi Arabia, at 'one-third or one-fourth' the price competitors charge. Besides referring to undercutting any supplier, he hinted at India offering weapons at friendship prices because, depending on the government's decision and with the larger geopolitical goals in mind, the 'export price' of hardware can be appreciably reduced.[73]

Saraswat rated the attitudes of the three services to technology sensitivity and to indigenous technology development thus: The navy officers are well educated, familiar with the latest technology and have a receptive outlook. The army is unchanging in that most of its officers still have only an NDA (National Defence Academy) qualification and don't have a technological outlook. The air force is in-between, but while dealing with advanced technology they put emphasis on flying and the force is run by pilots, not engineers, who have 'zero role', unlike in the navy, which is run by engineers and engineering officers can rise to Vice Chief of the Naval Staff-rank. IAF understands that war cannot be fought 'if you are not technologically savvy but its attitude is "I need this, you give it to me, or I'll buy from outside"'. But he indicated that the visceral distrust of the armed services to home-grown technology is lessening and mentioned in this regard how the IAF 'now vouches for DRDO-produced electronic warfare systems and doesn't hanker for imported systems'. He cited IAF's opting in 2011 for an indigenous surveillance and tracking radar–a sphere of defence electronics in which DRDO, he added, 'matches the performance of the best in the world'.[74]

Advanced defense electronics, however, require high-performance integrated circuits (microchips). So far, he said, India has managed by designing complete chips and having foreign companies fabricate them. The Department of Space, he revealed, has a 180 nanometer foundry—'which is good but not state-of-the-art, which is 45 nanometers'. While there are foundries abroad that can produce 13 nanometer chips crucial to cyber security DRDO, he revealed, hires 45 nanometer foundries. However, private sector companies are in the process of setting up fabs to produce 22 nanometer level chips, but it will still take some more years. 'Unless we build some of these strategic components in-house, we'll always be vulnerable. We need to have that investment done', he declared. 'Indian government has realized this more because of cyber security reasons than because of commercial reasons, and will pitch in with huge investments in this area'.[75] But excelling in military electronics and software is not the same thing as flying home-made combat aircraft, firing locally-produced artillery pieces, or mounting armored offensives with indigenous tanks (Shukla 2012). This will require sufficiency in 'aero-mechanical and electronic engineering based technologies' in which the dependency rates are high—64 per cent for HAL (with 47 per cent of the components of the Tejas LCA being 'still imported, not to speak of related materials'), 44 per cent for Bharat Dynamics Limited producing strategic and tactical missiles, and 39 per cent for Bharat Electronics Limited producing military electronics systems, such as radars, military telecommunications, sensors (Gopalaswamy and Reddy 2013: 84–85). The R&D record of the 56 DRDO laboratories suggests that the defence industrial deficiency, according to one recent analysis is at the manufacturing end owing to the negative economies of scale, amounting to a 'techno-industrial Achilles heel'. This weakness is attributed to 'imports of hundreds of varieties of raw materials (metals and non-metals) and thousands of small components in the aeronautics, electronics, and guided missile industries, worth billions of dollars, a historical legacy of the "licensed production" era with no determined, integrated, focused, time-bound efforts to find indigenous alternatives and solutions'. The country can become genuinely self-reliant within five years, concludes this analysis, if the government opts for 'public-private ventures' (Gopalaswamy and Reddy 2013 : 97). How severe the problem is may be gauged from the troubles being faced by 25 of the frontline warships in their normal maintenance and short and medium refit programmes docked in Mumbai and Visakhapatnam. It led the Comptroller and Auditor General to say in his report that the lack of availability of spares 'resulted in the postponement of essential routines and use of refurbished components, resulting in adverse impact on quality, reliability and longevity of equipment on board. In the absence of supply, the demands were met either by refurbishing old spares or by resorting to local purchases'.[76] 'Local purchases' suggests precisely the indigenous potential, which the Indian military continues to be sceptical about.

In contrast to the public sector, the budding private defence industrial sector is on the ball. For one, it is far more cost-conscious and operate their capacities for profit—ironically the reason why the socialist state does not consider them 'national' assets to be tapped to make India self-sufficient in arms. Consider this: The public sector shipyards have orders valued at $24 billion for some 60 warships of all types on their books; these require to be delivered to the navy within 12 years. At their current pace of work, it will take the DPSUs 30 years to produce these ships. In the context of the manifest incapacity of the public sector MoD is nevertheless loath to go in for competitive bids for ship-building contracts, or directly allot major contracts to private sector shipyards or help them become prime integrators. The private sector giant, Larsen and Toubro (L&T), has constructed the nuclear powered Arihant-class submarine and has built up its in-house engineering, tooling, and manufacturing expertise to the point where all it needs is a design blueprint and specifications for motors, pumps, etc., it can do the rest, starting with converting the design to detailed drawings. It learned to handle titanium metal and to engineer the titanium pressure hull and the stern shafting for the SSBN, developing the high-pressure plasma welding techniques for micron tolerances, and set up a laboratory in Mumbai where virtual reality is simulated to study the effect on the submarine of underwater manouevres and weapons launches as feedback to calibrate the basic ship design and, in the process, has won a high rating for the company's submarine production capability.[77] Despite, the 30-year Naval Plan approved in 1999 by the last BJP government, which envisioned 24 conventional submarines to be built in the 'Buy and Make' mode, not even a single boat has been delivered by MDL. This even as L&T with proven but idle capacity was given no contract to build any of these warships nor involved in the Scorpene submarine production. With the evidence of the four year delay by the DPSU, Mazgaon Dockyard Ltd, in producing six French Scorpene diesel submarines worth Rs 23,562 crores and its own private sector-weighted 'Make in India' policy in mind, the Modi government decided capable private companies—L&T and Pipavav Shipyard, could bid for the 75i contract.[78] This should ideally lead to more rational use of the available capacities irrespective of whether these are in the public or private sectors, and is a reasonable model to grow the defence industry, making it more capable, efficacious, and profitable. The public sector shipyards in Mumbai, Kolkata, Goa, Kochi, and Vishakhapatnam have bulging order books for some 41 surface combatants, but are unable to meet the navy's needs in time.[79] In the event, not transferring some of the current warship construction contracts to the private sector and keeping them out of the competition to build additional capital ships, such as seven additional stealth guided missile frigates and the second indigenous aircraft carrier, could prove fatal for private companies with large investments in shipbuilding facilities but meagre returns.[80] But defence production bureaucrats continue to shovel contracts to public sector shipyards saying private companies lack experience.

But this attitude cannot be maintained with regard to submarine manufacture, whence the MOD's attempts early in the Modi rule to channel the 75i submarine production to HSL or MDL failed. If the total order of 85 warships under construction and in the design pipeline were shared, with both private and public sector production lines working in parallel to meet time and cost parameters, it would mean more rapid induction of ships, a more modern navy, greater 'maritime density' and larger visibility in the surrounding and distant seas and a genuinely competitive shipbuilding industry. Instead, the navy has to make do with the DPSU schedule of a Kolkata-class missile destroyer being outputted by the DPSU Garden Reach Shipbuilders & Engineers in Kolkata every 4–5 years, for instance, resulting in progressive thinning out of the naval force because the attrition/phase-out rate of ships exceeds the induction rate of new vessels. In like vein, IAF is unhappy with the production delays at HAL. M.M. Pallam Raju, Minister of State for Defence in the Manmohan Singh government charged HAL with not meeting the expectations of the IAF and blamed it for getting 'involved in too many projects and… [in producing] every nut and bolt in aviation'.[81]

Imports are justified by the military in terms of meeting immediate need that only foreign suppliers can meet with readily available systems. No government has so far shown the will to call out the armed services on this count or restricted their purchases to domestic producers by denying them the import option. The recent decisions by the BJP government in tune with its 'Make in India' outlook have routed defence contracts to the private sector for Rs 65,000 crore worth of military procurements, with only Rs 10,000 crores set aside to 'buy global'.[82] In the short term, this will merely replace the DPSUs with private companies in the production cycle, with the former importing materials and technology from their foreign partners, with no requirement that any of the technologies be developed in-country.[83] The BJP government is apparently of the view that this halfway measure will help private sector capabilities evolve and mature, enabling it to emerge more fully as technology innovators and producers of whole systems.

Politicians of the old school (represented by the Congress party) were not motivated to bring the private sector at all into the defence industry because purchase of high-value weapons systems from abroad followed by licensed production in India provided them with access to a steady stream of unaccountable funds.[84] In the wake of recent initiatives, whether a ban on unlimited FDI in the private defence industrial companies will continue remains to be seen, given the entrenched view that this will help them to become rivals to the DPSUs.[85] In the decade 2004–2014, the Congress party government opposed increasing FDI in defence beyond the 26 per cent level because, then Defence Minister A.K. Antony, feared it will 'stymie the growth of indigenous design and development, and our dependence on foreign countries and [original equipment manufacturers] for modern weapons will get perpetuated'.[86] The irony and the political cost of sixty years of arms dependency that such thinking obtained escaped him, but it also capped India's potential as arms maker and exporter. The military is partial to increased FDI because 'Aviation industry is capital intensive [and] [t]here are long incubation periods', said Air Marshal P.P. Reddy in-charge of Flight Safety in the IAF, which FDI can help tide over (Sawant 2013). Tiring of the under-performing DPSUs the military too is looking to the private sector to meet its needs in aero-engines and avionics exceeding $10-$12 billion in value (or as much as 40 per cent of the 2012–13 defence budget).[87]

The cumulative experience and record of defence purchases and lack of defence industrial progress have finally begun to impact the government. There is greater willingness to concede that increased FDI to the extent even of 100 per cent may fire up the local defence industry.[88] Defence units fully owned by foreign majors could generate high-value employment, catalyze innovation in the country, upskill the Indian workforce and ease the adoption of best-practices by a process of osmosis by the Indian industry at large. Further, Indian engineers and managers exposed to First World working conditions and best practices could, in turn, accelerate the forming of an Indian mittelstand as has occurred with respect to the Agni missile and SSBN projects. In 2006, the Manmohan Singh government introduced the 'Make' category of weapons systems and mooted the possibility of the MOD bearing 80 per cent of the development cost of indigenously-produced military-use items. The BJP Defence Minister Manohar Parrikar, however, has heeded the concerns of the Federation of Indian Chambers of Commerce and Industry (FICCI) that existing rules may end up perversely favouring foreign vendors by providing them incentives to set up shop in the country. FICCI believes foreign arms companies would use the loopholes in the 2008 Defence Procurement Procedure (DPP) issued by MOD to establish joint ventures (JVs) with Indian business houses as sleeping partners on the permissible 40 per cent–51per cent basis and get the R&D funding from MOD as stipulated, and realize the fear expressed in the 2008 DPP that Indian Industry would thus become a 'conduit for entry of foreign companies without any significant value addition by the Indian partner'. FICCI, further apprehended that products sold by such JVs would come laden with end-use certification requirements and other oppressive conditions imposed by source countries to throttle the possibility of exporting these India-produced goods. It also sought modification in the MOD's disbursement method of the 80 per cent of the project cost keyed to companies meeting technology development milestones. FICCI has recommended that the 'tried and tested methodology' adopted by the Indian Space Research Organization (ISRO) for disbursing payments through escrow accounts be followed to alleviate the problem of high interest on working capital. Parrikar apparently sees merit in such arguments and has promised 'to make [a defence

industrial] policy more attractive for Indian [private] companies'
(Shukla 2014).

The new thinking coursing through the MOD notwithstanding,
the under-developed state of Indian defence industry continues to
provide the military with the prime rationale for importing foreign
hardware and for accusing critics of 'undermining national security'.[89] This agglomeration of political-bureaucratic-DPSU-military
interests preventing the rapid growth of the private sector Indian
defence industry as the means of attaining self-sufficiency in armaments, labelled the 'military-corruption complex' by a former MOD
bureaucrat, is still strong.[90]

How has China, which started with greater handicaps than India,
streak so far ahead? According to a recent study by a former IAF
officer comparing the Indian and Chinese industries, the Chinese
'leapfrogged' technology, 'optimized [their] resources by smartly
investing on R&D in the denial regime rather than trying to reinvent
the wheel by investing in the entire spectrum of technology', and by
securing technology 'developed elsewhere either through alliances or
by subterfuge and then bridging the gap through internal R&D on
that part of the technology spectrum not available through either
means'. Moreover, China, the study notes, has 'effectively leveraged
access to civil technology to spin in technology' into the military
sphere, and used 'Commercialization and expanding trade of low-
cost conventional arms [to] not only narrow the existing qualitative
gap but also to augment capability for future capacity development'.[91] In other words, it did everything right that India didn't
do. The one thing India can learn from the Chinese experience is
for DRDO, which is busy doing too many things, most of them
of the 're-inventing the wheel' variety, to do any particular thing
well. It wastes time and resources and ends up eliciting smirks, not
kudos, from the military. The BJP government is aware of DRDO's
spotty record over the years and seems determined to take corrective
measures. In his first address to the DRDO Prime Minister Modi's
messaging was stern: give up the 'chalta hai' (easygoing) attitude, he
warned, and set in train policies to 'weed out dead wood'.[92] A chas-
tened DRDO chief Avinash Chander said 'We hope to turn over a
new leaf' and indicated the organization's focus hereafter on 'defence
indigenization and exports' because of the new government's putting

a 'premium on' it.[93] The BJP government seems to mean business because even before this meeting with the defence scientists, industrial de-licensing was announced, and the list of items requiring prior government approval for manufacture in the country was slashed by 60 per cent. The private sector welcomed this move to prune the licensing list 'to the bare minimum', which Baba Kalyani, Chairman of the Committee on Defence Industry at the Confederation of Indian Industry and head of Bharat Forge Ltd, said would help India to rise from 'the bottom of the [defence industrial] value chain'.[94]

DRDO should perhaps restrict itself to funding high-value research in academic institutions and professional R&D centres in frontier areas of technology and be the 'catalyst of innovation' in the manner that DARPA (Defence Advanced Research Projects Agency) is in the United States, leaving the designing, developing and producing weapons and weapons platforms to private sector companies tapping into existing DPSU resources.[95] A start is being made to move DRDO in this direction. In Fiscal 2014, Rs 100–Rs 200 crores out of the DRDO budget of Rs 15,000 crores were spent on funding such research activity. Beginning in Fiscal 2015, fully 10 per cent of its annual budget will be set aside for cutting edge research projects carried out in nine 'centres of excellence' with the most advanced facilities for experimentation and research being constructed on the campuses of the Indian Institutes of Technology (IITs), the Indian Institute of Science, Bangalore, the National Institutes of Information Technology, and other select universities and regional engineering colleges. These centres are to become magnets for the best and the brightest among graduate students, including from abroad. Thus, Jadavpur University already has a metallurgy centre researching shape-changing metal skins for futuristic aerial combat vehicles, and IITs in Mumbai and Chennai are sharing a laboratory and other resources to develop pulse detonation propulsion systems.[96]

The fact is decades of schizophrenic policies have loaded India with curious capabilities. It is able to wage strategic war with home-grown nuclear weapons and long range delivery platforms more effectively than it can fight conventional conflict, in which foreign supplier states can obtain the outcome they want on the regional battlefield by calibrating the flow of spares and servicing support for imported weapons platforms employed by Indian forces.[97] But because the likelihood of conventional hostilities in proximal areas is infinitely higher than of strategic conflict or nuclear war, India's growing arms dependency makes the country vulnerable even as, paradoxically, it has grown stronger in terms of strategic weaponry. The state of the Indian defense industry is to blame for this situation and the government is responsible for it. But because it is a self-inflicted impairment, it can be rapidly righted by a guiding vision and coordinated policies. But the military's deep bias against Indian-made military goods won't easily disappear. The former DRDO head, Chander, alluded to this last saying that his organization 'is more challenged by lack of trust in its capabilities rather than lack of capability'. Whatever or whosoever is to blame for the present condition, the outcome of 'India's abject dependence on foreign sources for military hardware...every [imported] piece placing [the country] at the mercy of the seller nation for 30–40 years thereafter', wrote Admiral Prakash in the wake of the Agusta Westland deal implicating a former air force chief, is a 'threat to national security' 'more toxic' than the corruption related to defence deals. [98] Unwilling to mobilize the private sector and unable to improve the working of DPSUs, which enjoy powerful political patronage, the government has ended up piquantly with a poor country like India sustaining the defence industries of several advanced countries—Russia, Israel, France, U.K. Italy, and increasingly the United States, with an endless series of expensive buys.[99] In the process, the possibility of being jerked around at will by supplier states has only increased. Of course, by becoming such a large importer India has counter-leverage and, by withholding custom, can threaten the evisceration of certain sections of foreign defence industry. For example, Italy fell in line and returned two of its Marines to face trial in an Indian court for controversially killing Indian fisher-men, for fear that not doing so would jeopardize defense deals worth some $12 billion in the pipeline.[100] But it will not work in the face of the Indian military's desperate needs.

Reforms by Committee

Mindful of the ramifications of a floundering defence industry, the government set up a number of high-level committees to recommend correctives, such as the one chaired by former Finance Secretary Vijay

L. Kelkar. Its report submitted to government in April 2005 recommended preparation of a 15-year long-term acquisition plan, sharing this information with the industry at large, identifying entry points for the private sector in the acquisition process, evolving policy framework to promote participation of Small and Medium Enterprises in defence production, setting up a new professional agency for defence acquisition, providing defence research and development opportunities for DRDO and industry, promoting transparency in decision making, encouraging optimum utilization of existing capacity in the country, working out Request For Proposals (RFP) to include an Offset Clause for contracts valued over Rs. 300 crores, and re-replacing the concept of 'Negative List' overseen by MEA for Defence exports with an Export Marketing Organization. But it also advised accrediting and fostering of 'Raksha Udyog Ratnas' ('defence public sector diamonds') from among the DPSUs.[101] It therefore indicated an unwillingness to majorly shake up and change the prevailing procurement system reinforced by the bad work culture and low productivity levels in DPSUs. With some DPSUs designated as Ratnas (or jewels) and out of the pale of scrutiny, moreover, other DPSUs too resisted change. Persisting with the DPSUs, the Congress Party defence minister A.K. Antony's decision to invest Rs 15,000 crores into modernizing and technologically updating the Ordnance Factory Board (OFB) and its 41 factories, sent a chill through private sector companies which had erected new plants in the hope of getting spillover business the creaky OFB couldn't handle. The problems of high-staffing and low productivity in the public sector are accepted as liability and the explanation offered is that modernization would result in the trimming of the labour force to 50,000 from its current strength of 150,000, which last has resulted in 'abysmally low' worker productivity of Rs. 12.5 lakh per annum on sales mostly to the Indian military of Rs 11,214 crores ($2.04 billion). Injection by these means of new production technology is seen as lifebuoy by the DPSUs generally, except OFB units have found innovating foreign technology secured under Transfer of Technology (TOT) regimes beyond them. This is evident from their R&D spend of zero in Fiscal 2007–08 increasing to a mere Rs 39.95 crores by 2010–11, even as the monopoly provider to the Indian armed forces the OFB profits grew from Rs 590.01 crores on earnings of Rs 6,937.81 crores in

2007–08 to Rs 1,171.70 crores on earnings of Rs 11,214 crores four years later. The production infrastructure of the OFB, moreover is so antiquated, it is dangerous to the workers. The process of manually filling shell casings with chemical explosive material at the Gun and Shell Factory in Cossipore (near Kolkata), for example, has seemingly not changed from the time the British first set up this unit in 1802! The variable quality of the ammunition so produced, moreover, is a perennial peeve of the artillery.[102] But DPSUs are waking up to the coming competition; they know the private sector will make life difficult for them with 'severe unrealistic predatory pricing'. 'While deep pockets can replicate physical infrastructure', Rear Admiral Shekhar Mital (Retd), Managing Director of the Goa Shipyard Ltd. specializing in building offshore patrol vessels and recently modernized with a Rs 700 crore government subvention, was confident private sector competitors 'cannot generate the required knowledge set, which [GSL and other public sector shipyards have] gained over last 58 years'.[103] But this supposed strength is a fast depleting asset when confronted by more innovative firms bent on minimizing labour and operating costs and turning a profit to beat DPSUs burdened with a massive workforce and a languorous work ethic.

The license production oriented DPSUs ruling the roost are at once the reason for, and the result of, the import-driven procurement system in place. In the new millennium the Indian government, mindful that such a system ill-serves the national interest, constituted several committees (headed variously by Vijay Kelkar, N.S. Sisodia, Rama Rao, V.K. Misra, etc.) to chart a road map for a national defence industry in which the private sector is integrated into the procurement process. But the imperviousness of the extant system to change is such that MOD is yet to implement any of their recommendations, such as the Kelkar Committee's suggestion to use laid down criteria to accord the privileged 'Rashtra Udyog Ratna' status to private sector majors enabling them to bid for defence contracts, or the Sisodia committee's advice that the defence industry be brought in at the stage of writing the Qualitative Requirements of weapons systems by the armed services to escape the laughable practice of aggregating the best features of weapons systems available in the global market into QRs (Behera 2013: 64–66). The bureaucratic instinct to tinker and the tug of loyalty towards DPSUs has eventuated in the private sector's entry into defence production in fits and starts, even when the situation is crying out for reforms which is evident from figures showing the import dependency five decades into licensed production. In 2006–2011, the imported content of India-built weapons systems actually increased from 52.07 per cent to 61.49 per cent, in value from Rs. 10,071.36 crores to Rs 18,457.18 crores. In the same years, the sourcing of high-value avionics, assemblies and components by HAL, for example, went up from 67.04 per cent to a still heftier 69.65 per cent.[104] By 2014, the import content had reached an eye-popping 90 per cent plus level.[105] It bares the myth of growingly indigenized defence production. If the local share of the procurement budget is to increase from 58 per cent to 90 per cent in five years, which the Kelkar Committee thought eminently doable and if achieved would have large economic multiplier impact—acceleration in the manufacturing sector growth of 8–14 per cent, generation of 120,000 to 200,000 new jobs, and savings by way of import substitution adding up to as much as Rs. 4,000 crores annually (Behera 2013: 62). These were projected impact figures at the time the Kelkar Committee drafted its report in 2005–2006. Ten years later the desirable economic effects could be much larger.

Creating Competing Giant Defence-Industrial Complexes

Faced with hard choices, the Indian government invariably opts for the easier solution involving less rearranging of the prevailing order. In that case, New Delhi could choose to invest more monies in modernizing DPSUs in the hope they will become commercial-minded and productive. Except there is no indication the DPSU 'navratnas' and ordnance factories with flashier shop floors will not operate in the same old slovenly way, and fail to raise the military's confidence in indigenous wares and loosen the stranglehold of foreign arms suppliers. Alternative schemes for a refurbished defence industry have been detailed. A private research unit in Mumbai called the Planning & Design Lab, for instance, has proposed establishing six 'defence economic zones' along the lines of the exports-oriented Special Economic Zones enjoying similar financial incentives and tax-breaks. Located all over the country, they would emerge as regional industrial and talent hubs, and produce complex military hardware economically by mustering 'frugal engineering' methods (Puntambekar 2014). It isn't clear though how the existing DRDO facilities, ordnance factories, and other DPSUs are to be integrated into this model.

To obtain real synergy, however, private sector capacities and capabilities will have to be institutionally and physically merged with the more heavily built up and better endowed public sector DRDO, DPSUs, and Ordnance Factories. An ambitious plan for completely reordering the defence sector was drafted for the Technology Review sub-committee of the (first) National Security Advisory Board in 1998–99 as part of the first Strategic Review.[106] The proposal suggests dividing all defence-related R&D, manufacturing, and testing facilities in the public sector into two capability-wise roughly equal defence-industrial combines. The two largest and leading private sector firms—Tata and Larsen & Toubro—with the highest reputation, industrial versatility, and proven track records would be put in charge of them. The private sector leaders would be free to attach their own units and capacities as well as draw other private sector companies in the country into their respective folds to create two mega defence-industrial complexes with inherent economies of scale. They would then compete for procurement contracts, with MOD funding any new project to the stage of development of the prototype (something mooted in the 2008 Defence Production Procedure) when a run-off conducted by a newly founded agency within MOD with parliamentary oversight, and staffed by experts inclusive of armed service officers, would be held, with the winning Combine getting the contract. This new umpiring and selection agency would be along the lines of the French General Directorate of Armament (*Direction generale de l'armement*) that the Kelkar Committee recommended. The scoring system would be deliberately weighted to favour the prototype with more indigenized content by value. Other than participating in this agency as project managers and as liaison with the concerned armed service, the role of the military officers would be restricted to writing realistic General Staff Quality Requirements for the armaments the services require in cooperation with representatives from these two complexes. How and from where these two giant combines secure the technologies for any project—from within the country or abroad, will be solely their concern as would the choice of a foreign partner in case the combines deemed such partnership useful. The MOD will not otherwise involve itself in any way in the functioning of, or in the decision-making by, the combines. The significant aspect of this scheme is that the Indian state will continue to own the DPSU, DRDO, and OFB physical assets, facilities, and installations, inclusive of the land, and earn revenue from the rent to be negotiated for each of the public sector facility, and a commercially viable negotiated royalty payment, again negotiated, for the products manufactured. The private sector companies that create new technology and get patents would be allowed to fully retain them, and profit from them including by commercializing them. This is government in the role of an enlightened facilitator and landlord which, as owner of the physical plants, will be responsible for periodically upgrading the designing and production wherewithal, such as Computer-Aided Design/Computer-Aided-Manufacturing systems, multi-axes lathes, retooled production jigs, etc. In short, the government gets out of the defence business altogether, but stays on as a landlord and owner in perpetuity so the public investment in these properties does not pass into private hands. It will defang the Leftist arguments against privatizing the valuable DPSUs. This model is derived from the American defence industry where many of the most important defence industrial assets are government-owned, earning the U.S. Treasury rental and other revenue. The upside of this model is minimization of corruption, with the two corporate Combine leaders incentivized, under threat of stringent penalties, to zero it out by following ever more transparent practices and procedures. Because profit was scorned in socialist India the private sector in the country did not bother with creating the necessary defence industrial capacity and talent pool. That has now changed.

With market forces and the logic of fair competition becoming more acceptable, it will ensure low unit prices, beget the best technology for the defence rupee, encourage arms exports and, most importantly, generate profit to make these combines economically viable.[107] These complexes, moreover, will be free to import foreign engineering and managerial talent in order to upgrade the quality of the local managers and engineers. Skilled manpower in niche areas is now available in plenty in the United States and Europe where austerity measures have compelled companies to lay off employees. Over the past few years 160,000 jobs have been lost in the U.S. defence industry alone. Nearly 750,000 are connected directly with the defence industrial sector in the Western countries, which is experiencing a recession.[108] India would attract top engineering and managerial talent because the complexes would pay them top dollar. Foreign arms sales and exports by the two Combines would be facilitated by government policies, and the MEA tasked with assisting them to sell their goods in the Third World. There will be a ready market for India-made weapons systems because the militaries in many of these developing states look up to the Indian armed services, what with expanding Indian government programmes to train military officers from Asia, Africa, and Latin America. Exposed to Indian military equipment in the Indian military training institutions the visiting officers would be encouraged to consider acquiring them for their own services back home and which weaponry could be made available at economical cost.[109] This is a viable plan and will help the country reach self-sufficiency in arms fast. All it needs is a government with the foresight and the gumption to upend the extant system.[110] The Modi government seems to be displaying some such initiative by implementing, perhaps on an experimental basis, the model sketched above centering on competition and profit and involving two industrial consortia to develop and produce a 'battlefield management system' worth as much as Rs 50,000 crores.[111] It conforms with the thinking to optimize the indigenous capacities in private and public sectors, mooted by the L&T Group Executive Chairman A.M. Naik. He has talked about authorizing DRDO labs, DPSUs and individual ordnance factories 'to form partnerships with private organizations of their choice for cutting-edge technology development, while simultaneously allowing use of their facilities on commercial terms by companies in the field'.[112] For the more advanced markets, the combines could follow the path, as McKinsey Report advised, the Indian auto-components industry did to penetrate Western markets, by making and exporting spares and ancillaries.[113] Exports are essential because the projected outgo from arms imports are in excess of Rs 3,50,000 crores—money that could consolidate Indian industry, help it find markets abroad and spur the national economy instead of helping foreign defence industries prosper.[114]

A nation that does not make its own armaments will not only not be a great power, it will have its national interests and foreign and defence policies routinely infringed by big powers, and its security made hostage to the passing whims and interests of vendor states. Much has changed, but not this basic weakness in India's hard power standing. It also diminishes great power ambition. The country can 'buy its way' to an impressive military, but it will only be like putting up a façade. 'India's almost masochistic ability to snarl up foreign defence procurement—alongside the institutional hurdles to successful indigenous production', writes James Hardy of the *Jane's Defense Weekly* 'could have more serious side effects than just obvious reputational damage'.[115]

Notes

1. For the military's complaints against the civilian MOD bureaucracy, see Singh (2013: 314–23).

2. See Prakash. 'India as a 21st Century Power', available at: http://southasiamonitor.org/detail.php?type=emerging&nid=5147.

3. An innocuous instance of how this works: A new organization—National Intelligence Grid (NIG)—authorized at the highest level—has been established as a platform to scour social networks, process and collate terrorism and other internal security-related information and data coursing through them, and provide real-time alerts to police and intelligence agencies. It was provided a piece of land in the National Capital Region for its permanent facilities. The MOD officials, however, would not sanction funds for a two-level underground garage that was proposed by NIG command, who factored into the construction plans future growth of this outfit. It was ruled to be in 'excess of need' and additional funds were denied, despite express approval by the Home Minister. The civil servants who were bypassed cussedly kept exhuming the additional expenditure issue to stop the construction from getting underway until the Home Minister finally put his foot down with a direct and unequivocal order to the recalcitrant bureaucrats. A senior NIG official.

4. The ex-Cabinet Secretary Naresh Chandra chaired task force on national security recommended by way of reforming decision-making, the cross-staffing of military officers in MOD starting at the middle Director-level posts. It was rejected. See Pranabh Dhal Samanta 'Govt rejects Chandra panel proposal for a four-star general', *Indian Express*, May 3, 2014. A serving army General is quoted as saying that 'Civilian primacy over the military has,

unfortunately, morphed into bureaucratic control...the political leadership [meanwhile] twiddles its thumbs in masterly inaction.' Quote in Rajat Pandit, 'Civil-military ties worsening?', *Times of India*, October 7, 2013. 'The lack of bureaucratic expertise in defense affairs', writes Anit Mukherjee of the Nanyang Technological University, Singapore, 'is problem inherited from the colonial era, with its emphasis on a generalist cadre instead of a specialist one. [This means that] in the absence of in-depth knowledge and hindered by information asymmetries, most bureaucrats predictably, have focused on the process of decision-making instead of the outcome. Further, lacking the expertise to challenge the military on its logic makes it difficult to arbitrate between competing parochial [service] interests.' Quote in Shashank Joshi, 'India's Military Instrument: A Doctrine Stillborn', at http://shashankjoshifiles. wordpress.com/2011/09/indias-military-instrument-2011.pdf.

5. See Sharma (2013). Jaswant Singh, a cabinet member who in the Vajpayee government held many portfolios, including External Affairs, Defense, and Finance, blames this state of affairs on what he calls 'psychological disarming' as a result of Mahatma Gandhi's stress on nonviolence combining with 'a militarily illiterate and untrusting civilian control of the armed forces.'

6. Personal communication, a former service chief.

7. See Jaswant Singh. *India at Risk*, 236.

8. Chairman, HAL, R.K. Tyagi said 'more than 70% of manufacturing needs of IAF is done by HAL.' Quote in 'HAL and IAF to work for make in India', *Whispers in the Corridors.Com* (undated, but likely November-end, 2014), at http://www.whispersinthecorridors.in/ReadArticle. php?id=41404&table=whispers

9. Air Marshal A.L. Matheswaran (Retd), who retired as Deputy Chief of the Integrated Defence Staff, said the L-1 system 'had ruined the [Indian] defence industry'. See http://www.stratpost.com/ video-vayu-stratpost-air-power-roundtable-ii.

10. According to documents tabled in Parliament by Defence Minister Manohar Parrikar, Indian companies supplied goods amounting to only 3–4 per cent of the military's capital acquisitions budget in 2011–2013, compared to 56.69 per cent spent on imports, with the DPSUs in license manufacture mode making up the remaining 41.84 per cent. See Rajat Pandit, 'Private firms in India play a measly role in arming forces', *Times of India*, December 10, 2014.

11. 'Strength for Peace', Larsen & Toubro brochure.

12. Senior industry source.

13. See Shishir Arya, 'INSAS rifle may be on its way out; *Times of India*, November 15, 2012.

14. Yatish Yadav, 'Ministry's Glowing Tribute to Antony', *The Indian Express*, March 16, 2014.

15. Parthasarathi is a former Science & Technology adviser to Prime Minister Indira Gandhi.

16. Bharat Karnad, 'Zero for DRDO', *Asian Age*, April 26, 2013 and at www.bharatkarnad.com

17. Air Vice Marshal (Retd.) Manmohan Bahadur, 'How not to arm a nation', *Indian Express*, October 5, 2013.

18. A DRDO official at the senior most level.

19. Bharat Karnad, 'Parrikar's priority', *New Indian Express*, November 14, 2014 http://www.newindianexpress.com/columns/Parrikars-Priority/2014/11/14/article2521690.ece and on the author's blog, http://bharatkarnad.com/2014/11/15/parrikars-priority/.

20. Consider the 'high concurrency' U.S. Joint Strike Fighter F-35 Lightening II programme. See Vucetic (2014).

21. For a brief history of the Indian Navy's ship design capabilities, see Vice Admiral A.K. Singh (Retd), 'Indigenous Defence Production: No Quick Fixes', *Extraordinary and Plenipotentiary Diplomatist*, Annual edition, 2014.

22. 'Russia places Rs 54-crore order for procuring 34 radar computers', *Economic Times*, February 8, 2013.

23. This was when these laws were being tested at the U.S. testing facility at the Wright-Patterson Air Force base in Ohio, and which systems were confiscated by the U.S. government in the wake of the 1998 Indian nuclear tests. In the event, even more effective CLAWS have since been devised for the Tejas. See the interview of Dr. Kota Harinarayana, former director of the Tejas program at 'Tejas: India's Light Combat Aircraft', http://tejas.gov.in/featured_articles/dr_kota_harinarayana.html (undated).

24. When the land version of the Brahmos was first tested in 2008 the Indian Army officers couldn't believe the performance and called in Russian experts to witness the subsequent two tests held in Pokhran test range, and they too were 'dumbstruck' by the S-maneuver pulled by the missile on the way to hitting the targets dead-on. Source: Missile expert.

25. Personal communication, former head of the SSBN project.

26. Sources in the Agni missile programme. For an authoritative study on the Indian rocket and missile programmes, see Nagappa (2014).

27. Karnad, *India's Nuclear Policy*, 44–5.

28. Ibid, 77–83.

29. http://www.stratpost.com/video-vayu-stratpost-air-power-roundtable-ii

30. Senior military and bureaucratic sources.

31. For an account of how German talent spurred the U.S. and Soviet missile programs, see Stoiko (1970 : 70–77).

32. Karnad, *Nuclear Weapons and Indian Security*, 186.

33. The source for German interest in HF-24: B.M. Malik, who retired as a Manager, HAL.

34. 'Indian Air Force Darin Upgrades for Sepecat Jaguar', *Defence Aviation*, December 2011 at http://www.defenceaviation.com/2011/12/indian-air-force-darin-upgrades-for-sepecat-jaguar.html.

35. Dr Raj Mahindra, the lead Indian designer in the HF-24 project, interview, March 1991; B.M. Malik, Manager (ret.) HAL. Air Marshal (ret.) A.K. Singh vouches for the excellent low-level flying attributes of the Marut HF-24, which he flew as a young pilot; personal communication.

36. A former Air Marshal; one of the very few IAF brass keen on indigenous combat aircraft.

37. For the stepmotherly treatment accorded Tejas and its heavier MMRCA variant under development, see Bharat Karnad, 'Stop wasteful military deals', *New Indian Express*, November 1, 2013. This article set off a firestorm of criticism against the Indian government's attitude. For the learned, technical, responses to this article see www.bharatkarnad.com

38. Pushpindar Singh, agent in India for various German aviation companies including Dornier, at the *Vayu Aerospace Seminar* on 'Air Power 2014', for video in three parts, see http://www.stratpost.com/video-vayu-stratpost-air-power-roundtable-i, http://www.stratpost.com/video-vayu-stratpost-air-power-roundtable-ii, http://www.stratpost.com/video-vayu-stratpost-air-power-roundtable-iii.

39. http://www.stratpost.com/video-vayu-stratpost-air-power-roundtable-ii.

40. Senior DRDO official.

41. See his 'The Triple-Trap, Dual-Use and the Single Reform', paper presented at a seminar in Delhi on June 10, 2006; text emailed the author by Dr Siddhartha.

42. 'With eye on exports, Tejas on display in Bahrain air show', PTI, *Economic Times*, January 15, 2014.

43. Senior DRDO official.

44. See the revealing presentation by Air Marshal Matheswaran on this subject at a seminar in which Air Chief Marshal S.P. Tyagi participated and during whose tenure as IAF Chief, the MMRCA concept was created. Matheswaran was the Assistant Chief of the Air Staff (Plans) tasked with drawing up the MMRCA specs. http://www.stratpost.com/video-vayu-stratpost-air-power-roundtable-ii .

45. Interview.

46. Bharat Karnad, 'Impending MMRCA waste', *New Indian Express*, October 3, 2014, http://bharatkarnad.com/2014/10/03/impending-mmrca-waste/.

47. Dassault expects to have 50 per cent of the production of the 108 aircraft to be license produced in India to be actually sourced from some 500 French companies and involving 7,000 jobs. See Hassan (2012). Also see Bharat Karnad, 'Indian alternative to Rafale', *New Indian Express*, November 1, 2013.

48. For a comparison of the DPSUs and the private sector defense industry and the reason for the latter suffering stepchild treatment at the hands of the Indian MOD, see Sruthijith K.K., 'Private Sector Can Take Aim, But Can't Shoot', *Economic Times*, March 19, 2013.

49. Rajat Pandit, 'High cost of Mirage-2000 upgrade raises eyebrows', *Times of India*, March 5, 2013.

50. Karnad, *Nuclear Weapons and Indian Security*, pp. 185–6.

51. The opposition BJP leader Yashwant Sinha believes such costing is merely a device to raise the acquisition costs and to lock the country into purchasing inferior equipment. See 'Sinha questions change in defense procurement policy', *Times of India*, March 25, 2013.

52. Interview.

53. Interview.

54. http://www.stratpost.com/video-vayu-stratpost-air-power-roundta-ble-ii .

55. Interview.

56. Bharat Karnad, 'India's submarine production', *New Indian Express*, August 23, 2014, also at http://bharatkarnad.com/2013/08/23/indias-submarine-production/; Rahul Singh, 'India okays Rs 55,000 cr submarine purchase', *Hindustan Times*, December 5, 2012.

57. E-mail correspondence, April 30–August 3, 2013.

58. Personal communication.

59. In anticipation of winning a fairly conducted contest, L&T has already 'built a Rs 4,500-crore shipyard-cum-port at Katupalli, near Ennore in Tamil Nadu, with sufficient draught and capacity to build any size of submarine. It has also established a submarine design centre in Chennai and a virtual reality centre in Mumbai. For good measure, it created a Rs 500-crore fabrication unit at Talegaon, near Pune; and a Rs 350-crore unit at Coimbatore for engineering missile parts. Locating Katupalli shipyard on the east coast was a smart move by L&T, since that distributes the risk of disruption to production.' See Shukla (2014).

60. Senior DRDO official.

61. India successfully tested Nirbhay, able to fly at tree-top heights, that during its second test-firing climbed to an altitude of 4.8 kms before diving

to target at maximum range. See Y. Mallikarjun, 'India successfully tests fires cruise missile "Nirbhay"', *Hindu*, October 20, 2014.

62. Bharat Karnad, 'Parrikar's priority', *New Indian Express*, November 114, 2014.

63. Interview.

64. Senior DRDO, MOD, and military officials.

65. Personal communication.

66. For example, the case of the Pilatus trainer purchased from Switzerland by IAF. See Ajai Shukla, 'IAF to HAL: Build Swiss trainer aircraft, don't develop your own', *Business Standard*, October 14, 2013.

67. Meeting with author.

68. Seshadri Chatterji, 'Govt may divest 10 percent stake in HAL', *Hindustan Times*, November 8, 2012.

69. Senior DRDO official.

70. Senior DRDO official.

71. Senior DRDO official.

72. The order book for the $97 billion Tata Group with 14 defence companies, for instance, now totals $1.3 billion with defence sales going up from $283 million in 2013 by 40 per cent $400 million a year late, inclusive of a $260 million contract to upgrade and modernize IAF air fields (beating out Selex of Italy) and a $37 million sale by Tata Motors of specialized vehicles to the United Nations. See Raghuvanshi (2014).

73. 'India Can Export Fighter Planes, Missiles, Says Defence Research Chief', PTI, *NDTV News*, June 22, 2014, www.ndtv.com/article/india/india-can-export-gighter-planes-missiles-says-defence-research-chief/

74. Interview.

75. Interview.

76. N.C. Bipindra, 'No One to Spare a Thought for Naval Warship Upgrades', *New Indian Express*, April 6, 2014.

77. Bharat Karnad, 'Submarine import trap', *Asian Age*, February 4, 2013; Dassault Systems has rated L&T's submarine design center a 'Center of Excellence' for exploiting the CATIA design software suite, virtual reality software, product lifecycle management tools and aspects of intelligent modeling capability. Refer L&T brochure—*Meeting a Naval Challenge: Scale, Speed, Sophistication*, L&T Shipbuilding.

78. Rajat Pandit, 'Delays force Navy to drop demand for foreign submarines', *Times of India*, September 8, 2014.

79. The 41 warships under construction by type—1 aircraft carrier (INS Vikrant), 2 Kolkata-class missile destroyers, 4 Shivalik-class stealth missile destroyers, 6 Scorpene submarines, 3 anti-submarine corvettes, 8 landing craft utility (for amphibious/littoral warfare), 5 offshore patrol vessels, 3 training ships, 5 survey vessels, and 4 water-jet fast attack craft.

See 'Adding muscle to the maritime security', *Times of India*, December 4, 2014.

80. L&T, for instance, has invested some Rs 5,000 crore in its shipbuilding complexes. See Cukoo Paul, 'L&T: Armed but not commissioned', *Forbes India*, September 29, 2014, http://forbesindia.com/printcontent/38703

81. Quote in Anantha Krishnan M, 'Tyagi takes control of HAL; Pallam says "action"', *New Indian Express*, March 3, 2012.

82. See Rajat Pandit, 'Private firms in India play a measly role in arming forces', *Times of India*, December 10, 2014.

83. Thus, the Tata company will buy 16 Airbus C-295s—medium range turbo-prop planes for tactical airlift, and license produce 40 more in India, with this deal costing Rs 13,000 crores. See Rajat Pandit, 'Govt call on Tata-Airbus bid on Saturday', *Times of India*, November 20, 2014.

84. A former director of the Central Intelligence Bureau, A.P. Mukherjee, recounts that Prime Minister Rajiv Gandhi, who was tainted with the scam involving the Swedish Bofors gun, told him that his Congress party needed to divert commissions offered by foreign arm companies, that were previously grabbed by the 'collusive nexus' of corrupt 'middlemen, ministers, and bureaucrats', to meet its election and other expenses. See Ritu Sarin, 'Rajiv Gandhi told me to use arms deal payoffs for party funds: Ex-CBI chief', *Indian Express*, November 13, 2013.

85. Defense Minister A.K. Antony was of the view that 'Allowing foreign companies to set up manufacturing/assembly plants would be a retrograde step as it will stymie the indigenous design and development and our dependence on foreign countries…for modern weapons will get perpetuated.' See 'Antony opposes proposal to hike FDI in defence to 40 per cent', *Indian Express*, July 4, 2013.

86. 'Antony opposes proposal to hike FDI in defence to 49 per cent', *Indian Express*, July 4, 2014.

87. See the statements by Air Marshal P.P. Reddy, Director-General Flight Safety and Inspection, IAF in Sawant (2013).

88. Amitabh Kant, secretary, Department of Industrial Policy Promotions, said the government may be open to 100 per cent FDI in the defence sector. See his interview in *Economic Times*, April 21, 2014.

89. See the op/ed piece by Air Vice Marshal Arjun Subramaniam, 'Undermining national security', *New Indian Express*, November 7, 2013 at http://newindianexpress.com/opinion/Undermining-national-security/2013/11/07/article1876105.ece. It was in response to the author's article questioning the IAF's choice of the French Rafale as MMRCA when a bigger, heavier variant of the Tejas is under development but the IAF is not enthusiastic about. See 'Stop wasteful military deals', *New Indian Express*,

November 1, 2013 at http://newindianexpress.com/opinion/Stop-wasteful-military-deals/2013/11/01/article1866740.ece.

90. Amitabha Pande, 'The military-corruption complex', *Indian Express*, February 21, 2013.

91. Vishal Nigam, 'Decoding China's Aviation Industry—Comparative Narrative with India', 8, 12-13; text emailed to the author.

92. Bhavna Aurora, 'Prime Minister Favours Detailed Review of DRDO', *Economic Times*, August 23, 2014.

93. Rahul Singh, 'India focus on export of 15 arms systems', *Hindustan Times*, September 14, 2014.

94. 'Boost for Defence as Licensed Items List Cut by 60%', *Economic Times*, June 26, 2014.

95. Arati Prabhakar, an NRI and director of U.S. DARPA, explained that her agency's job is to work with 'science and technology across government agencies, universities and the private sector...pursuing efforts to catalyze the next generation' military-use technologies. For the text of her talk at the Center for International Security and Cooperation, Stanford University, May 14, 2014, http://cisac.stanford.edu/news/darpa_director_arati_prabhakar_we_are_catalyst_for_innovation_20140514/.

96. Senior DRDO official.

97. With the onset of the war with Pakistan in September 1965, the US government clamped an arms embargo on both countries, bringing the conflict to an abrupt end. See Wolpert (1990: 77). The Soviet Union pressured India against attacking West Pakistan after subduing East Pakistan in the 1971 War. See Dobrynin (1995: 236).

98. See Prakash. 2013. 'India's Achilles Heel', *Times of India*, March 14.

99. Frank Jack Daniel, 'Eyes on Defence Deals, Western Powers Court Modi', Reuters, *Economic Times*, June 30, 2014. The failure by the European aerospace consortium EADS to sell the Eurofighter as MMRCA especially to India may lead to its production close-down by 2018. See David Oliver, 'Another Peace Dividend for the Defence Inustry?', *Indian Defence Review*, March 23, 2014 at www.indiandefencereview.com/print/?print_post_id=14531.

100. Jayanth Jacob, 'Rs 60,000 crore arms business at stake, Italy sends back marines', *Hindustan Times*, March 23, 2013.

101. 'Kelkar Committee submits report on defence acquisition', Press Information Bureau, Government of India, April 5, 2005 at http://pib.nic.in/newsite/erelease.aspx?relid=8386.

102. 'MoD's massive Rs 15,000-cr upgrade for ordnance factories', Indian Defence, April 8, 2013, at http://indiandefence.com/threads/modas-massive-rs-15-000-cr-upgrade-for-ordnance-factories.25540/.

103. See his interview, *Hindustan Times*, July 14, 2014.

104. Ibid, Tables 2.3 & 2.4, 51–53.

105. A Senior HAL source.

106. It was a paper written by the author as member of the first NSAB and of the Technology Review sub-committee chaired by Dr Roddam Narsimhan, and created considerable interest at the time but was not followed-up by the government with any concrete decisions and actions.

107. A recent Pentagon report on the U.S. military procurement system pointed out several factors impacting the acquisitions process, chief among them being the centrality of the profit motive and the need for at least two bidders to obtain better cost, price, and schedule. See *Performance of the Defense Acquisition System: 2014 Annual Report* [Washington, DC: U.S. Department of Defense, June 13, 2013], http://www.acq.osd.mil/docs/ Performance-of-Defense-Acquisition-System-2014.pdf.

108. David Oliver, 'Another Peace Dividend for the Defence Industry?', *Indian Defence Review*, March 23, 2014 at www.indiandefencereview.com/ print/?print_post_id=14531. Importing foreign talent is a means recommended by the McKinsey Report ' "A bright future" to speedily ramp up and improve the indigenous talent pool.

109. Dipanjan Roy Chaudhury, 'Global strategic move: India increases defence trainings in Asia, Africa and Latin America', *Economic Times*, September 5, 2014.

110. The BJP leader Narendra Modi is clear the procurement system and the defence industry need a makeover. 'I think the time has come when domestic production of defence equipment and machinery needs to be seriously incentivized by the government in a carefully calibrated manner so that we move towards indigenous equipment and manufacturing in the medium term without compromising our preparedness in the short term', he said. 'DRDO has several decades of experience but India still imports most of its military hardware. We should involve the corporate in PPPs [Public-Private Partnerships] for defence manufacturing. We have the scientific and technical knowhow but the arms lobby has prevented indigenization…This must change, making Indian defence more self-reliant and also saving foreign exchange.' See his interview, *Times of India*, May 15, 2014.

111. Two combines led by the private sector L&T and the DPSU, Bharat Electronics Ltd, will be competing for this contract, with MOD paying for the development of competing systems to the prototype stage, with built-in financial incentives to seed an Indian mittelstand by favouring local micro, small, and medium-sized enterprises in the project. See 'L&T, BEL consortia set to get Rs 40,000 crore project', *Business Standard*, February 11, 2015.

112. See his 'Boost India's Strategic Independence', *Times of India*, June 30, 2014.

113. The Report said it could 'target three sets of components: highly varied, low-volume, and skill-intensive parts, such as aero-structures components and armor plates; those that require a higher degree of engineering, especially manufacturing engineering, such as complex castings, forgings, and fabricated part; and components with embedded software, such as communications and navigation electronics.' See Chibber (2013: 51).

114. Other than Rs 1,80,000 crore for the Rafale MMRCA and a minimum of Rs 20,000 crores for artillery—self-propelled and towed guns, howitzers, battlefield rocket systems (not mentioned in the following *Hindustan Times* article), Rs. 50,000 crore for the 75i submarine, Rs. 40,000 crore for 440 helicopters of all kinds for the military, and Rs. 20,000 crores for tanks and armoured combat vehicles. See Arnab Mitra and Tomsy Jaipuria, 'Govt may hike foreign direct investment in defence units to 74%', *Hindustan Times*, December 4, 2014.

115. James Hardy, 'India's Defense Procurement Bungles', *The Diplomat*, October 25, 2013 at http://thediplomat.com/2013/10/25/ondias-defense-procurement-bungles-2/

References

Behera, Laxman Kumar. 2013. *Indian Defence Industry: Issues of Self-Reliance*, Monograph Series No. 21.New Delhi: Institute of Defence Studies and Analyses, pp. 64–66.

Chatterjee Miller, Manjari. 2013. 'India's Feeble Foreign Policy', *Foreign Affairs*, May/June.

Chibber, Brajesh. 2013. *A Bright Future for India's Defence Industry?* McKinsey Report, 48.

Dobrynin, Anatoly . 1995. *In Confidence: Moscow's Ambassador to Six Cold War Presidents, 1962–1986*. New York: Crown.

Fallows, James. 1981. *National Defense*. New York: Random House.

Gopalaswamy, R. and Satheesh Reddy. 2013. 'Strategic Perspectives on Growth Phases and Long Term Techno-Economic Peformance of India's DRDO', *Journal of Defence Studies*, Vol 7, No 4.

Layak, Suman. 2014. 'Undersea bonanza', *Economic Times Magazine*, November 09–15.

Meddah, Hassan. 2012. 'La Rafale indien resterait largement produit en France', *L'Usine Nouvelle*. Available at www.usinenouvelle.com/article/le-rafale-indien-resterait-largement-produit-en-france.N180558.

Nagappa, Rajaram. 2014. *Evolution of Solid Propellant Rockets in India*. New Delhi: DRDO (DESIDOC), MOD.

Performance of the Defense Acquisition System: 2014 Annual Report. Washington, DC: U.S. Department of Defense. Available at http://www.acq.osd.mil/docs/Performance-of-Defense-Acquisition-System-2014.pdf.

Paul, Cuckoo. 2014. 'L&T: Armed but not commissioned', *Forbes India.* Available at http://forbesindia.com/printcontent/38703.

Puntambekar, Ashish. 2014. 'Defence Economic Zones: Transforming India's Military-Industrial Complex', The Planning & Design Lab, Mumbai, March 4.

Raghuvanshi, Vivek. 2014. 'Tata Officials Forecast Big Boost in '14 Defense Sales', *Defense News.* Available at http://www.defensenews.com/article/20140212/DEFREG03/302120040/Tata-Officials-Forecast-Big-Boost-14-Defense-Sales.

Sawant, Gaurav C. 2013. 'IAF miffed with HAL for failing to keep pace with changing times', *India Today.* Available at http://indiatoday.intoday.in/story/iaf-miffed-with-hal-for-failing-to-keep-pace-with-changing-times/1/321910.html.

Sharma, Nirbhay. 2013. *The Indigenisation of India's Defence Industry*, ORF Seminar Series, Vol. 1, Issue 12, April.

Shukla, Ajai. 2014.'Mr. Jaitley's Best Decision', *Business Standard*, October 27.

———. 2012. 'Army Scuttles Arjun Trials to Push through T-90 Purchase', *Business Standard*, November 26.

Singh, V.K. 2013. *Courage and Conviction: An Autobiography* . New Delhi: Aleph Book Company, pp. 314–23.

Soman, Appu, K. 2013.'The Failed Negotiations with Snecma for Engine Technology', *Centre Right India.* Available at www.centreright.in/2013/03/the-failed-negotiations-with-snecma-for-engine-technology/#, VHwdUNLF8XU.

Stoiko, Michael. 1970. *Soviet Rocketry: Past, Present and Future.* New York: Holt, Rinehart & Winston.

Tellis, Ashely, J. 2011. *Dogfight: India's Medium Multi-Role Combat Aircraft Decision.* Washington, DC: Carnegie Endowment for International Peace.

Unnithan, Sandeep. 2010. 'Indo-Israeli Missile Successfully Tested: DRDO Chief', *India Today.* Available at http://indiatoday.intoday.in/story/Indo-Israeli+missile+successfully+test-fired:+DRDO+chief/1/99283.html.

Valluri, S.R. 2007.'Restructuring Aeronautics', *Indian Defense Review*, July–Sept .

Vucetic, Srjdan. 2014. 'Aircraft Stories: The F-35 Joint Strike Fighter (Part I)', International Relations and Security Network, *ETH Zurich.* Available at http://isnblog.ethz.ch/government/aircraft-stories-the-f-35-joint-strike-fighter-part-i#.

Wolpert, Stanley. 1990. *India.* Berkeley & Los Angeles: University of California Press.

7

Internal Barriers

Independent India has been an ambitious experiment to see whether a large, very poor, country can take to constitutional democracy, whether a patchwork of diverse peoples of differing ethnicities, religions, caste, sub-cultures, and creed can live in peace and grow prosperous together, and whether this heterogeneous mix-as-nation can, in fact, rise to be a great power. The departing colonial overseers were not hopeful. Winston Churchill for one, having memorably described democracy as the worst possible political system bar the alternatives, must have been mortified to see Indian leaders he had biliously dismissed as 'rascals, rogues, freebooters,...of low caliber and men of straw', establish a federal democratic system, liberal in its fundaments, that has endured (Herman 2009).[1] The inherited system of administration and government was crafted to maintain order in the British Raj with London directing India's defence and external relations. It was not rejigged after independence to provide good governance at home nor optimized for conducting power politics abroad. The system has, however, evolved over the decades into a democratic polity that is meeting, albeit in slip-shod fashion, the aspirations of the masses for a better life. If the nature of the polity owes much to debate and discussion in the Constituent Assembly (1946–1949), the economic system was mostly something Nehru conjured up out of his conviction that a Soviet-style command economy, in the context of an undeveloped capital market, was the best means of frog-marching India industrially into the modern age but minus the excesses of the Stalinist state. In the event, what obtained was a well-meaning but badly functioning Nanny state. The system to administer and implement policies depended on the civil services, and with the apolitical Indian Army to rely on as last resort to maintain order, provided continuity and stability in a difficult period of transition. But the administrative structure has proved incapable of overseeing development policies efficiently or delivering social welfare benefits to the grassroots and has grown into a primary source of corruption and major obstacle to rapid economic growth. Nehru's Fabian Socialism resulted in topsy-turvy developments in the economic sphere. Thus, labour unions sprouted within and outside the public sector with government prompting before the indigenous industry could take flight becoming, in the process, a permanent brake on 'hire and fire' practices and on industrial advancement. However, the liberal political system empowering previously marginalized people at the bottom of the social and economic pyramid and a mixed economy with the state at the controls proved to be a boon, and also a bane. The growing political consciousness and assertion of rights by hitherto weaker sections of society led to a more genuinely democratic order, and created its own set of problems, as has the difficult transition in the new millennium of the Indian economy dominated by the public-sector into one led by the more productive private sector. Moreover, the over-reliance on the administrative structure for governance purposes and a decision-making system swaddled in red-tape—a legacy of the British Raj —combined with the Westminster type of parliamentary democracy where ministries are run autonomously has produced extreme compartmentalization of authority such that coordinated national policy seems hard for the Indian system to muster, especially in coalition governments as evidenced by the drift and paralysis in Prime Minister Manmohan Singh's second term. The differently motivated coalition partners running different ministries, exacerbated the clashing interests and contradictory policy impulses. The 2014 election mandate to the BJP is either a short-term departure from the norm of a patchwork ruling coalition, or it may be a harbinger of a two party system, with the innumerable parties coalescing around the right-of-centre BJP party and the left-of-centre Congress party or the regrouped Janata 'parivar'.[2] In either case, the complexities of governing a heterogeneous society with innumerable fault lines, will not be eased. The root problem in India, Timothy Garton-Ash, an

Oxford University researcher said, is one of 'managing extraordinary diversity in freedom (2013). The fact also is that India is a 'weak state' which is described by Susan Rice, President Obama's National Security Adviser, as one possessing 'critical capacity gaps, that [leaves it] unable to fulfill some or all of the four key government functions, including fostering equitable and sustainable economic growth, governing legitimately, ensuring physical security, and delivering basic, social services' (Rice 2007:191). This chapter will analyze a few of these gaps and the more enduring internal problems relating to the nature of politics, the governance structure, and policymaking that obstruct India's rise to great power.

Socially Fractured and Still Immature Polity

Called a 'deviant democracy', India has puzzled generations of experts who have wondered how, despite lacking the prerequisites— a high standard of living and literacy rate, a resilient democratic system has flourished in a setting of extreme diversity and just as extreme deprivation (McMillan 2008). The liberalism and inclusivist thinking of Nehru and his cohort at the time of Independence resulted in a Constitution that guaranteed adult franchise, individual rights, including of the press. In a federated system they conceived of divided responsibilities with certain policy jurisdictions, such as education, land, and law and order, as the responsibility of the provinces. This division of responsibility catering to the geographic spread and diversity of the country, gave the 29 states and seven centrally-controlled 'Union Territories' (such as the National Capital Region of Delhi) a substantive stake in the 'Union'. It was a complicated feat of constitutional engineering that did not, however, foresee problems inherent in this arrangement. 'I find that there are a large number of issues that, per our Constitution, is handled by the state governments. If you look at the overall picture where we are lagging behind in terms of providing basic amenities to our people, in terms of infrastructure, employment generation, you will find that most of these are with the state government', said Yashwant Sinha, Finance Minister in the BJP coalition government (1998–2004). 'And this is where a crucial issue has emerged that of the quality of governance at the state level. Where the quality of governance has been good, those states have progressed.'[3] So the peninsular states and Narendra Modi's Gujarat have fared better than the more backward states in the Gangetic plains – Bihar and Uttar Pradesh, or hinterland provinces in central India, such as Jharkhand, Madhya Pradesh, Chhattisgarh, and Odisha where long years of indifferent rule and the breakdown of the machinery of state have bred the Maoist guerilla (Naxalite) movement.

Governance also suffers owing to coalition governments at the center and in the provinces. Small party partners in ruling coalitions are more interested in politically consolidating themselves by servicing their specific constituency and sectional interests than worrying about how the resulting skewed policies hurt the economy, state or the nation at-large. Thus, the Indian Union Muslim League, a junior partner of the Congress Party-led coalition in Kerala, its support base comprising Muslim voters, especially Gulf-returned labour, has to soft-peddle the growing radicalization of Muslim youth in the state even though it has polarized the previously harmonious society along religious lines.[4] The tension arising out of different parties running the governments in the states and at the center, moreover, has got to a point where some of these states even hinder the conduct of foreign policy. Thus, the Trinamool Congress government in West Bengal headed by chief minister Mamata Banerjee, for instance, first stopped an agreement on sharing the Teesta River water with Bangladesh (in pre-Partition days 'East Bengal', later, 'East Pakistan') and then delayed an agreement to straighten out the squiggly border with the same country, protesting that one would cut water availability to the people of her state, and the other encourage illegal migrants from Bangladesh.[5] Likewise, the southern state of Tamil Nadu exercises a virtual veto over Indian relations with Sri Lanka, its population and government taking their role as guardians of the kindred Tamil people across the Palk Strait seriously.[6] On the positive side, the government of Punjab is canvassing for open border and easy trade with the entities in and government of Pakistani Punjab.[7] This element of domestic politics-induced uncertainties in the foreign policy arena, has miffed neighbouring countries, the resulting ill-will and frictions putting off realization of sensible regional initiatives such as the South Asian Free Trade Agreement and the South Asia Association for Regional Cooperation that New Delhi is keen on as means of obtaining a South Asian economic bloc. Even more problematic is the opposition of the provinces to economic measures pushed by the central government to obtain hassle-free movement of trade and commerce across state borders, such as the Goods and Services Tax (GST) that's expected to streamline tax collection from inter-state trade, because 'octroi taxes' levied by individual provinces are big revenue sources they are loath to lose, whence alarms are sounded about the centre expropriating state rights.[8] The GST 'has fallen victim to competitive politics', explained Jairam Ramesh, Minister for Rural Development in the Congress government who in his earlier role as Commerce Minister was in the thick of this issue. The main opposition Bharatiya Janata Party (BJP) proposed the GST when in power but, once in the opposition, opposed it. 'This is ironic [but it] is natural and only to be expected. It is difficult for parties to be in opposition and cede credit for something to the ruling party.'[9] With the BJP returned to power, GST has regained top priority.[10] Such competitive assertiveness by the provinces may be seen as part of the process of democratic consolidation. But it also accentuates the 'delicate balance between forces of centralization and de-centralization' that often produces bad governance because 'interests of the powerful [are] served without including the interests of the weaker sections of society' (Kohli 2009:4).

This latter aspect was sought to be addressed by the Representation of Peoples Act (RPA), which sanctifies the 'first past the post'-principle to decide election winners. It has hoisted parties into power at the center and in the states with support rarely exceeding 25 per cent of the popular vote. Thus, even though the BJP won a majority of the Lok Sabha seats in the 2014 general elections, it did so with only 31 per cent of the popular vote.[11] It exacerbates social and political fault lines, makes for unstable regimes at the center and in the states and gives the lesser parties representing the interests of small but mobilized sections of society a disproportionate say in government.[12] The process of politicization of the masses with each section and subsection of society seeking to corner state services and benefits has led to politics down to the grassroots level being perceived as a zero sum game activity where virtually anything goes, and the criminalization of the political process has ensued.[13] With more groups with discrete social/ethnic identities mobilizing to protect and advance sectional interests and gaining ground at the expense of the pan-Indian parties, the country has experienced inherently unstable coalition governments. Because survival depends on meeting the demands of a multitude of these coalition partners and because regimes cannot muster a consensus, a cohesive policy is difficult to achieve. Interminable discussion and negotiation between numerous interest groups and constituencies and gridlock often follow.

In the new millennium this has proved to be particularly hurtful to the 'India story'. The Economics Nobel laureate Michael Spence, for instance, surveying Manmohan Singh's India said it wasn't a 'good long-term growth bet' because 'it is one thing to have a healthy debate and another endless healthy debate'.[14] Jai Panda, a Member of Parliament from the provincial Biju Janata Dal from Odisha, faulted the two national parties—the Congress and the BJP around whom smaller parties collect for this state of affairs. He charged them with following the antiquated British parliamentary tradition of 'consensus' between the ruling and opposition parties as precondition for policy conceptualization and implementation, which convention the UK long ago discarded. Instead of legislating policies to realize promises in the ruling party's election manifesto, the onerous business of crafting a consensus consumes time and results in inefficient policy-making. Panda has labeled the cost of such inefficiency a 'democracy tax'.[15]

With the Preamble to the Constitution announcing the country as a 'Sovereign Socialist Secular Democratic Republic'—'Socialist' and 'Secular' being inserted by a Constitutional Amendment by the Leftist Prime Minister, Indira Gandhi, courtesy a captive Parliament during her dictatorial rule during the 'Emergency' in the mid-1970s when Constitutional rights and freedoms were suspended, and the socialist-populist economic straitjacket was tightened. It has constrained governments since then from openly switching economic tracks to make speedy progress along alternative development pathways. Such socialism is manifested in the public sector enterprises which grew from 5 in 1951 to 249 in 2010 and investment in them from Rs 29 crores to Rs 1,37,3526 crores.[16] A senior adviser to Manmohan Singh said the Prime Minister was for selling off the loss-making units but accepted that political will to create a transparent market for them, or for land, minerals, and other natural resources (owned by the state) was missing. This is in the main because the discretionary power of politicians to part with national assets to crony capitalists and supporters is at stake.[17] Populism, dressed up in socialist dogma, has led to subsidies and giveaway programmes for the poor even as 'political practice has been considerably more conservative, eschewing any decisive redistribution', avers Princeton University political scientist Atul Kohli. '[These] twin tendencies—radical in tone, conservative in practice may well have strengthened' the existing democratic system (Kohli 2009). This is because the lower castes, which comprise over 80 per cent of the population, growingly mobilized, forming their own separate parties, and electing their own representatives to power in the states and at the center, are less eager to change the system now that they are in a position to extract benefits from the state (Bose 2008).[18] It marks an India transiting from 'Brahmin raj' to the 'Sudra (a collective word for the lower castes) raj' and genuine majority rule (Rudolph and Rudolph 2008). With the enormous political flux that has followed, *jugaad* politics is the norm.[19] According to the Berkeley political economist Pranab Bardhan, 'When groups don't trust one another in the sharing of costs and benefits of long-term reform, there's the inevitable tendency', he writes, 'to opt instead for the "bird in hand" short-term subsidies and government handouts, which pile up as an enormous fiscal burden' (Bardhan 2010: 133). Subsidies accounted for 17 per cent of the budget deficit at an unsustainably high 5.6 per cent of GDP in 2012, which way lies fiscal ruin for the state (Bardhan 2010: 144–5). But populist measures (such as the National Rural Employment Guarantee scheme costing the exchequer some $8 billion annually) and a law guaranteeing food, many fear, will become entitlement programmes and a drain on the treasury in perpetuity. Except, these monies don't end up benefitting the poor as much as they do the petty officialdom and the ruling party apparatchiks at the grassroots level who expropriate large portions of the funds, food, and services. The grain meant for the poor, for instance, routinely finds itself diverted to the market by corrupt local politicians and state functionaries.[20] Hence, the talk from the Congress Party days of financial benefits and subsidies being directly channeled into the individual bank accounts of the intended beneficiaries, which is sought to be translated into delivery mechanisms. Whence, the drive by Prime Minister Modi to have banks open accounts for the poor without requiring them to deposit the mandatory sums of money.[21]

But good governance and effective delivery of services and benefits, according to Jairam Ramesh, is not what the more powerful social justice parties, such as the Bahujan Samaj Party [representing the lowest castes, collectively referred to as Dalits] or Samajwadi party [of the kulak or landed peasantry, middle castes] care for; they instead stress empowerment by sustaining the politics of identity, which has brought them electoral dividend. Caste is a uniquely resilient Hindu social ordering and stratification device that is supposedly immutable and occupation-linked, even affecting Muslim and Christian communities peopled by converts from Hinduism, and has its antecedents in religious myths and legends (Doniger 2010). Except, it turns out, it is not able to weather market reforms in a modernizing India. Caste and its social effects, a recent study finds, diminishes with people moving from their rural areas of origin to urban concentrations for work, and sending back remittances to raise the social stock of their families left behind in villages (Kapur et al. 2010). A class of Dalit capitalists has even emerged, which believes in meritocracy, not government handouts, and advocates free market, not Marx, to defeat the pernicious caste system.[22]

Accompanying such social transformation in the countryside is the change in the outlook of the people. Grown impatient with outmoded ideas and considering their experience over the years of the corruption-ridden government programmes doling out free food—in reality rotting, vermin-infested grain, free education—one room schools with missing teachers, the poor growingly see these measures as perpetuating their poverty, but support them and the parties promising more of the same because getting dribbles of state help is better than getting nothing at all. Successful political leaders, such as Narendra Modi, who implemented free market policies and oversaw relatively corruption-free development and social welfare programmes in their states, are gaining strong popular support, and awakening the people to opportunity outside the governmental ambit in an economic milieu freed of government controls. Modi's belief that 'Government has no business to be in business' won him the Prime Minister's post, forcing the socialist-minded Congress party government and Leftist parties to admit that 'freebies and subsidies' can neither replace nor spur economic growth.[23] An economic revolution in governance may thus be in the offing, but will take some time to take wing.

Demographic Bomb

If migration and accessibility to capital is the key to rendering caste irrelevant, education is the other factor, but progress in this sphere is disappointing. According to the erstwhile Planning Commission there is a shortage of 500,000 secondary schools in the country. Forty per cent of the population—some 500 million people, are in the 13–35 age bracket; by 2025 this section will comprise 25 per cent of the global workforce. With free and compulsory education programmes the enrollment is high—as much as 95 per cent, but 31 per cent of the students (150 million) drop out at the primary school stage, and only nine per cent complete secondary education.[24] Rakesh Mani, a sometime teacher in one of Mumbai's slum schools describes the appalling conditions—the open drains running by the one-room sized 'English language' school in which he taught, where most of the space is taken up by broken school desks and cupboards stacked along a wall. He identifies two major problems why the country may fail in educating its youth and imparting job skills needed in the twenty-first century employment market. 'As with most serious issues in India, the problem is not a lack of high-minded laws, but rather the failure to implement them effectively', writes Mani. The other issue concerns school curricula, which he declares are 'often hijacked by state governments to promote their ideological agendas [and] are largely inadequate for building skills'.[25] In 2000, the then President of India K.R. Narayanan, a Dalit, described the contradictions of the 'two Indias'—highly educated technically proficient personnel and the largest number of illiterates, world's largest middle class and also the largest number of people living below the 'poverty line'. A September 2010 study of the Indian education sector sponsored by the UK Department for International Development observed with a straight face just how the 'two Indias' coexist:

> What is clear is that in the highly politicized society in India, civil society groups will continue to call on government to do more for

elementary education. Central government will appeal to state government and local government bodies to do more. All will call on teachers and on parents to support the education of their children more. Poor parents will look to local, state and national government bodies to meet the Fundamental Rights of their children. Meanwhile the middle classes will use private means to look after the educational futures of their children...[who] will use the education to access growing economic opportunities in the modern sector of the economy lined with the global economy.

Thomas Macaulay in his famous 1835 Minute on Indian Education devised a colonial system of education that Middle School level up was in the English language medium and orientated to Western science and literature with a view to producing, he said, 'a class of persons Indian in blood and color but English in taste, in opinion, in morals, and in intellect (Little 2010). In a modified form that is still the system followed by one of these Indias, and making a success of it. The other India too aspires to the same standard, as vouched for by the great demand for 'English education' in the countryside and in city-slum clusters which the state is unable to meet.[26]

In any case, what education most youth do manage to get does not make them more employable.[27] Things have been going wrong at all levels with the state governments particularly culpable. The craving for good education and basic health services, for instance, is met by building colleges and hospitals in even remote areas but these are inadequately staffed and haphazardly equipped. In the countryside, 'science' colleges are established but have neither teachers nor laboratories, and health service centres boast of medical equipment but no doctors. This is because teachers and medical staff once recruited in the state educational and health service departments and posted to hinterland centres bribe local politicians and petty bureaucrats to arrange their transfers to bigger towns and cities, denying the people in these areas access to education and health services. 'After so many years', said M. Ramachandran, of the elite Indian Administrative Service (IAS), who retired as Chief Secretary (top bureaucrat) in the small mountain state of Uttarakhand, 'we are still talking the basics of development without being able to deliver on very much'.[28] Uttarakhand is a microcosm of things going wrong in the Indian states. By the time the country irons out such large kinks in the education sphere millions upon millions of youth will have entered adulthood with paper degrees but no competence to make it in a skills-demanding economy. In fact, the Congress Party Finance Minister P. Chidambaram alluded to the enormity of the problem. 'Only about 3 per cent of rural youth and 6 per cent of the urban youth in the age group of 15 to 29 years receive any kind of formal vocational training', he disclosed, and large numbers of engineering degree and diploma holders, he said, 'remain without jobs' because the outdated education they receive does not fit in with the requirements of modern industry, and most companies end up skilling entrant level engineers and technicians in the workforce.[29] The possibility of the disillusioned educated-unemployables roiling the law and order situation and of the 'demographic dividend' turning into a bomb is hinted at in a report by Ashish Puntambekar of the Nataraja Foundation in Mumbai. Co-relating population growth, employment prospects, and increase in crime, he concludes that with over 200 million ill-educated youth joining the job market by 2018, alongside the 112 million already unemployed as per the 2011 census, crime in the country will increase five-fold.[30] With the law and order machinery, especially in north India, already in tatters, this is a bad omen.[31]

The Modi government has conceived its flagship 'Make in India' policy as means of bulking up the manufacturing sector as stepping stone to India's becoming the 'workshop' to the world. But mostly it sees very fast manufacturing growth as the answer to the teeming millions without work and joining the labour market. An annual growth rate of 9–10 per cent over the next 30 years to take care of the projected youth bulge will require the manufacturing sector to grow by15–16 per cent on a sustained basis. The share of manufacturing in India's GDP has, however, stayed stuck at the 16 per cent level, providing work for only 12 per cent of the available manpower pool, and constituting half of the country's exports. This share will have to increase to 25 per cent to generate 100 million jobs, requiring this sector to grow yearly by 16 per cent. The small informal manufacturing firms account for 40 per cent of the jobs in the country (compared to 4 per cent in South Korea and 5.8 per cent in Japan). Amitabh Kant, secretary, Department of Industrial Policy & Promotion, attributes the malaise in manufacturing to the 'lack of global size and scale of physical infrastructure; and redundant and outdated labour laws'. But he expects that with the new government easing the rules and procedures for doing business and setting up 'industrial clusters' with an 'eco-system of supply chain responsiveness, lower logistics costs, availability of labour and technology upgrade', freight corridors, and the removal of constraints on coal and gas to improve the power sector, that the 'Make in India' initiative will make the country 'global champion' in 25 manufacturing areas. Kant also makes the case that for every manufacturing job created three jobs will be generated in the services sector.[32] As plans go, this roadmap to ensure a bright manufacturing future and employment scene makes sense. But converting this plan into policies in the face of roadblocks by opposition parties in Parliament and in the provinces won't be easy and will make for some stirring politics.[33]

Transitioning from Bad Economics

Milton Friedman, the guru of laissez faire economics, was commissioned in the 1960s by the International Cooperation Administration (in State Department) to tour India and assess Indian development projects. His conclusion, prophetically, was that economic growth will happen despite the economic system in place. Some 60 years later it is encapsulated in the phrase 'private success, public failure' to explain the state of the nation and the economy (Das 2012). Friedman's subsequent paper on 'Indian Economic Planning'—a comprehensive critique of India's economic approach was scathing and, in the context, of the hesitant economic liberalization undertaken by the Indian government since the early 1990s, still relevant. 'Unfortunately, Indian economic policy has not been producing the results that [were] hoped for', he wrote, 'I do not believe it can do so.' His view was that 'centralized economic planning' only works, as in China and the former Soviet Union, if there's a 'strong authoritarian government to extract a high fraction of the aggregate output of the people for governmental purposes'. Relying on the Indian government's figures and data, Friedman highlighted just how poorly the statist policies had fared.[34] He was unimpressed by the steel mills and dams which Nehru had called 'the temples of modern India', even implying that these were but Potemkinised fluff and make-believe development. '[T]he progress appears spotty, and some of the appearance of progress', he huffed, 'is misleading.' Friedman questioned the wisdom of the country seeking autarky, producing things in India at higher cost when the same could be procured at a much cheaper price from abroad. He rejected outright, what he said were 'frequently heard explanations' trotted out for India's dismal economic record, such as social institutions, the un-enterprising 'nature of the Indian people', 'a fatalistic philosophy', the caste system, and religious taboos, and even the hot and humid climate that induces torpor that is said to 'imprison the society in a straitjacket of custom and tradition'. To refute such arguments, he pointed to Indian migrants—and this was before the United States and the West discovered the economic value of talented Indian professionals—constituting in East Africa and Southeast Asia the entrepreneurial class and 'the dynamic element initiating and promoting economic progress' in those regions. He cited his personal experience of the small Punjab city of Ludhiana, a manufacturing hub, 'bursting at the seams', Friedman wrote, with 'a self confident, strident, raw capitalism'. 'If these tendencies…could be given full rein, and not hampered and hindered in every direction by governmental interference and control, India', he asserted, 'could achieve a growth rate that'd exceed today's fondest hopes.' Further, he discussed just why centralized planning was inimical to economic growth. 'Growth is a process of change, it requires flexibility, adaptability, and the willingness to experiment, above all else it is a process of trial and error that requires', he observed, 'an effective system for ruthlessly weeding out the errors and for generously backing the successful experiments.' These are attributes, he argued, centralized planning lacks because the plans made in advance are 'cumbersome and rigid' and difficult to modify with changing circumstances, and the tendency of such a system to not 'admit error' because of 'the political costs of doing so'. It leads to bad projects, ineffective programmes, and wasteful policies being persisted with— 'subsidized, protected, supported, and labeled successes'. Friedman then slammed state controls, 'apart from the economic harm they do', in terms of breeding '[c]orruption and petty bribery [which] have reach[ed] new heights in India'. He pointed out that socialist policies nurtured crony capitalism, referring to the politically-connected business houses which, far from having a strong central government shape their private conduct, were as 'powerful private groups' able 'through political and financial influence, to use governmental policy as an instrument to further their own interests'. Friedman repeated a common jest heard in the India of the 1960s that while the US was an 'affluent society', India was an 'influence society', adding parenthetically that the 'existing private entrepreneurs are in practice among the most effective enemies of free enterprise.' If controls are removed, 'an enormous reservoir of energy [would be released] and produce a dramatic accelerat[ion] of economic growth in India', he ventured, 'comparable to that which occurred in Japan after the Meiji Revolution.' A free enterprise economy, Friedman advised, is what is needed for India to be able to 'compress into decades what took other countries centuries'. Should New Delhi continue with its statist approach that eked out a miserable 1.5 per cent growth rate in the decade of the 1950s when the international situation was favourable for economic growth, it would take India, he feared, over 300 years to merely reach the per capita income levels of Japan [of 1963], and concluded that, 'The current danger is that India will stretch into centuries what took other countries decades'.[35]

Apparently, Nehru was not unaware that he had taken the wrong economic turn which would get India to the then current Western standard of living in another 600 years.[36] Except for her stab at liberalizing the economy in 1966–7, the government's control of the economy tightened during Indira Gandhi's helmsmanship with the nationalization of banks, life insurance companies, and natural resources, and other steps that solidified the position of the state on the 'commanding heights' and promoted socialism by enlarging the infamous 'license-control Raj' to throttle free enterprise. 'We were trying to marry the equity of the socialist framework, even though we had an underlying sub-strata that was capitalist, in agriculture, industry', explained Ramesh, a minister in Manmohan Singh's cabinet. 'We certainly had a notion of a developmental state, but were hindered by complex social and structural realities.' 'Why did we fail? Is it the failure of the Indian state alone?' he wondered. 'The good intentions were certainly there. The Indian state had many successes in its initial years but at a point in time when, perhaps, we should have switched [to the free market policies] we could not for a variety of reasons.' Ramesh thinks that had Indira Gandhi done in 1966–7 what Prime Minister Narasimha Rao did in 1991–1992, India might have been a very different place. Except, India faced a series of cataclysmic shocks—three consecutive monsoon failures, oil price hike, a variety of factors that conspired to make that particular episode of liberalization short-lived. This was roughly the time when the 'little dragons' of East Asia—Hongkong, South Korea, Taiwan, and Singapore—were taking-off with Japanese FDI, and the entry of multinational corporations into their economies. 'It was certainly missed opportunity,' rues Ramesh, 'One of the reasons is that the nature of our economic planning has always been multi-objective, it's never been unidirectional, it's never been focused on one over-riding objective.' For instance, in India, steel plants, he explained, are not just enterprises to make steel, they are large social enterprises to open up backward tribal areas, to provide employment. Referring to the massive public sector steel plants at Bhilai, Bokaro, Rourkela, in backward, tribal, regions, he says, 'The multi-objective nature of our economic planning meant the use of national resources to correct social and regional disparities.'

In fact, New Delhi resists changing the direction of any policy however disastrous until the country is pushed to the brink. It took the 1962 military debacle for New Delhi to wake up to the threat from China and to build up India's conventional military strength in the mountains to meet it. And in the early 1990s, it was imminent bankruptcy that impelled the government to shift the bullion it held to the Bank of England vaults in London to cover national debt and forced Prime Minister Narasimha Rao to change direction, rid the country of the license-permit system of controls, order a 'revolutionary' budget and implement the first set of economic reforms to begin globalizing the Indian economy. 'Most people', said a senior adviser to Prime Minister Manmohan Singh, 'believe that if we hadn't been in hock and in crisis, we wouldn't have changed. That probably is true'.[37] The outcome of freeing the economy was, as Professor Friedman had foreseen, dramatic—a galloping growth rate averaging 8–9 per cent in the following decade, an equally impressive reduction in poverty, and surging economic prospects for the private sector. The economic slowdown post-2008 happened because of the sudden collapse of political will of the Congress Party government to push the pedal on economic deregulation owing to the fear that without more populist policies and programmes it might lose the votes of the poor.[38] The economic head steam built up by the mid-2000s was thus frittered away post-2009, which may be the pattern in the future as well if the parties/coalitions in power fail to further loosen state controls on the economy and remove bureaucratic and procedural shackles slowing down the pace of industrial and infrastructure growth. Significantly, the private sector responded to a regressing Congress party government not with the usual pleadings to clear the bottlenecks as in times past, but with threats to invest more abroad as part of a 'hedging strategy' that New Delhi could not afford to ignore.[39] Direct investment, mostly in the West, by Indian companies leaped to over $107.3 billion by 2010–2011.[40] This aspect of a globalizing Indian economy has led to Indian companies buying out some 2000 foreign companies, including marquee names such as Corus Steel, Jaguar and Land Rover automobile firms in the UK, for instance, by Tata, the largest ($97 billion) Indian conglomerate.[41]

The shrinking of the government's role as the basis for economic growth and vitality is now widely accepted, particularly in the wake of the stellar advances by the Information Technology (IT) industry, responsible for 7.5 per cent of the country's GDP, with exports rocketing from $0.90 billion in 1990 to $70 billion by mid-2012 and, per a Nasscom-McKinsey study, expected to touch $225 billion by 2020.[42] The other leading area where India has established its credentials also relies on the amply skilled engineering and technically proficient manpower available in the country—the field of 'frugal engineering'—a phrase coined by an impressed Carlos Ghosn, CEO of Nissan-Renault, after he saw the novel methods Tata Motors had adopted to produce the low cost car, Nano. It is a concept multinational companies have taken to with General Electric, ABB, Siemens, Daimler Benz, among them, quickly setting up shop, opening their own Engineering Research and Development (ERD) centers and manufacturing facilities in India for products 'without frills' to cater to the needs of price-conscious consumers in India and rest of the developing world. Indian ERD sector has grown into a $10 billion industry, its revenue constituting 22 per cent of all global ERD revenues and saving its international customer organizations $20 billion in 2011. It has 'created deep impact' in the automotive, avionics, construction, heavy engineering, and telecommunications fields and is moving into 'complex, higher-end services'.[43] Frugal engineering has produced, for example, a simpler, more rugged truck for Daimler Benz in its $600 million factory in Chennai costing half as much as its Europe-made Astor model, with 85 per cent of the components sourced from 400 Indian suppliers. Twenty per cent of the production in this plant by 2018 is scheduled for exports. General Electric has come out with many low-cost medical diagnostic tools such as a compact digital X-ray machine; a CT scanner is in the pipeline. The German engineering company Siemens has developed low-cost transmission equipment—40 per cent cheaper than imported models. The Swiss engineering firm, ABB, has likewise invested heavily in R&D and manufacturing facilities.[44] The trouble is the talented Indians responsible for such technology innovations add only indirectly to national wealth because profits and patents accruing from their toil are harvested by the Western companies employing them.

The exceptional success of the IT/ ITeS (Information Technology-enabled Services), and ERD sectors brings into stark contrast the failure of the government and the public sector to create any of the technology needed to grow, prosper, and even defend itself (with an indigenous armaments industry). The country has the requisite skilled manpower and managerial skills to have a world-class high-technology industry but what it lacks, says Stanford electrical engineering professor, Arogyaswami J. Paulraj, is 'the right kind of investment capital—private capital [which] is hard to attract given the high levels of investment and very high risk. State capitalism—India's initial route to high technology by creating state funded public sector companies [such as the Indian Telephone Industries and the Semi-Conductor Corporation Ltd] have proved to be very disappointing.' India, wrote Paulraj, a former Commodore in the Indian Navy and celebrated designer of a powerful sonar equipping Indian warships and submarines, 'needs to attract private capital to build this sector. This will be possible if the government offers an adequate policy support to reduce the risk for private capital by a variety of measures including preferential market access, soft debt financing, R&D investments, spectrum policy geared to promote telecom technology and downside risk mitigation for venture capital'.[45]

Even the obvious, however, seems difficult for the Indian government to achieve, including in the flagship area of information technology, which could do with more comprehensive indigenous capability to manufacture micro-chips/semi-conductors—the building blocks of the IT and ITeS industries. Exasperated with the systemic constraints on critical technology acquisition, a senior policy adviser to Manmohan Singh outlined the convoluted thinking and misplaced priorities that dogged the Congress party government decisions. He alluded to an actual case regarding the decision to set up a world-class top-of-the-line microchip fabrication facility (fab) that required the government to ante up a grant of $2 billion. 'One simple approach would be to do a Singapore. Go to Japan, America, approach a company there, give it this amount of money, allow the hire of whoever they wanted, and set up the plant. This can't be done in India', he explained, 'because you can't give $2 billon to a foreign company. It'd have to be $2 billion to a joint venture which has an Indian partner, assuming you had the balls to decide to give the money to a joint venture in the private sector, in the first place.' Then the question, he said, would arise—whether to pit [the rival conglomerates] Tata against Reliance and have [the winner] compete against Mahindra & Mahindra [a third Indian conglomerate]. After each of these companies ties up with a global fab major, they would compete. Reliance might say it will do it for $1.9 billion, Tata would say they would do it for $1.8 billion, Mahindra would underbid at $1.7 billion, so it will go to Mahindra. At which point someone would get up and say that joint venture should be with the public sector, so why not Semi-Conductor Corporation, Chandigarh? The moment the role and capability of this PSU is questioned and the fact of the burning down of the fab unit in that plant is raised, PSU supporters will say, well, all the Reliance [offshore oil] guys have been taken from the public sector Oil & Natural Gas Commission, to make the point that public sector personnel are competent. So the decision will end up with the worst possible compromise—the grant will be cut in half and divided between the public sector and the private sector, ensuring that both fail. The options would be even more skewed were ArcelorMittal one of the most prominent steel companies in the world and owned by an Indian living in the UK, L.N. Mittal, for instance, to offer to erect a fab—it would be kept out of the running because of the prohibition on funding a foreign company. That is why, he said, more active government involvement in venture capital is needed but the distrust of private sector in government is so high, 'it would be a miracle' if a government gave $1 billion to a private sector firm for a fab. 'The government has to take a strategic view. You could get it wrong', he said. 'Equity does not help the company, a grant will in such a venture. You could have a loan at zero interest rate till the fab becomes profitable. The issue is the $2 billion as grant. The essential thing is giving the contract to whichever private party the cabinet decides on giving the grant to. That is the way the Chinese and the South Koreans do it.' He moreover thought it necessary for the government to 'totally change our research funding pattern', and base it on international peer review and achievements audit. In the event, a decision was finally taken in September 2013 by the Indian government to permit competing consortia led by IBM and STMicroelectronics to set up two fabs in Gujarat and outside Delhi, involving Israeli, Malaysian, and Indian companies (including the public sector Hindustan Semi-Conductor Manufacturing Corporation) to produce chips in the 48–22 nanometer range with an initial investment of $8 billion that could rise to $55 billion to service an Indian ESDM (Electronic System Design and Manufacturing) market projected to be $400 billion by 2020.[46]

However, for India to scale economic heights it is nowhere enough to be only a global IT/ITeS and ERD power. The country has to industrialize, become a hub for manufactures on a much bigger scale than it is now with the ability to snatch business away from China and Southeast Asia. P. Chidambaram, Finance Minister in the Congress government said plainly that 'Manufacturing is the Achilles heel of the Indian economy'. Of the GDP growth in 2013–14 of 4.9 per cent, manufacturing contributed only 1.1 per cent.[47] Historically, industrialization has been the main vehicle for generating employment and lifting masses of people into the middle class. In India, moreover, owing to the youth-bulge, creation of jobs is the prime concern of government. But official efforts have failed because the precursor conditions for the manufacturing sector to accelerate do not exist. There's no settled policy on land acquisition—a hot political issue, no rationalization of the tax regime such as General Sales Tax, no setting of environmental standards, no country-wide schemes for upskilling poorly educated youth, and to top it all, is the rank bad infrastructure. Hence, while establishing of National

Manufacturing Investment Zones for clustering production units was mooted as part of a general policy by the Congress regime, there wasn't the push necessary to make the concept work. When it moved fast, as in liberalizing the automotive sector in the 1990s, the results were encouraging. The multinational companies that stepped in improved capital and labour productivity manifold, until now when three million small cars are manufactured, with a quarter of this output exported. The states that prioritized manufacturing have done well; populous provinces in the cow-belt of Uttar Pradesh and Bihar that shied away from creating conditions receptive to industry have lagged behind, much as countries that failed to do so, India among them. Industrial production in India still makes up only 15 per cent of GDP growth compared to 30–40 per cent in the 'little dragon' economies of Asia.[48] Other than a conducive milieu, world-class roads, railways, ports, airports, fibre-optic network for communications and e-commerce, water and electricity are key requirements. Presently, the infrastructure is in dismal condition. The senior adviser to Prime Minister Manmohan Singh was certain India would not become a great power 'unless we have the balls to do all the second generation reforms and take decisions straightforwardly without letting extraneous factors intervene'. He was worried about the Indian government's inability to be proactive in any policy sphere instead of, as it is prone to, getting 'big things done' but only under extreme duress or in the wake of 'a major crisis or breakdown' suffered by the country.[49] It affects investor confidence. '[T]hough India is gradually taking part in the regional production networks, India's role has not been highly visible, and has focused on the low level of "value addition" in the region', writes a Taiwanese economist Kristy Hsu (2013). Were India to get its manufacturing policy in working order, it could be quickly integrated into the trans-regional manufacturing partnerships. 'These days an increasing number of Taiwanese firms', Hsu says, 'are relocating their manufacturing bases away from China, and consider India as a potential new "Asia Factory"'. But for India 'to develop diverse and strong manufacturing industries' and thus 'restructure' the economy for sustained growth, it will have to simplify its central and state level laws and tax systems, and overcome the infrastructure deficit (Hsu 2013).[50] Taiwanese industry and capital, it must be borne in mind, responsible for 80 per cent of the FDI in

China, is what sparked off China's galloping economic growth in the last 30 years. It could do the same for India if only New Delhi obtained the necessary conditions.

The infrastructure deficit is especially massive, estimated at anywhere up to a trillion dollars. $500 billion was roughly the size of investment in infrastructure Manmohan Singh promised in 2007–2012. But corruption and the characteristic inertia of the Indian government, and a 'revolving door democracy' with success in elections predicated on out-doing rival parties in populism, ensured snail-like progress and a trickle of FDI. According to Montek Ahluwalia, Deputy Chairman of the Planning Commission in the Congress decade 2004–2014, the void in quality infrastructure cannot be easily made up by FDI and foreign companies invited to bid for massive projects because of ideological antipathy of some political parties to adopting such a course. He also said that 'file procedures' (the requirement for bureaucrats at every level to make 'notings' on official documents) that waste time together with the enhanced public sensitivity to environmental damage is responsible for unconscionable delays in critical infrastructure projects. 'Essentially what happens', he said, 'is that a project may be important and contribute massively, letus us say, to meet the shortfall in power, which in turn will lead to more development in rural areas, more extension of electricity, more GDP, etc. But when it needs a particular clearance, these are not the issues before the officer at all. That officer follows his own silo mentality'.[51] Official clearances, because of ecological concerns, moreover, become grist for public ire. To overcome bureaucratic caution or motivated obstructionism a National Investment Board or Cabinet Committee on Investment chaired by the Prime Minister was proposed. An infrastructure project once approved by this body over-rode all objections against implementing it.[52] Until this Board/Committee begins working, power plants valued at $50 billion to produce 45,000 MW of acutely needed electricity, for example, remain in limbo. It is the slowness of the process, which is a liability. The fact of power shortages is not new, but it took the government 15 years to realize the need for one-window clearance for power plants.

The conspicuous shortfalls in urban infrastructure—antiquated sewerage systems, pot-holed roads, inadequate and poorly maintained public transport, irregular water supply, power outages, and woeful housing and the lack of plans factoring in migration into cities from the countryside has resulted in most Indian cities and even towns resembling vast shanty-towns, and proving an urban nightmare for people living in them. According to 2011 figures, 400 million people live in 7,935 urban agglomerations, which population is expected to rise by 200 million by 2030. But governments at all levels seem unprepared for an urbanized future for the country—a natural progression for a modernizing state on a growth trajectory.[53] As a result, the urban spread has been amoeba-like without a hint of town-planning and virtually no supportive infrastructure.[54] The neglect of urban areas is traceable to an institutional mindset traceable to Mahatma Gandhi's Luddite-like desire for India to be a collection of 'village republics'. This vision for the country resulted in an unofficial but firm policy, post-independence, to discourage and disincentivize the movement of people from the countryside into cities by not properly planning for their growth.[55] These migrants, unwilling to put up with the existential difficulties of living in cities were expected to wend their way back to their villages, but this did not happen. Lacking affordable housing, the poor, homeless migrants end up simply squatting on public land, putting up their lean-to's and, in next to no time, springs up another slum cluster.[56] Or, the poor migrants buy space on public land captured by the 'land mafia'.[57] To protect their meager possessions and illegally-occupied pieces of real estate the residents of these slums/shanty towns then court local politicians and win protection with the promise of bloc votes. Most of these 'unregulated colonies' in time end up getting 'regularized' and the legal rights of the inhabitants are secured. Except, other than a water tap for a slum cluster or a few latrines social services are absent and the shanty-towns remain an eyesore and health hazard.[58] Despite the challenges of surviving in urban areas, rural India continues to disgorge people at a faster rate because there's employment to be had in cities and towns, which produce 60–70 per cent of the country's GDP. It has led to a still wilder mushrooming of slums and 'unregularized colonies' to accommodate the inflow and ever greater pressure on land and on the existing creaky urban infrastructure. Urban India as a result daily grows more crowded and unlivable. According to M. Ramachandran, who retired as Secretary in the Urban Development Ministry, 40 per cent of the Indian urban population has no access to potable water, and one in six defecates in the open.[59] An embarrassed and angry Congress government minister for rural development Jairam Ramesh compared the defence budget of Rs 1.93 lakh crores ($37 billion) with Rs 99,000 crores ($20 billion) for his ministry, and demanded the diversion of defense funds to build toilets, keeping alive, in the process, the 'guns versus bread' debate. He made the point that the $30 billion expended on acquiring the French Rafale combat air-craft will make a thousand villages 'open defecation-free'.[60] Realizing the gravity of the problem, the new Prime Minister Narendra Modi of the BJP, which in the past has agitated for constructing a temple to Lord Rama on a disputed site, has voiced a different priority—'toilets first, temples later'.[61]

Indian and foreign companies attracted as much by the challenge as potential profits, are beginning to invest in private-public projects (PPP) in the infrastructure field, where private parties build and operate roads, etc. for a long enough period of time for the returns to satisfy the investor before handing over the same to government. The 11th Five Year Plan had sequestered 8 per cent of GDP for infrastructure development; the 12th Five Year Plan starting in 2012 has increased that to 9.95 per cent of GDP, with $30 billion as FDI.[62] On the infrastructure deficit official India confronts a dilemma—bad quality if public sector companies are tasked with construction, and 'gold-plating' when private sector is involved.[63]

That no aspect of government and public life is spared the mess that has been created all round is illustrated by the fact that even in the judicial sector, which is in relatively better condition, there is a backlog of over 31 million pending cases in all courts, which a High Court judge estimated would take 320 years to clear.[64] A Bench of the Supreme Court blamed the government for failing to make the promised ad hoc appointments of 5,000 judges to clear the backlog.[65] The policy adviser to Manmohan Singh attributed the difficulty of alighting on reasonable socio-economic policies to the penchant of even the younger lot of Indian politicians to stick with the redistributive language in public while talking free market in private. He was, however, optimistic that the importance of high growth rate as the predicate for 'inclusivist' (populist) programmes is now accepted by the political class, including the Left-led unionized labor.[66] Despite everything, there is optimism. BJP leader Yashwant

Sinha said: 'Notwithstanding all our problems, our noisy democracy, we have ...been able to generate momentum in our economic system and the fact that we have had some good entrepreneurs. It is still full of corrupt practices because when the license–permit-quota raj was replaced by a more liberal regime, the corporations and the politicians found another way of making huge sums of money by parceling out natural resources, such as the bandwidth (2G), coal, and iron ore, and this is what we are struggling with at this point in time. But now there's an increasing awareness that land, water, minerals, telecommunications spectrum, minerals, oil and gas, and other such natural resources should be auctioned rather than given as a favor to any corporate house.' He called 'crony capitalism' a stage advanced countries too had passed through in their economic development. This can be bypassed, he said, 'by auctioning through a transparent system'.[67] Raghuram Rajan, Governor of the Reserve Bank of India, seconded the view that transparency in government procedures and ways of doing business is the crucial factor to propel economic growth.[68]

Administrative Apparatus of State

The Hongkong-based Political and Economic Risk Consultancy rated Indian bureaucracy as the worst in Asia, scoring it 9.21 points out of 10, Singapore the best at 2.71, and China somewhere in the middle at 7.11.[69] Lant Pritchett of Harvard University describes India as a 'flailing state'—'in which the head, that is the elite institutions at the national level, remain sound and functional but that this head is no longer reliably connected via nerves and sinews to its own limbs.' Contradictions, he suggests, are aplenty—'a booming economy and active democracy with world-class elite institutions and yet chaotic conditions. The growing democracy lags behind in several key measures of development, including high rates of infant mortality and malnutrition rates and low immunization rates.' As far as the 'limbs of the state' are concerned, 'In police, tax collection, education, health, power, water supply—in nearly every routine service', writes Pritchett, with experience of having lived and worked in India, 'there is rampant absenteeism, indifference, incompetence, and corruption. In many parts of [the country] in many sectors, the everyday actions of the field level agents of the state—policemen, engineers, teachers, health workers—are increasingly beyond the control of the adminis-tration at the national or state level'.[70]

This is the India Indians live in and put up with and Pritchett's view of the infirmities is widely shared. Devesh Kapur of the University of Pennsylvania refers to the 'under-staffed, over-bureaucratized' Indian state as 'suffocating' and says the 'biggest challenge' the country faces is 'the Indian state itself' (Kapur 2015). The common man experi-ences the Indian state, writes political scientist Kohli, 'as relatively ineffective, corrupt, more an obstacle than a source of solutions, even venal, and more often than not, simply absent when needed'.[71] Jairam Ramesh believes the problem is not with over-manning in government—the federal government has just about three and half million employees, for a country with 1.2 billion people, which he doesn't think is excessive. What's to blame is the way governments at the center and in the states work, there being no incentive structures. 'I am all for the army system of promotion where at every level you go through a weeding out process', Ramesh said. 'Unfortunately, thanks to Article 311 in the Constitution, we can't fire anyone in government post. If you want to bring in accountability, Article 311 has to go'.

Government service, Ramesh stated, 'is a deeply hierarchical sys-tem. The bureaucracy has now got a stranglehold on the system and the left hand does not know what the right hand is doing.' It is a grip maintained by the Indian Administrative Service (IAS), said G. Parthasarathy, one of a rare breed of ex-military officers absorbed into the foreign service, who had a stint in the Prime Minister's Office. 'The IAS are control freaks, they want to control everything and they do. They permit only vertical integration and not horizontal integration.' This leads to severely compartmentalized functioning of government and absence of coordinated decisions and activity of the kind Ramesh decried.[72] The trouble, he said, is that the system only serves those on the inside; it doesn't serve anyone else. When there's executive inaction, there's judicial intervention. In the last 15 odd years, Ramesh disclosed, many of the systemic reforms happened because of court rulings. 'We have to admit that. Sometimes the executive deliberately lobs the ball to the judiciary because political leaders don't have the political courage to take decisions', he con-fessed. Thus, the government, he stated, doesn't want to settle any issue bilaterally. Over 60 per cent of all litigation and pending cases involve the government. 'Things that can be resolved across the table are not, but sent to the courts to decide instead. The executive is afraid that it'll be charged with favoritism or cronyism. That, 'he said, 'adds to the time.'[73] Much of what Ramesh says about the Indian governmental and legal system conforms to how American business-men, for instance, view the problems of dealing with the Indian bureaucracy and the legal system.[74]

Whether it is policies geared to obtain social and economic equity, or to implement economic liberalization and reforms, they all run up against the same inefficient, ineffective, and archaic over-bureaucra-tized administrative structure. Ponderous at its best, except in a crisis or the occasional dire situation when, magically, it works fast, clock-work-like, the administrative system is slow, sodden in corruption, and inept. Many senior bureaucrats fondly recall the 'Emergency' imposed by Indira Gandhi for a couple of years when habeas corpus and Constitutional rights (including Article 311 protecting the jobs of those on the public payroll) were suspended. Trains ran on time, and government offices worked smoothly. It was the fear of immediate dismissal from service that apparently did the trick. 'I'm reminded', said the retired civil servant Ramachandran, 'of what Lee Kwan Yew [the founding Prime Minister of Singapore] bluntly said that for countries like ours we should have limited democracy, because in a full democracy—while we appreciate its beauty and strength—any-one can do anything and that does not help'. He enumerated the other characteristics of the Indian bureaucracy: its willingness to be the handmaiden of rent-seeking politicians, to assist them in their corrupt practices by interpreting the plethora of confusing rules and regulations in facilitative ways, which secures for the IAS officers desirable and lucrative postings and a smoothly rising career path. 'It is always better', he said, 'to be a safe bureaucrat in a system like ours—don't initiate much, don't take decisions, shuttle it to another ministry or another level, and absent yourself from crucial meetings and ask subordinates to take decisions and the rap if the decision is subsequently deemed to be wrong'.[75] Honest bureaucrats are bent by politicians to the corruption facilitation task by threats of frequent transfers or transfers to punishment posts in the hinterland, embroil-ment in corruption cases, and other sorts of harassment.[76] These practices are aided by the fact that the investigation agency—the Central Bureau of Investigation, is controlled by the Home Ministry in the central government and often used to settle personal and political scores. Corruption has reached such pandemic proportions that in a 2010 survey by the Department of Administrative Reforms and Public Grievances, a majority of the Indian Administrative Service officers, who are the medium and, sometimes, beneficiaries of this system, when polled admitted 'there is no incentive to remain honest and the system is so designed that officer entering the service is forced to adapt to the corrupt system' and, further, that the 'weeding out of corrupt, inefficient, and nonperforming civil servants is not being done' (Civil Services Survey 2010).

Ahluwalia, the Manmohan Singh-era deputy chairman of the Planning Commission, which Modi has dismantled, blamed the '19th century file-based procedures' for the slovenly pace of bureaucratic functioning. He described these procedures as requiring 'every individual [in the bureaucratic hierarchy in a ministry] to pronounce sequentially on a file—all of which is open to questioning—Under Secretary wrote this, why did the Deputy Secretary write that, etc.— and it is absolutely impossible to fix responsibility in the system'. The only solution for this bureaucratic madness, he maintained, lies in 'abandoning the system and taking collective decisions and minuting them as speaking orders'. A Group of Ministers—a device often used by the Manmohan Singh government to push through potentially controversial policies, or to delay taking explosive decisions, he believes should do this so the bureaucracy feels protected, because 'the file system is extremely damaging——you write something and you don't know what the next fellow will write or what consideration he is going to bring to say that you are wrong'. With collective decision coming down from on high the 'administrative paralysis will end' because bureaucrats will merely have to implement decisions, not make them for the political masters.[77]

What has turned governmental processes so viscous is the impenetrable mass of opaquely worded rules and regulations, most of them of colonial vintage, which the Indian state, instead of dumping in 1947, has chosen to pad with layer upon layer of new laws, statutes, and rules. Depending on how far down or how extensively a bureaucrat cares to go into this corpus of legal constraints/provisions, he can justify or reject almost any decision to please his political master. Further, each ministry defines the existing rules variably and to its advantage, whence the 'silo mentality' mentioned by Ahluwalia, and the phenomenon of the different agencies of government separately carrying on with their sometimes clashing agendas. The rules were originally drafted by the British to standardize procedures, bring in 'a common system of law and a uniform code of government' that amalgamated the best features of the numerous 'native' systems. It produced, as a former British member of the Indian Civil Service (ICS), Percival Griffiths wrote, 'a large measure of [administrative] unity' to complement the cultural unity already prevailing in the subcontinent. Except, because the rules were weighted to enhance the ruler's image, it also instilled in the average Indian's mind the idea of the colonial government as provider of security and source of benefits, as *mai-baap sarkar*, literally 'mother-father government'—a benign entity looking out for the people's welfare—an impression the British overlords undoubtedly wished to embed in the Indian public's consciousness. 'The most serious adverse effect of British administration', observed Griffiths, 'was that it pressed too heavily on the people of India...engendering in the Indian mind an undue dependence upon the Government for everything...[P]rivate enterprise and charity in public fields were thus not stimulated. The District Officer became the father and mother of the district' (Griffiths 1965:229–30). The downside of such a dependency-promoting system was the public's deferential attitude to government combined with the 'give me' approach to the state. It was reinforced by Nehru's neo-socialism that begot a state that looked askance at individualism and private initiative, including private charitable activity. Indians politicians, who replaced the British as rulers, quickly exploited the value of having the unlettered masses perceive them as the fount of largesse and benefits. It explains the reluctance of the Indian political class to overhaul the system; persisting with the shell of a 'socialist' state that affords it control and the power of patronage.

The Indian members of the colonial era ICS, in turn imbued the successor IAS with their working habits and ethos. Except, as Zafar Hilaly, a retired Pakistani diplomat hailing from a well-known Muslim family from peninsular India that produced several ICS stalwarts, surveying the disaster they made of it in Pakistan, has written that the Indian members of the ICS 'had little intellectual heft... were not visionaries or statesmen...[and lived and worked] by the book...[were] unsuited to examine "national" problems and devise countrywide "modern" solutions...[and were trained mostly] to sit on the fence with respect to things that did not strictly concern their operational ambit directly, and wait for the lead from their colonial masters'. In Pakistan, with Jinnah dead in 1948, there was no one the ICS could look up to and take orders from, and became a law unto themselves.[78] In India, Nehru occupied the space vacated by the British and filled policy with his content. It explains why Nehruvian concepts and thinking continue to have currency in the Indian government and bureaucrat-heavy policy establishment.

Speedy decision-making is not what the ICS-derived IAS has excelled in. But corruption, which was prevalent at the petty official level in British times is now, as stated earlier, a pandemic. During the Centenary celebrations of the Congress party in 1985, the then Prime Minister Rajiv Gandhi famously bared the truth that fully 85 per cent of the funds meant for development and social welfare goes into maintaining the delivery structure itself, meaning paying the salaries of the armies of bureaucrats, and suffers from various kinds of 'leakages', including being siphoned off by the bureaucracy grassroots level up. A more honest appraisal of the system has not been made by a politician before or since. But, equally, no effort whatsoever has been made to makeover the administration of the country that everybody admits is broken, but whose repair has to be undertaken by the very people who most profit from it—the politicians and functionaries and the other agents of state actually interfacing with the public. Hence, there's no political will for a great big cleansing and reconfiguration of the administrative apparatus because too many people have too much to lose. Large financial allocations to people-pleasing populist programmes are actually cash-cows that are effortlessly milked by those within the system. Thus, in the Dudu District of Rajasthan, an investigative press report revealed, unemployed village folk built a road and were each supposed to get a remuneration of Rs. 133 per day as per the guidelines of the National Rural Employment Guarantee Scheme; what each of them actually received was Rs. 0.001.[79]

The system of omniscient corruption, it is generally agreed was installed by Prime Minister Indira Gandhi. She sought to match the financial support rightwing parties attracted from the corporate sector by tapping into 'commissions' available to middlemen in financially lucrative defence and other capital acquisitions deals, this money ostensibly filling the party coffers to fight elections. The Congress Party ever since has become associated with corruption in high-value deals.[80] The cascading effect of such corruption is the systematic and institutionalized delays endemic to everything the government undertakes to do. Thus, in the decade of Congress party rule, 2004–2010, Prime Minister Manmohan Singh talked incessantly about economic growth as panacea and infrastructure development as a prerequisite. Except in almost the same period, as the Planning Commission informed BJP Prime Minister Narendra Modi in November 2014, 83 per cent of the 707 central government projects have experienced cost-over-runs to the tune of Rs.1,90,000 crores (over $32 billion). More dishearteningly, it observed, that while over Rs 5.6 lakh crores had already been invested over the previous 12 years in these road, rail, airports, and inland waterways projects, another Rs 5.7 lakh crores will be needed to complete them.[81] Systemic discouragement hampered the growth of the private sector in the first four decades after independence which, other than the set of crony capitalists, subsided like the rest of the economy, into the shallows. With the fountainhead of corruption cemented since Indira Gandhi's days at the very top of the Indian government, corrupt practices downstream have become the norm.[82] It scares away foreign capital needed to perk up the infrastructure, manufacturing, and the defence industrial sectors.[83] Institutionalized corruption hits the poorest worst of all, with the funds allocated to populist schemes and as subsidies disappearing into the pockets of grassroots politicians and government service providers. The economist Surjit Bhalla contends that 0.5 per cent of GDP 'perfectly targeted' would remove poverty from the country. The government spends six times as much and 22 per cent of the country's population remains abjectly poor.[84]

In lieu of a totally reformed system, it is left to the initiative of individual ministers to implement 'band-aid' measures, which in some instances, have become major correctives. Thus, in the important Rural Development Ministry the fact of India's being the 'perennial late comer' has been turned to advantage by, for instance, using the latest technology, such as hand-held micro-automatic teller machines, to deliver government cash benefits directly to the poor in select parts of the country.[85] This is a technical means to eliminate corruption by cutting the petty bureaucracy, used to pocketing the funds meant for the poor, out of the delivery loop. A programme to directly transfer Rs. 300,000 crores ($6 billion) as subsidies and cash benefits to the poor with biometric identification cards developed for such use by Nandan Nilekani, one of the founders of the Indian IT major, Infosys, is underway.[86] The connectivity available to rural folks by cheap mobile telephony has led to a 'transformation' of the countryside with some 300,000 village-level 'panchayat' government cells exercising more and more of the powers devolved to them. The reservation of 50 per cent of the panchayat posts for women has meant gradually rising graph of women's rights and female empowerment and the ending, albeit slowly, of some of the ghastliest social practices prevalent in the countryside, among them female foeticide and 'honour killings' of girls.[87]

Increasingly, the Right To Information (RTI) Act—an Indian variant of, and inspired by, the US Freedom of Information Act, the law to protect whistle-blowers, and a horde of 24/7 television news channels, have made old style corruption of roads and bridges existing merely on paper and similar brazen exercises in channeling public funds into private pockets increasingly difficult to manage.[88] Corruption is nevertheless rampant and permeates all aspects of public life. The watchdog group Transparency International claims that truckers, for instance, pay some $5 billion in 'speed money'. The Delhi-based Center for Media Studies in 2010 calculated that rural households paid Rs 471.8 crores ($94 million) in bribes just to avail basic services, including subsidized rations, health, education, and water supply.[89]

Sustained misgovernance is also at the root of the Maoist insurgency in several provinces of Central India and in 165 of the 602 districts in the country, where the badly treated tribal population has taken up arms with some success.[90] The counterinsurgency measures are politically difficult to prosecute because the central and state governments are not certain how severely and with what amount of force to deal with these rebels, lest it fan more alienation and discontent, and lose them votes (Vira 2011). The resistance movement is sought to be doused with special development programmes and road building to increase connectivity, attract industry and employment opportunities for the alienated tribal youth.[91] Technology and empowerment of women is leading to the underway transformation of rural India. The 65 per cent of the population residing in the countryside, said BJP leader and former IAS officer Yashwant Sinha, will demand better governance from their elected representatives on the pain of being voted out, resulting in fast turnover of elected representatives. 'This is what gives me hope that we are bound to move forward', he says. 'We are still too much civil servant-oriented'.[92] It is this milieu Prime Minister Modi is seeking to change by propounding the revolutionary message that especially the rural folk 'need to give up the notion that it is the government that's the doer and they are only beneficiaries' and urged the youth to recognize their 'ability to shape their own destiny through their own entrepreneurial skills and hard work'.[93]

While the issue of corruption has galvanized public opinion, as serious a problem is the sheer multitude of government schemes that need implementation. There are over 250 government schemes floating around to be managed by the central and state governments. They end up clogging the delivery pipeline, affording the corrupt additional sources to tap into and divert public monies from, and few actual benefits for the people.[94] Efforts during the BJP regime in the early 2000s to prune these schemes to a dozen or so central programmes and a policy for the money thus saved to be transferred to the provinces failed because of the vested interests in the Planning Commission and the line ministries. The problem is compounded by the absence of a system of zero budgeting. 'So schemes continue year after year without monitoring. The approach to the allocation of funds to these numerous schemes is casual, absolutely ad hoc. This is no way to run a government', BJP leader Sinha fumed.[95]

The dysfunctional Indian system retarding economic growth and modernization of the country is attributed by the Indian Finance Minister P. Chidambaram in the Manmohan Singh government to the adoption of the '*dirigiste* model of economic development' with the state as the 'principal driver'. Dismantling even pieces of this 'monstrous and rapacious structure', he confessed, has proved difficult with the vested interests within and also outside the government opposing any change. He cited the example of what he called the 'trading mafia'. He charged it with joining the environmentalists and those seeking protection of tribal rights to mineral-rich but forested hinterland areas, against prospecting and mining licenses and FDI in this sector, which's preventing the development of employment-generating mining and allied industries. Chidambaram's take on why India is still poor and under-developed is both candid and revealing. Speaking at the Harvard Business School in 2007 he described India as 'a poor-rich country'. 'India is rich', he said, because of its 'natural resources', 'entrepreneurial talent', 'young population', 'traditional systems of medicine and its capacity to adopt modern medicine', 'strengths in concept and design of programs', and because its people are 'hardworking, resilient, and pragmatic', have a high saving-rate, and 'set great store by values and moral standards'. However, it is poor, he said, because 'it is unable to exploit its natural resources efficiently and profitably', its 'many policy and procedural hurdles stand in the way of entrepreneurs…[inability] to deliver quality education to all its children…'weaknesses in the system to deliver basic medical services to rural India…lack of accountability and reluctance to punish the wrongdoers…obsession with outlays rather than outcomes… declining standards in public life', and because 'often commonsense is devoured by ideology'.[96] The way out may be the disassembling of the socialist state, starting with disinvestment and selloff of public sector companies and industrial assets, something the BJP regime under Modi intends to do.[97]

Bad governance riding on the coattails of bad management practices has foreign policy repercussions. It has become an ingrained habit of the political class, even the strong and independent-minded among them, to look to bureaucrats for solutions when the bureaucracy itself is the main problem. Matters of national importance that fall fully within the purview of political decisions, such as economic 'transformation' and the budgetary means to achieve it, are farmed out to senior civil servants to make.[98] Robert Blake, the U.S. Assistant Secretary of State for South and Central Asia, for instance, confided to a Congressional committee in February 2013 that the booming bilateral relationship powered by spectacular growth in merchandise trade—of 1023.2 per cent in the previous 22 years—is at risk owing to the slowdown of the economic reforms and, consequently, of the Indian economy. This fact is reflected in the declining American investment in India, a situation exacerbated, he said, by 'Indian Parliament [being] tied up in knots about debates over corruption'.[99] The fact is India is struggling with two competing economic models and ideologies. The no-nonsense method of fixing accountability subscribed by Narendra Modi has resulted in fast-paced growth and speedy industrialization of Gujarat. The Gujarat model hews to Milton Friedman's nostrums of individual initiative and respon-sibility.[100] The other model is that of Nitish Kumar, chief minister of Bihar, who oversees delivery of social welfare to the deserving poor and has also done well. The Bihar experiment owes much to the Amartya Sen school of liberal development economics harking back to Nehru's socialist thinking, where the state is the instrument facilitating equitable growth (Dreze and Sen 2013) . That holding civil servants responsible for outcomes may be the better way to implement either model is evident from a recent example of startling bureaucratic performance that left government circles stunned as much as it did the people and foreign experts.

One of the worst-run and most backward states with a history of exorbitant corruption in government, Uttar Pradesh (UP), astonish-ingly, produced a minor miracle by flawlessly managing the gigantic Hindu religious fair, the Kumbh Mela, in 2013, held every 12 years at the confluence of the two main heartland rivers, Ganga and Jamuna, in Allahabad. In a state where $600 million allotted for building pub-lic latrines disappeared without a trace and without a single latrine actually being constructed, the state administration at the Mela used a work-force of 100,000 men to erect a tent city on the river bank inside of three months, to house 2 million people, with 100 miles of roads laid 'by placing steel plates on the sand', 18 pontoon bridges, 347 miles of water supply lines, 400 miles of electricity lines, 22,500 street lights, 200,000 power connections, 35,000 latrines, and some 275 food shops, topped by courteous and efficient policing that prevented incidents of any kind. A startled head of the World Bank in India, Otto Ruhl, called it 'an incredible logistical operation' and gushed, 'I have seen nothing like it in my life… If somehow we could translate that capacity to day-to-day business, you could transform U.P. It's a really powerful thought.' This success was attributed by the official in-charge to the fact that those working in it were held accountable for their actions and for the money spent.[101] The lesson many development experts are extracting from this experience is that the bureaucracy may not be as much a problem as it is made out to be, that it is more a management issue where, as also evidenced in the success of development programmes in Gujarat, the corrective is to make every functionary in the system responsible for delivery of government-mandated subsidies and services.

Indian Foreign Service as Retardant

A better, more effectively-administered, state can ensure internal peace, order, economic growth, and prosperity, but domestic progress cannot by itself turn a country into a big power if its diplomats—the standard-bearers of the country's interests to the outside world represent small-minded officialdom and are oblivious to the factors that can extend the reach and influence of India in the international community. Previous chapters have shown how the Indian Foreign Service is staffed mostly by persons with a view of the world that can be sourced to Nehru. They are oblivious, however, to his subterranean realpolitik thrust to policy that saw him nursing a nuclear weapons programme, building a jet fighter, and accepting the U.S. nuclear umbrella and, in case they were needed, conventional military forces to subdue the Communist Party menace at home and China abroad. And, like every other bunch of civil servants, the foreign service too is preoccupied with monopolizing foreign policy turf, limiting cadre strength, and protecting the service's perquisites. Taken together, these aspects have led to a palpable muting of the country's impact at a time when potentially India's diplomatic heft, influence, and leverage could have been increased in ever widening circles in Asia and the world. Thus, as the previous chapters have shown, the MEA has downplayed the importance of arms transfers and close military cooperation with countries in the extended region, vetoed the outreach initiatives by the armed services to countries in the Indian Ocean region and farther afield, declined strategy papers emanating from the military headquarters and denied the military any role and involvement in the shaping of foreign policy by, for instance, resisting the cross-posting of uniformed officers in MEA, and otherwise opposed the lateral entry at the middle and senior levels of domain experts from the industry and think-tanks to broad-base and flesh out Indian diplomacy and help it gain technical competence. It led a former Policy Planning staffer at the U.S. State Department, Daniel Markey, to analyze the 'software' shortfalls in India's foreign policy-making, implying that such weaknesses reduced India's potential utility as strategic partner to America and, by extension, to other countries interested in seeing India pull its weight in the international arena.[102]

India wants to be taken seriously as a coming power, in which case the conduct of its foreign policy too would have to be judged by standards applying to the most powerful countries. William Burns, who retired as U.S. Deputy Secretary of State and widely recognized as one of the best U.S. diplomats of recent times, mentioned ten principles for American diplomats to practice their craft by. To get a rough idea about the performance quality of Indian diplomats, it may help to judge them by the Burns standard. These principles are: knowing it is your country's interests that you represent and seeking to further them; being aware that 'It's not always about us'; mastery over fundamentals requiring that national interests be translated 'in ways that other governments can see as consistent with their own—or at least in ways that drive home the costs of alternative courses'; staying ahead of the curve and being 'ready to adapt to new challenges and innovations and ...to lead in emerging arenas of competition and cooperation'; promoting economic renewal with the diplomats playing 'a big role' in 'opening markets abroad, strengthening the economic rules of the road, ensuring a level playing field' for home companies; 'connecting ...concepts and goals to available instruments of national power, including military power'; being imaginative rather than cautious; speaking truth to power; accepting [personal] risk; and, convincing foreign governments that your country can be part of the solution even when it is seen not to be able to manage its own affairs too well.[103]

Based on the analysis in previous chapters and telescoping these numerous metrics, one can say that Indian diplomats are at their best and on top of their game when dealing with general, rather than technical, issues especially involving their counterparts from the West, whom they strive mightily to try and impress.[104] The quality of diplomatic interaction begins to slide when they assume superior airs in dealing with representatives from the Third World, tending to be downright pro-consular in attitude when talking to governments in the immediate neighbourhood.[105] And plainly, the tradition of the IFS officers posted abroad to view their remit in old diplomatic terms as evaluating developments in host countries and sending home lengthy dispatches in the modern era of instant communications and information overload is, as Prime Minister Modi pointed out soon after assuming office, anachronistic. Based on his experience as Gujarat chief minister and his attempts to sell Gujarat to the world, Modi's desire that Indian diplomats reorient themselves to doing something more useful, such as trade and economic cooperation facilitation, hints at the Indian diplomats' primary weakness. Modi also mooted the idea of 'paradiplomacy'—of the states marketing themselves directly in foreign countries as investment destinations and market-friendly environments. This will require diplomats posted abroad to be as familiar with the strengths of the Indian provinces as they are knowledgeable about the opportunities and challenges the state representatives may face in foreign capitals they are posted in.[106] But this Modi initiative will allow IAS—a competing service, to encroach on MEA's policy ground, with opportunities for officials from other ministries and even from the states canvassing for trade and foreign investment to occupy billets in Indian embassies abroad.[107] These cross-staffing initiatives along with recruiting young academics and think-tankers in the policy planning cell in MEA are compelled by prime ministerial directive. But it is also recognition that the world had grown too complex for professional diplomats alone to handle. The foreign service may be changing but not fast enough. For instance, promoting Indian export trade is the new mantra. But large Indian corporates and industrial houses with international presence are hardly likely to call on Indian embassies abroad to propel their business. Help will be sought by the less well known and unglamourous small and medium industries who may, however, find Indian diplomats, less responsive for the same reasons they turn their noses up when dealing with Third World countries to which they avoid postings.

The effectiveness of Indian diplomacy is, however, best assessed by the success or lack thereof of bilateral agreements with developing states because nearly 65 per cent of the MEA budget pertains to technical and commercial cooperation with fellow developing countries. In 2014–2015, this allocation is in excess of Rs 6,200 crores—not a small sum, but it hasn't pulled in the desired results.

This is evidenced in the inattention suffered by some 600 bilateral agreements the country has signed with countries in Asia and Africa, and the subcontinent, which the Modi government has had to remind MEA to honour. The lack of focus in the ten years of the previous Congress coalition government may be partially responsible, for this state of affairs, but it also shows up the disinterest of Indian diplomats in these matters. Thus, a 2012 understanding to transfer 17 fire-engines to Nepal was not followed up, and only $1 million of the $9 million budgetary support promised Palestine was actually disbursed. More worryingly, the 2008 accord with Yangon to develop the Kaladan multi-modal transport project to link the Indian northeast with Myanmar and Southeast Asia lay unattended until Prime Minister Modi came on the scene. Likewise, the long-ago agreement to invest and build up the Chahbahar port in Iran was dormant for a long time.[108] The Kaladan and Chahbahar cases, in particular, highlight MEA's neglect despite their geopolitical significance to India, and confirms the perception of Indian diplomats as not being particularly strategic-minded. It follows that they would also be less enamoured of India exercising hard power. In regional and international power politics where military prowess and interest in security cooperation can create useful leverages, Indian diplomats and missions abroad, by and large, have been slow. Juxtaposing the value of suasion by military means against the efficacy of diplomatic methods ends up merely reinforcing the bias Indian diplomats have institutionally nursed against military instruments of state even when they are seen to realize strategic ends. It was, perhaps, with such stunted Indian diplomacy in mind that the head of the Vietnamese Diplomatic Academy in April 2014, unable to keep the note of irritation out of his voice told an audience of Indian visitors, 'We have been waiting a long time for India to rise. Hope it rises soon'.[109]

Notes

1. For the interplay between Churchill and Indian leaders in the period 1940–7, see Herman (2009), Chapters 28 and 29.

2. The Janata 'parivar' of Mulayam Singh (Samajwadi Party), Lalu Prasad Yadav (Rahstriya Janata Dal), Nitish Kumar (Janata Dal United),

and Deve Gowda (Janata Dal Secular) getting together to form a front to fight Modi. See Smita Gupta, 'Janata Parivar meets, merger on the cards', *The Hindu*, November 7, 2014.

3. Interview.

4. Ullekh N.P., 2013. 'Gulf Money Gives Currency to Muslim Extremism in Kerala', *Economic Times*, 3 July.

5. Samanta, P. D. 2012. 'First Teesta, now Mamata objects to enclaves pact: Fear (sic) Bangla influx', *Sunday Express*, June 3 .

6. Sultana, G. 2012. 'The Tamil Nadu factor reappear in India-Sri Lanka Relations', *IDSA Comments*, September 12, available at www.idsa.in/idsacomments/.

The human rights excesses by the Sri Lankan military in bringing closure to the civil war waged by the secessionist LTTE (Liberation Tigers of Tamil Eelam) created a public furor in Tamil Nadu sufficient to pressure Prime Minister Manmohan Singh against attending the Commonwealth Heads of Government Meeting in Colombo. See 'PM to skip CHOGM', *The Hindu*, November 10, 2013.

7. 'Punjab pitches for trade with Pak', *Times of India*, April 25, 2014.

8. Gupta, S. 2012. 'GST rollout likely to miss 2013 April deadline', *Times of India*, August 22.

9. Interview, March 25, 2011.

10. 'Ambitious sell-off plans, GST top priority: FM', *Indian Express*, August 31, 2014.

11. 'BJP's 31% lowest vote share of any party to win majority', *Times of India*, May 19, 2014 at http://timesofindia.indiatimes.com/home/lok-sabha-elections-2014/news/BJPs-31-lowest-vote-share-of-any-party-to-win-majority/articleshow/35315930.cms.

12. Subhash Kashyap, former Secretary-General of the Lok Sabha; personal communication.

13. Fully 31 per cent of Members of Parliament have charges of rape, robbery, and murder against them. Talk on 'The Merits of Money and Muscle: Criminality, Elections and Democracy in India', by Milan Vaishnav of the Carnegie Endowment, Center for Policy Research, New Delhi, November 29, 2012.

14. 'India isn't a Good Long-term Growth Bet', *Economic Times*, November 21, 2013.

15. Jai Panda on 'Face the Nation' program, CNN-IBN TV channel, May 1, 2013.

16. *Public Sector Enterprises Survey, 2011–2012* [New Delhi: Department of Public Enterprises, Government of India, 2012], 26.

17. Interview.

18. A striking example is Mayawati, the powerful leader of the Dalits (the lowest castes, previously called 'untouchables'), head of the mainly lower caste Bahujan Samaj Party (BSP), and former chief minister of Uttar Pradesh, with a number of corruption cases lodged against her. For a glimpse into Dalit politics, see Bose (2008).

19. 'UPA is a "jugaad" expert, polls not before '14: Nitish', *Times of India*, September 18, 2012.

20. 'Rice meant for poor ends up in black market', *Business Standard*, May 2, 2014.

21. 'India Opens 15 Million Bank Accounts in Modi's Inclusion Drive', *Bloomberg News*, August 28, 2014, http://www.bloomberg.com/news/2014-08-28/india-opens-15-million-bank-accounts-in-modi-s-inclusion-drive.html.

22. A Dalit Indian Chamber of Commerce & Industry has paved the way for industrial estates and credit being made available to Dalit entrepreneurs at discounted rates. DICCI has over 3,000 Dalit entrepreneurs whose companies in 2012 had a combined turnover of Rs 27,000 crores ($5.4 billion). Source: Milind Kamble, Chairman, DICCI, personal communication, November 29, 2012. Kamble runs a successful civil engineering construction company. Chandra Bhan Prasad and Milind Kamble, 'Manifesto to end caste', *Times of India*, January 23, 2013.

23. 'Government has no business to be in business, PM must accept reality: Narendra Modi', *Economic Times*, June 7, 2012. 'Freebies, subsidies alone won't help development, says FM', PTI, *Indian Express*, February 3, 2013.

24. Puntambekar, A. 'Defence Economic Zones', 23

25. Mani, R (7 August 2012) 'Educating India', *Project Syndicate*, available at www.project-syndicate.org/.

26. Yashwant Sinha of the BJP refers to schools with names like 'St. Francis' that promise English language proficiency in his 'backward' constituency in the Bihar countryside and are choc-a-bloc full with students whose families pay lots more for their education even though the indifferent quality but free education is available in state-run schools in villages and towns. Interview. Also see Thakur and Pandey (2009: 348–50).

27. In a poll of 300,000 students in 29 provinces and seven Union territories, only 37 per cent of the graduates were found employable. See '"Only 37% grads employable, women beat men"', *Times of India*, November 10, 2014.

28. Interview, August 18, 2011.

29. P. Chidambaram, 'Poor-rich countries: The Challenge of Development', the Second Harish C. Mahindra Annual Endowed Lecture,

Harvard Business School, MA, 2007, available at http://www.mahindra. com/News/Press-Releases/1294210847.

30. Puntambekar, A. 'Rising Crime and the role of the Planning Commission', Nataraja Foundation, Mumbai, January 5, 2013.

31. 'Controlling law, order in UP is a challenge', *Millennium Post*, February 27, 2013 at http://millenniumpost.com.in/.

32. See his 'Spurring India's industrial power to new heights', *Hindustan Times*, November 17, 2014.

33. Crabtree, J (14 October 2014) 'Modi hits campaign trail with populist campaign to woo Indi anew', *Financial Times*, October 14, 2014, available at http://www.ft.com/intl/cms/s/0/7a139d7a-539e-11e4-929b-00144feab7de.html#axzz3Jbgx89xy.

34. Friedman, M. 'Indian Economic Policy', first draft, May 6, 1963 available at http://ebrowse.com/, 1, 9.

35. Ibid, 3–4, 6–7, 9, 14–17.

36. Lamont, J. 'Time to put the brakes on India's dreams', *Financial Times*, 29 April 2011.

37. Interview.

38. Bhalla, S. S. 'The kiss of socialism', *Indian Express*, 11 August 2012.

39. Crabtree, J. 'Bollygarchs at bay', *Financial Times*, 6 June 2012.

40. 'Have cash? Invest abroad: India Inc's 2012 deal mantra', Business Standard, January 1, 2012. In fact, 53.8 per cent of Indian foreign investment in 1999–2007 went to North America and Western Europe. See Anil Kumar Kanungo, 'Internationalization of Indian Firms: Overseas Investment A Key Strategy', Table 3, 14, (undated) available at www.freit. org/WorkingPapers/Papers/ForeignInvestment/FRIET384.pdf.

41. Bajaj, V. 'Tata Motors Finds Success in Jaguar, Land Rover', *New York Times*, 10 August 2012.

42. Joseph, L. 'Indian IT, ITS sectors have to change course to sustain the success story', *Economic Times*, June 21, 2012; 'India turns east for more tech success', *The National*, available at www.thenational.ae/,21 June 2012.

43. India Shining in the Global ER&D Space', Nasscom (undated, but probably early 2012) available at www.nasscom.org/.

44. 'India taking "Frugal Engineering" to the world', *Thomas White— Global Investing*, August 31, 2012 available at www.thomaswhite.com/.

45. Paulraj, A. J. 'Does India Need a High Technology Industry?', Center for Advanced Study of India, University of Pennsylvania, November 19, 2012 available at http://casi.ssc.upenn.edu/iit/paulraj.

46. Majumdar, A. 'IBM, STMicroelectronics to invest $8 billion in setting up Indian fab units', *Tech2*, September 16, 2013 available at http://tech2.

in.com/news/general/ibm-stmicroelectronics-to-invest-8-billion-in-setting-up-indian-fab-units/914750.

47. Das, G. 'Manufacturing sector is dragging down India's economic growth', *Business Today*, February 27, 2014 available at http://businesstoday.intoday.in/storyprint/203616.

48. Singh, S. 2014. 'Manufacturing sector cal pull us out of economic crisis', Telegraph (Kolkata).September 29. http://www.telegraphindia.com/1130929/jsp/bihar/story_17401448.jsp#.U2xXMoFdU8wnterview.

49. Interview.

50. Hsu, K. ' India-Taiwan Economic Partnership: Building a New Growth Model', *Indian Foreign Affairs Journal*, Vol. 8, No. 3, July–September 2013, pp. 298–300.

51. Interview, *Sunday Express*, September 23, 2012.

52. Singh, D.K. 'NIB on the way, will have power to approve', *Indian Express*, 29 November 2012.

53. Lakshmi, R. 'India unprepared for urban boom', *Washington Post*, 18 July 2011.

54. Raghu Dayal, 'Closing India's Infrastructure deficit', *Business Standard*, December 20, 2011.

55. Dr. Ajit Mazoomdar, IAS, former Secretary of Economic Affairs, Government of India; personal communication.

56. Nagarajan, R. 'Towns with shanties increased from 1,743 in 2001 to 2,613 in 2011.'33% of slum population live without basic facilities', *Times of India*, 3 October 2013.

57. Suresh Golani, 'Thanks to Mafia, slums mushroom on forest land', *Afternoon Despatch and Courier*, April 8, 2013 at http://www.afternoondc.in/city-news/thanks-to-mafia-slums-mushroom-on-forest-land/article_79795; 'Mumbai slums in the grip of land mafia', *NCHRO (National Confederation of Human Rights Organizations)*, undated but probably mid-2000s at http://nchro.org/index.php?option=com_content&view=article&id=2631:mumbai-slums-in-the-grip-of-land-mafia&catid=4:corruption&Itemid=12.

58. The Congress Party chief minister of Delhi, Sheila Dixit, for instance, confirmed this problem, saying 'There is a vested interest at work but now we need to do something about it.' See 'Politicians let slums grow as vote banks: CM', *Times of India*, June 29, 2013.

59. Interview, August 18, 2011

60. 'Reduce defense budget, fund toilets: Ramesh', *Times of India*, July 27, 2012.

61. 'Toilets first, temples later, says Narendra Modi', PTI, *Indian Express*, October 3, 2013.

62. An economic planner; communication.

63. Minister Ramesh cites the case of the private company built modern airport in New Delhi. Original estimate was Rs 9,000 crore ($1.8 billion), for which viability gap funding was promised by government; the second estimate was Rs 13,000 crore ($2.5 billion), and the third estimate rose to Rs 16,000 crore ($3.2 billion); interview. Montek Ahluwalia, Deputy Chairman of the Planning Commission and former World Bank functionary, counters infrastructure projects in the public sector too 'end up with costs that are 4–5 times higher than the original estimates'. See his Interview, *Sunday Express*, September 23, 2012.

64. 'Courts will take 320 years to clear backlog', *Times of India*, March 6, 2010.

65. Mahapatra, D. 'Supreme Court chides itself, govt for judicial backlog', *Times of India*. 12 January 2012.

66. Interview. For the first time since its founding in 1920 the Communist Party of India's labour unionizing arm, All India Trade Union Congress conceded at is 40th Congress that 'the role of private capital is not ruled out'. See Mohua Chatterjee, 'AITUC Warms up to Private Capital', *Times of India*, November 27, 2012.

67. Interview.

68. Interview, *Times of India*, September 27, 2012.

69. See www.asiarisk.com/

70. Lindsay Hodges Anderson, 'Lant Pritchett Argues India is Flailing, Underperforming', Harvard Kennedy School, June 8, 2009 at www.hks.harvard.edu/.

71. See his *Democracy and Development in India: From Socialism to Pro-Business*, 10.

72. Personal communication, February 26, 2013.

73. Interview.

74. For the views of many American businessmen, including Chip Jones, CEO of microchip-maker Intel India, see Prashant Duggal, 'India's slow bureaucracy restricting IT growth: American executives (Wikileaks)', June 9, 2011, at http://rtn.asia/990_foreign-it-firms-see-slow-bureaucracy-courts-indias-biggest-weakness-wikileaks.

75. Interview.

76. Nripendra Misra, 'Why Bureaucracy Baulks at Decisions', *Economic Times*, December 3, 2012.

77. Interview, *Sunday Express*, September 23, 2012.

78. Hilaly, Z. 'Our founders and guardians', *The News*, 26 February 2013.

79. Dutta, S. 'MNREGS mockery: Re. .001 per day', *Indian Express*, 26 March 2013.

80. 'Why are Gandhis always Linked to Def Deals: BJP', *Times of India*, April 9, 2013.

81. Siddhanta, P. 'Cost overruns, delays in 83% infra projects, plan panel tells Modi', *Indian Express.*, 12 November 2014.

82. Wikileaks documents suggest that Indira Gandhi's son, Rajiv Gandhi, who became prime minister in 1984, was the middleman for the Swedish company, Saab-Scania, trying to sell its Viggen combat aircraft to India, which deal might have gone through but for the US Government's veto owing to the Flygmotor Pratt & Whitney engine in it. See 'Rajiv was 'negotiator' for Swedish jet firm: Wiki', *Times of India*, April 9, 2013.

83. Says Robert Metzger, a defence contracts lawyer: 'You can't be in a situation where you go to India as a company subject to the (UK) Anti-Bribery Act or the US Foreign Corrupt Practices Act and have your Indian partner say: "Not to worry; everybody pays to get the government to do the work here." It just can't happen....What am I going to get for the risk I'm going to take? What [Indian partners] may think is ordinary could put you out of business.' See '"Companies choosing not to invest in India due to corruption" Robert Metzger', *Indian Defense Review*, March 6, 2013.

84. Bhalla, S.S. 'Where have all the subsidies gone?', *Indian Express.* 23 February 2013.

85. Rajashekhar, M. and Tiwari, D. 'Government plans micro-ATMs to transfer cash to poor', *Economic Times*, 1 December 2012.

86. Surabhi, 'Subsidies: Govt to roll out direct cash trasfers in 6 states by Jan 1', *Indian Express*, November 12, 2012.

87. Ramesh, J. Keynote address, 'Celebrating Twenty Years of the Center for the Advanced Study of India', New Delhi, November 29, 2012.

88. Belawadi, P. 'Indian political heirs', *Express Tribune*, 23 November 2012.

89. Singh, J., 'Venal leaders, vile babus', *Pioneer*, 23 January 2012.

90. Tharoor S., *Pax Indica*, 410.

91. Sinha, interview.

92. Interview.

93. 'PM adopts Jayapur village, assures region's development', *Tribune* (Chandigarh), available at http://www.tribuneindia.com/2014/20141107/latest-news.htm, 7 November 2014.

94. Rehana Jhabvala, heads SEVA, a women's self-help group in Ahmedabad, News at 9, *IBN-CNN TV*, November 26, 2012.

95. Yashwant Sinha, interview.

96. Chidambaram, 'Poor-rich countries: The Challenges of Development'

97. Sridhar, V. (31 October 2014) 'The Mega Sale', *Frontline*.

98. 'Suggest transformational budget ideas, act fearlessly, PM tells Secys', *Times of India*, November 2, 2014.

99. Raj, Y. 'India's slowing economy affecting ties with US', *Hindustan Times*, 28 February 2013.

100. Interview of Columbia University professor, Arvind Panagariya, *Economic Times*, July 17, 2013.

101. Mallet. V. (I March 2013) (*Financial Times*), 'Could Hindu festival "pop-up megacity" be an organizational model for India?', *Washington Post*.

102. See Daniel Markey. 2009. 'Developing India's Foreign Policy "Software"', *Asia Policy*, National Bureau of Asian Research, Number 8, July.

103. See William Burns. 2014.' 10 Parting Thoughts for America's Diplomats', *Foreign Policy*, October 23, available at http://www.foreignpolicy.com/articles/2014/10/23/10_important_lessons_for_america_s_diplomats_parting_thoughts_william_burns_state_department#trending.

104. A former U.S. diplomat, personal communication.

105. The Sri Lanka Foreign Minister in 1994–2001, Lakshman Kadirgamar, in a personal communication during a Washington thinktank event told the author about the Indian High Commissioner Mani Dixit's 'grating pro-consular' attitude before and during the Indian military's intervention in his country in the mid-1980s. The late Mr. Dixit was considered among the most able and effective of IFS officers. Diplomats of other states in the vicinity have similar perceptions of Indian diplomatic representatives.

106. 'Overseas missions need to boost trade: Narendra Modi', *Times of India*, May 26, 2014.

107. Siddhanta, P. 'Government trains focus on trade diplomacy in mission mode', *Indian Express*, 15 August 2014.

108. Jacob, J. 'UPA pacts under NDA lens', *Hindustan Times*, 21 November 2014.

109. Ambassador N.N. Jha, Valedictory Address, National Seminar on 'India's Foreign Policy and its Stance in Present Global Security Scenario', Centre for Policy Analysis (Patna), New Delhi, October 26, 2014.

References

Bose, A. 2008. *Behenji: A Political Biography of Mayawati*. New Delhi: Penguin India.

Civil Services Survey 2010: A Report. New Delhi: Dept. of Administrative Reforms, Government of India, 2010, 111, available at http://darpg.nic.in/darpgwebsite_cms/Document/file/Civil_Services_Survey_2010.pdf .

Das, G. 2012. *India Grows by Night: The Liberal Case for a Strong State*. New Delhi: Allen Lane.

Doniger, W. 2010. *The Hindus: An Alternative History*. New York: Penguin.

Dreze, J. and Sen, A. 2013. *An Uncertain Glory: India and Its Contradictions*. New Delhi: Allen Lane.

Garton-Ash, T. 2013. 'Europe and India Between America and China', Center for Policy Research: New Delhi.

Golani, S. 2013. 'Thanks to Mafia, Slums Mushroom on Forest Land', *Afternoon Despatch and Courier*, April 8, 2013 available at http://www.after-noondc.in/city-news/thanks-to-mafia-slums-mushroom-on-forest-land/article_79795.

'Mumbai slums in the grip of land mafia', *NCHRO (National Confederation of Human Rights Organizations)*, undated but probably mid-2000s available at http://nchro.org/index.php?option=com_content&view=article&id=2631:mumbai-slums-in-the-grip-of-land-mafia&catid=4:corruptio n&Itemid=12.

Griffiths, P. 1965. *The British Impact on India*. London: Frank Cass & Co. Ltd.

Herman, A. 2009. *Gandhi & Churchill: The Epic Rivalry that Destroyed an Empire and Forged our Age*. New York: Bantam Books.

Hsu, K. 2013. ' India-Taiwan Economic Partnership: Building a New Growth Model', *Indian Foreign Affairs Journal*, 8(3): 298–300.

Kapur, Devesh, Chandra Bhan Prasad, Lant Pritchett, and Shyam Babu. 2010. 'Rethinking Inequality: Dalits in Uttar Pradesh in the Market Reform Era', *Economic & Political Weekly*, Vol XLV, No. 35

Kapur, Devesh. 2015. 'India: The Suffocating State', Lecture, Nehru Memorial Mueseum and Library, July 8, 2015.

Kohli, A. 2009. *Democracy and Development in India: From Socialism to Pro-Business*. New Delhi: Oxford University Press.

Little, A. W. 2010. *Access to Elementary Education in India: Politics, Policies and Progress*, London: Consortium for Research on Access, Transitions, and Equity, U.K, 5, 55, 60 available at www.create-rpc-.org/pdf_documents/PTA44.pdf.

Lloyd Rudolf and Susan Hoeber Rudolf. 2010. 'Hope Under Fire: South Asia's Search for Stability', *Global Asia*, Vol. 3, No. 1, Spring 2008 at http://globalasia.org/Back_Issues/.

McMillan, Alister. 2008. 'Deviant Democratization in India', Democratization, Volume 15, No. 4, August 2008 available at http://faculty.washington.edu/

Pandey, S. and Thakur A.P. 2009. *21st Century India: View and Vision*. New Delhi: Global Vision Publishing House.

Rice, S. E. 2007. 'Strengthening Weak States: A Twenty-first Century Imperative'. In M. H. Halperin, J. Laurenti, P. Rundlet, and S. P. Boyer (Eds), *Power and Superpower: Global Leadership and Exceptionalism in the 21st Century*, New York: The Century Foundation Press, p 191.

Vira, V. 2011. 'Counterinsurgency in India: The Maoists', *Small Wars Journal*, available at www.smallwarsjournal.com/.

Conclusion

India is democratic to its roots, but has for most of its independent existence been misgoverned in one sense because it is not easily governable. It is saddled with a system of government virtually designed to work at cross purposes with itself; has big ambitions to affect international developments in Asia, Africa, and even Latin America; and boasts of many successful development aid and security assistance programmes underway in Asia and Africa that have fetched it enormous goodwill and established its bona fides as a strategically capable power with potentially global impact. However, it seems unable to connect the dots, lacks the single driving vision to get the various streams of foreign, economic, and military policies to cohere, or to do that extra bit to realize great power. Many of the debilities in Indian policy and posture, because self-inflicted, are correctible. But the lack of a comprehensive vision, strategy and game plan, and primarily political will, and a scatter-shot approach to marshalling national resources amounting to their gross misuse, give the impression of a country nearly clueless about what it wants and how to get it with what it has. So despite having a large and professional military that is modern in parts and a nuclear arsenal with distant reach that can be ramped up quickly quality and quantity-wise, India, like in the economic realm, has contrived a relatively small strategic impress for itself owing to short-sighted policies, bad choices, and loss of nerve.

Thus, the country has the industrial potential to become the 'workshop' of the world but remains a comparative laggard in manufacturing.[1] Rules and regulations, and political tilt favour defence public sector units, which have proved incapable of innovating foreign military technology transferred to them as part of large, expensive deals for high-value hardware. This is what the private sector excels at, except it is only in a small way part of the defence production cycle. The public rhetoric apart, arms imports are institutionally preferred as source of illicit funds for the ruling party-of-the-day and of contracts for licensed manufacture of foreign armaments to keep the inefficient public sector units, ordnance factories, and shipyards, who do little other than 'screwdriver' weapon systems, busy.[2] Consequently, India's large defence spend provides succor to the defence industries in the West and Russia, even as Indian private sector defence industrial companies with impressive production wherewithal wither away for want of custom. Arms dependency affects foreign policy and restricts the Indian military from becoming a major national security asset in the external sphere and curbs its ability to fight long wars to conclusion and maintain high levels of preparedness. The absurdity of this situation is such that India is self-sufficient in the strategic field, having designed and built advanced natural uranium-fuelled nuclear reactors, is getting a breeder reactor on stream and working an experimental thorium reactor, produces nuclear weapons and highly accurate ballistic and supersonic cruise missiles, nuclear-powered submarines, satellites, space launch vehicles, and even sends inexpensive space probes that have caught the attention of the world, but the government professes the country's inability to produce lower-technology conventional weaponry and buys them abroad.[3] The lack of foresight means high technology, skills, and managerial competence developed by indigenous programs in mission-mode (nuclear weapons, missiles, space vehicles) are not transferred to the industry in order to upgrade it and to commercialize these technologies as a way of amortizing public investment in these sensitive sectors.

India is an anachronism writ large. It was the first country outside the U.S. and Europe to design and develop a supersonic fighter plane (Marut HF-24) in the late 1960s, but has been procuring combat aircraft from foreign sources ever since. India has transited from surviving on American PL 480 food shipments to having food surpluses, but also has widespread malnutrition and mountains of grain rotting in government depots. It has great cities that are sliding into urban chaos for want of planning, political direction, and administrative accountability. The country generates globally acknowledged elite engineering and managerial talent, but fails to impart quality education to the masses at any level—primary school level up—and is, therefore, not in a position to optimally harness its rich human resources.[4] It has a thriving medical tourism industry, but cannot offer basic healthcare to its people. India is an information technology giant, hosts centres of cutting-edge science and technology R&D, but features shameful infrastructure; it has the necessary building blocks, but seems unable to summon the political spirit and the sense of purpose to use these for a grand, national mission. It has, as this book has tried to show, all the attributes, but is not a great power. India is truly unique in having so much but so little to show for it. The new right-of-centre government of Narendra Modi will have to undo what decades of ideologically blinkered policies have wrought. But it will take time for this change to show results.

With the Indian system getting so much wrong for so long, it is not surprising it exalts soft power as the means to reach great power because this is a way to escape making hard decisions. The fact is soft power can only embellish great power, not carry a country to that threshold. It can, however, be aligned with hard power which, if wielded with vigour, agility, and verve, can vault India to the top. India has partially secured the wherewithal of hard power, without acquiring the defence industrial means to maintain it. But significantly, it is the troika of the absences—the absence of a national vision, of the political will to realize it, and of the understanding of the utility of hard power—that has so far kept India down. Minus vision and will, hard power is useless and India is like a large, well-laden ship without a rudder—all buoyancy and drift, and no destination in sight. But it is a condition fit for New Delhi's rationale for risk averse foreign and military policy, namely, that the country's priority for the foreseeable future is economic growth. The trouble is, while the country transforms internally, the external world cannot be put on hold. Attempts to do which with a 'don't rock the boat' approach and an antiseptic foreign policy has only skewed the power imbalance in Asia and the world so completely as may leave India with few options when New Delhi finally determines it is ready to act. The over-bureaucratized

Indian system prides itself in muddling through, except as the Princeton political scientist Klaus Knorr long ago warned, only the strong can afford to do so. In policymaking, New Delhi betrays the mindset of a small power surviving on 'small margin of safety' and, therefore, instinctively opts for foreign and military policies of 'vigilant prudence' (Knorr 1975: 23). Such vigilance, however, only denotes a passive-reactive policy outlook. Nowhere is this more evident than in India's relations with China. This hasn't so far happened, but standing up to China and taking the fight to its periphery rather than responding tepidly to Chinese moves in its neighbourhood, could well define India as a great power in the twenty-first century. But the Indian government has remained oblivious to this aspect. On 10 April 2013, PLA intruded 19 kilometres inside Depsang Valley on the Indian side of the Line of Actual Control in western Ladakh. The Indian government turned down the army's entreaties for an assertive response, relied on diplomacy, and accepted a compromise to defuse the crisis by agreeing to dismantle a fortified observation post at Chumar on the Indian side of the LAC, which was not even contested, thereby accepting in principle that India would not erect military-use infrastructure, such as roads, on its side even as China has built a dense network of roads or 'shunts' (in military parlance) parallel to the Xinjiang Highway on the Tibetan plateau enabling it to mass its forces at will along the long disputed border, and concentrate in depth, on their side. Even though there was evidence that Beijing relented on the Depsang intrusion after the Indian government announced an extension of the trip in late May 2013 by Prime Minister Manmohan Singh to Japan. But instead of playing up the Japan angle to tip over the Chinese fear calculus, his government, in order not to rattle Beijing, abruptly cancelled the Indian Navy's participation in a joint war exercise off Okinawa, notwithstanding officers from the U.S. and Japanese navies being in New Delhi at the time to work out the details of the exercise.[5] Such infirmity frustrates Japan, the U.S., and other potential allies in Asia and hurts India's credibility. This attitude may be changing. A road grid on the LAC in Arunachal Pradesh has been approved and the Indian PM called China an 'expansionist' power whilst in Tokyo. And when President Xi Jinping's visit coincided with another PLA intrusion in Ladakh, Modi chided his visitor, who professed ignorance about such provocation, by telling him the Chinese Army was no better than the Pakistan Army—out of the government's control. It was a jibe that hit home; the PLA withdrew post-haste.[6]

Indian foreign policy is also handicapped by a beguiling naiveté of seeing the world in terms of friendly powers and states such as China that are geostrategic adversaries but who can be won over by the soft touch. A corollary is the belief that friendly powers mean no ill and will do India no harm. In the context of the Columbia University trade economist Jagdish Bhagwati talking of 'a climate of India-baiting' in Washington, D.C., New Delhi regularly fails to anticipate punitive US visa rules and industry regulations devised to hurt Indian software and pharmaceutical sectors, and initiatives by the US Congress to penalize India on the Intellectual Property Rights issue meant to stifle India in areas where it has comparative advantage.[7] Besides, mechanisms such as the US-sponsored Trans-Pacific Partnership, that India is kept out of, will directly affect Indian exports and access to the American market (Palit 2015). In a different setting, the Indian Defence Ministry does not care to twist France's arm, for instance, to obtain advanced collateral technology, such as for ceramic blade in aircraft jet engines, as part of the multi-billion dollar Rafale deal.[8] In contrast, China broke the European aviation technology embargo by threatening to cancel an $11 billion order for Airbus SAS passenger aircraft.[9] If the Indian government does not stand up for India's national interest, who will?

The influential Chinese policy analyst Hu Angang has enumerated six criteria for judging whether a country deserves recognition as great power. It might be useful to see the extent to which India fits the bill. Culturally, the would-be 'superpower', he writes, must be 'tolerant', making possible the survival and development of all civilizations; geographically 'feature vast land and sea territories'; economically and financially, be 'extraordinarily powerful'; demographically, boast of 'large number of well-educated citizens and well-developed infra-structure"; militarily, 'possess a unified military power that is relatively indestructible, capable of preventing or causing huge destruction, and able to project its influence across the globe'; and politically and ideologically, 'have a powerful political system capable of efficiently allocating resources to realize the political objectives and to exert influence via ideology'.[10] Other than culturally, geographically, and to a lesser extent militarily, India does not measure up. Culture is a social/anthropological construct and geography a natural attribute, and India has used neither very well in terms of blending government policies and private sector initiatives, as revealed in this study. Politically, India is evolving towards a more accountable participatory democracy, which is a good thing. The federated system of government, however, delays implementation of policy and freights centre-state relations with political baggage. And between serving their political masters and the people the bureaucrat–administrators choose the former to the detriment of society and nation. It is curious that in Gujarat, Bihar, and Tamil Nadu, the same genus of bureaucrats have delivered good governance who elsewhere resemble a pack of stumblebums. So, maybe, it is as much the existing system that is to blame as the political leaders at the controls. It only emphasizes the fact that there has been no strong leader at the centre to chart a new course and steer the country, mobilize the people and efficiently marshal the myriad resources to overcome challenges, and to mine the opportunities offered by the new millennium and a changing international milieu at once in flux and well-disposed to India's rise.

India's progress on the economic front has been tardy and hesitant with the system only very slowly shaking off the ideological underpinnings of socialist development.[11] It reveals the political uncertainty in the country and the extent to which economic globalization has become irreversible. Once the reverse thrusters are taken off, as promised by Modi, a surging Indian economy will increase government revenues, making more funds available for education, skilling, and social welfare programmes, and for discriminate expenditures to gain a consequential military, and rendering an open economy less of a political issue.

The sprucing up of the system to deliver better governance will then depend on whether the people will any longer countenance corruption at any level of government, lackadaisical political leadership, and slovenly administration. The evidence of recent elections and rapid changes in government in the states and at the centre indicate the people are out of patience and the central and provincial governments will have to get their acts together. Even so, political and administrative reforms and new accountability norms are unlikely to transform the ground reality in a trice. Though Prime Minister Modi's attempts to tidy up the political leader–bureaucrat interface, set goals, and whip the extant system into working seems to have perked up the government apparatus. Whether the initial enthusiasm translates into permanent change in the outlook and functioning of civil servants—the grit in the machine—is less certain. The country cannot long avoid a drastic pruning of the government's role in national life considering the growing social and political consciousness of the Indian people and their demand for smaller, more effective government. Once the system becomes more accountable, norms of good governance will tend to become a staple of administration. However, given the population size and the scale of the problems to be tackled and considering how many things it has to set right, Ruchir Sharma, head of Morgan Stanley Investment Management, for instance, gives India only a '50-50' chance of making it as a 'breakout nation' (Sharma 2012: 38). Based on some 15 criteria, including reform, where India has so far opted for 'soft bailouts' not 'tough' measures, and populist policies it 'can't afford' India, he claims, is failing to achieve what he calls, 'a Zen balance' required to build a 'European welfare state at an early stage of development'. He rates India as performing badly in six of the 15 criteria, doing good in five, and having a 'mixed' record in the remaining four.[12]

Assuming India somehow scrambles through with whatever result, it cannot afford to be detached from the international system which is tending towards bipolarity— after the short interregnum of U.S. dominance— with China the other pole.[13] To make sure the international system trends towards multipolarity instead and India is not swamped by China in Asia, New Delhi will have to utilize its hard power more strenuously, as this book has argued. The catch is the Indian government is reticent and hasn't displayed the wit to recognize the value of hard power and to deploy it to bolster the country's standing and to carve out an Indian sphere of influence or responsibility. This only underlines the need to address certain critical weaknesses dogging the Indian conventional military other than shortlegged weapons platforms and legacy forces and attitude, such as its organizational rigidity and inability to adapt to technological change. As dawdlers in transformation, Indian armed forces will face riskier confrontations against countries with more adaptive and advanced militaries. It is a situation that brings into sharp relief the need for proven high-yield thermonuclear weapons to deter such better endowed adversaries from prosecuting wars to decision. The Indian armed forces, moreover, are misaligned in terms of the gravity of threats, being geared principally to fight Pakistan while treating the more dangerous China lightly. The intent of the 2010 Operational Directive issued by the Defence Minister to the military services designating China as main threat was typically diluted by the then Minister for External Affairs, Salman Khurshid, in the Congress government, who referred to China as a 'major concern' and Pakistan as part of the Chinese 'picture', but also talked of China as being 'more important in terms of our global vision', adding that it 'can be an important partner in Asia, Africa and elsewhere.'[14] This sort of mixed messaging increased the confusion of the Indian armed services, but did not deter the Manmohan Singh regime from showing extreme reluctance to do other than try and conflate Indian interests with China's in order to avoid conflict that geo-strategic considerations indicate is inevitable. If hostilities do occur, the fighting qualities of the Indian armed forces would be impaired by policies perpetuating dependence on imported hardware, spares, and service support. This last may be undergoing change with the BJP government deciding on the 'Make in India' thrust to produce conventional submarines and medium transport aircraft, which is perhaps, a harbinger of in-country production of warships, combat aircraft, light helicopters, artillery, and tanks. But 'Make in India' in substance resembles assembling weapons and is not the same thing as 'Made in India'—design to delivery (Shukla 2015). The nuclear deterrent has been upgraded with nanotechnology to make weapons lighter and more lethal. But it still boasts of thermonuclear weapons of flawed design, to correct which will require nuclear testing. Unproven high-yield fusion armaments, 'no first use', and ruling out of nuclear warfighting (with small-yield weapons), weaken India's nuclear stance even as canisterization of weapons, accurate missiles, and SSBN ensure any initiator of a nuclear exchange will be fatally hurt. With its strategic deterrent and conventional military handicapped in different ways, and its slate of recessive foreign and security policies making the country look timid, India cannot emerge as an independent player and muscular counterweight to China, or become a great power.

To avoid such a denouement, India will have to discard its tendency to please Washington and Beijing, and become more disruptive in Asia and globally because that's what great powers and would-be great powers do—they break eggs to make the great power omelette for themselves. It will require, as has been contended in this book: (1) realization of an Indian Monroe Doctrine system; (2) resumption of thermonuclear tests until the military end-users are satisfied with the resulting high-yield and tailored-yield fusion and sub-kiloton warheads and weapons; (3) agreement with Mauritius to lease the North & South Agalega Islands as the western leg of the strategic tripod involving India's Andaman Command and the Nha Trang in Vietnam in the east; (4) consolidation of the Iran–Afghanistan–Central Asia trade–economic–security link-up to connect landwards with Russia and Europe and, in concert with Moscow, to outflank and stifle the Chinese power creep westward through Xinjiang, and southward through Gwadar; (5) initiation of an all-aspects policy to co-opt Pakistan while moving aggressively to secure South Asia by minimizing the Chinese role in Myanmar, Nepal, and in the Indian Ocean region; (6) arming Vietnam with strategic missiles, beyond the Brahmos cruise missile already approved for transfer, as tit-for-tat for the Chinese nuclear weapons and missile technology transfers to Pakistan, and beef up military-to-military ties with the ASEAN states; (7) arrange with Manila for regular use of the Subic Bay naval base by the Indian Navy and periodic visits by Indian squadrons of Su-30s to Clark air base in the Philippines; (8) explore a northern Australian basing option for Indian SSBNs to secure strategic presence and reach in China's backyard; (9) increase the frequency and complexity of joint naval and air battle drills and exercises with the Japanese, U.S., and littoral forces, and up-weight the Indian military presence in the Andaman and Nicobar sea territories to, in fact, make the so-called 'steel curtain' that some Chinese analysts apprehend coming down on the western side of the Malacca Strait, a reality and, by such measures, to flesh out a comprehensive and assertive military posture and strategy configured to heighten the uncertainties for China and to create a series of tactical, theatre-level, and strategic predicaments for Beijing it cannot easily overcome; and (10) promote cultural exchanges, trade, and commercial ties, encourage tourist traffic and Chinese investment in infrastructure projects—country-girdling road and high-speed rail networks (a Chinese specialty)—in effect, use the sort of non-linear, multi-pronged, multi-layered strategy Beijing has so deftly employed to keep India off-balance, against China.

The ring-fencing of China is best achieved on bilateral basis with the countries on its periphery, while keeping the US and Russia, friends with stakes in Asia, posted about these developments. But these actions, under no circumstances, should be contingent on any extra-Asian country's approval or participation. The United States is not in Asia and is only a distant maritime neighbour of China. How it wants to take care of the China threat it perceives as threatening its interests is its business. However, Washington would be more amenable to involving itself decisively in any confrontation with China in Asia if it sees the main effort being made by the Asian states themselves than, as has happened since 1945, if the US has to carry the can and the regional countries free-ride. How much the United States would be part of any collective effort to 'neutralize China' will depend on the stake it perceives in any given situation. Indo-US relations are stable but lack of trust still colours perceptions on both sides. In any case, India has to deal with the menace posed to it by China, preferably together with other Asian states desirous of seeing Beijing constrained.[15] With the conservative Liberal Democratic Party in power and Shinzo Abe, a Japanese nationalist and a friend who has been urging India to be more assertive in the defence of its interests, heading the government in Tokyo, the time is nigh for New Delhi to join with Japan in strategically squeezing China at the two ends of Asia.[16] India has the resources now to be outward thrusting—the most telling characteristic of great power—and fill out its ambition by expansive undertakings in Central Asia, Africa, the Gulf and Southeast Asia with financial and technical aid and assistance, with offers to train and build local militaries, set up trading bourses, build railways and energy pipelines, do whatever it takes to win these states over. It is imperative, as part of this exercise, for New Delhi to give the private sector-led defence industry its head in letting India emerge as militarily self-sufficient power able to sell arms, including sophisticated items like the 4.5 generation Tejas light combat aircraft—an almost perfect export product, warships, and submarines to countries in Asia, Africa, and Latin America. India has to capture the 'wei qi' space presently held by China with the aim of crowding it out. Or, India will slide back into the ranks of the also-rans in Asia validating, in the process, the Chinese strategy inspired by Sun Tzu of overwhelming an enemy without actually fighting him.

Going against the grain, devising policies driven to realize expansively defined geostrategic interests, and acting relentlessly in the realpolitik mode is what India will have to begin doing if it means to be taken seriously as a coming power. It will have to relegate universal peace, disarmament, and such other ideals that New Delhi has been enamoured of from Nehru's days to the realm of rhetoric and speeches in the UN, and ensure they do not intrude into actual policy space. It will increase India's leverage as a strategic spoiler and bolster its standing as a great power in the process of being.

The end-state of great power, however, is still some ways off because there are no signs the Indian government—pickled in doubt for decades and mired in indistinct ideas about the country's destiny, and unnerved by the country's enormous socio-economic problems and the incapacity of the existing system to deliver—can undertake the radical reorganization and administrative restructuring and reform that is required. What is needed is for a Meiji kind of spirit that catapulted Japan in the latter half of the nineteenth century, to be stoked in India.

India has missed many opportunities to stand up to China, burnish its image in Asia by publicly signalling its intent to cross swords with Beijing if need be, once it became apparent that the Chinese government was not interested in applying closure to the interminable rounds of talks to resolve the festering dispute over the land border. On the eve of Manmohan Singh's NSA Shivshankar Menon's trip to Beijing in December 2012 to touch base with the functionaries of the new Xi Jinping regime and to expedite a border solution, Beijing issued e-passports with Chinese maps showing the north eastern state of Arunachal Pradesh and Aksai Chin in the extreme west as inalienable Chinese territory, and followed up a few days later by formally informing New Delhi that the two sides were still very far apart on the issue of demarcating the border.[17] As has been the Indian government's wont, it once again acted as an apologist for Chinese actions, with Menon dismissing the Chinese contretemps as just differences over maps in the one case and, in the other case, the MEA said that Beijing's communication clarified the issues on which the two sides differed, as if it had learned of the differences for the first time.[18] Then, with Menon in Beijing, an inadvertent opportunity arose for New Delhi to signal steadfastness in protecting national interest, which it fluffed. In light of aggressive noises from Beijing, the Indian naval chief was asked by the press about how the navy would react to any Chinese attempt to board its warships deployed in the South China Sea to protect Indian energy assets jointly owned with Vietnam. Admiral D.K. Joshi forthrightly replied the Indian Navy had practised actions to thwart any such intervention and that these would be implemented. The usual 'rules of engagement' will apply, he added, 'whenever [one's] right of self-defense is impeded'.[19] Joshi had said the right thing, sent the right message, at a time when the new Xi Jinping dispensation was feeling its oats. But the effect was spoiled by Menon, a former ambassador to China, venting misinformation to placate his hosts, saying the Indian naval chief was 'misled' into making his statement, which the NSA feared, would hurt Chinese sensibilities.[20] It was followed a day later by the Foreign Office urging restraint on the Indian military, leading to the conclusion that New Delhi is more mindful of Chinese sensitivities than keen about safeguarding Indian interests.[21]

The tendency of reflexive kowtowing to Beijing is classic MEA-qua-Indian government behaviour and has to stop, because it speaks of the official intent to avoid giving offence to China even as the options available to the Indian military to send a message to Beijing by defying China in its own backyard languish. More than the armed forces, it seems it is Indian diplomats who are scarred by the 1962 military defeat, expecting a similar drubbing in the future should they fail to pacify a China that under President Xi is turning into a tantalizing adversary.[22] The fact is the Indian government has yet to digest the strategic import of India's 'self-powered economic rise' or to appreciate the emergence of the Indian military as a confident fighting force that can handle China and should be consciously used to achieve larger political goals.[23] Its approach, instead, seems to be to ride out the periodic storms deliberately created by China by doing nothing, each such incident leaving New Delhi more frazzled and seemingly less motivated to confront and counter it even as there's accretion in Beijing's confidence to keep pushing India into the corner. In this respect, even the Modi government erred. In order not to give offence to Xi, an important political leader from Arunachal Pradesh, which China claims as its own, and who is Minister of State for Home, Kiren Rijiju, was kept away from the banquet in Delhi for the visiting Xi.[24] This is not the sign of a newly bold India.

The incident happened, perhaps, because India's national security minders are still not convinced that in a twenty-first century world with 'a flatter distribution of power' 'friction or even conflict [is] inevitable'.[25] In the event, they think not so much about exercising hard or even soft power as dabbling in abstractions about them, something typified by the Congress party government. 'We must be conscious of the difference between weight, influence, and power', averred Menon, in a prepared statement for the Defence Services Staff College. 'Power is the ability to create and sustain outcomes. Weight we have, our influence is growing, but our power remains limited and constrained and should first be used for our domestic transformation.' It neatly encapsulates the absolute confusion of means and ends at the heart of Indian policymaking. But Menon did not amplify his ideas about how to use the Indian military for domestic development and 'transformation'. If as history and common sense suggest, comprehensive military capability can extend and consolidate India's influence in the world, then consistently to undercut the value of the coercive means of the state by discouraging the armed services from restating their primary mission and operational readiness, is vitally to hurt the country's standing and prospects. It is not surprising the Congress party government's National Security Adviser fumbled so basic a precept of statecraft. Most elaborations of policy by senior Manmohan Singh government officials appeared to be verbose rationales for a fatalistic brand of do-nothing-ism. Consider another statement by Menon—he was nothing if not prolix—this time about the world the great Hindu strategist from the third century BC, Kautilya, held sway in. 'In many ways it is India's historical experience of poly-centric multi-state systems, plurality, and of the omni-directional diplomacy and relativistic statecraft that it produced that is closer to the world we see today', he said. '[So] when we call for a plural, inclusive and open security architecture in the Indo-Pacific we are well within a tradition and culture of thought which was relativistic, idea-driven, and omni-directional.'[26] It is hard to interpret this as other than justifying India's fear of leading a collective security scheme in Asia—such as an Indian Monroe Doctrine system (as part of a triple Monroe Doctrine system) detailed earlier in this book that can keep China in its place—and, in terms of power politics, and to wheedle India into playing second fiddle. In a time of revived nationalism everywhere, Manmohan Singh's India, exceptionally, was seen marching to a different drumbeat.[27]

Perhaps, such views, tending to an inert policy and inaction, have less to do with the country's ancient history than with the more recent past. That India tends to be a low hurdler, unwilling to stray far from past policies and comfort zones or, strategically speaking, to look beyond its nose, to free-ride on security afforded by great powers as international public good whenever possible, to seek great power as an entitlement, to shirk great power responsibility, and generally to escape aiming high or doing anything big, has by now become a cliché.[28] New Delhi seems so thrilled with just being acknowledged as a country with some standing, so overwhelmed with inclusion in exclusive conclaves (G-3, G-8, G-20, etc.), and so satisfied with itself and the way things have gone so far in the new millennium, it doesn't see the need to raise its sights, put in the effort, and do the things that will in fact make India a genuine great power. Then again it may be a cultural trait reflected, for instance, in the bemused observation by a hard-charging Australian hired to coach the Indian Field Hockey team, that Indian players seemed happy with 'just turning up' at the Olympic Games rather than being keen to win medals.[29]

India has been down for so long in history, its leaders confuse small achievements and the slight recognition accorded the country as attaining great power. Such a low threshold of national self-esteem has, in turn, resulted in sustained under-achievement and lack of official desire for India to stamp the world with its presence in a big way. Such an attitude may be explained with references to the Hindu zeitgeist, but the fact is the Indian government still seems steeped in strategic reserve, perhaps, imbibed from the British in the waning days of their great power period. Admiral Sir Reginald Custance in the 1920s differentiated the 'will to security' he claimed the British nation displayed from the 'will to power' he said Germany exemplified (Karnad 2005: 455). India has never been short of the will to security, it is the grander will to power that's been conspicuously missing precisely because, from Nehru's days, power has improvidently been equated with bellicosity and aggression, and a 'tough' state with a 'dumb' state and as antithesis of a 'smart' state.[30] New Delhi by this reckoning seems satisfied with glorying in its information technology prowess, its talent for jugaad and 'frugal engineering', the Moon and Mars space missions, an unimaginative foreign policy bereft of geo-strategic imagination, and national security considerations centred on the subcontinent rather than on distant defence, a skewed conventional military unsupported by a credible thermonuclear arsenal and a comprehensively capable defence industry, in other words with just the show and symbolism of great power.

Modi seems more direct in addressing adversaries and in the exercise of power, and more confident about India's place in the world.[31] However, a national vision is still absent as is real appreciation of hard power. Moreover, rather than remaking the system, he is relying on the same old establishment to deliver on a new agenda. The danger is of the old ways of thinking influencing his policies. The country will then miss yet another opportunity to make good, and India will be fated to remain at least a while longer, as political analyst Pratap Bhanu Mehta said in another context, a 'nation of small strivings'.[32]

Notes

1. 'India to Be World's Factory Hub as China Loses Edge', *Economic Times*, 18 August 2014.

2. Peerzada Abrar and Biswaroop Gooptu, 'Facing Friendly Fire', *Economic Times*, 15 February 2013.

3. India's ability to produce SSBNs and yet the Indian Navy's indenting for yet another imported diesel submarine (in addition to the German HDW-209 and the French Scorpene submersibles already in its inventory) analysed in Bharat Karnad, 'Submarine Import Trap', *Asian Age*, 8 February 2013.

4. 'What a Waste: How India is Failing Its Young' and 'Wasting Time', *Economist*, 11–17 May 2013.

5. Parashar, S., 'PM Extends Japan Trip, Sends a Strong Message to China', *Times of India*, 5 May 2013. Gupta, S. & Chaudhuri, P. P., 'Fearing China, India Pulls Out of War Games with US, Japan', *Hindustan Times*, 13 May 2013.

6. Senior political source in the PM's Office.

7. Bhagwati, J., 'A Climate of India-Baiting', *Times of India*,11 May 2013; Thappil, D.A. McLain, S. and Yadron, D., 'Face-Off on Visa Curbs Pits U.S. Against India', *Wall Street Journal*, 25 April 2013; 'US Faces Pressure to Take India to WTO on Patent Rules', *Economic Times*, 8 May 2014.

8. Senior DRDO official.

9. 'Airbus to China: We Support You, Please Buy Our Jets', Reuters, *Live Mint*, 13 May 2013.

10. Hu Angang, *China in 2020: A New Type of Superpower* [Washington, D.C.: the Brookings Institution, 2011], p. 13.

11. This was reflected in the parliamentary vote in early December 2012 that saw the left-of-center Congress party and its partners pushing for the legislation allowing Foreign Direct Investment in the retail sector, for instance. See 'Govt Wins Vote in Retail FDI in Lok Sabha', *Reuters*, 5 December 2012.

12. Sharma, R. 2012. 'Can India Still Be a Breakout Nation?', *Economic Times*, 19 December.

13. On the possible Sino-American bipolar system, see the debate in the U.K. House of Lords on such a world in 'Lords Discussion on China & Multilateral Nuclear Disarmament, November 2012' available at www.acronym.org.uk/parliamentary-records/201211/lords-discussion-china-multilateral-nuclear-disarmament-november-2012?page=show. For a senior Chinese military officer's view of replacing the U.S. as superpower, see Hu Angang, *China in 2020*, pp. xxxiii–iv.

14. 'China Major Concern than Pakistan, says Khurshid', *Times of India*, 17 December 2012.

15. 'The interesting thing about Asia at the moment is that for first time in a very long time, you've got several Asian economies becoming strong at the same time. You've got China rising, India rising, you've got Japan, notwithstanding its economic problems, you've got Korea, Vietnam, Indonesia—all moving much faster than the global average on economic growth,' said the Australian Ambassador to India, Peter Varghese. 'All of us in the region want to ensure that economic growth does not spill over into strategic instability and therefore, we need to find ways to ensure that countries are part of a system and not standing outside of the system and that applies to China as much as it applies to anyone else.' Interview, *Sunday Express*, 9 December 2012.

16. Justin McCurry, 'Japanese Hawk's Election Victory Prompts Fear of Regional Tension', *Guardian*, 16 December 2012.

17. Pranab Dhal Samanta, 'India, China Long Way from Border Solution', *Sunday Express*, 2 December 2012.

18. 'NSA Shivshankar Menon Plays Down China Map Row, *Times of India*, 27 November 2012.

19. Rajat Pandit, 'Ready to Tackle China Sea Threat: Navy Chief', *Times of India*, 4 December 2012.

20. Saibal Dasgupta, 'Navy Chief Was Fed Words by Media: NSA', *Times of India*, 5 December 2012.

21. 'Navy Chief's Remarks: MEA Asks for Restraint', *Indian Express*, 6 December 2012.

22. 'Xi Jinping Calls for Powerful Strategic Missile Force', *Xinhua*, 5 December 2012 available at http://chinascope.org/main/conternt. view/5083/106.

23. On the subject of India's internally powered economic rise, see Tellis, A.J., 'Overview: The United States and Asia's Rising Powers' in *Strategic Asia 2011-12: Asia Responds to the Rising Powers—China and India* edited by Ashley J. Tellis, Travis Tanner, and Jessica Keough (Seattle & Washington, DC: Strategic Asia 2011-12, National Bureau of Asian Research, 2011), p. 4.

24. 'Arunachal MP Kiren Rijiju Absent from Xi Jinping's State Banquet', *Samachar.com*, 19 September 2014 available at http://www.samachar.com/ live-arunachal-mp-kiren-rijiju-absent-from-xi-jinping-s-state-banquet-ojtoQEafhei.html.

25. Indian NSA, Shivshankar Menon, 'Rising Powers and Global Governance', Munich Security Conference, 2 February 2013.

26. Menon, S., 'Kautilya Today', Institute of Defense Studies and Analyses, New Delhi, 18 October 2012.

27. Paul R. Pillar, 'The Age of Nationalism', *National Interest*, 1 September 2013 available at http://nationalinterest.org/article/ the-age-nationalism-8954.

28. See the Special Report on India titled 'Aim Higher', *Economist*, 29 September 2012.

29. The Australian coach of the Indian hockey team, Michael Nobbs, preparing for the 2012 London Olympics, said, 'The players need to make a decision whether they are satisfied just to be in the Olympics..., or are they willing to be tough and make the commitment for the nation's cause.' See 'Hockey Players' Lack of Commitment Shocks Coach Nobbs', *Sunday Hindustan Times*, 8 August 2012.

30. Shyam Saran, 'Is there Merit in India Turning into a Tough State?', *Business Standard*, 14 May 2014.

31. In the lead-up to the elections, Modi warned China against its 'expansionist mindset' and asked it to drop its claims on India's Arunachal Pradesh. It was the sort of blunt talk Beijing had never heard before. See Gottipati, S., 'Modi Says China Must Drop "Mindset of Expansionism" over Arunachal Pradesh',

Reuters, 22 February 2014 available at http://in.reuters.com/article/2014/02/22/india-modi-china-arunachal-idINDEEA1L03V20140222.

32. See his 'Nation of Small Strivings', *Indian Express*, 6 December, 2012.

References

Karnad, B. 2005 [First edition: 2002]. *Nuclear Weapons and Indian Security: The Realist Foundations of Strategy*. New Delhi: Macmillan India.

Knorr, K. 1975. *The Power of Nations: The Political Economy of International Relations*. New York: Basic Books.

Palit, Amalendu. 2015. 'Trans-Pacific Partnership, India and South Asia', *ISAS Insights*, No. 284, July 11, 2015, Institute of South Asian Studies, National University of Singapore available at http://www.isas.nus.edu.sg/Attachments/PublisherAttachment/ISAS_Insights_No._284_-_Trans-Pacific_Partnership_11072015232257.pdf.

Sharma, R. 2012. *Breakout Nations: In Search of the Next Economic Miracle*. London: Allen Lane.

Shukla, Ajay. 2015. 'Making "Make" Happen', *Business Standard*, March 16, 2015.

Index

About the Author

Bharat Karnad is Professor of National Security Studies, Centre for Policy Research, New Delhi, India. One of the foremost national security strategists of India, and author of *India's Nuclear Policy* (2008) and *Nuclear Weapons and Indian Security*, 2nd ed. (2005), he has been a member of the National Security Advisory Board, the Nuclear Doctrine Drafting Group, and Adviser, Defence Expenditure, (10th) Finance Commission, India. He has also been a Visiting Scholar at Princeton University, University of Pennsylvania, Shanghai Institutes of International Studies, and the Henry L. Stimson Center, Washington, DC.